Application Pa

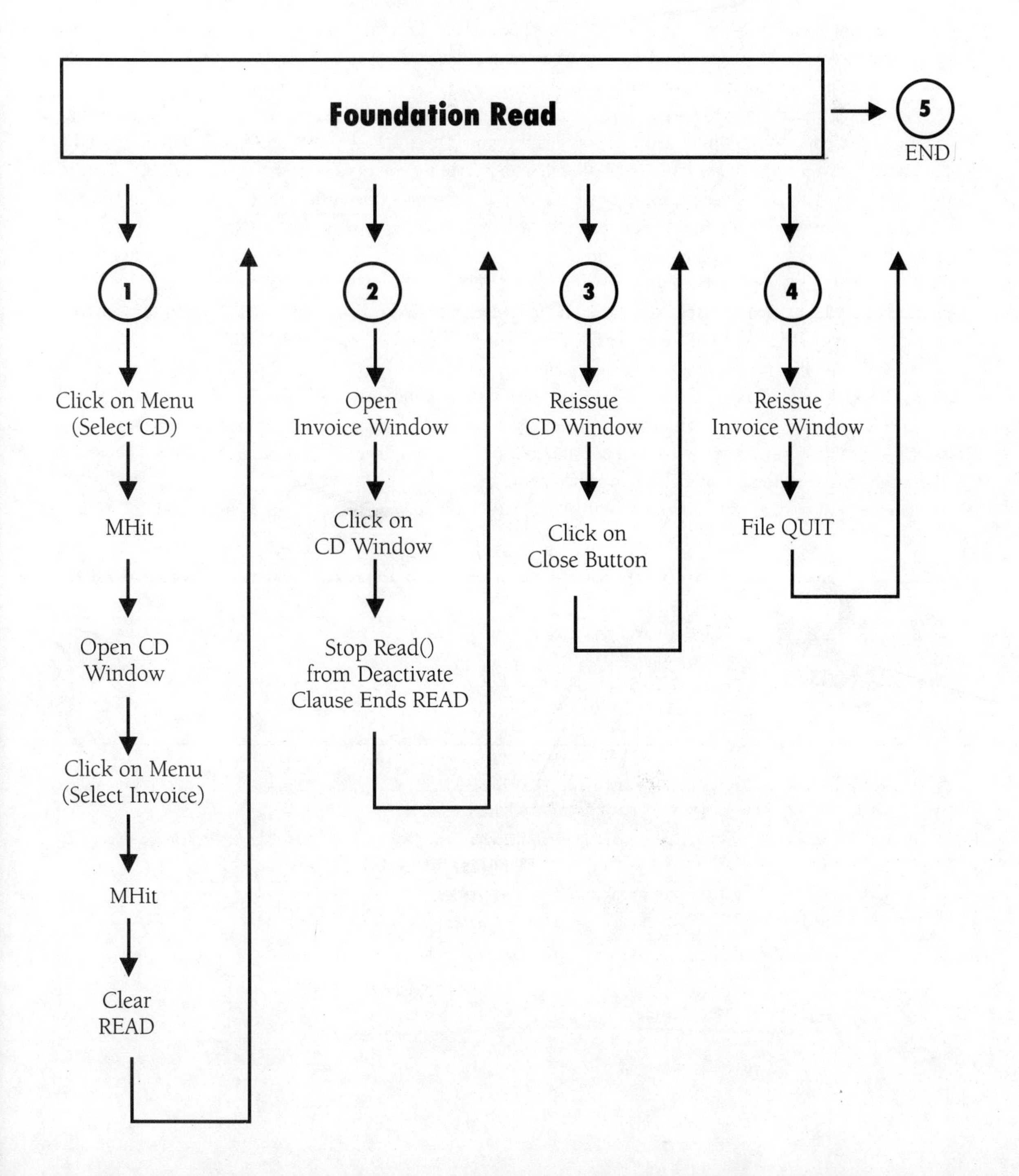
Foundation Read
5
END
1
Click on Menu (Select CD)
MHit
Open CD Window
Click on Menu (Select Invoice)
MHit
Clear READ
2
Open Invoice Window
Click on CD Window
Stop Read() from Deactivate Clause Ends READ
3
Reissue CD Window
Click on Close Button
4
Reissue Invoice Window
File QUIT

For every kind of computer user, there is a SYBEX book.

All computer users learn in their own way. Some need straightforward and methodical explanations. Others are just too busy for this approach. But no matter what camp you fall into, SYBEX has a book that can help you get the most out of your computer and computer software while learning at your own pace.

Beginners generally want to start at the beginning. The ABC's series, with its step-by-step lessons in plain language, helps you build basic skills quickly. Or you might try our Quick & Easy series, the friendly, full-color guide.

The Mastering and Understanding series will tell you everything you need to know about a subject. They're perfect for intermediate and advanced computer users, yet they don't make the mistake of leaving beginners behind.

If you're a busy person and are already comfortable with computers, you can choose from two SYBEX series—Up & Running and Running Start. The Up & Running series gets you started in just 20 lessons. Or you can get two books in one, a step-by-step tutorial and an alphabetical reference, with our Running Start series.

Everyone who uses computer software can also use a computer software reference. SYBEX offers the gamut—from portable Instant References to comprehensive Encyclopedias, Desktop References, and Bibles.

SYBEX even offers special titles on subjects that don't neatly fit a category—like Tips & Tricks, the Shareware Treasure Chests, and a wide range of books for Macintosh computers and software.

SYBEX books are written by authors who are expert in their subjects. In fact, many make their living as professionals, consultants or teachers in the field of computer software. And their manuscripts are thoroughly reviewed by our technical and editorial staff for accuracy and ease-of-use.

So when you want answers about computers or any popular software package, just help yourself to SYBEX.

For a complete catalog of our publications, please write:

SYBEX Inc.
2021 Challenger Drive
Alameda, CA 94501
Tel: (510) 523-8233/(800) 227-2346 Telex: 336311
Fax: (510) 523-2373

SYBEX is committed to using natural resources wisely to preserve and improve our environment. As a leader in the computer book publishing industry, we are aware that over 40% of America's solid waste is paper. This is why we have been printing the text of books like this one on recycled paper since 1982.

This year our use of recycled paper will result in the saving of more than 15,300 trees. We will lower air pollution effluents by 54,000 pounds, save 6,300,000 gallons of water, and reduce landfill by 2,700 cubic yards.

In choosing a SYBEX book you are not only making a choice for the best in skills and information, you are also choosing to enhance the quality of life for all of us.

The FoxPro® 2.6 Codebook

Yair Alan Griver

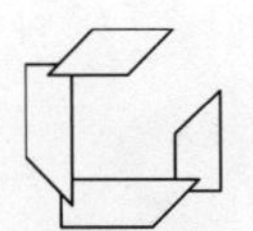

SYBEX® • *San Francisco* • *Paris* • *Düsseldorf* • *Soest*

Developmental Editor: David Peal
Editor and Typesetter: Guy Hart-Davis
Chapter Art: Charlotte Carter
Production Assistant: Lisa Haden
Indexer: Matthew Spence
Cover Design: The DesignSite
SYBEX is a registered trademark of SYBEX Inc.

Library of Congress Card Number: 94-65692
ISBN: 0-7821-1551-9

Manufactured in the United States of America

10 9 8 7 6 5 4 3 2 1

As before, this book is dedicated to my wife, Jan. She's made it through two books now and just knows that there may be a number three one day....

Foreword

Yair Alan Griver, known affectionately within the FoxPro community as YAG, has a long-running record of excellence and contribution to the database development community spanning more than eight years.

His articles in *Data Based Advisor*, *FoxPro Advisor*, and *FoxTalk* have offered many practical insights into database programming and design. He's developed many sophisticated applications for major corporations, and is a first-rate trainer. YAG is consistently rated by attendees as one of the best speakers at our Developer Conferences, and has been an active and helpful presence on our FoxForum and CompuServe. He's made many significant contributions to the product line during beta testing as well.

What made YAG's original *FoxPro Codebook* such a handy reference was the immensely practical approach he took. I'm pleased to see that this edition is just as packed with examples, useful tips, and methodology advice to give any programmer many useful constructs to consider. For example, the variable and field naming conventions YAG proposes are not merely pedantry; he extracts maximum utility from FoxPro functions by taking advantage of a clever scheme. His ideas on code reusability and cross-application standardization are worthwhile and will save you significant time and effort.

I think YAG is a class act, and so is this book. I expect you'll agree.

Dr. David Fulton
Vice President and Database Architect
Microsoft Corporation

Acknowledgments

There are *tons* of people to thank this time (like there weren't enough last time). I'm sure that I'll forget some people, so please consider yourselves mentioned.

My coworkers at Flash Creative Management: David Blumenthal, Menachem Bazian, Ed and Elise Ziv, Bill House, Lior Hod, Miriam Frisch, Annette Delli Santi, David Lederer (the original Codebook Kid), Ari Neugroschl, Leslie Koorhan, Avi Greengart, Dan Freeman (that's Beautiful Hackensack, Dan), Paul Bienick, Jonathan Silver, Ed Benison, David Kosowsky, Debra Wolff, Pablo Geralnik, David Fullerton, and Bryan Caplowitz. This book is theirs also. They all contributed ideas, code, text, and a fun place to return to when writing this book got to be too much. Thanks a lot, fellow Flashers.

To Diana Lichstein, who created all the bitmaps and icons for the Windows and Macintosh versions.

To everyone on CompuServe's Foxforum: There is no better or closer forum around. I especially have to thank all of the people who made suggestions, recommendations and just helped out with *Codebook* questions. These people include George Berotti, Steven Black, Ted Brousseau, Chaim Caron, Jose Constant, Doug Dodge, Eldor Gemst, Dale Gilstrap, Tamar Granor, Michael Gurr, Erhard C. Gust, Steve Kern (not Steven!), Tina Newton, John Noffsinger, Joe Paquette, Robert Petruzzelli, Tony Scarpelli and George Stevenson. There is also a large group of Foxforum friends to mention: Pat Adams, Randy Brown, GillyFlower Chesapeake, Chip Doolittle, Nancy Jacobsen, Lucy Lockwood, Tom Meeks (of restaurant-mapping fame), Jordan Powell, Tom Rettig, Ellen Sander, Alan Schwartz, Lisa Slater and Bill Speights.

To all the folks at Microsoft who helped with creating Microsoft FoxPro and help to support it. Sherri Bruhn Kennamer, Susan Graham, Morris Sim, Roger Bischoff, Chris Pudlicki, Blaise Mitsutama, Bob Fortner, Steve Murch, Tod Neilsen, Walt Kennamer, Janet Walker, Michael Mee, and of course, Dr. Dave Fulton.

To two friends no longer with us, Glenn Hart and Tom Kemm.

To my parents and brothers, who understood when I spent a trip home working on this book.

To my in-laws, who didn't fuss when I missed a few get-togethers working on this book.

To my friend Kory Kessel, the originator of the name YAG. You finally made it into a book.

To my editors, David Peal and Guy Hart-Davis. They worked incredibly hard under tight time constraints to make this book possible.

Finally, I have to mention my cat, Chushie, who now has the dubious distinction of having been mentioned in at least two FoxPro books, by two different authors.

Table of Contents

Introduction

I have made many changes and enhancements to the code since the original *FoxPro Codebook* appeared for FoxPro 2.0, and I have changed the focus of the book from developing event-driven applications to a discussion of an *approach* to developing PC applications that focuses on FoxPro.

The non–FoxPro-specific sections of the book provide guidance for any development environment—not just for FoxPro. Selecting a flexible methodology and sticking to the parts that work will improve any development system. This book discusses the process of developing applications and provides an approach that will enable you to create event-driven FoxPro applications faster and with fewer bugs.

Changes and Enhancements

The main change in the code for the sample application discussed in *The FoxPro 2.6 Codebook* involves applying object-oriented capabilities to the toolbar in FoxPro in order to reduce the amount of code necessary for the original application-specific portion by a significant amount—over 70 percent. Furthermore, I have added enhancements to the original system. These enhancements include the further modularization of the application both by creating new reusable procedures and by adding data-driven OPENDBF() capabilities and a default data-driven BROWSE for each screen.

The second major enhancement to the new code is that the application is now multiplatform, running on DOS, Windows, and Macintosh platforms. All the reusable code has been transported and modified to be platform-correct; for instance, the message box windows now call the native Windows or Macintosh messaging/alert functions.

The application is now fully multiuser and uses a parent-to-child-to-grandchild relation to demonstrate techniques for creating one-to-many screen sets. Moreover, the screens are interdependent now: If you select a specific client in the invoice window and then select a customer window, the customer window will display the client that you are billing. Finally, I have added state-saving code to the application to allow users to click from one window to another while editing and return to exactly where they were.

The FoxPro 2.6 Codebook

The FoxPro 2.6 Codebook focuses more on an *approach* to developing applications than on the development itself. This is for several reasons: First, the hardware we developers are using to develop applications on and for is becoming more powerful and less expensive. Second, the software tools available to us can create larger portions of applications for us. Third, the types of applications we are being called on to create are also becoming more complex as we develop applications for a user base that is comfortable with and understands the capabilities of computers.

Early applications tended to be monolithic structures geared toward solving an unchanging business problem by using a software-development methodology known as the *waterfall model*. In the waterfall model of software development, you performed and completed one phase before "falling into" the next.

The typical steps in a waterfall model look like this:

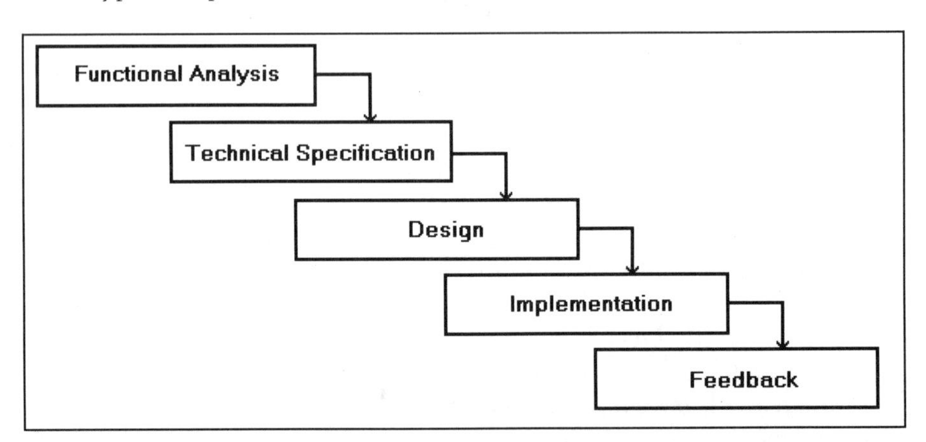

The development effort typically began with a functional analysis that focused on what the application had to do. The business issues were covered in this stage. Once the functional analysis was completed, the development group went off and developed a technical specification, including flow charts, database diagrams, and so on. Once the technical specification was finished, the application was developed, tested, and installed. After installation, feedback began, invariably necessitating extensive changes to the application.

The failings of the waterfall model brought developers to a better approach, one that involved constant communication with the end user. This approach can be seen as more of a spiral: It involves going through the same steps of functional analysis, technical analysis, and development, but in bite-sized chunks. The developer obtains a global view of the application first, then develops smaller pieces of it while keeping the user involved by using *prototyping* during analysis and *milestones* during installation.

Prototyping moves a portion of the development section into analysis. Using tools such as screen and menu builders, you can quickly develop the look of an application. Using core sets of reusable code, you may even be able to create a working model of the application, allowing the user to become more comfortable with the "look and feel" of the proposed system. Users can then relate their business needs to a sample application a lot more easily than to a paper sketch.

Using a prototyping approach has two other advantages: It allows you to get to the correct design and solution *before* doing the "guts" coding, and equally important, it achieves buy-in with the end users. They can see their recommendations coming to life, and will have an investment in the success of the software that you are creating.

The *milestone* approach to software delivery complements the prototyped analysis. The developer delivers milestones—working, completed sections of the application—over a span of time. Using this approach, the developer first installs a core set of functionality, such as a section that allows the maintenance of "setup" data (for instance, client information in an accounts receivable system), and trains the clients on that portion of the application. This allows the users to begin entry of data, become comfortable with the system, and suggest enhancements and changes to the application before it is completed and it becomes more difficult to modify. Finally, since the users are training and working with only a subset of the complete application, they do not get overwhelmed by the enormity of the entire product. Using the milestone approach, a user learns the entire process one task at a time, and actually enters useful data throughout, ensuring proper testing of all the application. All the test data in the world doesn't compare to real-world data entry.

Once the final milestone is delivered and the entire application is in place, the users can be confident that they have a system that they understand and that meets their needs, and the developers can be confident that they have reduced support calls and maintenance issues.

How This Book Is Organized

This book discusses how to keep communication flowing between members of a development group and between developers and their clients. The code portion of the book (which is still the main focus) stresses the use of object-oriented techniques and reusable code to enable the developer to quickly develop prototypes and finished applications, facilitating the development and delivery approaches explained above.

The book is divided into two parts. Part One discusses development issues in a global context, explaining the goals of the development approach. Part Two includes the code for a complete application and discusses the unique and desirable features in the code. Unlike the code sections in the original *FoxPro Codebook*, Part Two contains the code in only one format: a "picture" view that displays the screens, menus and reports object by object, allowing the developer to recreate the code using FoxPro's tools. To develop applications in FoxPro, one needs to use the tools—especially in a graphical environment, with its finer control over the look of an application—so we have provided a method of recreating the code using those tools.

Is This Book for You?

Part One of this book will benefit any developer, because it discusses the issues that arise in application development in today's fast-changing world.

Part Two is geared towards the intermediate-to-advanced FoxPro developer. It assumes that you have a basic knowledge of the FoxPro command set and the use of the Power Tools. The book discusses an approach to using the commands and tools rather than telling you what each command or tool does.

From reading this book, you will gain an understanding of the issues involved in developing large-scale applications. You will also gain a methodology that eases development in FoxPro by incorporating reusable code and object-oriented techniques.

Accessing the Sample Application via CompuServe

I have posted a copy of the running FoxPro application on the SYBEX forum on CompuServe, including selected reusable code modules from the book. The back of the book includes an order form for a diskette containing all of the book's code as well as an advanced version of the book's code, and some tools to make your FoxPro development easier.

FoxPro 2.6

During the final editing of this book, Microsoft began beta-testing on FoxPro 2.6. FoxPro 2.6 includes a number of wizards for end-users as well as enhanced dBASE IV compatibility. FoxPro 2.6 is compatible with all the code and methodologies detailed in this book.

New Capabilities in FoxPro 2.6

FoxPro 2.6 contains added commands, functions, and screen-generator directives of particular interest to the professional FoxPro developer (to whom this book is geared). These new capabilities do not, however, affect anything in this book.

These are the most useful of these new capabilities.

OBJVAR(<expN>) — This function returns the object name (with the full alias) of the current object or the object associated with the number that you can pass it.

BLANK — This command allows you to blank out a record. It can be used with ISBLANK() to provide for some NULL support.

ISBLANK() — This function differs from the EMPTY() command in that it returns a true only if the field is truly blank. For instance, EMPTY() returns a true if a numeric field contains a 0. ISBLANK() will only return a true if the field has no number in it. This can help in calculating averages where you want to ignore empty records, but include records where a 0 has been entered:

```
CALCULATE AVG(nAmt) FOR NOT ISBLANK(nAmt)
```

PRTINFO() — This function returns the page orientation and paper size for the currently selected printer in FoxPro for Windows.

SYS(1037) — This function calls up the Windows printer-selection dialog box.

SET FIELDS TO — This command allows you to limit the fields that the various FoxPro commands and functions work with.

SET KEY	This command allows you to limit the range of records that are acted upon by FoxPro. You define the key range (which must agree with the current index).
ISREADONLY()	This function returns true if the current table is opened NOUPDATE (in read-only mode).

PART 1

Developing FoxPro Applications

Chapter 1

Developing Applications: The Big Picture

In today's ever more powerful technological environment, businesses and corporations are looking to PCs and networks more and more to solve their business problems. As more mission-critical applications are planned, developed and implemented, the scope and complexity of these projects are growing to include business requirements never before considered manageable in a PC/network environment. The power of the PC/network environment has convinced many firms, from the Wall Street investment houses to many smaller organizations, that complex technology is now affordable. Downsizing is now the watchword as companies seek to increase the responsiveness of their development staff to business requirements and decrease the operating costs of their MIS operations.

Part of the lure of the PC environment has always been the relative ease with which applications can be developed. The tools available for the PC are more user friendly and feature-rich than those available for their "big iron" counterparts—mainframes, minis, and high-end servers. PC programmers have developed, to a great degree, as direct opposites of their control-oriented larger-system colleagues. Some programmers born and bred to the PC consider much of the documentation and controls accepted as normal in the larger-systems environment quite useless. Data Flow Diagrams, Entity Relationship Diagrams, Change Request Forms and all those other requirements so common in the larger systems arena have traditionally been viewed as hindrances in the PC environment.

But things are changing. Now that the sizes of applications and development projects have grown, the tricks and tools of old are becoming requirements in the PC environment. More and more firms are relying on the formal requirements so common in larger systems environments to help control the life cycles of their projects.

This chapter discusses some of the more common issues a developer and project leader must deal with when working on larger applications in FoxPro. It looks at both problems common to these tasks as well as possible solutions for dealing with the inevitable complexities inherent in the development of larger applications.

What Is a Large Application?

What is a "large application"? There really is no clear definition. Every person may have a different opinion about what constitutes a large application. But for the purposes of this book, let us define a large application as an application that:

- Has a large scope
- Typically takes longer than one month to develop

- May require multiple developers (and often does)
- Represents the core system for a business activity or entity

Remember, the guidelines and techniques discussed in this book apply to all applications that you can develop. Having a scientific, structured approach towards development will only help you in the long run. Such an approach becomes more important as the application grows in size or in number of developers, but the good habits that you learn to use will enable you to move towards large-scale development without having to change your way of thinking.

Key Issues in Application Development

When developing an application, you have to manage not only your technical staff—you must manage your client as well. Having a satisfied client is a matter of perceptions—theirs and yours. If you have knocked yourself out on a job, and are very happy with the results, but the client is upset because you haven't returned their phone calls promptly, you have not completed your responsibility and your engagement successfully. Similarly, if your client is happy, but your development staff has created an unmaintainable application, you again have not achieved your goal. One of the reasons that people dislike being told to maintain legacy applications is because such applications become full of spaghetti code, making it impossible to read the code or understand the logic involved. If your staff shares a commitment towards design and coding excellence, you will not encounter this problem. The upcoming chapters discuss approaches that enable you to enhance your client communications, and techniques that help you keep your staff focused and "on the same page."

Communicating with Clients

It would be impossible to compile a list of all the possible issues and problems that could arise when developing a large application—there is no limit to the issues that may arise during the development of *any* system. In all cases, however, problems that develop can usually be attributed to one basic issue: communication between the development staff and between the development staff and the client/user. You can avoid spending an inordinate amount of time by establishing suitable communication procedures between all the individuals involved in a development project.

There are many ways to improve communication during the development process. Here are four:

- Developing complete functional and technical specifications
- Implementing coding standards and naming conventions
- Requiring proper technical documentation both within the code and in printed form
- Establishing regular meetings with the development staff

In this section, I will discuss procedures to improve communications with our clients and users and enhance the design and development process of any large-scale application.

Some Basic Principles

What is a client? A client is anybody for whom you are writing an application or anybody to whom you are giving advice. Whether you are a consultant working for another company or a developer working in an organization, a large part of your job consists of dealing with client management.

Clients care about one thing: their business goals. They have a business to conduct and they want—rightly—to get it done in the most professional way that they can. If they wanted to do the development themselves, they would not call in professional developers like us to work with them in designing and creating systems to solve their business needs.

The key to maintaining effective communication with your clients is to make sure that they have considered all their business requirements and then to keep them involved in the development process. The client is the key to the development process. Clearly, we developers should not meet with the client only once, then disappear and develop our systems in a vacuum; we should keep the client, the ultimate user of our work, involved at all steps in the development process. Clients must have a hand in developing the functional specification of the system and agree to the technical design of the system; they should be kept updated on the development progress as well. The fewer surprises clients have, the fewer problems we developers will have.

The Needs Analysis (Functional Specification)

A *Needs Analysis* or Functional Specification is a review of the business requirements that will have to be solved by the application to be developed. This review must be complete and exhaustive. Bear in mind that, in many cases, the client may not be fully aware of all their requirements.

A Needs Analysis is the first step in determining how the client's business needs can best be met with an application. The Needs Analysis provides the development team and the client with a proper basis for determining the business requirements and the functionality needed in a system to automate procedures.

To complete a Needs Analysis, the developer should meet with the client's personnel to determine the current business process to be automated and enhanced. It is frequently more informative and certainly equally important to meet with the clerks and operators who actually perform the day-to-day work than with upper management. Upper management will know what they need for *their* decision-making purposes but may not be aware of the operational difficulties faced by the personnel who actually perform the work. Any complete system must service the needs of the entire organization, from the data-entry operator to the highest officer and manager.

The Needs Analysis process should result in a document that is reviewed by *all* involved parties. Only when all involved parties agree on the requirements of the organization can the the developer start designing the system and developing a technical specification.

In many cases, an off-the-shelf package can be found that fulfills the requirements of the organization. Performing the Needs Analysis allows you to efficiently search for existing software, possibly reducing the costs to your client. Often, however, existing software cannot be found, or only solves a portion of the problem. In these cases, the developer should draw up a Technical Specification that details what code must be written to accomplish the task.

The Software (Technical) Specification

The Software Specification contains the design of the software, and is the beginning of the development process. The Software Specification is a complete functional and design specification of the software as it will appear after development and includes menus, sample screens, a data dictionary with field-level help, and sample reports.

The developer should not simply mail the Software Specification to the client—the developer must meet with the client and review the document carefully with them. In this way, you can ensure that the client has reviewed the document carefully before signing off on it.

The Software Specification results in a:

- System prototype

Part of the Software Specification process calls for design of screens, reports, menus, and database structures. This is a prototype of the system. *This prototype is the basis for the completed system*. Thus, much of the work in the specification process is directly leveraged during the development process.

The core of the Software Specification process is to actually develop the menus, screens, and report layouts *as they will exist in the system*. The Software Specification results in a base of code that will be leveraged during the final development of the system. Since your prototype is actually done in FoxPro, the time spent on this portion of the system directly benefits the ultimate development effort. Furthermore, your client can be sure that what they signed off on in the Software Specification is what they will receive in the final product.

This is where the design tools built into FoxPro and using a design methodology (such as the one detailed in this book) become extremely important. Screen and Report Design, which represents the bulk of time spent in designing the look and feel of a system, can be done using the FoxPro Screen Builder, Menu Builder, and Report Writer. The menus, screens and reports created using these tools are then rolled into the system when the design is finalized and the development process begins. This represents an economical use of resources and time.

- Project design "bible"

All subsequent development is based on the specification. The software, when delivered, will look and behave as stated in the Software Specification. The Software Specification becomes the measure for determining status and completion of the project.

This is, perhaps, the most significant purpose of a Software Specification. Before the system is actually developed, the client has reviewed the entire design of the system and has signed off on the specification. Once the design is complete, all coding is done *to the requirements of the specification*. While business requirements may well change during the development of the system, at the very least the prototyping aspect of the Software Specification affords the developer the comfort of having a document that has been reviewed and approved by the client on which to base development of the system. The Software Specification thus eliminates questions as to what was agreed to and what is to be included in the final product.

An additional benefit of the system specification is that it allows the development team the ability to manage the dreaded "Scope Creep."

Managing "Scope Creep"

Scope Creep refers to that all-too-often–encountered phenomenon whereby a project scope begins to grow, seemingly of its own accord. Scope creep happens frequently when a system is designed and development begins—the client then begins to ask for additional features before the original design has even been implemented! Completing a Software Specification prior to developing the system forces the client to consider their requirements very carefully. Given the results of the Needs Analysis and the Software Specification, the client should, by that time, have considered most, if not all, of their requirements at the outset. As a result, the developers are less likely to be presented with requests for enlarging the scope of the system.

Here the Software Specification process shines. Clients rarely are fully aware of what actually goes into a systems-development project. Forcing them to define and specify what they need and want, as well as agreeing to the complete design of the system before the development is undertaken, results in their being more aware of what will actually go into the development of their software. This will tend to make them more understanding of the possible results of making significant changes to the scope of the project in midstream.

Changes to an application are inevitable. Business needs change and, as a result, the scope of the systems to handle those needs must change along with them. Most frequently, however, Scope Creep will rear its ugly head because the system was not properly planned in the first place. If the homework is done up front, major unforeseen scope changes are less likely to occur.

Furthermore, agreeing on a Software Specification helps to manage such changes as are deemed necessary. The Software Specification makes it easier to explain to a client that adding the newly requested feature will change the schedule in a certain way, and allows you to present (*in writing*) the cost and time estimates for the new feature.

Finally, good system documentation helps you to visualize where requested enhancements should go, which modules will be affected, and enables you to standardize an approach to application support.

The Update Process

At all times in the process of defining, designing and developing systems, the developer should keep the client informed of all significant developments. Depending on your relationship with the client, and the degree to which the client *wants* to be involved in the process, this procedure can range from regular phone calls to establishing a regular series of meetings for discussing the progress of the project.

Maintaining frequent contact with the client is crucial for many reasons. Here are just a few:

- Maintaining regular contact with the client avoids miscommunication.

Miscommunication is a developer's worst enemy—misinterpreting a client's statement and then designing the system around that misinterpretation can be disastrous. Despite the care of the Software Specification, there will always be issues that the developer will have to resolve during the development of the system. (Let's face it, we can't think of *everything* beforehand.) Maintain regular contact with your client to reduce the risks that this misinterpretation will get too far without being caught.

- Specification changes can be caught as quickly as possible.

Maintain constant contact with your client to stay in tune with the client's business and catch any possible scope creep or design changes earlier. Frequently, just by talking to your client, you will catch drifts of possible changes in their organization that can affect your system. Always remember that forewarned is forearmed.

- You can avoid nasty surprises.

Clients hate surprises. Then again, so do developers. When developers and clients do not maintain good communications, each side can easily make improper assumptions about what the other is doing. Keep the lines of communications open and you will avoid this nasty problem.

- Frequent contact minimizes difficulties.

Occasionally, any project can fall behind schedule. An unforeseen difficulty will arise, a developer will be called away for a family emergency, or something will alter the delivery schedule. Keeping in touch with your client minimizes the negative effects of these issues. This way, clients don't get the feeling that they hear from you only when something goes wrong, and your relationship stays friendly rather than becoming adversarial.

Software Development and Delivery

Managing the delivery of your software project is equally critical. You can frequently organize large applications into *milestones*, small portions of the application, such as the setup files, that you can deliver one by one to the client. Rather than developing the entire application in one piece, divide the project into milestones so that you can deliver it in independent components.

The milestone approach has significant advantages for both the developer and the client. It accomplishes the following key objectives:

- Allows the client to go "live" on the system in a shorter time frame.

Typically, setup tables and their maintenance routines are delivered in the first milestone. This allows the client to begin data entry. By the time the developer has delivered the last milestone, the client has finished their data entry and can go "live" almost immediately.

- Provides a second exceptionally effective tier of software testing.

The best way to fully test applications is with real data. The client who receives the software in milestones has the opportunity to enter their data and ensure that there are no coding difficulties. Bugs that the client discovers can be quickly traced and corrected. Furthermore, the developer benefits by virtually eliminating all technical support calls once the product has been delivered in full.

- Training provided with each milestone ensures that the client uses all software to its fullest capabilities.

Since the software is delivered in milestones, the client learns the appli cation in a more considered approach and time frame. They can visualize how components are linked together and do not face information overflow from having to learn too much in one sitting.

- The developer has a far better chance to change and modify the software in a simple and timely fashion.

If the client requires scope changes, the developer can implement the changes more easily earlier in the development process than later. The client who receives the software in milestones can work with the software and request and receive any necessary changes to the specification earlier than if they received the software in one unit.

This approach also lets the client discover more quickly any elements of the specification accidentally omitted from the software and the developer can add them more easily.

Communicating with Your Team

When working on a large application, proper communication between members of the development team is vital. Although each member of the team may be assigned to separate and distinct portions of the project, it is nonetheless critical for all members of the team to remain in constant contact as to progress, technical design, and programs created. The better you can keep communication between members of your team going, the easier it will be to manage the process.

The Specification Process

It is useful for the team leader (if not the whole team) to be in the "loop" during the development of the two specifications. We prefer to have the developers actually develop the Functional and Software Specification documents. The greater the involvement of the development team in the specification process, the better organized it will be come development time.

Always remember that developers rarely work well in a vacuum. The closer they are to the functional and design specifications, the more familiar they will be with the *reasons* behind the various requirements. Additionally, since the design specification includes a fairly complete prototype of the application, a developer should be involved in the creation of this prototype. This will lead to greater creativity from the developers and a *much* more efficient development phase.

Team Meetings

The best way to maintain communications between team members is to *talk*. Allow developers frequent opportunities to talk with each other. There is no substitute for this tried and true approach. Despite the fact that there are few enough hours in the day, even taking a half-hour or an hour out of a day for updates and meetings, especially when the heat is on, can save many hours of development time. The schedule of meetings will vary based on the project, the size of the team, and where you are in the development phase: The later you are in development, the more frequently you will need to have meetings.

Here's an approach to scheduling meetings during the development of a project. You may not want to schedule meetings this frequently, but the synergy produced by having all the team members communicate frequently cannot be underestimated.

Every morning, before everyone sits down to work, have a team meeting to review where everyone is and what work they feel that they will get done during the day. This meeting should *not* put people on the spot—rather it should ensure that everyone on the team knows where everyone else is concentrating their efforts. The developers can exchange ideas and discuss any problems that they are having; the team leader can make plans for testing the work and ensure that all the work will stay on schedule.

The morning meeting is also an ideal time for raising technical issues. Many developers, once they get into their work, are loath to break away for anything more than a cup of coffee. Technical questions and the problems of a colleague can inhibit creative flow and focus. The morning meeting lets developers raise issues that did not have to be raised the minute they presented themselves.

Team meetings are important not only for the *development* phase but also for all the other phases of a project, such as the various specification phases.

Design Specification

During the design specification stage, discuss with your development team how to handle things during the system's development. Having many eyes look at the design gives you the benefit of having many minds in on the process as well as the increased efficiency that comes from being familiar with the design specification from the inside.

Documentation

Define standard rules for system documentation that will allow new team members to get a running start when they join a project that is under way. Many of the coding conventions discussed in the *Technical Issues* chapter can be used to enhance communication between developers, but these don't take the place of having a central location where team members can look for the rules behind the application.

Chapter 2

Technical Standards and Guidelines

In any development situation, especially when you are dealing with multiple developers, it is extremely important to establish proper methodologies for reducing the amount of time required to code and debug your applications. You need to establish proper standards and guidelines, creating a base of reusable code that can be leveraged during the development process and properly establishing the procedures for testing the application under development.

All developers in an organization must be able to intelligently read and understand each other's code. Developers come and go, but the project must continue—indeed, the project often has a lengthy life of its own. Establishing a suite of standards and guidelines for developing applications is the key to this processing. Please note that I am not recommending standards for the sake of standards. In too many offices, when a new person is hired, they are given a 3,000-page book of "coding standards." This book simply collects dust because it is too overwhelming, and nobody is going to look up the proper rule to govern every situation, particularly when they're facing a deadline. When developing your own standards, make sure they can be understood immediately and that they provide a large enough gain to offset the use of the standard. Remember, conventions may seem restrictive. You must show your personnel that the standard actually enhances their day-to-day work by relieving drudgery from the coding that they must perform.

Some Standards

In this section, we will review some recommended standards.

Naming Conventions

This book will use a variation on Hungarian Notation as a naming convention. This convention has increased in popularity since the original FoxPro Codebook, and has become a favored standard among Xbase developers.

FoxPro has three essential problems with the way that variables are used.

1. They are limited to ten characters
2. There is no strong scoping capability
3. There is no strong typing capability

Due to FoxPro's limit of ten characters for field names and variable names, each character comes at a premium in identifying the object and providing clues to its type and behavior. Rather than using underscores to separate name elements, and thus wasting a needed character, we use capitalization instead to distinguish between parts of a name:

```
STORE "Griver" TO last_name
```

becomes

```
STORE "Griver" TO LastName
```

FoxPro provides two types of variable scopes: PUBLIC and PRIVATE. A PUBLIC variable is available throughout the application, and a PRIVATE variable is available in the current procedure *as well as all lower-level called procedures*. Creating a black-box routine becomes more difficult because a variable, if used in a lower procedure, will overwrite the same named variable from the higher procedure. Explicitly calling the black-box routine's variable PRIVATE creates a new instance of that variable and hides the higher version of that same named variable.

The fact that FoxPro uses weak typing is both one of its great strengths and one of its greater weaknesses. Every variable can have its type changed at will. This can lead to a maintenance nightmare:

```
PUBLIC ClientID
ClientID = 1
```

This is the code in the first module of an application. After a number of years, a routine is added to a month end closing process that includes the following line of code:

```
ClientID = STR(ClientID)
```

Your ClientID numeric variable has just become a string! This allows the developer to use it as needed in their routine, but upon exit from the routine, the code that had been in place for years will crash because it expects a numeric value. Worse yet, it becomes very difficult to trace where the variable type changed, since a month-end routine is only run twelve times a year, and if the client runs it and then exits the application to do something else, the bug will occur even more randomly.

As a result of the scoping and typing problems, we will use the first two characters of our variables to show the scope and type of the variable.

The first character indicates the SCOPE of the variable:

g	>	Public
l	>	Private
t	>	Parameter
j	>	Junk Variable—Used in a black-box routine. Procedure must start out with: PRIVATE ALL LIKE j*

The second character indicates the variable TYPE:

c	>	Character/Text
n	>	Numeric
d	>	Date
l	>	Logical
m	>	Memo
a	>	Array
h	>	Pushbutton
b	>	Menu Bar
u	>	Unknown (used for variables that may change types)

This will take care of both of our problems. If we start our black-box routine with

```
PRIVATE ALL LIKE j*
```

all variables beginning with the letter *j* will automatically be made PRIVATE for us, assuring us that they are hidden from higher routines. Please note that this syntax is somewhat slower than explicitly naming every variable PRIVATE, so I do recommend referencing each variable explicitly, but when developing the black box, it definitely makes things easier and assures that no mistakes will be made.

Explicitly typing the variable in the second character will automatically ensure that the typing problem shown above will not occur:

```
PUBLIC gnClientID
gnClientID = 1
```

If the new developer is following these standards, the new routine would create a private character instance of the variable:

```
lcClientID = STR(gnClientID)
```

Using this standard, our code becomes easier to read and much more maintainable. As I mentioned before, adhering to standards assures that developers in a group can read each other's code, and the development effort becomes easier.

Field Naming

Our field-naming standards follow the same convention as variables, except we only use the field type as the first character.

C > Character

D > Date

L > Logical

M > Memo

N > Numeric

B > General (BLOB—Binary Large OBject)

The table alias will be used (with the . separator) to indicate the table from which the field is taken. Therefore it is not necessary to include part of the table name in the field name (e.g., client.cAddress1).

Window Naming

The first character in a window name is always *w* to indicate a window as the "scope". The second character delineates the type of window that is being used.

R > READ (application) window

C > Control window

S > Status window (e.g., thermometer, status of a process)

M > MODAL window

The rest of the window name is the name of the generated SPR file. The type of window that you define will vary depending on why the window is created. You may have a longer list than the one presented here. The main issue here is to define the types of windows.

Adhering to these window-naming conventions allows us to determine the name of the program generated if we know the window name, and allows us to determine the window name from the name of the program.

```
wrCustomer  -  Customer.spr
wrInvoices  -  Invoices.spr
```

The code to do this check is straightforward:

```
IF UPPER(LEFT(<window name>,2)) = "WR"
   lcCurrSPR = SUBSTR(<window name>,3,8) + ".SPR"
ENDIF
```

Database Tables

We use an internal, unique key field on every dbf. This key is used to relate dbfs to each other. While there may be unique keys inherent in the table (such as a social security number), experience has shown that client-accessed unique keys do not always remain unique and unchanging. Furthermore, using the same field name (cID) for the unique key allows us to create black-box routines that reference the key ID, no matter which table we are working with.

Formatting Source Code

Adhering to standard formatting in source code can provide a large number of benefits. In particular, commenting standards allow you to create a set of routines that will automatically go through your source code, stripping out information from your comments and building developer's documentation for you.

Developers hate commenting code. For that reason, it becomes very important that you make it easy to do so. Provide a standard header file with a simple way to copy it into your program. If adding the comment is made relatively painless, and the gains in documentation are shown, then developers will do the commenting. Otherwise, sadly enough, all the standards in the world won't cause someone to do what they don't want to do.

Header Format

Standard programs use the following header identifying the author, project, description, and creation date and time.

```
*  Program...........: Prog1.Prg
*  Author............: Y. Alan Griver
*  Project...........: Common
*  Created...........: 03/08/93  20:14:06
*  Copyright.........: (c) Flash Creative Management, 1993
*) Description.......: Does something with something
*  Calling Samples...: m.lnTemp = Prog1()
*  Parameter List....: None
*  Major change list.:
```

Procedures and Functions use a modified version of the above as follows:

```
**********************************************
PROCEDURE proc1
**********************************************
 *  Procedure.........: xTabRpt
 *  Author............: Y. Alan Griver
 *  Project...........: Big Client Project 1
 *  Created...........: 03/08/93  23:11:27
 *  Copyright.........: (c) Flash Creative Management, 1993
 *) Description.......: Does something as a procedure
 *  Calling Samples...: Do xTabRpt WITH lcRepoName
 *  Parameter List....: tcReport—The report we are running
 *  Major change list.:
 PARAMETER tcReport
 PRIVATE ALL LIKE j*
```

Formatting Code

Code-format issues are, to a great degree, a matter of taste. This, in fact, is the heart of this issue. Since all developers have their own sense of aesthetics when it comes to formatting code, different procedures in the application will likely have different format conventions. Typical differences between formatting code deal with using tabs rather than spaces for indenting, the number of spaces to indent each level, how comments are formatted, and more.

Having different code formats in an application can be annoying, especially when one programmer has to change or leverage code that another has developed. It is important to establish standards that specify how code is to be formatted and commented. These standards will allow for a homogenous "look and feel" to the code in an organization.

Creating Reusable Code

Reusable code is any code module that does not make any assumptions about its environment. It takes care of itself, and can be "dropped" into any application, providing increased functionality with no necessary modifications. The key to reusable code is that it should only exist on one location on your drive/network, and should be called from multiple applications. In this manner, you have a core group of well-tested, bug-free code modules that you can rely on in your development effort. Furthermore, any enhancements to one of these modules will "ripple through" to every application that calls it, providing your users with enhanced capabilities with minimal effort on your part.

By creating reusable objects that you can drop into an application, you can significantly reduce the amount of time spent coding and debugging. One of the keys to creating reusable objects is that they must not affect the procedure that is calling them. For a more detailed discussion of various reusable code techniques, see Chapter 6, *Creating Reusable Objects*.

Interface Standards and Guidelines

Designing the user interface for an application in any language requires that the programmer be aware of the current standards in interface design, and their applicability to his or her own software. FoxPro 2.X enables the programmer to implement what is currently best known as either the Mac interface or the Windows interface. I will refer to this interface as a "mouse-driven" interface.

Much of the code in this book is devoted to "user-centric" application sections. Therefore, it is a good idea to review some of the objects available in a mouse-driven interface. These objects, combined with user-interface theory, can help us create easy-to-use, easy-to-learn, powerful applications.

A Description of Available Objects

The basic objects available in a mouse-driven interface are still new to some Fox programmers. Even some Windows applications do not necessarily adhere to the standards, most typically confusing a radio button and a check box. Therefore, a review of these objects is in order. A mouse-driven interface is typically composed of the following discrete objects.

Radio Buttons

Radio buttons are groups of choices where only one of the group is chosen. Selecting another in the group will move the marker, clearing the previous mark.

Radio buttons are similar to radio buttons on your car stereo. When you select one station, none of the others are tuned in. Likewise with this class of object. When you select one radio button, the other radio buttons are turned off.

Check Boxes

A check box is a single choice that is set ON or OFF.

Check boxes are like the check boxes on forms. Pressing the <spacebar> will insert or erase the X for you.

Pushbuttons

Pushbuttons are menu choices that initiate action of some type.

Pushbuttons can be assigned as the default "yes" option by preceding the prompt with the \! characters, and can be assigned as the default "no" option by preceding the prompt with the \? characters. The default "yes" option is automatically selectable by pressing Ctrl+Enter either in DOS or when KEYCOMP is set to DOS, and by pressing <ENTER > in Windows and Macintosh if KEYCOMP is set to Windows or Mac. The default "no" option is selectable by pressing <ESCAPE>.

FoxPro's sample code is full of pushbutton sets, groupings of pushbuttons that are connected to one variable. This practice forces the developer to use CASE statements throughout the snippets for those buttons. It also makes use of the message clause more difficult, and finally, forces all buttons to the same size, which can be a problem under DOS where screen real estate is more precious.

Making each pushbutton its own object allows you to place the action that should occur when that object is selected in that object. No CASE statements are required. It makes coding easier and allows you to move the buttons around and size them as necessary—all without modifying any code.

Scrolling Lists

Scrolling lists are boxes within a screen that, when activated, allow the user to scroll the list.

Scrolling lists are similar to the forms on which you have a choice of many selections and are asked to circle the one that you prefer.

One thing to remember about scrolling lists is that the "# of Elements" snippet points to the column that you wish to display, if you are using a two dimensional array to populate your screen object. Manipulating the "# of Elements" snippet can allow you to create left and right scrolling list objects.

Popups

Under DOS, popups consist of a boxed data field, with the selected choice displayed on screen. When activated, a popup list is displayed, allowing the selection of one of the bars.

DOS popups look like a deck of cards, with the top card showing. Pressing the <spacebar> will fan the cards, allowing you to place a new one on top.

FoxPro for Windows and FoxPro for the Mac display a popup as a pulldown. The information appears in a one line field, with a down arrow to the right. Clicking on the down arrow displays the list.

One nice trick that makes life easier for keyboard users is to KEYBOARD a {SpaceBar} in the WHEN of a POPUP. This causes the popup to open when the user enters the field, saving them a keystroke. Note that when KEYCOMP is set to Mac, you can only access popups with a mouse.

I have provided examples of these user interface elements in DOS, Windows, and Macintosh on the next two pages.

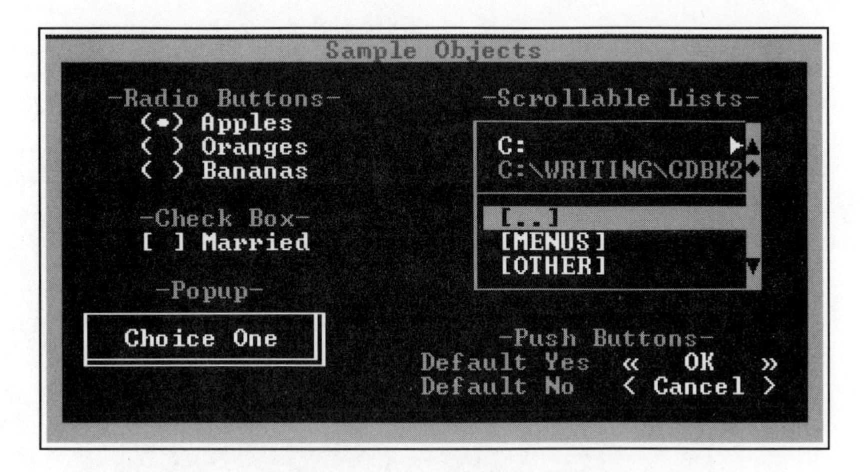

Sample FoxPro for DOS screen object

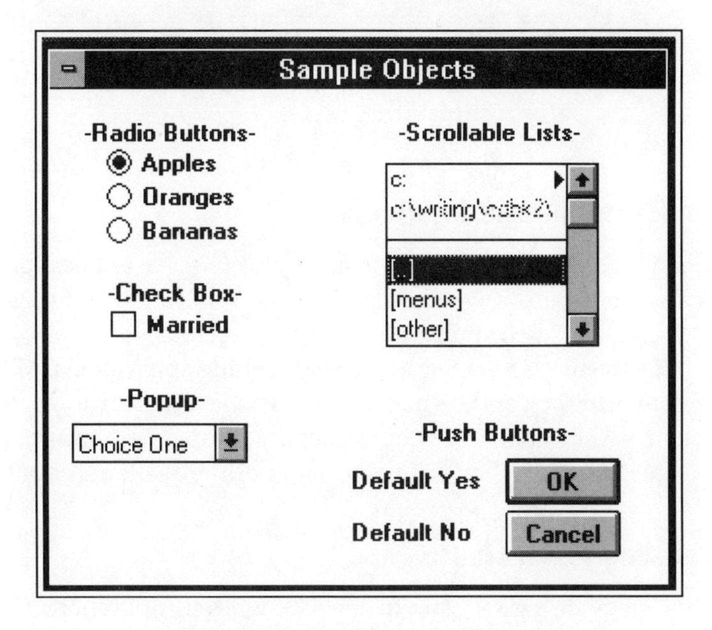

Sample FoxPro for Windows screen object

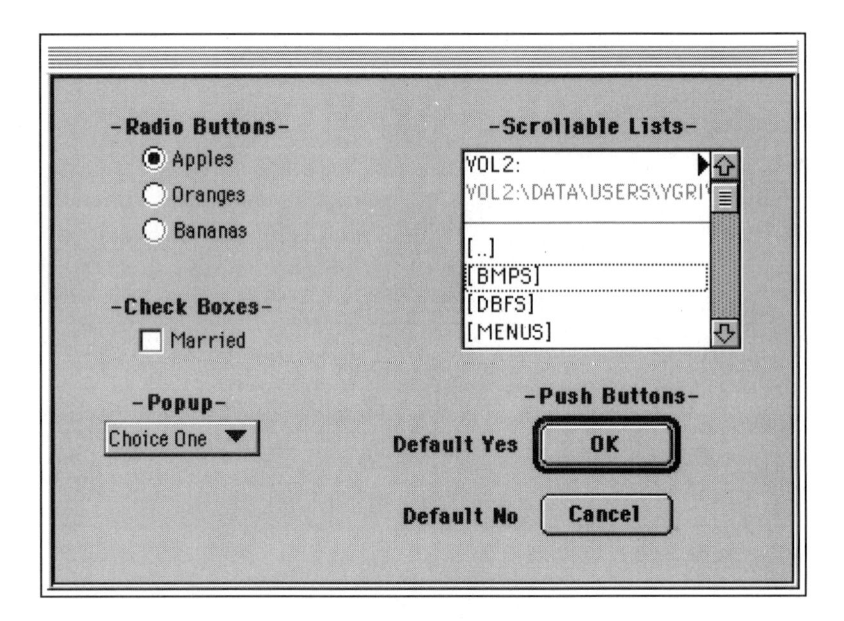

Sample FoxPro for the Mac screen object

Consistency in User Interfaces

Adhering to the published guidelines helps to make applications consistent with each other. A person who has learned one application that uses these interface guidelines will learn similar applications more quickly.

Consistency is also important in designing applications. Messages should always be displayed at the same screen position. Fatal error messages should be a specific set of colors, and should not vary throughout the application. Screens that are constantly changing colors and positions will only confuse the user.

Providing Visual Clues

Visual clues are a great asset to any well-written application. These clues let the user familiar with one part of the system quickly "pick up" or learn another section. These visual clues can take many forms including dimmed selections, screen-object design, and window design.

Dimmed Selections

This is a very powerful visual clue. It is also one of the easiest to explain. Anything that is dimmed is not currently available to the user.

Screen Objects

When the developer standardizes on the screen objects described above, a user can easily move from one application to another. For instance, a user can see a check box and immediately understand its function.

Dialog Boxes

Dialog boxes are used to communicate with the user. There are two types: *modal* and *nonmodal* (or *modeless*).

A modal dialog requires that the user perform some sort of action before the program will continue. An example would be a box that appears informing the user that the printer is off-line. The user is then instructed to put the printer on-line and press « OK » or <Cancel>.

A modeless dialog box does not require any action. For instance, during a pick list routine, a modeless dialog may pop up informing the user that he or she can "Use arrow keys to highlight a selection; press <ENTER> to select." Most data-entry windows are modeless.

A good visual clue for these types of dialogs is to select a "window type" for each one. Apple suggests using a double window with no shadow for a modal dialog, and a single-line window with a title for a modeless dialog box. The important thing here is to select one type for each and be consistent in your usage.

Menu Components

If a menu selection has submenus, place an arrowhead to the right of the item. If picking a menu item will result in a request for further information, put an ellipsis (...) to the right of the menu. Finally, if the menu is a selection that sets an attribute, put a checkmark to its left. These visual clues will help the user know what's going to happen.

Through the use of the menu builder, a menu can quickly be created with all of these features. The menu code generated will automatically handle submenus and markings. However, you must put the ellipsis into the prompt yourself.

Mixed Case	Research has proven that people recognize the patterns that mixed case provides better than ALLCAPS or all lowercase. Menu items should always be in mixed case.
Familiar Metaphors	If you are writing a Rolodex program, have the screen look like a Rolodex card. If you are writing a check-entry routine, try to mimic the look of a check. This is a *very* powerful technique. Users see these metaphors on-screen and say, "Oh, I know what that is—no problem."
Shortcuts	Provide keyboard shortcuts for the most frequently used functions. Your advanced users will love you for this. These shortcuts enable them to quickly access a menu function without having to take the extra step of accessing the menu.

Thinking about Your Users

Until recently, typical programs seemed to be written by computer people for computer people. This led to undecipherable help (if help is provided) and frightening error messages.

Help Systems	Help systems should have three levels: keys available, section description, and field-specific help. The first level of help is the one that tells the user what keys are available at the *current location in the program*. If users ever wonder, "What is the shortcut to apply a check?", they should be able to find this out quickly and easily. The second level of help is the section description. This is often associated with a menu item. It describes the office procedure that this menu item mimics. It explains what will happen when the user selects this menu item, and provides an overview of the selections that will follow. The final level of help is field specific help. This level describes the information that should be inputted into the field that the user has currently selected. It should not only describe what the field is, ("Selecting this radio button will specify that the information entered is

income information for the current applicant.") but should also describe any ramifications involved ("Once you select this button, you will be asked to enter the applicant's monthly income and the source of that income.").

Careful usage of FoxPro's MESSAGE command along with the SEE ALSO capabilities built into the FoxPro Help System, allow a programmer to quickly create a help system that meets all of the above criteria.

Error Messages

"FATAL ERROR", "INVALID HANDLE", "PROCEDURE ABORTED", "ILLEGAL USE OF NAME", "BAD DATE PROCESSED", "KILL THIS APPLICANT?"

All of the above are examples of hostile error messages. Try to avoid any of the negative words. Your messages should state what is wrong *and how to fix it.* The user will appreciate being told things in a calm and considered manner, and will also be quite happy to know what to do without having to telephone you.

A corollary to this guideline is the enhancement of your error-trapping routine to save a "picture" of your current STATUS and MEMORY to a database. This will allow you to know what the user was doing when the error occurred, without having to grill that user under a bare bulb in order to learn how to recreate the error.

Avoid Modes

Modes are restrictions that make life easier on the programmer, but harder on the user. A common example is the use of separate EDIT and ADD modes. The user can't add a record in the edit mode, and can't edit a record in the add mode. Picture what MODIFYing a STRUCTURE would be like if you had to use different commands when you wanted to add fields and edit them.

Ease-of-Use versus Power

Any system specification must be approached from two perspectives: the first-time user's and the power user's. A first-time user requires an easy-to-learn and easy-to-use system. Such a system will typically include various levels of help (overviews, menu sensitive, context sensitive), mouse support, pull-down windows, buttons and popups.

A user who has grown familiar with a system does *not* want to have to use a mouse or move through many menu selections and popups in order to do their jobs. The "power" data-entry person wants the computer to allow the quick entry of data, nothing more... hands on the keyboard at all times, no need to look at the monitor, just straight-ahead data entry.

A well-written program must accommodate both types of users. FoxPro includes an example of this type of capability. Any command that can be selected through the pull-down menus (for mouse users) can also be typed in the command window in order to speed up quick command work. Please note that I am not saying that only beginners use a mouse. I often find that certain functions are more efficient with a mouse, but a simple USE command to close a work area is quicker for me than calling up the view window and clicking on Close. FoxPro also maps common menu functions to keystroke equivalents. For instance, instead of selecting Edit and then Copy, the user can just hit ^C. Mapping common functions to a single keystroke is an easy way to provide enhanced ease of use for the advanced user.

In Conclusion

Please remember that all of the user interface books in the world are only meant to serve as *guidelines*. It is up to you, the software designer (note that I did not use the term programmer), to decide what is the best for your application. The important thing is to learn the principles behind all the research results. Designing a system that is easy to use and does not slow down a fast user, but at the same time helps the beginning user is not an easy thing to do. However, it *is* possible and does become easier with practice.

For Further Information

Here is a list of some books that you may want to read in order to further develop your design skills:

The Art of Human–Computer Interface Design (Brenda Laurel)

Addison-Wesley

A collection of articles by experts in the field, on everything from use of color to prototyping to on-line help systems.

The Design of Everyday Things (Donald A. Norman)

An extremely entertaining book that covers the design of everything from door handles to refrigerator controls to computer systems.

Human Interface Guidelines

Apple Computers

Addison Wesley

One of the best user-interface books, this explains the Macintosh interface in easy-to-understand terms.

Secrets of Effective GUI Design (Mark Minasi)

SYBEX Inc.

A short and engagingly written book that discusses how to plan and lay out your graphical user interfaces with style and clarity—the GUI equivalent of Strunk & White's *Elements of Style*.

The Windows Interface

Microsoft Press

The standards book for Microsoft Windows Development. The book comes with a diskette containing samples of different interface options.

Menu Standards

FoxPro allows the developer to create standard pull-down menus that have become the accepted standard in mouse-driven, window-based applications. While all platforms have evolved towards using pull-down menus, the text of the menus and the shortcut keys are different in each environment. The developer must decide what standards should be used in developing an application's menus.

Single-Platform Applications

The developer developing an application for a single platform should be careful to match the application's menus with the standards for that platform. The Macintosh and Windows environments have written guidelines for menu look and feel. DOS developers should choose the standards that are most familiar to their users, typically Windows.

Cross-Platform Applications

An application that must run across multiple environments (especially across Windows and Macintosh environments) poses an interesting puzzle for the developer. Do you develop your menus so that they are unique to each platform (thereby losing some of the cross-platform ease of FoxPro), or do you develop one look and feel that is the same across platforms?

The answer should depend on your users and how they interact with the machines that run your application. If your users run multiple applications on one platform, the first option (using a platform-correct menu) is the proper choice. If, on the other hand, your users will typically be running your application, or move between machines, having a consistent *in-application* menu is the proper choice.

In either case, do not fall into the multilevel submenu trap. FoxPro allows you to develop many levels of a menu hierarchy, which becomes very difficult for a user. It is better to have a menu option call a modal dialog box that is then used to launch your option. Note that FoxPro itself makes this choice: When you select File and then New, you are given a dialog allowing you to select the proper type of file to create. FoxPro's developers could have made the decision to create a nested submenu with the same selections, but did not. The rule of thumb to follow is that you rarely, if ever, want to go past a menu popup into a submenu.

Chapter 3

Multiuser Programming

One of the basic tenets of designing a multiuser application is to keep a record locked for as little time as possible. There have traditionally been three ways of looking at record locking:

- Direct reads
- Indirect reads
- Semaphore locking

Approach 1: Direct READs

FoxPro will automatically attempt a lock for you when you edit a record directly, and the lock will be kept in force until the end of the edit. The advantage of this method is that little programming needs to be done. It is all automatic. A copy of the record must be saved before the edit begins (either with a SCATTER MEMVAR [MEMO], or a COPY TO <tempfile>) in case the user decides to cancel the edit.

A modeless application creates further difficulties, however. A record is *always* showing on the screen, ready to be edited. In fact, with multiple windows, many records may be showing on the screen, ready to be edited. For instance, a customer information screen may be available at the same time as the CD entry screen. As software designers, we cannot allow all of these records to be locked at all times. FoxPro has provided an enhancement to the READ command, READ NOLOCK. Issuing a READ with the NOLOCK clause will allow FoxPro 2.5 to display the window without the capability of editing the fields until a lock is manually placed with a SHOW GETS LOCK. The SHOW GETS LOCK refreshes the screen and locks the record.

Approach 2: Indirect READs

Editing to a memory variable means that the record is never locked, and the user can do all the changes that are necessary. Cancelling the edit does not require that you do anything to the record because it was never changed. When the record is saved, you must lock the record and move the changes into the record (with a GATHER MEMVAR [MEMO] or an APPEND FROM <tempfile>). The problem with this method is that another user may have modified the record, and the current user's modifications may wipe out the first user's changes.

One solution is to lock the record immediately when beginning the edit, and to hold the lock until the edit is completed. The other solution is to compare the record to a second set of memory variables that have not been changed. If there is a match, the change may take place. If the two don't match, modifications to the record have taken place and you must program accordingly.

Approach 3: Semaphore Locking

A third approach that can be used involves a marker that lets you check whether or not someone has modified or locked your record. The simplest form of semaphore locking allows you to know that someone else has modified the record while you were editing (to memvars), without having to check every field to see if it has been modified. This form of logical locking involves the addition of an extra field to every dbf, in which you put a unique ID. When you wish to save your modifications, simply lock the record and check if the semaphore ID field has changed. If it has, you know that someone else has saved changes, and can act appropriately.

A more advanced form of logical locking would allow you to do edits to certain fields while other fields are being updated. For instance, if you have to globally update an inventory file with a new pricing scheme, you would normally have to lock the inventory file and change all of the records. While performing this update, nobody else could have access to the file. Using a semaphore locking scheme, however, you could let people know that you've locked the item price field, but allow them to update the on-hand field.

Concurrency Issues

The key thing to remember about multiuser programming in FoxPro is that *only the user that has the RLOCK() is viewing the current information*. FoxPro caches information at the local station, updating it as necessary. You can only assure that the user is seeing the most recent data if they have a lock on the record. Accordingly, you will want to perform an RLOCK() before allowing the user to edit the data.

Adding a New Record

I am a big believer in providing unique system-generated IDs for every record. Allowing the user to enter a unique ID for an employee (for instance, Social

Security Number) will only work until you hire the first person who doesn't have a social security number, or until you find two people with the same number (which has happened before). The key is that with a system-generated unique ID, you will *never* have to worry about duplication.

In a multiuser environment, we have to wrestle with the issues of concurrency. One accepted method of generating unique keys is to have a SYSTEM.DBF that has a field containing the next ID for a table. When you add a record, lock the SYSTEM.DBF, get the next ID, increment it, UNLOCK the record, and add your new data. In a large system this may cause a small amount of retries as two people try to add data at the same time.

The application in this book uses a unique approach. When a user logs on, they are given a unique ID for the login. When adding a record, the user's new ID is concatenated with the current date and time converted to base 207 (to reduce the amount of disk space that must be used), and that is used as the unique ID. Note that this procedure does not require *any* network traffic when creating a unique ID for a newly added record. Turn to Chapter 17, *Reusable Programs,* and see the sections titled METHODS.PRG, TRAFICOP.PRG, and NEXT207.PRG for examples of this function in use.

An enhancement to this function would be to save an audit table that connects the user name to all of their login IDs. In this manner, you can create a report showing the user that added the record, and the date and time that it occurred, simply by decomposing the unique ID of each record. Using a similar unique ID scheme for the semaphore field would allow you to view who changed the record last, and what date and time that person did so.

Event-Driven Environments

How can we handle locking issues in a multiwindow environment? There are a number of ways to address this situation. The easiest method is to force the user to select an <EDIT> button in order to begin an edit. This would either perform a SHOW GETS LOCK (if using direct editing), or would lock the record (if using locked record memvar editing). This method also requires that the event handler check to see if there is an edit in process, and to refuse any change of windows until the edit is completed. This will avoid keeping multiple records locked.

If you have decided to use the secondary memory variable-checking method before a record is modified, it is possible to allow the user to jump between windows, modifying memory variables (because the records are never locked), but the longer that the user doesn't save a record, the better chance that user has of coming back to an edit that will be refused due to another user's modifications. You must also provide a method for tracking the user's edits and saving them when they click between windows (there may be similarly named variables in two windows). A wonderful method of accomplishing this is to store the memory variables in a database table with the user's name, the window name and a memo field containing the memvars (use the SAVE TO MEMO command). This also allows you to keep the user in the application until all of their modifications have been approved or rejected. For a sample of how this is accomplished, see the TRAFICOP.PRG, SAVEMEM.PRG, and RESTMEM.PRG sections in Chapter 17.

In the application that we will be discussing, I have used the simple semaphore scheme described earlier. When a user edits a record, I check to see if it has been deleted by someone else. If so, I alert the user and go to another record. If the current record has not been deleted, I then attempt to lock the record. If the lock is successful, the record is moved into memvars and is unlocked, proceeding with the edit.

```
IF ! DelCheck()                         && Was record deleted?
   glEditable = .F.
   RETURN
ENDIF

IF RLOCK() OR NetLock()
   SCATTER MEMVAR MEMO                  && Refresh GETs
   UNLOCK
   _CUROBJ = 1
   glEditable = .T.
ELSE
   glEditable = .F.
ENDIF

RETURN
```

When the record is saved, the semaphore is checked to see if the data has changed. If so, the user is asked if they want to overwrite the changes. A more advanced check would actually show the user what fields have changed.

Chapter 4

Event-Driven Programming

It's buzzword time! Usability labs, horizontal management, graphical user interfaces, and mice are everywhere. What do all of these terms have in common? The concept of user empowerment. It is no longer enough to simply automate a task that the user performs; we are now being called upon to help the user make strategic decisions in their day-to-day work.

How can we use FoxPro 2.6 to accomplish this task? How do we use our knowledge of programming along with our knowledge of the business process that we are working with to provide a strategic partnership with that business?

The answer is to give the users power to do their job and give them power to analyze the information that is being collected. Many facets are involved in this approach. Two major ones include event-driven environments and FoxPro "tricks" that allow both you and the user to think beyond the edges.

Let's take a look at the concepts behind event-driven programming. In this type of environment, the user decides what they want to do, and they do it. This doesn't mean that there are no limits placed on the user—it is still possible (when necessary) to force them through a standard set of routines (for instance, when posting Accounts Receivable data to a General Ledger). This also doesn't mean that a user will *have* to open 50 windows at once—it only means that they have the *option* of doing so, *if they feel comfortable* working that way.

Think about how you and your co-workers work with FoxPro. You open as many windows as you can handle, closing some when you feel that too many are open. For instance, I can't handle having more than four windows open at a time. On the other hand, a coworker isn't comfortable unless he has a minimum of 70 windows open at once! We each find and work at our own level.

How are event-driven (or *modeless*) programs handled internally? Unlike standard applications that put the user in a menu and wait for a selection before running a subroutine that ends with the user back at the menu, event-driven programs wait for the user to do something (an *event*) and then a standard driver program (the *event handler*) is called that figures out where the user is coming from and where they are going to, and then takes the appropriate action. Note that the menu is always available in these applications, making it impossible to have the menu control the application (if the app stopped when the menu was active, the user couldn't call it while in the middle of a READ—for instance to cut or paste something).

Let's create a diagram of how an event-driven application would have to work:

1. Set up your environment (SET commands, USE your DBFs, etc.).
2. Tack your menu up on the screen (so it's ready when needed).

3. Provide some sort of wait state, so that the program is ready for the user's input.
4. Set up an event handler to deal with the input. The handler should look for (at the minimum) the following events:
   - The user exits the application.
   - The user clicks on a menu option to activate a window.
   - The user clicks from one window to another.
   - The user exits a window.
   - If you're using a toolbar/control panel, create it when the user pops up their first window, and remove it when the user closes the last window.
   - If the user closes a window with a control panel option, determine which window the control panel should now work with.

In general terms, that's all there is to it! Let's focus on some of the code that accomplishes the task of trapping events and handling them.

The Foundation READ

The Foundation READ is FoxPro's wait state. Menus created with the FoxPro menu builder cannot cause the application to wait whenever they are active, because they remain active all the time. Instead, the menus are tacked up on your screen, and don't do anything until they are selected. Once the menu program is run, the code execution continues. As a result, we can no longer write code that looks like this:

Set up environment

Open data files

Do the menu program ➟ Our app runs here

Close the environment

RETURN

If we did that, our application would end as soon as it began! We need a method of pausing our application, creating a "wait state" that will allow us to select something off the menu. The Foundation READ is a READ that is typically without GET commands attached. It has a VALID hooked onto it, allowing us to stay in the READ (as long as the VALID returns .F.) until we are ready to end the application. An interesting fact about the Foundation READ is that it is triggered whenever we fall back to its read level (typically level 1), allowing us to hook a user-defined function to it that determines what is happening at the time, and acts accordingly. This function is the event loop.

A benefit of using a Foundation READ instead of a DO WHILE loop is that a Foundation READ adds functionality in multitasking environments. While in the Foundation READ wait state, FoxPro returns control to the operating environment. For instance, using the Foundation READ on the Macintosh allows your user to click on the multifinder icon and select a different open application.

Coding the Event Loop

As we have seen, the event loop (or event handler) is called from the Foundation READ. What is the code that handles our events? Let's go through the event list mentioned earlier, and look at a simple example of the code that might be used.

The User Exits the Application

The first event that we need to test for is when the user wishes to exit the application. We test for this event first because there's no reason to spend time testing for other events in this case. Let's get the user out—fast! The code for this test involves the testing of a memory variable, glEndProg, that is set when the user actually picks the menu option that ends the application.

```
IF glEndProg
   RETURN .T.
ENDIF
```

The User Clicks on a Menu Option

This event also relies on the setting of a variable by the menu. The variable gcNextProg is set with the name of the screen program that the user wishes to run. We pass this name to the event handler so that all of the events are localized to this one area.

```
IF !EMPTY(gcNextProg)
   m.lcCurrSpr = gcNextProg
   gcNextProg = ""
   DO (m.lcCurrSpr)
   RETURN .F.
ENDIF
```

Note the use of FoxPro's named-expression capability in the line "DO (m.lcCurrSpr)." Since the memory variable contains a name, we can surround it with parentheses, in effect telling FoxPro that it should just DO the name inside the variable. This lets us refrain from using macro substitution (using the &), which would require FoxPro to compile the line at runtime. Named expression usage is much faster than macro substitution.

The User Clicks between Windows

This event requires a number of routines. One routine is called when the user clicks off a window, and the other is triggered when the user clicks on a window. Our event loop will handle the second of these two cases. We'll look at the routine to handle the first a little later.

Let's discuss what we are doing. FoxPro limits us to five read levels. We are using one for the Foundation READ, leaving four to work with. How do we allow the user to open any amount of screen sets, each controlled by a READ, when only four can be active at once? The answer is "magic." Just like a magician focuses an audience's attention on one hand while doing the real work with the other, we *end the READ of the window that we're leaving before we reissue the READ of the window we're entering*. In this way, all our windows remain at read level two.

The code for this event involves deciding what window we are clicking on and acting accordingly. This code can take the shape of a CASE statement, listing every window in the application as a separate case:

```
DO CASE
   CASE WONTOP("Customer")
      DO Customer.spr
   CASE WONTOP("Invoice")
      DO Invoice.spr
ENDCASE
```

The above code checks the top window, and runs the associated screen program. This causes the GETs to be reissued, and the READ takes place, putting us in an active window at read level two.

The problem with the above code is that it isn't reusable. Every window that we create has to be added to this CASE statement (and other statements below, as we'll see). Furthermore, any time we begin a new application, we'll have to create a new event handler. What we need to do is find a generic way to write this set of code.

Enter window-naming conventions. Since DOS limits us to eight characters for a file name, and Fox allows ten characters for a variable name, we can use the first two characters to give us the window "type." This turns the above code into:

```
IF UPPER(LEFT(WONTOP(),2)) = "WR"
   DO (SUBSTR(WONTOP(),3,8) + ".SPR")
ENDIF
```

The above code says that if the leftmost two characters of the top window are "WR" (for Read Window), DO the screen program that is defined by the last characters of the window name (after we've dropped the first two). We now have an event that will work for clicking on any window that is named with a "WR" naming convention.

The User Exits a Window

This routine is not part of our event loop, but is integral to keeping track of our read levels. Essentially, it is hooked into the DEACTIVATE clause of a "WR" window's READ, and makes the decision whether or not to end the READ when you have left the window. If there is code associated with the DEACTIVATE clause, it can decide whether or not the READ should end by returning a .T. (end the READ) or a .F. (keep the READ running).

In this routine, if you have left a "WR" window for a window in a different screen set, you would want to end the READ. However, if you have left it for another window that is participating in the current READ, you want to keep the READ going. The code to handle this function includes a test for when the user clicks on the close box of a window, forcing the window to disappear before you hit the test. In this case, we set a variable called glQuitting to .T.; this variable is used to designate that the user has decided to close the window.

Finally, the WREAD() function is used to let us know if we have clicked on a window that is part of the currently active READ or not. By returning a true if the user has decided to close the window (glQuitting is true) or if we are not clicking on a related window, the DEACTIVATE snippet properly ends the READ for us.

```
FUNCTION stopread
PARAMETER tcWindow
```

```
IF !WVISIBLE(tcWindow)      && Did the user close the window?
   glQuitting = .T.
   SHOW WINDOW wcControl TOP
ENDIF

RETURN glQuitting OR NOT WREAD()
```

Creating and Removing a Toolbar

To have the control panel appear when the user pops up the first window, simply include it in the screen set of all the "WR" type windows. When the "WR" window is closed, run a test to see if any other "WR" window is open (necessitating that we retain the control panel).

In order to do this, we make use of the WCHILD() function. The function takes two parameters, the parent window and the positioning number. The parent window is set to a null string, signifying that we wish to trace through the children of the desktop (in other words, all windows). Passing a zero tells FoxPro to begin with the oldest open window, and passing a one tells FoxPro to move up one in the list. In this way, we search through all of the open windows, from back to front, and when we find a "WR" window (which means that we still need the toolbar), we RETURN. If we loop through all open windows, we can release the toolbar.

```
PROCEDURE Efface
PRIVATE m.lcWindChck

m.lcWindChck = WCHILD("",0)
DO WHILE !EMPTY(m.lcWindChck)
   IF UPPER(LEFT(m.lcWindChck,2)) = "WR"
      RETURN
   ENDIF
   m.lcWindChck = WCHILD("",1)
ENDDO
RELEASE WINDOW (WONTOP())

RETURN
```

Closing an Application Window

When the user closes a window with a <Close> pushbutton, the WONTOP() becomes the control panel. This event requires that we discover which "WR" window was the last one manipulated (before the one that was just closed), so that we can reissue the screen program associated with that last manipulated window.

This function also makes use of the WCHILD() function. We search through all of the open windows, from back to front, and when we find a "WR" window (which may be the one to be run), we assign that "WR" window's screen program to a variable. When we are done looping, the variable will contain the screen program name for the last accessed "WR" window.

```
m.lcWindow = WCHILD("",0)
DO WHILE !EMPTY(m.lcWindow)
   IF UPPER(LEFT(m.lcWindow,2)) = "WR"
      m.lcProgram = SUBSTR(m.lcWindow,3,8) + ".spr"
   ENDIF
   m.lcWindow = WCHILD("",1)
ENDDO
IF !EMPTY(m.lcProgram)
   DO (m.lcProgram)
ENDIF
RETURN .F.
```

Putting the Final Pieces in Place

Now that we've looked at the code for our event handler, lets take a final look at the screens and menus that call the handler. The menu calls a generic routine whenever a user requests that a "WR" screen be run, and passes the screen program that is required.

```
PROCEDURE mhit
PARAMETER lcToBeDone

gcNextProg = lcToBeDone
CLEAR READ

RETURN
```

Setting gcNextProg primes the event handler to trap for a menu hit. The CLEAR READ command will end the read of any current "WR" window, falling us back to read level one, and triggering the event handler.

Our "WR" screens are set up as follows:

- The check box for [ ]Release Windows is turned OFF. *We will determine when to release the windows.* Fox would automatically do it when a READ ends, and we don't want that. We want the window released when the user closes a window—remember, we end READs when clicking from window to window, but we want those windows to stay open.
- We name the window following our naming convention: the screen program name with a prepended "WR."
- The DEACTIVATE snippet contains the expression: stopread("<window name>").
- The CLEANUP snippet contains the code:

```
IF glQuitting
   RELEASE WINDOW <<window name>>
   DO efface
ENDIF
```

If you prefer to, you can put this code in a procedure that is always called. For a look at our application's (more complete) event handler, see the section titled TRAFICOP.PRG in Chapter 17.

Chapter 5

Toolbars and Object-Oriented Programming

A control panel or toolbar provides a user with *interface consistency*. All the most commonly accessed functions of an application are called from one location, and work the same way no matter which window is on top. In this way, the user learns, for example, that the "Next" button moves to the next item in the current view, whether the window shows customer information or invoice information.

How do we create a toolbar that can "know" how to handle each window?

Consider two windows: Customer and Invoices. Customer only uses a single dbf file, and the code to perform a "Save" may be as simple as:

```
APPEND BLANK
GATHER MEMVAR
```

The Invoices window, however, consists of two dbf files, Header and Details. This window requires code along these lines:

```
APPEND BLANK
GATHER MEMVAR
INSERT INTO Details FROM ARRAY laDetails
```

Each window has different code associated with the same button, "Save". We need to discover a reusable approach to having the buttons know which routine to call.

Approach 1: CASE Statements

Let's begin with the simplest approach, a CASE statement. In this scenario, the "Save" button would check to see which window it's working with and runs the appropriate code. For this example, we'll assume that we've written a function, CurrWR(), that returns this window name:

```
DO CASE
   CASE CurrWR() = "Customer"
      APPEND BLANK
      GATHER MEMVAR
   CASE CurrWR() = "Invoices"
      APPEND BLANK
      GATHER MEMVAR
      INSERT INTO Details FROM ARRAY laDetails
ENDCASE
```

There are two problems with this approach:

- Every time you add a window, you have to add a CASE statement to each button on the toolbar.
- Every application needs its own unique toolbar—there's no reusability.

Approach 2: The IN Clause

This is the approach used in the original *FoxPro Codebook*. It uses our CurrWR() function to return the current application window, but then uses the IN clause of the DO command to call a standard procedure in the current window. The IN clause tells FoxPro to ignore its internal program queue and to use a procedure IN the specified file. Using this technique, each button would simply determine what window it is working with, and do a standard routine (for "Save", let's call the routine "SaveIt") IN the window itself. *Remember that earlier we showed that we can use a window-naming convention to find out what the screen program associated with it is.*

```
*-- First get the current screen program
lcCurrSPR = SUBSTR(CurrWR(),3,8)+".SPR"

DO SaveIt IN (lcCurrSPR)
```

In this case, each window's Cleanup snippet would contain a procedure called SaveIt that includes the code to handle the window's particular save function. This is better, as it allows us to create a generic toolbar for any application. Yet, it also has two failings:

- The IN clause slows things down.
- We have to duplicate code across windows. Every application has multiple single dbf windows. This approach requires that we add the same SaveIt code to all of them.

Approach 3: The Calling Stack

This approach takes advantage of the way that FoxPro generates code for screen sets. Our toolbar is part of every data-entry screen set. FoxPro *duplicates* the generated code from the toolbar into each of our resulting .SPR files. This means that when the Customer window is active, the toolbar code that is running is the code in the Customer screen program. We can now take advantage of the way that FoxPro looks for a program that you call. It searches its program stack in the following manner:

1. Current program file
2. SET PROCEDURE TO file
3. Another program in the stack (I'll explain this later)
4. A standalone PRG file

Looking at the above list, we see that there is no need to use the IN clause in our "Save" button's VALID snippet. Simply calling the standard SaveIt procedure will automatically find the one in the Cleanup of the current window because the toolbar code is duplicated in every SPR in which it is used. We can go further, however. Note that *if no procedure is found in the current program, FoxPro will keep searching for it along the stack.* This means that if we create a SAVEIT.PRG file, that contains the standard save routine for a single dbf, we can avoid putting a SaveIt procedure in the single dbf window's cleanup snippets, and FoxPro will run the PRG instead! Let's look at the code for the <Save> button:

```
*-- VALID of <Save> button
DO SaveIt
```

That's it! Now, let's look at what SAVEIT.PRG might contain:

```
*-- PROGRAM SaveIt
*-- Standard <SAVE> routine
APPEND BLANK
GATHER MEMVAR MEMO
RETURN
```

Finally, our Customer window's cleanup would be empty (causing the DO SaveIt to chain back to the standard SAVEIT.PRG), while our Invoices window's cleanup would contain:

```
*-- Cleanup for Invoice window
PROCEDURE SaveIt
APPEND BLANK
GATHER MEMVAR MEMO
INSERT INTO Details FROM ARRAY laDetails
```

We've solved the problems that we listed above. We now have a set of reusable toolbar buttons that properly call the necessary routines for each window. We've even set up a standard behavior for these buttons, and only have to *code the exceptions*. This is a very important feature, and a real timesaver when coding. Essentially, the minute we design a single dbf window and add the toolbar to the screen set, it becomes fully functional with no code! For multi-dbf windows, we only have to code the routines that may be different from our standard behavior.

There is one problem with this approach. Note that the SaveIt routine for the Details screen is essentially the same as the standard one, with one added line of code. Experience shows that most toolbar routines are similar. They adhere to the standard, but some have extra code that has to be run before or after it. It would be nice to be able to say, "Do the standard approach, and add this afterwards." Enter Approach Four.

Approach Four: The Methods Program

This approach takes advantage of the fact that FoxPro searches for a called procedure through all programs in its calling stack. If I have a program, TRAFICOP.PRG, which contains my Foundation READ, and the program stays in that program until the user quits, I can create another program, METHODS.PRG, which calls TRAFICOP. METHODS.PRG is set as the "Main" program in the Project Builder. Since METHODS.PRG doesn't end (it never hits the end of the file or a RETURN statement), it *and all procedures within it* remain in the FoxPro calling stack. Here's a sample of METHODS.PRG:

```
*-- Methods.prg
*-- Contains the methods for our toolbar
DO Traficop && Installs the Foundation READ
RETURN      && Doesn't hit here until after
            && the program ends

PROCEDURE SaveIt
*-- Standard method for <Save> buttons
APPEND BLANK
GATHER MEMVAR MEMO
RETURN
```

That's METHODS.PRG. It replaces the standalone .PRG files for every standard button routine. Now, since this procedure is in our calling path, we continue to simply say "DO SaveIt" from our button's VALID, knowing that it will be our default for single dbf entry screens like customer.

Our Invoice window's SaveIt procedure will look a little different than before, however:

```
*-- Cleanup for Invoice window
PROCEDURE SaveIt

* Call standard routine for header
DO SaveIt IN Methods.prg

* Add unique code for details
INSERT INTO Details FROM ARRAY laDetails
```

As you can see, this takes care of our last issue, that of duplicating standard code in our unique procedures. We've inherited the standard behavior and enhanced it. I'm sure that you've noticed the use of the IN clause, however. This is where we, as developers, have to make a decision. You can go with approach three, duplicating the standard code for the best speed, or you can go with approach four, which will give you the greatest code flexibility in the long run.

What do I mean by code flexibility? Let's suppose that one day, FoxPro adds a new command that saves all of the memory variables into the current table (just like APPEND BLANK/GATHER MEMVAR), but it is much faster on a network. The fourth approach allows you to simply modify your METHODS.PRG and *every program will now use this new command.* The third approach will require that you modify every unique SaveIt procedure in an application.

This fourth method is also useful in *incrementally upgrading* your applications. You write your standard SaveIt routine as it is listed above. Later, you realize that you want to perform a standard routine that notes the date and time of the save as well as the user name and data file (perhaps to see how many records each user is adding in a day) for every datafile in the systems that you write. You can now add that routine to your standard SaveIt function and you are done:

```
INSERT INTO SaveInfo ;
   VALUES (DATE(), TIME(), DBF(), gcUser)
```

For a look at our complete set of standard methods, please turn to the section titled METHODS.PRG in Chapter 17.

Chapter 6

Creating Reusable Objects

Writing Reusable Code

Writing reusable code is one of the biggest opportunities for developers to increase productivity and quality for new and existing development efforts. I'm going to focus on using the power tools (specifically the screen and project builder) to manage our reusable code for us. I'll also talk about different commands that you should watch out for when developing reusable code.

What Is Reusable Code and Why Use It?

As I mentioned earlier, reusable code is any code module that does not make any assumptions about its environment. It takes care of itself, and can be "dropped in" to any application, providing increased functionality with no necessary modifications. The key to reusable code is that it should only exist on one location on your drive/network, and should be called from multiple applications. In this manner, you have a core group of well-tested, bug-free code modules that you can rely on in your development effort. Furthermore, any enhancements to one of these modules will "ripple through" to every application that calls it, providing your users with enhanced capabilities with minimal effort on your part.

Coding Issues

One of the keys to creating reusable objects is that they must not affect the procedure that is calling them. This means you must make a few design decisions.

Calling Your Code

Any variables that are required from a higher-level procedure must be passed to your reusable code. Do not assume that what you need will be there. Remember, we are writing black box objects. You pass information to them, and they return information *without affecting the calling procedure*.

For instance, if you need a routine that squares a number for an application, you can code it specifically for the *current* application:

```
lnSquareMe = 9
lnSquared = sqr()

FUNCTION sqr
RETURN lnSquareMe * lnSquareMe
```

The above routine will work for the current application, but if you have to use it again in a future application, you'd better be sure to have a variable called lnSquareMe. It's much better to write the application this way:

```
lnSquareMe = 9
lnSquared = sqr2(lnSquareMe)

FUNCTION sqr2
PARAMETER tnValue
RETURN tnValue * tnValue
```

You now have a routine that will work in any application and for any value that is passed.

The PRIVATE Trap

When writing reusable code, you must be sure that you don't affect the higher procedure. This means that you must be sure that any variables that you use in the current procedure aren't used in a higher procedure. This can seem very difficult—you never know what may call this piece of code!

The solution is to be very careful about naming every variable PRIVATE. This will hide any instance of the variable that may have been created in a higher procedure.

I can't emphasize this point enough. Debugging an application that fails because a variable in a black box is changing a higher variable is one of the toughest things to do. Take the time to go back into the code for the object and make sure that every variable is declared PRIVATE.

SETting Your Environment

FoxPro's environment handling commands are very powerful. However, with power comes responsibility. For instance, you can't assume that an application will always have EXACT set ON. If your reusable object requires that one of the SET or ON commands be set a certain way, do it yourself. When you do so, save the previous setting, and restore it on exit.

For instance, if your routine requires that EXACT be ON for an ASCAN() on an array, do this:

```
PROCEDURE LookArry
*-- This procedure takes 3 parameters,
*--   taPassed = An array
*--   tcFind   = An expression to search for
*--   tnCol    = The column to return
*--
*-- Note:  After this proc, you must test for EMPTY(value)
*--        to see if it was found
PARAMETER taPassed, tcFind, tnCol
PRIVATE jcOldExact, jnFound, jnRow, jcRetVal

jcOldExact = SET("EXACT") && Save the old value of EXACT
SET EXACT ON
jcRetVal - ""

jnFound = ASCAN(taPassed, tcFind)
IF jnFound # 0
  jnRow = ASUBSCRIPT(taPassed,jnFound,1)
  jcRetVal = taPassed[jnRow,tnCol]
ENDIF

IF jcOldExact = "ON"        && We reset EXACT here
   SET EXACT ON
ELSE
   SET EXACT OFF
ENDIF

RETURN jcRetVal
```

Note that we save the original value of any modified SET commands, and set it back before exiting the function.

SET TALK is the one setting that must be handled differently due to the nature of the command. If SET TALK is ON, you can't directly test for the condition without messing up the screen with unwanted text. Remember that if TALK is ON, any assignment echoes to the current output window.

This echo does not occur with IF statements, so we code our standard routine for SET TALK saving as follows:

```
IF SET("TALK") = "ON"
   SET TALK OFF
   lcOldTalk = "ON"
ELSE
   lcOldTalk = "OFF"
ENDIF
```

Parameter Usage

Parameters in FoxPro provide a hidden boost in modifying and maintaining reusable code. FoxPro allows you to pass less parameters than are called for in the routine. The PARAMETER() function lets you test for the number of actually passed parameters. Using this ability, you can add new functions to existing objects *without changing their original purpose*.

In other words, if you have been using the LOOKARRY() routine that is listed above, and suddenly need to be able to (occasionally) force it to *not* change the EXACT setting, you can simply add a fourth parameter, llNoExact. If it's .F., don't change a thing. If it's .T., ignore the SET EXACT line. The beauty of this technique is that by adding the fourth parameter, and making its default (.F.) the same as things were, you don't have to change any of the calling lines in all of the applications that used LOOKARRY().

This is another maxim of writing reusable code. Don't break anything with your "enhancements."

The Screen Builder and Reusable Code

The screen builder makes it much easier to develop more complex reusable objects than ever. You can focus on what the object should do, rather than how it looks.

Here are a few rules to follow when writing a reusable screen:

- Put your PRIVATEs in the SETUP snippet.
- Save your SET and ON values in the SETUP snippet.
- Reset your SET and ON values in the CLEANUP snippet.
- Any RETURNed values have to go in the CLEANUP snippet.

We've found that screen design goes much quicker if you design in the following manner:

1. Draw your screen. Decide what it will look like before adding any code.
2. Ask yourself what your user should see when the screen first appears. Whatever code has to run before the screen appears goes in your SETUP.
3. Click on each screen object and decide what should happen when the user does so. Put that code in the VALID/WHEN snippets for the object.
4. Decide what has to happen when the screen goes away. Put that in the CLEANUP snippet.
5. Congratulate yourself on how easy it was to create the screen.

The Project Builder and Reusable Code

One of the key issues to remember when using reusable objects is that they may call other reusable objects. The project builder will automatically search for any referenced screens, procedures, etc., and will include the item in the project for you. This makes using reusable objects much easier—you don't have to worry about forgetting a necessary object. Just call it—if you're using the project builder (and you *should*), it will be there when you need it.

Using a specific directory structure on your network or PC makes managing reusable code much easier. Set up a COMMON directory. Underneath that directory create a number of other directories: SCREENS, MENUS, REPORTS, DBFS, PROGS, etc. This lets you compartmentalize the location of your reusable code. You can perform backups quickly and easily. If you are on a network, map one of the network drives to this COMMON directory to allow quick access to it when necessary.

Managing Reusable Code

Committing yourself or your company to using reusable code requires a commitment to *managing* that code. Having a reusable reporting engine is not very useful if you're the only one who knows about it. You need a way to disseminate information about these procedures to others in your group or company. You also have to create a method for adding new or modified routines to your COMMON set of directories. One approach is to create a PROPOSED subdirectory into which any developer can place new or enhanced reusable objects before they are tested, approved and moved to the correct COMMON subdirectory.

An Object Manager

An object manager is a focal point for tracking your reusable code. The object manager can be as simple as a dbf that contains the name of the object, what it does, some key words for searches, calling conventions and return value. It should also contain a field that tracks the changes to the object over time.

Here again, placing some structures in place can ease development. Using the COMMON directory structure described above, you can easily write a routine that automatically moves information into the object manager by looping through the directory tree, placing any information that it finds into the table. If you standardize on a commenting convention for the header, your routine can even fill in much of the information for you.

Data-Driven Reusable Objects

Data-driven reusable objects are more complex and more useful forms of reusable code. These typically perform a function used in multiple applications but vary the data that they act upon based on information in .DBF files.

For instance, you can store report information in a table, allowing you to create a generic reporting function that works in every application. Reporting is a common task in applications—only the reports themselves differ. Therefore, create a reusable reporting module, and have the information that varies by application (e.g., the report names, filters, etc.) change by storing that information separately.

A Practical Example

Let's look a little more closely at an example of a data-driven portion of code.

One typical case would be a routine that creates any dbfs that don't exist. In this manner, if the program is just being installed, or you forgot to give your user a dbf, your routine can create it for you. It would be nice if we could write the code once, and simply fill a dbf for each application. This way, we don't have to worry about bugs creeping into our code.

To create this routine, let's look at the data file that is needed:

```
Structure for database: C:\BOOK\CD\DBFS\DATADICT.DBF
Number of data records:      17
Date of last update   : 07/11/91
Memo file block size  :      64
   Field Name Type       Width   Dec   Index
1  FIELD_NAME Character  10            Asc
2  FIELD_TYPE Character   1            Asc
3  FIELD_LEN  Numeric     3
4  FIELD_DEC  Numeric     3
5  DBF_NAME      Character   8            Asc
** Total **      26
```

The first four fields can be quickly created through the COPY STRUCTURE EXTENDED command or AFIELDS() function. The fifth field contains the name of the dbf for the current FIELD_NAME. Note that with only these five fields, we can write a program that creates all of our dbfs on the fly if they don't exist:

```
PROCEDURE CreaDBF
*--
*-- Routine to create any missing dbfs
PRIVATE lnArryCnt, lcDBF

SELECT DISTINCT datadict.dbf_name ;
   FROM datadict ;
   INTO ARRAY laDbfList

FOR lnArryCnt = 1 TO ALEN(laDbfList)
   lcDBF = laDbfList[lnArryCnt]—'.DBF'
   IF NOT FILE(lcDBF)                  && DBF doesn't exist
      SELECT * ;
         FROM Datadict ;
         WHERE Datadict.dbf_name = laDBFList[lnArryCnt] ;
         INTO ARRAY laFields
      CREATE TABLE laDBFList[lnArryCnt] ;
         FROM ARRAY laFields
      RELEASE laFields
   ENDIF
ENDFOR
```

We can, of course, expand on this model, adding fields that store indexing information, and full field names. Using this additional information, we can create automatic reindexing routines, a window that allows the user to change the active index on the fly, and a simple query builder that allows the user to select fields for a query. This shows the power of data-driven design and reusable object: one DATADICT.DBF could be created, automatically enabling all four of the above functions.

One hint when creating reusable objects that use data-driven design techniques: Assign a default action to the object. In other words, write it so that it will work even without the data file. Even if it simply exits with a WAIT WINDOW "No data file found," at least it will not crash if called when you are originally prototyping an application.

Updating Data-Driven Routines

As you upgrade your data-driven modules, you may find that you want to add more fields to the tables that control those modules. At the same time, you don't want your code to break in older applications that may have the earlier version of your tables.

This is a case where using the FCOUNT() function can help. Basically, bracket your code with a check for the number of fields:

```
IF FCOUNT("DATADICT") = 8    && Old-style table
   *-- Do old style code
ELSE
   *-- Do new style routine
ENDIF
```

This approach is similar to using the PARAMETERS() function to modify the manner in which code executes.

In Conclusion

Writing reusable code affects the entire development organization. It increases productivity and decreases maintenance efforts. Using the techniques outlined above will help you to show a marked gain in the quality and quantity of applications that your organization can develop.

Chapter 7

Mover—a Sample Reusable Object

As we saw in the last section, one of the key techniques for developing applications quickly is to have a stable of reusable code. In this chapter, we'll look at the issues involved in creating a fairly complex reusable window that uses arrays. We'll explore the reusable window step by step, reviewing how the techniques that enable reusability (making variables PRIVATE, snippet usage, parameter management) are handled in this piece of code.

A Useful Reusable Object

Often during an application, we have to give our users the capability to pick multiple items from a list. For instance, in a mailing-list application, we may want to allow the user to set up groups of people that can be stored under one name. A window of this sort may look like this:

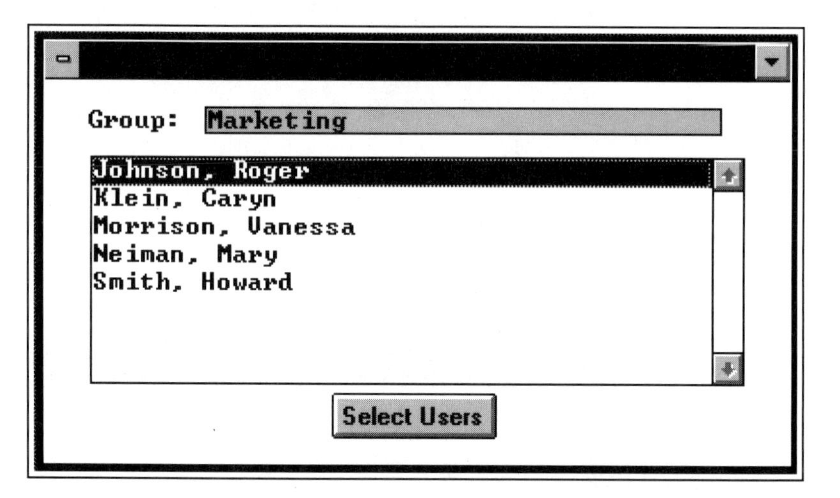

This window is created with a GET field, and a scrolling list that is based on an array called laUsers. What interests us is what happens when the user clicks on the Select Users pushbutton. At that time, the VALID of the pushbutton calls a window that allows our user to select as many people as necessary from a list of all personnel.

This capability, however, may be needed for multiple windows in our application, or in multiple applications. Selecting a number of people from a personnel list is no different from selecting multiple items from an inventory list. What we would like to do is create a window that can be called from all our applications, to which we pass the information for the full list and selected list, and have it return the items that were selected.

Designing Our Reusable Window

When creating any reusable piece of code, we have to map out how we want it to work, and what interface (if any) it should present to the user. In our case, our list of requirements might look like this:

- The interface should present two lists, allowing the user to move an item from one side to the other by double-clicking on it with the mouse.
- To accommodate those who don't like double-clicking, a set of buttons (Move, Move All, Remove, Remove All) should be included, allowing the user to click on an item and then select the action to be performed on it.
- To accommodate those who are using the keyboard, the <ENTER> key should act like a double-click, keeping the user in their list object.
- The application should accept two parameters, the full list and the selected list, passed as arrays.

Once we are done with the list of actions and interface issues, we can begin designing our reusable window in FoxPro's Screen Builder. It will look something like this (when actually in use):

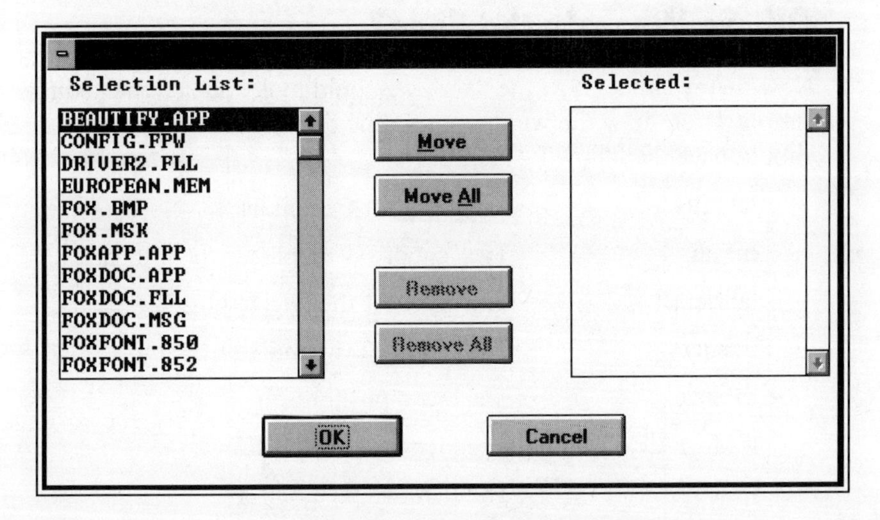

And once the first three items are moved across, the window will look like this:

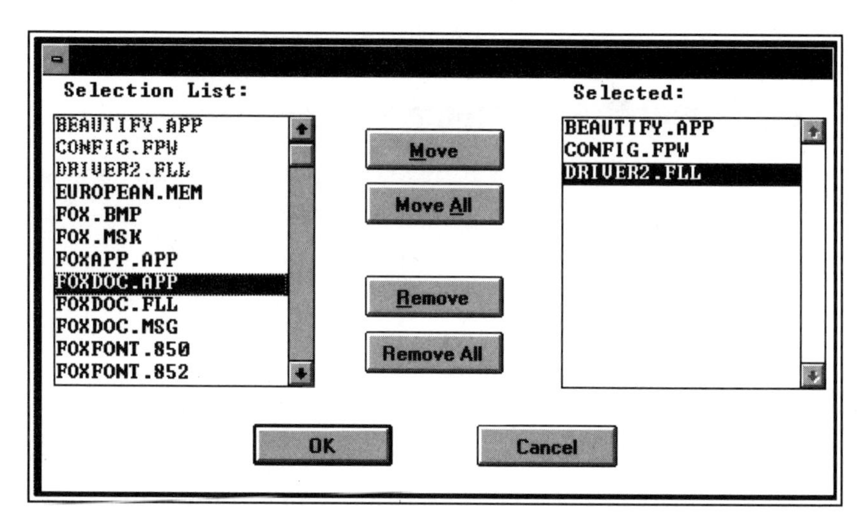

Note the use of dimming in the window. In the first example, there are no items in the selected list. We have, therefore, dimmed the Remove and Remove All pushbuttons. In the second example, those buttons are no longer dimmed, but the three moved items are dimmed in the full list, showing the user that they can no longer select those items.

OK, So Where's the Code?

Now that we know how the window should look and act, the coding is quite simple. First, draw the window using the design tools in FoxPro. The objects should have the following names:

laFullList	The array for the full list
lnFull	The "choose" variable for the full list
laSeleList	The array for the selected list
lnSelect	The "choose" variable for the selected list
lhMove	The Move pushbutton
lhMoveAll	The Move All pushbutton
lhRemove	The Remove pushbutton
lhRemoveAll	The Remove All pushbutton

lhOK	The OK pushbutton
lhCancel	The Cancel pushbutton

The Setup Snippet

Once the window is drawn, we begin with the Setup snippet. This snippet contains any code that we wish to run before the object appears on screen. In our case, we have to do the following things:

- Accept two parameters.
- Make sure the setting of EXACT is set to true (for later array comparisons).
- Initialize any necessary variables.
- If there are any items in the Selected List, dim the same item in the Full List.

The Setup snippet therefore contains the following code:

```
#SECTION 1
*  Program...........: MOVER Screen
*  Author............: yag
*  Project...........: COMMON
*  Created...........: 04/16/93
*  Copyright.........: (c) Flash Creative Mgt.
*) Description.......: Mover dialog.
*)                   : Accepts two arrays, and
*)                   : allows the user to move
*)                   : items from one to the other.
*)                   : This dialog displays the
*)                   : arrays vertically.
*  Calling Samples...: =mover(@laFull, @laSelect)
*  Parameter List....: laFullList-All items
*                    : laSeleList-Selected items
*  Major change list.:
PARAMETER laFullList, laSeleList

#SECTION 2
* lnSelect -Currently selected Selected List item
* lnFull   -Currently selected Full List item
* lnFullCnt-Number of un-moved items
* lnSeleCnt-Number of selected items
PRIVATE m.lnSelect, m.lnFull, m.lnFullCnt
PRIVATE m.lnSeleCnt, laOrigList
```

```
* To stop FoxPro Compiler Warnings
EXTERNAL ARRAY laFullList
EXTERNAL ARRAY laSeleList

* Copy arrays in case of <Cancel>
=ACOPY(laSeleList,laOrigList)
=ACOPY(laFullList,laOrigFull)

* Save SET commands
lcOldExact = SET("EXACT")
SET EXACT ON

* Highlight initial selections
STORE 1 TO m.lnFull, m.lnSelect

* Initialize counters for button dimming
m.lnFullCnt = sizearry(@laFullList)
m.lnSeleCnt = SizeArry(@laSeleList)

*- Dim already selected items
FOR i = 1 TO m.lnSeleCnt
  lnFound = ASCAN(laFullList,laSeleList[i,1])
  IF lnFound # 0
    lnFound = ASUBSCRIPT(laFullList,lnFound,1)
    laFullList[lnFound,1] = "\"+laFullList[lnFound,1]
    m.lnFullCnt = m.lnFullCnt-1
  ENDIF
ENDFOR
```

Let's take a look at the Setup snippet. We use FoxPro's #SECTION generator directives to tell FoxPro to put the PARAMETER statement at the top of the generated code. Normally, FoxPro places the code from the Setup snippet after the statements that define the window and set the environment. We need to have the PARAMETER statement at the top of the file, and anything in #SECTION 1 is placed there for us.

We then declare the variables that we will be using PRIVATE, so that they won't override any similarly named variables that may exist in a calling procedure. Remember, this is supposed to be a black-box routine, so we have to make it bulletproof.

Our next two lines of code use the EXTERNAL command to tell FoxPro that we have declared the two arrays, laFullList and laSeleList, externally to this routine. If we don't have these lines here, FoxPro will generate a warning when it compiles the code. Basically, FoxPro sees us using two arrays, but never sees them created (because these arrays are simply pointers to our application-specific arrays and are passed as parameters). Using this command allows us to turn off FoxPro's warnings for these arrays.

FoxPro's SET commands are very powerful and therefore can be very dangerous. They change the entire environment of our application, something that we don't want to do inside a black box. Yet this routine requires that SET EXACT be ON, so that we can do ASCANs of array elements when comparing lists. Therefore we save the current setting of EXACT before SETting it to ON, and we will reset it in the Cleanup snippet.

The STORE command is now used to initialize both scrolling list variables to one. This insures that the first item in the array will be highlighted if the user tabs into the list. The variable contains a number that references the selected array row. If we do not initialize it, FoxPro will default it to zero, causing no lines to be highlighted, and confusing our user.

The next two lines use a reusable program called Sizearry() that returns the number of *filled rows* in our array. These values are used to determine when we should dim the movement pushbuttons. Note the @ sign before the array names in the calls to Sizearry(). We use this sign to tell FoxPro to *pass the array by reference*. This causes FoxPro to pass a pointer to our actual array, and is in fact the only way to pass a whole array to a user defined function. Sizearry() looks like this:

```
*  Program...........: SIZEARRY.PRG
*  Author............: yag
*  Project...........: COMMON
*  Created...........: 12/09/92
*  Copyright.........: (c) Flash Creative Mgt.
*) Description.......: Returns the # of filled rows
*)                   :  of an array.
*  Calling Samples...: =sizearry( @laArray1 )
*  Parameter List....: taArry—array to be sized.
*  Major change list.:

PARAMETER taArry
PRIVATE m.lnCount

EXTERNAL ARRAY taArry
```

```
FOR m.lnCount = ALEN(taArry,1) TO 1 STEP -1
  IF NOT EMPTY(taArry[m.lnCount,1])
    EXIT           && Filled item
  ENDIF
ENDFOR

RETURN m.lnCount
```

Sizearry simply loops through the whole array, from bottom to top, and when it finds a non-empty element, it stops, returning the correct number of rows.

The last thing that we do in our Setup snippet is to dim any elements found in our selected list. The process for this is straightforward. We loop through the selected list. If the item is found in the full list, we prepend a \ to that item in the full list, automatically dimming it.

The ACTIVATE Snippet

The ACTIVATE snippet triggers after the GETs have been drawn, making it perfect for doing some initial dimming of the window objects, if necessary. In our code, if the full list is empty, we dim every object except for the Cancel pushbutton. If the selected list is empty, we dim the Remove and Remove All pushbuttons.

```
IF EMPTY(laFullList)
    SHOW GETS ONLY DISABLE
    SHOW GET lhCancel ENABLE
ENDIF

IF EMPTY(laSeleList)
     SHOW GET m.lhRemove DISABLE
     SHOW GET m.lhRemoveAll DISABLE
ENDIF
```

The Full List and Selected List Snippets

The scrolling lists, lnFull and lnSelect, use the *# of elements* snippet and the *VALID* snippet. The first of these snippets, when used with a two-dimensional array, tells FoxPro the number of rows to display in the list.

We attach the expression:

```
sizearry(@<name of array>)
```

to this snippet, which will cause FoxPro to show the number of filled rows in the array. In this manner, if there are some array rows at the bottom of the array with no information in them, we won't show our users a set of .F. values.

The VALID snippets for these objects are similar. The VALID for lnFull contains the following code:

```
lnLastKey = LASTKEY()
=ValMover()
IF lnLastKey = 13
  _CUROBJ = OBJNUM(m.lnFull)
ENDIF
```

The VALID for lnSelect contains:

```
lnLastKey = LASTKEY()
=ValRemove()
IF lnLastKey = 13
  _CUROBJ = OBJNUM(m.lnSelect)
ENDIF
```

This code saves the value of the last key pressed. It then calls a function that performs the move or remove. If the last key pressed was an <ENTER> key, we use the _CUROBJ system memory variable to keep this object as the current active object. FoxPro's default behavior for the <ENTER> key is to run the VALID and move to the next object. Keyboard users, however, would like to be able to select multiple items from the list object. Instead of forcing them to hit the spacebar twice in rapid succession (simulating a double click that stays on the current object), or forcing them to press <ENTER> and then <SHIFT+TAB> to move back one object, we check what key they pressed, keeping them in the list object if they hit <ENTER>. The user can then press <TAB> to leave the object.

ValMover()

ValMover() is the routine that actually moves the selected item from the full list to the selected list. Since we are going to call this routine from two locations (the VALID of the full list and the VALID of the Move pushbutton), we place this code in the Cleanup snippet, allowing any modifications to it to apply to both locations.

The code is fairly straightforward. We first check to see if we have any empty rows in the laSeleList array. If not, we create an empty row using the ALEN()

function to return the number of columns in the full list. In this way, we don't assume a set number of columns in our arrays.

We now use the highest empty row to store a copy of the select row from the laFullList array. We prepend a \ to the selected row in the laFullList array, dimming it. Finally, we issue a series of SHOW GET commands to redisplay only those objects that may have changed. This is a very powerful technique, especially in a graphical environment. FoxPro does not refresh the window until we tell it to. Instead of telling FoxPro to refresh the whole window, we can refresh pieces of it, speeding up the process. Additionally, by placing all of our SHOW GET commands in a row, they seem to refresh simultaneously to the user, making it seem as if our application is running faster.

```
FUNCTION ValMover

* Make sure that there is a selected item
*   and that it isn't dimmed already
IF (m.lnFull # 0) AND ;
      (LEFT(laFullList[m.lnFull,1],1) # "\")

  * If we have no extra rows, add one
  IF m.lnSeleCnt+1 > ALEN(laSeleList,1)
    DIMENSION laSeleList[m.lnSeleCnt+1, ;
                         ALEN(laFullList,2)]
  ENDIF

  * Fill the selected array row
  FOR i = 1 TO ALEN(laFullList,2)
     laSeleList[m.lnSeleCnt+1,i] = laFullList[m.lnFull,i]
  ENDFOR

  * Dim the full list row, and increment pointers
  laFullList[m.lnFull,1] = "\"+laFullList[m.lnFull,1]
  m.lnSeleCnt = m.lnSeleCnt + 1
  m.lnFullCnt = m.lnFullCnt-1

  * Redisplay the screen objects
  SHOW GET m.lnSelect
  SHOW GET m.lnFull
  SHOW GET m.lhRemove ENABLE
  IF m.lnFullCnt = 0
     SHOW GET m.lhMove DISABLE
  ENDIF
```

```
ENDIF
RETURN .T.
```

ValRemove()

ValRemove() is the function that removes an item from a selected list object and re-enables the item in the full list object. It makes sure that the user has selected an item in the selected list, then searches for that item in the full list (with a prepended \ of course). It then removes the \ from the full list item, deletes the row in the selected list, and resets all necessary counter values. Finally, the routine does a series of SHOW GET commands to redisplay the necessary objects with their new values.

```
FUNCTION ValRemove
IF m.lnSelect # 0

  * Find the item and delete it while
  *   restoring it in the full list
  lnFound = ASCAN(laFullList, ;
                "\"+laSeleList[m.lnSelect,1])
  IF lnFound # 0
    lnFound = ASUBSCRIPT(laFullList,lnFound,1)
    laFullList[lnFound,1] = ;
           SUBSTR(laFullList[lnFound,1],2)
    m.lnFullCnt = m.lnFullCnt + 1
  ENDIF
   =ADEL(laSeleList, m.lnSelect)
   m.lnSeleCnt = m.lnSeleCnt-1
   m.lnSelect = m.lnSeleCnt

   * Redisplay the window
   IF m.lnSeleCnt = 0
     SHOW GET m.lhRemove DISABLE
   ENDIF
   IF m.lnFullCnt > 0
     SHOW GET m.lhMove ENABLE
  ENDIF
   SHOW GET m.lnSelect
   SHOW GET m.lnFull
ENDIF
RETURN .T.
```

The Move and Remove Pushbuttons

Both of these pushbuttons simply have a VALID clause that calls the Cleanup Procedures ValMover() and ValRemove() appropriately.

The Move All Pushbutton

This pushbutton has a VALID clause attached that contains the following code:

```
* Dim all items in Full List
FOR i = 1 TO sizearry(@laFullList)
  IF LEFT(laFullList[i,1],1) # "\"
    laFullList[i,1] = "\"+laFullList[i,1]
   ENDIF
ENDFOR

* Dimension and fill selected list
DIMENSION laSeleList[ALEN(laOrigFull,1), ;
                     ALEN(laOrigFull,2)]
=ACOPY(laOrigFull,laSeleList)

* Reset counter variables
lnSeleCnt = sizearry(@laSeleList)
lnFullCnt = 0
m.lnSelect = m.lnSeleCnt

* Redisplay the window
SHOW GET m.lnSelect
SHOW GET m.lnFull
SHOW GET m.lhMove DISABLE
SHOW GET m.lhMoveAll DISABLE
SHOW GET m.lhRemove ENABLE
SHOW GET m.lhRemoveAll ENABLE
```

We know that we are moving all items from the full list to the selected list. Therefore, it is faster to dim all of the items in the full list in a loop, and then simply redimension the selected list and fill it from the copy of the full list that we made in the setup code. Again, please note the use of ALEN() when we re-dimension the array. Since this is a black box, we are not making any assumptions as to number of rows or columns. Redimensioning the array and using ACOPY()

cuts down on unnecessary loops to fill the selected array. Once again we set the counter variables and redisplay any appropriate objects.

The Remove All Pushbutton

This pushbutton does the opposite of the Move All pushbutton and requires even less code:

```
* Reinitialize the selected list and counters
laSeleList = .F.
m.lnSeleCnt = 0
m.lnSelect = 0
m.lnFullCnt = sizearry(@laFullList)

* Remove dimmed items from full list
FOR i = 1 TO m.lnFullCnt
  IF LEFT(laFullList[i,1],1) = "\"
    laFullList[i,1] = SUBSTR(laFullList[i,1],2)
  ENDIF
ENDFOR

* Redisplay the window
SHOW GET m.lnSelect
SHOW GET m.lnFull
SHOW GET m.lhMove ENABLE
SHOW GET m.lhMoveAll ENABLE
SHOW GET m.lhRemove DISABLE
SHOW GET m.lhRemoveAll DISABLE
```

This routine reinitializes the laSeleList array by setting it equal to .F., thereby resetting the whole array without resizing it (remember, we're using SizeArry() to return the number of filled rows). It then strips off any prepended \ characters from the full list and redisplays the window.

Our OK and Cancel Pushbuttons

Both of these pushbuttons are set as [X]Terminating pushbuttons so that clicking on them will end the READ. The OK pushbutton has no snippet code associated with it. The Cancel pushbutton, on the other hand, has to reset our selected list array to its original form. This is accomplished through a one line VALID snippet.

```
=ACOPY(laOrigList,laSeleList)
```

The Cleanup Snippet

Finally, the Cleanup snippet, in addition to having our ValMover() and ValRemove() procedures, includes a small amount of code that is run when the window is closed. The code resets the full list to the way it was upon entering the window (no need to return it with prepended \ characters). It also resets the setting of EXACT to the way it was before this black-box routine was run.

```
=ACOPY(laOrigFull,laFullList)
IF lcOldExact = "ON"
  SET EXACT ON
ELSE
  SET EXACT OFF
ENDIF
```

We use the IF statement instead of the SET EXACT &lcOldExact because it actually executes faster. Macro expansion tends to be slow and should be avoided when possible.

The Generate Options

When we include this object in a project, we will typically set the options as shown at the top of the next page.

We make the window MODAL so that the user has to put it away before continuing. We also set the output file (Screen Set Name) to be MOVER.PRG so that we can call it as a function:

```
=MOVER(@Array1,@Array2)
```

In Conclusion

The reusable window code that we've created allows us to provide an intuitive selection process for our users. It also has allowed us to explore many of the issues involved with creating a reusable screen using FoxPro's Screen Builder. FoxPro's capability of redimensioning arrays on the fly, and reinitializing them quickly were used by this object, as well as the capability of specifying how many rows should be shown from the array.

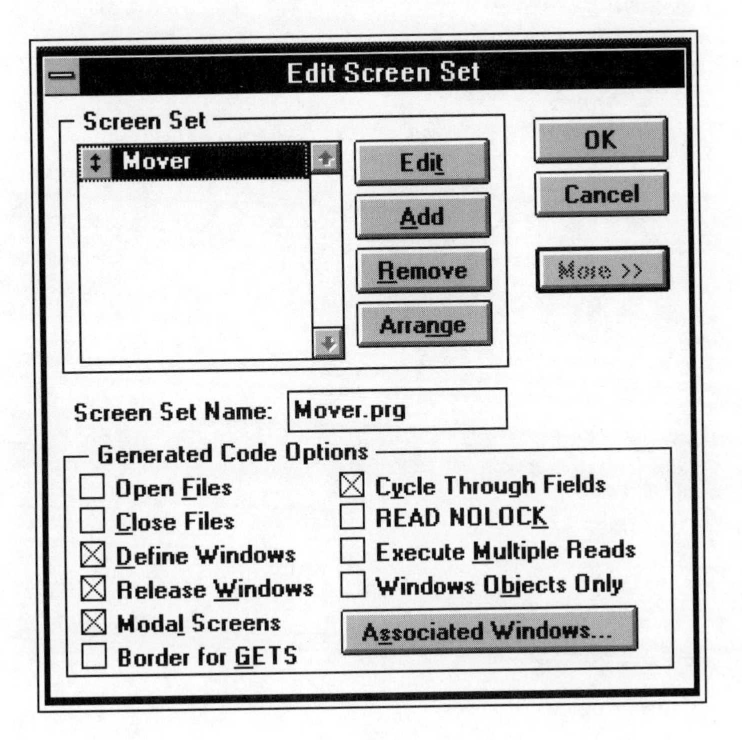
Edit Screen Set
Screen Set
Mover
Edit
Add
Remove
Arrange
OK
Cancel
More >>
Screen Set Name:
Mover.prg
Generated Code Options
Open Files
Close Files
Define Windows
Release Windows
Modal Screens
Border for GETS
Cycle Through Fields
READ NOLOCK
Execute Multiple Reads
Windows Objects Only
Associated Windows...

Chapter 8

Usability Techniques

In addition to techniques that enhance development, let's take a look at various methods of making our FoxPro applications more accessible to the user. This involves two types of approaches: usability tricks and information-enhancing techniques.

Usability tricks make the application easier for the user to control. The last few chapters were devoted to allowing the user access to functions in an order of their choosing and in a standard fashion. Usability tricks keep the learning curve to a minimum.

Information-enhancing techniques turn the raw data collected into the information that the user requires. These techniques make the user *want* to use the application. Capturing check information is boring, but if you allow users to easily graph their expense categories, with drill-down capabilities in the graph, they are willing to get through the boring part in order to get the information about their business.

Let's look at some techniques in both categories.

Usability Tricks

As I mentioned earlier, creating an event-driven application and providing a toolbar approach towards accessing common functions allow the users to decide what they want to do, when they want to do it, and give them a consistent way of accomplishing their task.

But toolbars have one major flaw—they require the use of a mouse. Many toolbars are not accessible without a mouse (particularly in graphical environments), and even if tabbing through fields eventually gets you to the toolbar, users do not often want to tab multiple times in order to do their work. They want to get it done—*now*.

The solution is to provide an alternate means of accessing the same functions contained in the toolbar. You can create a menu pad (called *Tools*) with a bar for every option on the toolbar. Alternately, you can place the toolbar options in various existing menus (for instance, a Cut option should go under the Edit menu pad). The user can now use the keyboard or mouse to access any of these menu options.

You can go further, however. Every option on the toolbar is, by definition, a commonly used function. Therefore, give every one of their menu options a *shortcut* (typically a control key combination) that when pressed, automatically runs the menu option. This lets the user access the function by pressing a single key combination. The user now has three separate methods for performing any commonly accessed function, and can choose whichever they find most comfortable.

To assign a shortcut key in FoxPro, simply open the menu builder and go to the menu bar to which you would like to assign a shortcut. Check the options checkbox, and select ShortCut from the dialog box. Press the key that you would like to assign as a shortcut and you're done! Think of menu shortcuts as global ON KEY LABELs that don't have any recursion problems.

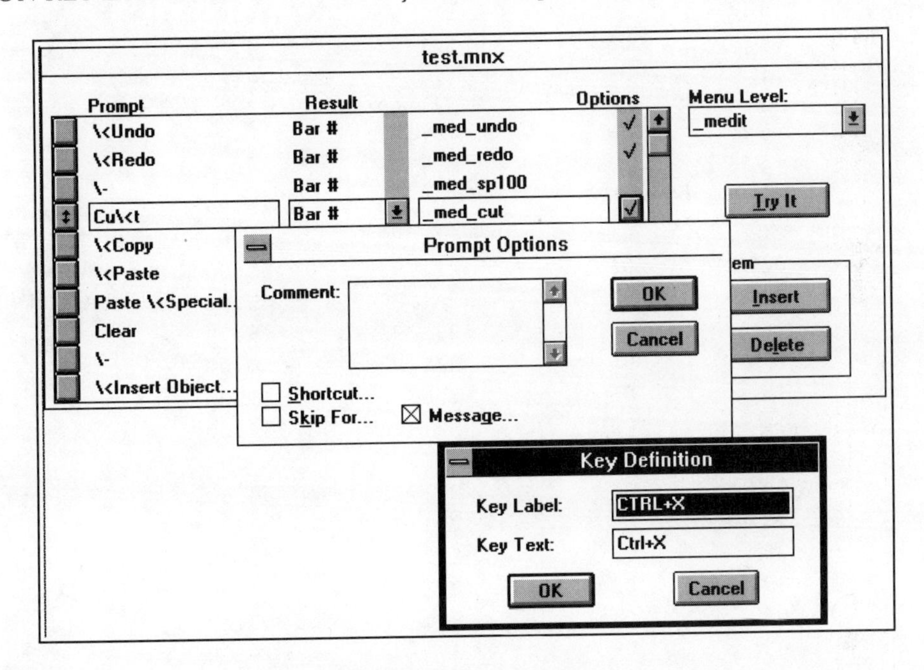

Sample FoxPro shortcut creation dialog

Information-Enhancing Techniques—Cross-Tabulation

One of the most commonly requested reports is that of a cross-tabulation. Cross-tabs allow your user to look at the essentially linear data captured by your application in a spreadsheet view. For instance, your application may create the following files and data (I know that these files are not fully normalized, but they're for demonstration purposes):

```
CUSTOMER.DBF
CCUSTID     CNAME
01          Alpha Associates
02          Beta Associates
04          Delta, Ltd.
05          Epsilon Group, Inc.
03          Gamma, Inc.
```

INVOICES.DBF

CINVID	CCUSTID	DDATE	NAMT
01	01	1/1/92	45.00
05	02	1/1/92	45.00
08	03	1/1/92	34.00
11	01	1/1/92	74.00
16	03	1/1/92	14.00
17	02	1/1/92	32.00
19	02	1/1/92	23.00
21	02	1/1/92	75.00
24	01	1/1/92	43.00
02	01	2/1/92	55.00
04	01	2/1/92	45.00
06	02	2/1/92	46.70
07	05	2/1/92	64.00
13	05	2/1/92	63.00
14	05	2/1/92	34.00
18	01	2/1/92	52.00
23	05	2/1/92	64.00
27	04	2/1/92	37.00
28	03	2/1/92	46.00
29	02	2/1/92	63.00
03	04	3/1/92	65.00
09	05	3/1/92	74.00
10	02	3/1/92	34.00
12	04	3/1/92	47.00
15	04	3/1/92	25.00
20	03	3/1/92	32.00
22	04	3/1/92	85.00
25	03	3/1/92	83.00
26	02	3/1/92	46.00

Storing the information in this manner is very useful to your application, but not so useful to the user that wants to see what a client was billed, by month and quarter. Enter cross tabs.

Cross tabs essentially work as follows:

1. Use the information that you want down the left side of the page as your first column (in our case, the client name)
2. Use the information that you want stretched across the columns as your second column (in our case, the month)

3. Use the information that you want tabulated as the third column (in our case, the SUM of the invoice amounts)
4. Do a SQL SELECT that GROUPs and ORDERs by the first and second columns
5. Run the GENXTAB program (that comes with FoxPro) against the results of the SQL SELECT

For the current example, the code would look like this:

```
SELECT CUSTOMER.CNAME, INVOICES.DDATE, SUM(INVOICES.NAMT);
 FROM INVOICES, CUSTOMER;
 WHERE CUSTOMER.CCUSTID = INVOICES.CCUSTID;
 GROUP BY CUSTOMER.CNAME, INVOICES.DDATE;
 ORDER BY CUSTOMER.CNAME, INVOICES.DDATE;
 INTO CURSOR SYS(2015)

DO sys(2004)+"GENXTAB" WITH 'XTAB'
```

The result of the query before the cross tab looks like this:

CNAME	DDATE	SUM_NAMT
Alpha Associates	1/1/92	162.00
Alpha Associates	2/1/92	152.00
Beta Associates	1/1/92	175.00
Beta Associates	2/1/92	109.70
Beta Associates	3/1/92	80.00
Delta, Ltd.	2/1/92	37.00
Delta, Ltd.	3/1/92	222.00
Epsilon Group, Inc.	2/1/92	225.00
Epsilon Group, Inc.	3/1/92	74.00
Gamma, Inc.	1/1/92	48.00
Gamma, Inc.	2/1/92	46.00
Gamma, Inc.	3/1/92	115.00

GENXTAB.PRG takes the results of this intermediate file and uses it to create the final results. Essentially it takes the unique values of the first column, and uses that as the first column in the result set. GENXTAB then takes the unique values of the second column, and uses them as the field names for the result set. Finally, GENXTAB places the information in the third column in the proper locations in the result set, placing the results where the first and second columns cross.

Once GENXTAB is run, we arrive at this final result set.

CNAME	D_19920101	D_19920201	D_19920301
Alpha Associates	162.00	152.00	
Beta Associates	175.00	109.70	80.00
Delta, Ltd.		37.00	222.00
Epsilon Group, Inc.		225.00	74.00
Gamma, Inc.	48.00	46.00	115.00

These results are nice, but it would be nicer if we could force the columns to show the headings that we want instead of things like "D_19920101". Let's take a look again at how GENXTAB works. The second column of the intermediate file is used to generate the field headings for the final results. What happens if we force the second column to something more Englishlike? Our SQL SELECT now becomes:

```
SELECT CUSTOMER.CNAME, ;
       PADR(CMONTH(INVOICES.DDATE),10) AS COLHEAD,
       SUM(INVOICES.NAMT);
 FROM INVOICES, CUSTOMER;
 WHERE CUSTOMER.CCUSTID = INVOICES.CCUSTID;
 GROUP BY CUSTOMER.CNAME, COLHEAD;
 ORDER BY CUSTOMER.CNAME, COLHEAD;
 INTO CURSOR SYS(2015)
```

The results now look more worthwhile:

CNAME	JANUARY	FEBRUARY	MARCH
Alpha Associates	162.00	152.00	
Beta Associates	175.00	109.70	80.00
Delta, Ltd.		37.00	222.00
Epsilon Group, Inc.		225.00	74.00
Gamma, Inc.	48.00	46.00	115.00

These results give the user information that they understand in an easily understood fashion. Let's see where else we can take these capabilities.

Information-Enhancing Techniques—A/R Reporting

As we've seen, the second column of our SQL SELECT is used to provide the columns for the final result set. If we provide a call to a UDF in the second column, it becomes very simple to create an A/R Aging Report (typically known as a 30/60/90 report). The second column simply calls a UDF called ColHead(), to which the invoice date is passed, and returns the values "Current," "Over30," "Over60," or "Over90," depending on the date of the invoice.

```
FUNCTION ColHead()
PARAMETER tdInvDate
PRIVATE jcRetVal, jnDays

jnDays = DATE()-tdInvDate
DO CASE
   CASE jnDays < 30
      jcRetVal = "Current"
   CASE jnDays < 60
      jcRetVal = "Over30"
   CASE jnDays < 90
      jcRetVal = "Over60"
   OTHERWISE
      jcRetVal = "Over90"
ENDCASE

RETURN jcRetVal
```

The possibilities available with this technique are virtually endless.

Information-Enhancing Techniques—On-the-Fly Client Balances

Here's a technique that has always pleased our clients. As part of our client information window, we provide a pushbutton labeled "Billings". When the client clicks on this button, we issue a query/cross tab for the current client, for all months in the current year, by month. Once that is completed, we SCATTER the results to memvars, and pop up a window that shows the balances, with quarterly subtotals (achieved by summing the proper months' memvars).

You'll see a sample of such a screen on the next page.

Let's look at the code involved after creating the cross tab:

```
STORE 0.00 TO m.january, m.february, m.march, ;
              m.april, m.may, m.june, m.july, ;
              m.august, m.september, m.october, ;
              m.november, m.december
SCATTER MEMVAR
m.Qtr1 = m.january + m.february + m.march
m.Qtr2 = m.april + m.may + m.june
```

```
m.Qtr3 = m.july + m.august + m.september
m.Qtr4 = m.october + m.november + m.december
DO ShowXTab.SPR                  && Call the screen
```

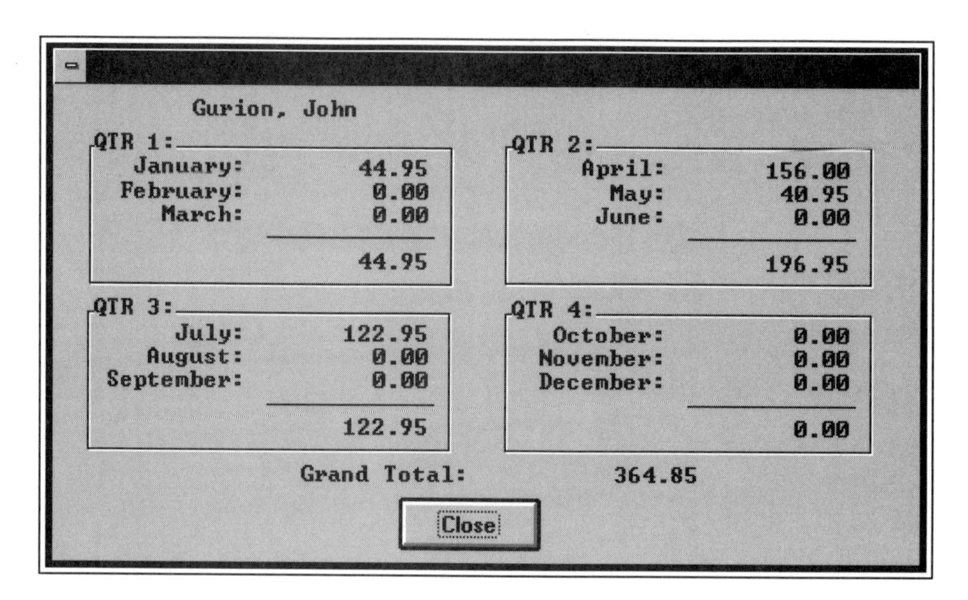

We have to initialize all of the twelve months' memvars because *GENXTAB only creates fields for months with data.* This means that if the current client had no billings in May, no May field would be created, therefore no May memvar would be SCATTERed, and the screen code would crash when it tried to display May. By initializing all months with zero, then overwriting the existing ones with the current data, we allow for this eventuality.

This method of instantly showing information in a highly readable form can be used to show not only billings, but unpaid billings information, inventory sold (by volume or by price), or basically anything that you'd like. All you have to do is change the SQL SELECT that drives the entire show.

Chapter 9

Testing Your Application

Developing proper testing methodologies is critical to completing any application. Even the best code has bugs in it. Bugs are inevitable. Even the most conscientious developer may miss a required feature in a system. It is crucial for any development effort to plan the testing methods properly.

When to Plan the Testing

A frequent question regarding developing testing methodologies relates to when the plan should be developed. There are two theories on this:

1. Plan the testing at the *outset.*

   The logic behind this theory says that only by planning everything at the outset can you properly put all your assets in place for the mammoth job ahead. Furthermore, testing takes place throughout the development process and therefore *should* be planned at the outset.

2. Plan the testing towards the *end* of development.

   This theory states that *planned* testing need occur only when the development of modules has reached a certain point. Until that point, when the modules are significantly completed, unit testing is done primarily by the developers. Planned testing is applicable, according to this theory, only during the *system* and *acceptance* testing phases. Accordingly, since you are not 100 percent sure of what your system will have until later in the development process, it is appropriate to plan the testing later in the development process when the design of the system is complete and development is substantially under way.

Our preferred approach is to develop test plans at the *outset* and to revisit them later in the development process. The reasoning is simple. The system specification document that has been agreed to with the client represents the design of the system. Since all development will be based on the specification, it makes sense to prepare the plans for that testing up front. This will allow you to "line up all your ducks" at the outset. If the design has to change, then the testing plan can be modified along with it.

A testing plan is a living document—it would be foolish to consider any document or plan as "carved in stone." It stands to reason that the testing plan will have to be reviewed towards the end of the development process, when system and acceptance testing are ready to begin. Still, it's better to have all your plans completed up front. It allows for more efficient management of all your personnel.

Testing Phases

There are three different phases of testing that occur during development:

1. Unit Testing

   Unit testing refers to the testing of each individual routine and module as they are created and completed. *Unit testing is usually completed by the developers.*

2. System Testing

   Systems testing, sometimes referred to as Integration Testing, deals with testing the application as a whole. All elements in the application should be tested to ensure that they are bug free and the application should be reviewed for completeness as well. *System Testing is normally performed by individuals other than the developers.* Having someone other than the developers test the application will introduce a more rigorous form of testing. In most cases, developers are so familiar with their work that they naturally test the application in a logical order. Individuals who have not been involved in the development of the application are more like to try "crazy" combinations that may uncover bugs and anomalies in the application.

   If no additional resources for testing are available other than the development team, testing of modules should *not* be performed by the individuals who created them. Where possible, the testing should be assigned to other members of the team.

   All system testing should be done based on a *testing script*. A script is a list of specific actions to take in order to test the application. The script is treated as a checklist of items to test. Each item is tested and the results are recorded in the script. If a bug is detected, it should be retested once the developers have certified it as repaired.

3. Acceptance Testing

   Acceptance Testing refers to the client's test of the software to ensure that the software is in accordance with the software specification. This is the final testing phase. In many cases, this type of testing is not done formally but occurs naturally as a result of the "milestone" delivery approach mentioned earlier.

Methods of Implementing Testing Procedures

There are two approaches that you should take when implementing testing of an application. They are *automatic* and *repetitive testing*. Automatic testing involves having your application automatically configure itself into a "testing mode" when you are developing at your site. Repetitive testing requires that you have a constant set of testing criteria that you use on all applications.

You can enhance automatic testing in DOS and Windows by using the FoxPro GETENV() function. You can set up an environmental variable (typically in AUTOEXEC.BAT) and have your application test for it. If the environmental variable exists, the application sets up certain ON KEY LABEL commands for your testing needs.

```
Autoexec.bat
    SET DEBUSER=FLASH

Your Application
    IF GETENV("DEBUSER") = "FLASH"
       <Set up your environment for testing>
    ENDIF
```

Another approach to take is to use FoxPro's new precompiler directives, #IF, #ELIF and #ENDIF. These allow you to place conditional code within your application code. This code is only included in your application if the test is passed *at compile time*. In this manner, you would not have your application testing the IF statement whenever it is run by the user.

```
Autoexec.bat
    SET DEBUSER=FLASH

Your Application
    #IF GETENV("DEBUSER") = "FLASH"
       <Set up your environment for testing>
    #ENDIF
```

On the Macintosh, you can either use the existence of a variable to decide whether or not you are debugging (for instance, glDebug), or you can check for the existence of a file on your machine with the FILE() function. I prefer the latter because the former requires that you remember to set the variable whenever you go into FoxPro.

A standard repetitive test that you should use on all portions of an application includes *bounds checking*. Bounds checking insures that your program will work at certain typical boundaries of data. For instance, you should test every application window to assure that it works with zero records, one record, one hundred records, and some upper bound depending on the application. If an application will have to handle 100,000 records, test your application with some factor greater than that amount of data.

In Conclusion

As PC development moves into the mission-critical arena, it becomes very important to "borrow" from the methodologies developed in big-iron development, and to adapt them to the capabilities of today's tools. By creating standards for coding and testing, we ensure that we can move development staff around multiple projects. However, the key is communication—both with developers and with the clients that you are servicing. Keeping a constant multi-directional flow of information in your development team will facilitate the necessary building of skills in the personnel, and will ensure the adherence to standards and use of reusable code. Letting a client know where you stand and calling to "keep in touch" will allow you to develop a rapport with your client, which will help to counteract any problems that may occur. Communication will allow you to be proactive with your clients, instead of reactive.

Using these approaches, along with the power tools available in and for FoxPro, will enable you to more easily create and maintain large-scale applications.

Chapter 10

Working with OLE

FoxPro for Windows and FoxPro for the Macintosh allow you to add multimedia and document tracking capabilities to your FoxPro applications. FoxPro does this by implementing the capability known as Object Linking and Embedding or OLE. As we'll see, OLE is more fully implemented under Windows, so I'll begin by describing the Windows implementation and then move on to the differences on the Macintosh.

What Is OLE?

Object Linking and Embedding (OLE) is a feature of Microsoft Windows 3.1 that allows the user to transfer and share information among Windows applications. There is no need to copy and paste in order to exchange data—using OLE, you can open up an application from within another application.

An *object* is anything created by a Windows application. There are two types of applications that use OLE—clients and servers. A *client* is an application that can take linked or embedded objects, while a *server* is an application that can be embedded in other applications. FoxPro can act only as an OLE client, accepting files from other documents.

Using OLE, you can write a report in your Windows word-processing application and embed within it a graph from a Windows spreadsheet application. You can then make changes to the graph by opening up the application used to create it and saving it from within your word-processing application. When you finish editing the graph, you return to your document with the updated graph in place.

OLE allows you to link or embed objects. When you *link* an object, you create a link to the source document. This is where the information is stored. Therefore, when you make a change to the source document, the changes are seen in the linked object. When you *embed* an object, a *copy* of the source document information is pasted to the destination document. Since there is no link between the two documents, you can modify one without affecting the other.

OLE information is stored in the Registration Database (REG.DAT), which can be modified using the Registration Editor.

What Is the Registration Database?

The registration database is a source of information regarding applications and their OLE and association capabilities. This information is used in three cases:

- By applications that support object linking and embedding.

- When you open or print a file from File Manager.
- For associating file name extentions with applications.

The registration database is set up and maintained by Windows and Windows applications. The database is located in the Windows directory under REG.DAT. This file should not be moved or deleted. If the file is moved or deleted, loss of functionality in File Manager, Program Manager, and applications that support object linking and embedding, may occur. The Registration Database is modified by running the Registration Editor, REGEDIT.EXE.

The Advanced Interface of REGEDIT

You access the advanced interface of REGEDIT by running REGEDIT with the /v option (REGEDIT /V). The advanced interface is designed to be used by application developers and system administrators, who modify the registration database to manipulate the OLE and Association properties in Windows.

When you run the Registration Information Editor with the /v option, the advanced Registration Editor screen is shown with all of the information in the database. The contents of the registration database is branched in a tree format like the directory tree in File Manager.

Each branch of the tree is identified by its key name, which is Windows' internal name for the program. You can select any key name in the Registration Information Editor window by typing the first letter of the key name, or by using the mouse or arrow keys. Select the key name you want to work with and then manipulate the information.

What Can We Do with REGEDIT?

REGEDIT contains the commands available to our application when dealing with OLE objects. For instance, let's look at a sample of the registration editor (illustrated at the top of the next page). We can see from this picture that the SoundRec OLE server (which plays sounds) has two possible actions (called VERBs in Windows): Play and Edit. Seeing this allows us to understand how FoxPro for Windows actually handles OLE objects within its General fields.

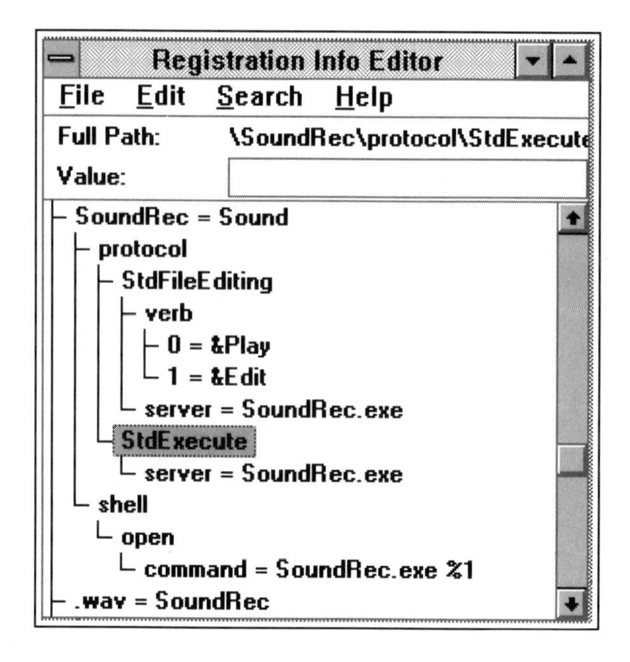

Registration Editor (REGEDIT /V)

Using OLE

To play a sound stored in a FoxPro table, we simply issue a SAY command with the proper VERB:

```
@ 0,0 SAY gSound VERB "Play"
```

To edit a sound stored in a FoxPro table, we simply issue the same SAY command, but with its proper VERB:

```
@ 0,0 SAY gSound VERB "Edit"
```

Most OLE objects support an Edit VERB.

In addition to the string version of the VERB keyword, we can call the value of the OLE verb. The default action of any OLE object is VERB 0. In the case of a Paintbrush picture, the following two commands are equivalent:

```
@ 0,0 SAY gPict VERB "Edit"
@ 0,0 SAY gPict VERB 0
```

In order to add an OLE object to FoxPro, we can either use the standard interactive Windows approach of forcing our users to cut and paste an object into a

General field (opened with the MODIFY GENERAL command), or we can use the new APPEND GENERAL command to add an item programmatically.

The APPEND GENERAL command works the same way as the APPEND MEMO command does. It takes the name of a file and puts a copy of that file into the general field. Adding the LINK keyword adds an OLE link instead of embedding a copy of the file. Finally, the CLASS option allows us to tell the environment what type of object it is. OLE servers have default file extensions (for instance, BMP for Paintbrush, DOC for Microsoft Word), so in most cases you don't have to use the CLASS keyword. If your object has a unique extension, however, you must use the CLASS option to specify what OLE server the object should call. This line of code adds a link to a Word for Windows document called YAGDEMO.XYZ:

```
APPEND GENERAL gDocs FROM Yagdemo.xyz LINK CLASS Winword
```

OLE on the Macintosh

Like Windows, FoxPro for the Macintosh implements Object Linking and Embedding (as a Shared Library Manager extension). Unfortunately, the Macintosh implementation is not as full as the Windows implementation.

The FoxPro for the Mac command syntax for working with OLE is the same as the syntax for FoxPro for Windows, but you do not have access to REGEDIT on the Macintosh, which keeps you from finding out which accepted verbs are available for a particular server. If you cannot find out what the verbs are from the server's documentation, the best idea is to use the numeric verbs, starting at 0, and experiment with the results.

In Conclusion

Using the OLE capabilities in FoxPro, we can begin to create useful business applications that employ multimedia capabilities, or that function as front ends to files created by other business software. Let us hope that, as Microsoft enhances OLE for the Macintosh, FoxPro for the Mac will benefit from a more robust implementation of OLE.

Chapter 11

Working with DDE

Dynamic Data Exchange (DDE) allows for data exchange between Windows applications. Using DDE, you can initiate an action with another Windows application. For example, you can use DDE with Word for Windows to create a mail merge with FoxPro 2.5 for Windows. A request is sent out to Word to initiate a mail merge using a Word document and a FoxPro address database. With the DDE commands, FoxPro can act as both a client and a server. FoxPro can manipulate a Word document and can be manipulated with the Word macro language.

There are three types of naming conventions used in all applications that support Dynamic Data Exchange Functions—service name, topic name, and item name.

- A *service name* is the name that the server responds to when called upon by the client. A server can have numerous service names. "EXCEL" is an example of a service.
- A *topic name* specifies a logical set of data. For file applications, topic names are usually file names. To access a server, the client must specify a topic name in addition to the server's service name. "C:\WKSHT1.XLS" is an example of a topic.
- An *item name* is a name that specifies a unit of data that the server can pass to the client requesting the data. "R1C1" (Row One, Column One) can be an example of an item.

Please note that all Windows programs have their own commands and functions in order to carry out a DDE conversation. This session will focus on the FoxPro for Windows commands and functions only.

DDE Basics

DDE is a standard protocol supported by Windows that allows one application (called the DDE Client) to communicate with, and even control, another application (called the DDE Server). For example, if we were to call Excel from within FoxPro, FoxPro would be the client and Excel would be the server.

A client can typically perform one of three basic operations once a link has been established:

- Send information to the server.
- Request information from the server.
- Tell the server to execute a command. This command may be any one that the server recognizes, including open a file, close a file, minimize, and much more.

Establishing a Link

Establishing a link is very much like making a phone call. The client application "calls" the server and asks it to discuss a certain topic. A "topic," in this case, will usually mean one of two things:

"System" — A special topic that all DDE servers recognize. This topic is typically used to discuss information regarding the server application. Typical items discussed could be "What other topics do you recognize?", "What file formats do you recognize?" and more. The rule here is that each system has its own items that it will recognize. Unfortunately, just because one application recognizes a particular item doesn't mean that another will. The only way to know is to consult each server application's manuals.

Other topics — These other topics will usually be the name of a document or spreadsheet. In the case of a spreadsheet, for example, the items recognized would be cell addresses. Again, there are no hard-and-fast rules for this; you will need to check the server application's manuals for more information on the topics and items the server will recognize.

The process whereby a link is established is very simple. All you need to do is initiate a link by specifying the name of the server application and the topic you want to discuss. Assuming that the server you want to talk to is available and the topic you want to discuss is recognized, you are in business.

Establishing a Link with FoxPro for Windows

Now that we have discussed the basics of establishing a link, let's take a look at the mechanics of establishing a link between FoxPro for Windows as a client and another application (once again, we'll use Excel as our example).

```
m.lnChannel = DDEInitiate("Excel","System")
```

This line of code will establish a link between FoxPro for Windows as a client and Excel as a server. You can look at it as calling up Excel and saying "I would like to discuss the System topic with you." The return value is numeric and represents the *channel* number. Any communications between FoxPro and the server application will take place over the link channel.

The first parameter represents the name of the server you want to link with. Here's another example showing a link with another application—in this case, Microsoft Word for Windows.

```
m.lnChannel = DDEInitiate("WinWord","System")
```

An attempt to establish a link between FoxPro and a DDE server may fail for one of two reasons. If you think of establishing a link in terms of making a phone call, it stands to reason that the person you are calling may not be in or they may not know anything about the topic you want to discuss. Similarly, an attempt to link to a DDE server may fail because the server application is not running or it does not understand the topic you are trying to discuss.

If the link fails because the server application is not running, FoxPro will pop up a dialog telling you that *"Remote data not accessible. Start application "EXCEL.EXE"?.* If you answer Yes, FoxPro will attempt to load Excel for you. If you are like us and prefer to control these things yourself, you can tell FoxPro not to prompt for this with the following function:

```
=DDESetoption("Safety",.F.)
```

In effect, this function is the equivalent to the SET SAFETY OFF command for DDE.

The second reason a link may fail is that the topic you are asking for may not be understood by the server application. In any event, if the link fails, DDEINITIATE returns -1.

Since Excel definitely understands the System topic, if the link fails, we can be pretty sure that Excel is not running. In that case, we can start it up ourselves. Here's a bit of code that shows this process:

```
=DDESetoption("SAFETY",.F.)
m.lnChannel = DDEinitiate("Excel","System")

*-- If the DDEINITIATE fails, lnChannel will
*-- equal -1. If it fails, open Excel with a
*-- RUN command. Note the /N which, in
*-- Fox/Win means we are opening another
*-- Windows application. It does NOT open an
*-- MSDOS window.
```

```
IF m.lnChannel < 0

    *-- This RUN command works because I have
    *-- EXCEL in my path. If you do not, you
    *-- will have to specifically address the
    *-- directory or the RUN command will fail.

    RUN /N EXCEL.EXE

    *-- Once it's open, set up the link.

    m.lnChannel = DDEInitiate("Excel", "System")
    = DDEExecute(m.lnChannel,'[APP.ACTIVATE("FoxPro",1)]')
ENDIF
```

The RUN command has a new parameter, /N. This parameter distinguishes an attempt to RUN a DOS command from a Windows application. If /N is included in FoxPro for Windows, FoxPro does not request a DOS session from Windows. Instead, it understands that you are attempting to open another Windows application. Since Windows is subject to the limitations of the DOS path, Excel will have to be in the path to execute if you do not want to specify the full path to Excel.Exe. The /N Parameter of the RUN command can take a number that specifies how the application should be opened. The following numbers are accepted:

1 Active and normal size

2 Active and minimized

3 Active and maximized

4 Inactivate and normal size

7 Inactivate and minimized

The above code could have started Excel with the RUN /N7 command, but in this way, the code that does the inactivation and minimization using native Excel command can be demonstrated. When Excel is started, it becomes the foremost application (i.e., it is on top). Issuing the DDEExecute function with the command [APP.ACTIVATE("FoxPro",1)] tells Excel to put FoxPro back on top. The DDEExecute function will be discussed in more detail later in this chapter.

Now that Excel is open and a link has been established, we are ready to get to work with it. In order to do anything really useful with it, we will need to work with a spreadsheet.

Working with a Spreadsheet

If you wanted to get data from a spreadsheet, or send data to it, you must establish a link between FoxPro and Excel to discuss the spreadsheet. Note that you *cannot* discuss a particular spreadsheet over a channel established to discuss the System topic. The spreadsheet is a topic unto itself. Here's how you establish the link between FoxPro and Excel to discuss a spreadsheet:

```
m.lnChannel = DDEINITIATE("Excel",SpreadSheet Name)
```

A key point to understand here is that the spreadsheet must be loaded before you can talk about it. A common method of establishing a link with a particular spreadsheet might be to initiate a link with Excel to discuss the System Topic and then execute a command that loads the spreadsheet into memory. Once the spreadsheet is loaded, you can initiate a new link between FoxPro and Excel to discuss the spreadsheet.

Executing Commands with DDE

The next question deals with how we can execute commands in the server application under FoxPro control. For example, as we just discussed, a common command sequence might be to open a file in the server application so that FoxPro can initiate a DDE link to discuss it. Here's an example that executes a File Open command in Excel:

```
m.llSuccess = DDEExecute(lnChannel,'[OPEN("C:\mortgage.xls")]')
```

This function sends the command to the DDE server to execute and returns a logical value indicating whether the attempt to execute the command was successful.

This line of code will open a file called *Mortgage.xls* located in the root directory of the C: drive. The DDEExecute function returns a logical value depending on whether the operation was successfully executed by the server. Once the file is opened, you can establish a link between FoxPro and Excel to discuss the spreadsheet.

One technical comment about the function and its syntax. You may note the use of quotes in the function. Although FoxPro does not care how the quotes are matched, Excel expects the name of the spreadsheet to be in double quotes. Other spreadsheet applications may have different requirements.

Every Windows application supports different command and syntax. For example, Microsoft Word for Windows (WinWord) has a programming language called WordBasic built in. To execute commands in WinWord, you would need to send WordBasic commands. The same function to open a WinWord document (assuming lnChannel holds the channel number to a link with WinWord), for example, would be:

```
? DDEExecute(lnChannel,'[FileOpen "c:\docs\ncscmemo.doc"]')
```

Discussing Items in the Spreadsheet

Once you have a spreadsheet open and a link established, you're ready to talk about different items. The next question is, what would you want to talk about? Typically, you will want to talk about individual cells in the spreadsheet. Each cell within the spreadsheet is an item unto itself. Cells are referenced by Row and Column subscripts with DDE. For example, the first row and column in the spreadsheet (cell "A1") would be referenced as "R1C1."

The discussions that you will have with a item within a spreadsheet will typically take the form of requesting the contents of that cell or placing (poking) data in the cell. There are two functions to accomplish these tasks: DDERequest and DDEPoke. A common task would be to poke a formula or value into a cell and to query the contents of a cell with DDERequest.

It is important to note that only character information can be passed through a DDE link. Thus, if you would like to POKE a numeric value into a cell, you would have to send it through as a character string. Similarly, numeric values are passed back to FoxPro in character format.

Another thing to be aware of is that data is returned from Excel in the *format in which it is displayed*. For example, if a cell is formatted to show numbers in currency format with no decimals, the number 10000 would come through the link as "$10,000". Lastly, if a numeric result in Excel exceeds the width of the column, it displays as pound signs (#######). If you request a value from a cell suffering from this condition, all you will get back is a string of pound signs.

Here's the syntax to the two functions:

```
m.llSuccess = DDEPoke(m.lnChannel,Item,Data_to_Transmit)
m.lcValue   = DDERequest(m.lnChannel,Item)
```

DDEPoke returns a logical indicating whether the action was successful. DDERequest returns the data in the item. If the item is unknown, DDERequest returns a null string.

Terminating a Link

It's always nice to be neat. Once you're done with a link, it's prudent to close it down. The function is simple and straightforward:

```
=DDETerminate(m.lnChannel)
```

DDE Function Listing

What follows is a table that lists all of the DDE functions available in FoxPro for Windows. Please note that unlike other FoxPro functions, you *cannot* limit the function name to four characters. You must type in the whole name.

DDEAbortTrans()	Aborts an asynchronous DDE transaction. In other words, if you set up a DDE transaction to wait for feedback from the other application, this will tell Fox to stop waiting.
DDEAdvise()	Creates a notify link or an automatic link. These links are used to set up asynchronous transactions and are often known as "warm" or "hot" links. A notify link notifies FoxPro when something happens, an automatic link notifies FoxPro and sends the changed information across immediately.
DDEEnabled()	Enables or disables DDE processing, or returns the current status of DDE processing.
DDEExecute()	Sends a command to the other application. Note that you must phrase the command in the other application's native language.
DDEInitiate()	Establishes a DDE link between FP/Win and another application.
DDELastError()	Returns an error number for the last DDE function processed.
DDEPoke()	Sends data from FoxPro for Windows to the other application.
DDERequest()	Requests data from the other application.
DDESetOption()	Sets or returns DDE settings. It is similar to the SET command and function in FoxPro.

DDESetService()	Creates, releases or modifies a service that is defined in FoxPro for Windows.
DDESetTopic()	Creates or releases a topic that is set from a service as defined in FoxPro for Windows.
DDETerminate()	Ends a DDE session.

PART 2

Our Sample Application

Chapter 12

Our Sample Application—An Introduction

What follows is a description of all of the items in our application with a printout of all the information from the metafiles (SCX, MNX etc.) that make up that item. This should allow you to rekey in all this information to duplicate the application if you don't wish to order the source code disk. Please note that the program that prints out this information will be made available on CompuServe's SYBEX forum and FOXFORUM and on the source-code diskette. Also, for readers of the original *FoxPro Codebook*, I have not included the generated code in this book. The printouts for the DOS, Windows, and Macintosh versions of the various metafiles take up enough pages, and there is no reason to hard-code any of that information.

Data Structures

I have included a short description and the structures of every table used in the application. Where a table is used internally, I have also included a list of indices and record information.

Compact Disc Inventory Information: CD.DBF

This table contains the inventory information about the compact discs that can be purchased.

```
Structure for table:     c:\book25\cd\cd.dbf
Number of data records:  24
Date of last update:     07/20/1993
Memo file block size:    33
Field  Field Name   Type        Width    Dec
    1  CID          Character       9
    2  CMUSICIAN    Character      30
    3  CTITLE       Character      40
    4  NCOST        Numeric         5      2
    5  NPRICE       Numeric         5      2
    6  MDESCRIPT    Memo           10
    7  CLASTUPD     Character       9
** Total **                       109
```

Application Resource Directory: CDRSRC.DBF

This table is a standard FoxPro resource file that is renamed and bound into the application. It can contain any application specific colors or other resources.

Customer Information: CUSTOMER.DBF

The Customer table contains information about the customers of our company.

```
Structure for table:     c:\book25\cd\customer.dbf
Number of data records: 13
Date of last update:     07/08/1993
Field  Field Name  Type          Width    Dec
    1  CID         Character         9
    2  CFIRSTNAME  Character        15
    3  CLASTNAME   Character        25
    4  CADDRESS1   Character        40
    5  CADDRESS2   Character        40
    6  CCITY       Character        20
    7  CSTATE      Character         2
    8  CZIP        Character         9
    9  CPHONE      Character        10
   10  CLASTUPD    Character         9
** Total **                        180
```

Field-Level Data Dictionary: DATADICT.DBF

This table contains basic information about our application's fields. It is used by a number of reusable windows including GETORDER, APPSRCH and DBFREIND.

```
Structure for table:     c:\book25\cd\dbfs\datadict.dbf
Number of data records: 23
Date of last update:     05/02/1993
Memo file block size:    33
Field  Field Name  Type          Width    Dec
    1  FIELD_NAME  Character        10
    2  FIELD_TYPE  Character         1
    3  FIELD_LEN   Numeric           3
    4  FIELD_DEC   Numeric           3
    5  DBF_NAME    Character         8
    6  LINDEX      Logical           1
```

```
    7  INDEX_KEY    Memo            10
    8  CTAG         Character       20
    9  LSHOW        Logical          1
** Total **                         58

  Structural CDX file:   C:\BOOK25\CD\DBFS\DATADICT.CDX
            Index tag:   FIELD_NAME    Key: FIELD_NAME
            Index tag:   FIELD_TYPE    Key: FIELD_TYPE
            Index tag:   DBF_NAME      Key: DBF_NAME
            Index tag:   LINDEX        Key: LINDEX
            Index tag:   CTAG          Key: CTAG
```

Table Contents:

FIELD_NAME	**TYPE**	**LEN**	**FLDDEC**	**DBF_NAME**	**LINDEX**	**CTAG**	**LSHOW**
CID	C	9	000	CD	.T.	CD Internal ID	.F.
CMUSICIAN	C	030	000	CD	.T.	Artist Name	.T.
CTITLE	C	040	000	CD	.T.	CD Title	.T.
NCOST	N	005	002	CD	.T.	Cost of CD	.T.
NPRICE	N	005	002	CD	.T.	Price of CD	.T.
MDESCRIPT	M	010	000	CD	.F.	CD Description	.F.
CCDID	C	9	000	PURCHASE	.T.	Internal CD Link	.F.
CID	C	9	000	CUSTOMER	.T.	Cust Internal ID	.F.
CFIRSTNAME	C	15	000	CUSTOMER	.T.	Customer First Name	.T.
CCITY	C	020	000	CUSTOMER	.T.	Customer City	.T.
CSTATE	C	002	000	CUSTOMER	.T.	Customer State	.T.
CZIP	C	010	000	CUSTOMER	.T.	Customer Zip	.T.
CPHONE	C	010	000	CUSTOMER	.T.	Customer Phone	.T.
CLASTNAME	C	25	000	CUSTOMER	.T.	Customer Last Name	.T.
CNAME				CUSTOMER	.T.	Customer Full Name	.F.
CINVID	C	9	0	PURCHASE	.T.	Internal Inv. Link	.F.

```
NCDAMT       N    5    2 PURCHASE   .T.   Cost When     .T.
                                          Purchased
NCDQTY       N    2    0 PURCHASE   .T.   # of CDs      .T.
                                          Purchased
CID          C    9      INVOICE    .T.   Invoice       .F.
                                          Internal ID
CCUSTID      C    9      INVOICE    .T.   Cust          .F.
                                          Internal Link
DORDERED     D    8      INVOICE    .T.   Invoice Date  .T.
CINVNUM      C   10      INVOICE    .T.   Invoice       .T.
                                          Number

Index_Key Contents:
       NCOST      STR(nCost,5,2)
       NPRICE     STR(nPrice,5,2)
       CNAME      cLastName + cFirstName
```

Invoice Line-Item Purchases: PURCHASE.DBF

The Purchase table contains the line item information for an invoice. This file contains the CD Price and Quantity at purchase time. The CD Price field in the CD table is the current CD Price, which may change over time, so we record that information at purchase time as well.

```
Structure for table:      c:\book25\cd\purchase.dbf
Number of data records: 34
Date of last update:      07/19/1993
Field  Field Name  Type         Width     Dec
    1  CINVID      Character        9
    2  CCDID       Character        9
    3  NCDAMT      Numeric          5       2
    4  NCDQTY      Numeric          2
** Total **                        26
```

Report Dictionary: REPOLIST.DBF

RepoList contains the information that drives our Reports reusable window. It contains the DOS file name of the report and connected .QPR file, and a full English name that the user sees. The mFRX and mFRT memo fields are used to hold a copy of the report itself, in case we grant the user rights to modify a report. If we do that, we want to have some method of resetting the report to its original specification just in case there is a problem. This technique makes this possible.

```
Structure for table:     c:\book25\cd\dbfs\repolist.dbf
Number of data records: 5
Date of last update:     04/29/1993
Memo file block size:    33
Field  Field Name   Type         Width    Dec
    1  CDOSNAME     Character        8
    2  CFULLNAME    Character       30
    3  MFRX         Memo            10
    4  MFRT         Memo            10
    5  CTYPE        Character        4
    6  LEDITABLE    Logical          1
    7  CSELECT      Character       10
    8  CWINDSHOW    Character        4
** Total **                         78

  Structural CDX file:   C:\BOOK25\CD\DBFS\REPOLIST.CDX
           Index tag:    CDOSNAME      Key: CDOSNAME
           Index tag:    CFULLNAME     Key: CFULLNAME
           Index tag:    CTYPE         Key: CTYPE
           Index tag:    LEDITABLE     Key: LEDITABLE
           Index tag:    CSELECT       Key: CSELECT
           Index tag:    CWINDSHOW     Key: CWINDSHOW

Table Contents:
```

CDOSNAME	CFULLNAME	CTYPE	LEDITABLE	CSELECT	CWINDSHOW
LISTCD	Compact Disc Listing	List	.F.	CD	List
LISTCUST	Customer Listing	List	.F.	CUSTOMER	List
ORDERS	Customer Orders	Repo	.F.		Repo
CUSTLBL	Customer Mailing Labels	Labe	.F.	CUSTOMER	Labe
ARREPO	30/60/90 Report	Repo	.F.		Repo

User Access File: SECURITY.DBF

The Security table is used to hold information about user's security rights. It is tied to the main menu's SKIP FOR clauses. If a user's ID and a menu option are found in this table, that option is automatically dimmed. For a more detailed explanation, please see Chapter 14, *Our Menu—MAIN.MNX*.

```
Structure for table:    c:\book25\cd\dbfs\security.dbf
Number of data records: 0
Date of last update:    07/12/1991
Field  Field Name  Type        Width    Dec
    1  CUSERID     Character       5
    2  CMENUID     Character       8
** Total **                       14

  Structural CDX file:    C:\BOOK25\CD\DBFS\SECURITY.CDX
            Index tag:    CUSERID       Key: CUSERID
            Index tag:    CMENUID       Key: CMENUID
```

State Validation: STATES.DBF

States is a straightforward table containing a state's abbreviation and its full name.

```
Structure for table:    c:\common25\dbfs\states.dbf
Number of data records: 51
Date of last update:    05/26/1991
Field  Field Name  Type        Width    Dec
    1  CSTATE      Character       2
    2  CFULLNAME   Character      20
** Total **                       23

  Structural CDX file:    C:\COMMON25\DBFS\STATES.CDX
       Index tag:    CFULLNAME    Collate: Machine   Key: CFULLNAME
       Index tag:    CSTATE       Collate: Machine   Key: CSTATE
```

Runtime Setup Information: SETUP.DBF

Setup contains application specific information for data driven routines including the ABOUT screen and our unique ID handler. For those of you who have the original *FoxPro Codebook*, please note that we no longer have a unique field for every table's ID. That is now handled by our NewID() function as described in Chapter 3, *Multiuser Programming*.

```
Structure for table:     c:\book25\cd\setup.dbf
Number of data records: 1
Date of last update:     07/20/1993
Field  Field Name  Type          Width     Dec
    1  CSESSIONID  Character         4
    2  CCURRPRINT  Character        10
    3  CSYSTNAME   Character        40
    4  CLONGNAME1  Character        40
    5  CLONGNAME2  Character        40
    6  CSHORTNAME  Character        10
** Total **                        145

Table Contents:
CSESSIONID      0029
CCURRPRINT
CSYSTNAME       Compact Disc Ordering Application
CLONGNAME1      Demonstration Source Code for
CLONGNAME2      The FoxPro 2.5 Codebook
CSHORTNAME      CDTrak...
```

Trapped Error Message: ONERROR.DBF

OnError is a table that stores basic error-handling information. It is called from the OnError screen set.

```
Structure for table:     c:\book25\cd\onerror.dbf
Number of data records: 2
Date of last update:     07/15/1993
Memo file block size:    64
Field  Field Name  Type          Width     Dec
    1  MMESSAGE    Memo             10
    2  MMESSAGE1   Memo             10
    3  NLINENO     Numeric           6
    4  NERROR      Numeric           4
    5  DDATE       Date              8
    6  CTIME       Character         8
    7  MPROC       Memo             10
** Total **                         57
```

Application Help File: CODEHELP.DBF

CodeHelp is a standard FoxPro help table containing help information for this application.

Invoice Header Information: INVOICE.DBF

The Invoice table contains the header information for any invoices. We use a ten character user-modifiable invoice number, many applications will have code to auto-increment this number.

```
Structure for table:    c:\book25\cd\invoice.dbf
Number of data records: 9
Date of last update:    07/19/1993
Field  Field Name  Type          Width    Dec
    1  CID         Character         9
    2  CCUSTID     Character         9
    3  DORDERED    Date              8
    4  CINVNUM     Character        10
    5  CLASTUPD    Character         9
** Total **                         46
```

Developer Information: INTSETUP.DBF

IntSetup contains information on the developers of the application. It is used in the ABOUT screens as well as by the BCKGRND screen in DOS.

```
Structure for table:    c:\common25\dbfs\intsetup.dbf
Number of data records: 1
Date of last update:    05/11/1993
Memo file block size:   33
Field  Field Name  Type          Width    Dec
    1  CCOMPANY    Character        40
    2  CADDRESS1   Character        40
    3  CADDRESS2   Character        40
    4  CCITY       Character        20
    5  CSTATE      Character         2
    6  CZIP        Character         9
    7  CPHONE      Character        10
    8  CFAX        Character        10
    9  MCOMPINFO   Memo             10
** Total **                        182
```

```
Table Contents:
CCOMPANY          Flash Creative Management, Inc.
CADDRESS1         1060 Main Street
CADDRESS2         Third Floor
CCITY             River Edge
CSTATE            NJ
CZIP              07661
CPHONE            2014892500
CFAX              2014896750
MCOMPINFO         Miscellaneous Company Information
```

Table-Level Data Dictionary: TABLDICT.DBF

TablDict is a dictionary file that contains information on the tables in the system. It is used to handle opening the proper files (by OPENDB.PRG) and to create a BROWSE in the ListIt routine. There is an extra memo field, mDelAlias, which can be used to add cascading delete information for a new reusable program at some point in time.

```
Structure for table:     c:\book25\cd\dbfs\tabldict.dbf
Number of data records:  4
Date of last update:     05/02/1993
Memo file block size:    64
Field  Field Name  Type        Width     Dec
    1  CDBFNAME    Character       8
    2  CALIAS      Character      10
    3  CINITORDER  Character      10
    4  NBROWSIZE   Numeric         2
    5  MBROWSE     Memo           10
    6  MDELALIAS   Memo           10
** Total **                       51

Table Contents:
  CDBFNAME CALIAS     CINITORDER NBROWSIZE MBROWSE MDELALIAS
  CD       CD                           66 Memo    memo
  CUSTOMER CUSTOMER                     60 Memo    memo
  INVOICE  INVOICE                      27 Memo    memo
  PURCHASE PURCHASE                        memo    memo
```

```
    mBrowse Contents:
CD        BROWSE FIELDS cMusician :25 :H='Musician', cTitle :30
          :H='Title', nPrice :05 :H="Price"
Customer  BROWSE FIELDS cName = TRIM(cLastName)+", "+cFirstName :35
          :H='Name', cState :5 :H="State", cPhone :14
          :P="@R (999) 999-9999" :H="Phone"
Invoice   BROWSE FIELDS cInvNum :10 :H="Invoice #", dOrdered :12
          :H="Invoice Date" FOR cCustID = laCustPick[lnCustPick,2]
```

Chapter 13

Our Project File—CODEBOOK.PJX

The project builder is the core of the FoxPro programmer's application development efforts. A programmer uses a project to access screen sets, menus, programs, databases, reports, labels, libraries, and anything involved in creating and modifying an application. FoxPro's project builder automatically assures that everything is maintained and kept current (even across multiple directories, if you want).

By "excluding" a file, you can make it available to the project builder, but it will not be bound into the APP/EXE file that you create to run your application. Typically, you would not exclude a help database or a database of state abbreviations used in state validation. These can be bound into the APP/EXE file, ensuring that they remain static and available to the application.

The project builder allows a programmer to look at a program as a series of "objects" that call each other in order to provide the functionality required. These objects can be recycled across applications, simply by including an object from one application in another's project. No duplication of code or wasted disk space occurs. This allows a programmer to quickly model new applications based on older ones.

Another benefit to developing in a project-centric approach is that the project builder knows what kind of file it is pointing to. Double-clicking on a database file will pop up a browse. Double-clicking on a menu will bring up the menu builder. The project builder insulates you from specifically calling the item.

Designing a Common Project Directory Structure

To use the project builder effectively, create a directory structure as follows:

```
COMMON (parent directory for your common code)
    BMPS (common bitmaps)
    SCREENS (common screen sets)
    MENUS  (common menus)
    DBFS (common databases and indexes)
    QUERIES (common SQL queries)
    REPORTS (common reports and labels)
    PROGS (common program files)
```

PROGS is used to replace the old SET PROCEDURE TO convention of programming. In FoxPro 1.02 and Foxbase+, a programmer would typically combine all common programs into one large procedure file, and issue a SET PROCEDURE TO <filename> command. The programs in the procedure file would now be available throughout the application. FoxPro's project builder manages all references to other programs when a project is rebuilt or an application is compiled. Therefore, divide your old procedure file into separate programs, and store them each in the COMMON\PROGS directory. Use these procedures in your program code as you did before. When FoxPro rebuilds the project or compiles your application, it will look for the file with the procedure that you've called. If it doesn't find it, FoxPro will ask you to locate it. Once you've done this, it will always know where to look for your program. This way, only the programs that you actually use will be bound into your APP/EXE file. There won't be any extra "baggage" in your application.

Designing an Application-Specific Directory Structure

When beginning a new application, create another parent subdirectory with the name of the application (in our case CD). It will have the same structure as the COMMON directory, but will contain code and data that is unique to this application. The parent directory will contain the project itself and any files distributed with the application. In other words, databases and indexes distributed separately to the user will stay in the parent directory, as will any reports that may be sent to the user for modification.

Remember, the project builder allows you to include reports in the APP/EXE file, making them usable but not modifiable. These reports can be placed in the REPORTS subdirectory, since they will not be shipped separately to the user.

By keeping all the files that are distributed in the root directory, you can easily write a program to automatically create a distribution diskette! The structure of the application directory tree is as follows:

```
CD (parent directory containing the project & distributed data)
    BMPS (application bitmaps)
    SCREENS (application screen sets)
    MENUS (application menus)
    DBFS (dbfs and indexes that are included in the APP/EXE)
    QUERIES (application SQL queries)
    REPORTS (reports and labels that are included in the APP/EXE)
    PROGS (programs that are included in the APP/EXE)
    OTHER (miscellaneous files)
```

The OTHER directory can contain any type of file that you want. One nice idea is to include a TODO.LST file in the OTHER directory, and to add it to the project as a "File". Now, whenever you have an idea, it is a simple matter to click on the TODO.LST in the project, and jot it down. Another file that is useful in this regard is BUGS.LST, which tracks any bugs and records when they have been fixed.

Chapter 14

Our Menu—MAIN.MNX

The menu used in our Codebook application is essentially a duplicate of the one in the original *FoxPro Codebook*. I haven't rewritten it to adhere to each platform's interface because I am assuming that some existing users of the DOS application will wish to move between platforms without retraining. This was a design decision. Creating a Windows- or Macintosh-adherent version of the menu takes only a few minutes' work in the menu builder.

FoxPro's menu builder allows you to quickly create pull-down menus that are available throughout your application. FoxPro's "Quick Menu" feature will place all the FoxPro system menu in the menu-building window, allowing you to modify it as necessary. Placing code in the setup for a specific popup will allow you to create *stubs* that are called if any of that popup's bars are selected and have no code associated with them. When prototyping an application, a common use for this stub is the command:

```
WAIT WINDOW NOWAIT "Not yet implemented"
```

This will allow you to quickly show the user which menu choices will be available. Selecting one of these stubs pops up a window showing *Not yet implemented* and lets you later add specific code to these choices at a later date.

A Common Beginning

In our COMMON/MENUS directory, we keep a "base" menu used to begin all our projects. We copy this menu into our application-specific MENUS subdirectory and add it to our project. We now have a place to begin work on our application.

The main menu bar begins with System, File, and Edit menu pads. It continues with Database, Record, Program, Output, and Window. Each menu pad has a defined purpose:

System	The System popup contains general system routines. The popup associated with this pad is static, and no changes have to be made from application to application.
File	We begin with the File pad that is placed through Quick Menu and remove items that do not apply to a typical application (like Print, which we move to Output). This pad also remains static from application to application.
Edit	The Edit popup is also taken from FoxPro's Quick Menu command. This offers our application full undo and redo, and

cut, copy, and paste capabilities with no coding. This pad remains static from application to application.

Database	The Database popup contains all the actions performed on an entire database. This pad remains static from application to application.
Record	The Record popup manages all of the common record manipulation for an application. This pad allows you to move from record to record, edit a record, save a record, etc. This pad remains static from application to application.
Program	The Program popup contains the code to bring up an entry screen or to bring a specific entry screen to the front of multiple windows. This pad changes from application to application, though the window-calling conventions do not.
Output	The Output popup manages all forms of output: listing, reports, mail-merge secondary files and customized reports. This pad remains static from application to application, though the database that drives the directory of available reports changes from application to application.
Window	The Window popup allows the user to manipulate the multiple windows available through a modeless application. While this pad appears to be similar to the one that FoxPro places into the menu builder with Quick Menu, it differs from it in that it places the window *title* in the window list, instead of the window name. This makes the pad easier for the user to understand (they see *Customer Entry Screen* instead of *wrCustome1*). This menu remains static from application to application.

As you can readily see, most of the menu remains static from application to application. This is made possible through naming conventions (explained in earlier chapters) that automate most of the process. Let's look at the menus in greater detail.

Our Application's Menus

In this section, we'll look at our application's menus in detail.

The System Pad

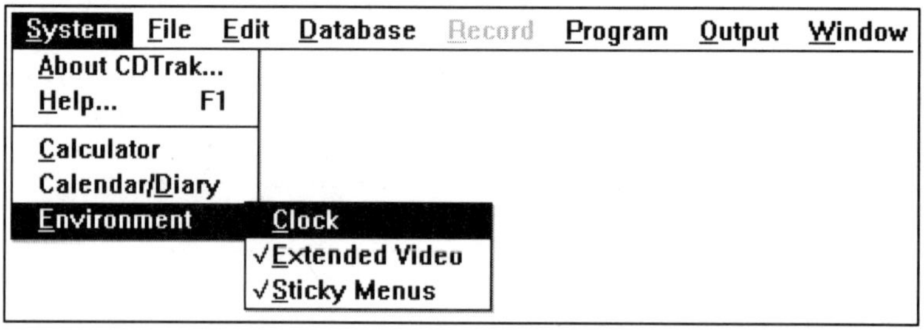

System File Edit Database Record Program Output Window
About CDTrak...
Help... F1
Calculator
Calendar/Diary
Environment
Clock
√Extended Video
√Sticky Menus

The system menu contains five bars and one submenu. The first two bars are separated from the other three by a line that groups similar functions together and makes the menu easier to read.

About <system name>...

This bar automatically calls up the four ABOUT windows that provide information on the application and the hardware running it. This bar is data driven from the Setup table. Note the expression used for the bar's prompt:

```
\About "+Setup.cShortName +"
```

This forces the generator to add the cShortName field from the Setup table into the About prompt.

Note that this pad is followed by an ellipsis (...). The user interface guidelines recommend this format because the window called requires user entry.

Help...

Selecting this bar brings up a window with the help topics available for this application. A hot key is added to this menu item, allowing a user to access it quickly.

Note that this pad is followed by an ellipsis (...). The user interface guidelines recommend this format because the window called requires user entry.

Calculator

Selecting Calculator from the System popup automatically brings forward FoxPro's built-in calculator. No work is required to provide this capability, so why not add it for our users?

Calendar/Diary

Selecting Calendar/Diary from the System popup automatically brings forward FoxPro's built-in calendar. If this application is multiuser, the users must each have their own resource file in order to access the Diary section. Again, no work is required to provide this capability, so we provide it willingly.

Environment — Selecting this bar from the System popup brings up a submenu to which we add as many environmental settings as we would like the user to access. In this case, we are providing access to three selections: clock, extended video, and sticky menus.

Selecting Clock toggles the appearance of FoxPro's built-in clock.

Selecting Extended Video toggles the monitor from 25-line to 43- or 50-line mode (depending on the monitor) under DOS.

Sticky Menus allow the mouse user to click on a menu pad and have the associated popup remain on the screen.

Note that these three menu bars make use of FoxPro's "mark" feature. They show a mark character when they are turned on. This allows a user to quickly see the option's status.

Note also that some of these options may not make sense in Windows or Macintosh applications. Placing a RELEASE PAD in a platform-checking CASE statement in the menu cleanup will allow you to remove these options.

The File Pad

The File menu contains three bars. The bars are separated from each other by lines because they each perform separate functions.

Close — Selecting this option will close the currently open window. This bar is kept "as is" from the Quick Menu selection.

Printer Setup — Selecting this option would normally bring up a window that allows the user to select which type of printer is being used. Our sample application uses this option as a sample of the "stub" code, and will activate a *Not yet implemented* window.

Quit — Selecting this option will end the program and exit the system.

The Edit Pad

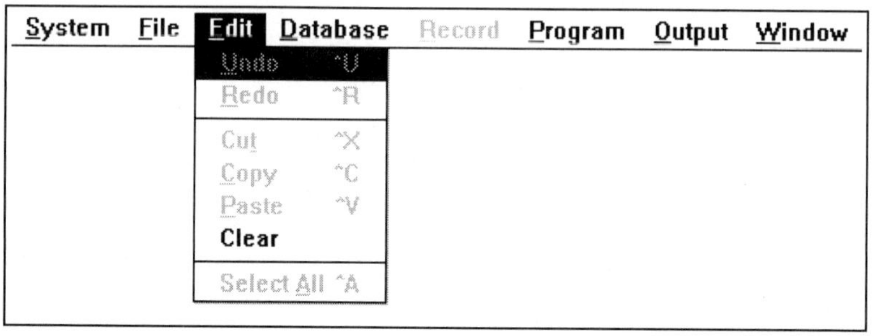

System File Edit Database Record Program Output Window

Undo ^U
Redo ^R
Cut ^X
Copy ^C
Paste ^V
Clear
Select All ^A

The Edit menu contains seven bars separated according to function by lines. These bars are all automatically created by the Quick Menus function. *Note that the hot keys assigned are the same hot keys used in the DOS environment in which this application was originally created. This will allow our application to be quickly ported to other environments and builds on the existing knowledge of our users.*

Undo — Selecting this option will undo any text modifications made. This is especially useful in memo field–intensive applications.

Redo — This option performs the opposite function of Undo. If the user has mistakenly undone a modification, selecting Redo will redo that modification.

Cut — Selecting this option will remove any text selected by the user, and will place it on the Clipboard for later use.

Copy — Selecting this will place a copy of the selected text on the Clipboard for later use.

Paste — This option will place the text from the Clipboard in the current field.

Clear — This option will clear any selected text without placing it on the Clipboard.

Select All — This option will select everything in the current field.

The Database Pad

The Database menu contains three bars separated by a line according to function. These functions perform global operations on the entire database.

Order... This option allows the user to select the order in which the data is displayed. Selecting this menu option calls one of our reusable screen objects, GETORDER.SPR.

Note that this pad is followed by an ellipsis (...). The user interface guidelines recommend this format because the window called requires user entry.

Reindex... Selecting this option brings up another of our reusable screen objects, DBFREIND.SPR. This window allows the user to reindex one or all of the databases, and keeps the user apprised of what is happening as the indexing operation continues.

Note that this pad is followed by an ellipsis (...). The user interface guidelines recommend this format because the window called requires user entry.

Compress... Selecting this option brings up yet another of our reusable screen objects, DBFPACK.SPR. This window allows the user to compress one or all of the existing databases that contain memo fields, and keeps the user apprised of what is happening as the PACK MEMO operation continues.

Note that this pad is followed by an ellipsis (...). The user interface guidelines recommend this format because the window called requires user entry.

The Record Pad

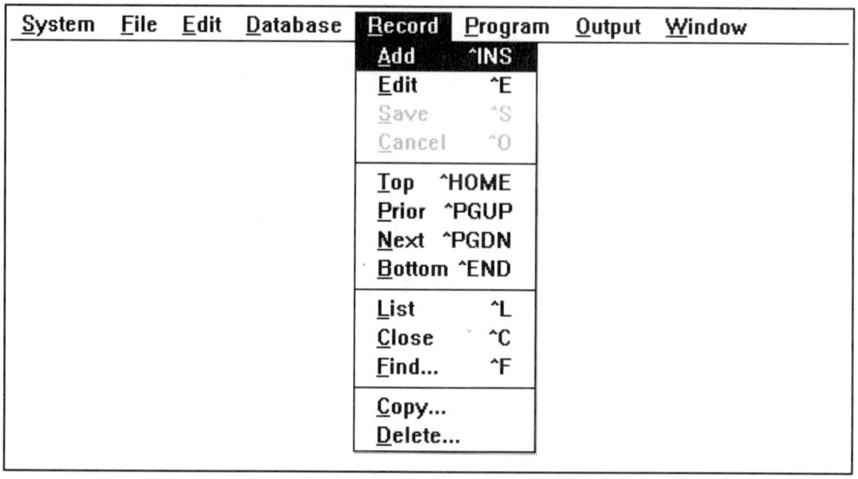

```
System  File  Edit  Database  Record  Program  Output  Window
                              Add      ^INS
                              Edit     ^E
                              Save     ^S
                              Cancel   ^O
                              Top    ^HOME
                              Prior  ^PGUP
                              Next   ^PGDN
                              Bottom ^END
                              List     ^L
                              Close    ^C
                              Find...  ^F
                              Copy...
                              Delete...
```

The Record menu contains thirteen bars separated according to their function. The first eleven of these bars duplicate the selections on the control window. This gives the user three ways of performing these common functions: clicking on the control window, selecting the menu option, or using the hot key associated with the option. In this manner, we have designed an easy-to-use system for the beginner and a quick system for the advanced user. *Note that Delete is found only on this menu and does not have an associated hot key. Delete is a destructive function, and making its selection a little "unfriendly" helps to protect the integrity of the overall system.*

Add	Selecting this option will allow the user to add a new item to whatever window the user is currently working with.
Edit	Selecting this option will allow the user to edit the current item. We force the user to select Edit because we do not want to lock the record (in a multiuser situation) until the user is ready to work with it. This system always shows information on the screen, but it cannot be modified until a user chooses the Edit option.
Save	This option saves the current modifications that the user has made. In our sample application, modifications are not made to the actual data until a user selects this option.

Cancel	Cancel allows the user to return the record to the last saved state. If the user realizes that a mistaken entry has been made, this selection allows them to backtrack and recapture the pre-existing data.
Top	Selecting this option takes the user to the first record, the "top" of the file.
Prior	Selecting this option allows the user to move to the previous record.
Next	Selecting this option allows the user to move to the next record.
Bottom	Selecting this option takes the user to the last record, the "bottom" of the file.
List	Selecting this option shows a listing of the entire database, allowing the user to quickly move to another record. When used in concert with the Order option in the Database menu, List is a very powerful tool for users.
Close	This option closes the current screen set.
Find...	Selecting this option brings up AppSrch.spr, our reusable screen program, and allows the user to find an item in the current database.
Copy...	This option will ask the user to verify that they want a copy to take place, and if so, will duplicate the current information with a new unique ID.
Delete...	The Delete option allows the user to remove a record from the data file. The record is not truly removed until the user select Pack is selected from the Database menu, but in the meantime the record remains invisible to the user. *Note that the Delete option calls up a window that forces the user to confirm the deletion of the record.* *Note that this pad is followed by an ellipsis (...). The user inter-face guidelines recommend this format because the window called requires user entry.*

The Program Pad

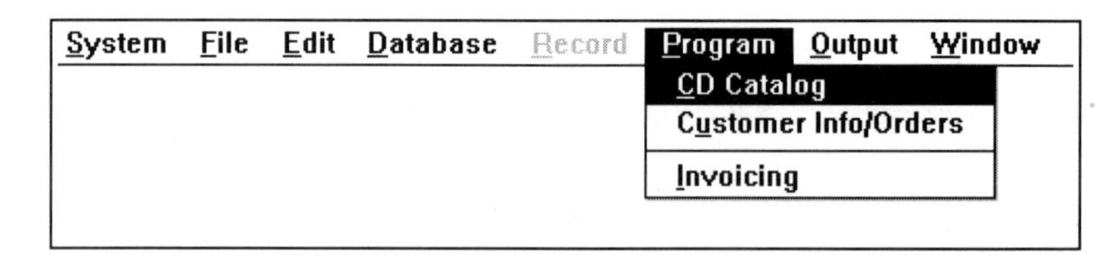

The Program pad is the heart of our application. From this popup the windows used in this application are opened.

CD Catalog...	Selecting this option allows the user to work with the list of CDs currently being handled by the company. Once a CD is listed in the window, it may be modified or deleted. New CDs can be added to the system from this window as well.
Customer Info/Orders...	This option allows the user to work with all the company's customers. The user can access basic information on the customer, including a list of CDs ordered.
Invoicing	This option calls up our invoice-entry window, which is an example of a one to many window.

The Output Pad

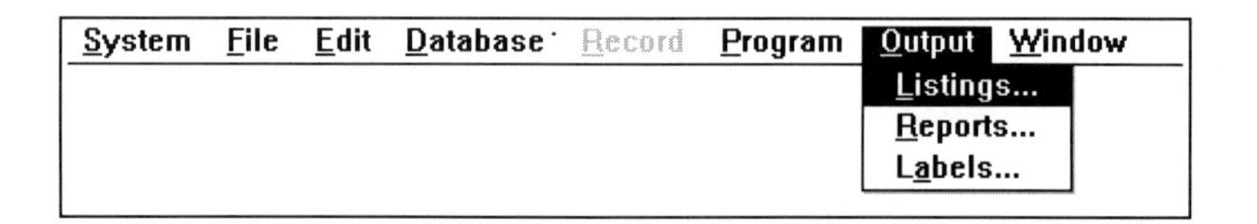

The Output popup controls all output options in our program. By default, the output menu runs from a data driven report handler (which will be discussed in detail later). It contains three pads.

Listings... Listings are simple lists of information, typically setup data.

Note that this pad is followed by an ellipsis (...). The user inter-face guidelines recommend this format because the window called requires user entry.

Reports... This menu pad allows the user to select a report to print.

Note that this pad is followed by an ellipsis (...). The user inter-face guidelines recommend this format because the window called requires user entry.

Labels... This option allows the user to select a label form to be printed.

Note that this pad is followed by an ellipsis (...). The user inter-face guidelines recommend this format because the window called requires user entry.

The Window Pad

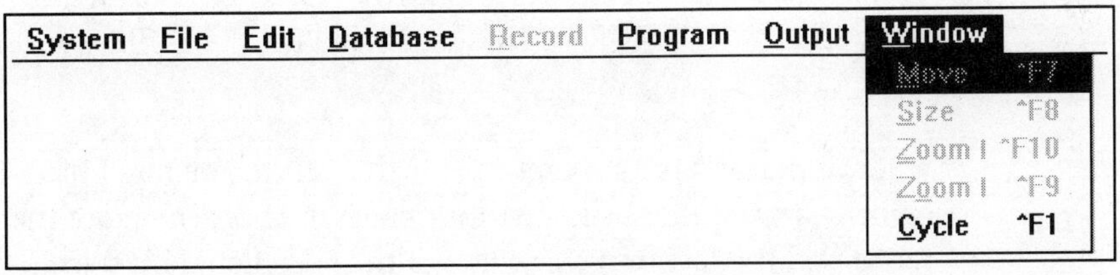

System File Edit Database Record Program Output Window

Move ^F7
Size ^F8
Zoom ↑ ^F10
Zoom ↓ ^F9
Cycle ^F1

The Window popup allows the user to manipulate the different windows on the screen. The upper part of the menu contains static options. The lower portion of the menu contains a listing of currently visible windows. Selecting one of these windows brings that window to the "front" of the screen, making it active. All these options have a hot key, allowing the advanced user to perform them quickly.

Move This option allows the user to move the window to another location on the screen—for example, if the viewer wishes to work in extended-video mode and to use the enlarged screen area.

Size Selecting this option allows the user to resize the current window. Typical entry windows will not be resizable, however BROWSE type windows can be resized to the user's preference.

Zoom Selecting this option zooms the window to full-screen size immediately. Typical entry windows cannot be zoomed, but BROWSE-type windows can be zoomed to display more information.

Zoom Selecting this option minimizes the window to a one-row by eighteen-character size. Typical entry windows cannot be minimized, but BROWSE type windows can be minimized to move them temporarily out of the way.

Cycle — This option activates windows sequentially, allowing the user to cycle between them, until the proper window is active. All windows except MODAL windows can be cycled.

Security Implementations

Using the menu builder in concert with a "Security" database makes creating a password-based application a snap. To implement a security system:

1. Create a database with two fields, cLogonID (C:5) and cMenuID (C:8).

2. When creating the menu, select the SKIP FOR check box in the menu bar options window. The SKIP FOR clause should use the SEEK() function like this:

   ```
   SEEK(Security,<cMenuID>)
   ```

   where cMenuID is a mnemonic for the current menu choice. I use an eight-character field, the first four characters of which are the main pad name and the last four the name of the specific menu selection. For example, if I am defining the bar for the calculator, I would type:

   ```
   SEEK(Security,"SYSTCALC")
   ```

   This code tells the system to check the Security database for a record with the current menu item in it. If this record is found, the function returns true, and the menu option is automatically dimmed.

3. When the user logs on, set a global variable, gcUserID, to that user's logon name (or to a group logon name, if you are providing protection by group, not by individual user).

4. Open the Security table, set the order to cMenuID, and set a FILTER to the current logged in user with a SET FILTER TO cLogonID = gcUserID. This causes the SEEK() command in the SKIP FOR clause to look only at the current user's records in the security database.

   To disable any menu option, one need only place a record in the Security database with the user's logon ID and the menu option to disable.

While this application does not require a security system, I have built a simple example into the code. I have hard-coded the user's ID (in the Menu Cleanup snippet) as YAG. If you USE the Security database and add some records for YAG, you will see that the appropriate menu items are dimmed once the application is rebuilt.

Chapter 15

Application-Specific Screens

Inventory Entry: CD.SCX

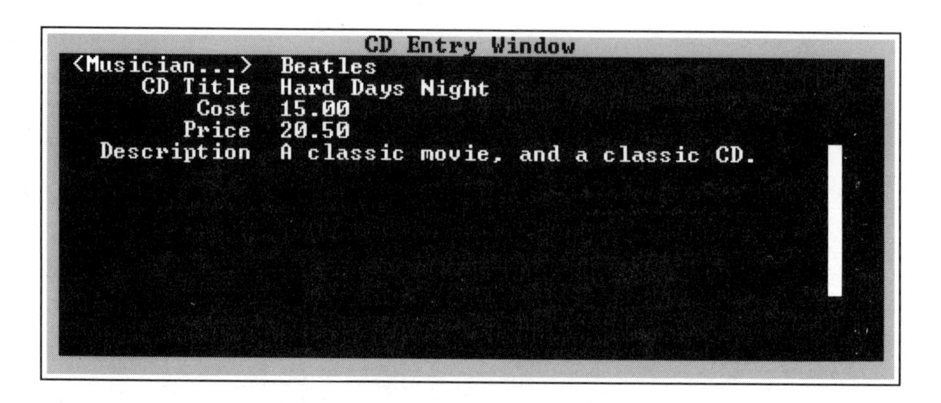

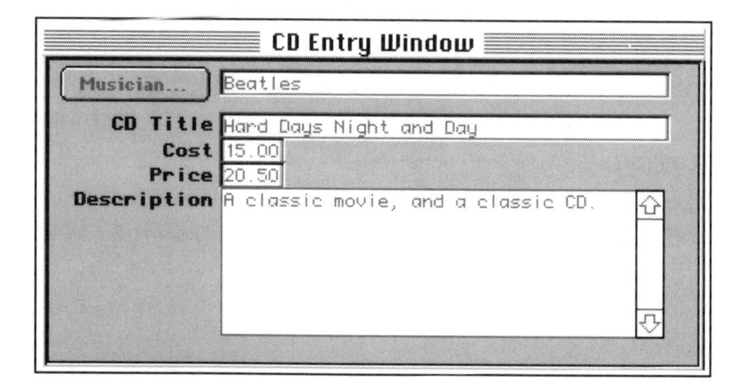

CD is the first screen in our application. It allows the entry of inventory information. Let's take a close look at the code snippets required for this window.

First, we name the window wrCD, following our naming conventions. This lets our event handler know that we are dealing with a modeless application window.

The Setup Snippet

The Setup snippet contains the #SECTION generator directives, which force FoxPro to generate anything in #SECTION 1 at the top of the generated code. The new #WCLAUSES directive allows us to add clauses to the FoxPro generated DEFINE WINDOW command. We use the command:

```
#WCLAUSES IN &gcMainWind
```

because FoxPro only allows one #WCLAUSES command per window, and we want to define the window IN SCREEN under DOS, and IN WINDOW wzMain under Windows and Macintosh. This allows us to create the toolbar effect. Since all application windows will be IN WINDOW wzMain, which is defined under the toolbar panel, every application window is forced to stay under the toolbar, thereby not allowing the user to drag them over the toolbar. The variable, gcMainWind, is defined in Traficop as either "SCREEN" or "WINDOW wzMain" depending on the platform. It is properly called at runtime thanks to the macro substitution.

We continue by selecting the workarea that this window requires, and putting the current information into memory. The reusable programs AddBar() and RestMem() are called with the title of the window. AddBar() adds the title of the window to the Window menu popup, allowing the user to select a window in that manner if necessary. The RestMem() function checks to see if the user last left this window in the middle of an edit. If so, it restores the memory variables that were in use, and makes sure that the correct record is selected.

The Deactivate Snippet

The Deactivate snippet contains our standard expression:

```
StopRead("wrCD")
```

As explained in Chapter 4, *Event-Driven Programming*, this function tests to see if the window's READ should end.

The Cleanup Snippet

The Cleanup snippet simply checks to see if the user has elected to close this window. If so, we call the KillBar() and KillWind() functions. The first of these removes the menu bar that was installed in the Window menu pad. The KillWind() function removes the current window and all related windows from memory. It then checks to see if the toolbar should be removed as well, and does so if necessary.

CD Window—A Summary

This window contains approximately ten lines of FoxPro code. That is all that is necessary in order to implement the full range of capabilities necessary. Since this is a relatively simple "setup" type of window, we can default to all of the common methods for the necessary data handling.

Note that the fact that we use the default procedures doesn't make this a poor window. It has full multiuser, modeless, state-saving capabilities, and the user can Add, Edit, Find, List, Copy, Delete, and navigate through this window.

This window shows the power of the object oriented approach to development in FoxPro. With relatively little code, we've created a fully functional window. Basically, we can prototype a functional window simply by drawing and naming it properly.

```
******************************************************************
**--    CD.SCX - DOS PLATFORM
******************************************************************
```

```
( ) DeskTop                          (·) Window

Name:    wrCD                        <Type...>
Title:   CD Entry Window
Footer:

Size:              Screen Code:

  Height:   16      [X] Setup...
  Width:    61      [X] Cleanup & Procs...          «   OK   »

Position:          READ Clauses:                    < Cancel >

  Row:        0     [ ] Activate...    [ ] Show...
  Column:     0     [ ] Valid...       [ ] When...
  [X] Center        [X] Deactivate...

Environment:                          [X] Add alias

      Environment NOT saved with screen.
```

```
Type:        User

Attributes:       Border:

  [ ] Close         ( ) None
  [X] Float         ( ) Single
  [ ] Shadow        ( ) Double      «   OK   »
  [X] Minimize      ( ) Panel
                    (·) System      < Cancel >

Color Schemes:

  Primary:          Popup:

  Windows           Window Pop
```

```
******************************************************************
*  SCREEN SETUP CODE
******************************************************************
#SECTION 1
#WCLAUSES IN &gcMainWind
#SECTION 2
SELECT CD
SCATTER MEMVAR MEMO
=addbar('wrCD')
=restmem('wrCD')
PRIVATE liCD
liCD = 0
------------------------------------------------------------------
```

```
*-- READ Deactivate Clause
-------------------------------------------------------------

  READ Deactivate
    (·) Procedure
    ( ) Expression

RETURN stopread('wrCD')
**************************************************************
*--    G E T    O B J E C T S
**************************************************************
*=============================================================
*  licd
*=============================================================
 @   0,   0
     SIZE  14,   59
 Spacing:    0

  Invisible Buttons #:   1
    (·) Horizontal     ( ) Vertical
    [ ] Terminating   <Spacing...>

  Variable:
                                        «   OK   »
    < Choose... > licd
                                        < Cancel >

  Options:
    [X] When...      [ ] Comment...
    [ ] Valid...     [ ] Disabled
    [ ] Message...

-------------------------------------------------------------
*-- licd When Clause
-------------------------------------------------------------

  When
    ( ) Procedure
    (·) Expression

When:   !glEditable
*=============================================================
*  lhMusician
*=============================================================
 @   0,   1
```

```
Spacing:     1

 Push Button Prompts:        (·) Horizontal    ( ) Vertical
                             [ ] Terminating  <Spacing...>
 Musician...
                            Variable:

                             < Choose... >  lhMusician

                            Options:

                             [ ] When...      [ ] Comment...
                             [X] Valid...     [X] Disabled
                             [X] Message...

                «   OK   »     < Cancel >
------------------------------------------------------------
*-- lhMusician Valid Clause
------------------------------------------------------------

   Valid
      (·) Procedure
      ( ) Expression

DO musician.spr
SHOW GET m.cMusician
------------------------------------------------------------
*-- lhMusician Message Clause
------------------------------------------------------------

   Message
      ( ) Procedure
      (·) Expression

Message:    "Enter the artist for this compact disc"
*===========================================================
*  Text: CD Title
*===========================================================
 @   1,   6
*===========================================================
*  Text: Cost
*===========================================================
 @   2,  10
*===========================================================
*  Text: Price
```

```
*=============================================================
 @   3,   9
*=============================================================
*  Text: Description
*=============================================================
 @   4,   3
*=============================================================
*  m.cmusician
*=============================================================
 @   0,  16

   Field:

   ( ) Say          (·) Get          ( ) Edit

   <  Get...    > m.cmusician
                                                   «   OK   »
   < Format... >
                                                   < Cancel >
   Range:

   [ ] Upper...                    [ ] Lower...

   [X] When...      [ ] Error...       [ ] Scroll bar
   [ ] Valid...     [ ] Comment...     [ ] Allow tabs
   [ ] Message...   [X] Disabled       [X] Refresh

-------------------------------------------------------------
*-- m.cmusician When Clause
-------------------------------------------------------------

   When

   ( ) Procedure
   (·) Expression

When:   .f.
*=============================================================
*  m.ctitle
*=============================================================
 @   1,  16
```

```
Field:
  ( ) Say          (·) Get          ( ) Edit

< Get...   > m.ctitle
                                          «   OK   »
< Format... >
                                          < Cancel >
Range:
  [ ] Upper...                 [ ] Lower...

[ ] When...       [ ] Error...      [ ] Scroll bar
[ ] Valid...      [ ] Comment...    [ ] Allow tabs
[X] Message...    [X] Disabled      [ ] Refresh
-----------------------------------------------------------------
*-- m.ctitle Message Clause
-----------------------------------------------------------------

Message
  ( ) Procedure
  (·) Expression

Message:   "Enter the title of this CD.  Do not start with 'The' or 'A'..."
*================================================================
*  m.ncost
*================================================================
 @   2,  16

Field:
  ( ) Say          (·) Get          ( ) Edit

< Get...   > m.ncost
                                          «   OK   »
< Format... >
                                          < Cancel >
Range:
  [ ] Upper...                 [ ] Lower...

[ ] When...       [ ] Error...      [ ] Scroll bar
[ ] Valid...      [ ] Comment...    [ ] Allow tabs
[X] Message...    [X] Disabled      [ ] Refresh
-----------------------------------------------------------------
```

```
*-- m.ncost Message Clause
--------------------------------------------------------------

  Message
  ( ) Procedure
  (·) Expression

Message:   "Enter OUR cost of purchasing this compact disc"
*=============================================================
*  m.nprice
*=============================================================
 @   3,  16

  Field:
  ( ) Say          (·) Get          ( ) Edit

  <  Get...   > m.nprice
                                              «   OK   »
  < Format... >
                                              < Cancel >
  Range:
  [ ] Upper...                    [ ] Lower...

  [ ] When...      [ ] Error...      [ ] Scroll bar
  [ ] Valid...     [ ] Comment...    [ ] Allow tabs
  [X] Message...   [X] Disabled      [ ] Refresh

--------------------------------------------------------------
*-- m.nprice Message Clause
--------------------------------------------------------------

  Message
  ( ) Procedure
  (·) Expression

Message:   "Enter the price at which we will be selling this CD"
*=============================================================
*  m.mdescript
*=============================================================
 @   4,  16
```

```
Field:
  ( ) Say        ( ) Get        (·) Edit

< Edit...   > m.mdescript
                                            «   OK   »
< Format... > @2
                                            < Cancel >
Range:
  [ ] Upper...                  [ ] Lower...

[ ] When...     [ ] Error...     [X] Scroll bar
[ ] Valid...    [ ] Comment...   [ ] Allow tabs
[X] Message...  [X] Disabled     [ ] Refresh
------------------------------------------------------------
*-- m.mdescript Message Clause
------------------------------------------------------------
Message
  ( ) Procedure
  (·) Expression

Message:   "Enter a description of this CD for our catalog"
************************************************************
*--  SCREEN CLEANUP CODE
************************************************************
IF glQuitting
   *-- Note, we can't store the BAR # as a regional value
   *-- and use that to release the BAR(), because the regional
   *-- is lost whenever the READ is exited (which happens when
   *-- we click between windows).  So instead, we do this...
   =KillBar('wrCD')
   =KillWind('wrCD')
ENDIF
*-----------------------------------------------------------
```

```
**************************************************************
**--      CD.SCX - MAC PLATFORM
**************************************************************

 ( ) DeskTop                          (·) Window

 Name:   wrCD                         <Type...>
 Title:  CD Entry Window
 Footer:

 Size:             Screen Code:

  Height:   13.250   [X] Setup...
  Width:    59.000   [X] Cleanup & Procs...             «   OK   »

 Position:         READ Clauses:                      < Cancel >

  Row:       0.000   [ ] Activate...    [ ] Show...
  Column:    0.000   [ ] Valid...       [ ] When...
  [X] Center         [X] Deactivate...

 Environment:                           [X] Add alias

        Environment NOT saved with screen.


  Type:        User

  Attributes:       Border:

   [ ] Close         ( ) None
   [X] Float         ( ) Single
   [ ] Shadow        ( ) Double        «   OK   »
   [X] Minimize      ( ) Panel
                     (·) System       < Cancel >

  Color Schemes:

   Primary:        Popup:

MAC       RGB Fill Color Scheme: (,,)
MAC       Font: Geneva,  10
 Screen Setup code above
 READ Deactivate code above
**************************************************************
*--     G E T    O B J E C T S
**************************************************************
*=============================================================
*  Text: CD Title
*=============================================================
 @   2.333,   5.833
MAC       RGB Color Scheme: (,,,,,)
```

```
MAC       Font: Monaco,    9
        Style: Bold
*============================================================
*  Text: Cost
*============================================================
 @   3.500,  10.500
MAC       RGB Color Scheme: (,,,,,)
MAC       Font: Monaco,    9
        Style: Bold
*============================================================
*  Text: Price
*============================================================
 @   4.583,   9.333
MAC       RGB Color Scheme: (,,,,,)
MAC       Font: Monaco,    9
        Style: Bold
*============================================================
*  Text: Description
*============================================================
 @   5.667,   2.333
MAC       RGB Color Scheme: (,,,,,)
MAC       Font: Monaco,    9
        Style: Bold
*============================================================
*  licd
*============================================================
 @   0.000,   0.000
     SIZE   0.333,   0.667
 Spacing:    1
```

```
  Invisible Buttons #:   1

  (·) Horizontal     ( ) Vertical
  [ ] Terminating  <Spacing...>

  Variable:
                                      «   OK   »
  < Choose... > licd
                                      < Cancel >

  Options:

  [X] When...      [ ] Comment...
  [ ] Valid...     [ ] Disabled
  [ ] Message...
```

```
 When code above
*============================================================
*  lhMusician
*============================================================
 @   0.250,   1.000
     SIZE   1.583,  13.833
 Spacing:    2
```

```
Push Button Prompts:        (·) Horizontal    ( ) Vertical
                            [ ] Terminating   <Spacing...>
Musician...
                            Variable:

                            < Choose... >  lhMusician

                            Options:

                            [ ] When...       [ ] Comment...
                            [X] Valid...      [X] Disabled
                            [X] Message...

              «   OK   »     < Cancel >
MAC      RGB Color Scheme: (,,,,,)
MAC      Font: Geneva,    9
        Style: Bold
 Valid code above
 Message code above
*============================================================
*  m.cmusician
*============================================================
 @   0.500,  16.167

  Field:

    ( ) Say          (·) Get          ( ) Edit

  <  Get...    > m.cmusician
                                              «   OK   »
  < Format... > @3
                                              < Cancel >
  Range:

    [ ] Upper...                 [ ] Lower...

  [X] When...      [ ] Error...     [ ] Scroll bar
  [ ] Valid...     [ ] Comment...   [ ] Allow tabs
  [ ] Message...   [X] Disabled     [X] Refresh
MAC      RGB Color Scheme: (,,,,,)
MAC      Font: monaco,    9
 When code above
*============================================================
*  m.ctitle
*============================================================
 @   2.417,  16.167
```

```
┌──────────────────────────────────────────────────────────┐
│                                                          │
│  Field:                                                  │
│  ┌────────────────────────────────────────┐              │
│  │ ( ) Say        (·) Get        ( ) Edit │              │
│  └────────────────────────────────────────┘              │
│                                                          │
│  <  Get...    > m.ctitle                                 │
│                                             «   OK   »   │
│  < Format... > @3                                        │
│                                             < Cancel >   │
│  Range:                                                  │
│  ┌────────────────────────────────────────┐              │
│  │ [ ] Upper...              [ ] Lower... │              │
│  └────────────────────────────────────────┘              │
│                                                          │
│  [ ] When...     [ ] Error...     [ ] Scroll bar         │
│  [ ] Valid...    [ ] Comment...   [ ] Allow tabs         │
│  [X] Message...  [X] Disabled     [ ] Refresh            │
│                                                          │
└──────────────────────────────────────────────────────────┘
MAC       RGB Color Scheme: (,,,,,)
MAC       Font: monaco,   9
 Message code above
*============================================================
*  m.ncost
*============================================================
 @   3.500,  16.167
┌──────────────────────────────────────────────────────────┐
│                                                          │
│  Field:                                                  │
│  ┌────────────────────────────────────────┐              │
│  │ ( ) Say        (·) Get        ( ) Edit │              │
│  └────────────────────────────────────────┘              │
│                                                          │
│  <  Get...    > m.ncost                                  │
│                                             «   OK   »   │
│  < Format... > @3                                        │
│                                             < Cancel >   │
│  Range:                                                  │
│  ┌────────────────────────────────────────┐              │
│  │ [ ] Upper...              [ ] Lower... │              │
│  └────────────────────────────────────────┘              │
│                                                          │
│  [ ] When...     [ ] Error...     [ ] Scroll bar         │
│  [ ] Valid...    [ ] Comment...   [ ] Allow tabs         │
│  [X] Message...  [X] Disabled     [ ] Refresh            │
│                                                          │
└──────────────────────────────────────────────────────────┘
MAC       RGB Color Scheme: (,,,,,)
MAC       Font: monaco,   9
 Message code above
*============================================================
*  m.nprice
*============================================================
 @   4.583,  16.167
```

```
 Field:
 ( ) Say          (·) Get          ( ) Edit

 <  Get...    > m.nprice
                                              «    OK    »
 < Format... > @3
                                              < Cancel >
 Range:
 [ ] Upper...                 [ ] Lower...

 [ ] When...     [ ] Error...     [ ] Scroll bar
 [ ] Valid...    [ ] Comment...   [ ] Allow tabs
 [X] Message...  [X] Disabled     [ ] Refresh

MAC       RGB Color Scheme: (,,,,,)
MAC       Font: monaco,   9
 Message code above
*============================================================
*  m.mdescript
*============================================================
 @   5.667,  16.167

 Field:
 ( ) Say          ( ) Get          (·) Edit

 < Edit...    > m.mdescript
                                              «    OK    »
 < Format... > @2
                                              < Cancel >
 Range:
 [ ] Upper...                 [ ] Lower...

 [ ] When...     [ ] Error...     [X] Scroll bar
 [ ] Valid...    [ ] Comment...   [ ] Allow tabs
 [X] Message...  [X] Disabled     [ ] Refresh

MAC       RGB Color Scheme: (,,,,,)
MAC       Font: monaco,   9
 Message code above
 Screen Cleanup and Procedures code above
*------------------------------------------------------------
*************************************************************
**--    CD.SCX - WINDOWS PLATFORM
*************************************************************
```

```
( ) DeskTop                          (·) Window

Name:   wrCD                         <Type...>
Title:  CD Entry Window
Footer:

Size:              Screen Code:

  Height:   13.250   [X] Setup...
  Width:    59.000   [X] Cleanup & Procs...          «   OK   »

Position:          READ Clauses:                     < Cancel >

  Row:        0.000  [ ] Activate...     [ ] Show...
  Column:     0.000  [ ] Valid...        [ ] When...
  [X] Center         [X] Deactivate...

Environment:                        [X] Add alias

        Environment NOT saved with screen.
```

```
 Type:       User

 Attributes:      Border:

  [ ] Close        ( ) None
  [X] Float        ( ) Single
  [ ] Shadow       ( ) Double       «   OK   »
  [X] Minimize     ( ) Panel
                   (·) System       < Cancel >

 Color Schemes:

  Primary:         Popup:
```

```
WINDOWS  RGB Fill Color Scheme: (,,)
WINDOWS  Font: Terminal,    9
 Screen Setup code above
 READ Deactivate code above
************************************************************
*--    G E T    O B J E C T S
************************************************************
*===========================================================
*  Text: CD Title
*===========================================================
 @   2.333,   6.000
WINDOWS  RGB Color Scheme: (,,,,,)
WINDOWS  Font: Terminal,   9
*===========================================================
*  Text: Cost
*===========================================================
```

```
 @   3.500,  10.000
WINDOWS  RGB Color Scheme: (,,,,,)
WINDOWS  Font: Terminal,   9
*==============================================================
*  Text: Price
*==============================================================
 @   4.583,   9.000
WINDOWS  RGB Color Scheme: (,,,,,)
WINDOWS  Font: Terminal,   9
*==============================================================
*  Text: Description
*==============================================================
 @   5.667,   3.000
WINDOWS  RGB Color Scheme: (,,,,,)
WINDOWS  Font: Terminal,   9
*==============================================================
*  licd
*==============================================================
 @   0.000,   0.000
     SIZE   0.333,   0.500
 Spacing:    1
```

```
  Invisible Buttons #:   1

   (·) Horizontal    ( ) Vertical
   [ ] Terminating  <Spacing...>

  Variable:
                                       «   OK   »
   < Choose... > licd
                                       < Cancel >
  Options:

   [X] When...     [ ] Comment...
   [ ] Valid...    [ ] Disabled
   [ ] Message...
```

```
 When code above
*==============================================================
*  lhMusician
*==============================================================
 @   0.000,   1.000
     SIZE   1.615,  19.500
 Spacing:    2
```

```
Push Button Prompts:        (·) Horizontal    ( ) Vertical
                            [ ] Terminating  <Spacing...>
Musician...
                           Variable:

                            < Choose... >  lhMusician

                           Options:

                            [ ] When...      [ ] Comment...
                            [X] Valid...     [X] Disabled
                            [X] Message...

              «   OK   »    < Cancel >

WINDOWS  RGB Color Scheme: (,,,,,)
WINDOWS  Font: MS Sans Serif,   8
         Style: Bold
 Valid code above
 Message code above
*============================================================
*  m.cmusician
*============================================================
 @   0.500,  16.125

  Field:

   ( ) Say          (·) Get          ( ) Edit

  <  Get...    > m.cmusician
                                               «   OK   »
  < Format... >
                                               < Cancel >
  Range:

   [ ] Upper...                 [ ] Lower...

  [X] When...      [ ] Error...      [ ] Scroll bar
  [ ] Valid...     [ ] Comment...    [ ] Allow tabs
  [ ] Message...   [X] Disabled      [X] Refresh

WINDOWS  RGB Color Scheme: (,,,,,)
WINDOWS  Font: Terminal,   9
 When code above
*============================================================
*  m.ctitle
*============================================================
 @   2.417,  16.125
```

```
Field:
 ( ) Say          (·) Get          ( ) Edit

< Get...    > m.ctitle
                                               «   OK   »
< Format... >
                                               < Cancel >
Range:
 [ ] Upper...                 [ ] Lower...

[ ] When...      [ ] Error...     [ ] Scroll bar
[ ] Valid...     [ ] Comment...   [ ] Allow tabs
[X] Message...   [X] Disabled     [ ] Refresh
```

```
WINDOWS  RGB Color Scheme: (,,,,,)
WINDOWS  Font: Terminal,   9
 Message code above
*==============================================================
*  m.ncost
*==============================================================
 @   3.500,  16.125
```

```
Field:
 ( ) Say          (·) Get          ( ) Edit

< Get...    > m.ncost
                                               «   OK   »
< Format... >
                                               < Cancel >
Range:
 [ ] Upper...                 [ ] Lower...

[ ] When...      [ ] Error...     [ ] Scroll bar
[ ] Valid...     [ ] Comment...   [ ] Allow tabs
[X] Message...   [X] Disabled     [ ] Refresh
```

```
WINDOWS  RGB Color Scheme: (,,,,,)
WINDOWS  Font: Terminal,   9
 Message code above
*==============================================================
*  m.nprice
*==============================================================
 @   4.583,  16.125
```

```
        Field:
        ( ) Say          (·) Get          ( ) Edit

        <  Get...     > m.nprice
                                                    «   OK   »
        < Format... >
                                                    < Cancel >
        Range:
        [ ] Upper...                  [ ] Lower...

        [ ] When...     [ ] Error...     [ ] Scroll bar
        [ ] Valid...    [ ] Comment...   [ ] Allow tabs
        [X] Message...  [X] Disabled     [ ] Refresh

WINDOWS  RGB Color Scheme: (,,,,,)
WINDOWS  Font: Terminal,   9
 Message code above
*==============================================================
*  m.mdescript
*==============================================================
 @   5.667,  16.125

        Field:
        ( ) Say          ( ) Get          (·) Edit

        < Edit...     > m.mdescript
                                                    «   OK   »
        < Format... > @2
                                                    < Cancel >
        Range:
        [ ] Upper...                  [ ] Lower...

        [ ] When...     [ ] Error...     [X] Scroll bar
        [ ] Valid...    [ ] Comment...   [ ] Allow tabs
        [X] Message...  [X] Disabled     [ ] Refresh

WINDOWS  RGB Color Scheme: (,,,,,)
WINDOWS  Font: Terminal,   9
 Message code above
 Screen Cleanup and Procedures code above
```

Application-Specific Screen—MUSICIAN.SCX

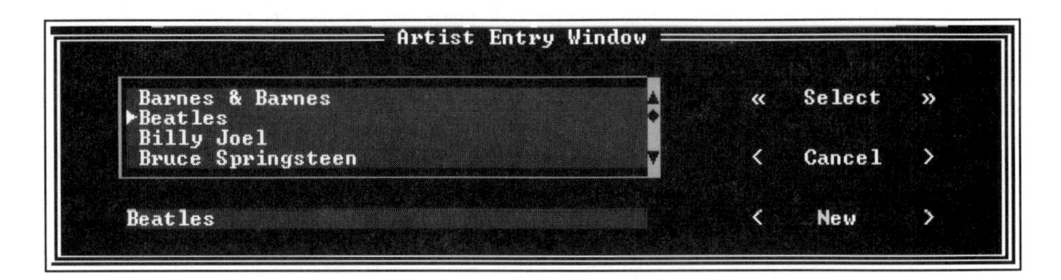

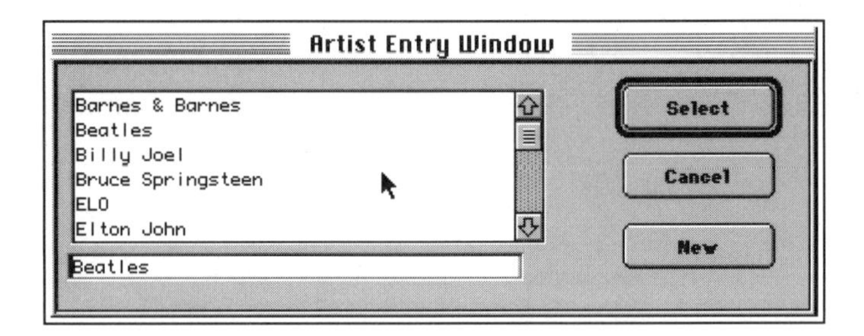

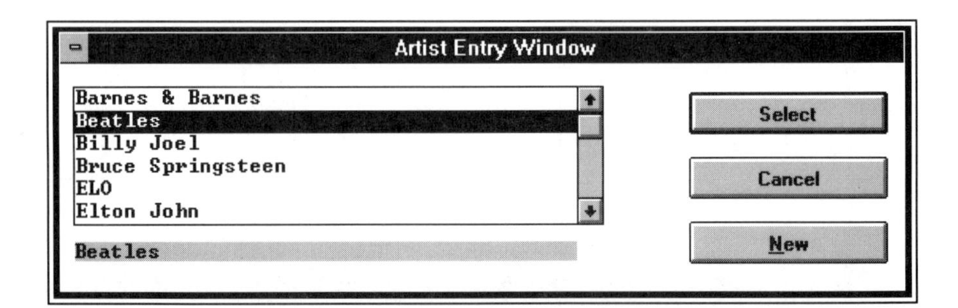

Musician is a modal window that is called from the CD window. It allows the user to select a new musician or add a new one. The CD window's lhMusician pushbutton simply calls this window with a DO Musician.spr, and then issues a SHOW GET m.cMusician afterwards to refresh that GET object.

The most interesting thing to note in the musician screen is the use of the _CUROBJ and OBJNUM() functions to position the cursor on the next correct input field. This is a very powerful ease-of-use feature for your user. An example of it is shown in the valid clause of the <New> push button.

```
SHOW GET m.cMusician ENABLE
_CUROBJ = OBJNUM(m.cMusician)
```

When the <New> push button is selected, it first enables the cMusician field, which is used to enter the new artist name. Instead of continuing on to the next field in the window, however, we force the cursor to the cMusician field. It is obvious that the user would really prefer to go to the field where the entry is to take place, so we force our program to take them there.

```
*------------------------------------------------------------
************************************************************
**--    MUSICIAN.SCX - DOS PLATFORM
************************************************************

 ( ) DeskTop                          (·) Window

 Name:                                <Type...>
 Title:  Artist Entry Window
 Footer:

 Size:             Screen Code:

  Height:   12      [X] Setup...
  Width:    74      [ ] Cleanup & Procs...            «    OK    »

 Position:         READ Clauses:                      < Cancel >

  Row:        0     [ ] Activate...    [ ] Show...
  Column:     0     [ ] Valid...       [ ] When...
  [X] Center        [ ] Deactivate...

 Environment:                         [X] Add alias

       Environment NOT saved with screen.
```

```
Type:  [ Dialog ]

Attributes:          Border:

[ ] Close            ( ) None
[X] Float            ( ) Single
[X] Shadow           (·) Double        «  OK  »
[ ] Minimize         ( ) Panel
                     ( ) System        < Cancel >

Color Schemes:

  Primary:           Popup:
  [ Dialogs ]        [ Dialog Pop ]
```

```
****************************************************************
*  SCREEN SETUP CODE
****************************************************************
m.lcOldMusic = m.cMusician
* Move current Musicians into an array for a pick list
SELECT DISTINCT cMusician ;
  FROM CD ;
  ORDER BY cMusician ;
  INTO ARRAY laMusician
IF _tally = 0
   DIMENSION laMusician[1]
ENDIF
lnMusician = ASCAN(laMusician, m.cMusician)
IF lnMusician = 0
   lnMusician = 1
ENDIF
****************************************************************
*--    G E T   O B J E C T S
****************************************************************
*==============================================================
*  lnmusician
*==============================================================
 @   1,   4
```

```
List Type:                                    Options:
 (·) From Array          laMusician           [ ] When...        [ ] Comment...
 ( ) From Popup                               [X] Valid...       [ ] Disabled
 ( ) Prompt Structure                         [X] Message...     [ ] 1st Element...
 ( ) Prompt Field                             [ ] Terminating    [X] # Elements...
 ( ) Prompt Files

Variable:
 < Choose... > lnmusician                         «   OK   »    < Cancel >

------------------------------------------------------------
*-- lnmusician Valid Clause
------------------------------------------------------------

 Valid
  (·) Procedure
  ( ) Expression

IF lnMusician # 0
   m.cMusician = laMusician(lnMusician)
ENDIF
SHOW GET m.cMusician
------------------------------------------------------------
*-- lnmusician Message Clause
------------------------------------------------------------

 Message
  ( ) Procedure
  (·) Expression

Message:   "Select a musician from this list"
*-- lnmusician # Elements Clause
------------------------------------------------------------

 # Elements
  ( ) Procedure
  (·) Expression

# Elements:   sizearry(@laMusician)
*============================================================
*  m.lhselect
```

```
*============================================================
 @    2,   53
 Spacing:     2

  Push Button Prompts:          ( ) Horizontal    (·) Vertical
                                [ ] Terminating  <Spacing...>
  \!Select
                               Variable:

                                < Choose... >  m.lhselect

                               Options:

                                [ ] When...      [ ] Comment...
                                [X] Valid...     [ ] Disabled
                                [X] Message...

                  «    OK    »    < Cancel >

------------------------------------------------------------
*-- m.lhselect Valid Clause
------------------------------------------------------------

  Valid

    (·) Procedure
    ( ) Expression

m.cMusician = laMusician(lnMusician)    && Show the selection
CLEAR READ
------------------------------------------------------------
*-- m.lhselect Message Clause
------------------------------------------------------------

  Message

    ( ) Procedure
    (·) Expression

Message:    "Select the current musician"
*============================================================
*  lhCancel
*============================================================
 @    5,   53
 Spacing:     2
```

```
+--------------------------------------------------------------+
| Push Button Prompts:       ( ) Horizontal   (·) Vertical     |
|                            [ ] Terminating  <Spacing...>     |
| \?Cancel                                                     |
|                           Variable:                          |
|                            < Choose... >  lhCancel           |
|                                                              |
|                           Options:                           |
|                            [ ] When...      [ ] Comment...   |
|                            [X] Valid...     [ ] Disabled     |
|                            [X] Message...                    |
|                                                              |
|              «   OK   »     < Cancel >                       |
+--------------------------------------------------------------+
------------------------------------------------------------
*-- lhCancel Valid Clause
------------------------------------------------------------

+--------------------------------------------+
| Valid                                      |
|   (·) Procedure                            |
|   ( ) Expression                           |
+--------------------------------------------+

m.cMusician = m.lcOldMusic
CLEAR READ
------------------------------------------------------------
*-- lhCancel Message Clause
------------------------------------------------------------

+--------------------------------------------+
| Message                                    |
|   ( ) Procedure                            |
|   (·) Expression                           |
+--------------------------------------------+

Message:   "Do not change the musician selection"
*============================================================
*  m.cmusician
*============================================================
 @   8,   5
```

```
Field:
 ( ) Say        (·) Get        ( ) Edit

< Get...   > m.cmusician
                                          «   OK   »
< Format... >
                                          < Cancel >
Range:
 [ ] Upper...                 [ ] Lower...

[ ] When...      [ ] Error...      [ ] Scroll bar
[X] Valid...     [ ] Comment...    [ ] Allow tabs
[X] Message...   [X] Disabled      [ ] Refresh
------------------------------------------------------------
*-- m.cmusician Valid Clause
------------------------------------------------------------
Valid
 (·) Procedure
 ( ) Expression

SHOW GET m.cMusician DISABLE
lnMusician = ASCAN(laMusician,m.cMusician)
IF lnMusician = 0
   lnMusician = sizearry(@laMusician) + 1
   DIMENSION laMusician[lnMusician]
   laMusician[lnMusician] = m.cMusician
   =ASORT(laMusician)
   lnMusician = ASCAN(laMusician,m.cMusician)
ENDIF
SHOW GET lnMusician
_CUROBJ = OBJNUM(lhSelect)
------------------------------------------------------------
*-- m.cmusician Message Clause
------------------------------------------------------------
Message
 ( ) Procedure
 (·) Expression

Message:   "Add a new musician to the list"
*============================================================
*   m.lhNew
```

```
*==============================================================
 @    8,  53
 Spacing:     2

 Push Button Prompts:         ( ) Horizontal    (·) Vertical
                              [ ] Terminating   <Spacing...>
 \<New
                             Variable:
                              < Choose... >  m.lhNew
                             Options:
                              [ ] When...     [ ] Comment...
                              [X] Valid...    [ ] Disabled
                              [X] Message...

               «   OK   »     < Cancel >
--------------------------------------------------------------
*-- m.lhNew Valid Clause
--------------------------------------------------------------
 Valid
   (·) Procedure
   ( ) Expression

SHOW GET m.cMusician ENABLE
_CUROBJ = OBJNUM(m.cMusician)
--------------------------------------------------------------
*-- m.lhNew Message Clause
--------------------------------------------------------------
 Message
   ( ) Procedure
   (·) Expression

Message:    "Enable the entry of a new musician"
```

```
*------------------------------------------------------------
************************************************************
**--     MUSICIAN.SCX - MAC PLATFORM
************************************************************
```

```
( ) DeskTop                          (·) Window

Name:                                <Type...>
Title:  Artist Entry Window
Footer:

Size:              Screen Code:

  Height:    11.636     [X] Setup...
  Width:     67.167     [ ] Cleanup & Procs...             «   OK   »

Position:          READ Clauses:                           < Cancel >

  Row:         0.000    [ ] Activate...    [ ] Show...
  Column:      0.000    [ ] Valid...       [ ] When...
  [X] Center            [ ] Deactivate...

Environment:                              [X] Add alias

        Environment NOT saved with screen.
```

```
 Type:        Dialog

 Attributes:       Border:

   [ ] Close         ( ) None
   [X] Float         ( ) Single
   [X] Shadow        (·) Double      «   OK   »
   [ ] Minimize      ( ) Panel
                     ( ) System      < Cancel >

 Color Schemes:

   Primary:          Popup:
```

```
MAC       RGB Fill Color Scheme: (,,)
MAC       Font: monaco,    9
 Screen Setup code above
************************************************************
*--    G E T    O B J E C T S
************************************************************
*===========================================================
*  lnmusician
*===========================================================
 @   1.182,    1.167
     SIZE   7.091,   42.000
```

```
List Type:                              Options:

 (·) From Array   laMusician |  [ ] When...       [ ] Comment...
 ( ) From Popup              |  [X] Valid...      [ ] Disabled
 ( ) Prompt Structure        |  [X] Message...    [ ] 1st Element...
 ( ) Prompt Field            |  [ ] Terminating   [X] # Elements...
 ( ) Prompt Files            |

Variable:

 < Choose... > lnmusician              «  OK  »     < Cancel >
```

```
MAC       RGB Color Scheme: (,,,,,)
MAC       Font: monaco,   9
 Valid code above
 Message code above
 # Elements code above
*============================================================
*  m.lhselect
*============================================================
 @   1.000,  50.667
     SIZE   2.000,  13.667
 Spacing:    2
```

```
Push Button Prompts:        ( ) Horizontal    (·) Vertical
                            [ ] Terminating   <Spacing...>
 \!Select
                           Variable:

                            < Choose... >  m.lhselect

                           Options:

                            [ ] When...      [ ] Comment...
                            [X] Valid...     [ ] Disabled
                            [X] Message...

             «  OK  »   < Cancel >
```

```
MAC       RGB Color Scheme: (,,,,,)
MAC       Font: Geneva,   9
          Style: Bold
 Valid code above
 Message code above
*============================================================
*  lhCancel
*============================================================
 @   4.273,  50.667
     SIZE   2.000,  13.667
 Spacing:    2
```

```
Push Button Prompts:            ( ) Horizontal    (·) Vertical
                                [ ] Terminating   <Spacing...>
\?Cancel
                                Variable:

                                < Choose... >  lhCancel

                                Options:

                                [ ] When...      [ ] Comment...
                                [X] Valid...     [ ] Disabled
                                [X] Message...

                 «   OK   »    < Cancel >
```

```
MAC       RGB Color Scheme: (,,,,,)
MAC       Font: Geneva,    9
          Style: Bold
 Valid code above
 Message code above
*==============================================================
*  m.cmusician
*==============================================================
 @    9.182,    1.333
```

```
Field:

 ( ) Say          (·) Get          ( ) Edit

<  Get...    > m.cmusician
                                                  «   OK   »
< Format... > @3
                                                  < Cancel >
Range:

 [ ] Upper...                    [ ] Lower...

[ ] When...      [ ] Error...     [ ] Scroll bar
[X] Valid...     [ ] Comment...   [ ] Allow tabs
[X] Message...   [X] Disabled     [ ] Refresh
```

```
MAC       RGB Color Scheme: (,,,,,)
MAC       Font: monaco,    9
 Valid code above
 Message code above
*==============================================================
*  m.lhNew
*==============================================================
 @    7.636,   50.667
      SIZE    2.000,   13.667
 Spacing:     2
```

```
Push Button Prompts:          ( ) Horizontal    (·) Vertical
                              [ ] Terminating   <Spacing...>
\<New
                              Variable:

                              < Choose... >  m.lhNew

                              Options:

                              [ ] When...      [ ] Comment...
                              [X] Valid...     [ ] Disabled
                              [X] Message...

              «   OK   »    < Cancel >
```

```
MAC       RGB Color Scheme: (,,,,,)
MAC       Font: Geneva,    9
        Style: Bold
 Valid code above
 Message code above
*------------------------------------------------------------
*************************************************************
**--    MUSICIAN.SCX - WINDOWS PLATFORM
*************************************************************
```

```
( ) DeskTop                            (·) Window

Name:                                  <Type...>
Title:  Artist Entry Window
Footer:

Size:              Screen Code:

 Height:   11.667   [X] Setup...
 Width:    67.125   [ ] Cleanup & Procs...          «   OK   »

Position:          READ Clauses:                    < Cancel >

 Row:        0.000  [ ] Activate...    [ ] Show...
 Column:     0.000  [ ] Valid...       [ ] When...
 [X] Center         [ ] Deactivate...

Environment:                         [X] Add alias

       Environment NOT saved with screen.
```

```
Type:  [ Dialog ]

Attributes:        Border:

[ ] Close          ( ) None
[X] Float          ( ) Single
[X] Shadow         (·) Double      «  OK  »
[ ] Minimize       ( ) Panel
                   ( ) System      < Cancel >

Color Schemes:

  Primary:         Popup:
  [          ]     [          ]

WINDOWS  RGB Fill Color Scheme: (,,)
WINDOWS  Font: Terminal,   9
 Screen Setup code above
***************************************************************
*--    G E T   O B J E C T S
***************************************************************
*==============================================================
*  lnmusician
*==============================================================
 @   1.167,   1.125
     SIZE   7.000,  42.000

List Type:                                  Options:

  (·) From Array    laMusician   [ ] When...        [ ] Comment...
  ( ) From Popup                 [X] Valid...       [ ] Disabled
  ( ) Prompt Structure           [X] Message...     [ ] 1st Element...
  ( ) Prompt Field               [ ] Terminating [X] # Elements...
  ( ) Prompt Files

Variable:

  < Choose... > lnmusician              «  OK  »     < Cancel >

WINDOWS  RGB Color Scheme: (,,,,,)
WINDOWS  Font: Terminal,   9
 Valid code above
 Message code above
 # Elements code above
*==============================================================
*  m.lhselect
*==============================================================
 @   1.500,  50.125
     SIZE   2.000,  21.000
```

```
Spacing:    2
╔══════════════════════════════════════════════════════════════╗
║                                                              ║
║  Push Button Prompts:       ┌──────────────────────────────┐ ║
║                             │ ( ) Horizontal   (·) Vertical│ ║
║  ┌──────────────────┐       │ [ ] Terminating <Spacing...> │ ║
║  │\!Select          │       └──────────────────────────────┘ ║
║  │                  │       Variable:                        ║
║  │                  │       ┌──────────────────────────────┐ ║
║  │                  │       │ < Choose... >  m.lhselect    │ ║
║  │                  │       └──────────────────────────────┘ ║
║  │                  │       Options:                         ║
║  │                  │       ┌──────────────────────────────┐ ║
║  │                  │       │ [ ] When...    [ ] Comment...│ ║
║  │                  │       │ [X] Valid...   [ ] Disabled  │ ║
║  │                  │       │ [X] Message...               │ ║
║  └──────────────────┘       └──────────────────────────────┘ ║
║                                                              ║
║               «   OK   »   < Cancel >                        ║
║                                                              ║
╚══════════════════════════════════════════════════════════════╝
WINDOWS  RGB Color Scheme: (,,,,,)
WINDOWS  Font: MS Sans Serif,   8
         Style: Bold
 Valid code above
 Message code above
*============================================================
*  lhCancel
*============================================================
 @   4.833,  50.125
     SIZE   2.000,  21.000
 Spacing:    2
╔══════════════════════════════════════════════════════════════╗
║                                                              ║
║  Push Button Prompts:       ┌──────────────────────────────┐ ║
║                             │ ( ) Horizontal   (·) Vertical│ ║
║  ┌──────────────────┐       │ [ ] Terminating <Spacing...> │ ║
║  │\?Cancel          │       └──────────────────────────────┘ ║
║  │                  │       Variable:                        ║
║  │                  │       ┌──────────────────────────────┐ ║
║  │                  │       │ < Choose... >  lhCancel      │ ║
║  │                  │       └──────────────────────────────┘ ║
║  │                  │       Options:                         ║
║  │                  │       ┌──────────────────────────────┐ ║
║  │                  │       │ [ ] When...    [ ] Comment...│ ║
║  │                  │       │ [X] Valid...   [ ] Disabled  │ ║
║  │                  │       │ [X] Message...               │ ║
║  └──────────────────┘       └──────────────────────────────┘ ║
║                                                              ║
║               «   OK   »   < Cancel >                        ║
║                                                              ║
╚══════════════════════════════════════════════════════════════╝
WINDOWS  RGB Color Scheme: (,,,,,)
WINDOWS  Font: MS Sans Serif,   8
         Style: Bold
 Valid code above
 Message code above
*============================================================
*  m.cmusician
*============================================================
 @   9.167,   1.250
```

```
Field:
 ( ) Say          (·) Get          ( ) Edit

< Get...   > m.cmusician
                                          «   OK   »
< Format... >
                                          < Cancel >
Range:
 [ ] Upper...                  [ ] Lower...

[ ] When...     [ ] Error...     [ ] Scroll bar
[X] Valid...    [ ] Comment...   [ ] Allow tabs
[X] Message...  [X] Disabled     [ ] Refresh
```

```
WINDOWS  RGB Color Scheme: (,,,,,)
WINDOWS  Font: Terminal,   9
 Valid code above
 Message code above
*============================================================
*  m.lhNew
*============================================================
 @   8.167,  50.125
     SIZE   2.000,  21.000
 Spacing:    2
```

```
Push Button Prompts:        ( ) Horizontal   (·) Vertical
                            [ ] Terminating  <Spacing...>
 \<New
                           Variable:

                            < Choose... >  m.lhNew

                           Options:

                            [ ] When...     [ ] Comment...
                            [X] Valid...    [ ] Disabled
                            [X] Message...

               «   OK   »    < Cancel >
```

```
WINDOWS  RGB Color Scheme: (,,,,,)
WINDOWS  Font: MS Sans Serif,   8
         Style: Bold
 Valid code above
 Message code above
```

Customer Information Entry: CUSTOMER.SCX

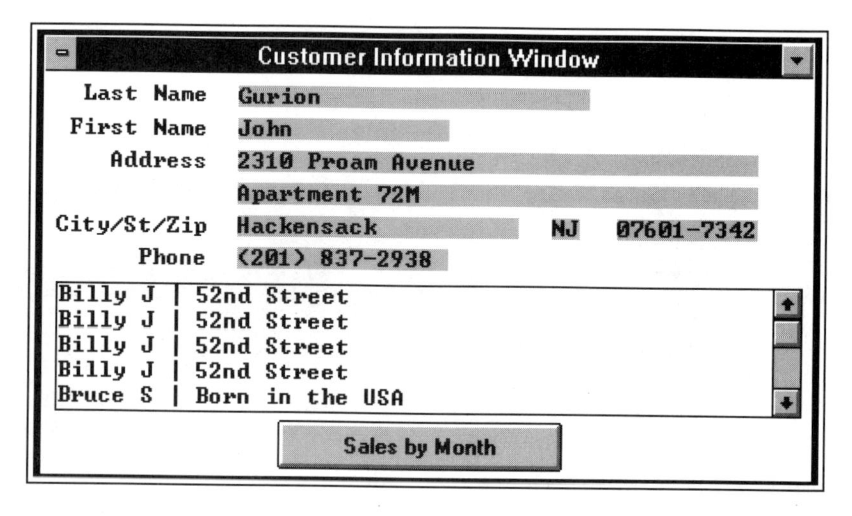

Customer is another example of the power of the Methods approach to development when creating modeless application windows. This window has a sample of a read-only 1:M relationship. When the user selects a customer, all purchased CDs for that customer show up in a list.

Setup Snippet

The Setup snippet is similar to the one for the CD screen, except that we add a SQL SELECT that creates an array containing the list of purchased information.

```
SELECT left(cd.cmusician,7)+" | "+cd.ctitle, cd.cid ;
 FROM INVOICE, CD, PURCHASE ;
 WHERE INVOICE.CCUSTID = m.cID;
   AND INVOICE.cID = PURCHASE.cInvID ;
   AND PURCHASE.CCDID = CD.CID ;
 ORDER BY 1 ;
 INTO ARRAY laCDPurch
```

Note that the SQL SELECT creates a column containing concatenated field information with a bar between the fields. This allows us to create the illusion of a BROWSE type window. In graphical environments like the Macintosh and Windows, we must be sure to select a nonproportional font so that the pseudo-columns will line up correctly.

After the SQL SELECT is run, we test _tally to see if any records were found. If none are found, we create the array with one empty row so that the objects based on that array will be successfully created.

Show Snippet

The Show snippet is used to refresh any information that must be refreshed when a new record is shown on the screen. Accordingly, it simply reissues the SQL select that creates the Purchased CD array.

Cleanup Snippet

The Cleanup snippet is similar to the CD screen, but we change the behavior of a number of our methods. Initit() is placed here in order to dimension an empty Purchased CD array when adding a new customer.

It accomplishes this with the following code:

```
DO InitIt IN Methods.prg
DIME laCDPurch[1,2]      && Reset the array to empty
laCDPurch = .F.
```

This function demonstrates the use of inheritance in FoxPro. We call the base InitIt() method and then add extra capabilities as necessary for this window.

The base DeleteIt() method is overridden by the DeleteIt() function in this screen. When we delete a customer, we want to make sure to delete all purchasing information for the customer as well. Therefore, we lock the current record, and all invoice records for this client. If the locking is successful, we delete all of the records in a second pass. Note that we do not have to lock the purchase records. These are only accessible by someone who has locked the associated invoice record, so we have placed a logical lock on them.

Finally, we inherit and add to the base DisableIt() method. Instead of disabling all items in this window when not editing, we want to allow the user to click on the "Sales By Month" pushbutton at any time. This is a read-only window, generated by a crosstab (see Chapter 8, *Usability Techniques*), so it should always be accessible.

Customer Window—A Summary

This window is one level of complexity higher than the CD window. It uses inheritance and overriding to modify the base behavior of a window. Note that we still require relatively little code. We simply *code the exceptions*. The base behavior of our windows is correct for most of the customer window—we only worry about the specific changes that are necessary for this window.

```
*--------------------------------------------------------------
**************************************************************
**--    CUSTOMER.SCX - DOS PLATFORM
**************************************************************
 ( ) DeskTop                          (·) Window

 Name:   wrCustome                    <Type...>
 Title:  Customer Information Window
 Footer:

 Size:              Screen Code:

  Height:   15       [X] Setup...
  Width:    57       [X] Cleanup & Procs...            « OK »

 Position:          READ Clauses:                      < Cancel >

  Row:        0      [ ] Activate...     [X] Show...
  Column:     0      [ ] Valid...        [ ] When...
  [X] Center         [X] Deactivate...

 Environment:                          [X] Add alias

        Environment NOT saved with screen.

 Type:        User

 Attributes:      Border:

  [ ] Close        ( ) None
  [X] Float        ( ) Single
  [ ] Shadow       ( ) Double       « OK »
  [X] Minimize     ( ) Panel
                   (·) System       < Cancel >

 Color Schemes:

  Primary:         Popup:
   Windows          Window Pop
**************************************************************
*  SCREEN SETUP CODE
**************************************************************
#SECTION 1
#WCLAUSES IN &gcMainWind
#SECTION 2
SELECT Customer
SCATTER MEMVAR MEMO
m.cID = CUSTOMER.cID
SELECT left(cd.cmusician,7)+" | "+cd.ctitle, cd.cid ;
 FROM INVOICE, CD, PURCHASE ;
```

```
 WHERE INVOICE.CCUSTID = m.cID;
   AND INVOICE.cID = PURCHASE.cInvID ;
   AND PURCHASE.CCDID = CD.CID ;
 ORDER BY 1 ;
 INTO ARRAY laCDPurch
IF _tally = 0
  DIMENSION laCDPurch[1]
ENDIF
=AddBar("wrCustome")
=restmem('wrCustome')
-----------------------------------------------------------
*-- READ Deactivate Clause
-----------------------------------------------------------

 READ Deactivate

   (·) Procedure
   ( ) Expression

RETURN stopread("wrCustome")
-----------------------------------------------------------
*-- READ Show Clause
-----------------------------------------------------------

 READ Show

   (·) Procedure
   ( ) Expression

m.cID = CUSTOMER.cID
DIME laCDPurch[1,2]       && Reset the array to empty
=ADEL(laCDPurch,1)
SELECT left(cd.cmusician,7)+" | "+cd.ctitle, cd.cid ;
 FROM INVOICE, CD, PURCHASE ;
 WHERE INVOICE.CCUSTID = m.cID;
   AND INVOICE.cID = PURCHASE.cInvID ;
   AND PURCHASE.CCDID = CD.CID ;
 ORDER BY 1 ;
 INTO ARRAY laCDPurch
lnCD = 0
SHOW GET lnCD
***********************************************************
*--   G E T   O B J E C T S
***********************************************************
*==========================================================
*  Text: Address
*==========================================================
 @   2,   5
*==========================================================
*  Text: City/St/Zip
*==========================================================
 @   4,   1
*==========================================================
*  Text: Phone
```

```
*==============================================================
 @   5,   7
*==============================================================
*  Text: Last Name
*==============================================================
 @   0,   3
*==============================================================
*  Text: First Name
*==============================================================
 @   1,   2
*==============================================================
*  m.clastname
*==============================================================
 @   0,  14
```

```
  Field:

  ( ) Say          (·) Get          ( ) Edit

  <  Get...    > m.clastname
                                               «   OK   »
  < Format... >
                                               < Cancel >
  Range:

  [ ] Upper...                   [ ] Lower...

  [ ] When...      [ ] Error...       [ ] Scroll bar
  [ ] Valid...     [ ] Comment...     [ ] Allow tabs
  [X] Message...   [X] Disabled       [ ] Refresh
```

```
--------------------------------------------------------------
*-- m.clastname Message Clause
--------------------------------------------------------------
```

```
  Message

  ( ) Procedure
  (·) Expression
```

```
Message:   "Enter the customer's last name"
*==============================================================
*  m.cfirstname
*==============================================================
 @   1,  14
```

```
 Field:
  ( ) Say         (·) Get         ( ) Edit

 <  Get...    > m.cfirstname
                                           «   OK   »
 < Format... >
                                          < Cancel >
 Range:
  [ ] Upper...                [ ] Lower...

 [ ] When...      [ ] Error...      [ ] Scroll bar
 [ ] Valid...     [ ] Comment...    [ ] Allow tabs
 [X] Message...   [X] Disabled      [ ] Refresh
----------------------------------------------------------
*-- m.cfirstname Message Clause
----------------------------------------------------------
 Message
  ( ) Procedure
  (·) Expression

Message:   "Enter the customer's first name"
*=========================================================
*  m.caddress1
*=========================================================
 @   2,  14

 Field:
  ( ) Say         (·) Get         ( ) Edit

 <  Get...    > m.caddress1
                                           «   OK   »
 < Format... >
                                          < Cancel >
 Range:
  [ ] Upper...                [ ] Lower...

 [ ] When...      [ ] Error...      [ ] Scroll bar
 [ ] Valid...     [ ] Comment...    [ ] Allow tabs
 [X] Message...   [X] Disabled      [ ] Refresh
----------------------------------------------------------
```

```
*-- m.caddress1 Message Clause
-------------------------------------------------------------

 Message

   ( ) Procedure
   (·) Expression

Message:   "Enter the first line of the customer's street address"
*============================================================
*  m.caddress2
*============================================================
 @   3,  14

 Field:

   ( ) Say          (·) Get          ( ) Edit

 <  Get...   > m.caddress2
                                                «   OK   »
 < Format... >
                                                < Cancel >
 Range:

   [ ] Upper...                   [ ] Lower...

 [ ] When...     [ ] Error...     [ ] Scroll bar
 [ ] Valid...    [ ] Comment...   [ ] Allow tabs
 [X] Message...  [X] Disabled     [ ] Refresh

-------------------------------------------------------------
*-- m.caddress2 Message Clause
-------------------------------------------------------------

 Message

   ( ) Procedure
   (·) Expression

Message:   "Enter the second line of the customer's street address"
*============================================================
*  m.ccity
*============================================================
 @   4,  14
```

```
Field:
 ( ) Say          (·) Get          ( ) Edit

< Get...    > m.ccity
                                           «   OK   »
< Format... >
                                           < Cancel >
Range:
 [ ] Upper...                   [ ] Lower...

[ ] When...       [ ] Error...       [ ] Scroll bar
[ ] Valid...      [ ] Comment...     [ ] Allow tabs
[X] Message...    [X] Disabled       [ ] Refresh
------------------------------------------------------------
*-- m.ccity Message Clause
------------------------------------------------------------
Message
 ( ) Procedure
 (·) Expression

Message:   "Enter the customer's city of residence"
*===========================================================
*  m.cstate
*===========================================================
 @   4,  36

Field:
 ( ) Say          (·) Get          ( ) Edit

< Get...    > m.cstate
                                           «   OK   »
< Format... > @A!
                                           < Cancel >
Range:
 [ ] Upper...                   [ ] Lower...

[ ] When...       [X] Error...       [ ] Scroll bar
[X] Valid...      [ ] Comment...     [ ] Allow tabs
[X] Message...    [X] Disabled       [ ] Refresh
------------------------------------------------------------
```

```
*-- m.cstate Valid Clause
------------------------------------------------------------

 Valid
  (·) Procedure
  ( ) Expression

PRIVATE lnTemp
IF !SEEK(m.cState,"States")
   lnTemp = States(ROW(),COL())
   m.cState = gaStates(lnTemp,1)
ENDIF
------------------------------------------------------------
*-- m.cstate Message Clause
------------------------------------------------------------

 Message
  ( ) Procedure
  (·) Expression

Message:   "Enter the customer's state"
------------------------------------------------------------
*-- m.cstate Error Clause
------------------------------------------------------------

 Error
  ( ) Procedure
  (·) Expression

Error:   "Invalid State - try again"
*===========================================================
*  m.czip
*===========================================================
 @   4,  41
```

```
Field:
 ( ) Say         (·) Get         ( ) Edit

< Get...  > m.czip
                                          «   OK   »
< Format... > @R 99999-9999
                                          < Cancel >
Range:
 [ ] Upper...                    [ ] Lower...

[ ] When...      [ ] Error...      [ ] Scroll bar
[ ] Valid...     [ ] Comment...    [ ] Allow tabs
[X] Message...   [X] Disabled      [ ] Refresh
---------------------------------------------------------------
*-- m.czip Message Clause
---------------------------------------------------------------
Message
 ( ) Procedure
 (·) Expression

Message:   "Enter the customer's zip code (5 or 9 digits)"
*==============================================================
*  m.cphone
*==============================================================
 @   5,  14

Field:
 ( ) Say         (·) Get         ( ) Edit

< Get...  > m.cphone
                                          «   OK   »
< Format... > @R (999) 999-9999
                                          < Cancel >
Range:
 [ ] Upper...                    [ ] Lower...

[ ] When...      [ ] Error...      [ ] Scroll bar
[ ] Valid...     [ ] Comment...    [ ] Allow tabs
[X] Message...   [X] Disabled      [ ] Refresh
---------------------------------------------------------------
```

```
*-- m.cphone Message Clause
------------------------------------------------------------

  Message

    ( ) Procedure
    (•) Expression

Message:   "Enter the customer's phone number (area code first)"
*============================================================
*  lnCD
*============================================================
 @   6,   1

  List Type:                           Options:

    (•) From Array       laCDPurch       [ ] When...      [ ] Comment...
    ( ) From Popup                       [ ] Valid...     [ ] Disabled
    ( ) Prompt Structure                 [X] Message...   [ ] 1st Element...
    ( ) Prompt Field                     [ ] Terminating  [X] # Elements...
    ( ) Prompt Files

  Variable:

    < Choose... > lnCD                       «   OK   »     < Cancel >

------------------------------------------------------------
*-- lnCD Message Clause
------------------------------------------------------------

  Message

    ( ) Procedure
    (•) Expression

Message:   "View the purchase history of the client"
------------------------------------------------------------
*-- lnCD # Elements Clause
------------------------------------------------------------

  # Elements

    ( ) Procedure
    (•) Expression

# Elements:   SizeArry(@laCDPurch)
```

```
*==============================================================
*  lhSales
*==============================================================
 @  12,  18
 Spacing:    1

  Push Button Prompts:         (·) Horizontal    ( ) Vertical
                               [ ] Terminating  <Spacing...>
   Sales by Month
                              Variable:

                               < Choose... >  lhSales

                              Options:

                               [ ] When...      [ ] Comment...
                               [X] Valid...     [ ] Disabled
                               [ ] Message...

                  «   OK   »    < Cancel >
--------------------------------------------------------------
*-- lhSales Valid Clause
--------------------------------------------------------------

  Valid

    (·) Procedure
    ( ) Expression

SELECT Invoice.cCustID, ;
       PADR(CMONTH(dOrdered),10) AS InvMonth, ;
       nCdQty * nCdAmt AS InvTotal;
  FROM Invoice, Purchase ;
 WHERE Invoice.cID = Purchase.cInvID ;
   AND Invoice.cCustID = m.cID ;
   AND YEAR(Invoice.dOrdered) = YEAR(DATE()) ;
  INTO CURSOR SYS(2015)
IF _tally = 0
   WAIT WINDOW "No sales to this customer in the current year"
ELSE
   DO GENXTAB WITH "CustSales"
   DO YearShow.spr WITH TRIM(cLastName)+", "+TRIM(cFirstName)
   USE IN CustSales
ENDIF
SELECT Customer
**************************************************************
*--  SCREEN CLEANUP CODE
**************************************************************
IF glQuitting
   *-- Check out Getbar()
   =killbar('wrCustome')
   =killwind('wrCustome')
ENDIF
```

```
PROCEDURE InitIt
*-- Called when "ADD" selected
*-- Performs necessary initialization
      DO InitIt IN Methods.prg
      DIME laCDPurch[1,2]     && Reset the array to empty
      laCDPurch = .F.
RETURN
PROCEDURE DeleteIt
*-- Called when "DELETE" selected from the menu
*-- Checks to see if the user *really* wants to
*--   delete, then does it.
   PRIVATE jcOldOrder, jcInvID, jlNoLock, jcOldPOrder, jnNewRec
   jlNoLock = .F.

   IF !DelCheck()
      RETURN
   ENDIF
   SKIP
   jnNewRec = IIF(EOF(),-1,RECNO())
   SKIP -1

   IF (IsLocked() OR RLOCK() OR NetLock()) AND DelRec()  && Lock Customer record
      jcErrMsg = "Someone has modified this data. Do you want to delete " + ;
                 "this information anyway? Doing so will destroy the other " + ;
                 "person's changes. "
      IF cLastUpd # m.cLastUpd AND !AreUSure(jcErrMsg)
         WAIT WINDOW TIMEOUT 2 "Refreshing Other User's Changes..."
         SCATTER MEMVAR MEMO
         jlNoLock = .T.
      ELSE
         *-- Set up all ORDERs at the top
         jcOldOrder  = ORDER("Invoice")
         jcOldPOrder = ORDER("Purchase")
         SET ORDER TO cCustID IN Invoice
         SET ORDER TO cInvID  IN Purchase

         *-- Lock Invoice Headers
         SELECT Invoice
         SEEK m.cID
         SCAN WHILE cCustID = m.cID
            IF NOT (IsLocked() OR RLOCK() OR NetLock())
               jlNoLock = .T.
            ENDIF
         ENDSCAN
      ENDIF
   ELSE
      UNLOCK
      RETURN
   ENDIF

   IF !jlNoLock
      SELECT Customer
      DELETE
      SELECT Invoice
      SEEK m.cID
      SCAN WHILE cCustID = m.cID
         m.jcInvID = Invoice.cID
         DELETE
         SELECT Purchase
```

```
         DO WHILE SEEK(jcInvID)
              DELETE
         ENDDO
      ENDSCAN
      *-- Reset the ORDERs
      SET ORDER TO (jcOldOrder)  IN Invoice
      SET ORDER TO (jcOldPOrder) IN Purchase

      SELECT Customer
      IF jnNewRec = -1
         GO BOTTOM
      ELSE
         GO jnNewRec
      ENDIF
   ELSE                     && No lock obtained
      ?? CHR(7)
      WAIT WINDOW "Customer data is in use. Cannot delete. Press any key..."
   ENDIF

   SCATTER MEMVAR MEMO
   UNLOCK ALL

RETURN
PROCEDURE DisableIt
   DO DisableIt IN methods.prg
   SHOW GET lnCD ENABLE
   SHOW GET lhSales ENABLE
RETURN
*------------------------------------------------------------
*************************************************************
**--    CUSTOMER.SCX - MAC PLATFORM
*************************************************************
```

```
( ) DeskTop                            (·) Window

Name:    wrCustome                     <Type...>
Title:   Customer Information Window
Footer:

Size:              Screen Code:

 Height:   18.333   [X] Setup...
 Width:    55.833   [X] Cleanup & Procs...              «   OK   »

Position:          READ Clauses:                        < Cancel >

 Row:        0.000  [ ] Activate...    [X] Show...
 Column:     0.000  [ ] Valid...       [ ] When...
 [X] Center         [X] Deactivate...

Environment:                      [X] Add alias

      Environment NOT saved with screen.
```

```
Type:      [ User ]

Attributes:          Border:

[ ] Close            ( ) None
[X] Float            ( ) Single
[ ] Shadow           ( ) Double        «   OK   »
[X] Minimize         ( ) Panel
                     (·) System        < Cancel >

Color Schemes:

Primary:          Popup:
[          ]      [          ]
```

```
MAC       RGB Fill Color Scheme: (,,)
MAC       Font: Geneva,  10
 Screen Setup code above
 READ Deactivate code above
 READ Show code above
************************************************************
*--    G E T    O B J E C T S
************************************************************
*===========================================================
*  Text: Address
*===========================================================
 @   2.833,   6.667
MAC       RGB Color Scheme: (,,,,,)
MAC       Font: Monaco,   9
          Style: Bold
*===========================================================
*  Text: City/St/Zip
*===========================================================
 @   5.250,   2.000
MAC       RGB Color Scheme: (,,,,,)
MAC       Font: Monaco,   9
          Style: Bold
*===========================================================
*  Text: Phone
*===========================================================
 @   6.500,   9.000
MAC       RGB Color Scheme: (,,,,,)
MAC       Font: Monaco,   9
          Style: Bold
*===========================================================
*  Text: Last Name
*===========================================================
 @   0.417,   4.333
MAC       RGB Color Scheme: (,,,,,)
MAC       Font: Monaco,   9
          Style: Bold
*===========================================================
*  Text: First Name
```

```
*=================================================================
 @   1.667,   3.167
MAC       RGB Color Scheme: (,,,,,)
MAC       Font: Monaco,   9
          Style: Bold
*=================================================================
*  m.clastname
*=================================================================
 @   0.500,  16.000

   Field:
    ( ) Say          (·) Get          ( ) Edit

   <  Get...    > m.clastname
                                                  «    OK    »
   < Format... > @3
                                                  < Cancel >
   Range:
    [ ] Upper...                   [ ] Lower...

   [ ] When...      [ ] Error...     [ ] Scroll bar
   [ ] Valid...     [ ] Comment...   [ ] Allow tabs
   [X] Message...   [X] Disabled     [ ] Refresh

MAC       RGB Color Scheme: (,,,,,)
MAC       Font: monaco,   9
 Message code above
*=================================================================
*  m.cfirstname
*=================================================================
 @   1.667,  16.000

   Field:
    ( ) Say          (·) Get          ( ) Edit

   <  Get...    > m.cfirstname
                                                  «    OK    »
   < Format... > @3
                                                  < Cancel >
   Range:
    [ ] Upper...                   [ ] Lower...

   [ ] When...      [ ] Error...     [ ] Scroll bar
   [ ] Valid...     [ ] Comment...   [ ] Allow tabs
   [X] Message...   [X] Disabled     [ ] Refresh

MAC       RGB Color Scheme: (,,,,,)
MAC       Font: monaco,   9
```

```
 Message code above
*==========================================================
*  m.caddress1
*==========================================================
 @   2.833,  16.000
╔══════════════════════════════════════════════════════════╗
║                                                          ║
║  Field:                                                  ║
║  ┌────────────────────────────────────────┐              ║
║  │ ( ) Say       (•) Get        ( ) Edit  │              ║
║  └────────────────────────────────────────┘              ║
║                                                          ║
║  <  Get...   > m.caddress1                               ║
║                                            «   OK   »    ║
║  < Format... > @3                                        ║
║                                            < Cancel >    ║
║  Range:                                                  ║
║  ┌────────────────────────────────────────┐              ║
║  │ [ ] Upper...              [ ] Lower... │              ║
║  └────────────────────────────────────────┘              ║
║                                                          ║
║  [ ] When...     [ ] Error...    [ ] Scroll bar          ║
║  [ ] Valid...    [ ] Comment...  [ ] Allow tabs          ║
║  [X] Message...  [X] Disabled    [ ] Refresh             ║
║                                                          ║
╚══════════════════════════════════════════════════════════╝
MAC       RGB Color Scheme: (,,,,,)
MAC       Font: monaco,   9
 Message code above
*==========================================================
*  m.caddress2
*==========================================================
 @   4.083,  16.000
╔══════════════════════════════════════════════════════════╗
║                                                          ║
║  Field:                                                  ║
║  ┌────────────────────────────────────────┐              ║
║  │ ( ) Say       (•) Get        ( ) Edit  │              ║
║  └────────────────────────────────────────┘              ║
║                                                          ║
║  <  Get...   > m.caddress2                               ║
║                                            «   OK   »    ║
║  < Format... > @3                                        ║
║                                            < Cancel >    ║
║  Range:                                                  ║
║  ┌────────────────────────────────────────┐              ║
║  │ [ ] Upper...              [ ] Lower... │              ║
║  └────────────────────────────────────────┘              ║
║                                                          ║
║  [ ] When...     [ ] Error...    [ ] Scroll bar          ║
║  [ ] Valid...    [ ] Comment...  [ ] Allow tabs          ║
║  [X] Message...  [X] Disabled    [ ] Refresh             ║
║                                                          ║
╚══════════════════════════════════════════════════════════╝
MAC       RGB Color Scheme: (,,,,,)
MAC       Font: monaco,   9
 Message code above
*==========================================================
*  m.ccity
```

```
*==============================================================
 @   5.250,  16.000
+--------------------------------------------------------------+
|                                                              |
|  Field:                                                      |
|  +-------------------------------------------+               |
|  | ( ) Say        (·) Get        ( ) Edit    |               |
|  +-------------------------------------------+               |
|                                                              |
|  <  Get...    > m.ccity                                      |
|                                             «    OK    »      |
|  < Format... > @3                                            |
|                                             < Cancel >      |
|  Range:                                                      |
|  +-------------------------------------------+               |
|  | [ ] Upper...                [ ] Lower...  |               |
|  +-------------------------------------------+               |
|                                                              |
|  [ ] When...      [ ] Error...     [ ] Scroll bar            |
|  [ ] Valid...     [ ] Comment...   [ ] Allow tabs            |
|  [X] Message...   [X] Disabled     [ ] Refresh               |
|                                                              |
+--------------------------------------------------------------+
MAC      RGB Color Scheme: (,,,,,)
MAC      Font: monaco,   9
 Message code above
*==============================================================
*  m.cstate
*==============================================================
 @   5.250,  34.167
+--------------------------------------------------------------+
|                                                              |
|  Field:                                                      |
|  +-------------------------------------------+               |
|  | ( ) Say        (·) Get        ( ) Edit    |               |
|  +-------------------------------------------+               |
|                                                              |
|  <  Get...    > m.cstate                                     |
|                                             «    OK    »      |
|  < Format... > @3A!                                          |
|                                             < Cancel >      |
|  Range:                                                      |
|  +-------------------------------------------+               |
|  | [ ] Upper...                [ ] Lower...  |               |
|  +-------------------------------------------+               |
|                                                              |
|  [ ] When...      [X] Error...     [ ] Scroll bar            |
|  [X] Valid...     [ ] Comment...   [ ] Allow tabs            |
|  [X] Message...   [X] Disabled     [ ] Refresh               |
|                                                              |
+--------------------------------------------------------------+
MAC      RGB Color Scheme: (,,,,,)
MAC      Font: monaco,   9
 Valid code above
 Message code above
 Error code above
*==============================================================
*  m.czip
*==============================================================
 @   5.250,  38.500
```

```
 Field:
  ( ) Say          (•) Get          ( ) Edit

 <  Get...    > m.czip
                                          «   OK   »
 < Format... > @3R 99999-9999
                                          < Cancel >
 Range:
  [ ] Upper...                [ ] Lower...

 [ ] When...     [ ] Error...     [ ] Scroll bar
 [ ] Valid...    [ ] Comment...   [ ] Allow tabs
 [X] Message...  [X] Disabled     [ ] Refresh

MAC      RGB Color Scheme: (,,,,,)
MAC      Font: monaco,   9
 Message code above
*============================================================
*  m.cphone
*============================================================
 @   6.500,  16.000

 Field:
  ( ) Say          (•) Get          ( ) Edit

 <  Get...    > m.cphone
                                          «   OK   »
 < Format... > @3R (999) 999-9999
                                          < Cancel >
 Range:
  [ ] Upper...                [ ] Lower...

 [ ] When...     [ ] Error...     [ ] Scroll bar
 [ ] Valid...    [ ] Comment...   [ ] Allow tabs
 [X] Message...  [X] Disabled     [ ] Refresh

MAC      RGB Color Scheme: (,,,,,)
MAC      Font: monaco,   9
 Message code above
*============================================================
*  lnCD
*============================================================
 @   8.250,   1.833
     SIZE   7.091,  52.500
```

```
 List Type:                                   Options:

  (·) From Array       laCDPurch              [ ] When...        [ ] Comment...
  ( ) From Popup                              [ ] Valid...       [ ] Disabled
  ( ) Prompt Structure                        [X] Message...     [ ] 1st Element...
  ( ) Prompt Field                            [ ] Terminating    [X] # Elements...
  ( ) Prompt Files

 Variable:

  < Choose... > lnCD                              «   OK   »     < Cancel >

MAC      RGB Color Scheme: (,,,,,)
MAC      Font: monaco,   9
 Message code above
 # Elements code above
*============================================================
*  lhSales
*============================================================
 @  15.917,  14.333
     SIZE   2.182,  27.000
 Spacing:    1

 Push Button Prompts:           (·) Horizontal   ( ) Vertical
                                [ ] Terminating  <Spacing...>
 Sales by Month
                               Variable:

                                < Choose... >  lhSales

                               Options:

                                [ ] When...     [ ] Comment...
                                [X] Valid...    [ ] Disabled
                                [ ] Message...

                 «   OK   »    < Cancel >

MAC      RGB Color Scheme: (,,,,,)
MAC      Font: monaco,   9
 Valid code above
 Screen Cleanup and Procedures code above
```

```
*------------------------------------------------------------
*************************************************************
**--    CUSTOMER.SCX - WINDOWS PLATFORM
*************************************************************
 ( ) DeskTop                        (·) Window

 Name:   wrCustome                  <Type...>
 Title:  Customer Information Window
 Footer:

 Size:            Screen Code:

   Height:   14.867     [X] Setup...
   Width:    55.000     [X] Cleanup & Procs...             «   OK   »

 Position:        READ Clauses:                             < Cancel >

   Row:         0.000   [ ] Activate...     [X] Show...
   Column:      0.000   [ ] Valid...        [ ] When...
   [X] Center           [X] Deactivate...

 Environment:                           [X] Add alias

        Environment NOT saved with screen.

  Type:        User

  Attributes:     Border:

   [ ] Close       ( ) None
   [X] Float       ( ) Single
   [ ] Shadow      ( ) Double      «   OK   »
   [X] Minimize    ( ) Panel
                   (·) System      < Cancel >

  Color Schemes:

   Primary:        Popup:

WINDOWS  RGB Fill Color Scheme: (,,)
WINDOWS  Font: Fixedsys,   9
 Screen Setup code above
 READ Deactivate code above
 READ Show code above
*************************************************************
*--    G E T   O B J E C T S
*************************************************************
*============================================================
*  Text: Address
*============================================================
```

```
 @   2.867,   5.000
WINDOWS  RGB Color Scheme: (,,,,,)
WINDOWS  Font: Terminal,   9
*=============================================================
*  Text: City/St/Zip
*=============================================================
 @   5.267,   1.000
WINDOWS  RGB Color Scheme: (,,,,,)
WINDOWS  Font: Terminal,   9
*=============================================================
*  Text: Phone
*=============================================================
 @   6.467,   7.000
WINDOWS  RGB Color Scheme: (,,,,,)
WINDOWS  Font: Terminal,   9
*=============================================================
*  Text: Last Name
*=============================================================
 @   0.400,   3.000
WINDOWS  RGB Color Scheme: (,,,,,)
WINDOWS  Font: Terminal,   9
*=============================================================
*  Text: First Name
*=============================================================
 @   1.667,   2.000
WINDOWS  RGB Color Scheme: (,,,,,)
WINDOWS  Font: Terminal,   9
*=============================================================
*  m.clastname
*=============================================================
 @   0.467,  14.125

  Field:
   ( ) Say         (·) Get         ( ) Edit

  <  Get...   > m.clastname
                                          «   OK   »
  < Format... >
                                          < Cancel >
  Range:
   [ ] Upper...                [ ] Lower...

  [ ] When...       [ ] Error...      [ ] Scroll bar
  [ ] Valid...      [ ] Comment...    [ ] Allow tabs
  [X] Message...    [X] Disabled      [ ] Refresh

WINDOWS  RGB Color Scheme: (,,,,,)
WINDOWS  Font: Terminal,   9
 Message code above
*=============================================================
*  m.cfirstname
*=============================================================
 @   1.667,  14.125
```

```
╔════════════════════════════════════════════════════════════════╗
║                                                                ║
║  Field:                                                        ║
║  ┌──────────────────────────────────────────┐                 ║
║  │ ( ) Say        (·) Get         ( ) Edit  │                 ║
║  └──────────────────────────────────────────┘                 ║
║                                                                ║
║  <  Get...   > m.cfirstname                                    ║
║                                                  «   OK   »    ║
║  < Format... >                                                 ║
║                                                  < Cancel >    ║
║  Range:                                                        ║
║  ┌──────────────────────────────────────────┐                 ║
║  │ [ ] Upper...                 [ ] Lower...│                 ║
║  └──────────────────────────────────────────┘                 ║
║                                                                ║
║  [ ] When...     [ ] Error...     [ ] Scroll bar               ║
║  [ ] Valid...    [ ] Comment...   [ ] Allow tabs               ║
║  [X] Message...  [X] Disabled     [ ] Refresh                  ║
║                                                                ║
╚════════════════════════════════════════════════════════════════╝
WINDOWS  RGB Color Scheme: (,,,,,)
WINDOWS  Font: Terminal,   9
 Message code above
*==============================================================
*  m.caddress1
*==============================================================
 @   2.867,  14.125
╔════════════════════════════════════════════════════════════════╗
║                                                                ║
║  Field:                                                        ║
║  ┌──────────────────────────────────────────┐                 ║
║  │ ( ) Say        (·) Get         ( ) Edit  │                 ║
║  └──────────────────────────────────────────┘                 ║
║                                                                ║
║  <  Get...   > m.caddress1                                     ║
║                                                  «   OK   »    ║
║  < Format... >                                                 ║
║                                                  < Cancel >    ║
║  Range:                                                        ║
║  ┌──────────────────────────────────────────┐                 ║
║  │ [ ] Upper...                 [ ] Lower...│                 ║
║  └──────────────────────────────────────────┘                 ║
║                                                                ║
║  [ ] When...     [ ] Error...     [ ] Scroll bar               ║
║  [ ] Valid...    [ ] Comment...   [ ] Allow tabs               ║
║  [X] Message...  [X] Disabled     [ ] Refresh                  ║
║                                                                ║
╚════════════════════════════════════════════════════════════════╝
WINDOWS  RGB Color Scheme: (,,,,,)
WINDOWS  Font: Terminal,   9
 Message code above
*==============================================================
*  m.caddress2
*==============================================================
 @   4.067,  14.125
```

```
  Field:
  ( ) Say          (·) Get          ( ) Edit

  <  Get...   > m.caddress2
                                              «    OK    »
  < Format... >
                                              < Cancel >
  Range:
  [ ] Upper...                    [ ] Lower...

  [ ] When...       [ ] Error...      [ ] Scroll bar
  [ ] Valid...      [ ] Comment...    [ ] Allow tabs
  [X] Message...    [X] Disabled      [ ] Refresh

WINDOWS  RGB Color Scheme: (,,,,,)
WINDOWS  Font: Terminal,   9
 Message code above
*===============================================================
*  m.ccity
*===============================================================
 @   5.267,  14.125

  Field:
  ( ) Say          (·) Get          ( ) Edit

  <  Get...   > m.ccity
                                              «    OK    »
  < Format... >
                                              < Cancel >
  Range:
  [ ] Upper...                    [ ] Lower...

  [ ] When...       [ ] Error...      [ ] Scroll bar
  [ ] Valid...      [ ] Comment...    [ ] Allow tabs
  [X] Message...    [X] Disabled      [ ] Refresh

WINDOWS  RGB Color Scheme: (,,,,,)
WINDOWS  Font: Terminal,   9
 Message code above
*===============================================================
*  m.cstate
*===============================================================
 @   5.267,  36.500
```

```
 Field:
 ( ) Say          (·) Get          ( ) Edit

 <  Get...    > m.cstate
                                             «   OK   »
 < Format... > @A!
                                             < Cancel >
 Range:
 [ ] Upper...                 [ ] Lower...

 [ ] When...     [X] Error...     [ ] Scroll bar
 [X] Valid...    [ ] Comment...   [ ] Allow tabs
 [X] Message...  [X] Disabled     [ ] Refresh

WINDOWS  RGB Color Scheme: (,,,,,)
WINDOWS  Font: Terminal,   9
 Valid code above
 Message code above
 Error code above
*============================================================
*  m.czip
*============================================================
 @   5.267,  41.125

 Field:
 ( ) Say          (·) Get          ( ) Edit

 <  Get...    > m.czip
                                             «   OK   »
 < Format... > @R 99999-9999
                                             < Cancel >
 Range:
 [ ] Upper...                 [ ] Lower...

 [ ] When...     [ ] Error...     [ ] Scroll bar
 [ ] Valid...    [ ] Comment...   [ ] Allow tabs
 [X] Message...  [X] Disabled     [ ] Refresh

WINDOWS  RGB Color Scheme: (,,,,,)
WINDOWS  Font: Terminal,   9
 Message code above
*============================================================
*  m.cphone
*============================================================
 @   6.467,  14.125
```

```
 Field:
 ( ) Say          (·) Get          ( ) Edit

 <  Get...    > m.cphone
                                          «   OK   »
 < Format... > @R (999) 999-9999
                                          < Cancel >
 Range:
 [ ] Upper...                 [ ] Lower...

 [ ] When...      [ ] Error...      [ ] Scroll bar
 [ ] Valid...     [ ] Comment...    [ ] Allow tabs
 [X] Message...   [X] Disabled      [ ] Refresh

WINDOWS  RGB Color Scheme: (,,,,,)
WINDOWS  Font: Terminal,   9
 Message code above
*===========================================================
*  lnCD
*===========================================================
 @   7.800,   1.000
     SIZE   5.833,  53.125

 List Type:                          Options:
 (·) From Array      laCDPurch       [ ] When...        [ ] Comment...
 ( ) From Popup                      [ ] Valid...       [ ] Disabled
 ( ) Prompt Structure                [X] Message...     [ ] 1st Element...
 ( ) Prompt Field                    [ ] Terminating    [X] # Elements...
 ( ) Prompt Files

 Variable:
 < Choose... > lnCD                      «   OK   »    < Cancel >

WINDOWS  RGB Color Scheme: (,,,,,)
WINDOWS  Font: Terminal,   9
 Message code above
 # Elements code above
*===========================================================
*  lhSales
*===========================================================
 @  12.867,  17.125
     SIZE   2.077,  27.000
 Spacing:   1
```

```
Push Button Prompts:          (·) Horizontal    ( ) Vertical
                              [ ] Terminating   <Spacing...>
 Sales by Month
                              Variable:

                              < Choose... >  lhSales

                              Options:

                              [ ] When...       [ ] Comment...
                              [X] Valid...      [ ] Disabled
                              [ ] Message...

                    «   OK   »    < Cancel >
```

```
WINDOWS  RGB Color Scheme: (,,,,,)
WINDOWS  Font: MS Sans Serif,   8
         Style: Bold
 Valid code above
 Screen Cleanup and Procedures code above
```

Invoice Entry: INVOICE.SCX

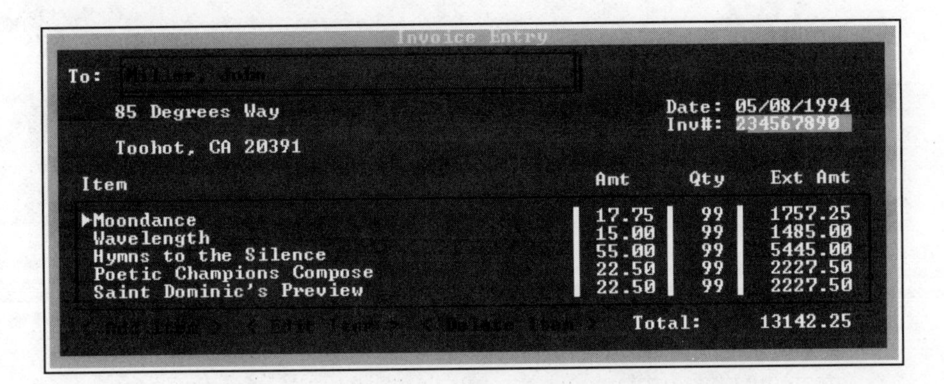

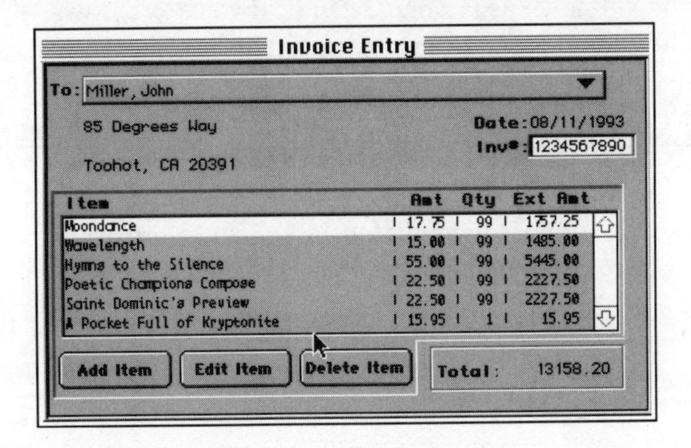

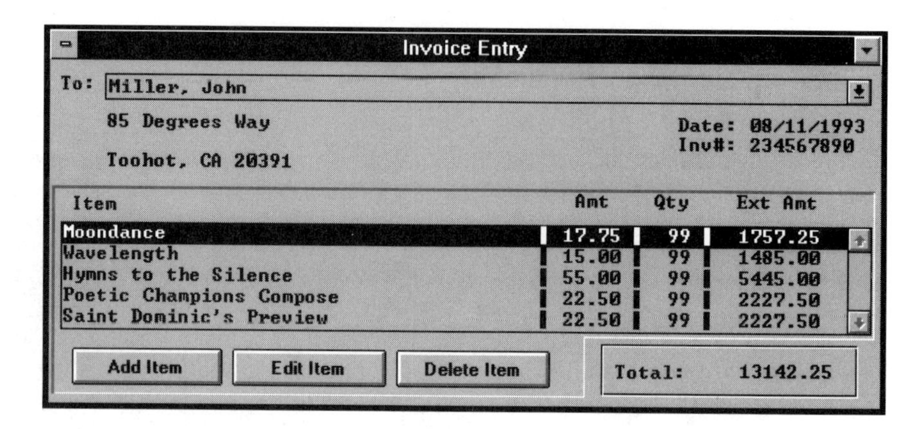

One of the more common types of window that database developers are asked to create involve displaying a one-to-many relationship. These types of windows are most often known as Header/Detail or Invoice Windows.

There are three basic approaches that can be used when developing this type of entry capability. They include:

1. Allow header entry and then bring up a modal window that is used to enter the detail information.
2. Use a READ window for the header information and a BROWSE window for the detail entry.
3. Use one READ window that accomodates both the header and the detail information.

Making the Design Decision

Which of the approaches should we use when developing an invoice window? We should use whichever approach is most in tune with our user's expectations. In the particular case of an invoice-entry window, I would opt for the third option, because it allows us, the developers, to most closely imitate the look of a typical invoice form.

While designing a single window with our header/detail information, how can we place the detail information *in the window*? We use a scrolling list, which allows the user to scroll through the detail items, and is a full READ object, that works within our window (as opposed to a BROWSE, which must be placed within its own window).

Our Data Structure

As we have seen from our data structure, this window requires a 1:M:M relation. One customer may have many invoices, each of which may have many purchase records.

Our invoice window allows the user to select a customer while not editing, and then brings up the first invoice for that user with a list of all purchased items in the invoice. Once the user decides to edit, they can place header information in the top of the invoice window, and modify detail information at will.

Creating Our Window

Let's take a moment to discuss the *behavior* of our window. We want to create an invoice entry window that allows a keyboard user to access all of the functions during data entry without having to use a mouse. Invoice entry is typically a typing intensive routine, and we want to facilitate the user's entry of information. At the same time, we will provide a mouse-driven method of accomplishing as much data entry as possible. In this way, we provide for all of our users.

Providing the mouse-driven entry is easy. We simply provide push buttons for adding, editing and deleting line items. How do we provide the same capabilities for our keyboard user? We take advantage of familiar metaphors and the behavior of scrolling lists.

The VALID clause of a scrolling list object is triggered when the user presses <ENTER> or double clicks. We will attach the line item edit procedure to our scrolling list's VALID snippet. The add and delete line item capability will be accomplished through the use of ON KEY LABELs that are only available while in the list itself. The <Ins> key will add a new line item, and the <Del> key will delete the current item.

Coding the Screen

How do we implement the interface that we discussed above? Let's take a look at all of the snippets involved, and see how they are used by this window.

The Window's Setup Snippet

The Setup snippet is used to set up our data files and variables. As written, this snippet assumes that all of the data files are currently open. We select our header table, and copy the information into memory. We then grab the detail information for the current header into an array. Note that the array consists of four columns:

- A string with concatenated information that is shown to the user.

- The unique ID of the item selected in the current detail row.
- The amount charged for the current item.
- The quantity purchased of the item.

The scrolling list will display the first column, and we will use the <Choose> variable (lnLineItem) to find which array row the user is pointing to. The second, third, and fourth columns can then be used in an entry window where the user can modify the information.

The READ WHEN Snippet

This snippet runs once at the beginning of the READ. Therefore, it is a perfect location to place code that we need to run just before the window starts becoming active. In this code, we set up our keyboard handler. We put a copy of any current ON KEY LABEL commands onto a stack, and set up the <INS> and <DEL> key.

```
PUSH KEY
ON KEY LABEL INS DO OnKeys WITH "INS"
ON KEY LABEL DEL DO OnKeys WITH "DEL"
```

OnKeys() is a routine (located in the Cleanup Snippet) that actually performs our key handling. It turns off the ON KEY LABELs, preventing recursive calling, and performs our add and delete routines *if we are currently in the scrolling list*. If we are not in the scrolling list, we KEYBOARD the character back into the buffer, causing the key to act as usual.

```
************************************************
PROCEDURE OnKeys
************************************************
*  Procedure.........: OnKeys
*  Author............: yag
*  Project...........: CodeBook 2.5
*  Created...........: 04/11/1993
*  Copyright.........: (c) Flash Creative Management, 1993
*) Description.......: Procedure run when ON KEY LABELs hit
*)                   : Mimics <ADD> <DELETE> lineitem buttons.
*)                   : Only effective when in lnLineItem List.
*  Calling Samples...: DO OnKeys WITH "INS"
*  Parameter List....: tcKey = "INS" or "DEL"
*  Major change list.:
PARAMETER tcKey
PUSH KEY CLEAR
tcKey = UPPER(tcKey)
```

```
IF UPPER(VARREAD()) = "LNLINEITEM"
   DO CASE
      CASE tcKey = "INS"
         DO AddItem
      CASE tcKey = "DEL"
         DO DelItem
   ENDCASE
ELSE             && Do the normal action
   jcKey = "{" + tcKey + "}"
   KEYBOARD jcKey PLAIN
ENDIF
POP KEY
RETURN
```

The Objects' VALID Snippets

The list object (lnLineItem) contains a VALID that simply says DO FillItem. Each of the pushbuttons (Add, Edit and Delete) contain DO AddItem, DO FillItem and DO DelItem respectively.

The three procedures AddItem, FillItem and DelItem perform appropriately for the application. For instance, AddItem and FillItem bring up a window (FillItem.scx) allowing the user to enter information into the array columns as appropriate, recreate the first array column and redisplay the scrolling list. The DelItem procedure will do an ADEL() on the currently selected array row, removing it.

The Cleanup Snippet

This snippet contains the code to handle the line item routines detailed above (since they are called from multiple locations, we put the code here), and inherited versions of AddIt(), SaveIt(), DeleteIt() and DisableIt(). The first three routines make sure to not only add/save/delete the invoice header information (done automatically by the base method) but add code to do the same for the purchase detail information. DisableIt() is used to allow the user to select the customer popup before editing takes place. Selecting a specific customer simply sets a filter in the invoice header table that limits us to seeing only the specific customer's invoices. Other approaches to filtering the invoice information could include performing a SQL SELECT of appropriate invoice IDs and relating the resulting cursor to the actual invoice table, or using an override of the TopIt(), NextIt(), PriorIt() and BottomIt() methods to only allow the user to move within the current customer's data set.

```
*----------------------------------------------------------------
******************************************************************
**--    INVOICE.SCX - DOS PLATFORM
******************************************************************

( ) DeskTop                               (·) Window

Name:   wrInvoice                         <Type...>
Title:  Invoice Entry
Footer:

Size:              Screen Code:

  Height:   18      [X] Setup...
  Width:    73      [X] Cleanup & Procs...                 «  OK  »

Position:          READ Clauses:                           < Cancel >

  Row:        0     [X] Activate...      [X] Show...
  Column:     0     [ ] Valid...         [X] When...
  [X] Center        [X] Deactivate...

Environment:                          [X] Add alias

       Environment saved with this screen.


  Type:     User

  Attributes:      Border:

  [ ] Close         ( ) None
  [X] Float         ( ) Single
  [ ] Shadow        ( ) Double        «  OK  »
  [X] Minimize      ( ) Panel
                    (·) System        < Cancel >

  Color Schemes:

    Primary:        Popup:

    Windows         Window Pop

******************************************************************
*  SCREEN SETUP CODE
******************************************************************
#SECTION 1
#WCLAUSES IN &gcMainWind
#SECTION 2
*-- Code for Invoice Window
#DEFINE dcLineDesc        1
#DEFINE dcID              2
#DEFINE dnCdAmt           3
#DEFINE dnCdQty           4
```

```
#DEFINE dnLineTtl         5
#DEFINE dcTitle           6
#DEFINE dnLineItem        6
SELECT Invoice
SCATTER MEMVAR
STORE "" TO m.cLastName, m.cFirstName, ;
   m.cAddress1, m.cAddress2, ;
   m.cCity, m.cState, m.cZip
STORE 0 TO m.lnCustPick

DIMENSION laLineItem[1,dnLineItem]
m.gbCopy = .T.                && Disable Copy Capability
*-- Code for Customer Popup
#DEFINE dcCustName    1
#DEFINE dcCustID      2
#DEFINE dnCustPick    2
SELECT TRIM(Customer.cLastName)+", "+Customer.cFirstName, ;
       Customer.cID ;
  FROM Customer ;
 ORDER BY Customer.cLastName ;
  INTO ARRAY laCustPick
IF _tally = 0
   DIMENSION laCustPick[1,dnCustPick]
ENDIF
=restmem('wrInvoice')
IF !glRestEdit
   *-- Initialize to last used customer
   lnCurCust = ASCAN(laCustPick, Customer.cID)
   IF lnCurCust # 0
      lnCustPick = ASUBSCRIPT(laCustPick,lnCurCust,1)
   ELSE
      lnCustPick = 1
   ENDIF
   DO ShoCustInv
   =addbar("wrInvoice")
ENDIF
-------------------------------------------------------------
*-- READ Activate Clause
-------------------------------------------------------------
```

```
READ Activate

  (·) Procedure
  ( ) Expression
```

```
DO ShowBtns
-------------------------------------------------------------
*-- READ Deactivate Clause
-------------------------------------------------------------
```

```
READ Deactivate

( ) Procedure
(·) Expression

READ Deactivate:   stopread('wrInvoice')
------------------------------------------------------------
*-- READ Show Clause
------------------------------------------------------------

READ Show

(·) Procedure
( ) Expression

IF !glRestEdit
   IF !EMPTY( ;
      LOOKUP(Customer.cID,laCustPick[lnCustPick,dcID],Customer.cID,"CID"))
      SELECT Customer
      SCATTER MEMVAR FIELDS ;
         cLastName, cFirstName, ;
         cAddress1, cAddress2, ;
         cCity, cState, cZip
      SELECT Invoice
   ENDIF

   SELECT CD.cTitle + " | " + STR(Purchase.nCdAmt,5,2) ;
      + " |  " + STR(Purchase.nCdQty,2,0) + ;
      + " |  " + STR(Purchase.nCdAmt * Purchase.nCDQty,7,2), ;
      CD.cID, Purchase.nCdAmt, Purchase.nCdQty, ;
      Purchase.nCdAmt * Purchase.nCdQty, ;
      CD.cTitle ;
      FROM CD, Purchase ;
    WHERE CD.cID = Purchase.cCdID ;
      AND Purchase.cInvID = m.cID ;
     INTO ARRAY laLineItem

   IF _tally = 0
      DIMENSION laLineItem[1,dnLineItem]
      laLineItem = .F.
   ENDIF
ENDIF
------------------------------------------------------------
*-- READ When Clause
------------------------------------------------------------
```

```
 ┌──────────────────────────────────────────┐
 │                                          │
 │  READ When                               │
 │   ┌────────────────────────────────────┐ │
 │   │ (·) Procedure                      │ │
 │   │ ( ) Expression                     │ │
 │   └────────────────────────────────────┘ │
 │                                          │
 └──────────────────────────────────────────┘
PUSH KEY
ON KEY LABEL INS DO OnKeys WITH "INS"
ON KEY LABEL DEL DO OnKeys WITH "DEL"
***********************************************************
*--   G E T    O B J E C T S
***********************************************************
*==========================================================
*  lnCustPick
*==========================================================
 @   0,   5
 ┌──────────────────────────────────────────────────────────────────┐
 │                                                                  │
 │  ( ) List Popup          (·) Array Popup  laCustPick             │
 │  ┌──────────────────┐                                            │
 │  │                  │    Variable:                               │
 │  │                  │    ┌───────────────────────────────────┐   │
 │  │                  │    │ < Choose... > lnCustPick          │   │
 │  │                  │    └───────────────────────────────────┘   │
 │  │                  │    Options:                                │
 │  │                  │    ┌───────────────────────────────────┐   │
 │  │                  │    │ [X] When...    [ ] Comment...     │   │
 │  │                  │    │ [X] Valid...   [ ] Disabled       │   │
 │  │                  │    │ [ ] Message... [ ] 1st Element... │   │
 │  │                  │    │                [X] # Elements...  │   │
 │  └──────────────────┘    └───────────────────────────────────┘   │
 │                                                                  │
 │  Initial: ┌──────────┐      «  OK  »     < Cancel >              │
 │           └──────────┘                                           │
 └──────────────────────────────────────────────────────────────────┘
-----------------------------------------------------------
*-- lnCustPick When Clause
-----------------------------------------------------------
 ┌──────────────────────────────────────────┐
 │                                          │
 │  When                                    │
 │   ┌────────────────────────────────────┐ │
 │   │ ( ) Procedure                      │ │
 │   │ (·) Expression                     │ │
 │   └────────────────────────────────────┘ │
 │                                          │
 └──────────────────────────────────────────┘
When:   NOT glEditable
-----------------------------------------------------------
*-- lnCustPick Valid Clause
-----------------------------------------------------------
```

```
 Valid

  (·) Procedure
  ( ) Expression

DO ShoCustInv
DO DimNavigat
------------------------------------------------------------
*-- lnCustPick # Elements Clause
------------------------------------------------------------

 # Elements

  ( ) Procedure
  (·) Expression

# Elements:   sizearry(@laCustPick)
*============================================================
*  Text: To:
*============================================================
 @   1,   1
*============================================================
*  Text: Date:
*============================================================
 @   3,  52
*============================================================
*
*============================================================
 @   3,  58

 Field:

  (·) Say          ( ) Get          ( ) Edit

 <  Say...   > m.dOrdered
                                                 «   OK   »
 < Format... >
                                                 < Cancel >
 Range:

  [ ] Upper...                     [ ] Lower...

 [ ] When...      [ ] Error...      [ ] Scroll bar
 [ ] Valid...     [ ] Comment...    [ ] Allow tabs
 [ ] Message...   [ ] Disabled      [X] Refresh

*============================================================
*
```

```
*==============================================================
 @   3,   5

 Field:
   (·) Say          ( ) Get          ( ) Edit

 <  Say...    > m.caddress1
                                                  «    OK    »
 < Format... >
                                                  < Cancel >
 Range:
   [ ] Upper...                   [ ] Lower...

 [ ] When...      [ ] Error...      [ ] Scroll bar
 [ ] Valid...     [ ] Comment...    [ ] Allow tabs
 [ ] Message...   [ ] Disabled      [X] Refresh
*==============================================================
*
*==============================================================
 @   4,   5

 Field:
   (·) Say          ( ) Get          ( ) Edit

 <  Say...    > m.cAddress2
                                                  «    OK    »
 < Format... >
                                                  < Cancel >
 Range:
   [ ] Upper...                   [ ] Lower...

 [ ] When...      [ ] Error...      [ ] Scroll bar
 [ ] Valid...     [ ] Comment...    [ ] Allow tabs
 [ ] Message...   [ ] Disabled      [X] Refresh
*==============================================================
*
*==============================================================
 @   5,   5
```

```
 Field:
 ┌──────────────────────────────────────────────┐
 │ (•) Say          ( ) Get          ( ) Edit    │
 └──────────────────────────────────────────────┘

 <  Say...   > csz(m.cCity,m.cState,m.cZip)
                                                   «   OK   »
 < Format... >
                                                   < Cancel >
 Range:
 ┌──────────────────────────────────────────────┐
 │ [ ] Upper...                  [ ] Lower...    │
 └──────────────────────────────────────────────┘

 [ ] When...      [ ] Error...      [ ] Scroll bar
 [ ] Valid...     [ ] Comment...    [ ] Allow tabs
 [ ] Message...   [ ] Disabled      [X] Refresh
```

```
*===============================================================
*  Text: Inv#:
*===============================================================
 @   4,  52
*===============================================================
*  m.cInvNum
*===============================================================
 @   4,  58
```

```
 Field:
 ┌──────────────────────────────────────────────┐
 │ ( ) Say          (•) Get          ( ) Edit    │
 └──────────────────────────────────────────────┘

 <  Get...   > m.cInvNum
                                                   «   OK   »
 < Format... >
                                                   < Cancel >
 Range:
 ┌──────────────────────────────────────────────┐
 │ [ ] Upper...                  [ ] Lower...    │
 └──────────────────────────────────────────────┘

 [ ] When...      [ ] Error...      [ ] Scroll bar
 [ ] Valid...     [ ] Comment...    [ ] Allow tabs
 [ ] Message...   [ ] Disabled      [ ] Refresh
```

```
*===============================================================
*  lnLineItem
*===============================================================
 @   8,   1
```

```
List Type:                                       Options:

  (·) From Array          laLineItem              [X] When...        [ ] Comment...
  ( ) From Popup                                  [X] Valid...       [ ] Disabled
  ( ) Prompt Structure                            [ ] Message...     [ ] 1st Element...
  ( ) Prompt Field                                [ ] Terminating    [X] # Elements...
  ( ) Prompt Files

Variable:

  < Choose... > lnLineItem                             «   OK   »      < Cancel >
------------------------------------------------------------
*-- lnLineItem When Clause
------------------------------------------------------------

When

  (·) Procedure
  ( ) Expression

IF sizearry(@laLineItem) = 0
   KEYBOARD "{INS}"
ENDIF
------------------------------------------------------------
*-- lnLineItem Valid Clause
------------------------------------------------------------

Valid

  (·) Procedure
  ( ) Expression

DO FillItem
------------------------------------------------------------
*-- lnLineItem # Elements Clause
------------------------------------------------------------

# Elements

  ( ) Procedure
  (·) Expression

# Elements:   sizearry(@laLineItem)
*===========================================================
*  Text: Total:
```

```
*==============================================================
 @  15,  49
*==============================================================
*  Text: Item
*==============================================================
 @   7,   2
*==============================================================
*  Text: Amt
*==============================================================
 @   7,  46
*==============================================================
*  Text: Qty
*==============================================================
 @   7,  54
*==============================================================
*  Text: Ext Amt
*==============================================================
 @   7,  61
*==============================================================
*
*==============================================================
 @  15,  56

  Field:
  (·) Say           ( ) Get           ( ) Edit

  <  Say...    > sumarry(@laLineItem,dnLineTtl)
                                                     «    OK    »
  < Format... >
                                                     < Cancel >
  Range:
  [ ] Upper...                    [ ] Lower...

  [X] When...      [ ] Error...      [ ] Scroll bar
  [ ] Valid...     [ ] Comment...    [ ] Allow tabs
  [ ] Message...   [ ] Disabled      [X] Refresh
-------------------------------------------------------------
*--  When Clause
-------------------------------------------------------------

  When
  ( ) Procedure
  (·) Expression

When:    .f.
*==============================================================
*  lhAddItem
*==============================================================
```

```
@  15,   2
Spacing:    1

  Push Button Prompts:          (·) Horizontal   ( ) Vertical
                                [ ] Terminating  <Spacing...>
  Add Item
                               Variable:

                                < Choose... >  lhAddItem

                               Options:

                                [ ] When...      [ ] Comment...
                                [X] Valid...     [ ] Disabled
                                [ ] Message...

                  «   OK   »    < Cancel >
--------------------------------------------------------------
*-- lhAddItem Valid Clause
--------------------------------------------------------------

  Valid

    (·) Procedure
    ( ) Expression

DO AddItem
*=============================================================
*  lhEditItem
*=============================================================
 @  15,  16
 Spacing:    1

  Push Button Prompts:          (·) Horizontal   ( ) Vertical
                                [ ] Terminating  <Spacing...>
  Edit Item
                               Variable:

                                < Choose... >  lhEditItem

                               Options:

                                [ ] When...      [ ] Comment...
                                [X] Valid...     [ ] Disabled
                                [ ] Message...

                  «   OK   »    < Cancel >
--------------------------------------------------------------
*-- lhEditItem Valid Clause
```

```
--------------------------------------------------------------
 ╔══════════════════════════════════════════════╗
 ║                                              ║
 ║  Valid                                       ║
 ║  ┌───────────────────────────────────────┐   ║
 ║  │ (•) Procedure                         │   ║
 ║  │ ( ) Expression                        │   ║
 ║  └───────────────────────────────────────┘   ║
 ║                                              ║
 ╚══════════════════════════════════════════════╝
DO FillItem
*=============================================================
*  lhDelItem
*=============================================================
 @  15,  31
 Spacing:    1
 ╔════════════════════════════════════════════════════════════════╗
 ║                                                                ║
 ║  Push Button Prompts:    ┌─────────────────────────────────┐   ║
 ║                          │ (•) Horizontal   ( ) Vertical   │   ║
 ║  ┌──────────────────────┐│ [ ] Terminating  <Spacing...>   │   ║
 ║  │Delete Item           │└─────────────────────────────────┘   ║
 ║  │                      │Variable:                             ║
 ║  │                      │┌─────────────────────────────────┐   ║
 ║  │                      ││ < Choose... >  lhDelItem        │   ║
 ║  │                      │└─────────────────────────────────┘   ║
 ║  │                      │Options:                              ║
 ║  │                      │┌─────────────────────────────────┐   ║
 ║  │                      ││ [ ] When...     [ ] Comment...  │   ║
 ║  │                      ││ [X] Valid...    [ ] Disabled    │   ║
 ║  │                      ││ [ ] Message...                  │   ║
 ║  └──────────────────────┘└─────────────────────────────────┘   ║
 ║                                                                ║
 ║              «   OK   »     < Cancel >                         ║
 ║                                                                ║
 ╚════════════════════════════════════════════════════════════════╝
--------------------------------------------------------------
*-- lhDelItem Valid Clause
--------------------------------------------------------------
 ╔══════════════════════════════════════════════╗
 ║                                              ║
 ║  Valid                                       ║
 ║  ┌───────────────────────────────────────┐   ║
 ║  │ (•) Procedure                         │   ║
 ║  │ ( ) Expression                        │   ║
 ║  └───────────────────────────────────────┘   ║
 ║                                              ║
 ╚══════════════════════════════════════════════╝
DO DelItem
**************************************************************
*--  SCREEN CLEANUP CODE
**************************************************************
m.gbCopy = .F.
SET FILTER TO
POP KEY
IF glQuitting
   *-- Note, we can't store the BAR # as a regional value
   *-- and use that to release the BAR(), because the regional
   *-- is lost whenever the READ is exited (which happens when
   *-- we click between windows).  So instead, we do this...
```

```
   =KillBar('wrInvoice')
   =KillWind('wrInvoice')
ENDIF
************************************************
PROCEDURE ShoCustInv
************************************************
*) Procedure.........: ShoCustInv
*  Author............: yag
*  Project...........: Codebook 2.5
*  Created...........: 05/11/93  04:20:49
*  Copyright.........: (c) Flash Creative Management, 1993
*) Description.......: Redisplay the customer's invoices when a new
*)                   : customer is selected.
*  Calling Samples...: DO ShoCustInv
*  Parameter List....:
*  Major change list.:
=LOOKUP(Invoice.cCustID, ;
      laCustPick[lnCustPick,dcCustID], ;
      Invoice.cCustID, ;
      "cCustID" )
IF !EOF()
   SCATTER MEMVAR
ELSE
   SCATTER MEMVAR BLANK
ENDIF
SET FILTER TO Invoice.cCustID = ;
            laCustPick[lnCustPick,dcID]
SKIP 0
SHOW GETS
RETURN
************************************************
PROCEDURE FillItem
************************************************
*  Procedure.........: FillItem
*  Author............: yag
*  Project...........: Codebook
*  Created...........: 04/04/1993
*  Copyright.........: (c) Flash Creative Management, 1993
*) Description.......: Edits the current array elements
*  Calling Samples...: DO FillItem
*  Parameter List....:
*  Major change list.:
DO FillItem.spr                                  && Let user pick item
IF EMPTY(laLineItem[lnLineItem,dnCdAmt])         && Cancelled on ADD
   =ADEL(laLineItem,lnLineItem)
   IF sizearry(@laLineItem) > 1                  && If not on 1st item
      DIMENSION laLineItem[ ALEN(laLineItem,1)-1, ALEN(laLineItem,2) ]
   ENDIF
ELSE
   laLineItem[lnLineItem,dcLineDesc] = ;
      laLineItem[lnLineItem,dcTitle] + " | " ;
      + STR(laLineItem[lnLineItem,dnCdAmt],5,2) ;
      + " |  " + STR(laLineItem[lnLineItem,dnCdQty],2,0) ;
      + " |  " + STR(laLineItem[lnLineItem,dnLineTtl],7,2)
   SHOW GET lnLineItem
ENDIF
RETURN
************************************************
PROCEDURE ShowBtns
************************************************
```

```
*  Procedure.........: ShowBtns
*  Author............: yag
*  Project...........: CodeBook 2.5
*  Created...........: 04/11/1993
*  Copyright.........: (c) Flash Creative Management, 1993
*) Description.......: Procedure run to refresh buttons when
*)                   :   LineItem is added or deleted
*  Calling Samples...: DO ShowBtns
*  Parameter List....:
*  Major change list.:
IF glEditable AND (sizearry(@laLineItem) > 0)
   SHOW GET lhEditItem ENABLE
   SHOW GET lhDelItem ENABLE
ELSE
   SHOW GET lhEditItem DISABLE
   SHOW GET lhDelItem DISABLE
ENDIF
***********************************************
PROCEDURE OnKeys
***********************************************
*  Procedure.........: OnKeys
*  Author............: yag
*  Project...........: CodeBook 2.5
*  Created...........: 04/11/1993
*  Copyright.........: (c) Flash Creative Management, 1993
*) Description.......: Procedure run when ON KEY LABELs hit
*)                   : Mimics <ADD> <DELETE> lineitem buttons.
*)                   : Only effective when in lnLineItem List.
*  Calling Samples...: DO OnKeys WITH "INS"
*  Parameter List....: tcKey = "INS" or "DEL"
*  Major change list.:
PARAMETER tcKey
PUSH KEY CLEAR
tcKey = UPPER(tcKey)
IF UPPER(VARREAD()) = "LNLINEITEM"
   DO CASE
      CASE tcKey = "INS"
         DO AddItem
      CASE tcKey = "DEL"
         DO DelItem
   ENDCASE
ELSE                                         && Do the normal action
   jcKey = "{" + tcKey + "}"
   KEYBOARD jcKey PLAIN
ENDIF
POP KEY
RETURN
***********************************************
PROCEDURE AddItem
***********************************************
*  Procedure.........: AddItem
*  Author............: yag
*  Project...........: Codebook 2.5
*  Created...........: 04/11/1993
*  Copyright.........: (c) Flash Creative Management, 1993
*) Description.......: Procedure called when adding lineitem
*  Calling Samples...: DO AddItem
*  Parameter List....:
*  Major change list.:
```

```
PRIVATE jnFilled
jnFilled = sizearry(@laLineItem)
IF jnFilled > 0                 && If not on 1st item
   DIMENSION laLineItem[ jnFilled+1, ALEN(laLineItem,2) ]
ENDIF
lnLineItem = ALEN(laLineItem,1)
DO FillItem
IF sizearry(@laLineItem) = 0                   && Cancelled add
   _curobj = OBJNUM(lhAddItem)
ENDIF
Do ShowBtns
RETURN
**********************************************
PROCEDURE DelItem
**********************************************
*  Procedure.........: DelItem
*  Author............: yag
*  Project...........: Codebook 2.5
*  Created...........: 04/11/1993
*  Copyright.........: (c) Flash Creative Management, 1993
*) Description.......: Procedure called when deleting lineitem
*  Calling Samples...: DO DelItem
*  Parameter List....:
*  Major change list.:
IF delrec("Are you sure you want to delete the order for " + ;
   TRIM(laLineItem[lnLineItem,dcTitle]) + "?")
   =ADEL(laLineItem,lnLineItem)

   PRIVATE jnItemRows
   jnItemRows = ALEN(laLineItem,1)

   IF jnItemRows > 1
      DIMENSION laLineItem[ jnItemRows-1, ALEN(laLineItem,2) ]
      lnLineItem = 1
   ENDIF
   SHOW GET lnLineItem
   DO ShowBtns
ENDIF
RETURN
**********************************************
PROCEDURE initit
**********************************************
*) Procedure.........: initit
*  Author............:
*  Project...........:
*  Created...........: 04/29/1993  11:38:47
*  Copyright.........: (c) Flash Creative Management, 1993
*) Description.......:
*  Calling Samples...:
*  Parameter List....:
*  Major change list.:
DO InitIt IN Methods.prg
m.cCustID = laCustPick[lnCustPick,2]
DIMENSION laLineItem[1,dnLineItem]
laLineItem = .F.
m.dOrdered = DATE()
RETURN
**********************************************
PROCEDURE AddIt
**********************************************
```

```
*) Procedure.........: AddIt
*  Author............:
*  Project...........:
*  Created...........: 04/29/1993  11:38:14
*  Copyright.........: (c) Flash Creative Management, 1993
*) Description.......:
*  Calling Samples...:
*  Parameter List....:
*  Major change list.:
DO AddIt IN Methods.prg
PRIVATE i
FOR i = 1 TO sizearry(@laLineItem)
*    =InsRec(" Purchase ;
      (cInvId, cCdId, nCdAmt, ncdQty) ;
      VALUES (m.cID, laLineItem[i,dcID], ;
                  laLineItem[i,dnCdAmt], ;
                  laLineItem[i,dnCdQty])" )
   =InsRec(" Purchase ;
      (cInvId, cCdId, nCdAmt, ncdQty) ;
      VALUES (m.cID, laLineItem[i,2], ;
                  laLineItem[i,3], ;
                  laLineItem[i,4])" )
ENDFOR
RETURN
*************************************************
PROCEDURE SaveIt
*************************************************
*) Procedure.........: SaveIt
*  Author............: yag
*  Project...........: CODEBOOK 2.5
*  Created...........: 04/29/1993  12:07:50
*  Copyright.........: (c) Flash Creative Management, 1993
*) Description.......:
*  Calling Samples...:
*  Parameter List....:
*  Major change list.:
PRIVATE i, jcOldOrder
DO SaveIt IN Methods.PRG
IF glOKToSave
   SELECT Purchase
   jcOldOrder = ORDER()
   SET ORDER TO TAG cInvId
   SEEK m.cID
   SCAN WHILE cInvId = m.cID
      DELETE
   ENDSCAN
   SET ORDER TO (jcOldOrder)
   SELECT Invoice
   FOR i = 1 TO sizearry(@laLineItem)
*       =InsRec("Purchase ;
         (cInvId, cCdId, nCdAmt, ncdQty) ;
         VALUES (m.cID, laLineItem[i,dcID], ;
                  laLineItem[i,dnCdAmt], ;
                  laLineItem[i,dnCdQty]) ")
      =InsRec("Purchase ;
         (cInvId, cCdId, nCdAmt, ncdQty) ;
         VALUES (m.cID, laLineItem[i,2], ;
                  laLineItem[i,3], ;
                  laLineItem[i,4]) ")
```

```
   ENDFOR
ENDIF
RETURN
***********************************************
PROCEDURE DeleteIt
***********************************************
*) Procedure.........: DeleteIt
*  Author............:
*  Project...........:
*  Created...........: 05/10/93  01:44:51
*  Copyright.........: (c) Flash Creative Management, 1993
*) Description.......:
*  Calling Samples...:
*  Parameter List....:
*  Major change list.:
PRIVATE jcInvID, jcOldPOrd
m.jcInvID = m.cID
DO DeleteIt IN Methods.prg
IF m.cID # m.jcInvID          && On different record, so delete took place
   SELECT Purchase
   jcOldPOrd = ORDER()
   SET ORDER TO cInvID
   DO WHILE SEEK(jcInvID)
      DELETE
   ENDDO
   SET ORDER TO (jcOldPOrd) IN Purchase
ENDIF
UNLOCK ALL

SELECT Invoice
RETURN
***********************************************
PROCEDURE DisableIt
***********************************************
*) Procedure.........: DisableIt
*  Author............: yag
*  Project...........: Codebook 2.5
*  Created...........: 05/11/93  04:25:51
*  Copyright.........: (c) Flash Creative Management, 1993
*) Description.......: Unique Disable code for Invoice
*)                   : Leaves customer pick list available
*  Calling Samples...: DO DisableIt (from ControlPrc)
*  Parameter List....:
*  Major change list.:
DO DisableIt IN Methods.PRG
SHOW GET lnCustPick ENABLE
*-----------------------------------------------------------
```

```
*************************************************************
**--     INVOICE.SCX - MAC PLATFORM
*************************************************************
```

```
( ) DeskTop                         (·) Window

Name:   wrInvoice                   <Type...>
Title:  Invoice Entry
Footer:

Size:              Screen Code:

  Height:   19.455    [X] Setup...
  Width:    75.400    [X] Cleanup & Procs...          «   OK   »

Position:          READ Clauses:                      < Cancel >

  Row:       0.000    [X] Activate...    [X] Show...
  Column:    0.000    [ ] Valid...       [X] When...
  [X] Center          [X] Deactivate...

Environment:                          [X] Add alias

     Environment saved with this screen.
```

```
 Type:        User

 Attributes:       Border:

  [ ] Close         ( ) None
  [X] Float         ( ) Single
  [ ] Shadow        ( ) Double       «   OK   »
  [X] Minimize      ( ) Panel
                    (·) System       < Cancel >

 Color Schemes:

  Primary:        Popup:
```

```
MAC      RGB Fill Color Scheme: (200,200,200)
MAC      Font: Terminal,   9
 Screen Setup code above
 READ Activate code above
 READ Deactivate code above
 READ Show code above
 READ When code above
*************************************************************
*--   G E T   O B J E C T S
*************************************************************
*============================================================
*  Text: Qty
```

```
*==============================================================
 @   7.182,  52.400
MAC      RGB Color Scheme: (,,,,,)
MAC      Font: Monaco,    9
         Style: Bold
*==============================================================
*  Box
*==============================================================
 @  15.909,  48.000
 SIZE   2.545,  24.800
MAC      RGB Color Scheme: (,,,,,)
           Pen: 2
*==============================================================
*  lnCustPick
*==============================================================
 @   0.545,   4.400
     SIZE   1.500,  66.200

  ( ) List Popup            (·) Array Popup  laCustPick

                            Variable:

                             < Choose... > lnCustPick

                            Options:

                              [X] When...     [ ] Comment...
                              [X] Valid...    [ ] Disabled
                              [ ] Message...  [ ] 1st Element...
                                              [X] # Elements...

  Initial: [          ]          «   OK   »     < Cancel >

MAC      RGB Color Scheme: (,,,200,200,200)
MAC      Font: Geneva,    9
 When code above
 Valid code above
 # Elements code above
*==============================================================
*  Text: To:
*==============================================================
 @   0.818,   0.400
MAC      RGB Color Scheme: (,,,,,)
MAC      Font: Monaco,    9
         Style: Bold
*==============================================================
*  Text: Date:
*==============================================================
 @   2.909,  54.000
MAC      RGB Color Scheme: (,,,,,)
MAC      Font: Monaco,    9
         Style: Bold
*==============================================================
*
*==============================================================
 @   2.909,  61.000
```

```
  Field:
   (·) Say          ( ) Get          ( ) Edit

  <  Say...    > m.dOrdered
                                                 «    OK    »
  < Format... >
                                                 < Cancel >
  Range:
   [ ] Upper...                  [ ] Lower...

  [ ] When...      [ ] Error...     [ ] Scroll bar
  [ ] Valid...     [ ] Comment...   [ ] Allow tabs
  [ ] Message...   [ ] Disabled     [X] Refresh

MAC      RGB Color Scheme: (,,,,,)
MAC      Font: monaco,   9
*============================================================
*
*============================================================
 @   2.909,    4.600

  Field:
   (·) Say          ( ) Get          ( ) Edit

  <  Say...    > m.caddress1
                                                 «    OK    »
  < Format... >
                                                 < Cancel >
  Range:
   [ ] Upper...                  [ ] Lower...

  [ ] When...      [ ] Error...     [ ] Scroll bar
  [ ] Valid...     [ ] Comment...   [ ] Allow tabs
  [ ] Message...   [ ] Disabled     [X] Refresh

MAC      RGB Color Scheme: (,,,,,)
MAC      Font: monaco,   9
*============================================================
*
*============================================================
 @   4.000,    4.600
```

```
┌─────────────────────────────────────────────────────────┐
│                                                         │
│  Field:                                                 │
│  ┌───────────────────────────────────────┐              │
│  │ (·) Say       ( ) Get       ( ) Edit  │              │
│  └───────────────────────────────────────┘              │
│                                                         │
│  <  Say...    > m.cAddress2                             │
│                                          «   OK   »     │
│  < Format... >                                          │
│                                          < Cancel >     │
│  Range:                                                 │
│  ┌───────────────────────────────────────┐              │
│  │ [ ] Upper...              [ ] Lower...│              │
│  └───────────────────────────────────────┘              │
│                                                         │
│  [ ] When...     [ ] Error...     [ ] Scroll bar        │
│  [ ] Valid...    [ ] Comment...   [ ] Allow tabs        │
│  [ ] Message...  [ ] Disabled     [X] Refresh           │
│                                                         │
└─────────────────────────────────────────────────────────┘
MAC      RGB Color Scheme: (,,,,,)
MAC      Font: monaco,   9
*============================================================
*
*============================================================
 @   5.091,   4.600
┌─────────────────────────────────────────────────────────┐
│                                                         │
│  Field:                                                 │
│  ┌───────────────────────────────────────┐              │
│  │ (·) Say       ( ) Get       ( ) Edit  │              │
│  └───────────────────────────────────────┘              │
│                                                         │
│  <  Say...    > csz(m.cCity,m.cState,m.cZip)            │
│                                          «   OK   »     │
│  < Format... >                                          │
│                                          < Cancel >     │
│  Range:                                                 │
│  ┌───────────────────────────────────────┐              │
│  │ [ ] Upper...              [ ] Lower...│              │
│  └───────────────────────────────────────┘              │
│                                                         │
│  [ ] When...     [ ] Error...     [ ] Scroll bar        │
│  [ ] Valid...    [ ] Comment...   [ ] Allow tabs        │
│  [ ] Message...  [ ] Disabled     [X] Refresh           │
│                                                         │
└─────────────────────────────────────────────────────────┘
MAC      RGB Color Scheme: (,,,,,)
MAC      Font: monaco,   9
*============================================================
*  Text: Inv#:
*============================================================
 @   4.273,  54.000
MAC      RGB Color Scheme: (,,,,,)
MAC      Font: Monaco,   9
         Style: Bold
*============================================================
*  m.cInvNum
*============================================================
```

```
 @   4.273,  61.200
+------------------------------------------------------------+
|                                                            |
|  Field:                                                    |
|  +-----------------------------------------+               |
|  | ( ) Say         (·) Get         ( ) Edit |               |
|  +-----------------------------------------+               |
|                                                            |
|  <  Get...   > m.cInvNum                                   |
|                                              «   OK   »    |
|  < Format... > @3                                          |
|                                              < Cancel >    |
|  Range:                                                    |
|  +-----------------------------------------+               |
|  | [ ] Upper...               [ ] Lower... |               |
|  +-----------------------------------------+               |
|                                                            |
|  [ ] When...     [ ] Error...     [ ] Scroll bar           |
|  [ ] Valid...    [ ] Comment...   [ ] Allow tabs           |
|  [ ] Message...  [ ] Disabled     [ ] Refresh              |
|                                                            |
+------------------------------------------------------------+
MAC      RGB Color Scheme: (,,,,,)
MAC      Font: monaco,   9
*=============================================================
*  lnLineItem
*=============================================================
 @   8.364,   1.600
     SIZE   7.200,  69.800
+-------------------------------------------------------------------------------+
|                                                                               |
|  List Type:                            Options:                               |
|  +----------------------------------+  +--------------------------------------+ |
|  | (·) From Array       laLineItem  |  | [X] When...       [ ] Comment...     | |
|  | ( ) From Popup                   |  | [X] Valid...      [ ] Disabled       | |
|  | ( ) Prompt Structure             |  | [ ] Message...    [ ] 1st Element... | |
|  | ( ) Prompt Field                 |  | [ ] Terminating   [X] # Elements...  | |
|  | ( ) Prompt Files                 |  +--------------------------------------+ |
|  +----------------------------------+                                         |
|                                                                               |
|  Variable:                                                                    |
|  +----------------------------------+                                         |
|  | < Choose... > lnLineItem         |     «   OK   »    < Cancel >            |
|  +----------------------------------+                                         |
|                                                                               |
+-------------------------------------------------------------------------------+
MAC      RGB Color Scheme: (,,,200,200,200)
MAC      Font: Monaco,   8
 When code above
 Valid code above
 # Elements code above
*=============================================================
*  Text: Total:
*=============================================================
 @  16.818,  49.000
MAC      RGB Color Scheme: (,,,,,)
MAC      Font: Monaco,   9
        Style: Bold
*=============================================================
```

```
*  Text: Item
*==============================================================
 @   7.182,   2.200
MAC      RGB Color Scheme: (,,,,,)
MAC      Font: Monaco,   9
        Style: Bold
*==============================================================
*  Text: Amt
*==============================================================
 @   7.182,  45.800
MAC      RGB Color Scheme: (,,,,,)
MAC      Font: Monaco,   9
         Style: Bold
*==============================================================
*  Text: Ext Amt
*==============================================================
 @   7.182,  58.800
MAC      RGB Color Scheme: (,,,,,)
MAC      Font: Monaco,   9
         Style: Bold
*==============================================================
*
*==============================================================
 @  16.727,  56.600

  Field:

  (·) Say         ( ) Get         ( ) Edit

  <  Say...    > sumarry(@laLineItem,dnLineTtl)
                                                   «   OK   »
  < Format... >
                                                   < Cancel >
  Range:

  [ ] Upper...                  [ ] Lower...

  [X] When...      [ ] Error...      [ ] Scroll bar
  [ ] Valid...     [ ] Comment...    [ ] Allow tabs
  [ ] Message...   [ ] Disabled      [X] Refresh

MAC      RGB Color Scheme: (,,,,,)
MAC      Font: monaco,   9
 When code above
*==============================================================
*  lhAddItem
*==============================================================
 @  16.000,   1.200
    SIZE   1.917,  11.833
 Spacing:    2
```

```
Push Button Prompts:          (·) Horizontal    ( ) Vertical
                              [ ] Terminating   <Spacing...>
Add Item
                              Variable:

                              < Choose... >  lhAddItem

                              Options:

                              [ ] When...      [ ] Comment...
                              [X] Valid...     [ ] Disabled
                              [ ] Message...

              «    OK    »    < Cancel >

MAC      RGB Color Scheme: (,,,,,)
MAC      Font: Geneva,   9
         Style: Bold
 Valid code above
*===========================================================
*  lhEditItem
*===========================================================
 @  16.000,  16.400
     SIZE   1.917,  11.833
 Spacing:    2
```

```
Push Button Prompts:          (·) Horizontal    ( ) Vertical
                              [ ] Terminating   <Spacing...>
Edit Item
                              Variable:

                              < Choose... >  lhEditItem

                              Options:

                              [ ] When...      [ ] Comment...
                              [X] Valid...     [ ] Disabled
                              [ ] Message...

              «    OK    »    < Cancel >

MAC      RGB Color Scheme: (,,,,,)
MAC      Font: Geneva,   9
         Style: Bold
 Valid code above
*===========================================================
*  lhDelItem
*===========================================================
 @  16.000,  31.600
     SIZE   1.917,  11.833
 Spacing:    2
```

```
Push Button Prompts:          (·) Horizontal   ( ) Vertical
                              [ ] Terminating  <Spacing...>
Delete Item
                              Variable:

                              < Choose... >  lhDelItem

                              Options:

                              [ ] When...     [ ] Comment...
                              [X] Valid...    [ ] Disabled
                              [ ] Message...

             «   OK   »    < Cancel >
```

```
MAC      RGB Color Scheme: (,,,,,)
MAC      Font: Geneva,   9
         Style: Bold
 Valid code above
*============================================================
*  Line
*============================================================
 @   7.000,   0.400
MAC      RGB Color Scheme: (135,135,135,135,135,135)
           Pen: 2
*============================================================
*  Line
*============================================================
 @   6.909,  72.600
MAC      RGB Color Scheme: (255,255,255,255,255,255)
           Pen: 1
*============================================================
*  Line
*============================================================
 @  15.545,  46.200
MAC      RGB Color Scheme: (255,255,255,255,255,255)
           Pen: 1
*============================================================
*  Line
*============================================================
 @  15.545,  46.200
MAC      RGB Color Scheme: (255,255,255,255,255,255)
           Pen: 1
*============================================================
*  Line
*============================================================
 @  18.545,   0.600
MAC      RGB Color Scheme: (255,255,255,255,255,255)
           Pen: 1
*============================================================
*  Line
*============================================================
 @   7.000,   0.400
MAC      RGB Color Scheme: (135,135,135,135,135,135)
           Pen: 2
 Screen Cleanup and Procedures code above
```

```
*--------------------------------------------------------------
**************************************************************
**--     INVOICE.SCX - WINDOWS PLATFORM
**************************************************************

 ( ) DeskTop                          (·) Window

 Name:   wrInvoice                    <Type...>
 Title:  Invoice Entry
 Footer:

 Size:            Screen Code:

  Height:   19.000    [X] Setup...
  Width:    71.250    [X] Cleanup & Procs...             «   OK   »

 Position:        READ Clauses:                          < Cancel >

  Row:         0.000   [X] Activate...    [X] Show...
  Column:      0.000   [ ] Valid...       [X] When...
  [X] Center           [X] Deactivate...

 Environment:                              [X] Add alias

      Environment saved with this screen.


 Type:        User

 Attributes:      Border:

  [ ] Close        ( ) None
  [X] Float        ( ) Single
  [ ] Shadow       ( ) Double      «   OK   »
  [X] Minimize     ( ) Panel
                   (·) System      < Cancel >

 Color Schemes:

  Primary:         Popup:


WINDOWS  RGB Fill Color Scheme: (192,192,192)
WINDOWS  Font: Terminal,   9
 Screen Setup code above
 READ Activate code above
 READ Deactivate code above
 READ Show code above
 READ When code above
**************************************************************
*--    G E T    O B J E C T S
**************************************************************
*=============================================================
```

```
*  lnCustPick
*===========================================================
 @   0.750,   4.875
     SIZE   1.500,  65.625
```

```
( ) List Popup              (·) Array Popup  laCustPick

                            Variable:
                            < Choose... > lnCustPick

                            Options:
                            [X] When...     [ ] Comment...
                            [X] Valid...    [ ] Disabled
                            [ ] Message...  [ ] 1st Element...
                                            [X] # Elements...

Initial: [          ]         «   OK   »    < Cancel >
```

```
WINDOWS  RGB Color Scheme: (,,,192,192,192)
WINDOWS  Font: Terminal,   9
 When code above
 Valid code above
 # Elements code above
*===========================================================
*  Text: To:
*===========================================================
 @   0.833,   1.000
WINDOWS  RGB Color Scheme: (,,,,,)
WINDOWS  Font: Terminal,   9
*===========================================================
*  Text: Date:
*===========================================================
 @   2.917,  54.000
WINDOWS  RGB Color Scheme: (,,,,,)
WINDOWS  Font: Terminal,   9
*===========================================================
*
*===========================================================
 @   2.917,  60.125
```

```
Field:
 ( ·) Say          ( ) Get          ( ) Edit

<  Say...   > m.dOrdered
                                              «   OK   »
< Format... >
                                              < Cancel >
Range:
 [ ] Upper...                   [ ] Lower...

[ ] When...      [ ] Error...      [ ] Scroll bar
[ ] Valid...     [ ] Comment...    [ ] Allow tabs
[ ] Message...   [ ] Disabled      [X] Refresh
```

```
WINDOWS  RGB Color Scheme: (,,,,,)
WINDOWS  Font: Terminal,   9
*============================================================
*
*============================================================
 @   2.917,   5.125
```

```
Field:
 ( ·) Say          ( ) Get          ( ) Edit

<  Say...   > m.caddress1
                                              «   OK   »
< Format... >
                                              < Cancel >
Range:
 [ ] Upper...                   [ ] Lower...

[ ] When...      [ ] Error...      [ ] Scroll bar
[ ] Valid...     [ ] Comment...    [ ] Allow tabs
[ ] Message...   [ ] Disabled      [X] Refresh
```

```
WINDOWS  RGB Color Scheme: (,,,,,)
WINDOWS  Font: Terminal,   9
*============================================================
*
*============================================================
 @   4.000,   5.125
```

```
 ┌──────────────────────────────────────────────────────────────┐
 │                                                              │
 │  Field:                                                      │
 │  ┌──────────────────────────────────────────┐                │
 │  │ (·) Say        ( ) Get        ( ) Edit   │                │
 │  └──────────────────────────────────────────┘                │
 │                                                              │
 │  <  Say...    > m.cAddress2                                  │
 │                                                 «   OK    »  │
 │  < Format... >                                               │
 │                                                 < Cancel >   │
 │  Range:                                                      │
 │  ┌──────────────────────────────────────────┐                │
 │  │ [ ] Upper...               [ ] Lower...  │                │
 │  └──────────────────────────────────────────┘                │
 │                                                              │
 │  [ ] When...     [ ] Error...     [ ] Scroll bar             │
 │  [ ] Valid...    [ ] Comment...   [ ] Allow tabs             │
 │  [ ] Message...  [ ] Disabled     [X] Refresh                │
 │                                                              │
 └──────────────────────────────────────────────────────────────┘
WINDOWS  RGB Color Scheme: (,,,,,)
WINDOWS  Font: Terminal,   9
*============================================================
*
*============================================================
 @   5.083,   5.125
 ┌──────────────────────────────────────────────────────────────┐
 │                                                              │
 │  Field:                                                      │
 │  ┌──────────────────────────────────────────┐                │
 │  │ (·) Say        ( ) Get        ( ) Edit   │                │
 │  └──────────────────────────────────────────┘                │
 │                                                              │
 │  <  Say...    > csz(m.cCity,m.cState,m.cZip)                 │
 │                                                 «   OK    »  │
 │  < Format... >                                               │
 │                                                 < Cancel >   │
 │  Range:                                                      │
 │  ┌──────────────────────────────────────────┐                │
 │  │ [ ] Upper...               [ ] Lower...  │                │
 │  └──────────────────────────────────────────┘                │
 │                                                              │
 │  [ ] When...     [ ] Error...     [ ] Scroll bar             │
 │  [ ] Valid...    [ ] Comment...   [ ] Allow tabs             │
 │  [ ] Message...  [ ] Disabled     [X] Refresh                │
 │                                                              │
 └──────────────────────────────────────────────────────────────┘
WINDOWS  RGB Color Scheme: (,,,,,)
WINDOWS  Font: Terminal,   9
*============================================================
*  Text: Inv#:
*============================================================
 @   4.000,  54.000
WINDOWS  RGB Color Scheme: (,,,,,)
WINDOWS  Font: Terminal,   9
*============================================================
*  m.cInvNum
*============================================================
 @   4.000,  60.125
```

```
Field:
 ( ) Say          (·) Get          ( ) Edit

< Get...    > m.cInvNum
                                          «   OK   »
< Format... >
                                          < Cancel >
Range:
 [ ] Upper...                  [ ] Lower...

[ ] When...      [ ] Error...      [ ] Scroll bar
[ ] Valid...     [ ] Comment...    [ ] Allow tabs
[ ] Message...   [ ] Disabled      [ ] Refresh
```

```
WINDOWS  RGB Color Scheme: (,,,,,)
WINDOWS  Font: Terminal,   9
*==============================================================
*  lnLineItem
*==============================================================
 @   9.000,   1.000
     SIZE   5.833,  69.375
```

```
List Type:                                Options:
 (·) From Array       laLineItem          [X] When...       [ ] Comment...
 ( ) From Popup                           [X] Valid...      [ ] Disabled
 ( ) Prompt Structure                     [ ] Message...    [ ] 1st Element...
 ( ) Prompt Field                         [ ] Terminating   [X] # Elements...
 ( ) Prompt Files

Variable:
 < Choose... > lnLineItem                   «   OK   »    < Cancel >
```

```
WINDOWS  RGB Color Scheme: (,,,192,192,192)
WINDOWS  Font: Terminal,   9
 When code above
 Valid code above
 # Elements code above
*==============================================================
*  Text: Total:
*==============================================================
 @  16.667,  48.750
WINDOWS  RGB Color Scheme: (,,,,,)
WINDOWS  Font: Terminal,   9
*==============================================================
*  Text: Item
*==============================================================
```

```
 @   7.500,    2.000
WINDOWS  RGB Color Scheme: (,,,,,)
WINDOWS  Font: Terminal,    9
*==============================================================
*  Text: Amt
*==============================================================
 @   7.167,  45.250
WINDOWS  RGB Color Scheme: (,,,,,)
WINDOWS  Font: Terminal,    9
*==============================================================
*  Text: Qty
*==============================================================
 @   7.167,  52.000
WINDOWS  RGB Color Scheme: (,,,,,)
WINDOWS  Font: Terminal,    9
*==============================================================
*  Text: Ext Amt
*==============================================================
 @   7.167,  59.000
WINDOWS  RGB Color Scheme: (,,,,,)
WINDOWS  Font: Terminal,    9
*==============================================================
*
*==============================================================
 @  16.583,  55.375

  Field:
   (·) Say          ( ) Get          ( ) Edit

  <  Say...   > sumarry(@laLineItem,dnLineTtl)
                                                   «   OK   »
  < Format... >
                                                   < Cancel >
  Range:
   [ ] Upper...                    [ ] Lower...

  [X] When...      [ ] Error...      [ ] Scroll bar
  [ ] Valid...     [ ] Comment...    [ ] Allow tabs
  [ ] Message...   [ ] Disabled      [X] Refresh

WINDOWS  RGB Color Scheme: (,,,,,)
WINDOWS  Font: Terminal,    9
 When code above
*==============================================================
*  lhAddItem
*==============================================================
 @  16.000,    2.000
     SIZE   1.923,  17.500
 Spacing:     2
```

```
Push Button Prompts:        (·) Horizontal    ( ) Vertical
                            [ ] Terminating   <Spacing...>
Add Item
                            Variable:

                            < Choose... >  lhAddItem

                            Options:

                            [ ] When...       [ ] Comment...
                            [X] Valid...      [ ] Disabled
                            [ ] Message...

              «   OK   »     < Cancel >
```

```
WINDOWS  RGB Color Scheme: (,,,,,)
WINDOWS  Font: MS Sans Serif,   8
         Style: Bold
 Valid code above
*==============================================================
*  lhEditItem
*==============================================================
 @  16.000,  16.000
     SIZE   1.923,  17.500
 Spacing:    2
```

```
Push Button Prompts:        (·) Horizontal    ( ) Vertical
                            [ ] Terminating   <Spacing...>
Edit Item
                            Variable:

                            < Choose... >  lhEditItem

                            Options:

                            [ ] When...       [ ] Comment...
                            [X] Valid...      [ ] Disabled
                            [ ] Message...

              «   OK   »     < Cancel >
```

```
WINDOWS  RGB Color Scheme: (,,,,,)
WINDOWS  Font: MS Sans Serif,   8
         Style: Bold
 Valid code above
*==============================================================
*  lhDelItem
*==============================================================
 @  16.000,  30.000
     SIZE   1.923,  17.500
 Spacing:    2
```

```
Push Button Prompts:          (·) Horizontal    ( ) Vertical
                              [ ] Terminating  <Spacing...>
Delete Item
                              Variable:

                              < Choose... >  lhDelItem

                              Options:

                              [ ] When...      [ ] Comment...
                              [X] Valid...     [ ] Disabled
                              [ ] Message...

               «  OK  »    < Cancel >
```

```
WINDOWS  RGB Color Scheme: (,,,,,)
WINDOWS  Font: MS Sans Serif,   8
         Style: Bold
 Valid code above
*==============================================================
*  Line
*==============================================================
 @   7.000,   0.250
WINDOWS  RGB Color Scheme: (128,128,128,128,128,128)
          Pen: 2
*==============================================================
*  Line
*==============================================================
 @   7.083,  70.750
WINDOWS  RGB Color Scheme: (255,255,255,255,255,255)
          Pen: 1
*==============================================================
*  Line
*==============================================================
 @  15.167,  46.000
WINDOWS  RGB Color Scheme: (255,255,255,255,255,255)
          Pen: 1
*==============================================================
*  Line
*==============================================================
 @  15.167,  46.000
WINDOWS  RGB Color Scheme: (255,255,255,255,255,255)
          Pen: 1
*==============================================================
*  Line
*==============================================================
 @  18.500,   0.375
WINDOWS  RGB Color Scheme: (255,255,255,255,255,255)
          Pen: 1
*==============================================================
*  Line
*==============================================================
 @   7.000,   0.250
WINDOWS  RGB Color Scheme: (128,128,128,128,128,128)
          Pen: 2
*==============================================================
```

```
*   Box
*==============================================================
 @  15.583,  47.500
 SIZE   2.833,  21.875
WINDOWS  RGB Color Scheme: (,,,,,)
           Pen: 1
*==============================================================
*   Box
*==============================================================
 @  15.667,  47.625
 SIZE   2.833,  21.875
WINDOWS  RGB Color Scheme: (255,255,255,,,)
           Pen: 1
 Screen Cleanup and Procedures code above
```

Line-Item Modification: FILLITEM.SCX

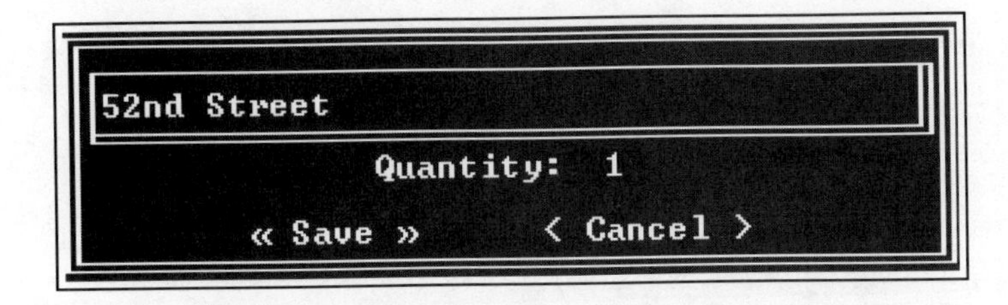

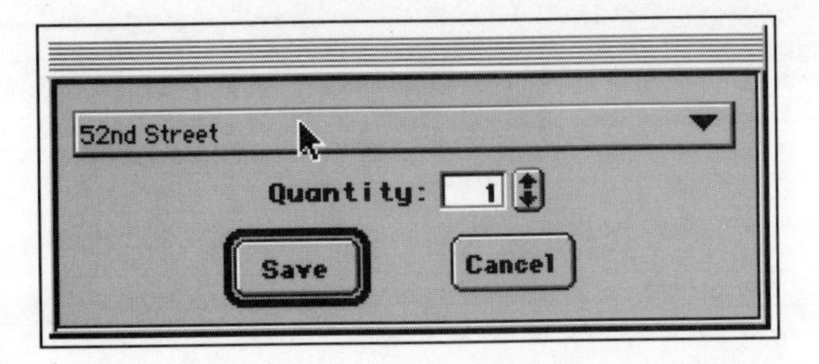

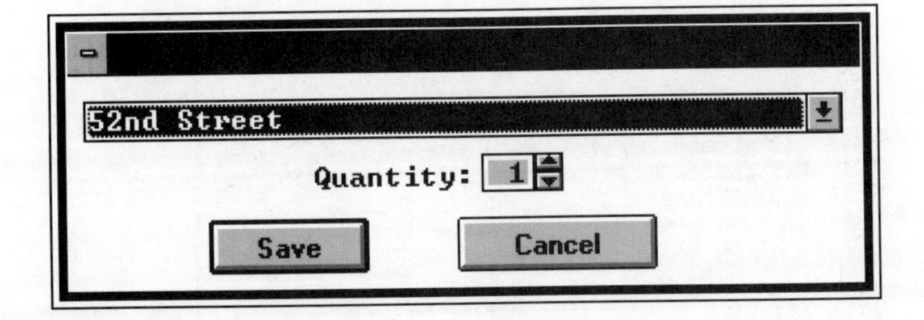

FillItem() is the screen set that allows the user to add or edit an invoice line item. It automatically dims the CD selection pulldown when the user is editing, only allowing a modification to the number of discs purchased.

Note the use of directives to make the array handling more legible to the developer.

```
*-----------------------------------------------------------------
******************************************************************
**--    FILLITEM.SCX - DOS PLATFORM
******************************************************************
```

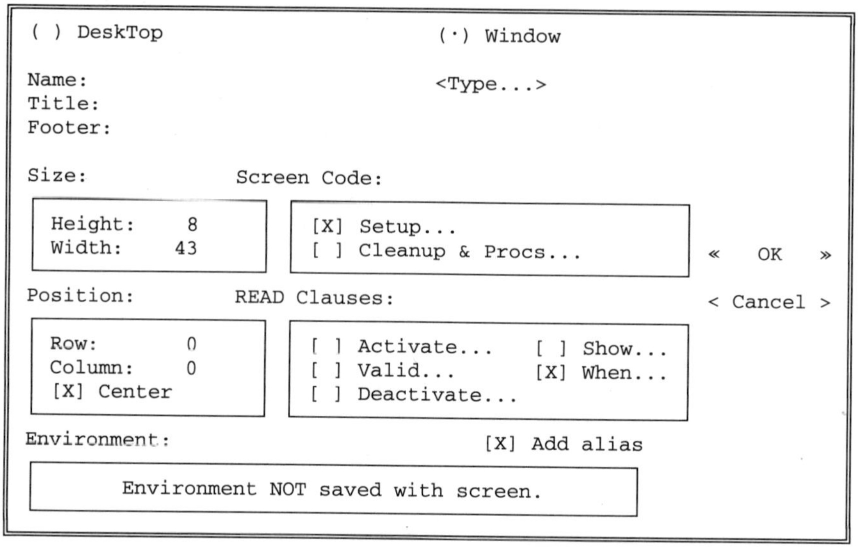

```
 ( ) DeskTop                          (·) Window

 Name:                                <Type...>
 Title:
 Footer:

 Size:               Screen Code:
 ┌──────────────────┐ ┌────────────────────────────────┐
 │ Height:    8     │ │ [X] Setup...                   │
 │ Width:    43     │ │ [ ] Cleanup & Procs...         │   «   OK   »
 └──────────────────┘ └────────────────────────────────┘
 Position:           READ Clauses:                          < Cancel >
 ┌──────────────────┐ ┌────────────────────────────────┐
 │ Row:          0  │ │ [ ] Activate...     [ ] Show...│
 │ Column:       0  │ │ [ ] Valid...        [X] When...│
 │ [X] Center       │ │ [ ] Deactivate...              │
 └──────────────────┘ └────────────────────────────────┘
 Environment:                          [X] Add alias
 ┌────────────────────────────────────────────────┐
 │       Environment NOT saved with screen.       │
 └────────────────────────────────────────────────┘
```

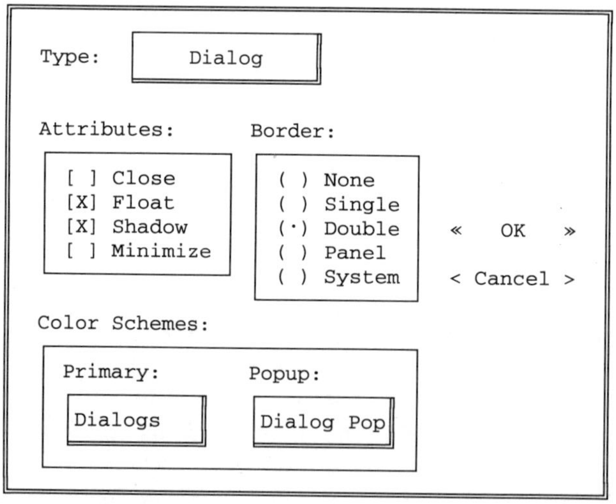

```
 Type:   │    Dialog    │

 Attributes:       Border:
 ┌──────────────┐  ┌────────────┐
 │ [ ] Close    │  │ ( ) None   │
 │ [X] Float    │  │ ( ) Single │
 │ [X] Shadow   │  │ (·) Double │   «   OK   »
 │ [ ] Minimize │  │ ( ) Panel  │
 └──────────────┘  │ ( ) System │   < Cancel >
                   └────────────┘
 Color Schemes:
 ┌─────────────────────────────┐
 │ Primary:       Popup:       │
 │ │ Dialogs  │   │Dialog Pop│ │
 └─────────────────────────────┘
```

```
******************************************************************
*  SCREEN SETUP CODE
******************************************************************
*  Program...........: FILLITEM
*  Author............: yag
*  Project...........: Codebook 2.5
*  Created...........: 04/11/1993
*  Copyright.........: (c) Flash Creative Management, 1993
*) Description.......: This screen allows editing of a line item.
*)                   : It assumes the existence of an array: laLineItem
*  Calling Samples...: DO FillItem.spr
```

```
*  Parameter List....:
*  Major change list.:
PRIVATE ALL LIKE j*
EXTERNAL ARRAY laLineItem
#DEFINE dcLineDesc    1
#DEFINE dcID          2
#DEFINE dnCdAmt       3
#DEFINE dnCdQty       4
#DEFINE dnLineTtl     5
#DEFINE dcTitle       6
#DEFINE dnLineItem    6
PRIVATE jlAdding
jlAdding = .F.
SELECT cTitle, cID ;
  FROM CD ;
  ORDER BY cTitle ;
  INTO ARRAY laCD
IF _tally = 0
   WAIT WINDOW "No Discs on File" TIMEOUT 4
   RETURN
ENDIF
jnFound = ASCAN(laCD,laLineItem[lnLineItem,dcID])
IF jnFound # 0
   lnCd = ASUBSCRIPT(laCD,jnFound,1)
ELSE
   jlAdding = .T.
ENDIF
PRIVATE jnQty
IF NOT jlAdding
   jnQty = laLineItem[lnLineItem,dnCdQty]
ELSE
   jnQty = 1
ENDIF
------------------------------------------------------------
*-- READ When Clause
------------------------------------------------------------
```

```
READ When

  (·) Procedure
  ( ) Expression
```

```
IF jlAdding
   SHOW GET lnCD ENABLE
ENDIF
************************************************************
*--    G E T    O B J E C T S
************************************************************
*===========================================================
*  Text: Quantity:
*===========================================================
 @   3,  14
*===========================================================
*  lnCD
*===========================================================
 @   0,   0
```

```
( ) List Popup                (·) Array Popup  laCD

                              Variable:

                              < Choose... > lnCD

                              Options:

                              [ ] When...     [ ] Comment...
                              [ ] Valid...    [X] Disabled
                              [ ] Message...  [ ] 1st Element...
                                              [ ] # Elements...

Initial:                         «  OK  »    < Cancel >
```

```
*=============================================================
*  jnQty
*=============================================================
 @  3, 24
```

```
Field:

( ) Say          (·) Get          ( ) Edit

<  Get...    > jnQty
                                                 «  OK  »
< Format... > @K 99
                                                 < Cancel >
Range:

[X] Upper...                     [X] Lower...

[ ] When...      [ ] Error...      [ ] Scroll bar
[ ] Valid...     [ ] Comment...    [ ] Allow tabs
[ ] Message...   [ ] Disabled      [ ] Refresh
```

```
-------------------------------------------------------------
*-- jnQty RangeHi Clause
-------------------------------------------------------------
```

```
╔══════════════════════════════════════════╗
║                                          ║
║  RangeHi                                 ║
║  ┌────────────────────────────────────┐  ║
║  │ ( ) Procedure                      │  ║
║  │ (·) Expression                     │  ║
║  └────────────────────────────────────┘  ║
║                                          ║
╚══════════════════════════════════════════╝
RangeHi:   99
----------------------------------------------------------
*-- jnQty RangeLo Clause
----------------------------------------------------------
╔══════════════════════════════════════════╗
║                                          ║
║  RangeLo                                 ║
║  ┌────────────────────────────────────┐  ║
║  │ ( ) Procedure                      │  ║
║  │ (·) Expression                     │  ║
║  └────────────────────────────────────┘  ║
║                                          ║
╚══════════════════════════════════════════╝
RangeLo:   1
*==========================================================
*  lhSave
*==========================================================
 @   5,    8
 Spacing:    1
╔═════════════════════════════════════════════════════════════╗
║                                                             ║
║  Push Button Prompts:    ┌──────────────────────────────┐   ║
║                          │ (·) Horizontal   ( ) Vertical│   ║
║  ┌────────────────────┐  │ [X] Terminating <Spacing...>│   ║
║  │\!Save              │  └──────────────────────────────┘   ║
║  │                    │  Variable:                          ║
║  │                    │  ┌──────────────────────────────┐   ║
║  │                    │  │ < Choose... >  lhSave        │   ║
║  │                    │  └──────────────────────────────┘   ║
║  │                    │  Options:                           ║
║  │                    │  ┌──────────────────────────────┐   ║
║  │                    │  │ [ ] When...     [ ] Comment...│  ║
║  │                    │  │ [X] Valid...    [ ] Disabled │   ║
║  │                    │  │ [ ] Message...               │   ║
║  └────────────────────┘  └──────────────────────────────┘   ║
║                                                             ║
║                  «   OK   »    < Cancel >                   ║
║                                                             ║
╚═════════════════════════════════════════════════════════════╝
----------------------------------------------------------
*-- lhSave Valid Clause
----------------------------------------------------------
╔══════════════════════════════════════════╗
║                                          ║
║  Valid                                   ║
║  ┌────────────────────────────────────┐  ║
║  │ (·) Procedure                      │  ║
║  │ ( ) Expression                     │  ║
║  └────────────────────────────────────┘  ║
║                                          ║
╚══════════════════════════════════════════╝
laLineItem[lnLineItem,dcID] = laCD[lnCD,2]
```

```
laLineItem[lnLineItem,dnCdQty] = jnQty
laLineItem[lnLineItem,dcTitle] = laCD[lnCD,1]
laLineItem[lnLineItem,dnCdAmt] = ;
   LOOKUP(cd.nPrice,laCD[lnCD,2],cd.cID,"CID")
laLineItem[lnLineItem,dnLineTtl] = ;
   laLineItem[lnLineItem,dnCdQty] * ;
   laLineItem[lnLineItem,dnCdAmt]
*==============================================================
*  lhCancel
*==============================================================
 @   5,  22
 Spacing:    1

  Push Button Prompts:        (·) Horizontal    ( ) Vertical
                              [X] Terminating  <Spacing...>
  \?Cancel
                             Variable:

                              < Choose... >  lhCancel

                             Options:

                              [ ] When...     [ ] Comment...
                              [ ] Valid...    [ ] Disabled
                              [ ] Message...

                 «   OK   »    < Cancel >

*-------------------------------------------------------------
**************************************************************
**--    FILLITEM.SCX - MAC PLATFORM
**************************************************************

 ( ) DeskTop                          (·) Window

 Name:                                <Type...>
 Title:
 Footer:

 Size:              Screen Code:

  Height:    8.273   [X] Setup...
  Width:    45.167   [ ] Cleanup & Procs...         «   OK   »

 Position:          READ Clauses:                   < Cancel >

  Row:        0.000  [ ] Activate...    [ ] Show...
  Column:     0.000  [ ] Valid...       [X] When...
  [X] Center         [ ] Deactivate...

 Environment:                          [X] Add alias

        Environment NOT saved with screen.
```

```
Type:    Dialog

Attributes:       Border:

[ ] Close         ( ) None
[X] Float         ( ) Single
[X] Shadow        (·) Double       «   OK    »
[ ] Minimize      ( ) Panel
                  ( ) System       < Cancel >

Color Schemes:

  Primary:          Popup:
```

```
MAC        RGB Fill Color Scheme: (,,)
MAC        Font: monaco,   9
 Screen Setup code above
 READ When code above
************************************************************
*--   G E T    O B J E C T S
************************************************************
*===========================================================
*  Text: Quantity:
*===========================================================
 @   3.364,  13.667
MAC        RGB Color Scheme: (,,,,,)
MAC        Font: Monaco,   9
           Style: Bold
*===========================================================
*  jnQty
*===========================================================
 @   3.364,  25.000
```

```
Spinner:
 Min:    1     Max:   99      Incr:    1

<Variable...> jnQty
                                            «   OK   »
< Format... > @3K 99
                                            < Cancel >
Range:
 [X] Upper...                 [X] Lower...

[ ] When...      [ ] Error...
[ ] Valid...     [ ] Comment...
[ ] Message...   [ ] Disabled
```

```
 RangeHi code above
 RangeLo code above
*============================================================
*  lnCD
*============================================================
 @   0.909,   1.000
     SIZE   1.500,  51.600
```

```
( ) List Popup          (·) Array Popup  laCD

                        Variable:

                         < Choose... > lnCD

                        Options:

                         [ ] When...     [ ] Comment...
                         [ ] Valid...    [X] Disabled
                         [ ] Message...  [ ] 1st Element...
                                         [ ] # Elements...

Initial:                   «   OK   »    < Cancel >
```

```
MAC      RGB Color Scheme: (,,,,,)
MAC      Font: Geneva,   9
*============================================================
*  lhSave
*============================================================
 @   5.455,  11.333
     SIZE   1.833,   8.167
 Spacing:    2
```

```
+---------------------------------------------------------------------+
|                                                                     |
|  Push Button Prompts:         (·) Horizontal    ( ) Vertical        |
|                               [X] Terminating   <Spacing...>        |
|  \!Save                                                             |
|                              Variable:                              |
|                                                                     |
|                               < Choose... >  lhSave                 |
|                                                                     |
|                              Options:                               |
|                                                                     |
|                               [ ] When...      [ ] Comment...       |
|                               [X] Valid...     [ ] Disabled         |
|                               [ ] Message...                        |
|                                                                     |
|                 «   OK   »    < Cancel >                            |
+---------------------------------------------------------------------+
MAC       RGB Color Scheme: (,,,,,)
MAC       Font: Geneva,   9
          Style: Bold
 Valid code above
*==============================================================
*  lhCancel
*==============================================================
 @   5.364,  25.333
     SIZE   1.833,   8.167
 Spacing:    2

+---------------------------------------------------------------------+
|                                                                     |
|  Push Button Prompts:         (·) Horizontal    ( ) Vertical        |
|                               [X] Terminating   <Spacing...>        |
|  \?Cancel                                                           |
|                              Variable:                              |
|                                                                     |
|                               < Choose... >  lhCancel               |
|                                                                     |
|                              Options:                               |
|                                                                     |
|                               [ ] When...      [ ] Comment...       |
|                               [ ] Valid...     [ ] Disabled         |
|                               [ ] Message...                        |
|                                                                     |
|                 «   OK   »    < Cancel >                            |
+---------------------------------------------------------------------+
MAC       RGB Color Scheme: (,,,,,)
MAC       Font: Geneva,   9
          Style: Bold
*--------------------------------------------------------------
```

```
************************************************************
**--     FILLITEM.SCX - WINDOWS PLATFORM
************************************************************
```

```
 ( ) DeskTop                        (·) Window

 Name:                              <Type...>
 Title:
 Footer:

 Size:             Screen Code:

  Height:    7.833   [X] Setup...
  Width:    45.000   [ ] Cleanup & Procs...            «   OK   »

 Position:         READ Clauses:                        < Cancel >

  Row:       0.000   [ ] Activate...     [ ] Show...
  Column:    0.000   [ ] Valid...        [X] When...
  [X] Center         [ ] Deactivate...

 Environment:                           [X] Add alias

        Environment NOT saved with screen.
```

```
  Type:       Dialog

  Attributes:      Border:

   [ ] Close        ( ) None
   [X] Float        ( ) Single
   [X] Shadow       (·) Double      «   OK   »
   [ ] Minimize     ( ) Panel
                    ( ) System      < Cancel >

  Color Schemes:

   Primary:        Popup:
```

```
WINDOWS  RGB Fill Color Scheme: (,,)
WINDOWS  Font: Terminal,   9
 Screen Setup code above
 READ When code above
************************************************************
*--    G E T   O B J E C T S
************************************************************
*==========================================================
*  Text: Quantity:
*==========================================================
 @   3.333,  14.000
WINDOWS  RGB Color Scheme: (,,,,,)
```

```
WINDOWS  Font: Terminal,   9
*==========================================================
*  lnCD
*==========================================================
 @   0.917,   1.000
     SIZE   1.500,  43.000

  ( ) List Popup              (·) Array Popup  laCD

                              Variable:
                                < Choose... > lnCD

                              Options:
                                [ ] When...     [ ] Comment...
                                [ ] Valid...    [X] Disabled
                                [ ] Message...  [ ] 1st Element...
                                                [ ] # Elements...

  Initial:                       «   OK   »    < Cancel >

WINDOWS  RGB Color Scheme: (,,,,,)
WINDOWS  Font: Terminal,   9
*==========================================================
*  jnQty
*==========================================================
 @   3.250,  23.750

  Spinner:
    Min:    1    Max:   99    Incr:    1

  <Variable...> jnQty
                                                «   OK   »
  < Format... > @K 99
                                                < Cancel >
  Range:
    [X] Upper...                  [X] Lower...

  [ ] When...       [ ] Error...
  [ ] Valid...      [ ] Comment...
  [ ] Message...    [ ] Disabled

 RangeHi code above
 RangeLo code above
*==========================================================
*  lhSave
*==========================================================
 @   5.333,   8.000
     SIZE   1.846,  12.000
 Spacing:    2
```

```
Push Button Prompts:          (·) Horizontal     ( ) Vertical
                              [X] Terminating   <Spacing...>
\!Save
                              Variable:

                              < Choose... >  lhSave

                              Options:

                              [ ] When...        [ ] Comment...
                              [X] Valid...       [ ] Disabled
                              [ ] Message...

              «   OK   »    < Cancel >
```

```
WINDOWS  RGB Color Scheme: (,,,,,)
WINDOWS  Font: MS Sans Serif,   8
         Style: Bold
 Valid code above
*============================================================
*  lhCancel
*============================================================
 @   5.333,  22.000
     SIZE   1.846,  15.000
 Spacing:    2
```

```
Push Button Prompts:          (·) Horizontal     ( ) Vertical
                              [X] Terminating   <Spacing...>
\?Cancel
                              Variable:

                              < Choose... >  lhCancel

                              Options:

                              [ ] When...        [ ] Comment...
                              [ ] Valid...       [ ] Disabled
                              [ ] Message...

              «   OK   »    < Cancel >
```

```
WINDOWS  RGB Color Scheme: (,,,,,)
WINDOWS  Font: MS Sans Serif,   8
        Style: Bold
```

Chapter 16

Application-Specific Reports

Customer Mailing Labels: CUSTLBL.LBX

```
MaryAnne Tillson
2938 Modson Lane
Dallas TX 75237


Jackie Smith
542 Rambling Lane
Dallas TX 75230
```

CustLbl is a simple form that prints customer labels.

```
Customer.cFirstName, Customer.cLastName;
Customer.cAddress1;
Customer.cAddress2;
Customer.cCity, Customer.cState, Customer.cZip;
therm()
```

Inventory Listing: LISTCD.FRX

CD Listing

Artist	CD Title	Cost	Price	Description
Barnes & Barnes	Fish Heads and other hits	45.00	65.00	A truly warped CD
Beatles	Hard Days Night	15.00	20.50	A classic movie, and a classic CD.
Beatles	HELP!	25.00	50.00	Good movie - better soundtrack
Beatles	White Album	20.00	55.00	Actually called "The Beatles" by the way.
Beatles	Yellow Submarine	20.00	30.30	
Billy Joel	52nd Street	15.00	25.00	
Billy Joel	Songs in the Attic	25.00	40.00	Live concert
Billy Joel	Piano Man	5.00	15.00	
Bruce Springsteen	Darkness on the Edge of Town	25.00	55.00	Classic
Bruce Springsteen	Born in the USA	13.00	26.00	Monster smash for Bruce. First time he used a synthesizer.

ListCD is a simple form that prints a list of existing compact discs.

```
***********************************************************
**--    LISTCD.FRX
***********************************************************
```

```
Page Layout:              < Options... >

  Page length      (rows):   66
  Top margin       (rows):    0
  Bottom margin    (rows):    0
                                          «   OK   »
  Printer indent    (columns):     0
  Right margin column:    80              < Cancel >

Environment:

  Environment saved with this report.
```

```
Options:

  [X] Page eject before printing
  [ ] Page eject after printing
                                          «   OK   »
  [ ] Plain page
  [ ] Summary report                      < Cancel >
  [ ] Suppress blank lines

  [ ] Add alias

 Printer Driver Setup:
------------------------------------------------------------
Work Area:    1
File Name:   ..\CD.DBF
    Alias:   CD
************************************************************
  Report Title:

  [X] Title Band
  [ ] New Page

------------------------------------------------------------
Row:   1  Col:  35
 Text:  CD Listing
      SIZE   1,  10

  [X] Style...                    «   OK   »
  [ ] Comment...
  [ ] Float as band stretches     < Cancel >

  Style                     Alignment
  [X] Bold                  (•) Left
  [ ] Italic                ( ) Center
  [X] Underline             ( ) Right
  [ ] Superscript
  [ ] Subscript
                            «   OK   »
  Code
  UB                        < Cancel >

************************************************************
  Page Header:
------------------------------------------------------------
Row:   4  Col:   0
 Text:  Artist
      SIZE   1,   6
```

```
[X] Style...                  «   OK   »
[ ] Comment...
[ ] Float as band stretches   < Cancel >
```

```
┌ Style ──────────────┐   ┌ Alignment ┐
│ [ ] Bold            │   │ (·) Left  │
│ [X] Italic          │   │ ( ) Center│
│ [ ] Underline       │   │ ( ) Right │
│ [ ] Superscript     │   └───────────┘
│ [ ] Subscript       │
└─────────────────────┘    «   OK   »
┌ Code ───────────────┐
│ I                   │    < Cancel >
└─────────────────────┘
```

```
Row:   4  Col:  22
 Text:  CD Title
     SIZE   1,   8
Row:   4  Col:  49
 Text:  Cost
     SIZE   1,   4
Row:   4  Col:  56
 Text:  Price
     SIZE   1,   5
Row:   4  Col:  63
 Text:  Description
     SIZE   1,  11
Row:   5  Col:   0
 Field - Full Expression:
     showpage()
     SIZE   1,   1
```

```
Report Expression:

<  Expr...  > showpage()

< Format... >                       Width:   1

[ ] Style...       [ ] Suppress...
[ ] Calculate...   [ ] Stretch Vertically
[ ] Comment...     [ ] Float as Band Stretches

         «   OK   »    < Cancel >
```

```
==================== Print When ====================
  Print Repeated Values
     ( ) Yes                            «   OK   »
     (·) No
                                        < Cancel >
  Also Print
   [ ] In First Whole Band of New Page/Col
   [ ] When This Group Changes
   [ ] When Detail Overflows to New Page/Col


   [ ] Print Only When Expression is True...

   [ ] Remove Line If Blank
************************************************************
  Detail:
------------------------------------------------------------
Row:   6  Col:   0
 Field - Full Expression:
      cmusician
      SIZE   1,  20

   Report Expression:

   <  Expr...  > cmusician

   < Format... >                          Width:  20

   [X] Style...      [ ] Suppress...
   [ ] Calculate...  [X] Stretch Vertically
   [ ] Comment...    [X] Float as Band Stretches

             «   OK   »    < Cancel >

  Style                 Alignment
   [ ] Bold              (·) Left
   [X] Italic            ( ) Center
   [ ] Underline         ( ) Right
   [ ] Superscript
   [ ] Subscript
                          «   OK   »
  Code
   I                      < Cancel >
```

```
═══════════════════ Print When ═══════════════════
  ┌ Print Repeated Values ┐
  │   ( ) Yes              │          «   OK   »
  │   (·) No               │
  └────────────────────────┘          < Cancel >
  ┌ Also Print ──────────────────────────────────┐
  │ [ ] In First Whole Band of New Page/Col      │
  │ [ ] When This Group Changes                  │
  │ [ ] When Detail Overflows to New Page/Col    │
  └──────────────────────────────────────────────┘

    [ ] Print Only When Expression is True...

    [ ] Remove Line If Blank
Row:   6  Col:  22
 Field - Full Expression:
     ctitle
     SIZE   1,  25
```

```
  Report Expression:

  <  Expr...  > ctitle

  < Format... >                         Width:  25

  [ ] Style...       [ ] Suppress...
  [ ] Calculate...  [X] Stretch Vertically
  [ ] Comment...    [X] Float as Band Stretches

            «   OK   »    < Cancel >
```

```
═══════════════════ Print When ═══════════════════
  ┌ Print Repeated Values ┐
  │   ( ) Yes              │          «   OK   »
  │   (·) No               │
  └────────────────────────┘          < Cancel >
  ┌ Also Print ──────────────────────────────────┐
  │ [ ] In First Whole Band of New Page/Col      │
  │ [ ] When This Group Changes                  │
  │ [ ] When Detail Overflows to New Page/Col    │
  └──────────────────────────────────────────────┘

    [ ] Print Only When Expression is True...

    [ ] Remove Line If Blank
Row:   6  Col:  49
 Field - Full Expression:
     ncost
     SIZE   1,   5
```

```
Report Expression:

<  Expr...  > ncost

< Format... >                    Width:   5

[ ] Style...     [ ] Suppress...
[ ] Calculate... [X] Stretch Vertically
[ ] Comment...   [X] Float as Band Stretches

          «   OK   »    < Cancel >
```

```
==================== Print When ====================
┌ Print Repeated Values ┐
    ( ) Yes                         «    OK    »
    (·) No
└───────────────────────┘
                                    < Cancel >
┌ Also Print ─────────────────────────────────┐
  [ ] In First Whole Band of New Page/Col
  [ ] When This Group Changes
  [ ] When Detail Overflows to New Page/Col
└─────────────────────────────────────────────┘

  [ ] Print Only When Expression is True...

  [ ] Remove Line If Blank
```

```
Row:   6  Col:  56
 Field - Full Expression:
      nprice
      SIZE   1,   5
```

```
Report Expression:

<  Expr...  > nprice

< Format... >                    Width:   5

[ ] Style...     [ ] Suppress...
[ ] Calculate... [X] Stretch Vertically
[ ] Comment...   [X] Float as Band Stretches

          «   OK   »    < Cancel >
```

```
                    Print When
  Print Repeated Values
     ( ) Yes                         «   OK   »
     (·) No
                                     < Cancel >
  Also Print
  [ ] In First Whole Band of New Page/Col
  [ ] When This Group Changes
  [ ] When Detail Overflows to New Page/Col

  [ ] Print Only When Expression is True...

  [ ] Remove Line If Blank

Row:   6  Col:  63
 Field - Full Expression:
      mdescript
      SIZE   1,  17

  Report Expression:

  <  Expr...  > mdescript

  < Format... >                 Width:  17

  [ ] Style...       [ ] Suppress...
  [ ] Calculate...   [X] Stretch Vertically
  [ ] Comment...     [X] Float as Band Stretches

          «   OK   »    < Cancel >

                    Print When
  Print Repeated Values
     ( ) Yes                         «   OK   »
     (·) No
                                     < Cancel >
  Also Print
  [ ] In First Whole Band of New Page/Col
  [ ] When This Group Changes
  [ ] When Detail Overflows to New Page/Col

  [ ] Print Only When Expression is True...

  [ ] Remove Line If Blank
************************************************************
  Page Footer:
------------------------------------------------------------
Row:  11  Col:   0
 Field - Full Expression:
      DATE()
      SIZE   1,   8
```

```
Report Expression:

<  Expr...  > DATE()

< Format... >                           Width:   8

[ ] Style...      [ ] Suppress...
[ ] Calculate...  [ ] Stretch Vertically
[ ] Comment...    [ ] Float as Band Stretches

          «   OK   »     < Cancel >
```

```
                    Print When
  Print Repeated Values
     ( ) Yes                                «   OK   »
     (·) No
                                            < Cancel >
  Also Print
   [ ] In First Whole Band of New Page/Col
   [ ] When This Group Changes
   [ ] When Detail Overflows to New Page/Col


   [ ] Print Only When Expression is True...

   [ ] Remove Line If Blank
```

```
Row:  11  Col:  71
 Text:  Page
     SIZE   1,   5
Row:  11  Col:  76
 Field - Full Expression:
     _PAGENO
     SIZE   1,   4
```

```
Report Expression:

<  Expr...  > _PAGENO

< Format... >                           Width:   4

[ ] Style...      [ ] Suppress...
[ ] Calculate...  [ ] Stretch Vertically
[ ] Comment...    [ ] Float as Band Stretches

          «   OK   »     < Cancel >
```

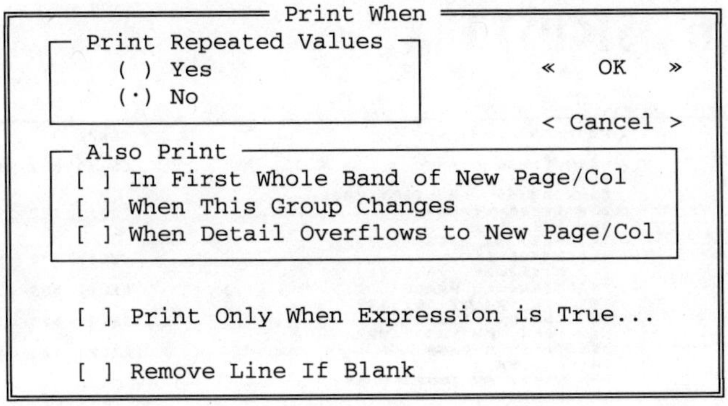

```
╔══════════════════ Print When ══════════════════╗
║ ┌ Print Repeated Values ┐                        ║
║ │   ( ) Yes             │        «  OK  »        ║
║ │   (·) No              │                        ║
║ └───────────────────────┘      < Cancel >        ║
║ ┌ Also Print ──────────────────────────────────┐ ║
║ │[ ] In First Whole Band of New Page/Col       │ ║
║ │[ ] When This Group Changes                   │ ║
║ │[ ] When Detail Overflows to New Page/Col     │ ║
║ └──────────────────────────────────────────────┘ ║
║                                                  ║
║  [ ] Print Only When Expression is True...       ║
║                                                  ║
║  [ ] Remove Line If Blank                        ║
╚══════════════════════════════════════════════════╝
```

Customer List: LISTCUST.FRX

Customer	Address	Phone
Gurion, John	2310 Proam Avenue Apartment 72M Hackensack, NJ 07601-7342	(201) 837-2938
Berger, David	234 Fifth Street Apt. 32 Teaneck, NJ 07666-5282	(201) 835-3523
Hodgson, Leo	551 Beach Street Far Rockaway, PA 10385	(718) 336-4864
Barretson, Ann	2938 Seventh Avenue Teaneck, NJ 07666-5389	(201) 823-4337
Garritson, John	95 Cabrini Blvd #3 New York, NY 10302-7278	(212) 823-4346
Sternberg, Max	293 Fifth Avenue Suite 1504 New York, NY 10023-5283	(212) 823-4343
Stern, Terri	20 Jerusalem Lane Irion, IA 23038-1273	(203) 234-3482
Miller, John	85 Degrees Way Toohot, CA 20391	(415) 293-8291
Johnson, John	23 Pragma Lane Jacksonville, NJ 07555-6238	(201) 837-2894
Tillson, MaryAnne	2938 Hodson Lane Dallas, TX 75237	(214) 293-8592
Smith, Jackie	542 Rambling Lane Dallas, TX 75230	(214) 920-5929

ListCust is a simple form that prints a list of customers.

```
*****************************************************
**--    LISTCUST.FRX
*****************************************************
```

```
Page Layout:              < Options... >

  Page length      (rows):    66
  Top margin       (rows):     0
  Bottom margin    (rows):     0
                                              «   OK   »
  Printer indent    (columns):     0
  Right margin column:    80                  < Cancel >

Environment:

Environment saved with this report.
```

```
Options:

  [X] Page eject before printing
  [ ] Page eject after printing
                                        «   OK   »
  [ ] Plain page
  [ ] Summary report                    < Cancel >
  [X] Suppress blank lines

  [X] Add alias
```

```
 Printer Driver Setup:
------------------------------------------------------------
Work Area:    1
File Name:  ..\CUSTOMER.DBF
    Alias:  CUSTOMER
************************************************************
  Page Header:
------------------------------------------------------------
Row:   0  Col:   0
 Text:  Customer
      SIZE   1,   8
Row:   0  Col:  25
 Text:  Address
      SIZE   1,   7
Row:   0  Col:  66
 Text:  Phone
      SIZE   1,   5
Row:   1  Col:   0
 Field - Full Expression:
      showpage()
      SIZE   1,   1
```

```
Report Expression:

<  Expr...   > showpage()

< Format... >                          Width:   1

[ ] Style...        [ ] Suppress...
[ ] Calculate...    [ ] Stretch Vertically
[ ] Comment...      [ ] Float as Band Stretches

          «   OK   »    < Cancel >
```

```
                     Print When
  Print Repeated Values
     ( ) Yes                                  «    OK    »
     (·) No
                                              < Cancel >
  Also Print
   [ ] In First Whole Band of New Page/Col
   [ ] When This Group Changes
   [ ] When Detail Overflows to New Page/Col

   [ ] Print Only When Expression is True...

   [ ] Remove Line If Blank
*************************************************************
  Detail:
-------------------------------------------------------------
Row:   2  Col:   0
 Field - Full Expression:
      ALLTRIM(cLastName-(", "+cFirstName))
      SIZE   1,  23

   Report Expression:

   <  Expr...   > ALLTRIM(cLastName-(

   < Format... >                         Width:  23

   [ ] Style...       [ ] Suppress...
   [ ] Calculate...  [X] Stretch Vertically
   [ ] Comment...    [X] Float as Band Stretches

            «    OK    »    < Cancel >

                     Print When
  Print Repeated Values
     ( ) Yes                                  «    OK    »
     (·) No
                                              < Cancel >
  Also Print
   [ ] In First Whole Band of New Page/Col
   [ ] When This Group Changes
   [ ] When Detail Overflows to New Page/Col

   [ ] Print Only When Expression is True...

   [ ] Remove Line If Blank
Row:   2  Col:  25
 Field - Full Expression:
      customer.caddress1
      SIZE   1,  40
```

```
Report Expression:

<  Expr...   > customer.caddress1

< Format... >                      Width:  40

[ ] Style...        [ ] Suppress...
[ ] Calculate... [X] Stretch Vertically
[ ] Comment...    [X] Float as Band Stretches

          «   OK    »     < Cancel >
```

```
═══════════════════ Print When ═══════════════════
 ┌ Print Repeated Values ┐
 │   ( ) Yes             │              «   OK   »
 │   (·) No              │
 └───────────────────────┘              < Cancel >
 ┌ Also Print ─────────────────────────────────┐
 │ [ ] In First Whole Band of New Page/Col     │
 │ [ ] When This Group Changes                 │
 │ [ ] When Detail Overflows to New Page/Col   │
 └─────────────────────────────────────────────┘

   [ ] Print Only When Expression is True...

   [ ] Remove Line If Blank
```

```
Row:   2  Col:  66
 Field - Full Expression:
      customer.cphone
      SIZE   1,  14
```

```
Report Expression:

<  Expr...   > customer.cphone

< Format... > @R (999) 999-9999    Width:  14

[ ] Style...        [ ] Suppress...
[ ] Calculate... [X] Stretch Vertically
[ ] Comment...    [X] Float as Band Stretches

          «   OK    »     < Cancel >
```

```
                    Print When
 Print Repeated Values
     ( ) Yes                            «   OK   »
     (·) No
                                        < Cancel >
 Also Print
  [ ] In First Whole Band of New Page/Col
  [ ] When This Group Changes
  [ ] When Detail Overflows to New Page/Col

  [ ] Print Only When Expression is True...

  [ ] Remove Line If Blank
Row:   3  Col:  25
 Field - Full Expression:
     customer.caddress2
     SIZE   1,  40
```

```
 Report Expression:

 <  Expr...  > customer.caddress2

 < Format... >                      Width:  40

 [ ] Style...      [ ] Suppress...
 [ ] Calculate...  [X] Stretch Vertically
 [ ] Comment...    [X] Float as Band Stretches

          «   OK   »    < Cancel >
```

```
                    Print When
 Print Repeated Values
     ( ) Yes                            «   OK   »
     (·) No
                                        < Cancel >
 Also Print
  [ ] In First Whole Band of New Page/Col
  [ ] When This Group Changes
  [ ] When Detail Overflows to New Page/Col

  [ ] Print Only When Expression is True...

  [ ] Remove Line If Blank
Row:   4  Col:  25
 Field - Full Expression:
     csz( customer.ccity, customer.cstate, customer.czip)
     SIZE   1,  40
```

```
Report Expression:

<  Expr...  > csz( customer.ccity

< Format... >                    Width:  40

[ ] Style...       [ ] Suppress...
[ ] Calculate...   [ ] Stretch Vertically
[ ] Comment...     [ ] Float as Band Stretches

         «   OK   »     < Cancel >
```

```
═══════════════ Print When ═══════════════
┌ Print Repeated Values ┐
    ( ) Yes                          «   OK   »
    (·) No
                                      < Cancel >
┌ Also Print
 [ ] In First Whole Band of New Page/Col
 [ ] When This Group Changes
 [ ] When Detail Overflows to New Page/Col

 [ ] Print Only When Expression is True...

 [ ] Remove Line If Blank
```

```
************************************************************
  Page Footer:
------------------------------------------------------------
Row:   8  Col:   0
 Field - Full Expression:
      DATE()
      SIZE    1,    8
```

```
Report Expression:

<  Expr...  > DATE()

< Format... >                    Width:   8

[ ] Style...       [ ] Suppress...
[ ] Calculate...   [ ] Stretch Vertically
[ ] Comment...     [ ] Float as Band Stretches

         «   OK   »     < Cancel >
```

```
═══════════════════ Print When ════════════════════
  ┌ Print Repeated Values ┐
  │   ( ) Yes             │           «   OK   »
  │   (•) No              │
  └───────────────────────┘          < Cancel >
  ┌ Also Print ─────────────────────────────────┐
  │ [ ] In First Whole Band of New Page/Col      │
  │ [ ] When This Group Changes                  │
  │ [ ] When Detail Overflows to New Page/Col    │
  └──────────────────────────────────────────────┘

  [ ] Print Only When Expression is True...

  [ ] Remove Line If Blank
```

```
Row:   8  Col:  71
 Text:  Page
      SIZE   1,   5
Row:   8  Col:  76
 Field - Full Expression:
      _PAGENO
      SIZE   1,   4
```

```
Report Expression:

<  Expr...  > _PAGENO

< Format... >                        Width:   4

[ ] Style...       [ ] Suppress...
[ ] Calculate...   [ ] Stretch Vertically
[ ] Comment...     [ ] Float as Band Stretches

         «   OK   »    < Cancel >
```

```
═══════════════════ Print When ════════════════════
  ┌ Print Repeated Values ┐
  │   ( ) Yes             │           «   OK   »
  │   (•) No              │
  └───────────────────────┘          < Cancel >
  ┌ Also Print ─────────────────────────────────┐
  │ [ ] In First Whole Band of New Page/Col      │
  │ [ ] When This Group Changes                  │
  │ [ ] When Detail Overflows to New Page/Col    │
  └──────────────────────────────────────────────┘

  [ ] Print Only When Expression is True...

  [ ] Remove Line If Blank
```

Orders by Customer Report: ORDERS.FRX

Orders is a form that prints the orders sent in by each customer, with subtotals.

As with all reports, this report's data is created through a SQL SELECT. Note that if we wanted, we could call a screen from this program and limit the selection as requested by the user.

Query

```
SELECT CD.CMUSICIAN, CD.CTITLE, CD.NPRICE,;
       ALLTRIM(CLASTNAME-(" "+CFIRSTNAME)) AS CustName, ;
       INVOICE.cInvNum, Purchase.nCdAmt, Purchase.nCdQty ;
  FROM CD, INVOICE, PURCHASE, CUSTOMER;
 WHERE PURCHASE.CCDID = CD.CID;
   AND Invoice.CID = PURCHASE.CInvID;
   AND Customer.cID = Invoice.cCustID ;
 ORDER BY CustName, Invoice.cInvNum, CD.CTITLE;
  INTO CURSOR ORDERS
```

Report

```
01/15/19                                                      Page     1

                              Customer Orders
                                                      Item             Extended
                                                      Price   Qty        Amount
                                                      -----   ---      --------

Customer: Gurion John

Inv: 11111
      Billy Joel               52nd Street             25.00    1         25.00
      Bruce Springsteen        Born in the USA         26.00    3         78.00
      Pink Floyd               Dark Side of the Moon   19.95    1         19.95
                                                               ---     --------
                      Subtotal for Invoice: 11111               5        122.95
Inv: 2983982398
      Billy Joel               52nd Street             25.00    4        100.00
      Bruce Springsteen        Born in the USA         26.00    1         26.00
      Elton John               Captain Fantastic...    30.00    1         30.00
                                                               ---     --------
                      Subtotal for Invoice: 2983982398          6        156.00
Inv: 46535
      Billy Joel               52nd Street             25.00    1         25.00
      Pink Floyd               Dark Side of the Moon   19.95    1         19.95
                                                               ---     --------
                      Subtotal for Invoice: 46535               2         44.95
```

```
************************************************************
**--    ORDERS.FRX
************************************************************
```

```
Page Layout:              < Options... >

 Page length      (rows):   66
 Top margin       (rows):    0
 Bottom margin    (rows):    0
                                                    «   OK   »
 Printer indent    (columns):    0
 Right margin column:  132                          < Cancel >

Environment:

Environment NOT saved with report.
```

```
Options:

 [X] Page eject before printing
 [ ] Page eject after printing
                                          «   OK   »
 [ ] Plain page
 [ ] Summary report                       < Cancel >
 [ ] Suppress blank lines

 [ ] Add alias
```

```
 Printer Driver Setup:
************************************************************
  Page Header:
------------------------------------------------------------
Row:   0  Col:   0
 Field - Full Expression:
      DATE()
      SIZE   1,   8
```

```
Report Expression:

<  Expr...   > DATE()

< Format... >                          Width:   8

[ ] Style...      [ ] Suppress...
[ ] Calculate...  [ ] Stretch Vertically
[ ] Comment...    [ ] Float as Band Stretches

         «   OK   »    < Cancel >
```

```
╔═══════════════════ Print When ════════════════════╗
║ ┌ Print Repeated Values ──┐                       ║
║ │   ( ) Yes               │     «   OK    »       ║
║ │   (·) No                │                       ║
║ └─────────────────────────┘     < Cancel >        ║
║ ┌ Also Print ────────────────────────────────┐    ║
║ │[ ] In First Whole Band of New Page/Col     │    ║
║ │[ ] When This Group Changes                 │    ║
║ │[ ] When Detail Overflows to New Page/Col   │    ║
║ └────────────────────────────────────────────┘    ║
║                                                   ║
║  [ ] Print Only When Expression is True...        ║
║                                                   ║
║  [ ] Remove Line If Blank                         ║
╚═══════════════════════════════════════════════════╝
Row:   0  Col:  71
 Text:  Page
     SIZE   1,   5
Row:   0  Col:  76
 Field - Full Expression:
     _PAGENO
     SIZE   1,   4
╔═══════════════════════════════════════════════════╗
║                                                   ║
║ Report Expression:                                ║
║                                                   ║
║ <  Expr...  > _PAGENO                             ║
║                                                   ║
║ < Format... >                        Width:   4   ║
║                                                   ║
║ [ ] Style...       [ ] Suppress...                ║
║ [ ] Calculate...   [ ] Stretch Vertically         ║
║ [ ] Comment...     [ ] Float as Band Stretches    ║
║                                                   ║
║          «   OK   »    < Cancel >                 ║
║                                                   ║
╚═══════════════════════════════════════════════════╝
╔═══════════════════ Print When ════════════════════╗
║ ┌ Print Repeated Values ──┐                       ║
║ │   ( ) Yes               │     «   OK    »       ║
║ │   (·) No                │                       ║
║ └─────────────────────────┘     < Cancel >        ║
║ ┌ Also Print ────────────────────────────────┐    ║
║ │[ ] In First Whole Band of New Page/Col     │    ║
║ │[ ] When This Group Changes                 │    ║
║ │[ ] When Detail Overflows to New Page/Col   │    ║
║ └────────────────────────────────────────────┘    ║
║                                                   ║
║  [ ] Print Only When Expression is True...        ║
║                                                   ║
║  [ ] Remove Line If Blank                         ║
╚═══════════════════════════════════════════════════╝
Row:   1  Col:   0
 Field - Full Expression:
     showpage()
     SIZE   1,   1
```

```
Report Expression:

<  Expr...  > showpage()

< Format... >                         Width:   1

[ ] Style...      [ ] Suppress...
[ ] Calculate... [ ] Stretch Vertically
[ ] Comment...    [ ] Float as Band Stretches

         «   OK   »    < Cancel >
```

```
                    Print When
 Print Repeated Values
     ( ) Yes                               «   OK   »
     (·) No
                                           < Cancel >
 Also Print
  [ ] In First Whole Band of New Page/Col
  [ ] When This Group Changes
  [ ] When Detail Overflows to New Page/Col


  [ ] Print Only When Expression is True...

  [ ] Remove Line If Blank
```

```
Row:   2  Col:  32
 Text:  Customer Orders
      SIZE   1,  15
Row:   3  Col:  68
 Text:  Item
      SIZE   1,   4
Row:   3  Col:  83
 Text:  Extended
      SIZE   1,   8
Row:   4  Col:  68
 Text:  Price
      SIZE   1,   5
Row:   4  Col:  76
 Text:  Qty
      SIZE   1,   3
Row:   4  Col:  85
 Text:  Amount
      SIZE   1,   6
Row:   5  Col:  68
  Line - Height:   1  Width:   5
```

```
Box:

(·) Single line
( ) Double line          «   OK    »
( ) Panel
( ) Character...         < Cancel >

[ ] Comment...
[ ] Float as band stretches

Row:   5  Col:  76
  Line - Height:   1  Width:   3

Box:

(·) Single line
( ) Double line          «   OK    »
( ) Panel
( ) Character...         < Cancel >

[ ] Comment...
[ ] Float as band stretches

Row:   5  Col:  83
  Line - Height:   1  Width:   8

Box:

(·) Single line
( ) Double line          «   OK    »
( ) Panel
( ) Character...         < Cancel >

[ ] Comment...
[ ] Float as band stretches
****************************************************************
```

```
Group  1 Info:

< Group... > custname

Options:
                                              «    OK    »
  [ ] New Page
  [ ] Swap Page Header                        < Cancel >
  [ ] Swap Page Footer
  [ ] Reprint Header
  [ ] Reset Page Number

# of rows following header:   0
-------------------------------------------------------------
Row:   8  Col:   0
 Text:  Customer:
      SIZE   1,   9
Row:   8  Col:  10
 Field - Full Expression:
      custname
      SIZE   1,  24

Report Expression:

<  Expr...  > custname

< Format... >                                  Width:  24

[ ] Style...      [ ] Suppress...
[ ] Calculate...  [ ] Stretch Vertically
[ ] Comment...    [ ] Float as Band Stretches

          «   OK   »    < Cancel >

                     Print When
  Print Repeated Values
     ( ) Yes                                   «   OK   »
     (·) No
                                               < Cancel >
  Also Print
   [ ] In First Whole Band of New Page/Col
   [ ] When This Group Changes
   [ ] When Detail Overflows to New Page/Col

   [ ] Print Only When Expression is True...

   [ ] Remove Line If Blank
*************************************************************
```

```
Group  2 Info:

< Group... > cinvnum

Options:
                                        «    OK    »
 [ ] New Page
 [ ] Swap Page Header                   < Cancel >
 [ ] Swap Page Footer
 [ ] Reprint Header
 [ ] Reset Page Number

# of rows following header:   0
-----------------------------------------------------------
Row:  10  Col:   0
 Text:  Inv:
     SIZE   1,   4
Row:  10  Col:   5
 Field - Full Expression:
     cinvnum
     SIZE   1,  10
```

```
Report Expression:

<  Expr...  > cinvnum

< Format... >                          Width:  10

[ ] Style...       [ ] Suppress...
[ ] Calculate...   [ ] Stretch Vertically
[ ] Comment...     [ ] Float as Band Stretches

          «   OK   »    < Cancel >
```

```
================ Print When ================
 Print Repeated Values
    ( ) Yes                              «   OK   »
    (·) No
                                         < Cancel >
 Also Print
 [ ] In First Whole Band of New Page/Col
 [ ] When This Group Changes
 [ ] When Detail Overflows to New Page/Col

 [ ] Print Only When Expression is True...

 [ ] Remove Line If Blank
***********************************************************
  Detail:
-----------------------------------------------------------
Row:  11  Col:   6
```

```
Field - Full Expression:
     cmusician
     SIZE   1,  27

Report Expression:

<  Expr...   > cmusician

< Format... >                           Width:  27

[ ] Style...      [ ] Suppress...
[ ] Calculate...  [ ] Stretch Vertically
[ ] Comment...    [ ] Float as Band Stretches

          «   OK   »     < Cancel >

                 Print When
 Print Repeated Values
    ( ) Yes                                «   OK   »
    (·) No
                                           < Cancel >
 Also Print
  [ ] In First Whole Band of New Page/Col
  [ ] When This Group Changes
  [ ] When Detail Overflows to New Page/Col


  [ ] Print Only When Expression is True...

  [ ] Remove Line If Blank
Row:  11  Col:  35
 Field - Full Expression:
     ctitle
     SIZE   1,  29

Report Expression:

<  Expr...   > ctitle

< Format... >                           Width:  29

[ ] Style...      [ ] Suppress...
[ ] Calculate...  [ ] Stretch Vertically
[ ] Comment...    [ ] Float as Band Stretches

          «   OK   »     < Cancel >
```

```
                 ═══════════════ Print When ═══════════════
     ┌ Print Repeated Values ┐
        ( ) Yes                          «   OK   »
        (·) No
     └───────────────────────┘           < Cancel >
     ┌ Also Print ──────────────────────────────────┐
       [ ] In First Whole Band of New Page/Col
       [ ] When This Group Changes
       [ ] When Detail Overflows to New Page/Col
     └──────────────────────────────────────────────┘

       [ ] Print Only When Expression is True...

       [ ] Remove Line If Blank

Row:  11  Col:  68
 Field - Full Expression:
      ncdamt
      SIZE   1,   5
```

```
   Report Expression:

   <  Expr...  > ncdamt

   < Format... >                          Width:   5

   [ ] Style...       [ ] Suppress...
   [ ] Calculate...   [ ] Stretch Vertically
   [ ] Comment...     [ ] Float as Band Stretches

             «   OK   »    < Cancel >
```

```
                 ═══════════════ Print When ═══════════════
     ┌ Print Repeated Values ┐
        ( ) Yes                          «   OK   »
        (·) No
     └───────────────────────┘           < Cancel >
     ┌ Also Print ──────────────────────────────────┐
       [ ] In First Whole Band of New Page/Col
       [ ] When This Group Changes
       [ ] When Detail Overflows to New Page/Col
     └──────────────────────────────────────────────┘

       [ ] Print Only When Expression is True...

       [ ] Remove Line If Blank

Row:  11  Col:  77
 Field - Full Expression:
      ncdqty
      SIZE   1,   2
```

```
Report Expression:

<  Expr...   > ncdqty

< Format... >                        Width:   2

[X] Style...       [ ] Suppress...
[ ] Calculate... [ ] Stretch Vertically
[ ] Comment...     [ ] Float as Band Stretches

          «   OK   »   < Cancel >

Style                  Alignment
 [ ] Bold               ( ) Left
 [ ] Italic             ( ) Center
 [ ] Underline          (·) Right
 [ ] Superscript
 [ ] Subscript
                        «   OK   »
Code
 J                      < Cancel >

               Print When
 Print Repeated Values
    ( ) Yes                         «   OK   »
    (·) No
                                    < Cancel >
 Also Print
  [ ] In First Whole Band of New Page/Col
  [ ] When This Group Changes
  [ ] When Detail Overflows to New Page/Col

  [ ] Print Only When Expression is True...

  [ ] Remove Line If Blank
Row:  11  Col:  83
 Field - Full Expression:
      ncdamt * ncdqty
      SIZE   1,   8
```

```
Report Expression:

<  Expr...  > ncdamt * ncdqty

< Format... >                  Width:   8

[X] Style...     [ ] Suppress...
[ ] Calculate... [ ] Stretch Vertically
[ ] Comment...   [ ] Float as Band Stretches

        «   OK   »     < Cancel >

┌ Style ──────────┐   ┌ Alignment ┐
  [ ] Bold              ( ) Left
  [ ] Italic            ( ) Center
  [ ] Underline         (·) Right
  [ ] Superscript
  [ ] Subscript
                         «   OK   »
┌ Code ───────────┐
  J                      < Cancel >

═══════════════ Print When ═══════════════
  ┌ Print Repeated Values ┐
       ( ) Yes                 «   OK   »
       (·) No
                               < Cancel >
  ┌ Also Print ─────────────────────────┐
   [ ] In First Whole Band of New Page/Col
   [ ] When This Group Changes
   [ ] When Detail Overflows to New Page/Col

   [ ] Print Only When Expression is True...

   [ ] Remove Line If Blank
**********************************************************
 Group  2 Footer:
----------------------------------------------------------
Row:  12  Col:  77
 Line - Height:   1  Width:   2
```

```
Box:

(·) Single line
( ) Double line              «   OK    »
( ) Panel
( ) Character...             < Cancel >

[ ] Comment...
[ ] Float as band stretches

Row:  12  Col:  83
  Line - Height:   1  Width:   8

Box:

(·) Single line
( ) Double line              «   OK    »
( ) Panel
( ) Character...             < Cancel >

[ ] Comment...
[ ] Float as band stretches

Row:  13  Col:  26
 Text:  Subtotal for Invoice:
      SIZE   1,  21
Row:  13  Col:  48
 Field - Full Expression:
      cinvnum
      SIZE   1,  10

Report Expression:

<  Expr...  > cinvnum

< Format... >                        Width:  10

[ ] Style...      [ ] Suppress...
[ ] Calculate... [ ] Stretch Vertically
[ ] Comment...    [ ] Float as Band Stretches

          «   OK   »     < Cancel >
```

```
                     Print When
  Print Repeated Values
     ( ) Yes                            «   OK   »
     (·) No
                                        < Cancel >
  Also Print
    [ ] In First Whole Band of New Page/Col
    [ ] When This Group Changes
    [ ] When Detail Overflows to New Page/Col

    [ ] Print Only When Expression is True...

    [ ] Remove Line If Blank
```

```
Row:  13  Col:  76
 Field - Full Expression:
     ncdqty
     SIZE   1,   3
```

```
  Report Expression:

  <  Expr...  > ncdqty

  < Format... >                      Width:   3

  [X] Style...       [ ] Suppress...
  [X] Calculate...   [ ] Stretch Vertically
  [ ] Comment...     [ ] Float as Band Stretches

          «   OK   »    < Cancel >
```

```
  Style                   Alignment
  [ ] Bold                ( ) Left
  [ ] Italic              ( ) Center
  [ ] Underline           (·) Right
  [ ] Superscript
  [ ] Subscript
                          «   OK   »
  Code
  J                       < Cancel >
```

```
Reset:        cinvnum

Calculate:   ( ) Nothing
             ( ) Count                 «   OK   »
             (·) Sum
             ( ) Average               < Cancel >
             ( ) Lowest
             ( ) Highest
             ( ) Std. Deviation
             ( ) Variance
```

```
                    Print When
  Print Repeated Values
     ( ) Yes                               «   OK   »
     (·) No
                                           < Cancel >
  Also Print
   [ ] In First Whole Band of New Page/Col
   [ ] When This Group Changes
   [ ] When Detail Overflows to New Page/Col

   [ ] Print Only When Expression is True...

   [ ] Remove Line If Blank
```

```
Row:  13  Col:  82
 Field - Full Expression:
      ncdamt * ncdqty
      SIZE   1,   9
```

```
Report Expression:

<  Expr...  > ncdamt * ncdqty

< Format... >                     Width:   9

[X] Style...       [ ] Suppress...
[X] Calculate...   [ ] Stretch Vertically
[ ] Comment...     [ ] Float as Band Stretches

          «   OK   »     < Cancel >
```

```
┌ Style ──────────────────┐  ┌ Alignment ┐
│ [ ] Bold                │  │ ( ) Left   │
│ [ ] Italic              │  │ ( ) Center │
│ [ ] Underline           │  │ (·) Right  │
│ [ ] Superscript         │  └────────────┘
│ [ ] Subscript           │
└─────────────────────────┘      «  OK  »
┌ Code ───────────────────┐
│ J                       │    < Cancel >
└─────────────────────────┘
```

```
Reset:        cinvnum

Calculate:  ( ) Nothing
            ( ) Count                «  OK  »
            (·) Sum
            ( ) Average              < Cancel >
            ( ) Lowest
            ( ) Highest
            ( ) Std. Deviation
            ( ) Variance
```

```
                    Print When
 ┌ Print Repeated Values ──┐
 │   ( ) Yes               │            «  OK  »
 │   (·) No                │
 └─────────────────────────┘            < Cancel >
 ┌ Also Print ─────────────────────────────────┐
 │ [ ] In First Whole Band of New Page/Col     │
 │ [ ] When This Group Changes                 │
 │ [ ] When Detail Overflows to New Page/Col   │
 └─────────────────────────────────────────────┘

   [ ] Print Only When Expression is True...

   [ ] Remove Line If Blank
```

```
************************************************************
  Group  1 Footer:
------------------------------------------------------------
Row:  15  Col:  26
 Text:  Subtotal for:
      SIZE   1,  13
Row:  15  Col:  40
 Field - Full Expression:
      custname
      SIZE   1,  24
```

```
Report Expression:

<  Expr...   > custname

< Format... >                        Width:  24

[ ] Style...      [ ] Suppress...
[ ] Calculate...  [ ] Stretch Vertically
[ ] Comment...    [ ] Float as Band Stretches

          «   OK   »    < Cancel >
```

```
=================== Print When ===================
 ┌ Print Repeated Values ┐
 │   ( ) Yes             │        «   OK   »
 │   (·) No              │
 └───────────────────────┘        < Cancel >
 ┌ Also Print ───────────────────────────────┐
 │ [ ] In First Whole Band of New Page/Col   │
 │ [ ] When This Group Changes               │
 │ [ ] When Detail Overflows to New Page/Col │
 └───────────────────────────────────────────┘

  [ ] Print Only When Expression is True...

  [ ] Remove Line If Blank
```

```
Row:  15  Col:  76
 Field - Full Expression:
      ncdqty
      SIZE   1,   3
```

```
Report Expression:

<  Expr...   > ncdqty

< Format... >                        Width:   3

[X] Style...      [ ] Suppress...
[X] Calculate...  [ ] Stretch Vertically
[ ] Comment...    [ ] Float as Band Stretches

          «   OK   »    < Cancel >
```

```
┌ Style ──────────────────┐   ┌ Alignment ┐
  [ ] Bold                      ( ) Left
  [ ] Italic                    ( ) Center
  [ ] Underline                 (·) Right
  [ ] Superscript
  [ ] Subscript
                                «   OK   »
┌ Code ───────────────────┐
  J                             < Cancel >
```

```
Reset:          custname

Calculate:    ( ) Nothing
              ( ) Count              «   OK   »
              (·) Sum
              ( ) Average            < Cancel >
              ( ) Lowest
              ( ) Highest
              ( ) Std. Deviation
              ( ) Variance
```

```
═══════════════════ Print When ═══════════════════
  ┌ Print Repeated Values ┐
      ( ) Yes                         «   OK   »
      (·) No
                                      < Cancel >
  ┌ Also Print ───────────────────────────────────┐
   [ ] In First Whole Band of New Page/Col
   [ ] When This Group Changes
   [ ] When Detail Overflows to New Page/Col

   [ ] Print Only When Expression is True...

   [ ] Remove Line If Blank
```

```
Row:  15  Col:  82
 Field - Full Expression:
      ncdamt * ncdqty
      SIZE   1,   9
```

```
Report Expression:

<  Expr...  > ncdamt * ncdqty

< Format... >                       Width:   9

[X] Style...      [ ] Suppress...
[X] Calculate... [ ] Stretch Vertically
[ ] Comment...    [ ] Float as Band Stretches

          «   OK   »    < Cancel >
```

```
┌ Style ──────────────┐  ┌ Alignment ─┐
│ [ ] Bold            │  │ ( ) Left   │
│ [ ] Italic          │  │ ( ) Center │
│ [ ] Underline       │  │ (·) Right  │
│ [ ] Superscript     │  └────────────┘
│ [ ] Subscript       │
└─────────────────────┘   «   OK   »
┌ Code ───────────────┐
│ J                   │   < Cancel >
└─────────────────────┘
```

```
Reset:        custname

Calculate:    ( ) Nothing
              ( ) Count               «   OK   »
              (·) Sum
              ( ) Average             < Cancel >
              ( ) Lowest
              ( ) Highest
              ( ) Std. Deviation
              ( ) Variance
```

```
═══════════════════ Print When ═══════════════════
┌ Print Repeated Values ─┐
│   ( ) Yes              │          «   OK   »
│   (·) No               │
└────────────────────────┘          < Cancel >
┌ Also Print ──────────────────────────────────┐
│ [ ] In First Whole Band of New Page/Col      │
│ [ ] When This Group Changes                  │
│ [ ] When Detail Overflows to New Page/Col    │
└──────────────────────────────────────────────┘

  [ ] Print Only When Expression is True...

  [ ] Remove Line If Blank
```

```
*************************************************************
  Page Footer:
-------------------------------------------------------------
Row:  18  Col:  52
   Box - Height:   5  Width:  29

  Box:

   (·) Single line
   ( ) Double line                «   OK   »
   ( ) Panel
   ( ) Character...               < Cancel >

   [ ] Comment...
   [ ] Float as band stretches

*************************************************************
  Report Summary:

   [X] Summary Band
   [ ] New Page

-------------------------------------------------------------
Row:  19  Col:  60
 Text:  GRAND TOTALS
      SIZE   1,  12
Row:  20  Col:  54
 Text:  CDs Purchased:
      SIZE   1,  14
Row:  20  Col:  75
 Field - Full Expression:
      ncdqty
      SIZE   1,   3

  Report Expression:

  <  Expr...  > ncdqty

  < Format... >                      Width:   3

  [X] Style...      [ ] Suppress...
  [X] Calculate...  [ ] Stretch Vertically
  [ ] Comment...    [ ] Float as Band Stretches

            «   OK   »   < Cancel >
```

```
┌ Style ──────────────────┐  ┌ Alignment ┐
  [ ] Bold                     ( ) Left
  [ ] Italic                   ( ) Center
  [ ] Underline                (·) Right
  [ ] Superscript
  [ ] Subscript
                                «   OK   »
┌ Code ───────────────────┐
  J                            < Cancel >


  Reset:        End of Report

  Calculate:    ( ) Nothing
                ( ) Count              «   OK   »
                (·) Sum
                ( ) Average            < Cancel >
                ( ) Lowest
                ( ) Highest
                ( ) Std. Deviation
                ( ) Variance

═══════════════════ Print When ═══════════════════
  ┌ Print Repeated Values ┐
      ( ) Yes                          «   OK   »
      (·) No
                                       < Cancel >
  ┌ Also Print ─────────────────────────────┐
    [ ] In First Whole Band of New Page/Col
    [ ] When This Group Changes
    [ ] When Detail Overflows to New Page/Col

    [ ] Print Only When Expression is True...

    [ ] Remove Line If Blank
Row:  21  Col:  55
 Text:  Total $ Sold:
      SIZE   1,  13
Row:  21  Col:  69
 Field - Full Expression:
      ncdamt * ncdqty
      SIZE   1,   9
```

```
Report Expression:

<  Expr...  > ncdamt * ncdqty

< Format... >                         Width:   9

[X] Style...       [ ] Suppress...
[X] Calculate...   [ ] Stretch Vertically
[ ] Comment...     [ ] Float as Band Stretches

          «   OK   »    < Cancel >
```

```
┌ Style ──────────────┐  ┌ Alignment ─┐
│ [ ] Bold            │  │ ( ) Left   │
│ [ ] Italic          │  │ ( ) Center │
│ [ ] Underline       │  │ (·) Right  │
│ [ ] Superscript     │  └────────────┘
│ [ ] Subscript       │
└─────────────────────┘    «   OK   »
┌ Code ───────────────┐
│ J                   │   < Cancel >
└─────────────────────┘
```

```
Reset:          End of Report

Calculate:    ( ) Nothing
              ( ) Count              «   OK   »
              (·) Sum
              ( ) Average            < Cancel >
              ( ) Lowest
              ( ) Highest
              ( ) Std. Deviation
              ( ) Variance
```

```
═══════════════ Print When ═══════════════
┌ Print Repeated Values ┐
│    ( ) Yes            │          «   OK   »
│    (·) No             │
└───────────────────────┘          < Cancel >
┌ Also Print ─────────────────────────────────┐
│ [ ] In First Whole Band of New Page/Col     │
│ [ ] When This Group Changes                 │
│ [ ] When Detail Overflows to New Page/Col   │
└─────────────────────────────────────────────┘

  [ ] Print Only When Expression is True...

  [ ] Remove Line If Blank
```

Accounts Receivable Aging Report: ARREPO.FRX

This report is created with a SQL SELECT to originally create our crosstab of 30/60/90 information (see Chapter 8, *Usability Techniques*). Since a crosstab will only include valid columns (if no customer currently owes us money for over 90 days, that column will never be created), we create a cursor with the proper columns that we require and APPEND FROM the crosstab.

Query

```
SELECT TRIM(Customer.cLastName) + ", " ;
       + TRIM(Customer.cFirstName) AS CustName, ;
       arcolhed(Invoice.dOrdered,DATE()) AS ColHead, ;
       SUM(purchase.ncdQty * Purchase.nCdAmt) AS Amount ;
  FROM CUSTOMER, INVOICE, PURCHASE, CD;
 WHERE INVOICE.CCUSTID = CUSTOMER.CID;
   AND PURCHASE.CINVID = INVOICE.CID;
   AND CD.CID = PURCHASE.CCDID;
 GROUP BY 1, 2;
 ORDER BY 1, 2;
  INTO CURSOR SYS(2015)

 DO GENXTAB WITH 'TEMP'

CREATE CURSOR ARREPO ;
    (CustName C(40), Current N(10,2), Over30 N(10,2), ;
     Over60 N(10,2), Over90 N(10,2), Future N(10,2) )

APPEND FROM DBF("TEMP")

USE IN Temp
```

Report

Customer Name	Current	Over Thirtv	Over Sixtv	Over Ninetv	Total
Gurion. John	44.95	0.00	0.00	0.00	44.95
Miller. John	0.00	0.00	0.00	0.00	0.00
	44.95	0.00	0.00	0.00	44.95

```
************************************************************
**--    ARREPO.FRX
************************************************************

  Page Layout:            < Options... >

   Page length      (rows):   66
   Top margin       (rows):    0
   Bottom margin    (rows):    0
                                               «   OK   »
   Printer indent    (columns):     0
   Right margin column:    80                  < Cancel >

  Environment:

   Environment NOT saved with report.


  Options:

    [X] Page eject before printing
    [ ] Page eject after printing
                                           «   OK   »
    [ ] Plain page
    [ ] Summary report                     < Cancel >
    [ ] Suppress blank lines

    [X] Add alias

 Printer Driver Setup:
************************************************************
  Page Header:
------------------------------------------------------------
Row:   1  Col:   0
 Field - Full Expression:
      showpage()
      SIZE   1,    1

  Report Expression:

  <  Expr...   > showpage()

  < Format... >                          Width:   1

  [ ] Style...       [ ] Suppress...
  [ ] Calculate...   [ ] Stretch Vertically
  [ ] Comment...     [ ] Float as Band Stretches

            «   OK   »    < Cancel >
```

```
                    Print When
  Print Repeated Values
     ( ) Yes                              «    OK    »
     (·) No
                                          < Cancel >
  Also Print
   [ ] In First Whole Band of New Page/Col
   [ ] When This Group Changes
   [ ] When Detail Overflows to New Page/Col

   [ ] Print Only When Expression is True...

   [ ] Remove Line If Blank
```

```
Row:   1  Col:  46
 Text:  Over
      SIZE   1,   4
Row:   1  Col:  56
 Text:  Over
      SIZE   1,   4
Row:   1  Col:  66
 Text:  Over
      SIZE   1,   4
Row:   2  Col:   0
 Text:  Customer Name
      SIZE   1,  13
Row:   2  Col:  33
 Text:  Current
      SIZE   1,   7
Row:   2  Col:  44
 Text:  Thirty
      SIZE   1,   6
Row:   2  Col:  55
 Text:  Sixty
      SIZE   1,   5
Row:   2  Col:  64
 Text:  Ninety
      SIZE   1,   6
Row:   2  Col:  75
 Text:  Total
      SIZE   1,   5
Row:   3  Col:   0
  Line - Height:   1  Width:  30
```

```
 Box:

  (·) Single line
  ( ) Double line               «    OK    »
  ( ) Panel
  ( ) Character...              < Cancel >

 [ ] Comment...
 [ ] Float as band stretches
```

```
Row:   3  Col:  33
  Line - Height:   1  Width:   7
```

```
Box:

 (·) Single line
 ( ) Double line            «   OK   »
 ( ) Panel
 ( ) Character...           < Cancel >


 [ ] Comment...
 [ ] Float as band stretches
```

```
Row:   3  Col:  43
  Line - Height:   1  Width:   7
```

```
Box:

 (·) Single line
 ( ) Double line            «   OK   »
 ( ) Panel
 ( ) Character...           < Cancel >


 [ ] Comment...
 [ ] Float as band stretches
```

```
Row:   3  Col:  53
  Line - Height:   1  Width:   7
```

```
Box:

 (·) Single line
 ( ) Double line            «   OK   »
 ( ) Panel
 ( ) Character...           < Cancel >


 [ ] Comment...
 [ ] Float as band stretches
```

```
Row:   3  Col:  63
  Line - Height:   1  Width:   7
```

```
Box:

  (·) Single line
  ( ) Double line          «    OK    »
  ( ) Panel
  ( ) Character...         < Cancel >

[ ] Comment...
[ ] Float as band stretches

Row:   3  Col:  73
  Line - Height:   1  Width:   7

Box:

  (·) Single line
  ( ) Double line          «    OK    »
  ( ) Panel
  ( ) Character...         < Cancel >

[ ] Comment...
[ ] Float as band stretches

************************************************************
  Detail:
------------------------------------------------------------
Row:   5  Col:   0
 Field - Full Expression:
      arrepo.custname
      SIZE   1,  30

Report Expression:

< Expr...  > arrepo.custname

< Format... >                          Width:  30

[ ] Style...      [ ] Suppress...
[ ] Calculate...  [ ] Stretch Vertically
[ ] Comment...    [ ] Float as Band Stretches

          «   OK   »    < Cancel >
```

```
╔═══════════════ Print When ═══════════════════╗
║ ┌ Print Repeated Values ─┐                   ║
║ │   ( ) Yes              │       «  OK  »    ║
║ │   (·) No               │                   ║
║ └────────────────────────┘     < Cancel >    ║
║ ┌ Also Print ──────────────────────────────┐ ║
║ │ [ ] In First Whole Band of New Page/Col  │ ║
║ │ [ ] When This Group Changes              │ ║
║ │ [ ] When Detail Overflows to New Page/Col│ ║
║ └──────────────────────────────────────────┘ ║
║                                              ║
║   [ ] Print Only When Expression is True...  ║
║                                              ║
║   [ ] Remove Line If Blank                   ║
╚══════════════════════════════════════════════╝
```

```
Row:   5  Col:  32
 Field - Full Expression:
     arrepo.current
     SIZE   1,   8
```

```
╔══════════════════════════════════════════════╗
║                                              ║
║  Report Expression:                          ║
║                                              ║
║  <  Expr...  > arrepo.current                ║
║                                              ║
║  < Format... >                   Width:   8  ║
║                                              ║
║  [X] Style...      [ ] Suppress...           ║
║  [ ] Calculate...  [ ] Stretch Vertically    ║
║  [ ] Comment...    [ ] Float as Band Stretches║
║                                              ║
║          «  OK  »    < Cancel >              ║
║                                              ║
╚══════════════════════════════════════════════╝
```

```
╔═════════════════════════════════════════╗
║ ┌ Style ──────────┐  ┌ Alignment ─┐     ║
║ │ [ ] Bold        │  │ ( ) Left   │     ║
║ │ [ ] Italic      │  │ ( ) Center │     ║
║ │ [ ] Underline   │  │ (·) Right  │     ║
║ │ [ ] Superscript │  └────────────┘     ║
║ │ [ ] Subscript   │                     ║
║ └─────────────────┘    «  OK  »         ║
║ ┌ Code ───────────┐                     ║
║ │ J               │    < Cancel >       ║
║ └─────────────────┘                     ║
╚═════════════════════════════════════════╝
```

```
                    Print When
  Print Repeated Values
     ( ) Yes                              «   OK   »
     (·) No
                                          < Cancel >
  Also Print
   [ ] In First Whole Band of New Page/Col
   [ ] When This Group Changes
   [ ] When Detail Overflows to New Page/Col

   [ ] Print Only When Expression is True...

   [ ] Remove Line If Blank
```

```
Row:   5  Col:  42
 Field - Full Expression:
      arrepo.over30
      SIZE   1,   8
```

```
 Report Expression:

 <  Expr...   > arrepo.over30

 < Format... >                        Width:   8

 [X] Style...      [ ] Suppress...
 [ ] Calculate...  [ ] Stretch Vertically
 [ ] Comment...    [ ] Float as Band Stretches

           «   OK   »    < Cancel >
```

```
  Style                     Alignment
  [ ] Bold                  ( ) Left
  [ ] Italic                ( ) Center
  [ ] Underline             (·) Right
  [ ] Superscript
  [ ] Subscript
                            «   OK   »
  Code
  J                         < Cancel >
```

```
Print When
  Print Repeated Values                     «    OK    »
     ( ) Yes
     (·) No                                 < Cancel >

  Also Print
   [ ] In First Whole Band of New Page/Col
   [ ] When This Group Changes
   [ ] When Detail Overflows to New Page/Col

   [ ] Print Only When Expression is True...

   [ ] Remove Line If Blank
```

```
Row:   5  Col:  52
 Field - Full Expression:
      arrepo.over60
      SIZE   1,   8
```

```
Report Expression:

<  Expr...  > arrepo.over60

< Format... >                        Width:   8

[X] Style...       [ ] Suppress...
[ ] Calculate...   [ ] Stretch Vertically
[ ] Comment...     [ ] Float as Band Stretches

        «   OK   »    < Cancel >
```

```
Style                  Alignment
 [ ] Bold               ( ) Left
 [ ] Italic             ( ) Center
 [ ] Underline          (·) Right
 [ ] Superscript
 [ ] Subscript
                        «   OK   »
Code
 J                      < Cancel >
```

```
                    Print When
  Print Repeated Values
     ( ) Yes                            «   OK   »
     (·) No
                                        < Cancel >
  Also Print
   [ ] In First Whole Band of New Page/Col
   [ ] When This Group Changes
   [ ] When Detail Overflows to New Page/Col

   [ ] Print Only When Expression is True...

   [ ] Remove Line If Blank
Row:   5  Col:  62
 Field - Full Expression:
      arrepo.over90
      SIZE   1,   8
```

```
  Report Expression:

  <  Expr...  > arrepo.over90

  < Format... >                      Width:   8

  [X] Style...       [ ] Suppress...
  [ ] Calculate... [ ] Stretch Vertically
  [ ] Comment...     [ ] Float as Band Stretches

           «   OK   »    < Cancel >
```

```
  Style                   Alignment
  [ ] Bold                 ( ) Left
  [ ] Italic               ( ) Center
  [ ] Underline            (·) Right
  [ ] Superscript
  [ ] Subscript
                           «   OK   »
  Code
  J                        < Cancel >
```

```
╔═══════════════════ Print When ════════════════════╗
║ ┌ Print Repeated Values ┐                         ║
║ │   ( ) Yes             │         «   OK   »      ║
║ │   (·) No              │                         ║
║ └───────────────────────┘        < Cancel >       ║
║ ┌ Also Print ────────────────────────────────┐    ║
║ │[ ] In First Whole Band of New Page/Col     │    ║
║ │[ ] When This Group Changes                 │    ║
║ │[ ] When Detail Overflows to New Page/Col   │    ║
║ └────────────────────────────────────────────┘    ║
║                                                   ║
║  [ ] Print Only When Expression is True...        ║
║                                                   ║
║  [ ] Remove Line If Blank                         ║
╚═══════════════════════════════════════════════════╝
Row:   5  Col:  72
 Field - Full Expression:
      current+over30+over60+over90
      SIZE   1,   8
```

```
╔═══════════════════════════════════════════════════╗
║                                                   ║
║  Report Expression:                               ║
║                                                   ║
║  <  Expr...  > current+over30+over                ║
║                                                   ║
║  < Format... >                       Width:   8   ║
║                                                   ║
║  [X] Style...      [ ] Suppress...                ║
║  [ ] Calculate...  [ ] Stretch Vertically         ║
║  [ ] Comment...    [ ] Float as Band Stretches    ║
║                                                   ║
║           «   OK   »    < Cancel >                ║
║                                                   ║
╚═══════════════════════════════════════════════════╝
```

```
╔═════════════════════════════════════════╗
║ ┌ Style ─────────────┐ ┌ Alignment ┐    ║
║ │ [ ] Bold           │ │ ( ) Left  │    ║
║ │ [ ] Italic         │ │ ( ) Center│    ║
║ │ [ ] Underline      │ │ (·) Right │    ║
║ │ [ ] Superscript    │ └───────────┘    ║
║ │ [ ] Subscript      │                  ║
║ └────────────────────┘   «   OK   »     ║
║ ┌ Code ──────────────┐                  ║
║ │ J                  │   < Cancel >     ║
║ └────────────────────┘                  ║
╚═════════════════════════════════════════╝
```

```
                    Print When
  Print Repeated Values
      ( ) Yes                          «   OK   »
      (·) No
                                       < Cancel >
  Also Print
   [ ] In First Whole Band of New Page/Col
   [ ] When This Group Changes
   [ ] When Detail Overflows to New Page/Col

   [ ] Print Only When Expression is True...

   [ ] Remove Line If Blank
************************************************************
  Page Footer:
------------------------------------------------------------
Row:   9  Col:    0
 Field - Full Expression:
      DATE()
      SIZE   1,   8

  Report Expression:

  <  Expr...   > DATE()

  < Format... >                       Width:   8

  [ ] Style...       [ ] Suppress...
  [ ] Calculate...   [ ] Stretch Vertically
  [ ] Comment...     [ ] Float as Band Stretches

          «   OK   »    < Cancel >

                    Print When
  Print Repeated Values
      ( ) Yes                          «   OK   »
      (·) No
                                       < Cancel >
  Also Print
   [ ] In First Whole Band of New Page/Col
   [ ] When This Group Changes
   [ ] When Detail Overflows to New Page/Col

   [ ] Print Only When Expression is True...

   [ ] Remove Line If Blank
Row:   9  Col:  71
 Text:  Page
      SIZE   1,   5
Row:   9  Col:  76
 Field - Full Expression:
      _PAGENO
      SIZE   1,   4
```

```
Report Expression:

<  Expr...  > _PAGENO

< Format... >                        Width:   4

[X] Style...        [ ] Suppress...
[ ] Calculate...    [ ] Stretch Vertically
[ ] Comment...      [ ] Float as Band Stretches

         «   OK   »    < Cancel >

 Style                     Alignment
  [ ] Bold                  ( ) Left
  [ ] Italic                ( ) Center
  [ ] Underline             (·) Right
  [ ] Superscript
  [ ] Subscript
                           «   OK   »
 Code
  J                        < Cancel >

                  Print When
  Print Repeated Values
      ( ) Yes                          «   OK   »
      (·) No
                                       < Cancel >
  Also Print
   [ ] In First Whole Band of New Page/Col
   [ ] When This Group Changes
   [ ] When Detail Overflows to New Page/Col

   [ ] Print Only When Expression is True...

   [ ] Remove Line If Blank
*************************************************************
 Report Summary:

   [X] Summary Band
   [ ] New Page

-------------------------------------------------------------
Row:  10  Col:  33
 Line - Height:   1  Width:   7
```

```
Box:

  ( ) Single line
  (·) Double line            «    OK    »
  ( ) Panel
  ( ) Character...           < Cancel >

[ ] Comment...
[ ] Float as band stretches
```

```
Row:  10  Col:  43
  Line - Height:   1  Width:   7
```

```
Box:

  ( ) Single line
  (·) Double line            «    OK    »
  ( ) Panel
  ( ) Character...           < Cancel >

[ ] Comment...
[ ] Float as band stretches
```

```
Row:  10  Col:  53
  Line - Height:   1  Width:   7
```

```
Box:

  ( ) Single line
  (·) Double line            «    OK    »
  ( ) Panel
  ( ) Character...           < Cancel >

[ ] Comment...
[ ] Float as band stretches
```

```
Row:  10  Col:  63
  Line - Height:   1  Width:   7
```

```
Box:

 ( ) Single line
 (·) Double line                  «    OK    »
 ( ) Panel
 ( ) Character...                 < Cancel >

 [ ] Comment...
 [ ] Float as band stretches
```

```
Row:  10  Col:  73
  Line - Height:   1  Width:   7
```

```
Box:

 ( ) Single line
 (·) Double line                  «    OK    »
 ( ) Panel
 ( ) Character...                 < Cancel >

 [ ] Comment...
 [ ] Float as band stretches
```

```
Row:  11  Col:  32
 Field - Full Expression:
      arrepo.current
      SIZE   1,   8
```

```
Report Expression:

<  Expr...   > arrepo.current

< Format... >                            Width:  8

 [X] Style...       [ ] Suppress...
 [X] Calculate...   [ ] Stretch Vertically
 [ ] Comment...     [ ] Float as Band Stretches

          «   OK   »    < Cancel >
```

```
┌ Style ───────────────────┐   ┌ Alignment ─┐
│ [ ] Bold                 │   │ ( ) Left   │
│ [ ] Italic               │   │ ( ) Center │
│ [ ] Underline            │   │ (·) Right  │
│ [ ] Superscript          │   └────────────┘
│ [ ] Subscript            │
└──────────────────────────┘    «   OK   »

┌ Code ────────────────────┐
│ J                        │    < Cancel >
└──────────────────────────┘
```

```
Reset:        [ End of Report ]

Calculate:    ( ) Nothing
              ( ) Count                «   OK   »
              (·) Sum
              ( ) Average              < Cancel >
              ( ) Lowest
              ( ) Highest
              ( ) Std. Deviation
              ( ) Variance
```

```
═══════════════ Print When ═══════════════
┌ Print Repeated Values ──────┐
│   ( ) Yes                   │        «   OK   »
│   (·) No                    │
└─────────────────────────────┘        < Cancel >
┌ Also Print ─────────────────────────────────────┐
│ [ ] In First Whole Band of New Page/Col         │
│ [ ] When This Group Changes                     │
│ [ ] When Detail Overflows to New Page/Col       │
└─────────────────────────────────────────────────┘

  [ ] Print Only When Expression is True...

  [ ] Remove Line If Blank
```

```
Row:  11  Col:  42
 Field - Full Expression:
      arrepo.over30
      SIZE   1,   8
```

```
Report Expression:

<  Expr...   > arrepo.over30

< Format... >                    Width:   8

[X] Style...       [ ] Suppress...
[X] Calculate...   [ ] Stretch Vertically
[ ] Comment...     [ ] Float as Band Stretches

          «   OK   »     < Cancel >
```

```
┌ Style ──────────────┐  ┌ Alignment ┐
│ [ ] Bold            │  │ ( ) Left  │
│ [ ] Italic          │  │ ( ) Center│
│ [ ] Underline       │  │ (·) Right │
│ [ ] Superscript     │  └───────────┘
│ [ ] Subscript       │
└─────────────────────┘   «   OK   »
┌ Code ───────────────┐
│ J                   │   < Cancel >
└─────────────────────┘
```

```
Reset:        End of Report

Calculate:   ( ) Nothing
             ( ) Count              «   OK   »
             (·) Sum
             ( ) Average            < Cancel >
             ( ) Lowest
             ( ) Highest
             ( ) Std. Deviation
             ( ) Variance
```

```
═══════════════ Print When ═══════════════
┌ Print Repeated Values ┐
│   ( ) Yes             │     «   OK   »
│   (·) No              │
└───────────────────────┘     < Cancel >
┌ Also Print ──────────────────────────────┐
│ [ ] In First Whole Band of New Page/Col  │
│ [ ] When This Group Changes              │
│ [ ] When Detail Overflows to New Page/Col│
└──────────────────────────────────────────┘

  [ ] Print Only When Expression is True...

  [ ] Remove Line If Blank
```

```
Row:  11  Col:  52
 Field - Full Expression:
      arrepo.over60
      SIZE   1,   8
```

```
Report Expression:

<  Expr...   > arrepo.over60

< Format... >                         Width:   8

[X] Style...      [ ] Suppress...
[X] Calculate... [ ] Stretch Vertically
[ ] Comment...    [ ] Float as Band Stretches

          «   OK   »    < Cancel >
```

```
┌ Style ─────────────┐   ┌ Alignment ┐
 [ ] Bold                ( ) Left
 [ ] Italic              ( ) Center
 [ ] Underline           (·) Right
 [ ] Superscript
 [ ] Subscript
                          «   OK   »
┌ Code ──────────────┐
 J                        < Cancel >
```

```
Reset:         End of Report

Calculate:     ( ) Nothing
               ( ) Count               «   OK   »
               (·) Sum
               ( ) Average             < Cancel >
               ( ) Lowest
               ( ) Highest
               ( ) Std. Deviation
               ( ) Variance
```

```
                  Print When
 Print Repeated Values
    ( ) Yes                          «   OK   »
    (·) No
                                     < Cancel >
 Also Print
  [ ] In First Whole Band of New Page/Col
  [ ] When This Group Changes
  [ ] When Detail Overflows to New Page/Col

  [ ] Print Only When Expression is True...

  [ ] Remove Line If Blank
```

```
Row:  11  Col:  62
 Field - Full Expression:
     arrepo.over90
     SIZE   1,   8
```

```
 Report Expression:

 <  Expr...  > arrepo.over90

 < Format... >                     Width:   8

 [X] Style...       [ ] Suppress...
 [X] Calculate...   [ ] Stretch Vertically
 [ ] Comment...     [ ] Float as Band Stretches

          «   OK   »    < Cancel >
```

```
 Style                    Alignment
 [ ] Bold                 ( ) Left
 [ ] Italic               ( ) Center
 [ ] Underline            (·) Right
 [ ] Superscript
 [ ] Subscript
                          «   OK   »
 Code
 J                        < Cancel >
```

```
Reset:        End of Report

Calculate:    ( ) Nothing
              ( ) Count                 «   OK   »
              (·) Sum
              ( ) Average               < Cancel >
              ( ) Lowest
              ( ) Highest
              ( ) Std. Deviation
              ( ) Variance
```

```
                    Print When
  Print Repeated Values
     ( ) Yes                              «   OK   »
     (·) No
                                          < Cancel >
  Also Print
   [ ] In First Whole Band of New Page/Col
   [ ] When This Group Changes
   [ ] When Detail Overflows to New Page/Col

   [ ] Print Only When Expression is True...

   [ ] Remove Line If Blank
```

```
Row:  11  Col:  72
 Field - Full Expression:
      current+over30+over60+over90
      SIZE   1,   8
```

```
 Report Expression:

 <  Expr...   > current+over30+over

 < Format... >                         Width:   8

 [X] Style...      [ ] Suppress...
 [X] Calculate... [ ] Stretch Vertically
 [ ] Comment...    [ ] Float as Band Stretches

          «   OK   »    < Cancel >
```

```
Style                       Alignment
[ ] Bold                    ( ) Left
[ ] Italic                  ( ) Center
[ ] Underline               (·) Right
[ ] Superscript
[ ] Subscript
                            «   OK   »
Code
J                           < Cancel >
```

```
Reset:          End of Report

Calculate:      ( ) Nothing
                ( ) Count                «   OK   »
                (·) Sum
                ( ) Average              < Cancel >
                ( ) Lowest
                ( ) Highest
                ( ) Std. Deviation
                ( ) Variance
```

```
                    Print When
 Print Repeated Values
    ( ) Yes                              «   OK   »
    (·) No
                                         < Cancel >
 Also Print
 [ ] In First Whole Band of New Page/Col
 [ ] When This Group Changes
 [ ] When Detail Overflows to New Page/Col

 [ ] Print Only When Expression is True...

 [ ] Remove Line If Blank
```

Chapter 17

Reusable Programs

About the Screen Handler: ABOUT.PRG

This program allows the calling of the various ABOUT screens without using multiple READs, and without the flashing that occurs when screens are displayed. It allows the application to have a system name passed to it (to maintain conformity to Codebook 2.0) and sets up a DO WHILE loop to keep calling the various screens beginning with ABOUT.SPR. The EXTERNAL SCREEN command is used to make FoxPro add the proper screens to our project (FoxPro cannot tell that we are using these screens because of the named expression used in calling them). We have to hard code the @...CLEAR command so that we clear everything in the window that is above the pushbuttons.

```
*  Program...........: ABOUT.PRG
*  Author............: yag
*  Project...........: common
*  Created...........: 12/09/92
*  Copyright.........: (c) Flash Creative Management, 1992
*) Description.......: Main control program for ABOUT screens
*)                   : Allows the user to loop through them indefinitely
*  Calling Samples...: DO About WITH Setup.cSystem
*  Parameter List....: lcSystem - Name of application
*  Major change list.:
PARAMETER lcSystem
PRIVATE llEndAbout, lcNext
llEndAbout = .F.
lcNext = "ABOUT.SPR"
EXTERNAL SCREEN About           && Forces their joining in the project
EXTERNAL SCREEN AboutMem
EXTERNAL SCREEN AboutGen
EXTERNAL SCREEN AboutFil
EXTERNAL SCREEN AboutCom
DO WHILE ! llEndAbout
   DO (lcNext)
   IF ! llEndAbout
      DO CASE                   && Clear the about window
         CASE _WINDOWS
            @ 0.530, 0.570 CLEAR TO 12.600, 57.700
         CASE _DOS
            @ 0,0 CLEAR TO 10, 58
      ENDCASE
   ENDIF
ENDDO
RETURN
```

Adding a Window Title to the Menu: ADDBAR.PRG

This program adds a menu bar containing the title of the passed window to the *window* popup. It first checks to see if the window is already visible. If so, it does nothing (the window has been previously defined, and is therefore already listed on the popup). If the window is new, however, it assigns the new bar a bar number by performing a check to see if the last window bar is a native FoxPro menu option (GETBAR() returns a negative number). If it is a FoxPro bar, it uses the bar's position in the popup, otherwise, it uses the number that is one higher than the highest existing menu option.

```
*  Program...........: ADDBAR.PRG
*  Author............: yag
*  Project...........: COMMON
*  Created...........: 04/16/93
*  Copyright.........: (c) Flash Creative Management, 1993
*) Description.......: Auto-add a menu bar to the Window popup
*)                   : Typically called in SETUP of "WR" windows
*)                   :
*)                   : This routine accepts a window name, and
*)                   : adds the *title* of that window.
*  Calling Samples...: =autobar('wrCD')
*  Parameter List....: tcWindName   -   Name of the window
*  Major change list.:
PARAMETER tcWindName
*-- Add the proper BAR to the Window POPUP
IF NOT WVISIBLE(tcWindName)
   IF GETBAR("Window",CNTBAR("Window")) < 0   && At a Fox System BAR
      lnMenuNum = CNTBAR("Window") + 1
   ELSE
      lnMenuNum = GETBAR("Window",CNTBAR("Window")) + 1
   ENDIF
   DEFINE BAR lnMenuNum OF Window  PROMPT WTITLE(tcWindName) AFTER _MLAST
   ON SELECTION BAR lnMenuNum OF Window ACTIVATE Window &tcWindName
ENDIF
RETURN
```

Calculating an Accounts Receivable Aging: ARCOLHED.PRG

This reusable program returns the column headings for a standard A/R Aging Report. It compares the passed invoice date to another date (which defaults to the current date) and returns proper column headings. Note the use of the fact that a developer can pass less parameters than FoxPro is expecting. If only one parameter is passed, this routine will automatically default the second parameter to the current date. This way, the developer doesn't have to always type in two parameters when calling this routine.

```
*  Program...........: ARCOLHED.PRG
*  Author............: yag
*  Project...........: COMMON
*  Created...........: 04/29/1993  16:31:01
*  Copyright.........: (c) Flash Creative Management, 1993
*) Description.......: Returns column headings for an A/R 30/60/90 report
*)                   : Pass it the invoice date and "today's" date and it
*)                   : returns "Current","Over30","Over60","Over90"
*)                   : Note: If "today's" date is *before* the invoice date
*)                   :         this routine will return "Future".
*  Calling Samples...: Typically used as second parameter in SQL SELECT
*                    : that is going into a crosstab.
*  Parameter List....: tdInv   -   Invoice Date
*                    : tdNow   -   Today's Date
*  Major change list.:
PARA tdInv, tdNow
PRIVATE lnNumDays, lcRetVal
IF EMPTY(tdNow)
   tdNow = DATE()
ENDIF
lnNumDays = tdNow - tdInv
DO CASE
   CASE lnNumDays < 0
      lcRetVal = "Future "
   CASE lnNumDays <= 30
      lcRetVal = "Current"
   CASE lnNumDays <= 60
      lcRetVal = "Over30 "
   CASE lnNumDays <= 90
      lcRetVal = "Over60 "
   OTHERWISE
      lcRetVal = "Over90 "
ENDCASE
RETURN lcRetVal
```

Formatting a City, State, Zip Output Field: CSZ.PRG

This function correctly formats a city, state, and zip code for the last line of an address. It is a good example of a simple reusable program that is called in almost every application you may write.

```
*  Program...........: CSZ.PRG
*  Author............: yag
*  Project...........: COMMON
*  Created...........: 12/09/92
*  Copyright.........: (c) Flash Creative Management, 1992
*) Description.......: This function correctly formats a city, state
*)                   : zip line. It handles 5 or 9 character zip codes.
*  Calling Samples...: lcCSZ = CSZ(cCity,cState,cZip)
*  Parameter List....: tcCity  - City
*                    : tcState - State
*                    : tcZip   - Zip Code
*  Major change list.: 1/7/93 yag Modified code for Legibility.
FUNCTION CSZ
PARAMETERS tcCity, tcState, tcZip
PRIVATE jcRetVal, jcZip2
jcRetVal = ALLTRIM(tcCity)
jcRetVal = jcRetVal + ;
           IIF(EMPTY(tcCity), " ", ", ")
jcRetVal = jcRetVal + ;
           tcState + " "
IF LEN(ALLTRIM(tcZip)) = 5
   jcZip2 = ALLTRIM(tcZip)
ELSE
   jcZip2 = LEFT(tcZip,5) + IIF(EMPTY(tcZip)," ","-") + ;
              RIGHT(tcZip,4)
ENDIF
RETURN jcRetVal + jcZip2
```

Multiuser Deletion Check: DELCHECK.PRG

When creating multiuser applications in which you do not keep the record locked while working with it, there is always the possibility that someone else may delete the record that you are working on (or, in a modeless environment, coming back to). This UDF checks to see if the record has been deleted, and if so, alerts the user, and goes to a nearby record.

```
*  Program...........: DELCHECK.PRG
*  Author............: yag
*  Project...........: COMMON
*  Created...........: 05/09/1993  13:01:27
*  Copyright.........: (c) Flash Creative Management, 1993
*) Description.......: Check if current record deleted. If so, go to
*)                   : a new one. Return .T. if not deleted.
*  Calling Samples...: IF NOT DelCheck()
*                    :   RETURN
*)                   : ENDIF
*  Parameter List....:
*  Major change list.:
PRIVATE jlRetVal
IF (IsLocked() OR RLOCK() OR NetLock()) AND DELETED()
   UNLOCK
   ?? CHR(7)
   WAIT WINDOW "This record has already been deleted. Moving to new info.
Press any key..."
   SKIP
   IF EOF()
      SKIP -1
   ENDIF
   SCATTER MEMVAR MEMO
   jlRetVal = .F.
ELSE
   jlRetVal = .T.
ENDIF

RETURN jlRetVal
```

Creating a Cross Tabulation: GENXTAB.PRG

This is a program provided by Microsoft that ships with FoxPro (therefore, it is not replicated here). You will find it in your FoxPro root directory. A description of GENXTAB's behavior can be found in Chapter 8, *Usability Techniques*.

Multiuser Record Insertion: INSREC.PRG

This is a sample of a routine that performs a standard FoxPro command, INSERT INTO. So why not just call the FoxPro INSERT INTO command directly? The FoxPro INSERT INTO command will fail if another user has a file lock or is adding a record at the same split second. Unlike RLOCK(), which returns a value, INSERT INTO (like APPEND BLANK) is a command, and will simply trigger an error message. Our application never does a file lock—therefore we can simply loop until the record can be added.

The more important reason to separate out the data manipulation command is so that we can, if we wish, add more capabilities to this routine at a later date. For instance, if we are using FoxPro's Connectivity Kit and working from server information, this routine could issue an INSERT INTO in the manner that the server expects. Separating out all data manipulation functions in this manner would, theoretically, allow us to switch to a server platform fairly easily, and with minimal code modification.

```
*  Program...........: INSREC.PRG
*  Author............: YAG
*  Project...........: CODEBOOK2.5
*  Created...........: 08/15/1993  17:26:37
*  Copyright.........: (c) Flash Creative Management, 1993
*) Description.......: Does an INSERT INTO while managing all
*)                   : record locking.
*)                   : It defaults to MEMVAR if only a table
*)                   : name is passed.
*)                   : Basically, pass this function everything
*)                   : after the INSERT INTO command. Currently
*)                   : will handle FP-based locking. Can be
*)                   : later modified to handle other back ends.
*  Calling Samples...: =InsRec("Hello")
*                    :   like INSERT INTO Hello FROM MEMVAR
*                    : =InsRec("Hello FROM ARRAY Howdy")
*                    :   like INSERT INTO Hello FROM ARRAY Howdy
*  Parameter List....: tcClause - INSERT INTO clause
*  Major change list.:
PARAMETER tcClause
PRIVATE jcOldErr, jnErrNum
IF AT(" ",ALLTRIM(tcClause)) = 0  && Only tablename passed
   tcClause = tcClause + " FROM MEMVAR"
ENDIF
tcClause = CHRTRAN(tcClause,CHR(9)," ")
jcOldErr = ON("ERROR")
ON ERROR m.jnErrNum=ERROR()
```

```
DO WHILE .T.
   m.jnErrNum=0
   INSERT INTO &tcClause
   DO CASE
     CASE m.jnErrNum = 0
       EXIT
     CASE m.jnErrNum # 108
       IF EMPTY(jcOldErr)
         WAIT WINDOW "Error Detected: " + ;
            MESSAGE() + " Press Any Key..."
         SUSPEND
       ELSE
         &jcOldErr
       ENDIF
     ENDCASE
ENDDO
ON ERROR &jcOldErr
RETURN
```

Checking Record Locking: ISLOCKED.PRG

This function simply checks to see whether or not the user currently has the record locked. It uses the SYS(2011) function, which does the check without releasing any currently active locks. This allows us to bypass a record locking attempt in a reusable piece of code when the lock already has taken place.

```
*  Program...........: ISLOCKED.PRG
*  Author............: YAG
*  Project...........: COMMON
*  Created...........: 08/06/92  12:20:08
*  Copyright.........: (c) Flash Creative Management, 1993
*) Description.......: Checks if a record is already locked
*)                   : We do it as a function in case FoxPro
*)                   : begins returning a different text when
*)                   : locking.
*  Calling Samples...: IF IsLocked() OR RLOCK() OR NetLock()
*  Parameter List....:
*  Major change list.:
RETURN "Locked" $ SYS(2011)
```

Checking for an Index Tag: ISTAG.PRG

This function checks to see whether or not a tag currently exists on a table. An example of its use can be found in the DBFREIND.SPR chapter. In that reusable window, we need to check if a tag called DelRec exists. If not, we can create it.

Note the parameter validity check (using the PARAMETERS() and TYPE() functions) at the beginning of the routine. If the developer forgets to pass a parameter, or passes the wrong type of parameter to IsTag() we RETURN a false.

```
*  Program...........: ISTAG.PRG
*  Author............: Menachem Bazian, CPA
*  Project...........: COMMON
*  Created...........: 04/15/93
*  Copyright.........: (c) Flash Creative Management, 1993
*) Description.......: Looks for a TAG in the CDX file attached to
*)                   : the CURRENTLY OPEN database
*)                   : This UDF very useful when you are not sure
*)                   : whether a tag exists in a .CDX file. Back in the
*)                   : old days we could check for the existence
*)                   : of an index with the FILE() function.
*)                   : Since .CDX tags are all in one
*)                   : file, we need to loop through the
*)                   : tags looking for the tag specified as a
*)                   : parameter.
*)                   :  NOTE: In order for a match to be recorded,
*)                   :        the tag names must match EXACTLY,
*)                   :        character for character. Extra spaces
*)                   :        are trimmed and case is not important.
*  Calling Samples...: ISTAG(<expC>)
*  Parameter List....: tcTagName    -   Name of the TAG to find
*  Major change list.: 11/18/92 by MB to conform to FCM naming conventions
PARAMETER tcTagName
PRIVATE ALL LIKE j*
IF SET("TALK") = 'ON'
   SET TALK OFF
   jcOldTalk = 'ON'
ELSE
   jcOldTalk = 'OFF'
ENDIF
jlRetVal = .f.
IF PARAMETERS()=0 OR TYPE("tcTagName")#'C'
  RETURN .f.
ELSE
  tcTagName = UPPER(ALLTRIM(tcTagName))
ENDIF
jcTagFound = 'NADA'
jnTagNum = 1
DO WHILE !EMPTY(jcTagFound)
  jcTagFound = TAG(jnTagNum)
  IF UPPER(ALLTRIM(jcTagFound)) == tcTagName
    jlRetVal = .t.
    EXIT
  ENDIF
  jnTagNum = jnTagNum + 1
ENDDO
RETURN (jlRetVal)
```

Removing a Window from a Menu: KILLBAR.PRG

KillBar() is the other side of AddBar(). It loops through the prompts of the bars in the Window popup, and compares them to the title of the window that has been passed to it. Once it finds a match, it removes that bar from the popup.

```
*  Program...........: KILLBAR.PRG
*  Author............: yag
*  Project...........: COMMON
*  Created...........: 04/16/93
*  Copyright.........: (c) Flash Creative Management, 1993
*) Description.......: Auto-kill a menu bar in the Window popup
*)                   : Typically called in CLEANUP of "WR" windows
*)                   : when they are going to be removed.
*)                   :
*)                   : This routine accepts a window name, and
*)                   : removes the *title* of that window.
*  Calling Samples...: =killbar('wrCD')
*  Parameter List....: tcWindName   -   The window that should be removed
*  Major change list.:
PARAMETER tcWindName
FOR i = CNTBAR("Window") TO 1 STEP -1
   IF PRMBAR("Window",GETBAR("Window",i)) = WTITLE(tcWindName)
      RELEASE BAR GETBAR("Window",i) OF Window
      EXIT
   ENDIF
ENDFOR
RETURN
```

Removing a Window from the Screen: KILLWIND.PRG

KillWind() is called from the CLEANUP code of "WR" windows. It removes all windows associated with the "WR" window. Note the FOR loop that checks for multiwindow screen sets, removing all windows until it finds none left, at which point it exits.

```
*  Program...........: KILLWIND.PRG
*  Author............: yag
*  Project...........: COMMON
*  Created...........: 04/16/93
*  Copyright.........: (c) Flash Creative Management, 1993
*) Description.......: Removes a "WR" window and all associated windows.
*)                   : Typically called in CLEANUP of "WR" windows
*)                   : when they are going to be removed.
*  Calling Samples...: =killwind('wrCD')
*  Parameter List....: tcWindName   -   The window that should be removed
*  Major change list.:
PARAMETER tcWindName
PRIVATE lcWindName, i
RELEASE WINDOW (tcWindName)
*-- Check for "WT" version of the window
*-- Only changes the first found "wr"
lcWindName = STRTRAN(tcWindName,"wr","wt",1,1)
IF WEXIST(lcWindName)
   RELEASE WINDOW (lcWindName)
ENDIF
FOR i = 1 TO 9
   lcWindName = tcWindName - STR(i,1)
   IF WEXIST(lcWindName)
      RELEASE WINDOW (lcWindName)
   ELSE
      EXIT
   ENDIF
ENDFOR
DO efface
```

Standard Toolbar Behavior: METHODS.PRG

Methods is the program that contains our standard methods for our toolbar and base window functions. Methods consists of a number of procedures that control the default behavior of our application windows. The default methods contained in this program are for single dbf entry windows since these windows tend to occur multiple times in an application, and the routines that handle them form the base of most one-to-many entry windows.

Initit() is the routine called when <Add> is selected by the user. It initializes the current window's memory variables.

Addit() is called when <Save> is selected after the user finishes adding a new item. It uses the NetID() function to create a new unique ID for the item and saves that ID in both the cID field (which will never change) and the cLastUpd semaphore field (which changes as people use the record). It then uses the INSERT INTO command to add the information. Note that the INSERT INTO (a SQL command) is faster on a network than the older APPEND BLANK/GATHER MEMVAR combination.

EditIt() is the method used when the user selects <Edit>. It first checks to see if the record was deleted by another user. If so, it returns a message to the user (in the DelCheck() function) and returns in non-edit mode. If the record still exists, it then attempts to lock the record. Note the use of the line

```
IF RLOCK() OR NetLock()
```

We attempt to lock the record using the native FoxPro function. If the lock is not granted, we move into our NetLock() function, which allows the user to keep trying the lock for thirty seconds. If the lock is granted, FoxPro never evaluates the right side of the OR statement (because the left side is true). Once the record lock is achieved, we SCATTER to memory variables, forcing the screen to be updated with the most current information. Remember, until we have a record lock, we don't necessarily have the most current information. We then UNLOCK the record and set glEditable to true, allowing the user to edit the memory variables.

CopyIt() is a method that allows the record information that the user is currently looking at to be duplicated with a new unique ID. We ask the user to confirm the copy, and then get a new unique ID and add the record. Note the lack of a lock on the record. This is a design decision. The user is looking at a certain piece of information that they wish to duplicate. The current record they are looking at may have been changed by someone else, but that is not what the user wishes to duplicate. Therefore, we *do not* get the most recent information, choosing instead to duplicate what the user sees.

SaveIt() is the routine that saves edited information. It locks the record and then checks the semaphore. If the semaphore has changed (meaning that someone else has modified the record) it asks if the user wants to overwrite those changes. If not, it SCATTERs the other users changes and shows the new information. If the user wishes to overwrite the changes, it puts in a new semaphore in cLastUpd and saves the information.

Note the use of the fact that FoxPro only checks as much of an IF statement as is necessary. The line:

```
cLastUpd # m.cLastUpd AND !AreUSure(jcErrMsg)
```

checks to see if the semaphore field has changed. If it hasn't (the two values are equal), then FoxPro never runs the AreUSure() screen function. Since we are using an AND to connect them, once the left side is shown to be false, there is no need to evaluate the right side of the IF statement.

OopsIt() is a function that simply resets all memory variables when the user selects to cancel the current edits.

DeleteIt() deletes the current record. It checks to see if the record has already been deleted. If not, it goes to the next record, and saves it (so that it has a record to go to after the delete). We then lock the record and ask the user if they want to delete it with the DelRec screen function. Next, we make sure the the data is current, and if not we give the user one last chance to cancel the delete function. Finally, we delete the record and go to the next record, showing the user that information.

Note the use of the line:

```
jnNextRec = IIF(EOF(),-1,RECNO())
```

We check to make sure that we aren't at EOF(). If we are, we flag it with a -1, so that we can act appropriately when moving the record pointer.

FindIt() is a base method that allows a simple search for information.

NextIt(), *PriorIt()*, *TopIt()* and *BottomIt()* simply move the record pointer to the appropriate record. The reason we use these as methods is that it allows us to override the actions on a window by window basis (in case we have a custom approach to moving the record pointer). Note the use of LOCATE for the TopIt() method. LOCATE is faster than a GO TOP in FoxPro 2.x.

CloseIt() sets our glQuitting variable to true, queueing our exit from the current window, and CLEARs the current READ.

ListIt() is a method that uses BROWSE to show a list of our current window's information. Note that BROWSE is used here because a BROWSE window's behavior (which is unlike that of any FoxPro window) works to our advantage. We are creating a pick list, allowing our users to select an item. By default, a BROWSE window closes if you click on any other window. This is the exact behavior that we would like from a pick list. Therefore, we can use BROWSE.

The routine saves the current record number in case the user escapes out of the BROWSE. It then checks to see if we have data driven our BROWSE by creating and filling in the TablDict DBF. We use the LOOKUP() function to find the current alias in the TablDict. Note that the fourth parameter (which turns the LOOKUP() into a SEEK, speeding things up) is not used. The TablDict DBF has no indices attached, but is small, so a LOCATE should be fast enough. If you wish to speed up this routine, simply add an index called cAlias to the cAlias field in TablDict and add "cAlias" as the fourth parameter to the LOOKUP() function.

The routine continues by creating the BROWSE command, and adding a factor to handle a large font in Windows. We then DEFINE the WINDOW with a AT...SIZE clause instead of the FROM...TO clause (this is cleaner in Windows) and MOVE the window to the center of the screen (in this way, we don't care what video mode the user is currently using). We continue by KEYBOARDing a dummy character. This is necessary so that LASTKEY() will not be 27 (Escape) in case the user selected <Cancel> (which is mapped to an escape key) before clicking on <List>.

We use ON KEY LABEL to set the <Enter> key as a key that will close the BROWSE and finally call the BROWSE. Once the BROWSE ends, we reset the <Enter> key, and if the user didn't escape out, we SCATTER MEMVAR MEMO to show the user the selected information.

EnableIt() is the function that is called to enable all of the fields in the current entry windows. It performs a SHOW GETS WINDOW to enable the current window, and then loops through the numbers one through nine, and if a window with the same name as the main one ending with a number exists, it enables that window as well. In this way, we can have up to ten window screen sets automatically enabled. Note that the routine counts from one to nine, and once a window is not found, it exits, enhancing the application's speed. We then add "li" to the name of the window and DISABLE that button. The "li" button can be used to bring the focus to a window that is totally disabled. An example of this can be found in the CD window.

DisableIt() is the reverse of EnableIt(). It disables all current windows and enables the invisible button.

For more information on the uses of the Methods approach, see Chapter 5, *Toolbars and Object-Oriented Programming*.

```
*  Program...........: METHODS.PRG
*  Author............: yag
*  Project...........: COMMON
*  Created...........: 01/17/93
*  Copyright.........: (c) Flash Creative Management, 1993
*) Description.......: This program instantiates all of the
*)                   : METHODS that will be called by the different
*)                   : tools in the toolbar. To put it in plain
*)                   : English: this file contains the default
*)                   : procedures for the input screens.
*  Calling Samples...: Typically "MAIN" program in project
*  Parameter List....:
*  Major change list.:
DO Traficop          && Run the application
RETURN
*---------
* Toolbar Methods Begin Here
*---------
************************************************
PROCEDURE INITIT
************************************************
*) Procedure.........: INITIT
*  Author............: yag
*  Project...........: COMMON
*  Created...........: 12/09/92
*  Copyright.........: (c) Flash Creative Management, 1992
*) Description.......: PROCEDURE InitIt
*)                   : Initializes variables for a window
*  Calling Samples...: DO InitIt
*  Parameter List....:
*  Major change list.:

SCATTER MEMVAR MEMO BLANK
RETURN
************************************************
PROCEDURE ADDIT
************************************************
*) Procedure.........: ADDIT
*  Author............: yag
*  Project...........: COMMON
*  Created...........: 12/09/92
*  Copyright.........: (c) Flash Creative Management, 1992
*) Description.......: PROCEDURE AddIt
*)                   : Called when "SAVE" selected after "ADD"
*)                   : Performs necessary saving
*  Calling Samples...: DO AddIt
*  Parameter List....:
*  Major change list.: Changed code to use INSERT INTO - Faster on a network
m.cID = NetID()
m.cLastUpd = m.cID
=InsRec("(ALIAS()) FROM MEMVAR")
glRestEdit = .F.
RETURN
************************************************
PROCEDURE EDITIT
************************************************
*) Procedure.........: EDITIT
*  Author............: yag
*  Project...........: COMMON
```

```
*  Created...........: 12/09/92
*  Copyright.........: (c) Flash Creative Management, 1992
*) Description.......: PROCEDURE EditIt
*)                   : Called when "EDIT" pressed
*  Calling Samples...: DO EditIt
*  Parameter List....:
*  Major change list.:
IF ! DelCheck()
   glEditable = .F.
   RETURN
ENDIF
IF IsLocked() OR RLOCK() OR NetLock()
   SCATTER MEMVAR MEMO             && Refresh GETs
   UNLOCK
   _CUROBJ = 1
   glEditable = .T.
ELSE
   glEditable = .F.
ENDIF
RETURN
************************************************
PROCEDURE COPYIT
************************************************
*) Procedure.........: COPYIT
*  Author............: yag
*  Project...........: COMMON
*  Created...........: 12/09/92
*  Copyright.........: (c) Flash Creative Management, 1992
*) Description.......: PROCEDURE CopyIt
*)                   : Called when "Copy" selected
*  Calling Samples...: DO CopyIt
*  Parameter List....:
*  Major change list.:
IF AreUSure("Are you sure that you want to duplicate this information?")
   m.cID=NetID()                           && Get new unique ID
   m.cLastUpd = m.cID
   =InsRec("(ALIAS()) FROM MEMVAR")
ENDIF
RETURN
************************************************
PROCEDURE SAVEIT
************************************************
*) Procedure.........: SAVEIT
*  Author............: yag
*  Project...........: COMMON
*  Created...........: 12/09/92
*  Copyright.........: (c) Flash Creative Management, 1992
*) Description.......: PROCEDURE SaveIt
*)                   : Called when "SAVE" selected after "EDIT". Performs
*)                   : necessary saving.
*  Calling Samples...: DO SaveIt
*  Parameter List....:
*  Major change list.:
PRIVATE jcErrMsg
jcErrMsg = "Someone has modified this data. Do you want to save " + ;
           "your changes anyway? Doing so will destroy the other " + ;
           "person's changes. "
IF (IsLocked() OR RLOCK() OR NetLock()) AND DelCheck()
   IF cLastUpd # m.cLastUpd AND !AreUSure(jcErrMsg)
```

```
      WAIT WINDOW "Refreshing Other User's Changes..." TIMEOUT 2
      SCATTER MEMVAR MEMO
      glOKToSave = .F.
   ELSE
      m.cLastUpd = NetID()
      GATHER MEMVAR MEMO
      glOKToSave = .T.
      glRestEdit = .F.
   ENDIF
ENDIF
UNLOCK
RETURN
***********************************************
PROCEDURE OOPSIT
***********************************************
*) Procedure.........: OOPSIT
*  Author............: yag
*  Project...........: COMMON
*  Created...........: 12/09/92
*  Copyright.........: (c) Flash Creative Management, 1992
*) Description.......: PROCEDURE OopsIt
*)                   : Called when "OOPS!" selected. Performs necessary
*)                   : reset.
*  Calling Samples...: DO OopsIt
*  Parameter List....:
*  Major change list.:

SCATTER MEMVAR MEMO
glRestEdit = .F.
RETURN
***********************************************
PROCEDURE DELETEIT
***********************************************
*) Procedure.........: DELETEIT
*  Author............: yag
*  Project...........: COMMON
*  Created...........: 12/09/92
*  Copyright.........: (c) Flash Creative Management, 1992
*) Description.......: PROCEDURE DeleteIt
*)                   : Called when "DELETE" selected from the menu
*)                   : Checks to see if the user *really* wants to delete,
*)                   : then does it.
*  Calling Samples...: DO DeleteIt
*  Parameter List....:
*  Major change list.:

PRIVATE jnNextRec
IF ! DelCheck()
   RETURN
ENDIF
*-- Save next record before delete
SKIP
jnNextRec = IIF(EOF(),-1,RECNO())
SKIP -1
IF (IsLocked() OR RLOCK() OR NetLock()) AND DelRec()
   jcErrMsg = "Someone has modified this data. Do you want to delete " + ;
              "this information anyway? Doing so will destroy the other " + ;
              "person's changes. "
   IF cLastUpd # m.cLastUpd AND !AreUSure(jcErrMsg)
```

```
      WAIT WINDOW TIMEOUT 2 "Refreshing Other User's Changes..."
      SCATTER MEMVAR MEMO
   ELSE
      DELETE
      UNLOCK
      IF jnNextRec = -1                             && Go to next record
         GO BOTTOM
      ELSE
         GO jnNextRec
      ENDIF
      SCATTER MEMVAR MEMO
      WAIT WINDOW NOWAIT "Information Deleted"
   ENDIF
ENDIF
RETURN
**********************************************
PROCEDURE FINDIT
**********************************************
*) Procedure.........: FINDIT
*  Author............: yag
*  Project...........: COMMON
*  Created...........: 12/09/92
*  Copyright.........: (c) Flash Creative Management, 1992
*) Description.......: PROCEDURE FindIt
*)                   : Called when "FIND" selected
*  Calling Samples...: DO FindIt
*  Parameter List....:
*  Major change list.:
DO AppSrch.spr
SCATTER MEMVAR MEMO
RETURN
**********************************************
PROCEDURE NEXTIT
**********************************************
*) Procedure.........: NEXTIT
*  Author............: yag
*  Project...........: COMMON
*  Created...........: 12/09/92
*  Copyright.........: (c) Flash Creative Management, 1992
*) Description.......: PROCEDURE NextIt
*)                   : Default for <next>
*  Calling Samples...: DO NextIt
*  Parameter List....:
*  Major change list.:

SKIP
SCATTER MEMVAR MEMO
RETURN
**********************************************
PROCEDURE PRIORIT
**********************************************
*) Procedure.........: PRIORIT
*  Author............: yag
*  Project...........: COMMON
*  Created...........: 12/09/92
*  Copyright.........: (c) Flash Creative Management, 1992
*) Description.......: PROCEDURE PriorIt
*)                   : Default for Prior
*  Calling Samples...: DO PriorIt
```

```
*  Parameter List....:
*  Major change list.:

SKIP -1
SCATTER MEMVAR MEMO
RETURN
**********************************************
PROCEDURE BOTTOMIT
**********************************************
*) Procedure.........: BOTTOMIT
*  Author............: yag
*  Project...........: COMMON
*  Created...........: 12/09/92
*  Copyright.........: (c) Flash Creative Management, 1992
*) Description.......: PROCEDURE BottomIt
*)                   : Default for <Bottom>
*  Calling Samples...: DO BottomIt
*  Parameter List....:
*  Major change list.:

GO BOTTOM
SCATTER MEMVAR MEMO
**********************************************
PROCEDURE TOPIT
**********************************************
*) Procedure.........: TOPIT
*  Author............: yag
*  Project...........: COMMON
*  Created...........: 12/09/92
*  Copyright.........: (c) Flash Creative Management, 1992
*) Description.......: PROCEDURE TopIt
*)                   : Default for <Top>
*  Calling Samples...: DO TopIt
*  Parameter List....:
*  Major change list.:

LOCATE                     && Faster than GO TOP
SCATTER MEMVAR MEMO
RETURN
**********************************************
PROCEDURE CLOSEIT
**********************************************
*) Procedure.........: CLOSEIT
*  Author............: yag
*  Project...........: COMMON
*  Created...........: 12/09/92
*  Copyright.........: (c) Flash Creative Management, 1992
*) Description.......: PROCEDURE CloseIt
*)                   : Default for <CLOSE>
*  Calling Samples...: DO CloseIt
*  Parameter List....:
*  Major change list.:

glQuitting = .T.
CLEAR READ
RETURN
**********************************************
PROCEDURE LISTIT
**********************************************
*) Procedure.........: LISTIT
```

```
*  Author............: yag
*  Project...........: COMMON
*  Created...........: 12/09/92
*  Copyright.........: (c) Flash Creative Management, 1992
*) Description.......: PROCEDURE ListIt
*)                   : Called when "LIST" selected. Performs necessary
*)                   : BROWSE code, including setup of {ENTER} as
*)                   : selection key.
*  Calling Samples...: DO ListIt
*  Parameter List....:
*  Major change list.:

PRIVATE jnOldRec, jcBrowse
jnOldRec = RECNO()
jcBrowse = ""
IF !USED("TablDict")
   IF FILE("TABLDICT.DBF")
      USE TablDict IN SELECT(1)
   ENDIF
ENDIF
IF USED("TablDict")
   jcBrowse = LOOKUP(TablDict.mBrowse,ALIAS(),TablDict.cAlias)
ENDIF
IF EMPTY(jcBrowse)
   jcBrowse = "BROWSE NORMAL TITLE 'Complete Listing' NOAPPEND" + ;
              " NODELETE NOEDIT WINDOW wBrowse "
   jnWindSize = 60
ELSE
   jcBrowse = jcBrowse + " NORMAL TITLE 'Complete Listing' " + ;
              " NOAPPEND NODELETE NOEDIT WINDOW wBrowse "
   jnWindSize = TablDict.nBrowSize
ENDIF
DO CASE
   CASE _WINDOWS
      jnWindSize = jnWindSize * 1.2      && To handle larger font
ENDCASE
DEFINE WINDOW wBrowse AT 0,0 SIZE 10,jnWindSize ;
     CLOSE ZOOM SYSTEM FLOAT GROW ;
     FONT "MS Sans Serif",8 STYLE "B"
MOVE WINDOW wBrowse CENTER
*-- We PUSH the MENU here due to a Fox/Win bug
*-- that causes a duplicate menu to appear
*-- this doesn't resolve it, but the menu gets
*-- reset after the BROWSE
PUSH MENU _MSYSMENU
KEYBOARD Chr(0)       && To clear out LASTKEY()
PUSH KEY CLEAR
ON KEY LABEL ENTER KEYBOARD "{CTRL+W}" PLAIN
&jcBrowse
ON KEY LABEL ENTER
POP KEY
POP MENU _MSYSMENU
RELEASE WINDOW wBrowse
IF LASTKEY() # 27
   SCATTER MEMVAR MEMO
ELSE
   GO jnOldRec
ENDIF
RETURN
```

```
***********************************************
PROCEDURE ENABLEIT
***********************************************
*) Procedure.........: ENABLEIT
*  Author............: yag
*  Project...........: COMMON
*  Created...........: 12/09/92
*  Copyright.........: (c) Flash Creative Management, 1992
*) Description.......: PROCEDURE EnableIt
*)                   : Default ENABLE routine. Called when glEditable
*  Calling Samples...: DO ENABLEIT
*  Parameter List....:
*  Major change list.:
PRIVATE jnWindCnt, jcOthWind

SHOW GETS WINDOW (lcReadWind) ENABLE ONLY && no need to rerun READ SHOW
FOR jnWindCnt = 1 TO 9
   jcOthWind = lcReadWind - STR(jnWindCnt,1)
   IF WEXIST(jcOthWind)
      SHOW GETS WINDOW (jcOthWind) ENABLE ONLY
   ELSE
      EXIT
   ENDIF
ENDFOR
RETURN
***********************************************
PROCEDURE DISABLEIT
***********************************************
*) Procedure.........: DISABLEIT
*  Author............: yag
*  Project...........: COMMON
*  Created...........: 12/09/92
*  Copyright.........: (c) Flash Creative Management, 1992
*) Description.......: PROCEDURE DisableIt
*)                   : Default DISABLE routine. Called when !glEditable
*  Calling Samples...: DO DISABLEIT
*  Parameter List....:
*  Major change list.:
PRIVATE jcOthWind, jnWindCnt
SHOW GETS WINDOW (lcReadWind) DISABLE
SHOW GET ('li' + SUBSTR(lcReadWind,3)) ENABLE
FOR jnWindCnt = 1 TO 9
jcOthWind = lcReadWind - STR(jnWindCnt,1)
   IF WEXIST(jcOthWind)
      SHOW GETS WINDOW (jcOthWind) DISABLE
      SHOW GET ('li' + SUBSTR(jcOthWind,3)) ENABLE
   ELSE
      EXIT
   ENDIF
ENDFOR
RETURN
```

Multiuser Incrementing of Unique IDs: NETID.PRG

NetId is a program that contains all of the subroutines for creating a new unique ID. It contains a few techniques that bear further examination. First, it declares four default values at the top of the file. This allows a future developer to modify them easily, or, better yet, to place them as parameters to the program, keeping these values as defaults.

Also note the routine to turn a number into a base 207 character. Base 207 is used because it allows us to compress more information into less characters, and yet doesn't use any of the low or high ASCII characters that can be difficult to debug (for instance, CHR(7) rings the PC bell).

```
*  Program...........: NETID.PRG
*  Author............: Bill House
*  Project...........: COMMON
*  Created...........: 04/16/93  12:53:15
*  Copyright.........: (c) Flash Creative Management, 1993
*) Description.......: Driver for ID generation. Uses no network I/O
*  Calling Samples...: m.cID = NetID()
*  Parameter List....:
*  Major change list.:
* gcSession       - Login session ID number generated by Next207().
*                Set in TRAFICOP()
* lnPlaces       - Time resolution for IDs. 0-3 (seconds to milliseconds).
* lnCodeLen     - Time code length
* lnDCodeLen     - Day code length
* ldSeedDate    - Day to start counting days from using Julian daynumbers
ldSeedDate    = {01/01/80} && Set day to start counting from
lnPlaces      = 2 && Set time resolution to 1/100th of a second
lnCodeLen     = 3 && Set time code length
lnDCodeLen    = 2 && Set day code length
PRIVATE lcResult
lcResult = gcSession + ;
        Dec2B207(VAL(SYS(1))-VAL(SYS(11,ldSeedDate)),lnDCodeLen) + ;
           Dec2B207(TimeNum(lnPlaces),lnCodeLen)
RETURN lcResult
*----------------------------------------------------------------------
**********************************************
FUNCTION Dec2B207
**********************************************
*) Function..........: Dec2B207
*  Author............: Bill House
*  Project...........: COMMON
*  Created...........: 04/16/93  13:09:17
*  Copyright.........: (c) Flash Creative Management, 1993
*) Description.......: Converts a number or numeric string tnParm
*)                   : into base 207 code. Left pads the result with
*)                   : "0" chars to the length of param tnLen.
*  Calling Samples...: lcCode = Dec2B207(lcNum,lnLen)
*  Parameter List....: tnParm - number to be converted
*                    : tnLen  - left-pad with "0" to this length if needed
*  Major change list.:
PARAMETERS tnParm, tnLen
PRIVATE lnPower, lcArray, i, lcResult
```

```
* Convert to number if char parameter
IF TYPE("tnParm") = "C"
  tnParm = VAL(tnParm)
ENDIF
* Size and declare work buffer
STORE 1 TO lnPower
DO WHILE tnParm / 207^lnPower >= 1
  lnPower = lnPower + 1
ENDDO
DECLARE lcArray[lnPower]
* Convert decimal to base 207 number
FOR i = lnPower TO 2 step -1
  lcArray[i] = INT( tnParm / 207^(i-1))
  tnParm = tnParm - (lcArray[i] * 207^(i-1))
  lcArray[i] = CHR(48+lcArray[i])
ENDFOR
lcArray[1] = CHR(48+tnParm)
* Initialize and build result variable
lcResult = ''
FOR i = lnPower TO 1 step -1
  lcResult = lcResult + lcArray[i]
ENDFOR
* Format returned result
RETURN PADL(lcResult,tnLen,'0')
*-----------------------------------------------------------------------
**********************************************
FUNCTION TimeNum
**********************************************
*) Function..........: TimeNum
*  Author............: Bill House
*  Project...........: COMMON
*  Created...........: 04/16/93  13:13:14
*  Copyright.........: (c) Flash Creative Management, 1993
*) Description.......: Returns seconds since midnight as a code
*)                   : with no decimal. If 200.123 seconds has
*)                   : passed and TimeNum(2) is called,
*)                   : 20012 will be returned.
*  Calling Samples...: ? TimeNum(2)
*  Parameter List....: tnPlaces   -   # of places to be moved
*  Major change list.:
PARAMETER tnPlaces
PRIVATE lcResult
lcResult = LTRIM(STR(SECONDS(),10,3))
IF tnPlaces = 0
  lcResult = LEFT(lcResult,AT('.',lcResult)-1)
ELSE
  IF tnPlaces > 3
    tnPlaces = 3
  ENDIF
  lcResult = SUBS(lcResult,1,AT('.',lcResult)-1)+;
           SUBS(lcResult,AT('.',lcResult)+1,tnPlaces)
ENDIF
RETURN lcResult
```

Record Locking: NETLOCK.PRG

NetLock is a routine that handles record locking in a simple manner. It tries locking a record for up to thirty seconds and asks the user if they want to keep on trying. Note that we give the user a running counter of the number of seconds left in the attempt, so that they know that something is happening, and also can determine if they have waited long enough.

```
*  Program...........: NETLOCK.PRG
*  Author............: yag
*  Project...........: COMMON
*  Created...........: 04/02/1992  03:12:24
*  Copyright.........: (c) Flash Creative Management, 1993
*) Description.......: Simple Record locking routine. Tries for 30
*)                   : seconds, then asks if the user wants to try
*)                   : again.
*  Calling Samples...: IF RLOCK() OR NetLock()
*  Parameter List....:
*  Major change list.:
PRIVATE ALL LIKE j*
jcMessage = "Waiting for another user to release their lock"
jlRetVal = .F.
IF RLOCK()
   jlRetVal = .T.
ELSE
   DO WHILE .T.
      jnSecs = 30
      DO WHILE jnSecs > 0 AND LASTKEY() # 27
         WAIT WINDOW jcMessage + " - " + STR(jnSecs,2,0) NOWAIT
         =INKEY(1)          && Wait one second
         IF RLOCK()
            jlRetVal = .T.
            EXIT
         ENDIF
         IF LASTKEY() = 27
            EXIT
         ENDIF
         jnSecs = jnSecs - 1
      ENDDO
      IF AreUSure("Cannot get lock. Try again?")
         LOOP
      ENDIF
      EXIT
   ENDDO
ENDIF
WAIT CLEAR
RETURN jlRetVal
```

Compressing Unique IDs: NEXT207.PRG

This routine increments a field to a new base 207 number and returns the resulting number. This routine is called when the user begins using the system, and gives the unique session ID.

```
*  Program...........: NEXT207.PRG
*  Author............: Bill House
*  Project...........: COMMON
*  Created...........: 04/16/93  13:02:02
*  Copyright.........: (c) Flash Creative Management, 1993
*) Description.......: Increments a field as a base 207 number
*)                   : and returns the result.
*  Calling Samples...: gcSession = Next207("Setup","Session_ID")
*  Parameter List....: lcSysAlias   -   ALIAS of incremented field
*                    : lcSysFld     -   Name of incremented field
*  Major change list.:
PARAMETERS lcSysAlias, lcSysFld

PRIVATE lcOldAlias, lnKeyLen, lcResult
STORE ALIAS() TO lcOldAlias
SELECT (lcSysAlias)
* Obtain lock on system record
IF IsLocked() OR RLOCK() OR NetLock()
  STORE LEN(&lcSysFld) TO lnKeyLen
  STORE &lcSysFld TO lcResult
  * Test variable and init to 0s if full, or if empty
  IF OCCURS(CHR(255),lcResult) = lnKeyLen .OR. lcResult = SPACE(lnKeyLen)
    lcResult = REPLICATE("0",lnKeyLen)
  ELSE
    * Increment Result variable
    FOR I = lnKeyLen TO 1 STEP -1
      IF SUBS( lcResult, I, 1) < CHR(255)
        lcResult = STUFF(lcResult, I, 1, CHR( ASC( SUBS( lcResult, I, 1) ) + 1 ) )
        EXIT
      ELSE
        lcResult = STUFF(lcResult, I, 1, "0")
      ENDIF
    ENDFOR
  ENDIF
  * Save results and unlock
  REPLACE (lcSysFld) WITH lcResult
  UNLOCK
ELSE
  * Set Result to error code
  lcResult = "ERROR"
ENDIF
SELECT (lcOldAlias)
RETURN lcResult
```

Data-Driven Table Opening: OPENDB.PRG

This routine opens all appropriate application tables. It is a simple example of data driven design. If the file TablDict exists, it is used to determine what files are opened. If not, all data files in the current directory are opened. Note the use of the #DEFINE precompiler directives to make the use of array handling easier for the maintenance programmer. Instead of seeing laTables[i,1], the developer sees laTables[i,dcDbfName], showing that we are working with the array column that contains the DBF file's name.

Note the use of SYS(2011) in the TablOpen() function. This SYS() function checks whether the current user has the table in shared or exclusive mode and is used so that we only reopen the table if we don't currently have it in the correct state.

```
*  Program...........: OPENDB.PRG
*  Author............: yag
*  Project...........: COMMON
*  Created...........: 06/02/1992
*  Copyright.........: (c) Flash Creative Management, 1993
*) Description.......: Opens all tables in an application.
*)                   : If TABLDICT exists, it uses that to decide
*)                   : what files will be opened. Otherwise, it
*)                   : does an ADIR() and opens files there.
*)                   : Note, it does no checking to assure that you
*)                   : have enough FILES= or workareas.
*)                   : Also note that it always opens SETUP, ONERROR,
*)                   : and Security.
*  Calling Samples...: DO OpenDb
*  Parameter List....: tcMode -  SHARED/EXCLUSIVE
*                    :           Only first letter used.
*                    :           Defaults to SHARED.
*                    : tcFile -  File name for a specific
*                    :           table.
*                    : tcAlias - Alias for a specific table.
*                    : tcOrder - Order for a specific table.
*  Major change list.:
PARAMETER tcMode, tcFile, tcAlias, tcOrder
PRIVATE jcOldExact, jcOldError, jlNoError
WAIT WINDOW NOWAIT "Opening data files..."
jcOldExact = SET("EXACT")
SET EXACT OFF
jlNoError = .T.
jcOldError = ON("ERROR")
ON ERROR jlNoError = .F.
DO CASE
   CASE PARAMETER() < 1
      tcMode = 'SHARED'
      STORE "" TO tcFile, tcAlias, tcOrder
   CASE PARAMETER() = 2
      tcAlias = tcFile
      tcOrder = ""
   CASE PARAMETER() = 3
      tcOrder = ""
```

```
ENDCASE
*-- Check out the passed parameters
IF UPPER(tcMode) = 'E'
   tcMode = "EXCLUSIVE"
ELSE
   tcMode = 'SHARED'
ENDIF
IF EMPTY(tcFile)
   RELEASE laTables                && Just in case
   PRIVATE i
   #DEFINE dcDbfName   1
   #DEFINE dcAlias      2
   #DEFINE dcInitOrder   3
   IF FILE("TablDict.dbf")
      SELECT cDbfName, cAlias, cInitOrder ;
         FROM TablDict ;
         INTO ARRAY laTables
   ELSE
      _TALLY = ADIR(laInitTable,"*.DBF")
      IF _TALLY # 0
         DIMENSION laTables[_TALLY,3]
         FOR i = 1 TO ALEN(laInitTable,1)
            laTables[i,dcDbfName] = laInitTable[i,1]
            laTables[i,dcAlias]   = STRIPEXT(laInitTable[i,1])
            laTables[i,dcInitOrder] = ""
         ENDFOR
      ENDIF
   ENDIF
   IF _TALLY = 0
      ?? CHR(7)
      WAIT WINDOW "No files found. Press any key..."
      RETURN
   ENDIF
   FOR i = 1 TO ALEN(laTables,1)
      =TablOpen( ;
         TRIM(laTables[i,dcDbfName]), ;
         TRIM(laTables[i,dcAlias]), ;
         TRIM(laTables[i,dcInitOrder]), ;
         tcMode )
   ENDFOR
   =TablOpen("Setup","Setup","",tcMode)
   =TablOpen("OnError","OnError","",tcMode)
   =TablOpen("Security","Security","cMenuID",tcMode)
   IF USED("Security")
      SET FILTER TO cUSERID = m.gcUserID
   ENDIF
   *-- Set up cursor for window tracking
   IF !USED("SaveStat")
      CREATE CURSOR SaveStat ;
         (cWindow C(10), mMemvars M(10), cSaveID C(9), ;
         cOldAlias C(10), cOldOrder C(10) )
   ENDIF
ELSE
      =TablOpen(tcFile,tcAlias,tcOrder,tcMode)
ENDIF
IF jcOldExact = "ON"
   SET EXACT ON
ELSE
   SET EXACT OFF
ENDIF
```

```
ON ERROR &jcOldError
WAIT CLEAR
RETURN jlNoError
*********************************************
PROCEDURE tablopen
*********************************************
*) Procedure.........: tablopen
*  Author............: YAG
*  Project...........: CODEBOOK2.5
*  Created...........: 08/12/1993  12:42:29
*  Copyright.........: (c) Flash Creative Management, 1993
*) Description.......:
*  Calling Samples...:
*  Parameter List....:
*  Major change list.:
PARAMETER tcTable, tcAlias, tcOrder, tcOpenMode
IF USED(tcAlias)
   SELECT (tcAlias)
   IF tcOpenMode = 'EXCLUSIVE' AND SYS(2011) # "Exclusive"
      USE (tcTable) ;
         ALIAS (tcAlias) ;
         EXCLUSIVE
   ENDIF
   IF tcOpenMode = 'SHARED' AND SYS(2011) = "Exclusive"
      USE (tcTable) ;
         ALIAS (tcAlias) ;
         SHARED
   ENDIF
   SET ORDER TO (tcOrder)
ELSE
   USE (tcTable) AGAIN ;
      ALIAS (tcAlias) ;
      IN 0 ;
      ORDER (tcOrder) ;
      &tcOpenMode
ENDIF
SELECT (tcAlias)
RETURN
```

Variable State Restoring: RESTMEM.PRG

RestMem() restores our saved state information when we enter a previously exited window. It checks the SaveStat cursor to see if there is a record that contains the current window name. If so, it knows that the user was in the midst of an edit when they left the window, and restores everything to its original state. Note that we check to see if the record we left was deleted by another user, and if so, alert the current user.

```
*  Program...........: RESTMEM.PRG
*  Author............: YAG
*  Project...........: CODEBOOK2.5
*  Created...........: 06/06/93  05:06:45
*  Copyright.........: (c) Flash Creative Management, 1993
*) Description.......: Restores memvars saved in SaveStat Cursor
*  Calling Samples...: DO RestMem
*  Parameter List....: tcWindow - Window whose memvars should be restored
*  Major change list.:
PARAMETER tcWindow
PRIVATE jcSaveAlias, jcSaveOrder, jcSaveID
jcSaveAlias = ALIAS()
jcSaveOrder = ORDER()
SELECT SaveStat
LOCATE FOR UPPER(SaveStat.cWindow) = UPPER(m.tcWindow)
IF FOUND()
   RESTORE FROM MEMO SaveStat.mMemvars ADDITIVE
   glEditable  = .T.
   glRestEdit  = .T.
   jcSaveAlias = TRIM(SaveStat.cOldAlias)
   jcSaveOrder = TRIM(SaveStat.cOldOrder)
   jcSaveID    = SaveStat.cSaveID
   DELETE
   IF EMPTY(jcSaveID)
      m.gcLastTool = "Add"
   ELSE
      jcIdField = jcSaveAlias+'.cID'
      IF EMPTY(LOOKUP(&jcIdField, jcSaveID, &jcIDField, "cID"))
* Record Deleted
         ?? CHR(7)
         WAIT WINDOW "This record has already been deleted. " +;
"Moving to new info. Press any key..."
         SCATTER MEMVAR MEMO
         glEditable = .F.
      ENDIF
   ENDIF
ELSE
   glEditable = .F.
   glRestEdit = .F.
ENDIF

SELECT (jcSaveAlias)
SET ORDER TO (jcSaveOrder)

RETURN
```

Variable State Saving: SAVEMEM.PRG

SaveMem() is called whenever the user moves from one window to an unrelated window while in the midst of an edit. It saves the state of the current memory variables, as well as the current key ID in a cursor that is created at startup of the application. This routine inserts into the SaveStat cursor the current window name, key id, alias and index order, and then uses the command

```
SAVE TO MEMO SaveStat.mMemvars ALL EXCEPT g*
```

to save all memory variables except PUBLIC ones into the cursor's memo field. Note that this routine and RestMem() use the following techniques:

- The capability of saving memory variables into memo fields.
- We use our naming conventions to ease the saving of the memory variables.
- Since we are saving the information only if the user is in the midst of an edit, if we find information in this cursor (when running the RestMem() routine) we know to set the user up in edit mode again.

This is a sample of a simple state saving routine. You can further enhance this routine as the need arises to provide other capabilities. For instance, you may want to save the value of _curobj in order to place the user back in the field that they were in when exiting the window.

```
*  Program...........: SAVEMEM.PRG
*  Author............: YAG
*  Project...........: COMMON
*  Created...........: 06/06/93  04:21:37
*  Copyright.........: (c) Flash Creative Management, 1993
*) Description.......: Save memory state when switching windows
*  Calling Samples...: DO SaveMem
*  Parameter List....: tcSaveWind - Window to save info for
*  Major change list.:
PARAMETER tcSaveWind
PRIVATE jcSaveAlias, jcSaveOrder, jcSaveID
IF USED("SaveStat")
   jcSaveAlias = ALIAS()
   jcSaveOrder = ORDER()
   =InsRec(" SaveStat ;
      (cWindow, mMemvars, cSaveID, cOldAlias, cOldOrder) ;
      VALUES (tcSaveWind, '', m.cID, jcSaveAlias, jcSaveOrder) ")
   SAVE TO MEMO SaveStat.mMemvars ALL EXCEPT g*
ENDIF
```

Initializing FoxPro's Environment: SETSETS.PRG

SetSets() is essentially unchanged from the original FoxPro Codebook. It sets the FoxPro environmental variables. Two changes have been made, however: _WRAP has been set to .F. to enable the ?? CHR(7) function to ring the bell (with _WRAP set to .T., the bell will not ring), and FULLPATH has been set ON, to make sure that FoxPro for Windows can find any cursors that we create. FoxPro for Windows does not create temporary files in the current directory (if TMPFILES is not used), it places them in the directory used for Windows temp files. Therefore, commands like:

```
APPEND FROM DBF("CursorName")
```

fail under FoxPro for Windows with FULLPATH set OFF.

```
*  Program...........: SETSETS.PRG
*  Author............: yag
*  Project...........: COMMON
*  Created...........: 12/09/92
*  Copyright.........: (c) Flash Creative Management, 1992
*) Description.......: Sets all environmental settings
*  Calling Samples...: DO SetSets
*  Parameter List....:
*  Major change list.: 10/15/92 Changed _WRAP to .F. so that bell would
*                    :             ring with ? CHR(7).
* Set up Global Variables
SET ALTERNATE OFF
SET ALTERNATE TO
SET ANSI OFF
SET AUTOSAVE OFF
SET BELL OFF
SET BLINK OFF
SET BLOCKSIZE TO 33
SET BORDER TO SINGLE
SET BRSTATUS OFF
SET CARRY OFF
SET CENTURY ON
SET CLEAR ON
SET CLOCK OFF
SET COMPATIBLE FOXPLUS
SET CONFIRM ON
IF SET('CONSOLE') = 'OFF'
  SET CONSOLE ON
ENDIF (SET('CONSOLE') = 'OFF')
SET CURRENCY LEFT
SET CURSOR ON
SET DATE AMERICAN
*  SET DEBUG                                  && Moved to IF FLASH section
SET DECIMALS TO 2
*  SET DEFAULT TO                                         && LEAVE SET TO CURRENT
DEFAULT DRIVE
SET DELETED ON
SET DELIMITERS OFF
IF GETENV("USER") = gcEnvUser                             && .T. if at the office
```

```
  SET DEBUG ON
  SET DEVELOPMENT ON
  SET LOGERRORS ON
ELSE
  SET DEBUG OFF
  SET DEVELOPMENT OFF
  SET LOGERRORS OFF
ENDIF (GETENV("USER") = gcEnvUser
SET DEVICE TO SCREEN
SET DOHISTORY OFF
SET ECHO OFF
SET ESCAPE OFF
SET EXACT OFF
SET EXCLUSIVE OFF                   && For Multi-user use - 08/04/92
SET FIELDS OFF
SET FIXED OFF
SET FORMAT TO
SET FULLPATH ON                 && To fix DBF() return value
SET HEADING ON
SET HELP ON
SET HELPFILTER TO
SET HOURS TO 12
SET HISTORY OFF
SET INTENSITY ON
DO CASE
   CASE _WINDOWS
      SET LIBRARY TO SYS(2004)+'foxtools.fll' ADDITIVE
   OTHERWISE
      SET LIBRARY TO
ENDCASE
SET LOCK OFF
*    SET LOGERROR OFF                          && Moved w/ SET DEVELOPMENT
SET MARGIN TO 0
SET MARK TO "/"
SET MEMOWIDTH TO 65
SET MENU ON
SET MESSAGE TO 24 CENTER
SET MOUSE ON
SET MULTILOCKS ON
SET NEAR OFF
SET NOTIFY ON
SET ODOMETER TO 100
SET OPTIMIZE ON
SET PATH TO
SET POINT TO "."
SET PRECISION TO 3
SET PRINT OFF
SET PRINTER TO Lpt1
SET PROCEDURE TO
SET REFRESH TO 0
*SET REPROCESS TO Automatic
SET REPROCESS TO 1
SET SAFETY OFF
IF SET('SCOREBOARD') = 'ON'
  SET SCOREBOARD OFF
ENDIF (SET('SCOREBOARD') = 'ON')
SET SEPARATOR TO  ","
SET SHADOWS ON
SET SPACE OFF
```

```
IF SET('STATUS')    = 'ON'
  SET STATUS OFF
ENDIF (SET('STATUS')    = 'ON')
SET STEP OFF
SET STICKY ON
SET SYSMENU AUTOMATIC
SET TALK OFF
SET TEXTMERGE OFF
SET TOPIC TO
SET TYPEAHEAD TO 0
SET TYPEAHEAD TO 25
SET UNIQUE OFF
* SET THE INSERT / CAPS / NUMLOCK KEYS
= INSMODE(.T.)
= CAPSLOCK(.F.)
= NUMLOCK(.T.)
* SYSTEM VARIABLE SETTINGS
_ALIGNMENT =   "LEFT"
_BOX =         .T.
_INDENT =      0
_LMARGIN =     0
_PADVANCE =    "FORMFEED"
_PAGENO =      1
_PBPAGE =      1
_PCOPIES =     1
_PECODE =      ""
_PEJECT =      "AFTER"
_PEPAGE =      32767
_PFORM =       ""
_PLENGTH =     66
_PLOFFSET =    0
_PPITCH =      "PICA"
_PQUALITY =    .T.
_PSCODE =      ""
_PSPACING =    1
_PWAIT =       .F.
_RMARGIN =     80
_TABS =        "10, 20, 30, 40, 50, 60, 70"
_WRAP =        .F.                   && Changed to .F. to enable bell
RETURN
```

Displaying a Page Number while Reporting: SHOWPAGE.PRG

This routine is used in place of Therm() when longer reports are run. Since it is much simpler than the thermometer routine, it takes less time to run and the user feels less of a time hit. The routine places a message at the top right of the screen, showing which page is currently printing.

```
*  Program...........: SHOWPAGE.PRG
*  Author............: yag
*  Project...........: COMMON
*  Created...........: 12/09/92
*  Copyright.........: (c) Flash Creative Management, 1992
*) Description.......: Place in page header of a report to provide status
*)                   : window without the time hit of thermometer.
*  Calling Samples...: =showpage()
*  Parameter List....:
*  Major change list.:
WAIT WINDOW NOWAIT "Now outputting page #: " + STR(_pageno,3,0)
RETURN ""
```

Calculating the Filled Size of an Array: SIZEARRY.PRG

SizeArry() is a routine that returns the number of filled rows in an array. It makes the assumption that the first column is not of a logical type, and simply counts through all the first column, from the bottom to the top, checking for a filled element. Once that element is found, it returns the row number.

This function is very useful for scrolling lists in which the array size may vary. It allows FoxPro to handle dimensioning the number of rows of the array that should be shown. Note the use of EXTERNAL ARRAY to let FoxPro know that we are creating the array externally to this procedure. This allows us to keep FoxPro from generating compiler warnings when it builds an application.

```
*  Program...........: SIZEARRY.PRG
*  Author............: yag
*  Project...........: COMMON
*  Created...........: 12/09/92
*  Copyright.........: (c) Flash Creative Management, 1992
*) Description.......: Returns the size of the array.
*  Calling Samples...: =sizearry( @laArray1 )
*  Parameter List....: taArry - array to be sized.
*  Major change list.:

PARAMETER taArry
PRIVATE m.lnCount

EXTERNAL ARRAY taArry

FOR m.lnCount = ALEN(taArry,1) TO 1 STEP -1
  IF NOT EMPTY(taArry[m.lnCount,1])
    EXIT                                    && Filled item
  ENDIF
ENDFOR

RETURN m.lnCount
```

File Extension Manipulation: STRIPEXT.PRG

StripExt() is a function that removes the extension from a file name.

```
*  Program...........: STRIPEXT.PRG
*  Author............: yag
*  Project...........: COMMON
*  Created...........: 12/09/92
*  Copyright.........: (c) Flash Creative Management, 1992
*) Description.......: Strip the extension from a file name. Use the
*)                   : algorithm employed by FoxPRO itself to strip a
*)                   : file of an extension (if any): Find the
*)                   : rightmost dot in the filename.  If this dot occurs
*)                   : to the right of a "\" or ":", then treat everything
*)                   : from the dot rightward as an extension.
*)                   : Of course, if we found no dot, we just hand back
*)                   : the filename unchanged.
*)                   : Courtesy of Fox Software.
*  Calling Samples...: stripext(lcFileName)
*  Parameter List....: tcFileName - character string representing a file
*  Major change list.: Modified to use Flash naming conventions.
*
FUNCTION stripext
PARAMETER m.tcFileName
PRIVATE m.lndotpos, m.lnTermintr
   m.lndotpos = RAT(".", m.tcFileName)
   m.lnTermintr = MAX(RAT("\", m.tcFileName), RAT(":", m.tcFileName))
   IF m.lndotpos > m.lnTermintr
      m.tcFileName = LEFT(m.tcFileName, m.lndotpos-1)
   ENDIF
RETURN m.tcFileName
```

File Path Manipulation: STRIPPAT.PRG

Like StripExt(), this is a handy function that strips the path off a file name.

```
*  Program...........: STRIPPAT.PRG
*  Author............: yag
*  Project...........: COMMON
*  Created...........: 12/09/92
*  Copyright.........: (c) Flash Creative Management, 1992
*) Description.......: Strip the path from a file name. Find positions of
*)                   : backslash in the name of the file.  If there is one
*)                   : take everything to the right of its position
*)                   : and make it the new file name.  If there
*)                   : is no slash look for colon.  Again if found, take
*)                   : everything to the right of it as the new name.
*)                   : If neither slash nor colon are found then
*)                   : return the name unchanged.
*  Calling Samples...: strippat(lcFileName)
*  Parameter List....: tcfilename - character string representing a file name
*  Major change list.:
FUNCTION strippat
PARAMETER m.tcFileName
PRIVATE m.lnSlashPos, m.lnNameLen, m.lnColonPos
   m.lnSlashPos = RAT("\", m.tcFileName)
   IF m.lnSlashPos <> 0
      m.lnNameLen  = LEN(m.tcFileName) - m.lnSlashPos
      m.tcFileName = RIGHT(m.tcFileName, m.lnNameLen)
   ELSE
      m.lnColonPos = RAT(":", m.tcFileName)
      IF m.lnColonPos <> 0
         m.lnNameLen  = LEN(m.tcFileName) - m.lnColonPos
         m.tcFileName = RIGHT(m.tcFileName, m.lnNameLen)
      ENDIF
   ENDIF
RETURN m.tcFileName
```

Adding Array Columns: SUMARRY.PRG

SumArry() is a function that is often used in invoice windows. It will sum a column of an array (for instance, the line items of an invoice). Note that it tests to make sure that an array was passed, and if not, it fails gracefully. If no column is passed, it will automatically make a best guess and add the first numeric column that it can find.

```
*  Program...........: SUMARRY.PRG
*  Author............: yag
*  Project...........: COMMON
*  Created...........: 03/29/93
*  Copyright.........: (c) Flash Creative Management, 1993
*) Description.......: Sums one column of an array
*)                   : If no column passed, it sums the first
*)                   : numeric column it finds.
*  Calling Samples...: lnSum = sumarry(@laInv,4)
*  Parameter List....: taSumArry - Array to be summed
*                    : tnColNum  - Column to be summed
*  Major change list.:

PARA taSumArry, tnColNum
PRIVATE jnRetVal, jnNumParam, jnCurCol, jcCurRow
EXTERNAL ARRAY taSumArry

jnNumParam = PARAMETER()
STORE 0 TO jnRetVal

*-- Check for proper call of function
IF jnNumParam = 0 OR TYPE('taSumArry[1]') = "U"
       WAIT WINDOW "Error in summing array - no array passed"
       RETURN 0
ENDIF

*-- Initialize to first numeric column if no number passed
IF jnNumParam = 1
       FOR jnCurCol = 1 TO ALEN(taSumArry,2)
              IF TYPE('taSumArry[1,jnCurCol]') = "N"
                     tnColNum = jnCurCol
             EXIT
       ENDIF
       ENDFOR
ENDIF

IF tnColNum = 0
  WAIT WINDOW "Error in summing array - no numeric column"
  RETURN 0
ENDIF

*-- Sum the column
FOR jnCurRow = 1 TO Sizearry(@taSumArry)
  jnRetVal = jnRetVal + taSumArry[jnCurRow,tnColNum]
ENDFOR
RETURN jnRetVal
```

A Useful Thermometer: THERM.PRG

This routine adds a self-maintaining thermometer to the screen during processing.

```
*  Program...........: THERM.PRG
*  Author............: yag
*  Project...........: COMMON
*  Created...........: 12/09/92
*  Copyright.........: (c) Flash Creative Management, 1992
*) Description.......: Emulates a thermometer
*)                   : In 1.02 can be used in a REPORT FORM, SCAN etc.
*)                   : In 2.0 can be used in INDEX as well (but requires
*)                   : a call to CDXSTRIP() afterwards
*  Calling Samples...:  1.  Place therm() in a report and call it with
*                           REPORT FORM TEST TO FILE TEMP.REP OFF
*                       2.  =Therm("This is a message")
*  Parameter List....: lcMessage - Message to print on top line of the
*                                  thermometer - optional.
*  Major change list.:
*
* NOTE:
*     If lcScope exists, it is used to automatically adjust for a
*     scoped command, such as FOR/WHILE etc.
*
* Thanks to Lisa Slater and Chip Doolittle for CIS thread
*-----------------------
FUNCTION therm
PARAMETERS lcMessage
IF TYPE("lnPercDone") = "U"
  PUBLIC lnRecsDone, lnRecsToDo, lnWinLngth, lnStartRec, lnPercDone
  lnStartRec = RECNO()
  DO CASE
     CASE _DOS
     DEFINE WINDOW wvTherm FROM 11,4 TO 16,76 SHADOWS DOUBLE;
       TITLE 'Processing Records'
    CASE _WINDOWS OR _MAC
     DEFINE WINDOW wvTherm FROM 11,4 TO 17,76 SHADOWS DOUBLE;
       TITLE 'Processing Records' FONT "FoxFont",10
  ENDCASE
  GOTO lnStartRec
  IF TYPE("lcScope") = "U"
    lcScope = "ALL"
  ENDIF (TYPE("lcScope") = "U"                       && Didn't add a scope)
  COUNT TO lnRecsToDo &lcScope
  GOTO lnStartRec
  STORE 0 TO lnRecsDone, lnPercDone
  ACTIVATE WINDOW wvTherm
  lnWinLngth = WCOLS()-4
  lnPercent = INT(WCOLS()/5)
  @ 1,1 SAY '0%'
  @ 1,lnPercent-1 SAY '20%'
  @ 1,(lnPercent-1)*2 SAY '40%'
  @ 1,(lnPercent-1)*3 SAY '60%'
```

```
  @ 1,(lnPercent-1)*4 SAY '80%'
  @ 1,(lnPercent-1)*5 SAY '100%'
ENDIF (TYPE("lnPercDone") = "U")
IF PARAMETERS() = 1
  @ 0,0 SAY PADC(lcMessage,WCOLS()," ")
ENDIF (PARA() = 1)
lnTempPerc = lnRecsDone / lnRecsToDo
IF (INT(lnPercDone*lnWinLngth) <> INT(lnTempPerc*lnWinLngth)) .OR. ;
    RECNO() = lnStartRec
  @ 2,1 SAY REPLICATE(CHR(177),INT(lnTempPerc*lnWinLngth))
  lnPercDone = lnTempPerc
ENDIF ((INT(lnPercDone*lnWinLngth) <> INT(lnTempPerc*lnWinLngth)) .OR. ;)
lnRecsDone = lnRecsDone + 1
IF lnRecsDone = lnRecsToDo
  RELEASE WINDOW wvTherm
  RELEASE lnPercDone, lnRecsDone, lnRecsToDo, lnWinLngth, lnStartRec
ENDIF (lnRecsDone = lnRecsToDo)
RETURN ""
```

Event Handler: TRAFICOP.PRG

Traficop is the heart of our event-driven foundation. It is based on the concepts found in Chapter 4, *Event-Driven Programming*. It is also the program that has changed the most from the original *FoxPro Codebook*.

The changes to Traficop encompass three major functions:

Platform-specific enhancements	Traficop now sets up the approach that causes the control panel to act like a toolbar when in a graphical environment. In Windows and Macintosh systems it also calls a startup window during setup, and saves and restores font information in the main window.
Data-driven enhancements	Traficop now loads in developer information from the IntSetup table if it is available. This information is used to drive the background window in DOS, and the ABOUT screens in all platforms.
State-saving enhancements	Traficop's functions now call the SaveMem() function to save the state of a window if it is being edited.

Let's take a look at how Traficop works. We begin by initializing our FoxPro environment, and if we are in Windows or Macintosh, we run the Startup screen program.

We continue by setting up PUBLIC memory variables that contain our basic information on windows, buttons, security, user information and developer information. We then initialize our developer information, set our SET commands, and save various resource, help and error settings. The lines

```
IF GETENV("USER") # gcEnvUser
   ON ERROR DO OnError WITH ...
ENDIF
```

are used to change the way that processing continues based on where the application is being run. One problem with development is that you often want to turn off the error handler while working on an application. Unfortunately, too many developers opt to comment out the error handler, which is then never placed back into the code, causing our clients grief. The GETENV() function allows us to check a DOS environmental variable, and if it is set (as it is by our network login script at the office), it ignores the error handler. Traficop defaults to checking for the first word in the development company name.

We continue by saving the old menu state, setting up a CURSOR for state saving (we use a CURSOR because it will automatically be removed at the end of the application, and we don't need to save states among multiple users), tacking our menu on top of the screen and clearing the background.

We then do some platform-specific startup work. If we are running under a graphical environment, we save font information using the WFONT() function, use the MODIFY WINDOW SCREEN command to change the title of the main window to our application's name, and we define a window, wzMain, as a no-border window that begins just below our toolbar. Every application window ("wr" window) will be IN WINDOW wzMain, therefore the user will not be able to move that window over the toolbar.

Finally, we set a variable, gcMainWind, to either "WINDOW wzMain" if we are running under Windows or the Macintosh, or to "SCREEN" if we are running under DOS. Each of our "wr" windows will contain the line

```
#WCLAUSE IN &wzMain
```

in the Setup snippet of the window. This causes the IN clause to be appended to the end of the DEFINE WINDOW command, forcing a Windows/Macintosh window to appear IN WINDOW wzMain, and a DOS window to appear IN SCREEN. This allows our control panel to automatically act as a toolbar when running under a graphical environment, with no code modifications necessary.

We continue by running the BckGrnd screen program, which issues our Foundation READ. We remain in this window until the user exits, at which point we reset everything to its initial state.

MyHandler() is a function that contains the event loop for the application. As discussed in Chapter 4, *Event-Driven Programming*, we trap for the major events in an application.

- We check to see if glEndProg is set to true. If so, we return a true to the Foundation READ and the application ends.
- We then check to see if something was placed in gcNextProg, signifying that a menu hit took place. If so, we check to see if that window is already open, and if it is, we activate it. Otherwise we run the proper screen program.
- If the top window is an application ("wr" type) window, we know that the user clicked on it from another window. We then get the name of the screen program associated with that window and run it.
- If the top window is a control panel, we check to see which window should be working with the control panel, and run the screen program associated with that window.

Efface() controls whether or not the control panel should be put away. It checks through every window, and if no "wr" windows are found, it RELEASEs the control window. Note that this function checks for WCHILD("",0) under

DOS, and WCHILD("wzMain",0) under Windows and the Macintosh. We are creating our own desktop window in the graphical environments, so we check all children of wzMain.

StopREAD() is triggered whenever a "wr" window's DEACTIVATE is triggered. It checks to see if the window has been manually closed by the user (by clicking on the close box) and if so, it closes any associated windows. It then checks to see if the user is leaving for an unrelated window (for instance, from CD to Invoices) and if so, if the user is still editing, we call SaveMem() to save the information about the window that we're leaving (so that it can later be restored). Finally, we return a true or a false depending on whether we want to end the READ of the window that the user is leaving.

CurrSPR() loops through all open windows and returns the screen program of the current READ window by stripping off the "wr" and appending a ".SPR" to the end.

CurrWR() loops through all open windows and returns the name of the current application window.

ControlPrc() is our message sender function. It is called from every tool in our toolbar/control panel and controls what function is called as a result. It does this by appending an "IT" to the end of the passed tool name (e.g. "NEXT" calls "NextIt"). For more information on how this works, please read the chapter titled *Toolbars and OOPS*.

DimNavigat() turns on and off the buttons in our toolbar and their corresponding menu selections. It checks to see where we are in a DBF, and dims items accordingly. Note the use of the "gb" variables. When they are set to true, their corresponding items on the toolbar and on the menu are dimmed. For example, note that the "COPY" function is dimmed in the Invoice Window because gbCopy is set to true in the Setup code of that window.

```
*  Program...........: TRAFICOP.PRG
*  Author............: yag
*  Project...........: COMMON
*  Created...........: 04/16/93
*  Copyright.........: (c) Flash Creative Management, 1993
*) Description.......: Main window event handler for all apps
*)                   : It uses naming conventions to handle the
*)                   : window types, and the way that they behave
*)                   : (they inherit their behavior from their type).
*)                   :
*)                   : WR = READ Window
*)                   : WM = MODAL Window
*)                   : WC = CONTROL Panel
*)                   : WT = WR-specific ConTrol panel
*)                   :
*)                   : Note:  Special code has been added for FoxPro's
*)                   :          Calculator and Calendar accessories.
*  Calling Samples...: DO Traficop
*  Parameter List....:
*  Major change list.:
CLOSE ALL
CLEAR ALL
CLEAR
SET TALK OFF
DO CASE
   CASE _WINDOWS OR _MAC       && Windows Splash Window while booting
      PRIVATE laOldFont, i
      DIMENSION laOldFont[3]
      FOR i = 1 TO 3
            laOldFont[i] = WFONT(i)
      ENDFOR
      DO Startup.spr
ENDCASE
*--PUBLIC memvars that track window/program switching information
PUBLIC glEndProg, gcNextProg, glQuitting, glRestEdit, glOpenErr
*--PUBLIC memvars that track window status information
PUBLIC glEditable, glOKtoSave, gcLastTool, gcMainWind
*--PUBLIC memvars to enable/disable directional menus
PUBLIC gbTop, gbPrior, gbNext, gbBottom, gbList, gbFind
*--PUBLIC memvars to enable/disable record changing menus
PUBLIC gbAdd, gbEdit, gbSave, gbOops, gbDelete, gbCopy
*-- PUBLIC memvars that contain user and application information
PUBLIC gcSession, gcSpread
*-- PUBLIC memvars that contain development company information
PUBLIC gcCompany, gcAddress1, gcAddress2, gcCity, gcState, gcZip
PUBLIC gcPhone, gcFax, gcEnvUser
*-- Add development company specific information
IF !USED("Intsetup")
   IF FILE("Intsetup.dbf")
      USE IntSetup IN SELECT(1)
      gcCompany  = TRIM(intsetup.ccompany)
      gcAddress1 = TRIM(intsetup.caddress1)
      gcAddress2 = TRIM(intsetup.caddress2)
      gcCity     = TRIM(intsetup.cCity)
      gcState    = TRIM(intsetup.cState)
      gcZip      = TRIM(intsetup.cZip)
      gcPhone    = TRIM(intsetup.cPhone)
      gcFax      = TRIM(intsetup.cFax)
      gcEnvUser  = UPPER(SUBSTR(gcCompany,1,AT("",gcCompany)-1))
```

```
      *-- Load company information
      SELECT IntSetup
      =AFIELDS(laFields)
      IF ASCAN(laFields,"MCOMPINFO") > 0
         gmCompInfo = mCompInfo
      ELSE
         gmCompInfo = ""
      ENDIF
      RELEASE laFields
      USE IN IntSetup
   ELSE
      STORE "" TO gcCompany, gcAddress1, gcAddress2, gcCity, gcState
      STORE "" TO gcZip, gcPhone, gcFax, gmCompInfo
      STORE "FLASH" TO gcEnvUser
   ENDIF
ENDIF
DO SetSets                          && Sets all the SET commands and sysvars
*-- Save the old ERROR, RESOURCE and HELP settings
lcOldError = ON("ERROR")
lcOldReso  = SET("RESOURCE",1)
lcOldResoS = SET("RESOURCE")
lcOldHelp  = SET("HELP",1)
lcOldHelpS = SET("HELP")
IF GETENV("USER") # gcEnvUser
   ON ERROR DO OnError WITH MESSAGE(), MESSAGE(1), PROGRAM(), LINENO(),
ERROR()
ENDIF
PUSH MENU _MSYSMENU                           && Save the old menu
SET SYSMENU AUTOMATIC
glQuitting = .T.   && in case we have no control windows, close when new
&& one is opened.
STORE .F. TO glEndProg, glEditable
gcNextProg=""
glOKtoSave = .T.
DO main.mpr
IF glOpenErr
   DO CASE
      CASE _WINDOWS OR _MAC
         RELEASE WINDOW wsStartup
   ENDCASE
   DO Alert.SPR WITH "Data could not be opened. Closing Application"
ELSE
   *-- Do platform specific startup
   DO CASE
      CASE _WINDOWS
         MODIFY WINDOW SCREEN ;
            TITLE ALLTRIM(Setup.cSystName) ;
            FONT "FoxFont",9 ;
            ICON FILE CHRTRAN(Setup.cShortName,' .-','')+".ICO" ;
            MINIMIZE NOCLOSE GROW
         ZOOM WINDOW SCREEN MAX
         DEFINE WINDOW wzMain ;
            FROM 3.7,0 TO SROWS()-1,SCOLS() ;
            NONE
         ACTIVATE WINDOW wzMain
         gcMainWind = "WINDOW wzMain"
      CASE _MAC
         MODIFY WINDOW SCREEN ;
            TITLE ALLTRIM(Setup.cSystName) ;
            FONT "FoxFont",9 ;
```

```
            ICON FILE CHRTRAN(Setup.cShortName,' .-','')+".ICO" ;
            MINIMIZE NOCLOSE GROW
         ZOOM WINDOW SCREEN MAX
         DEFINE WINDOW wzMain ;
            FROM 4.5,0 TO SROWS()-1,SCOLS() ;
            NONE
         ACTIVATE WINDOW wzMain
         gcMainWind = "WINDOW wzMain"
      CASE _DOS
         gcMainWind = "SCREEN"
   ENDCASE
   *-- Get unique session ID for ID fields
   gcSession = Next207("Setup","cSessionID")

   *-- Get spreadsheet name from SETUP dbf
   PRIVATE i
   gcSpread = ""
   DO CASE
      CASE _DOS
         FOR i = 1 TO FCOUNT("Setup")
            IF FIELD(i,"Setup") = "CDSPREAD"
               gcSpread  = SETUP.cDSpread         && Spreadsheet Name
               gcSpPath  = SETUP.cDSpPath         && Spreadsheet Path
            ENDIF
         ENDFOR
      CASE _WINDOWS
         FOR i = 1 TO FCOUNT("Setup")
            IF FIELD(i,"Setup") = "CWSPREAD"
               gcSpread  = SETUP.cWSpread         && Spreadsheet Name
               gcSpPath  = SETUP.cWSpPath         && Spreadsheet Path
            ENDIF
         ENDFOR
   ENDCASE
   DO CASE
      CASE _WINDOWS OR _MAC
         RELEASE WINDOW wsStartup
   ENDCASE
   DO BckGrnd.SPR           && Lets user know that they can start.
   && Calls Foundation READ
ENDIF
CLEAR WINDOW ALL
CLOSE DATABASES
POP KEY
IF GETENV("USER") = "FLASH"
   *-- Reset to former HELP, RESOURCE and ERROR if in the office
   IF !EMPTY(lcOldHelp)
      SET HELP TO &lcOldHelp
      SET HELP &lcOldHelpS
   ENDIF
   IF !EMPTY(lcOldReso)
      SET RESOURCE TO &lcOldReso
      SET RESOURCE &lcOldResoS
   ENDIF
   ON ERROR &lcOldError
ENDIF
*-- Reset platform specific environment
DO CASE
   CASE _WINDOWS OR _MAC
      IF laOldFont[3] = "N"
```

```
         MODIFY WINDOW SCREEN FONT laOldFont[1],laOldFont[2]
      ELSE
          MODIFY WINDOW SCREEN FONT laOldFont[1],laOldFont[2] STYLE
laOldFont[3]
      ENDIF
      RELEASE WINDOW wzMain
      MODIFY WINDOW SCREEN
ENDCASE
POP MENU _MSYSMENU
CLEAR
*-- End program
**********************************************
FUNCTION MyHandler
**********************************************
*  Procedure.........: MyHandler
*  Author............: yag
*  Project...........: COMMON
*  Created...........: 04/16/93
*  Copyright.........: (c) Flash Creative Management, 1993
*) Description.......: FUNCTION MyHandler
*)                   : Event Loop
*)                   : The Foundation READ terminates when this
*)                   : routine returns .T.  As long as it returns
*)                   : .F. execution of the Foundation READ continues
*  Calling Samples...: Called from Foundation READ's VALID
*  Parameter List....:
*  Major change list.:
PRIVATE m.lcCurrSPR, llRetVal, lcOldAlias
llRetVal = .F.                          && Initialize our RETURN value
IF glEndProg
   RETURN .T.                           && Only when 'Exit' is selected
ENDIF                                   && from the menu.
DO CASE                                 && Handles all other cases
   CASE !EMPTY(gcNextProg)              && Menu Hit
      lcWindow = "WR"+STRIPEXT(gcNextProg)
      IF WVISIBLE(lcWindow)
         =ResetWin(lcWindow)
         gcNextProg = ""
         KEYBOARD "{RIGHTARROW}"
         ACTIVATE WINDOW (lcWindow)
      ELSE
         m.lcCurrSPR = gcNextProg        && specified from the menu
         gcNextProg = ""
         DO (m.lcCurrSPR)
      ENDIF
   CASE UPPER(LEFT(WONTOP(),2)) = "WT"   && READ Window specific control panel
      lcProg = TRIM(SUBSTR(WONTOP(),3,8))
      lcProg = lcProg + ".SPR"
      DO (lcProg)
   CASE UPPER(LEFT(WONTOP(),2)) = "WR"          && READ Window
      lcProg = TRIM(SUBSTR(WONTOP(),3,8))
      IF RIGHT(lcProg,1) $ "1,2,3,4,5,6,7,8,9,0"
         lcProg = LEFT(lcProg,LEN(lcProg)-1)
      ENDIF
      lcProg = lcProg + ".SPR"
      =ResetWin(WONTOP())
      DO (lcProg)
   CASE LEFT(WONTOP(),2) = "WC"
      *
      *   Following code finds the foremost application window,
```

```
      *   then launches the .SPR which controls that window.  If none
      *   is found, nothing happens.
      *
      *   It is executed when the control panel is foremost.
      *
      m.lcProgram = CurrSPR()
      IF !EMPTY(m.lcProgram)
         =ResetWin("wr"+STRIPEXT(lcProgram))
         DO (m.lcProgram)          && Launch code to handle foremost
      ENDIF                                  && application screen
ENDCASE
RETURN llRetVal
**************************************************
PROCEDURE Efface
**************************************************
*  Procedure.........: Efface
*  Author............: yag
*  Project...........: COMMON
*  Created...........: 04/16/93
*  Copyright.........: (c) Flash Creative Management, 1993
*) Description.......: PROCEDURE Efface
*)                   : Routine to decide whether or not to release the
*)                   : control panel.
*)                   :
*)                   : EFFACE is called when either the 'Quit' button has
*)                   : been pressed or a READ window has been manually
*)                   : closed by clicking in the close box or by selecting
*)                   : 'Close' from the 'File' menu.
*)                   :
*)                   : It looks through all the windows that are open,
*)                   : from back to front. If it finds any of the user
*)                   : application windows (which will require the
*)                   : control panel) it simply exits.
*)                   :
*)                   : Otherwise, it concludes we're finished with the
*)                   : control panel and releases it.
*)                   :
*)                   : The surrounding application insures that WONTOP()
*)                   : is the control panel.
*  Calling Samples...: DO efface
*  Parameter List....:
*  Major change list.:
PRIVATE lcWindChck
IF _WINDOWS   OR _MAC                  && Hoping for XPlatform #WSETUP
   m.lcWindChck = UPPER(WCHILD("WZMAIN",0))
ELSE
   m.lcWindChck = UPPER(WCHILD("",0))
ENDIF
DO WHILE !EMPTY(m.lcWindChck)
   IF LEFT(m.lcWindChck,2) = "WR"
      RETURN
   ENDIF
   IF _WINDOWS OR _MAC
      m.lcWindChck = UPPER(WCHILD("WZMAIN",1))
   ELSE
      m.lcWindChck = UPPER(WCHILD("",1))
   ENDIF
ENDDO
DO CASE
```

```
   CASE _DOS
      IF !EMPTY(WONTOP())              && Release a control window if one
exists.
         RELEASE WINDOW (WONTOP())
         lnMesgLine = SROWS() - 1
         @ lnMesgLine,0 CLEAR TO lnMesgLine,79  && Turn off the "ghost" message
      ENDIF
   CASE _WINDOWS OR _MAC
      m.lcWindChck = WCHILD("",0)    && WC Windows are in Main area
      DO WHILE !EMPTY(m.lcWindChck)
         IF UPPER(LEFT(m.lcWindChck,2)) = "WC"
            RELEASE WINDOW (m.lcWindChck)
            EXIT
         ELSE
            m.lcWindChck = WCHILD("",1)
         ENDIF
      ENDDO
ENDCASE
************************************************
FUNCTION StopREAD
************************************************
*  Procedure.........: StopREAD
*  Author............: yag
*  Project...........: COMMON
*  Created...........: 04/16/93
*  Copyright.........: (c) Flash Creative Management, 1993
*) Description.......: FUNCTION StopREAD
*)                   : Routine executed when the DEACTIVATE clause
*)                   : of one of the application READs is triggered.
*)                   : If it returns .T., the READ terminates.  Otherwise,
*)                   : it returns .F.
*)                   :
*)                   : NOTE:  the value of 'glQuitting' may have been set
*)                   : to .T. prior to entering this routine if the user
*)                   : pressed the 'Quit' button to terminate the read.
*  Calling Samples...: RETURN stopread('wrCD')
*  Parameter List....: tcWindow    -   The Window we want to possibly leave
*  Major change list.:
PARAMETER m.tcWindow
PRIVATE m.lcWindChck
IF NOT WVISIBLE(m.tcWindow)           && Did window get closed manually?
   m.lcWindChck = UPPER(WCHILD("",0))
   DO WHILE !EMPTY(m.lcWindChck)
      IF m.lcWindChck = "WT"+UPPER(RIGHT(m.tcWindow,LEN(m.tcWindow)-2))
         RELEASE WINDOW ('wt'+RIGHT(m.tcWindow,LEN(m.tcWindow)-2))
      ENDIF
      IF LEFT(m.lcWindChck,2) = "WC"
         SHOW WINDOW (m.lcWindChck) TOP
      ENDIF
      m.lcWindChck = UPPER(WCHILD("",1))
   ENDDO
   glQuitting = .T.                  && and act as if 'Quit' was pressed
ENDIF
*--- Test for a return from the Calculator/Calendar (includes German)
llWREAD = WREAD()
```

```
IF !WREAD()
   IF LEFT(UPPER(WONTOP()),8) $ "CALCULATOR/CALENDAR/RECHNER/KALENDAR"
      llWREAD = .T.
   ELSE
      IF glEditable
         IF USED("SaveStat")            && If using state saving
            DO SaveMem WITH m.tcWindow
            llWREAD = .F.
         ELSE
            ?? CHR(7)
            WAIT WINDOW NOWAIT "Cannot exit this window until <SAVE> or <OOPS!> selected"
            lcTempWind = WLAST()
            SHOW WINDOW (lcTempWind) TOP
            llWREAD = .T.
         ENDIF
      ELSE
         llWREAD = .F.
      ENDIF
   ENDIF
ENDIF
RETURN glQuitting OR NOT llWREAD      && Stop if 'quitting', or
&& if WONTOP() isn't in current READ
**********************************************
FUNCTION CurrSPR
**********************************************
*  Procedure.........: CurrSPR
*  Author............: yag
*  Project...........: COMMON
*  Created...........: 04/16/93
*  Copyright.........: (c) Flash Creative Management, 1993
*) Description.......: FUNCTION CurrSPR
*)                   : This routine finds the current READ and returns
*)                   : the .SPR file to run.  If there is no READ window
*)                   : it returns a blank.
*  Calling Samples...: lcSpr = currspr()
*  Parameter List....:
*  Major change list.:
PRIVATE m.lcProgram, m.lcWindow
m.lcProgram = ""
IF _WINDOWS OR _MAC
   m.lcWindow = UPPER(WCHILD("WZMAIN",0))
ELSE
   m.lcWindow = UPPER(WCHILD("",0))
ENDIF
DO WHILE !EMPTY(m.lcWindow)
   IF UPPER(LEFT(m.lcWindow,2)) $ "WR/WT"
      m.lcProgram = TRIM(SUBSTR(m.lcWindow,3,8))
      IF RIGHT(m.lcProgram,1) $ "1,2,3,4,5,6,7,8,9,0"
         lcProgram = LEFT(lcProgram,LEN(lcProgram)-1)
      ENDIF
      m.lcProgram = m.lcProgram+".SPR"
   ENDIF
   IF _WINDOWS OR _MAC
      m.lcWindow = WCHILD("WZMAIN",1)
   ELSE
      m.lcWindow = WCHILD("",1)
   ENDIF
ENDDO
RETURN m.lcProgram
```

```
*********************************************
FUNCTION CurrWR
*********************************************
*  Procedure.........: CurrWR
*  Author............: yag
*  Project...........: COMMON
*  Created...........: 04/16/93
*  Copyright.........: (c) Flash Creative Management, 1993
*) Description.......: FUNCTION CurrWR
*)                   : This routine finds the current READ and returns
*)                   : the window name associated with it. If there is
*)                   : no READ window it returns a blank.
*  Calling Samples...: lcWR = currwr()
*  Parameter List....:
*  Major change list.:
PRIVATE m.lcWindow, m.lcReadWind
IF _WINDOWS OR _MAC
   m.lcWindow = UPPER(WCHILD("WZMAIN",0))
ELSE
   m.lcWindow = UPPER(WCHILD("",0))
ENDIF
DO WHILE !EMPTY(m.lcWindow)
   IF UPPER(LEFT(m.lcWindow,2)) = "WR"
      m.lcReadWind = m.lcWindow
      IF RIGHT(m.lcReadWind,1) $ "1,2,3,4,5,6,7,8,9,0"
         m.lcReadWind = LEFT(m.lcReadWind,LEN(m.lcReadWind)-1)
      ENDIF
   ENDIF
   IF _WINDOWS OR _MAC
      m.lcWindow = WCHILD("WZMAIN",1)
   ELSE
      m.lcWindow = WCHILD("",1)
   ENDIF
ENDDO
RETURN m.lcReadWind
*********************************************
PROCEDURE ControlPrc
*********************************************
*  Procedure.........: ControlPrc
*  Author............: yag
*  Project...........: COMMON
*  Created...........: 12/09/92
*  Copyright.........: (c) Flash Creative Management, 1992
*) Description.......: PROCEDURE ControlPrc
*)                   : Manages the calling of Methods. Typically by adding
*)                   : "it" to the passed name.
*  Calling Samples...: DO ControlPrc WITH "Add"
*  Parameter List....: tcTool   -   The tool chosen from the toolbar
*  Major change list.:
PARAMETER tcTool
=ResetWin(CurrWR())
DO CASE
   CASE tcTool = "Add"
      gcLastTool = tcTool
      glEditable = .T.
      _CUROBJ = 1
      DO InitIt
   CASE tcTool = "Save"
      IF gcLastTool = "Add"
         DO ADDIT
```

```
      ELSE
         DO SaveIt
      ENDIF
      IF glOkToSave                    && the valid checking for the
                                       &&   screen checked ok
         WAIT WINDOW NOWAIT "Information saved"
         glEditable = .F.
      ENDIF
   CASE tcTool = "Oops!" OR tcTool = "Cancel"
      glOkToSave = .T.
      DO OopsIt
      WAIT WINDOW NOWAIT "Information reset to previous status"
      glEditable = .F.
   OTHERWISE
      gcLastTool = tcTool
      glEditable = .F.
      DO (ALLTRIM(CHRTRAN(tcTool,'.','')) + "It")
ENDCASE
IF !glQuitting
   DO dimnavigat
   IF _WINDOWS
      _CUROBJ = 1
   ENDIF
ENDIF
RETURN
*********************************************
PROCEDURE DimNavigat
*********************************************
*  Procedure.........: DimNavigat
*  Author............: yag
*  Project...........: COMMON
*  Created...........: 12/09/1992
*  Copyright.........: (c) Flash Creative Management, 1992
*) Description.......: PROCEDURE DimNavigat
*)                   : Dims navigational buttons appropriately
*  Calling Samples...: DO DimNavigat
*  Parameter List....:
*  Major change list.:
PRIVATE lnOldRec, llRecords
IF EOF()
   GO TOP
ENDIF
lnOldRec = RECNO()
LOCATE
llRecords = !EOF()
IF llRecords                              && if we have records
   GO lnOldRec
   IF !glEditable                         && not editing
      SHOW GET m.lhAdd ENABLE
      SHOW GET m.lhEdit ENABLE
      SHOW GET m.lhSave DISABLE
      SHOW GET m.lhOops DISABLE
      SHOW GET m.lhClose ENABLE
      SHOW GET m.lhList ENABLE
      SHOW GET m.lhFind ENABLE
      STORE .F. TO m.gbList, m.gbFind
      SKIP -1                             && test for bof()
      IF BOF()                            && and disable properly
         SHOW GET m.lhTop DISABLE
```

```
         SHOW GET m.lhPrior DISABLE
         STORE .T. TO m.gbTop, m.gbPrior
      ELSE
         SHOW GET m.lhTop ENABLE
         SHOW GET m.lhPrior ENABLE
         STORE .F. TO m.gbTop, m.gbPrior
      ENDIF
      GO lnOldRec
      SKIP
      IF EOF()                                 && test for eof()
         SHOW GET m.lhNext DISABLE             && and disable properly
         SHOW GET m.lhBottom DISABLE
         STORE .T. TO m.gbNext, m.gbBottom
      ELSE
         SHOW GET m.lhNext ENABLE
         SHOW GET m.lhBottom ENABLE
         STORE .F. TO m.gbNext, m.gbBottom
      ENDIF
      GO lnOldRec
   ELSE                                        && we are editing
      SHOW GET m.lhAdd DISABLE
      SHOW GET m.lhEdit DISABLE
      SHOW GET m.lhSave ENABLE
      SHOW GET m.lhOops ENABLE
      SHOW GET m.lhClose DISABLE
      SHOW GET m.lhTop DISABLE
      SHOW GET m.lhPrior DISABLE
      SHOW GET m.lhNext DISABLE
      SHOW GET m.lhBottom DISABLE
      SHOW GET m.lhList DISABLE
      SHOW GET m.lhFind DISABLE
      STORE .T. TO m.gbTop, m.gbPrior, m.gbNext, m.gbBottom, m.gbList,
m.gbFind
   ENDIF
   STORE .F. TO m.gbEdit, m.gbDelete
ELSE                                           && there are no records
   SHOW GET m.lhTop DISABLE
   SHOW GET m.lhPrior DISABLE
   SHOW GET m.lhNext DISABLE
   SHOW GET m.lhBottom DISABLE
   SHOW GET m.lhList DISABLE
   SHOW GET m.lhEdit DISABLE
   SHOW GET m.lhFind DISABLE
   IF GlEditable                               && We are adding a record
      SHOW GET m.lhAdd  DISABLE
      SHOW GET m.lhClose DISABLE
      SHOW GET m.lhSave ENABLE
      SHOW GET m.lhOops ENABLE
   ELSE
      SHOW GET m.lhAdd  ENABLE
      SHOW GET m.lhClose ENABLE
      SHOW GET m.lhSave DISABLE
      SHOW GET m.lhOops DISABLE
   ENDIF
   STORE .T. TO m.gbTop, m.gbPrior, m.gbNext, m.gbBottom, m.gbList, m.gbEdit,
m.gbDelete, m.gbFind
ENDIF
* Dim the button based on the Security database
IF SEEK("RecoAdd ","Security")
   SHOW GET m.lhAdd DISABLE
```

```
ENDIF
IF SEEK("RecoEdit","Security")
   SHOW GET m.lhEdit DISABLE
ENDIF
IF SEEK("RecoSave","Security")
   SHOW GET m.lhSave DISABLE
ENDIF
IF SEEK("RecoRese","Security")
   SHOW GET m.lhOops DISABLE
ENDIF
IF SEEK("RecoTop ","Security")
   SHOW GET m.lhTop DISABLE
ENDIF
IF SEEK("RecoPrio","Security")
   SHOW GET m.lhPrior DISABLE
ENDIF
IF SEEK("RecoNext","Security")
   SHOW GET m.lhNext DISABLE
ENDIF
IF SEEK("RecoBott","Security")
   SHOW GET m.lhBottom DISABLE
ENDIF
IF SEEK("RecoList","Security")
   SHOW GET m.lhList DISABLE
ENDIF
IF SEEK("RecoFind","Security")
   SHOW GET m.lhFind DISABLE
ENDIF
IF SEEK("RecoClos","Security")
   SHOW GET m.lhClose DISABLE
ENDIF
* Dim the current READ Window if not in EDIT mode
lcReadWind = currwr() && current read window
IF !glEditable
   DO DisableIT
ELSE
   DO EnableIt
ENDIF
RETURN
*************************************************
PROCEDURE ResetWin
*************************************************
*  Procedure.........: ResetWin
*  Author............: yag
*  Project...........: COMMON
*  Created...........: 12/09/1992
*  Copyright.........: (c) Flash Creative Management, 1992
*) Description.......: PROCEDURE ResetWin
*)                   : Resets a window to its normal size and
*)                   : position if it is minimized.
*  Calling Samples...: =ResetWin(<Window>)
*  Parameter List....: tcWindName - Window to be reset
*  Major change list.:
PARAMETER tcWindName
IF WMINIMUM(tcWindName)
   ZOOM WINDOW (tcWindName) NORM
ENDIF
RETURN
```

Chapter 18

Reusable Screens

Initial Information Screen: ABOUT.SCX

As I discussed in the original *FoxPro Codebook*, one of the cardinal rules of user-friendly design is to make it easy for the user to accomplish their tasks, including contacting you when necessary. It is also important to make any information that you may require easily available to your user so that they can get it to you when necessary. This is accomplished through a series of windows attached to the About... menu bar under the System menu pad.

Compact Disc Ordering Application

(c) Flash Creative Management, Inc.

1060 Main Street
Third Floor
River Edge, NJ 07661

(201) 489-2500

< Prior > « Done » < Next >

These windows are standardized and do not change between applications. This version of the About screens are data driven, taking their information from the global memory variables set up in Traficop.

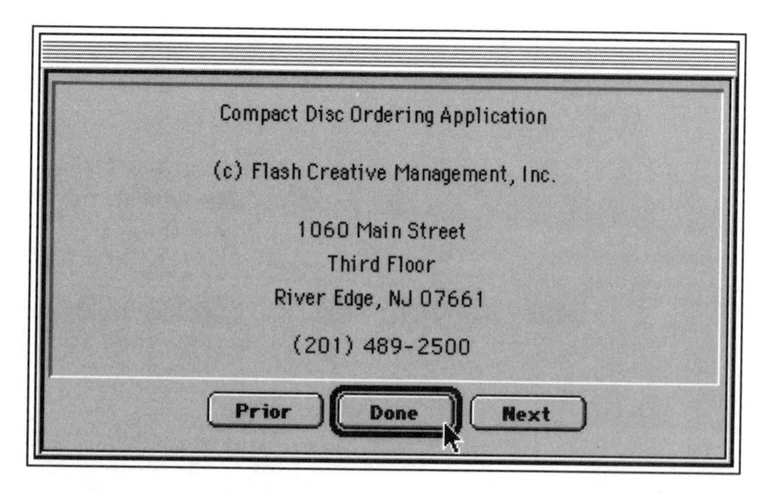

As before, we do not have FoxPro automatically release the window for us. We use the same window in all of the screen sets. In this manner, we prevent any window "flickering" that would occur if the window is being constantly erased and redrawn. We name the window (instead of allowing FoxPro to name it for us), so that we can release it explicitly when the user selects <DONE>.

Note that the ABOUT program is actually called by the menu, so that we can now provide a <NEXT> and <PREVIOUS> capability that can be continuously called without nesting our calls.

This window lists the name of the application, the copyright holder, the address and phone number. It provides users with the information that will allow them to easily get in touch with you, should the need arise.

The push buttons on the bottom of the window allow the user to access more system information or to close the window.

```
*-------------------------------------------------------------
**************************************************************
**--    ABOUT.SCX - DOS PLATFORM
**************************************************************
```

```
( ) DeskTop                           (·) Window

Name:   wmAbout                       <Type...>
Title:
Footer:

Size:               Screen Code:

 Height:   14        [X] Setup...
 Width:    61        [ ] Cleanup & Procs...          «  OK  »

Position:           READ Clauses:                   < Cancel >

 Row:        0       [ ] Activate...     [ ] Show...
 Column:     0       [ ] Valid...        [ ] When...
 [X] Center          [ ] Deactivate...

Environment:                          [X] Add alias

     Environment NOT saved with screen.
```

```
Type:    Dialog

Attributes:      Border:

 [ ] Close        ( ) None
 [X] Float        ( ) Single
 [X] Shadow       (·) Double       «  OK  »
 [ ] Minimize     ( ) Panel
                  ( ) System       < Cancel >

Color Schemes:

 Primary:         Popup:

 Dialogs          Dialog Pop
```

```
**************************************************************
*  SCREEN SETUP CODE
**************************************************************
*  Program...........: ABOUT Screen
*  Author............: yag
*  Project...........: COMMON
*  Created...........: 04/16/93
*  Copyright.........: (c) Flash Creative Management, 1993
*) Description.......: Main ABOUT Screen
*)                   : Shows information about Flash and phone
*)                   : #'s for support
```

```
*  Calling Samples...: Called from About.prg automatically
*  Parameter List....:
*  Major change list.:
#SECTION 1
PARAMETER lcSystem
IF EMPTY(lcSystem)
  IF FILE("Setup.dbf")
     lcSystem = ALLTRIM(Setup.cSystName)
  ELSE
     lcSystem = "Undefined System"
  ENDIF
ENDIF
#SECTION 2
************************************************************
*--    G E T   O B J E C T S
************************************************************
*===========================================================
*
*===========================================================
 @   1,   1
```

```
Field:

  (·) Say         ( ) Get        ( ) Edit

< Say...   > PADC(lcSystem,57)
                                             «   OK   »
< Format... > @I
                                             < Cancel >
Range:

  [ ] Upper...                  [ ] Lower...

[ ] When...     [ ] Error...     [ ] Scroll bar
[ ] Valid...    [ ] Comment...   [ ] Allow tabs
[ ] Message...  [ ] Disabled     [ ] Refresh
```

```
*===========================================================
*
*===========================================================
 @   3,   1
```

```
Field:
  (·) Say          ( ) Get          ( ) Edit

<  Say...    > PADC('(c) '+m.gccompany,57)
                                              «   OK   »
< Format... > @I
                                              < Cancel >
Range:
  [ ] Upper...                  [ ] Lower...

[ ] When...     [ ] Error...     [ ] Scroll bar
[ ] Valid...    [ ] Comment...   [ ] Allow tabs
[ ] Message...  [ ] Disabled     [ ] Refresh

*==============================================================
*
*==============================================================
 @   5,   1

Field:
  (·) Say          ( ) Get          ( ) Edit

<  Say...    > PADC(m.gcaddress1,57)
                                              «   OK   »
< Format... > @I
                                              < Cancel >
Range:
  [ ] Upper...                  [ ] Lower...

[ ] When...     [ ] Error...     [ ] Scroll bar
[ ] Valid...    [ ] Comment...   [ ] Allow tabs
[ ] Message...  [ ] Disabled     [ ] Refresh

*==============================================================
*
*==============================================================
 @   6,   1
```

```
 Field:
 (·) Say        ( ) Get        ( ) Edit

 <  Say...   > m.gcaddress2
                                          «   OK   »
 < Format... > @TI
                                          < Cancel >
 Range:
 [ ] Upper...                 [ ] Lower...

 [ ] When...     [ ] Error...      [ ] Scroll bar
 [ ] Valid...    [ ] Comment...    [ ] Allow tabs
 [ ] Message...  [ ] Disabled      [ ] Refresh
*============================================================
*
*============================================================
 @   7,   1

 Field:
 (·) Say        ( ) Get        ( ) Edit

 <  Say...   > IIF(EMPTY(m.gcCity),"",PADC(csz(m.gcCity,m
                                          «   OK   »
 < Format... > @I
                                          < Cancel >
 Range:
 [ ] Upper...                 [ ] Lower...

 [ ] When...     [ ] Error...      [ ] Scroll bar
 [ ] Valid...    [ ] Comment...    [ ] Allow tabs
 [ ] Message...  [ ] Disabled      [ ] Refresh
*============================================================
*
*============================================================
 @   9,   22
```

```
Field:
 (·) Say          ( ) Get          ( ) Edit

<  Say...    > m.gcphone
                                              «   OK   »
< Format... > @RI (999) 999-9999
                                              < Cancel >
Range:
 [ ] Upper...                 [ ] Lower...

[ ] When...     [ ] Error...     [ ] Scroll bar
[ ] Valid...    [ ] Comment...   [ ] Allow tabs
[ ] Message...  [ ] Disabled     [ ] Refresh
*============================================================
*  m.lhNext
*============================================================
 @  11,  39
 Spacing:    5

 Push Button Prompts:     (·) Horizontal   ( ) Vertical
                          [X] Terminating  <Spacing...>
 \<Next                  Variable:
                          < Choose... >  m.lhNext
                         Options:
                          [ ] When...     [ ] Comment...
                          [X] Valid...    [ ] Disabled
                          [ ] Message...

              «   OK   »    < Cancel >
------------------------------------------------------------
*-- m.lhNext Valid Clause
------------------------------------------------------------

 Valid
  (·) Procedure
  ( ) Expression

lcNext =  'aboutgen.spr'
*============================================================
```

```
*  m.lhPrior
*==============================================================
 @  11,   9
 Spacing:    5

 Push Button Prompts:     (·) Horizontal    ( ) Vertical
                          [X] Terminating  <Spacing...>
 \<Prior
                          Variable:

                          < Choose... >  m.lhPrior

                          Options:

                          [ ] When...     [ ] Comment...
                          [X] Valid...    [ ] Disabled
                          [ ] Message...

           «   OK   »    < Cancel >
--------------------------------------------------------------
*-- m.lhPrior Valid Clause
--------------------------------------------------------------

 Valid

  (·) Procedure
  ( ) Expression

lcNext = 'aboutcom.spr'
*==============================================================
*  m.lhDone
*==============================================================
 @  11,  24
 Spacing:    5

 Push Button Prompts:     (·) Horizontal    ( ) Vertical
                          [X] Terminating  <Spacing...>
 \!\?\<Done
                          Variable:

                          < Choose... >  m.lhDone

                          Options:

                          [ ] When...     [ ] Comment...
                          [X] Valid...    [ ] Disabled
                          [ ] Message...

           «   OK   »    < Cancel >
```

```
--------------------------------------------------------------
*-- m.lhDone Valid Clause
--------------------------------------------------------------

 Valid
   ( ) Procedure
   ( ) Expression

RELEASE WINDOW wmAbout
llEndAbout = .T.
*-------------------------------------------------------------
**************************************************************
**--    ABOUT.SCX - MAC PLATFORM
**************************************************************

 ( ) DeskTop                          (·) Window

 Name:    wmAbout                     <Type...>
 Title:
 Footer:

 Size:              Screen Code:

  Height:   15.667   [X] Setup...
  Width:    58.333   [ ] Cleanup & Procs...          «   OK   »

 Position:          READ Clauses:                    < Cancel >

  Row:       0.000   [ ] Activate...    [ ] Show...
  Column:    0.000   [ ] Valid...       [ ] When...
  [X] Center         [ ] Deactivate...

 Environment:                        [X] Add alias

        Environment NOT saved with screen.
```

```
Type:  [ Dialog ]

Attributes:        Border:

[ ] Close          ( ) None
[X] Float          ( ) Single
[X] Shadow         (·) Double        «  OK  »
[ ] Minimize       ( ) Panel
                   ( ) System        < Cancel >

Color Schemes:

  Primary:         Popup:
  [          ]     [          ]
```

```
MAC      RGB Fill Color Scheme: (201,201,201)
MAC      Font: Geneva,  10
 Screen Setup code above
************************************************************
*--   G E T     O B J E C T S
************************************************************
*===========================================================
*
*===========================================================
 @   1.083,   5.833
```

```
Field:
  (·) Say          ( ) Get          ( ) Edit

< Say...    > PADC(lcSystem,57)
                                              «  OK  »
< Format... > @I
                                              < Cancel >
Range:
  [ ] Upper...                 [ ] Lower...

[ ] When...      [ ] Error...      [ ] Scroll bar
[ ] Valid...     [ ] Comment...    [ ] Allow tabs
[ ] Message...   [ ] Disabled      [ ] Refresh
```

```
MAC      RGB Color Scheme: (,,,,,)
MAC      Font: Geneva,  10
*===========================================================
*
*===========================================================
 @   3.500,   5.833
```

```
Field:
  (·) Say          ( ) Get          ( ) Edit

<  Say...    > PADC('(c) '+m.gccompany,57)
                                                  «   OK   »
< Format... > @I
                                                  < Cancel >
Range:
  [ ] Upper...                  [ ] Lower...

[ ] When...     [ ] Error...     [ ] Scroll bar
[ ] Valid...    [ ] Comment...   [ ] Allow tabs
[ ] Message...  [ ] Disabled     [ ] Refresh

MAC       RCB Color Scheme: (,,,,,)
MAC       Font: Geneva,  10
*============================================================
*
*============================================================
 @   5.917,    5.833

Field:
  (·) Say          ( ) Get          ( ) Edit

<  Say...    > PADC(m.gcaddress1,57)
                                                  «   OK   »
< Format... > @I
                                                  < Cancel >
Range:
  [ ] Upper...                  [ ] Lower...

[ ] When...     [ ] Error...     [ ] Scroll bar
[ ] Valid...    [ ] Comment...   [ ] Allow tabs
[ ] Message...  [ ] Disabled     [ ] Refresh

MAC       RGB Color Scheme: (,,,,,)
MAC       Font: Geneva,  10
*============================================================
*
*============================================================
 @   7.333,    5.833
```

```
Field:
 (·) Say          ( ) Get          ( ) Edit

< Say...    > m.gcaddress2
                                               «   OK   »
< Format... > @TI
                                               < Cancel >
Range:
 [ ] Upper...                 [ ] Lower...

[ ] When...      [ ] Error...      [ ] Scroll bar
[ ] Valid...     [ ] Comment...    [ ] Allow tabs
[ ] Message...   [ ] Disabled      [ ] Refresh

MAC       RGB Color Scheme: (,,,,,)
MAC       Font: Geneva,  10
*==============================================================
*
*==============================================================
 @   8.750,   5.833

Field:
 (·) Say          ( ) Get          ( ) Edit

< Say...    > IIF(EMPTY(m.gcCity),"",PADC(csz(m.gcCity,m
                                               «   OK   »
< Format... > @I
                                               < Cancel >
Range:
 [ ] Upper...                 [ ] Lower...

[ ] When...      [ ] Error...      [ ] Scroll bar
[ ] Valid...     [ ] Comment...    [ ] Allow tabs
[ ] Message...   [ ] Disabled      [ ] Refresh

MAC       RGB Color Scheme: (,,,,,)
MAC       Font: Geneva,  10
*==============================================================
*
*==============================================================
 @  10.750,  20.833
```

```
Field:
   (·) Say          ( ) Get          ( ) Edit

< Say...   > m.gcphone
                                          «  OK  »
< Format... > @RI (999) 999-9999
                                          < Cancel >
Range:
   [ ] Upper...                [ ] Lower...

[ ] When...      [ ] Error...     [ ] Scroll bar
[ ] Valid...     [ ] Comment...   [ ] Allow tabs
[ ] Message...   [ ] Disabled     [ ] Refresh

MAC      RGB Color Scheme: (,,,,,)
MAC      Font: Geneva,  10
*============================================================
*  m.lhNext
*============================================================
 @  13.250,  36.667
     SIZE   1.500,  10.000
 Spacing:    5

 Push Button Prompts:        (·) Horizontal   ( ) Vertical
                             [X] Terminating  <Spacing...>
 \<Next
                            Variable:
                             < Choose... >  m.lhNext
                            Options:
                             [ ] When...     [ ] Comment...
                             [X] Valid...    [ ] Disabled
                             [ ] Message...

              «  OK  »    < Cancel >

MAC      RGB Color Scheme: (,,,,,)
MAC      Font: Geneva,   9
        Style: Bold
 Valid code above
*============================================================
*  m.lhPrior
*============================================================
 @  13.250,  14.167
     SIZE   1.500,  10.000
 Spacing:    5
```

```
Push Button Prompts:        (·) Horizontal    ( ) Vertical
                            [X] Terminating  <Spacing...>
\<Prior
                            Variable:

                            < Choose... >  m.lhPrior

                            Options:

                            [ ] When...       [ ] Comment...
                            [X] Valid...      [ ] Disabled
                            [ ] Message...

              «   OK   »    < Cancel >
```

```
MAC      RGB Color Scheme: (,,,,,)
MAC      Font: Geneva,   9
        Style: Bold
 Valid code above
*============================================================
*  m.lhDone
*============================================================
 @  13.250,  25.333
     SIZE   1.500,  10.000
 Spacing:    5
```

```
Push Button Prompts:        (·) Horizontal    ( ) Vertical
                            [X] Terminating  <Spacing...>
\!\?\<Done
                            Variable:

                            < Choose... >  m.lhDone

                            Options:

                            [ ] When...       [ ] Comment...
                            [X] Valid...      [ ] Disabled
                            [ ] Message...

              «   OK   »    < Cancel >
```

```
MAC      RGB Color Scheme: (,,,,,)
MAC      Font: Geneva,   9
        Style: Bold
 Valid code above
*============================================================
*  Line
*============================================================
 @   0.333,   0.333
MAC      RGB Color Scheme: (137,137,137,137,137,137)
            Pen: 2
*============================================================
*  Line
```

```
*==============================================================
 @   0.417,  57.833
MAC       RGB Color Scheme: (255,255,255,255,255,255)
            Pen: 1
*==============================================================
*  Line
*==============================================================
 @   0.333,   0.333
MAC       RGB Color Scheme: (137,137,137,137,137,137)
            Pen: 2
*==============================================================
*  Line
*==============================================================
 @  12.667,   0.500
MAC       RGB Color Scheme: (255,255,255,255,255,255)
            Pen: 1
*--------------------------------------------------------------
**************************************************************
**--     ABOUT.SCX - WINDOWS PLATFORM
**************************************************************
```

```
( ) DeskTop                          (•) Window

Name:   wmAbout                      <Type...>
Title:
Footer:

Size:             Screen Code:

 Height:   15.667   [X] Setup...
 Width:    58.250   [ ] Cleanup & Procs...           «  OK  »

Position:         READ Clauses:                      < Cancel >

 Row:       0.000   [ ] Activate...    [ ] Show...
 Column:    0.000   [ ] Valid...       [ ] When...
 [X] Center         [ ] Deactivate...

Environment:                        [X] Add alias

        Environment NOT saved with screen.
```

```
Type:          Dialog

Attributes:        Border:

 [ ] Close          ( ) None
 [X] Float          ( ) Single
 [X] Shadow         (·) Double      «   OK   »
 [ ] Minimize       ( ) Panel
                    ( ) System      < Cancel >

Color Schemes:

 Primary:           Popup:

WINDOWS  RGB Fill Color Scheme: (192,192,192)
WINDOWS  Font: Terminal,   9
 Screen Setup code above
************************************************************
*--    G E T   O B J E C T S
************************************************************
*===========================================================
*
*===========================================================
 @   1.167,   1.125

 Field:

  (·) Say            ( ) Get            ( ) Edit

 <  Say...    > PADC(lcSystem,57)
                                                    «   OK   »
 < Format... > @I
                                                    < Cancel >
 Range:

  [ ] Upper...                    [ ] Lower...

 [ ] When...       [ ] Error...      [ ] Scroll bar
 [ ] Valid...      [ ] Comment...    [ ] Allow tabs
 [ ] Message...    [ ] Disabled      [ ] Refresh

WINDOWS  RGB Color Scheme: (,,,,,)
WINDOWS  Font: Terminal,   9
*===========================================================
*
*===========================================================
 @   3.583,   1.125
```

```
Field:

  (·) Say           ( ) Get           ( ) Edit

<  Say...    > PADC('(c) '+m.gccompany,57)
                                                  «    OK    »
< Format... > @I
                                                  < Cancel >
Range:

  [ ] Upper...                    [ ] Lower...

[ ] When...      [ ] Error...     [ ] Scroll bar
[ ] Valid...     [ ] Comment...   [ ] Allow tabs
[ ] Message...   [ ] Disabled     [ ] Refresh

WINDOWS  RGB Color Scheme: (,,,,,)
WINDOWS  Font: Terminal,   9
*============================================================
*
*============================================================
 @   6.000,   1.125

Field:

  (·) Say           ( ) Get           ( ) Edit

<  Say...    > PADC(m.gcaddress1,57)
                                                  «    OK    »
< Format... > @I
                                                  < Cancel >
Range:

  [ ] Upper...                    [ ] Lower...

[ ] When...      [ ] Error...     [ ] Scroll bar
[ ] Valid...     [ ] Comment...   [ ] Allow tabs
[ ] Message...   [ ] Disabled     [ ] Refresh

WINDOWS  RGB Color Scheme: (,,,,,)
WINDOWS  Font: Terminal,   9
*============================================================
*
*============================================================
 @   7.417,   1.125
```

```
Field:
 (·) Say        ( ) Get        ( ) Edit

< Say...    > m.gcaddress2
                                          «   OK   »
< Format... > @TI
                                          < Cancel >
Range:
 [ ] Upper...                 [ ] Lower...

[ ] When...      [ ] Error...     [ ] Scroll bar
[ ] Valid...     [ ] Comment...   [ ] Allow tabs
[ ] Message...   [ ] Disabled     [ ] Refresh

WINDOWS  RGB Color Scheme: (,,,,,)
WINDOWS  Font: Terminal,   9
*==========================================================
*
*==========================================================
 @   8.833,   1.125

Field:
 (·) Say        ( ) Get        ( ) Edit

< Say...    > IIF(EMPTY(m.gcCity),"",PADC(csz(m.gcCity,m
                                          «   OK   »
< Format... > @I
                                          < Cancel >
Range:
 [ ] Upper...                 [ ] Lower...

[ ] When...      [ ] Error...     [ ] Scroll bar
[ ] Valid...     [ ] Comment...   [ ] Allow tabs
[ ] Message...   [ ] Disabled     [ ] Refresh

WINDOWS  RGB Color Scheme: (,,,,,)
WINDOWS  Font: Terminal,   9
*==========================================================
*
*==========================================================
 @  10.833,  22.000
```

```
Field:
 ( ) Say          ( ) Get          ( ) Edit

< Say...    > m.gcphone
                                            «   OK   »
< Format... > @RI (999) 999-9999
                                            < Cancel >
Range:
 [ ] Upper...               [ ] Lower...

[ ] When...      [ ] Error...      [ ] Scroll bar
[ ] Valid...     [ ] Comment...    [ ] Allow tabs
[ ] Message...   [ ] Disabled      [ ] Refresh
WINDOWS  RGB Color Scheme: (,,,,,)
WINDOWS  Font: Terminal,   9
*=============================================================
*  m.lhNext
*=============================================================
 @  13.250,  36.625
     SIZE   1.769,  10.000
 Spacing:    5

 Push Button Prompts:     ( ) Horizontal    ( ) Vertical
                          [X] Terminating   <Spacing...>
 \<Next
                         Variable:

                          < Choose... >  m.lhNext

                         Options:

                          [ ] When...     [ ] Comment...
                          [X] Valid...    [ ] Disabled
                          [ ] Message...

              «   OK   »    < Cancel >
WINDOWS  RGB Color Scheme: (,,,,,)
WINDOWS  Font: MS Sans Serif,   8
         Style: Bold
 Valid code above
*=============================================================
*  m.lhPrior
*=============================================================
 @  13.250,  14.125
     SIZE   1.769,  10.000
 Spacing:    5
```

```
┌──────────────────────────────────────────────────────────────┐
│                                                              │
│  Push Button Prompts:     ┌────────────────────────────────┐ │
│                           │ (·) Horizontal    ( ) Vertical │ │
│  ┌──────────────────┐     │ [X] Terminating  <Spacing...>  │ │
│  │ \<Prior          │     └────────────────────────────────┘ │
│  │                  │     Variable:                          │
│  │                  │     ┌────────────────────────────────┐ │
│  │                  │     │ < Choose... >  m.lhPrior       │ │
│  │                  │     └────────────────────────────────┘ │
│  │                  │     Options:                           │
│  │                  │     ┌────────────────────────────────┐ │
│  │                  │     │ [ ] When...      [ ] Comment...│ │
│  │                  │     │ [X] Valid...     [ ] Disabled  │ │
│  │                  │     │ [ ] Message...                 │ │
│  └──────────────────┘     └────────────────────────────────┘ │
│                                                              │
│              «   OK   »    < Cancel >                        │
│                                                              │
└──────────────────────────────────────────────────────────────┘
WINDOWS  RGB Color Scheme: (,,,,,)
WINDOWS  Font: MS Sans Serif,    8
        Style: Bold
 Valid code above
*============================================================
*  m.lhDone
*============================================================
 @  13.250,  25.375
    SIZE   1.769,  10.000
 Spacing:    5
┌──────────────────────────────────────────────────────────────┐
│                                                              │
│  Push Button Prompts:     ┌────────────────────────────────┐ │
│                           │ (·) Horizontal    ( ) Vertical │ │
│  ┌──────────────────┐     │ [X] Terminating  <Spacing...>  │ │
│  │ \!\?\<Done       │     └────────────────────────────────┘ │
│  │                  │     Variable:                          │
│  │                  │     ┌────────────────────────────────┐ │
│  │                  │     │ < Choose... >  m.lhDone        │ │
│  │                  │     └────────────────────────────────┘ │
│  │                  │     Options:                           │
│  │                  │     ┌────────────────────────────────┐ │
│  │                  │     │ [ ] When...      [ ] Comment...│ │
│  │                  │     │ [X] Valid...     [ ] Disabled  │ │
│  │                  │     │ [ ] Message...                 │ │
│  └──────────────────┘     └────────────────────────────────┘ │
│                                                              │
│              «   OK   »    < Cancel >                        │
│                                                              │
└──────────────────────────────────────────────────────────────┘
WINDOWS  RGB Color Scheme: (,,,,,)
WINDOWS  Font: MS Sans Serif,    8
        Style: Bold
 Valid code above
*============================================================
*  Line
*============================================================
 @   0.333,   0.375
WINDOWS  RGB Color Scheme: (128,128,128,128,128,128)
           Pen: 2
*============================================================
*  Line
```

```
*=============================================================
 @   0.417,   57.875
WINDOWS  RGB Color Scheme: (255,255,255,255,255,255)
           Pen: 1
*=============================================================
*  Line
*=============================================================
 @   0.333,   0.375
WINDOWS  RGB Color Scheme: (128,128,128,128,128,128)
           Pen: 2
*=============================================================
*  Line
*=============================================================
 @  12.667,   0.500
WINDOWS  RGB Color Scheme: (255,255,255,255,255,255)
           Pen: 1
```

About...: A Summary

The About... dialog is a good example of creating a reusable set of windows. We write them once, and can now call them from every application. The windows automatically function without any necessary "tweaking" from application to application. Any enhancements that we may care to make will automatically find their way into every application that we have made. No extra work is required.

Developer Information Screen: ABOUTCOM.SCX

This window did not appear in the original FoxPro Codebook. It is an example of blatant self promotion in an application. Essentially, this window allows the developer to put an unlimited amount of information about their company or the application in the About... screens, so that the user can always find it.

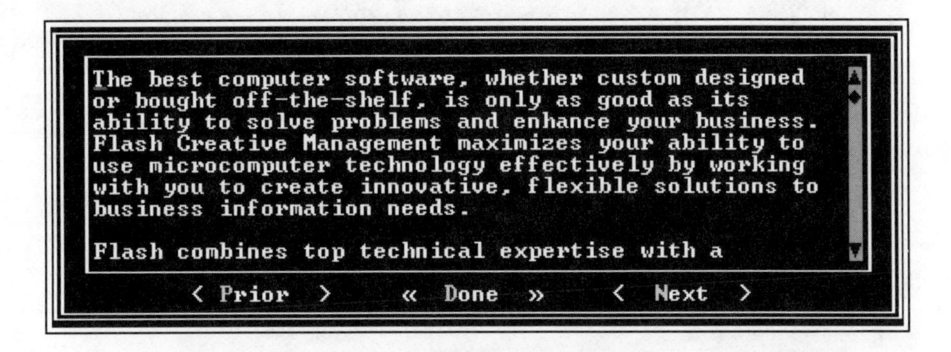

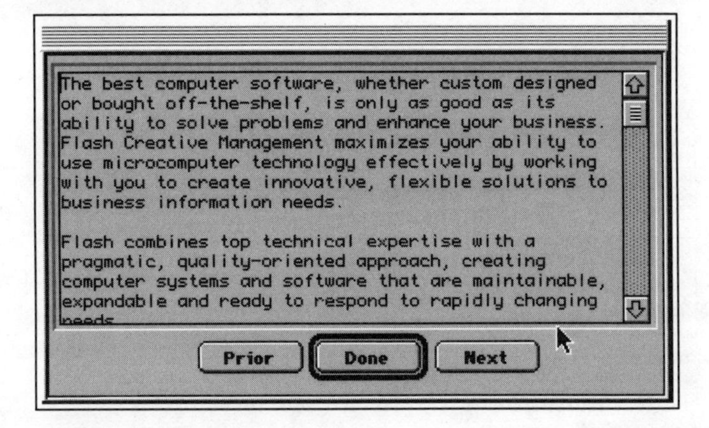

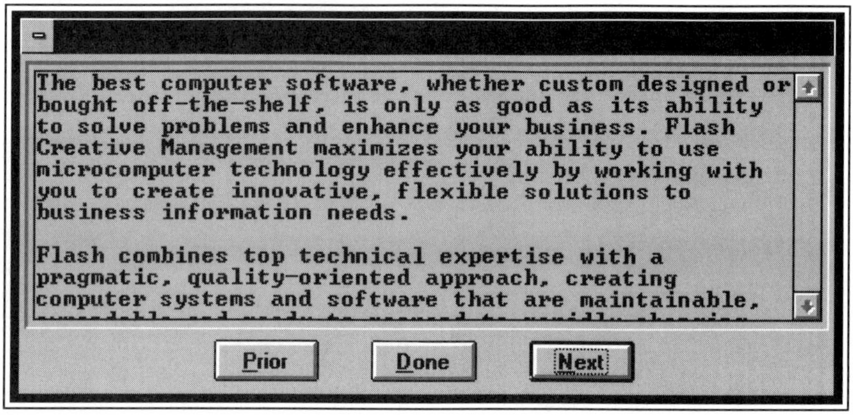

```
The best computer software, whether custom designed or
bought off-the-shelf, is only as good as its ability
to solve problems and enhance your business. Flash
Creative Management maximizes your ability to use
microcomputer technology effectively by working with
you to create innovative, flexible solutions to
business information needs.

Flash combines top technical expertise with a
pragmatic, quality-oriented approach, creating
computer systems and software that are maintainable,

        Prior        Done        Next
```

```
*--------------------------------------------------------------
***************************************************************
**--    ABOUTCOM.SCX - DOS PLATFORM
***************************************************************

 ( ) DeskTop                          (•) Window

 Name:    wmAbout                     <Type...>
 Title:
 Footer:

 Size:              Screen Code:

  Height:   14       [X] Setup...
  Width:    61       [X] Cleanup & Procs...              «   OK   »

 Position:          READ Clauses:                        < Cancel >

  Row:        0      [ ] Activate...    [ ] Show...
  Column:     0      [ ] Valid...       [ ] When...
  [X] Center         [ ] Deactivate...

 Environment:                          [X] Add alias

        Environment NOT saved with screen.
```

```
 Type:  [ Dialog ]

 Attributes:       Border:

 [ ] Close         ( ) None
 [X] Float         ( ) Single
 [X] Shadow        (·) Double      «  OK  »
 [ ] Minimize      ( ) Panel
                   ( ) System      < Cancel >

 Color Schemes:

   Primary:        Popup:
   [ Dialogs ]     [ Dialog Pop ]
```

```
************************************************************
*  SCREEN SETUP CODE
************************************************************
*  Program...........: ABOUTMEM Screen
*  Author............: yag
*  Project...........: COMMON
*  Created...........: 04/16/93
*  Copyright.........: (c) Flash Creative Management, 1993
*) Description.......: ABOUT COMPANY Screen
*)                   : Shows information about development company
*)                   : that is taken from IntSetup.dbf
*  Calling Samples...: Called from About.prg automatically
*  Parameter List....:
*  Major change list.:
PRIVATE jcPair, jcOldPair
jcPair      = SCHEME(5,1)
jcOldPair   = SCHEME(5,2)
SET COLOR OF SCHEME 5 TO ,&jcPair
************************************************************
*--    G E T    O B J E C T S
************************************************************
*===========================================================
*  Box
*===========================================================
 @   0,   1
 SIZE  11,  57
*===========================================================
*  m.lhNext
*===========================================================
 @  11,  39
 Spacing:    5
```

```
╔══════════════════════════════════════════════════════════════╗
║  Push Button Prompts:     ┌──────────────────────────────────┐║
║                           │ (•) Horizontal    ( ) Vertical   │║
║  ┌────────────────────┐   │ [X] Terminating  <Spacing...>    │║
║  │\<Next              │   └──────────────────────────────────┘║
║  │                    │   Variable:                           ║
║  │                    │   ┌──────────────────────────────────┐║
║  │                    │   │ < Choose... >  m.lhNext          │║
║  │                    │   └──────────────────────────────────┘║
║  │                    │   Options:                            ║
║  │                    │   ┌──────────────────────────────────┐║
║  │                    │   │ [ ] When...     [ ] Comment...   │║
║  │                    │   │ [X] Valid...    [ ] Disabled     │║
║  │                    │   │ [ ] Message...                   │║
║  └────────────────────┘   └──────────────────────────────────┘║
║                                                              ║
║              «   OK   »    < Cancel >                        ║
╚══════════════════════════════════════════════════════════════╝
------------------------------------------------------------
*-- m.lhNext Valid Clause
------------------------------------------------------------
╔════════════════════════════════════════╗
║ Valid                                  ║
║  ┌──────────────────────────────────┐  ║
║  │ (•) Procedure                    │  ║
║  │ ( ) Expression                   │  ║
║  └──────────────────────────────────┘  ║
╚════════════════════════════════════════╝
lcNext =  'about.spr'
*============================================================
*  m.lhPrior
*============================================================
 @  11,   9
 Spacing:    5
╔══════════════════════════════════════════════════════════════╗
║  Push Button Prompts:     ┌──────────────────────────────────┐║
║                           │ (•) Horizontal    ( ) Vertical   │║
║  ┌────────────────────┐   │ [X] Terminating  <Spacing...>    │║
║  │\<Prior             │   └──────────────────────────────────┘║
║  │                    │   Variable:                           ║
║  │                    │   ┌──────────────────────────────────┐║
║  │                    │   │ < Choose... >  m.lhPrior         │║
║  │                    │   └──────────────────────────────────┘║
║  │                    │   Options:                            ║
║  │                    │   ┌──────────────────────────────────┐║
║  │                    │   │ [ ] When...     [ ] Comment...   │║
║  │                    │   │ [X] Valid...    [ ] Disabled     │║
║  │                    │   │ [ ] Message...                   │║
║  └────────────────────┘   └──────────────────────────────────┘║
║                                                              ║
║              «   OK   »    < Cancel >                        ║
╚══════════════════════════════════════════════════════════════╝
```

```
----------------------------------------------------------------
*-- m.lhPrior Valid Clause
----------------------------------------------------------------

   Valid
     (·) Procedure
     ( ) Expression

lcNext = 'aboutmem.spr'
*===============================================================
*  m.lhDone
*===============================================================
 @  11,  24
 Spacing:    5

   Push Button Prompts:          (·) Horizontal    ( ) Vertical
                                 [X] Terminating  <Spacing...>
    \!\?\<Done
                                Variable:
                                 < Choose... >  m.lhDone
                                Options:
                                 [ ] When...     [ ] Comment...
                                 [X] Valid...    [ ] Disabled
                                 [ ] Message...

                  «   OK    »    < Cancel >

----------------------------------------------------------------
*-- m.lhDone Valid Clause
----------------------------------------------------------------

   Valid
     (·) Procedure
     ( ) Expression

RELEASE WINDOW wmAbout
llEndAbout = .T.
*===============================================================
*  gmCompInfo
*===============================================================
 @   1,   2
```

```
Field:
 ( ) Say          ( ) Get          (·) Edit

< Edit...    > gmCompInfo
                                            «   OK   »
< Format... >
                                            < Cancel >
Range:
 [ ] Upper...                   [ ] Lower...

[X] When...       [ ] Error...      [X] Scroll bar
[ ] Valid...      [ ] Comment...    [ ] Allow tabs
[ ] Message...    [ ] Disabled      [ ] Refresh
-------------------------------------------------------------
*-- gmCompInfo When Clause
-------------------------------------------------------------

When
 ( ) Procedure
 (·) Expression

When:   .T. NOMODIFY
*************************************************************
*--  SCREEN CLEANUP CODE
*************************************************************
SET COLOR OF SCHEME 5 TO ,&jcOldPair
```

```
*------------------------------------------------------------
*************************************************************
**--    ABOUTCOM.SCX - MAC PLATFORM
*************************************************************
```

```
( ) DeskTop                              (·) Window

Name:   wmAbout                          <Type...>
Title:
Footer:

Size:             Screen Code:

 Height:  15.667   [X] Setup...
 Width:   58.333   [X] Cleanup & Procs...            «   OK   »

Position:         READ Clauses:                      < Cancel >

 Row:       0.000  [ ] Activate...    [ ] Show...
 Column:    0.000  [ ] Valid...       [ ] When...
 [X] Center        [ ] Deactivate...

Environment:                          [X] Add alias

      Environment NOT saved with screen.
```

```
 Type:     Dialog

 Attributes:      Border:

  [ ] Close        ( ) None
  [X] Float        ( ) Single
  [X] Shadow       (·) Double       «   OK   »
  [ ] Minimize     ( ) Panel
                   ( ) System       < Cancel >

 Color Schemes:

  Primary:         Popup:
```

```
MAC      RGB Fill Color Scheme: (194,194,194)
MAC      Font: Geneva,  10
 Screen Setup code above
*************************************************************
*--    G E T    O B J E C T S
*************************************************************
*============================================================
*  m.lhNext
*============================================================
```

```
@  13.250,  36.667
    SIZE   1.500,  10.000
Spacing:    5

 Push Button Prompts:          (·) Horizontal    ( ) Vertical
                               [X] Terminating  <Spacing...>
 \<Next
                              Variable:

                               < Choose... >  m.lhNext

                              Options:

                               [ ] When...      [ ] Comment...
                               [X] Valid...     [ ] Disabled
                               [ ] Message...

                 «  OK  »    < Cancel >

MAC      RGB Color Scheme: (,,,,,)
MAC      Font: Geneva,   9
        Style: Bold
 Valid code above
*============================================================
*  m.lhPrior
*============================================================
 @  13.250,  14.167
     SIZE   1.500,  10.000
 Spacing:    5

 Push Button Prompts:          (·) Horizontal    ( ) Vertical
                               [X] Terminating  <Spacing...>
 \<Prior
                              Variable:

                               < Choose... >  m.lhPrior

                              Options:

                               [ ] When...      [ ] Comment...
                               [X] Valid...     [ ] Disabled
                               [ ] Message...

                 «  OK  »    < Cancel >

MAC      RGB Color Scheme: (,,,,,)
MAC      Font: Geneva,   9
        Style: Bold
 Valid code above
*============================================================
```

```
*  m.lhDone
*==============================================================
@  13.250,  25.333
    SIZE   1.500,  10.000
 Spacing:    5

 Push Button Prompts:          (·) Horizontal    ( ) Vertical
                               [X] Terminating  <Spacing...>
 \!\?\<Done
                               Variable:

                               < Choose... >  m.lhDone

                               Options:

                               [ ] When...      [ ] Comment...
                               [X] Valid...     [ ] Disabled
                               [ ] Message...

                  «   OK   »    < Cancel >

MAC      RGB Color Scheme: (,,,,,)
MAC      Font: Geneva,   9
         Style: Bold
 Valid code above
*==============================================================
*  gmCompInfo
*==============================================================
 @   0.833,   1.333

  Field:

   ( ) Say          ( ) Get          (·) Edit

  < Edit...    > gmCompInfo
                                                «   OK   »
  < Format... > @2
                                                < Cancel >
  Range:

   [ ] Upper...                     [ ] Lower...

  [X] When...      [ ] Error...      [X] Scroll bar
  [ ] Valid...     [ ] Comment...    [ ] Allow tabs
  [ ] Message...   [ ] Disabled      [ ] Refresh

MAC      RGB Color Scheme: (,,,194,194,194)
MAC      Font: monaco,   9
 When code above
*==============================================================
```

```
*  Line
*============================================================
 @   0.333,   0.333
MAC       RGB Color Scheme: (130,130,130,130,130,130)
            Pen: 2
*============================================================
*  Line
*============================================================
 @   0.417,  57.833
MAC       RGB Color Scheme: (255,255,255,255,255,255)
            Pen: 1
*============================================================
*  Line
*============================================================
 @   0.333,   0.333
MAC       RGB Color Scheme: (130,130,130,130,130,130)
            Pen: 2
*============================================================
*  Line
*============================================================
 @  12.667,   0.500
MAC       RGB Color Scheme: (255,255,255,255,255,255)
            Pen: 1
 Screen Cleanup and Procedures code above
*------------------------------------------------------------
*************************************************************
**--    ABOUTCOM.SCX - WINDOWS PLATFORM
*************************************************************
```

```
 ( ) DeskTop                          (·) Window

 Name:   wmAbout                      <Type...>
 Title:
 Footer:

 Size:             Screen Code:

 Height:   15.667   [X] Setup...
 Width:    58.250   [X] Cleanup & Procs...            «   OK   »

 Position:         READ Clauses:                      < Cancel >

 Row:       0.000   [ ] Activate...    [ ] Show...
 Column:    0.000   [ ] Valid...       [ ] When...
 [X] Center         [ ] Deactivate...

 Environment:                         [X] Add alias

        Environment NOT saved with screen.
```

```
Type:  [ Dialog ]

Attributes:          Border:

 [ ] Close            ( ) None
 [X] Float            ( ) Single
 [X] Shadow           (·) Double        «  OK  »
 [ ] Minimize         ( ) Panel
                      ( ) System        < Cancel >

Color Schemes:

 Primary:             Popup:
 [          ]         [          ]
```

```
WINDOWS  RGB Fill Color Scheme: (192,192,192)
WINDOWS  Font: Terminal,   9
 Screen Setup code above
*************************************************************
*--   G E T   O B J E C T S
*************************************************************
*============================================================
*  m.lhNext
*============================================================
 @  13.250,  36.625
     SIZE  1.769,  10.000
 Spacing:   5
```

```
Push Button Prompts:        (·) Horizontal    ( ) Vertical
                            [X] Terminating   <Spacing...>
 \<Next
                           Variable:

                            < Choose... >  m.lhNext

                           Options:

                            [ ] When...       [ ] Comment...
                            [X] Valid...      [ ] Disabled
                            [ ] Message...

             «  OK  »    < Cancel >
```

```
WINDOWS  RGB Color Scheme: (,,,,,)
WINDOWS  Font: MS Sans Serif,   8
       Style: Bold
 Valid code above
*============================================================
```

```
*  m.lhPrior
*===============================================================
 @  13.250,  14.125
     SIZE   1.769,  10.000
 Spacing:    5

     Push Button Prompts:          (·) Horizontal    ( ) Vertical
                                   [X] Terminating  <Spacing...>
     \<Prior
                                   Variable:

                                   < Choose... >  m.lhPrior

                                   Options:

                                    [ ] When...      [ ] Comment...
                                    [X] Valid...     [ ] Disabled
                                    [ ] Message...

                     «   OK   »     < Cancel >

WINDOWS  RGB Color Scheme: (,,,,,)
WINDOWS  Font: MS Sans Serif,   8
         Style: Bold
 Valid code above
*===============================================================
*  m.lhDone
*===============================================================
 @  13.250,  25.375
     SIZE   1.769,  10.000
 Spacing:    5

     Push Button Prompts:          (·) Horizontal    ( ) Vertical
                                   [X] Terminating  <Spacing...>
     \!\?\<Done
                                   Variable:

                                   < Choose... >  m.lhDone

                                   Options:

                                    [ ] When...      [ ] Comment...
                                    [X] Valid...     [ ] Disabled
                                    [ ] Message...

                     «   OK   »     < Cancel >

WINDOWS  RGB Color Scheme: (,,,,,)
WINDOWS  Font: MS Sans Serif,   8
         Style: Bold
```

```
 Valid code above
*==============================================================
*  gmCompInfo
*==============================================================
 @   0.833,   1.250
+--------------------------------------------------------------+
|                                                              |
|  Field:                                                      |
|  +---------------------------------------------+             |
|  |  ( ) Say          ( ) Get          (·) Edit |             |
|  +---------------------------------------------+             |
|                                                              |
|  < Edit...    > gmCompInfo                                   |
|                                               «    OK    »   |
|  < Format... >                                               |
|                                               < Cancel >     |
|  Range:                                                      |
|  +---------------------------------------------+             |
|  |  [ ] Upper...                  [ ] Lower... |             |
|  +---------------------------------------------+             |
|                                                              |
|  [X] When...      [ ] Error...      [X] Scroll bar           |
|  [ ] Valid...     [ ] Comment...    [ ] Allow tabs           |
|  [ ] Message...   [ ] Disabled      [ ] Refresh              |
|                                                              |
+--------------------------------------------------------------+
WINDOWS  RGB Color Scheme: (,,,192,192,192)
WINDOWS  Font: Terminal,   9
 When code above
*==============================================================
*  Line
*==============================================================
 @   0.333,   0.375
WINDOWS  RGB Color Scheme: (128,128,128,128,128,128)
         Pen: 2
*==============================================================
*  Line
*==============================================================
 @   0.417,  57.875
WINDOWS  RGB Color Scheme: (255,255,255,255,255,255)
         Pen: 1
*==============================================================
*  Line
*==============================================================
 @   0.333,   0.375
WINDOWS  RGB Color Scheme: (128,128,128,128,128,128)
         Pen: 2
*==============================================================
*  Line
*==============================================================
 @  12.667,   0.500
WINDOWS  RGB Color Scheme: (255,255,255,255,255,255)
         Pen: 1
 Screen Cleanup and Procedures code above
```

File Information Screen: ABOUTFIL.SCX

The third window in the About... section displays information on the hardware currently in use. It displays the total disk size, and the amount of room currently available. It also displays the network machine number (if the user is on a network) and the status of any attached printers or spoolers. It also displays the type of keyboard that is attached to the computer, and the type of graphics available to the user.

The pushbuttons on the bottom of the window allow the user to access more system information or to close the window.

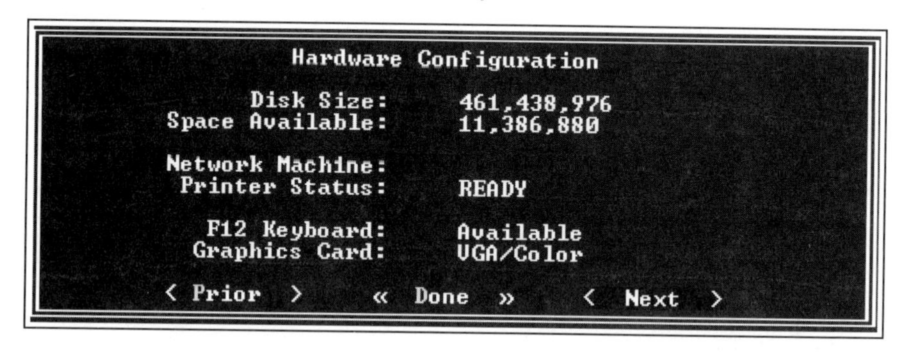

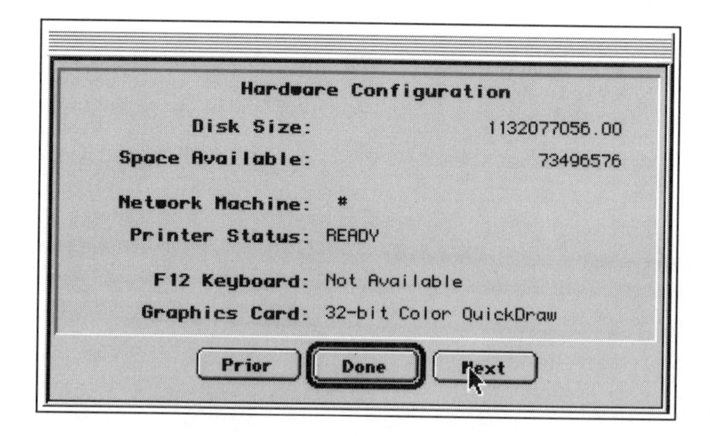

```
Hardware Configuration
           Disk Size:    456,220,672
     Space Available:    15,220,736

     Network Machine:                        # 0
      Printer Status:    READY

         F12 Keyboard:   Available
        Graphics Card:   VGA/Color

      [ Prior ]    [ Done ]    [ Next ]
```

```
*-----------------------------------------------------------
************************************************************
**--     ABOUTFIL.SCX - DOS PLATFORM
************************************************************
```

```
( ) DeskTop                        (·) Window

Name:   wmAbout                    <Type...>
Title:
Footer:

Size:              Screen Code:

  Height:   14     [X] Setup...
  Width:    61     [ ] Cleanup & Procs...            «   OK   »

Position:          READ Clauses:                     < Cancel >

  Row:       0     [ ] Activate...    [ ] Show...
  Column:    0     [ ] Valid...       [ ] When...
  [ ] Center       [ ] Deactivate...

Environment:                     [X] Add alias

     Environment NOT saved with screen.
```

```
Type:    [ Dialog ]

Attributes:          Border:

 [ ] Close            ( ) None
 [X] Float            ( ) Single
 [X] Shadow           (·) Double      «  OK  »
 [ ] Minimize         ( ) Panel
                      ( ) System      < Cancel >

Color Schemes:

 Primary:             Popup:

 [ Dialogs ]          [ Dialog Pop ]
```

```
************************************************************
*  SCREEN SETUP CODE
************************************************************
*  Program...........: ABOUTFIL Screen
*  Author............: yag
*  Project...........: COMMON
*  Created...........: 04/16/93
*  Copyright.........: (c) Flash Creative Management, 1993
*) Description.......: ABOUT FILES Screen
*)                   : Shows information about available
*)                   : hardware.
*  Calling Samples...: Called from About.prg automatically
*  Parameter List....:
*  Major change list.:
************************************************************
*--   G E T    O B J E C T S
************************************************************
*===========================================================
*
*===========================================================
 @   3,  30
```

```
Field:
  (·) Say          ( ) Get          ( ) Edit

< Say...    > DISKSPACE()
                                            «   OK   »
< Format... > @B 999,999,999,999
                                           < Cancel >
Range:
  [ ] Upper...                 [ ] Lower...

[ ] When...       [ ] Error...      [ ] Scroll bar
[ ] Valid...      [ ] Comment...    [ ] Allow tabs
[ ] Message...    [ ] Disabled      [ ] Refresh
*============================================================
*  Text: Disk Size:
*============================================================
 @   2,  15
*============================================================
*  Text: Space Available:
*============================================================
 @   3,   9
*============================================================
*  Text: Network Machine:
*============================================================
 @   5,   9
*============================================================
*
*============================================================
 @   5,  30
Field:
  (·) Say          ( ) Get          ( ) Edit

< Say...    > SYS(0)
                                            «   OK   »
< Format... >
                                           < Cancel >
Range:
  [ ] Upper...                 [ ] Lower...

[ ] When...       [ ] Error...      [ ] Scroll bar
[ ] Valid...      [ ] Comment...    [ ] Allow tabs
[ ] Message...    [ ] Disabled      [ ] Refresh
*============================================================
*  Text: Printer Status:
```

```
*==============================================================
 @   6,  10
*==============================================================
*
*==============================================================
 @   6,  30
```

```
 Field:

 ( ) Say          ( ) Get          ( ) Edit

 <  Say...    > SYS(13)
                                            «   OK   »
 < Format... >
                                            < Cancel >
 Range:

 [ ] Upper...                 [ ] Lower...

 [ ] When...      [ ] Error...     [ ] Scroll bar
 [ ] Valid...     [ ] Comment...   [ ] Allow tabs
 [ ] Message...   [ ] Disabled     [ ] Refresh
```

```
*==============================================================
*  Text: Graphics Card:
*==============================================================
 @   9,  11
*==============================================================
*
*==============================================================
 @   9,  30
```

```
 Field:

 ( ) Say          ( ) Get          ( ) Edit

 <  Say...    > SYS(2006)
                                            «   OK   »
 < Format... >
                                            < Cancel >
 Range:

 [ ] Upper...                 [ ] Lower...

 [ ] When...      [ ] Error...     [ ] Scroll bar
 [ ] Valid...     [ ] Comment...   [ ] Allow tabs
 [ ] Message...   [ ] Disabled     [ ] Refresh
```

```
*==============================================================
*  Text: F12 Keyboard:
*==============================================================
```

```
 @   8,  12
*==============================================================
*
*==============================================================
 @   8,  30

   Field:
    (·) Say          ( ) Get          ( ) Edit

   <  Say...    > IIF(FKMAX()>10,"","Not ") + "Available"
                                                 «    OK    »
   < Format... >
                                                 < Cancel >
   Range:
    [ ] Upper...                  [ ] Lower...

   [ ] When...      [ ] Error...     [ ] Scroll bar
   [ ] Valid...     [ ] Comment...   [ ] Allow tabs
   [ ] Message...   [ ] Disabled     [ ] Refresh

*==============================================================
*
*==============================================================
 @   2,  30

   Field:
    (·) Say          ( ) Get          ( ) Edit

   <  Say...    > VAL(SYS(2020))
                                                 «    OK    »
   < Format... > @B 999,999,999,999
                                                 < Cancel >
   Range:
    [ ] Upper...                  [ ] Lower...

   [ ] When...      [ ] Error...     [ ] Scroll bar
   [ ] Valid...     [ ] Comment...   [ ] Allow tabs
   [ ] Message...   [ ] Disabled     [ ] Refresh

*==============================================================
*  Text: Hardware Configuration
*==============================================================
 @   0,  18
*==============================================================
*  m.lhNext
*==============================================================
 @  11,  39
 Spacing:    5
```

```
Push Button Prompts:          (·) Horizontal    ( ) Vertical
                              [X] Terminating   <Spacing...>
\<Next
                              Variable:

                              < Choose... >  m.lhNext

                              Options:

                              [ ] When...       [ ] Comment...
                              [X] Valid...      [ ] Disabled
                              [ ] Message...

              «   OK   »    < Cancel >
-------------------------------------------------------------
*-- m.lhNext Valid Clause
-------------------------------------------------------------

 Valid

  (·) Procedure
  ( ) Expression

lcNext =  'aboutmem.spr'
*============================================================
*  m.lhPrior
*============================================================
 @  11,   9
 Spacing:    5

Push Button Prompts:          (·) Horizontal    ( ) Vertical
                              [X] Terminating   <Spacing...>
\<Prior
                              Variable:

                              < Choose... >  m.lhPrior

                              Options:

                              [ ] When...       [ ] Comment...
                              [X] Valid...      [ ] Disabled
                              [ ] Message...

              «   OK   »    < Cancel >
-------------------------------------------------------------
*-- m.lhPrior Valid Clause
-------------------------------------------------------------
```

```
Valid
  (·) Procedure
  ( ) Expression

lcNext = 'aboutgen.spr'
*==============================================================
*  m.lhDone
*==============================================================
 @  11,  24
 Spacing:     5

 Push Button Prompts:        (·) Horizontal    ( ) Vertical
                             [X] Terminating  <Spacing...>
 \!\?\<Done
                            Variable:

                             < Choose... >  m.lhDone

                            Options:

                             [ ] When...     [ ] Comment...
                             [X] Valid...    [ ] Disabled
                             [ ] Message...

                 «   OK   »    < Cancel >
--------------------------------------------------------------
*-- m.lhDone Valid Clause
--------------------------------------------------------------

Valid
  (·) Procedure
  ( ) Expression

RELEASE WINDOW wmAbout
llEndAbout = .T.
```

```
*-----------------------------------------------------------
************************************************************
**--    ABOUTFIL.SCX - MAC PLATFORM
************************************************************
 ( ) DeskTop                          (·) Window

 Name:   wmAbout                      <Type...>
 Title:
 Footer:

 Size:              Screen Code:

  Height:   15.692   [X] Setup...
  Width:    58.333   [ ] Cleanup & Procs...          «   OK   »

 Position:          READ Clauses:                    < Cancel >

  Row:       0.000   [ ] Activate...    [ ] Show...
  Column:    0.000   [ ] Valid...       [ ] When...
  [ ] Center         [ ] Deactivate...

 Environment:                          [X] Add alias

        Environment NOT saved with screen.

  Type:       Dialog

  Attributes:       Border:

   [ ] Close         ( ) None
   [X] Float         ( ) Single
   [X] Shadow        (·) Double      «   OK   »
   [ ] Minimize      ( ) Panel
                     ( ) System      < Cancel >

  Color Schemes:

   Primary:         Popup:

MAC      RGB Fill Color Scheme: (193,193,193)
MAC      Font: Geneva,  10
 Screen Setup code above
************************************************************
*--    G E T    O B J E C T S
************************************************************
*===========================================================
*
*===========================================================
 @   3.923,  26.500
```

```
 Field:
 ┌──────────────────────────────────────────┐
 │ (·) Say        ( ) Get        ( ) Edit   │
 └──────────────────────────────────────────┘

 <  Say...   > DISKSPACE()
                                              «   OK   »
 < Format... >
                                              < Cancel >
 Range:
 ┌──────────────────────────────────────────┐
 │ [ ] Upper...               [ ] Lower...  │
 └──────────────────────────────────────────┘

 [ ] When...      [ ] Error...     [ ] Scroll bar
 [ ] Valid...     [ ] Comment...   [ ] Allow tabs
 [ ] Message...   [ ] Disabled     [ ] Refresh
```

```
MAC      RGB Color Scheme: (,,,,,)
MAC      Font: monaco,   9
*============================================================
*  Text: Disk Size:
*============================================================
 @   2.538,  13.500
MAC      RGB Color Scheme: (,,,,,)
MAC      Font: Monaco,   9
        Style: Bold
*============================================================
*  Text: Space Available:
*============================================================
 @   4.000,   6.500
MAC      RGB Color Scheme: (,,,,,)
MAC      Font: Monaco,   9
        Style: Bold
*============================================================
*  Text: Network Machine:
*============================================================
 @   6.077,   6.500
MAC      RGB Color Scheme: (,,,,,)
MAC      Font: Monaco,   9
        Style: Bold
*============================================================
*
*============================================================
 @   6.000,  26.500
```

```
Field:
  (·) Say          ( ) Get           ( ) Edit

< Say...    > SYS(0)
                                              «   OK   »
< Format... >
                                              < Cancel >
Range:
  [ ] Upper...                  [ ] Lower...

[ ] When...     [ ] Error...     [ ] Scroll bar
[ ] Valid...    [ ] Comment...   [ ] Allow tabs
[ ] Message...  [ ] Disabled     [ ] Refresh
```

```
MAC      RGB Color Scheme: (,,,,,)
MAC      Font: monaco,   9
*==============================================================
*  Text: Printer Status:
*==============================================================
 @   7.615,    7.667
MAC      RGB Color Scheme: (,,,,,)
MAC      Font: Monaco,   9
        Style: Bold
*==============================================================
*
*==============================================================
 @   7.538,  26.500
```

```
Field:
  (·) Say          ( ) Get           ( ) Edit

< Say...    > SYS(13)
                                              «   OK   »
< Format... >
                                              < Cancel >
Range:
  [ ] Upper...                  [ ] Lower...

[ ] When...     [ ] Error...     [ ] Scroll bar
[ ] Valid...    [ ] Comment...   [ ] Allow tabs
[ ] Message...  [ ] Disabled     [ ] Refresh
```

```
MAC      RGB Color Scheme: (,,,,,)
MAC      Font: monaco,   9
*==============================================================
*  Text: Graphics Card:
```

```
*==============================================================
 @  11.154,   8.833
MAC       RGB Color Scheme: (,,,,,)
MAC       Font: Monaco,    9
         Style: Bold
*==============================================================
*
*==============================================================
 @  11.077,  26.500
╔══════════════════════════════════════════════════════════════╗
║                                                              ║
║  Field:                                                      ║
║  ┌──────────────────────────────────────────┐                ║
║  │ (·) Say        ( ) Get        ( ) Edit   │                ║
║  └──────────────────────────────────────────┘                ║
║                                                              ║
║  <  Say...    > SYS(2006)                                    ║
║                                               «   OK    »    ║
║  < Format... >                                               ║
║                                               < Cancel >     ║
║  Range:                                                      ║
║  ┌──────────────────────────────────────────┐                ║
║  │ [ ] Upper...              [ ] Lower...   │                ║
║  └──────────────────────────────────────────┘                ║
║                                                              ║
║  [ ] When...     [ ] Error...     [ ] Scroll bar             ║
║  [ ] Valid...    [ ] Comment...   [ ] Allow tabs             ║
║  [ ] Message...  [ ] Disabled     [ ] Refresh                ║
║                                                              ║
╚══════════════════════════════════════════════════════════════╝
MAC       RGB Color Scheme: (,,,,,)
MAC       Font: monaco,    9
*==============================================================
*  Text: F12 Keyboard:
*==============================================================
 @   9.692,  10.000
MAC       RGB Color Scheme: (,,,,,)
MAC       Font: Monaco,    9
         Style: Bold
*==============================================================
*
*==============================================================
 @   9.615,  26.500
```

```
╔══════════════════════════════════════════════════════════════════╗
║                                                                  ║
║  Field:                                                          ║
║  ┌─────────────────────────────────────────────┐                 ║
║  │ (·) Say          ( ) Get          ( ) Edit  │                 ║
║  └─────────────────────────────────────────────┘                 ║
║                                                                  ║
║  <  Say...   > IIF(FKMAX()>10,"","Not ") + "Available"           ║
║                                                  «   OK    »     ║
║  < Format... >                                                   ║
║                                                  < Cancel >      ║
║  Range:                                                          ║
║  ┌─────────────────────────────────────────────┐                 ║
║  │ [ ] Upper...                [ ] Lower...    │                 ║
║  └─────────────────────────────────────────────┘                 ║
║                                                                  ║
║  [ ] When...     [ ] Error...     [ ] Scroll bar                 ║
║  [ ] Valid...    [ ] Comment...   [ ] Allow tabs                 ║
║  [ ] Message...  [ ] Disabled     [ ] Refresh                    ║
║                                                                  ║
╚══════════════════════════════════════════════════════════════════╝
MAC       RGB Color Scheme: (,,,,,)
MAC       Font: monaco,   9
*==============================================================
*
*==============================================================
 @   2.385,  26.500
╔══════════════════════════════════════════════════════════════════╗
║                                                                  ║
║  Field:                                                          ║
║  ┌─────────────────────────────────────────────┐                 ║
║  │ (·) Say          ( ) Get          ( ) Edit  │                 ║
║  └─────────────────────────────────────────────┘                 ║
║                                                                  ║
║  <  Say...   > VAL(SYS(2020))                                    ║
║                                                  «   OK    »     ║
║  < Format... >                                                   ║
║                                                  < Cancel >      ║
║  Range:                                                          ║
║  ┌─────────────────────────────────────────────┐                 ║
║  │ [ ] Upper...                [ ] Lower...    │                 ║
║  └─────────────────────────────────────────────┘                 ║
║                                                                  ║
║  [ ] When...     [ ] Error...     [ ] Scroll bar                 ║
║  [ ] Valid...    [ ] Comment...   [ ] Allow tabs                 ║
║  [ ] Message...  [ ] Disabled     [ ] Refresh                    ║
║                                                                  ║
╚══════════════════════════════════════════════════════════════════╝
MAC       RGB Color Scheme: (,,,,,)
MAC       Font: monaco,   9
*==============================================================
*  Text: Hardware Configuration
*==============================================================
 @   0.769,  18.167
MAC       RGB Color Scheme: (,,,,,)
MAC       Font: Monaco,   9
         Style: Bold
*==============================================================
*  m.lhNext
```

```
*=================================================================
 @  13.231,  36.667
     SIZE   1.500,  10.000
 Spacing:    5
```

```
  Push Button Prompts:        (·) Horizontal    ( ) Vertical
                              [X] Terminating  <Spacing...>
  \<Next
                             Variable:

                              < Choose... >  m.lhNext

                             Options:

                              [ ] When...     [ ] Comment...
                              [X] Valid...    [ ] Disabled
                              [ ] Message...

                 «   OK   »    < Cancel >
```

```
MAC       RGB Color Scheme: (,,,,,)
MAC       Font: Geneva,   9
         Style: Bold
 Valid code above
*=================================================================
*  m.lhPrior
*=================================================================
 @  13.231,  14.167
     SIZE   1.500,  10.000
 Spacing:    5
```

```
  Push Button Prompts:        (·) Horizontal    ( ) Vertical
                              [X] Terminating  <Spacing...>
  \<Prior
                             Variable:

                              < Choose... >  m.lhPrior

                             Options:

                              [ ] When...     [ ] Comment...
                              [X] Valid...    [ ] Disabled
                              [ ] Message...

                 «   OK   »    < Cancel >
```

```
MAC       RGB Color Scheme: (,,,,,)
MAC       Font: Geneva,   9
         Style: Bold
 Valid code above
*=================================================================
*  m.lhDone
*=================================================================
 @  13.231,  25.333
```

```
    SIZE   1.500,  10.000
 Spacing:    5

  Push Button Prompts:        (·) Horizontal   ( ) Vertical
                              [X] Terminating  <Spacing...>
  \!\?\<Done
                             Variable:

                              < Choose... >  m.lhDone

                             Options:

                              [ ] When...      [ ] Comment...
                              [X] Valid...     [ ] Disabled
                              [ ] Message...

                  «   OK   »    < Cancel >

MAC       RGB Color Scheme: (,,,,,)
MAC       Font: Geneva,   9
         Style: Bold
 Valid code above
*============================================================
*  Line
*============================================================
 @   0.308,   0.333
MAC       RGB Color Scheme: (129,129,129,129,129,129)
            Pen: 2
*============================================================
*  Line
*============================================================
 @   0.385,  57.833
MAC       RGB Color Scheme: (255,255,255,255,255,255)
            Pen: 1
*============================================================
*  Line
*============================================================
 @   0.308,   0.333
MAC       RGB Color Scheme: (129,129,129,129,129,129)
            Pen: 2
*============================================================
*  Line
*============================================================
 @  12.692,   0.500
MAC       RGB Color Scheme: (255,255,255,255,255,255)
            Pen: 1
*------------------------------------------------------------
```

```
***********************************************************
**--    ABOUTFIL.SCX - WINDOWS PLATFORM
***********************************************************
```

```
( ) DeskTop                         (·) Window

Name:   wmAbout                     <Type...>
Title:
Footer:

Size:              Screen Code:

 Height:   15.667   [X] Setup...
 Width:    58.250   [ ] Cleanup & Procs...           « OK »

Position:          READ Clauses:                  < Cancel >

 Row:       0.000   [ ] Activate...   [ ] Show...
 Column:    0.000   [ ] Valid...      [ ] When...
 [ ] Center         [ ] Deactivate...

Environment:                         [X] Add alias

       Environment NOT saved with screen.
```

```
 Type:       Dialog

 Attributes:      Border:

  [ ] Close        ( ) None
  [X] Float        ( ) Single
  [X] Shadow       (·) Double     «  OK  »
  [ ] Minimize     ( ) Panel
                   ( ) System     < Cancel >

 Color Schemes:

  Primary:         Popup:
```

```
WINDOWS  RGB Fill Color Scheme: (192,192,192)
WINDOWS  Font: Terminal,   9
 Screen Setup code above
***********************************************************
*--    G E T    O B J E C T S
***********************************************************
*==========================================================
*
*==========================================================
 @   3.917,  26.500
```

```
Field:
 ┌──────────────────────────────────────────────┐
 │ (·) Say          ( ) Get          ( ) Edit   │
 └──────────────────────────────────────────────┘

< Say...    > DISKSPACE()
                                                  «    OK    »
< Format... > @B 999,999,999,999
                                                  < Cancel >
Range:
 ┌──────────────────────────────────────────────┐
 │ [ ] Upper...                 [ ] Lower...    │
 └──────────────────────────────────────────────┘

[ ] When...      [ ] Error...      [ ] Scroll bar
[ ] Valid...     [ ] Comment...    [ ] Allow tabs
[ ] Message...   [ ] Disabled      [ ] Refresh
```

```
WINDOWS  RGB Color Scheme: (,,,,,)
WINDOWS  Font: Terminal,   9
*============================================================
*  Text: Disk Size:
*============================================================
 @   2.500,  12.875
WINDOWS  RGB Color Scheme: (,,,,,)
WINDOWS  Font: Terminal,   9
*============================================================
*  Text: Space Available:
*============================================================
 @   4.000,   6.875
WINDOWS  RGB Color Scheme: (,,,,,)
WINDOWS  Font: Terminal,   9
*============================================================
*  Text: Network Machine:
*============================================================
 @   6.083,   6.875
WINDOWS  RGB Color Scheme: (,,,,,)
WINDOWS  Font: Terminal,   9
*============================================================
*
*============================================================
 @   6.000,  26.500
```

```
 Field:

 (·) Say          ( ) Get          ( ) Edit

 <  Say...    > SYS(0)
                                          «    OK    »
 < Format... >
                                          < Cancel >
 Range:

 [ ] Upper...                  [ ] Lower...

 [ ] When...       [ ] Error...      [ ] Scroll bar
 [ ] Valid...      [ ] Comment...    [ ] Allow tabs
 [ ] Message...    [ ] Disabled      [ ] Refresh
```

```
WINDOWS  RGB Color Scheme: (,,,,,)
WINDOWS  Font: Terminal,   9
*==============================================================
*  Text: Printer Status:
*==============================================================
 @   7.583,   7.875
WINDOWS  RGB Color Scheme: (,,,,,)
WINDOWS  Font: Terminal,   9
*==============================================================
*
*==============================================================
 @   7.500,  26.500
```

```
 Field:

 (·) Say          ( ) Get          ( ) Edit

 <  Say...    > SYS(13)
                                          «    OK    »
 < Format... >
                                          < Cancel >
 Range:

 [ ] Upper...                  [ ] Lower...

 [ ] When...       [ ] Error...      [ ] Scroll bar
 [ ] Valid...      [ ] Comment...    [ ] Allow tabs
 [ ] Message...    [ ] Disabled      [ ] Refresh
```

```
WINDOWS  RGB Color Scheme: (,,,,,)
WINDOWS  Font: Terminal,   9
*==============================================================
*  Text: Graphics Card:
*==============================================================
 @  11.167,   8.875
```

```
WINDOWS  RGB Color Scheme: (,,,,,)
WINDOWS  Font: Terminal,   9
*============================================================
*
*============================================================
 @  11.083,  26.500
╔════════════════════════════════════════════════════════════╗
║                                                            ║
║  Field:                                                    ║
║  ┌──────────────────────────────────────────┐              ║
║  │ (·) Say         ( ) Get         ( ) Edit │              ║
║  └──────────────────────────────────────────┘              ║
║                                                            ║
║  <  Say...    > SYS(2006)                                  ║
║                                                 «   OK   » ║
║  < Format... >                                             ║
║                                                 < Cancel > ║
║  Range:                                                    ║
║  ┌──────────────────────────────────────────┐              ║
║  │ [ ] Upper...                [ ] Lower... │              ║
║  └──────────────────────────────────────────┘              ║
║                                                            ║
║  [ ] When...     [ ] Error...     [ ] Scroll bar           ║
║  [ ] Valid...    [ ] Comment...   [ ] Allow tabs           ║
║  [ ] Message...  [ ] Disabled     [ ] Refresh              ║
║                                                            ║
╚════════════════════════════════════════════════════════════╝
WINDOWS  RGB Color Scheme: (,,,,,)
WINDOWS  Font: Terminal,   9
*============================================================
*  Text: F12 Keyboard:
*============================================================
 @   9.667,   9.875
WINDOWS  RGB Color Scheme: (,,,,,)
WINDOWS  Font: Terminal,   9
*============================================================
*
*============================================================
 @   9.583,  26.500
╔════════════════════════════════════════════════════════════╗
║                                                            ║
║  Field:                                                    ║
║  ┌──────────────────────────────────────────┐              ║
║  │ (·) Say         ( ) Get         ( ) Edit │              ║
║  └──────────────────────────────────────────┘              ║
║                                                            ║
║  <  Say...    > IIF(FKMAX()>10,"","Not ") + "Available"    ║
║                                                 «   OK   » ║
║  < Format... >                                             ║
║                                                 < Cancel > ║
║  Range:                                                    ║
║  ┌──────────────────────────────────────────┐              ║
║  │ [ ] Upper...                [ ] Lower... │              ║
║  └──────────────────────────────────────────┘              ║
║                                                            ║
║  [ ] When...     [ ] Error...     [ ] Scroll bar           ║
║  [ ] Valid...    [ ] Comment...   [ ] Allow tabs           ║
║  [ ] Message...  [ ] Disabled     [ ] Refresh              ║
║                                                            ║
╚════════════════════════════════════════════════════════════╝
```

```
WINDOWS  RGB Color Scheme: (,,,,,)
WINDOWS  Font: Terminal,   9
*============================================================
*
*============================================================
 @   2.417,  26.500

  Field:

   (·) Say        ( ) Get        ( ) Edit

  <  Say...   > VAL(SYS(2020))
                                          «   OK    »
  < Format... > @B 999,999,999,999
                                          < Cancel >
  Range:

   [ ] Upper...               [ ] Lower...

  [ ] When...      [ ] Error...     [ ] Scroll bar
  [ ] Valid...     [ ] Comment...   [ ] Allow tabs
  [ ] Message...   [ ] Disabled     [ ] Refresh

WINDOWS  RGB Color Scheme: (,,,,,)
WINDOWS  Font: Terminal,   9
*============================================================
*  Text: Hardware Configuration
*============================================================
 @   0.750,  18.125
WINDOWS  RGB Color Scheme: (,,,,,)
WINDOWS  Font: Terminal,   9
*============================================================
*  m.lhNext
*============================================================
 @  13.250,  36.625
    SIZE   1.769,  10.000
 Spacing:    5

  Push Button Prompts:         (·) Horizontal    ( ) Vertical
                               [X] Terminating  <Spacing...>
   \<Next
                              Variable:

                               < Choose... >  m.lhNext

                              Options:

                               [ ] When...     [ ] Comment...
                               [X] Valid...    [ ] Disabled
                               [ ] Message...

                   «   OK   »   < Cancel >
```

```
WINDOWS  RGB Color Scheme: (,,,,,)
WINDOWS  Font: MS Sans Serif,   8
        Style: Bold
 Valid code above
*==========================================================
*  m.lhPrior
*==========================================================
 @  13.250,  14.125
     SIZE   1.769,  10.000
 Spacing:    5
```

```
 Push Button Prompts:          (·) Horizontal    ( ) Vertical
                               [X] Terminating   <Spacing...>
 \<Prior
                              Variable:
                               < Choose... >  m.lhPrior
                              Options:
                               [ ] When...     [ ] Comment...
                               [X] Valid...    [ ] Disabled
                               [ ] Message...

              «   OK   »     < Cancel >
```

```
WINDOWS  RGB Color Scheme: (,,,,,)
WINDOWS  Font: MS Sans Serif,   8
        Style: Bold
 Valid code above
*==========================================================
*  m.lhDone
*==========================================================
 @  13.250,  25.375
     SIZE   1.769,  10.000
 Spacing:    5
```

```
 Push Button Prompts:          (·) Horizontal    ( ) Vertical
                               [X] Terminating   <Spacing...>
 \!\?\<Done
                              Variable:
                               < Choose... >  m.lhDone
                              Options:
                               [ ] When...     [ ] Comment...
                               [X] Valid...    [ ] Disabled
                               [ ] Message...

              «   OK   »     < Cancel >
```

```
WINDOWS  RGB Color Scheme: (,,,,,)
```

```
WINDOWS  Font: MS Sans Serif,   8
       Style: Bold
 Valid code above
*=========================================================
*  Line
*=========================================================
 @   0.333,   0.375
WINDOWS  RGB Color Scheme: (128,128,128,128,128,128)
          Pen: 2
*=========================================================
*  Line
*=========================================================
 @   0.417,  57.875
WINDOWS  RGB Color Scheme: (255,255,255,255,255,255)
          Pen: 1
*=========================================================
*  Line
*=========================================================
 @   0.333,   0.375
WINDOWS  RGB Color Scheme: (128,128,128,128,128,128)
          Pen: 2
*=========================================================
*  Line
*=========================================================
 @  12.667,   0.500
WINDOWS  RGB Color Scheme: (255,255,255,255,255,255)
          Pen: 1
```

Miscellaneous Information Screen: ABOUTGEN.SCX

AboutGen is the second About... window. It shows the user information about the application's current environment. It displays the current version of DOS, how many file handles are available to the application, the version of FoxPro that the application was coded in (handy in case of FoxPro bugs), the resource file that is being used (handy for network debugging), any CONFIG.FP file that may be used, and the directory information for the application and the work files.

The pushbuttons on the bottom of the window allow the user to access more system information or to close the window.

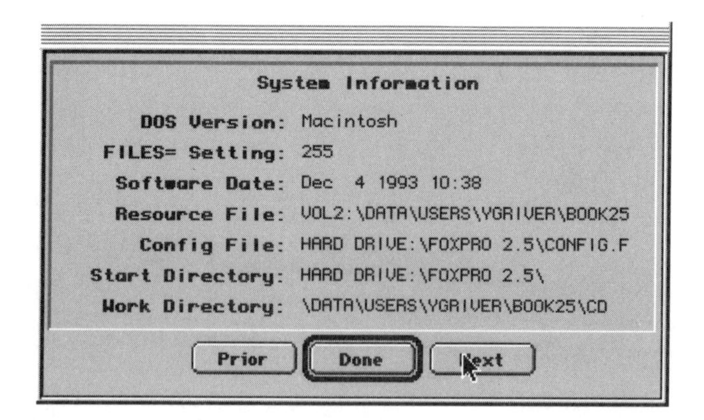

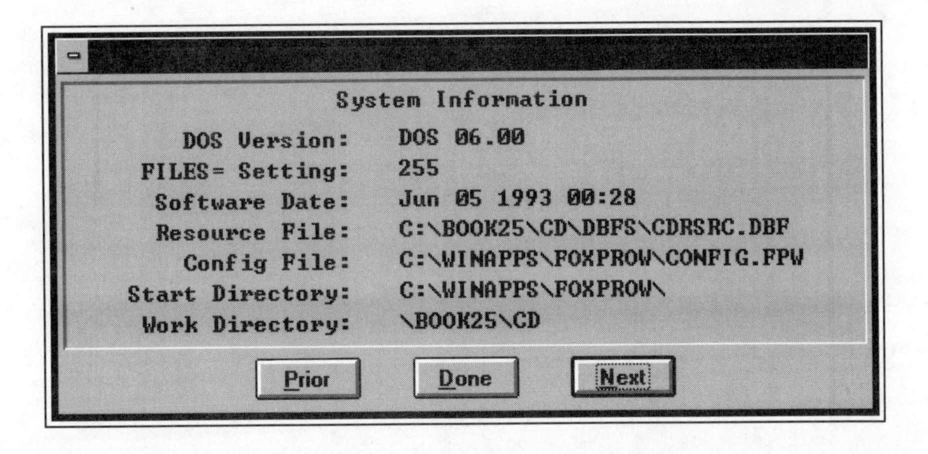


```
*------------------------------------------------------------
************************************************************
**--    ABOUTGEN.SCX - DOS PLATFORM
************************************************************
```

```
( ) DeskTop                              (·) Window

Name:   wmAbout                          <Type...>
Title:
Footer:

Size:              Screen Code:

 Height:   14       [X] Setup...
 Width:    61       [ ] Cleanup & Procs...            «   OK   »

Position:          READ Clauses:                      < Cancel >

 Row:        0      [ ] Activate...    [ ] Show...
 Column:     0      [ ] Valid...       [ ] When...
 [X] Center         [ ] Deactivate...

Environment:                         [X] Add alias

       Environment NOT saved with screen.
```

```
Type:     [ Dialog ]

Attributes:        Border:

 [ ] Close          ( ) None
 [X] Float          ( ) Single
 [X] Shadow         (·) Double        «   OK   »
 [ ] Minimize       ( ) Panel
                    ( ) System        < Cancel >

Color Schemes:

 Primary:          Popup:

 [ Dialogs ]       [ Dialog Pop ]
```

```
***************************************************************
*  SCREEN SETUP CODE
***************************************************************
*  Program...........: ABOUTGEN Screen
*  Author............: yag
*  Project...........: COMMON
*  Created...........: 04/16/93
*  Copyright.........: (c) Flash Creative Management, 1993
*) Description.......: General System Info ABOUT Screen
*)                   : Shows information about current
*)                   : system (e.g. CONFIG.FP, etc.)
*  Calling Samples...: Called from About.prg automatically
*  Parameter List....:
*  Major change list.:
lcVersDate = VERSION(1)
lnBegString = AT("[",lcVersDate)
lnEndString = AT("]",lcVersDate)
lnLenString = lnEndString - lnBegString
lcVersDate = SUBSTR(lcVersDate,lnBegString+1,lnLenString)
***************************************************************
*--   G E T   O B J E C T S
***************************************************************
*==============================================================
*  Text: Resource File:
*==============================================================
 @   5,   3
*==============================================================
*  Text: Config File:
*==============================================================
 @   6,   5
*==============================================================
*
*==============================================================
 @   4,  18
```

```
Field:
  (·) Say          ( ) Get          ( ) Edit

<  Say...    > lcVersDate
                                              «   OK   »
< Format... >
                                              < Cancel >
Range:
  [ ] Upper...                 [ ] Lower...

[ ] When...      [ ] Error...      [ ] Scroll bar
[ ] Valid...     [ ] Comment...    [ ] Allow tabs
[ ] Message...   [ ] Disabled      [ ] Refresh

*===============================================================
*
*===============================================================
@   5,  18

Field:
  (·) Say          ( ) Get          ( ) Edit

<  Say...    > SYS(2005)
                                              «   OK   »
< Format... >
                                              < Cancel >
Range:
  [ ] Upper...                 [ ] Lower...

[ ] When...      [ ] Error...      [ ] Scroll bar
[ ] Valid...     [ ] Comment...    [ ] Allow tabs
[ ] Message...   [ ] Disabled      [ ] Refresh

*===============================================================
*
*===============================================================
@   6,  18
```

```
+------------------------------------------------------------------+
| Field:                                                           |
| +----------------------------------------------+                 |
| | (·) Say          ( ) Get          ( ) Edit   |                 |
| +----------------------------------------------+                 |
|                                                                  |
| <  Say...    > SYS(2019)                                         |
|                                                 «   OK   »       |
| < Format... >                                                    |
|                                                 < Cancel >       |
| Range:                                                           |
| +----------------------------------------------+                 |
| | [ ] Upper...                 [ ] Lower...    |                 |
| +----------------------------------------------+                 |
|                                                                  |
| [ ] When...     [ ] Error...     [ ] Scroll bar                  |
| [ ] Valid...    [ ] Comment...   [ ] Allow tabs                  |
| [ ] Message...  [ ] Disabled     [ ] Refresh                     |
+------------------------------------------------------------------+
*==============================================================
*
*==============================================================
 @   9,  18
+------------------------------------------------------------------+
| Field:                                                           |
| +----------------------------------------------+                 |
| | (·) Say          ( ) Get          ( ) Edit   |                 |
| +----------------------------------------------+                 |
|                                                                  |
| <  Say...    > SYS(2003)                                         |
|                                                 «   OK   »       |
| < Format... >                                                    |
|                                                 < Cancel >       |
| Range:                                                           |
| +----------------------------------------------+                 |
| | [ ] Upper...                 [ ] Lower...    |                 |
| +----------------------------------------------+                 |
|                                                                  |
| [ ] When...     [ ] Error...     [ ] Scroll bar                  |
| [ ] Valid...    [ ] Comment...   [ ] Allow tabs                  |
| [ ] Message...  [ ] Disabled     [ ] Refresh                     |
+------------------------------------------------------------------+
*==============================================================
*  Text: Start Directory:
*==============================================================
 @   8,   1
*==============================================================
*
*==============================================================
 @   8,  18
```

```
Field:
  (·) Say          ( ) Get          ( ) Edit

< Say...    > SYS(2004)
                                             «   OK   »
< Format... >
                                             < Cancel >
Range:
  [ ] Upper...                  [ ] Lower...

[ ] When...      [ ] Error...      [ ] Scroll bar
[ ] Valid...     [ ] Comment...    [ ] Allow tabs
[ ] Message...   [ ] Disabled      [ ] Refresh
*==============================================================
*  Text: Software Date:
*==============================================================
 @   4,   3
*==============================================================
*  Text: DOS Version:
*==============================================================
 @   1,   5
*==============================================================
*  Text: Work Directory:
*==============================================================
 @   9,   2
*==============================================================
*
*==============================================================
 @   1,  18

Field:
  (·) Say          ( ) Get          ( ) Edit

< Say...    > OS()
                                             «   OK   »
< Format... >
                                             < Cancel >
Range:
  [ ] Upper...                  [ ] Lower...

[ ] When...      [ ] Error...      [ ] Scroll bar
[ ] Valid...     [ ] Comment...    [ ] Allow tabs
[ ] Message...   [ ] Disabled      [ ] Refresh
*==============================================================
*
```

```
*==============================================================
 @   2,  18

 Field:

   (·) Say          ( ) Get           ( ) Edit

 <  Say...    > SYS(2010)
                                                «   OK    »
 < Format... >
                                                < Cancel >
 Range:

   [ ] Upper...                      [ ] Lower...

 [ ] When...      [ ] Error...      [ ] Scroll bar
 [ ] Valid...     [ ] Comment...    [ ] Allow tabs
 [ ] Message...   [ ] Disabled      [ ] Refresh
*==============================================================
*  Text: FILES= Setting:
*==============================================================
 @   2,   2
*==============================================================
*  Text: System Information
*==============================================================
 @   0,  20
*==============================================================
*  m.lhNext
*==============================================================
 @  11,  39
 Spacing:    5

  Push Button Prompts:        (·) Horizontal    ( ) Vertical
                              [X] Terminating   <Spacing...>
  \<Next
                             Variable:

                              < Choose... >  m.lhNext

                             Options:

                              [ ] When...      [ ] Comment...
                              [X] Valid...     [ ] Disabled
                              [ ] Message...

                 «   OK    »    < Cancel >
--------------------------------------------------------------
*-- m.lhNext Valid Clause
--------------------------------------------------------------
```

```
 Valid
  (·) Procedure
  ( ) Expression

lcNext = 'aboutfil.spr'
*==========================================================
*  m.lhPrior
*==========================================================
 @  11,   9
 Spacing:    5

 Push Button Prompts:      (·) Horizontal    ( ) Vertical
                           [X] Terminating  <Spacing...>
 \<Prior
                          Variable:
                           < Choose... >  m.lhPrior

                          Options:
                           [ ] When...      [ ] Comment...
                           [X] Valid...     [ ] Disabled
                           [ ] Message...

              «   OK   »    < Cancel >
----------------------------------------------------------
*-- m.lhPrior Valid Clause
----------------------------------------------------------

 Valid
  (·) Procedure
  ( ) Expression

lcNext = 'about.spr'
*==========================================================
*  m.lhDone
*==========================================================
 @  11,  24
 Spacing:    5
```

```
Push Button Prompts:          (·) Horizontal    ( ) Vertical
                              [X] Terminating   <Spacing...>
\!\?\<Done
                              Variable:

                              < Choose... >  m.lhDone

                              Options:

                              [ ] When...       [ ] Comment...
                              [X] Valid...      [ ] Disabled
                              [ ] Message...

              «   OK   »     < Cancel >
--------------------------------------------------------------
*-- m.lhDone Valid Clause
--------------------------------------------------------------

  Valid

   (·) Procedure
   ( ) Expression

RELEASE WINDOW wmAbout
llEndAbout = .T.
*-------------------------------------------------------------
**************************************************************
**--    ABOUTGEN.SCX - MAC PLATFORM
**************************************************************
( ) DeskTop                           (·) Window

Name:    wmAbout                      <Type...>
Title:
Footer:

Size:              Screen Code:

 Height:   15.692   [X] Setup...
 Width:    58.333   [ ] Cleanup & Procs...          «  OK  »

Position:          READ Clauses:                    < Cancel >

 Row:        0.000   [ ] Activate...     [ ] Show...
 Column:     0.000   [ ] Valid...        [ ] When...
 [X] Center          [ ] Deactivate...

Environment:                           [X] Add alias

     Environment NOT saved with screen.
```

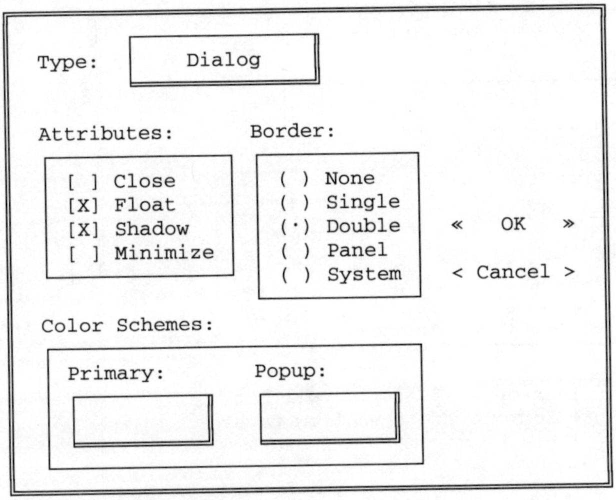

```
┌──────────────────────────────────────────────┐
│                                              │
│  Type:    ┌──────────────┐                   │
│           │    Dialog    │                   │
│           └──────────────┘                   │
│                                              │
│  Attributes:       Border:                   │
│  ┌──────────────┐ ┌────────────┐             │
│  │ [ ] Close    │ │ ( ) None   │             │
│  │ [X] Float    │ │ ( ) Single │             │
│  │ [X] Shadow   │ │ (·) Double │  «  OK   »  │
│  │ [ ] Minimize │ │ ( ) Panel  │             │
│  └──────────────┘ │ ( ) System │ < Cancel >  │
│                   └────────────┘             │
│  Color Schemes:                              │
│  ┌─────────────────────────────┐             │
│  │ Primary:        Popup:      │             │
│  │ ┌──────────┐   ┌──────────┐ │             │
│  │ └──────────┘   └──────────┘ │             │
│  └─────────────────────────────┘             │
└──────────────────────────────────────────────┘
MAC       RGB Fill Color Scheme: (193,193,193)
MAC       Font: Geneva,  10
 Screen Setup code above
************************************************************
*--     G E T     O B J E C T S
************************************************************
*===========================================================
*  Text: Resource File:
*===========================================================
 @   6.923,    6.833
MAC       RGB Color Scheme: (,,,,,)
MAC       Font: Monaco,    9
        Style: Bold
*===========================================================
*  Text: Config File:
*===========================================================
 @   8.308,    9.167
MAC       RGB Color Scheme: (,,,,,)
MAC       Font: Monaco,    9
        Style: Bold
*===========================================================
*
*===========================================================
 @   5.385,  24.500
```

```
 Field:
  ┌──────────────────────────────────────────────────────┐
  │ (·) Say            ( ) Get            ( ) Edit       │
  └──────────────────────────────────────────────────────┘

 <  Say...    > lcVersDate
                                                « OK »
 < Format... >
                                                < Cancel >
 Range:
  ┌──────────────────────────────────────────────────────┐
  │ [ ] Upper...                      [ ] Lower...       │
  └──────────────────────────────────────────────────────┘

 [ ] When...      [ ] Error...      [ ] Scroll bar
 [ ] Valid...     [ ] Comment...    [ ] Allow tabs
 [ ] Message...   [ ] Disabled      [ ] Refresh

MAC      RGB Color Scheme: (,,,,,)
MAC      Font: monaco,   9
*============================================================
*
*============================================================
 @   6.846,  24.500

 Field:
  ┌──────────────────────────────────────────────────────┐
  │ (·) Say            ( ) Get            ( ) Edit       │
  └──────────────────────────────────────────────────────┘

 <  Say...    > SYS(2005)
                                                « OK »
 < Format... >
                                                < Cancel >
 Range:
  ┌──────────────────────────────────────────────────────┐
  │ [ ] Upper...                      [ ] Lower...       │
  └──────────────────────────────────────────────────────┘

 [ ] When...      [ ] Error...      [ ] Scroll bar
 [ ] Valid...     [ ] Comment...    [ ] Allow tabs
 [ ] Message...   [ ] Disabled      [ ] Refresh

MAC      RGB Color Scheme: (,,,,,)
MAC      Font: monaco,   9
*============================================================
*
*============================================================
 @   8.231,  24.500
```

```
 Field:
 +------------------------------------------------+
 | (·) Say          ( ) Get          ( ) Edit    |
 +------------------------------------------------+

 <  Say...    > SYS(2019)
                                                    «   OK   »
 < Format... >
                                                    < Cancel >
 Range:
 +------------------------------------------------+
 | [ ] Upper...                    [ ] Lower...   |
 +------------------------------------------------+

 [ ] When...      [ ] Error...      [ ] Scroll bar
 [ ] Valid...     [ ] Comment...    [ ] Allow tabs
 [ ] Message...   [ ] Disabled      [ ] Refresh

MAC      RGB Color Scheme: (,,,,,)
MAC      Font: monaco,   9
*==============================================================
*
*==============================================================
 @  11.077,  24.500

 Field:
 +------------------------------------------------+
 | (·) Say          ( ) Get          ( ) Edit    |
 +------------------------------------------------+

 <  Say...    > SYS(2003)
                                                    «   OK   »
 < Format... >
                                                    < Cancel >
 Range:
 +------------------------------------------------+
 | [ ] Upper...                    [ ] Lower...   |
 +------------------------------------------------+

 [ ] When...      [ ] Error...      [ ] Scroll bar
 [ ] Valid...     [ ] Comment...    [ ] Allow tabs
 [ ] Message...   [ ] Disabled      [ ] Refresh

MAC      RGB Color Scheme: (,,,,,)
MAC      Font: monaco,   9
*==============================================================
*  Text: Start Directory:
*==============================================================
 @   9.769,   4.500
MAC      RGB Color Scheme: (,,,,,)
MAC      Font: Monaco,   9
       Style: Bold
*==============================================================
*
*==============================================================
```

```
 @   9.692,  24.500
 ╔══════════════════════════════════════════════════════════════╗
 ║                                                              ║
 ║  Field:                                                      ║
 ║  ┌──────────────────────────────────────────┐                ║
 ║  │ (·) Say         ( ) Get         ( ) Edit │                ║
 ║  └──────────────────────────────────────────┘                ║
 ║                                                              ║
 ║  <  Say...   > SYS(2004)                                     ║
 ║                                              «   OK    »     ║
 ║  < Format... >                                               ║
 ║                                              < Cancel >      ║
 ║  Range:                                                      ║
 ║  ┌──────────────────────────────────────────┐                ║
 ║  │ [ ] Upper...               [ ] Lower...  │                ║
 ║  └──────────────────────────────────────────┘                ║
 ║                                                              ║
 ║  [ ] When...      [ ] Error...     [ ] Scroll bar            ║
 ║  [ ] Valid...     [ ] Comment...   [ ] Allow tabs            ║
 ║  [ ] Message...   [ ] Disabled     [ ] Refresh               ║
 ║                                                              ║
 ╚══════════════════════════════════════════════════════════════╝
MAC      RGB Color Scheme: (,,,,,)
MAC      Font: monaco,   9
*==============================================================
*  Text: Software Date:
*==============================================================
 @   5.538,   6.833
MAC      RGB Color Scheme: (,,,,,)
MAC      Font: Monaco,   9
        Style: Bold
*==============================================================
*  Text: DOS Version:
*==============================================================
 @   2.692,   9.167
MAC      RGB Color Scheme: (,,,,,)
MAC      Font: Monaco,   9
        Style: Bold
*==============================================================
*  Text: Work Directory:
*==============================================================
 @  11.154,   5.667
MAC      RGB Color Scheme: (,,,,,)
MAC      Font: Monaco,   9
        Style: Bold
*==============================================================
*
*==============================================================
 @   2.615,  24.500
```

```
  Field:
  ┌────────────────────────────────────────────┐
  │ (·) Say          ( ) Get         ( ) Edit  │
  └────────────────────────────────────────────┘

  <  Say...    > OS()
                                                 «   OK   »
  < Format... >
                                                 < Cancel >
  Range:
  ┌────────────────────────────────────────────┐
  │ [ ] Upper...                 [ ] Lower...  │
  └────────────────────────────────────────────┘

  [ ] When...      [ ] Error...      [ ] Scroll bar
  [ ] Valid...     [ ] Comment...    [ ] Allow tabs
  [ ] Message...   [ ] Disabled      [ ] Refresh

MAC        RGB Color Scheme: (,,,,,)
MAC        Font: monaco,    9
*============================================================
*
*============================================================
 @   4.000,  24.500

  Field:
  ┌────────────────────────────────────────────┐
  │ (·) Say          ( ) Get         ( ) Edit  │
  └────────────────────────────────────────────┘

  <  Say...    > SYS(2010)
                                                 «   OK   »
  < Format... >
                                                 < Cancel >
  Range:
  ┌────────────────────────────────────────────┐
  │ [ ] Upper...                 [ ] Lower...  │
  └────────────────────────────────────────────┘

  [ ] When...      [ ] Error...      [ ] Scroll bar
  [ ] Valid...     [ ] Comment...    [ ] Allow tabs
  [ ] Message...   [ ] Disabled      [ ] Refresh

MAC        RGB Color Scheme: (,,,,,)
MAC        Font: monaco,    9
*============================================================
*  Text: FILES= Setting:
*============================================================
 @   4.077,    5.667
MAC        RGB Color Scheme: (,,,,,)
MAC        Font: Monaco,    9
          Style: Bold
*============================================================
*  Text: System Information
*============================================================
```

```
 @   0.846,  20.167
MAC      RGB Color Scheme: (,,,,,)
MAC      Font: Monaco,   9
        Style: Bold
*==============================================================
*  m.lhNext
*==============================================================
 @  13.231,  36.667
     SIZE   1.500,  10.000
 Spacing:    5
```

```
  Push Button Prompts:          (·) Horizontal    ( ) Vertical
                                [X] Terminating   <Spacing...>
  \<Next
                               Variable:

                                < Choose... >  m.lhNext

                               Options:

                                [ ] When...     [ ] Comment...
                                [X] Valid...    [ ] Disabled
                                [ ] Message...

                 «   OK   »    < Cancel >
```

```
MAC      RGB Color Scheme: (,,,,,)
MAC      Font: Geneva,   9
        Style: Bold
 Valid code above
*==============================================================
*  m.lhPrior
*==============================================================
 @  13.231,  14.167
     SIZE   1.500,  10.000
 Spacing:    5
```

```
  Push Button Prompts:          (·) Horizontal    ( ) Vertical
                                [X] Terminating   <Spacing...>
  \<Prior
                               Variable:

                                < Choose... >  m.lhPrior

                               Options:

                                [ ] When...     [ ] Comment...
                                [X] Valid...    [ ] Disabled
                                [ ] Message...

                 «   OK   »    < Cancel >
```

```
MAC      RGB Color Scheme: (,,,,,)
```

```
MAC      Font: Geneva,   9
        Style: Bold
 Valid code above
*===========================================================
*  m.lhDone
*===========================================================
 @  13.231,  25.333
    SIZE   1.500,  10.000
 Spacing:    5
```

```
Push Button Prompts:        (·) Horizontal    ( ) Vertical
                            [X] Terminating  <Spacing...>
 \!\?\<Done
                            Variable:

                            < Choose... >  m.lhDone

                            Options:

                            [ ] When...     [ ] Comment...
                            [X] Valid...    [ ] Disabled
                            [ ] Message...

              «  OK  »    < Cancel >
```

```
MAC      RGB Color Scheme: (,,,,,)
MAC      Font: Geneva,   9
        Style: Bold
 Valid code above
*===========================================================
*  Line
*===========================================================
 @   0.308,   0.333
MAC      RGB Color Scheme: (129,129,129,129,129,129)
           Pen: 2
*===========================================================
*  Line
*===========================================================
 @   0.385,  57.833
MAC      RGB Color Scheme: (255,255,255,255,255,255)
           Pen: 1
*===========================================================
*  Line
*===========================================================
 @   0.308,   0.333
MAC      RGB Color Scheme: (129,129,129,129,129,129)
           Pen: 2
*===========================================================
*  Line
*===========================================================
 @  12.692,   0.500
MAC      RGB Color Scheme: (255,255,255,255,255,255)
           Pen: 1
*-----------------------------------------------------------
```

```
***********************************************************
**--    ABOUTGEN.SCX - WINDOWS PLATFORM
***********************************************************

( ) DeskTop                          (·) Window

Name:   wmAbout                      <Type...>
Title:
Footer:

Size:            Screen Code:

  Height:   15.667    [X] Setup...
  Width:    58.250    [ ] Cleanup & Procs...         «   OK   »

Position:        READ Clauses:                       < Cancel >

  Row:       0.000    [ ] Activate...   [ ] Show...
  Column:    0.000    [ ] Valid...      [ ] When...
  [X] Center          [ ] Deactivate...

Environment:                        [X] Add alias

      Environment NOT saved with screen.


 Type:      Dialog

 Attributes:      Border:

  [ ] Close        ( ) None
  [X] Float        ( ) Single
  [X] Shadow       (·) Double      «   OK   »
  [ ] Minimize     ( ) Panel
                   ( ) System      < Cancel >

 Color Schemes:

  Primary:        Popup:

WINDOWS  RGB Fill Color Scheme: (192,192,192)
WINDOWS  Font: Terminal,   9
 Screen Setup code above
***********************************************************
*--    G E T   O B J E C T S
***********************************************************
*==========================================================
*  Text: Resource File:
*==========================================================
 @   6.917,   7.125
WINDOWS  RGB Color Scheme: (,,,,,)
WINDOWS  Font: Terminal,   9
```

```
*==============================================================
*  Text: Config File:
*==============================================================
 @   8.333,   9.125
WINDOWS  RGB Color Scheme: (,,,,,)
WINDOWS  Font: Terminal,   9
*==============================================================
*
*==============================================================
 @   5.417,  24.500

   Field:
   (·) Say         ( ) Get         ( ) Edit

   <  Say...    > lcVersDate
                                                 «   OK   »
   < Format... >
                                                 < Cancel >
   Range:
   [ ] Upper...                 [ ] Lower...

   [ ] When...      [ ] Error...     [ ] Scroll bar
   [ ] Valid...     [ ] Comment...   [ ] Allow tabs
   [ ] Message...   [ ] Disabled     [ ] Refresh

WINDOWS  RGB Color Scheme: (,,,,,)
WINDOWS  Font: Terminal,   9
*==============================================================
*
*==============================================================
 @   6.833,  24.500

   Field:
   (·) Say         ( ) Get         ( ) Edit

   <  Say...    > SYS(2005)
                                                 «   OK   »
   < Format... >
                                                 < Cancel >
   Range:
   [ ] Upper...                 [ ] Lower...

   [ ] When...      [ ] Error...     [ ] Scroll bar
   [ ] Valid...     [ ] Comment...   [ ] Allow tabs
   [ ] Message...   [ ] Disabled     [ ] Refresh

WINDOWS  RGB Color Scheme: (,,,,,)
WINDOWS  Font: Terminal,   9
```

```
*==============================================================
*
*==============================================================
 @   8.250,  24.500

   Field:

     (·) Say          ( ) Get          ( ) Edit

   <  Say...   > SYS(2019)
                                              «   OK   »
   < Format... >
                                              < Cancel >
   Range:

     [ ] Upper...                  [ ] Lower...

   [ ] When...     [ ] Error...     [ ] Scroll bar
   [ ] Valid...    [ ] Comment...   [ ] Allow tabs
   [ ] Message...  [ ] Disabled     [ ] Refresh

WINDOWS  RGB Color Scheme: (,,,,,)
WINDOWS  Font: Terminal,   9
*==============================================================
*
*==============================================================
 @  11.083,  24.500

   Field:

     (·) Say          ( ) Get          ( ) Edit

   <  Say...   > SYS(2003)
                                              «   OK   »
   < Format... >
                                              < Cancel >
   Range:

     [ ] Upper...                  [ ] Lower...

   [ ] When...     [ ] Error...     [ ] Scroll bar
   [ ] Valid...    [ ] Comment...   [ ] Allow tabs
   [ ] Message...  [ ] Disabled     [ ] Refresh

WINDOWS  RGB Color Scheme: (,,,,,)
WINDOWS  Font: Terminal,   9
*==============================================================
*  Text: Start Directory:
*==============================================================
 @   9.750,   5.125
WINDOWS  RGB Color Scheme: (,,,,,)
```

```
WINDOWS  Font: Terminal,   9
*============================================================
*
*============================================================
 @   9.667,  24.500
```

```
  Field:
  ┌──────────────────────────────────────────┐
  │ (·) Say        ( ) Get        ( ) Edit   │
  └──────────────────────────────────────────┘

  <  Say...   > SYS(2004)
                                            «   OK   »
  < Format... >
                                            < Cancel >
  Range:
  ┌──────────────────────────────────────────┐
  │ [ ] Upper...                [ ] Lower... │
  └──────────────────────────────────────────┘

  [ ] When...      [ ] Error...     [ ] Scroll bar
  [ ] Valid...     [ ] Comment...   [ ] Allow tabs
  [ ] Message...   [ ] Disabled     [ ] Refresh
```

```
WINDOWS  RGB Color Scheme: (,,,,,)
WINDOWS  Font: Terminal,   9
*============================================================
*  Text: Software Date:
*============================================================
 @   5.500,   7.125
WINDOWS  RGB Color Scheme: (,,,,,)
WINDOWS  Font: Terminal,   9
*============================================================
*  Text: DOS Version:
*============================================================
 @   2.667,   9.125
WINDOWS  RGB Color Scheme: (,,,,,)
WINDOWS  Font: Terminal,   9
*============================================================
*  Text: Work Directory:
*============================================================
 @  11.167,   6.125
WINDOWS  RGB Color Scheme: (,,,,,)
WINDOWS  Font: Terminal,   9
*============================================================
*
*============================================================
 @   2.583,  24.500
```

```
╔═════════════════════════════════════════════════════════════╗
║                                                             ║
║  Field:                                                     ║
║  ┌──────────────────────────────────────────┐               ║
║  │ (·) Say          ( ) Get          ( ) Edit│               ║
║  └──────────────────────────────────────────┘               ║
║                                                             ║
║  <  Say...    > OS()                                        ║
║                                                 «   OK   »  ║
║  < Format... >                                              ║
║                                                 < Cancel >  ║
║  Range:                                                     ║
║  ┌──────────────────────────────────────────┐               ║
║  │ [ ] Upper...                [ ] Lower... │               ║
║  └──────────────────────────────────────────┘               ║
║                                                             ║
║  [ ] When...     [ ] Error...     [ ] Scroll bar            ║
║  [ ] Valid...    [ ] Comment...   [ ] Allow tabs            ║
║  [ ] Message...  [ ] Disabled     [ ] Refresh               ║
║                                                             ║
╚═════════════════════════════════════════════════════════════╝
WINDOWS  RGB Color Scheme: (,,,,,)
WINDOWS  Font: Terminal,   9
*============================================================
*
*============================================================
 @   4.000,  24.500
╔═════════════════════════════════════════════════════════════╗
║                                                             ║
║  Field:                                                     ║
║  ┌──────────────────────────────────────────┐               ║
║  │ (·) Say          ( ) Get          ( ) Edit│               ║
║  └──────────────────────────────────────────┘               ║
║                                                             ║
║  <  Say...    > SYS(2010)                                   ║
║                                                 «   OK   »  ║
║  < Format... >                                              ║
║                                                 < Cancel >  ║
║  Range:                                                     ║
║  ┌──────────────────────────────────────────┐               ║
║  │ [ ] Upper...                [ ] Lower... │               ║
║  └──────────────────────────────────────────┘               ║
║                                                             ║
║  [ ] When...     [ ] Error...     [ ] Scroll bar            ║
║  [ ] Valid...    [ ] Comment...   [ ] Allow tabs            ║
║  [ ] Message...  [ ] Disabled     [ ] Refresh               ║
║                                                             ║
╚═════════════════════════════════════════════════════════════╝
WINDOWS  RGB Color Scheme: (,,,,,)
WINDOWS  Font: Terminal,   9
*============================================================
*  Text: FILES= Setting:
*============================================================
 @   4.083,    6.125
WINDOWS  RGB Color Scheme: (,,,,,)
WINDOWS  Font: Terminal,   9
*============================================================
*  Text: System Information
*============================================================
```

```
 @   0.833,  20.125
WINDOWS  RGB Color Scheme: (,,,,,)
WINDOWS  Font: Terminal,   9
*==============================================================
*  m.lhNext
*==============================================================
 @  13.250,  36.625
    SIZE   1.769,  10.000
 Spacing:    5
```

```
Push Button Prompts:        (·) Horizontal    ( ) Vertical
                            [X] Terminating   <Spacing...>
 \<Next
                           Variable:

                            < Choose... >  m.lhNext

                           Options:

                            [ ] When...      [ ] Comment...
                            [X] Valid...     [ ] Disabled
                            [ ] Message...

                «  OK  »    < Cancel >
```

```
WINDOWS  RGB Color Scheme: (,,,,,)
WINDOWS  Font: MS Sans Serif,   8
        Style: Bold
 Valid code above
*==============================================================
*  m.lhPrior
*==============================================================
 @  13.250,  14.125
    SIZE   1.769,  10.000
 Spacing:    5
```

```
Push Button Prompts:        (·) Horizontal    ( ) Vertical
                            [X] Terminating   <Spacing...>
 \<Prior
                           Variable:

                            < Choose... >  m.lhPrior

                           Options:

                            [ ] When...      [ ] Comment...
                            [X] Valid...     [ ] Disabled
                            [ ] Message...

                «  OK  »    < Cancel >
```

```
WINDOWS  RGB Color Scheme: (,,,,,)
WINDOWS  Font: MS Sans Serif,   8
        Style: Bold
```

```
 Valid code above
*==============================================================
*  m.lhDone
*==============================================================
 @  13.250,  25.375
     SIZE   1.769,  10.000
 Spacing:    5
```

```
  Push Button Prompts:         (·) Horizontal    ( ) Vertical
                               [X] Terminating  <Spacing...>
  \!\?\<Done
                              Variable:

                               < Choose... >  m.lhDone

                              Options:

                               [ ] When...     [ ] Comment...
                               [X] Valid...    [ ] Disabled
                               [ ] Message...

                 «   OK   »    < Cancel >
```

```
WINDOWS  RGB Color Scheme: (,,,,,)
WINDOWS  Font: MS Sans Serif,   8
         Style: Bold
 Valid code above
*==============================================================
*  Line
*==============================================================
 @   0.333,   0.375
WINDOWS  RGB Color Scheme: (128,128,128,128,128,128)
           Pen: 2
*==============================================================
*  Line
*==============================================================
 @   0.417,  57.875
WINDOWS  RGB Color Scheme: (255,255,255,255,255,255)
           Pen: 1
*==============================================================
*  Line
*==============================================================
 @   0.333,   0.375
WINDOWS  RGB Color Scheme: (128,128,128,128,128,128)
           Pen: 2
*==============================================================
*  Line
*==============================================================
 @  12.667,   0.500
WINDOWS  RGB Color Scheme: (255,255,255,255,255,255)
           Pen: 1
```

Memory Information Screen: ABOUTMEM.SCX

The fourth window in the set displays information on the application's memory utilization. It display the regular memory available, the current amount of memory being taken up by the applications objects (windows, popups, etc.), and the amount of memory available to the application. It also displays the amount of expanded memory that is currently being utilized by the application, and any limit placed on expanded memory usage. Finally, it displays the type of processor that is available in the current computer.

The pushbuttons on the bottom of the window allow the user to access more system information or to close the window.

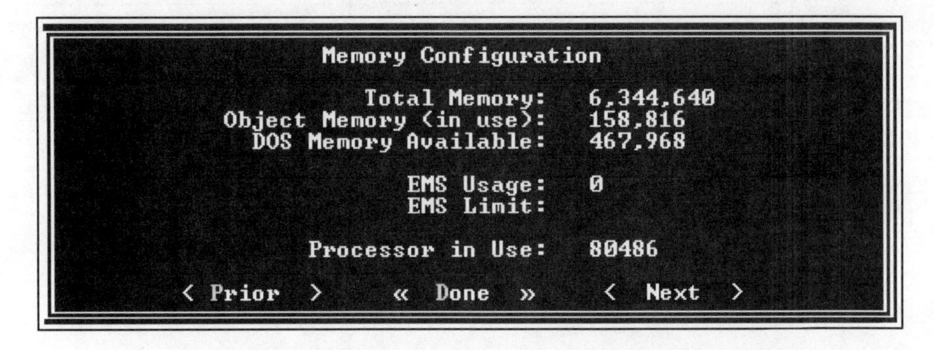

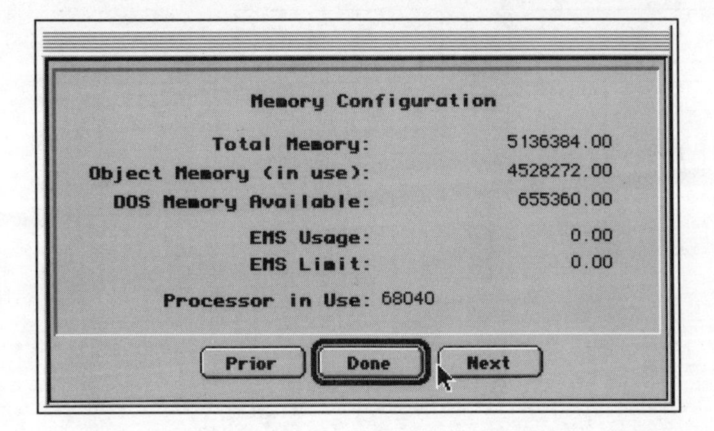

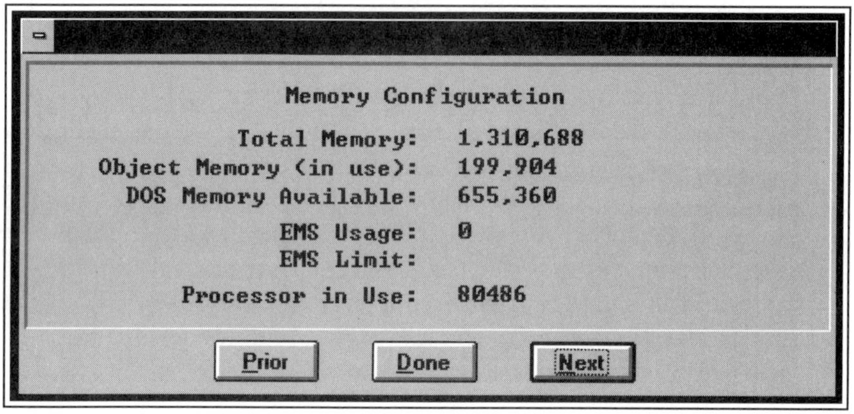

```
Memory Configuration

             Total Memory:   1,310,688
  Object Memory (in use):    199,904
     DOS Memory Available:   655,360

               EMS Usage:    0
               EMS Limit:

         Processor in Use:   80486

      Prior      Done      Next
```

```
*-------------------------------------------------------------
**************************************************************
**--    ABOUTMEM.SCX - DOS PLATFORM
**************************************************************
```

```
( ) DeskTop                         (·) Window

Name:   wmAbout                     <Type...>
Title:
Footer:

Size:               Screen Code:

 Height:   15        [X] Setup...
 Width:    61        [ ] Cleanup & Procs...            «   OK   »

Position:           READ Clauses:                      < Cancel >

 Row:        0       [ ] Activate...    [ ] Show...
 Column:     0       [ ] Valid...       [ ] When...
 [X] Center          [ ] Deactivate...

Environment:                            [X] Add alias

        Environment NOT saved with screen.
```

```
Type:  [ Dialog ]

Attributes:          Border:

 [ ] Close            ( ) None
 [X] Float            ( ) Single
 [X] Shadow           (·) Double       «   OK   »
 [ ] Minimize         ( ) Panel
                      ( ) System       < Cancel >

Color Schemes:

 Primary:             Popup:
 [ Dialogs ]          [ Dialog Pop ]
```

```
*************************************************************
*  SCREEN SETUP CODE
*************************************************************
*  Program...........: ABOUTMEM Screen
*  Author............: yag
*  Project...........: COMMON
*  Created...........: 04/16/93
*  Copyright.........: (c) Flash Creative Management, 1993
*) Description.......: ABOUT MEMORY Screen
*)                   : Shows information about available
*)                   : system memory.
*  Calling Samples...: Called from About.prg automatically
*  Parameter List....:
*  Major change list.:
*************************************************************
*--   G E T   O B J E C T S
*************************************************************
*============================================================
*
*============================================================
 @  4,  38
```

```
Field:
  (·) Say          ( ) Get          ( ) Edit

< Say...    > VAL(SYS(12))
                                                   «   OK   »
< Format... > @B 999,999,999
                                                   < Cancel >
Range:
  [ ] Upper...                      [ ] Lower...

[ ] When...      [ ] Error...      [ ] Scroll bar
[ ] Valid...     [ ] Comment...    [ ] Allow tabs
[ ] Message...   [ ] Disabled      [ ] Refresh
*==============================================================
*
*==============================================================
 @   6,  38

Field:
  (·) Say          ( ) Get          ( ) Edit

< Say...    > VAL(SYS(23))*1024
                                                   «   OK   »
< Format... > @B 999,999,999
                                                   < Cancel >
Range:
  [ ] Upper...                      [ ] Lower...

[ ] When...      [ ] Error...      [ ] Scroll bar
[ ] Valid...     [ ] Comment...    [ ] Allow tabs
[ ] Message...   [ ] Disabled      [ ] Refresh
*==============================================================
*
*==============================================================
 @   3,  38
```

```
Field:
  (·) Say          ( ) Get          ( ) Edit

< Say...    > VAL(SYS(1016))
                                              «   OK   »
< Format... > @B 999,999,999
                                              < Cancel >
Range:
  [ ] Upper...                 [ ] Lower...

[ ] When...      [ ] Error...      [ ] Scroll bar
[ ] Valid...     [ ] Comment...    [ ] Allow tabs
[ ] Message...   [ ] Disabled      [ ] Refresh
*============================================================
*  Text: EMS Usage:
*============================================================
 @   6,  25
*============================================================
*  Text: EMS Limit:
*============================================================
 @   7,  25
*============================================================
*
*============================================================
 @   7,  38
Field:
  (·) Say          ( ) Get          ( ) Edit

< Say...    > VAL(SYS(24))
                                              «   OK   »
< Format... > @BZ 999,999,999
                                              < Cancel >
Range:
  [ ] Upper...                 [ ] Lower...

[ ] When...      [ ] Error...      [ ] Scroll bar
[ ] Valid...     [ ] Comment...    [ ] Allow tabs
[ ] Message...   [ ] Disabled      [ ] Refresh
*============================================================
*
*============================================================
 @   9,  38
```

```
Field:
  (·) Say          ( ) Get          ( ) Edit

< Say...     > SYS(17)
                                                  «   OK    »
< Format... >
                                                  < Cancel >
Range:
  [ ] Upper...                  [ ] Lower...

[ ] When...      [ ] Error...      [ ] Scroll bar
[ ] Valid...     [ ] Comment...    [ ] Allow tabs
[ ] Message...   [ ] Disabled      [ ] Refresh

*============================================================
*  Text: Processor in Use:
*============================================================
 @   9,  18
*============================================================
*
*============================================================
 @   2,  38

Field:
  (·) Say          ( ) Get          ( ) Edit

< Say...     > VAL(SYS(1001))
                                                  «   OK    »
< Format... > @B 999,999,999
                                                  < Cancel >
Range:
  [ ] Upper...                  [ ] Lower...

[ ] When...      [ ] Error...      [ ] Scroll bar
[ ] Valid...     [ ] Comment...    [ ] Allow tabs
[ ] Message...   [ ] Disabled      [ ] Refresh

*============================================================
*  Text: Object Memory (in use):
*============================================================
 @   3,  12
*============================================================
*  Text: DOS Memory Available:
*============================================================
 @   4,  14
*============================================================
```

```
*  Text: Memory Configuration
*==============================================================
 @   0,  19
*==============================================================
*  Text: Total Memory:
*==============================================================
 @   2,  22
*==============================================================
*  m.lhNext
*==============================================================
 @  11,  39
 Spacing:    5
```

```
Push Button Prompts:          (·) Horizontal     ( ) Vertical
                              [X] Terminating   <Spacing...>
\<Next
                             Variable:

                              < Choose... >  m.lhNext

                             Options:

                              [ ] When...      [ ] Comment...
                              [X] Valid...     [ ] Disabled
                              [ ] Message...

                  «   OK   »    < Cancel >
```

```
--------------------------------------------------------------
*-- m.lhNext Valid Clause
--------------------------------------------------------------
```

```
Valid

  (·) Procedure
  ( ) Expression
```

```
lcNext =  'aboutcom.spr'
*==============================================================
*  m.lhPrior
*==============================================================
 @  11,   9
 Spacing:    5
```

```
Push Button Prompts:        (·) Horizontal    ( ) Vertical
                            [X] Terminating  <Spacing...>
\<Prior
                           Variable:

                            < Choose... >  m.lhPrior

                           Options:

                            [ ] When...     [ ] Comment...
                            [X] Valid...    [ ] Disabled
                            [ ] Message...

                  «   OK   »    < Cancel >
------------------------------------------------------------
*-- m.lhPrior Valid Clause
------------------------------------------------------------

  Valid

   (·) Procedure
   ( ) Expression

lcNext = 'aboutfil.spr'
*===========================================================
*  m.lhDone
*===========================================================
 @  11,  24
 Spacing:    5

Push Button Prompts:        (·) Horizontal    ( ) Vertical
                            [X] Terminating  <Spacing...>
\!\?\<Done
                           Variable:

                            < Choose... >  m.lhDone

                           Options:

                            [ ] When...     [ ] Comment...
                            [X] Valid...    [ ] Disabled
                            [ ] Message...

                  «   OK   »    < Cancel >
------------------------------------------------------------
*-- m.lhDone Valid Clause
------------------------------------------------------------
```

```
Valid

  (·) Procedure
  ( ) Expression

RELEASE WINDOW wmAbout
llEndAbout = .T.
*------------------------------------------------------------
*************************************************************
**--    ABOUTMEM.SCX - MAC PLATFORM
*************************************************************

( ) DeskTop                           (·) Window

Name:   wmAbout                       <Type...>
Title:
Footer:

Size:              Screen Code:

  Height:   15.692   [X] Setup...
  Width:    58.333   [ ] Cleanup & Procs...          «  OK  »

Position:          READ Clauses:                     < Cancel >

  Row:       0.000   [ ] Activate...    [ ] Show...
  Column:    0.000   [ ] Valid...       [ ] When...
  [X] Center         [ ] Deactivate...

Environment:                          [X] Add alias

      Environment NOT saved with screen.

Type:        Dialog

Attributes:        Border:

  [ ] Close          ( ) None
  [X] Float          ( ) Single
  [X] Shadow         (·) Double     «  OK  »
  [ ] Minimize       ( ) Panel
                     ( ) System     < Cancel >

Color Schemes:

  Primary:         Popup:

MAC      RGB Fill Color Scheme: (193,193,193)
```

```
MAC       Font: Geneva,  10
 Screen Setup code above
************************************************************
*--    G E T    O B J E C T S
************************************************************
*===========================================================
*
*===========================================================
 @   6.000,  31.500

 Field:
   (·) Say          ( ) Get          ( ) Edit

 <  Say...    > VAL(SYS(12))
                                                 «   OK   »
 < Format... >
                                                 < Cancel >
 Range:
   [ ] Upper...                   [ ] Lower...

 [ ] When...      [ ] Error...     [ ] Scroll bar
 [ ] Valid...     [ ] Comment...   [ ] Allow tabs
 [ ] Message...   [ ] Disabled     [ ] Refresh

MAC       RGB Color Scheme: (,,,,,)
MAC       Font: monaco,   9
*===========================================================
*
*===========================================================
 @   7.692,  31.500

 Field:
   (·) Say          ( ) Get          ( ) Edit

 <  Say...    > VAL(SYS(23))*1024
                                                 «   OK   »
 < Format... >
                                                 < Cancel >
 Range:
   [ ] Upper...                   [ ] Lower...

 [ ] When...      [ ] Error...     [ ] Scroll bar
 [ ] Valid...     [ ] Comment...   [ ] Allow tabs
 [ ] Message...   [ ] Disabled     [ ] Refresh

MAC       RGB Color Scheme: (,,,,,)
MAC       Font: monaco,   9
```

```
*==========================================================
*
*==========================================================
 @   4.692,  31.500
┌────────────────────────────────────────────────────────┐
│                                                        │
│  Field:                                                │
│  ┌──────────────────────────────────────┐              │
│  │ (·) Say      ( ) Get        ( ) Edit │              │
│  └──────────────────────────────────────┘              │
│                                                        │
│  <  Say...   > VAL(SYS(1016))                          │
│                                          «   OK   »    │
│  < Format... >                                         │
│                                          < Cancel >    │
│  Range:                                                │
│  ┌──────────────────────────────────────┐              │
│  │ [ ] Upper...            [ ] Lower... │              │
│  └──────────────────────────────────────┘              │
│                                                        │
│  [ ] When...     [ ] Error...     [ ] Scroll bar       │
│  [ ] Valid...    [ ] Comment...   [ ] Allow tabs       │
│  [ ] Message...  [ ] Disabled     [ ] Refresh          │
│                                                        │
└────────────────────────────────────────────────────────┘
MAC       RGB Color Scheme: (,,,,,)
MAC       Font: monaco,   9
*==========================================================
*  Text: EMS Usage:
*==========================================================
 @   7.769,  19.000
MAC       RGB Color Scheme: (,,,,,)
MAC       Font: Monaco,   9
         Style: Bold
*==========================================================
*  Text: EMS Limit:
*==========================================================
 @   9.000,  19.000
MAC       RGB Color Scheme: (,,,,,)
MAC       Font: Monaco,   9
         Style: Bold
*==========================================================
*
*==========================================================
 @   8.923,  31.500
```

```
 ┌─────────────────────────────────────────────────────────────┐
 │ Field:                                                      │
 │ ┌──────────────────────────────────────────┐               │
 │ │ (·) Say        ( ) Get        ( ) Edit   │               │
 │ └──────────────────────────────────────────┘               │
 │                                                             │
 │ <  Say...   > VAL(SYS(24))                                 │
 │                                               «   OK   »    │
 │ < Format... >                                               │
 │                                               < Cancel >    │
 │ Range:                                                      │
 │ ┌──────────────────────────────────────────┐               │
 │ │ [ ] Upper...               [ ] Lower...  │               │
 │ └──────────────────────────────────────────┘               │
 │                                                             │
 │ [ ] When...     [ ] Error...     [ ] Scroll bar             │
 │ [ ] Valid...    [ ] Comment...   [ ] Allow tabs             │
 │ [ ] Message...  [ ] Disabled     [ ] Refresh                │
 │                                                             │
 └─────────────────────────────────────────────────────────────┘
MAC      RGB Color Scheme: (,,,,,)
MAC      Font: monaco,   9
*==============================================================
*
*==============================================================
 @  10.615,  31.500
 ┌─────────────────────────────────────────────────────────────┐
 │ Field:                                                      │
 │ ┌──────────────────────────────────────────┐               │
 │ │ (·) Say        ( ) Get        ( ) Edit   │               │
 │ └──────────────────────────────────────────┘               │
 │                                                             │
 │ <  Say...   > SYS(17)                                      │
 │                                               «   OK   »    │
 │ < Format... >                                               │
 │                                               < Cancel >    │
 │ Range:                                                      │
 │ ┌──────────────────────────────────────────┐               │
 │ │ [ ] Upper...               [ ] Lower...  │               │
 │ └──────────────────────────────────────────┘               │
 │                                                             │
 │ [ ] When...     [ ] Error...     [ ] Scroll bar             │
 │ [ ] Valid...    [ ] Comment...   [ ] Allow tabs             │
 │ [ ] Message...  [ ] Disabled     [ ] Refresh                │
 │                                                             │
 └─────────────────────────────────────────────────────────────┘
MAC      RGB Color Scheme: (,,,,,)
MAC      Font: monaco,   9
*==============================================================
*  Text: Processor in Use:
*==============================================================
 @  10.692,  10.833
MAC      RGB Color Scheme: (,,,,,)
MAC      Font: Monaco,   9
       Style: Bold
*==============================================================
*
```

```
*==============================================================
 @   3.308,  31.500

  Field:
   ( ) Say          ( ) Get          ( ) Edit

  <  Say...    > VAL(SYS(1001))
                                              «   OK   »
  < Format... >
                                              < Cancel >
  Range:
   [ ] Upper...                  [ ] Lower...

   [ ] When...       [ ] Error...       [ ] Scroll bar
   [ ] Valid...      [ ] Comment...     [ ] Allow tabs
   [ ] Message...    [ ] Disabled       [ ] Refresh

MAC       RGB Color Scheme: (,,,,,)
MAC       Font: monaco,    9
*==============================================================
*  Text: Object Memory (in use):
*==============================================================
 @   4.769,   3.833
MAC       RGB Color Scheme: (,,,,,)
MAC       Font: Monaco,    9
         Style: Bold
*==============================================================
*  Text: DOS Memory Available:
*==============================================================
 @   6.077,   6.167
MAC       RGB Color Scheme: (,,,,,)
MAC       Font: Monaco,    9
         Style: Bold
*==============================================================
*  Text: Total Memory:
*==============================================================
 @   3.385,  15.500
MAC       RGB Color Scheme: (,,,,,)
MAC       Font: Monaco,    9
         Style: Bold
*==============================================================
*  Text: Memory Configuration
*==============================================================
 @   1.385,  19.167
MAC       RGB Color Scheme: (,,,,,)
MAC       Font: Monaco,    9
         Style: Bold
*==============================================================
*  m.lhNext
*==============================================================
 @  13.231,  36.667
     SIZE   1.500,  10.000
 Spacing:    5
```

```
Push Button Prompts:          (·) Horizontal    ( ) Vertical
                              [X] Terminating   <Spacing...>
\<Next
                              Variable:

                              < Choose... >  m.lhNext

                              Options:

                              [ ] When...     [ ] Comment...
                              [X] Valid...    [ ] Disabled
                              [ ] Message...

              «  OK  »     < Cancel >
MAC       RGB Color Scheme: (,,,,,)
MAC       Font: Geneva,    9
         Style: Bold
 Valid code above
*==============================================================
*  m.lhPrior
*==============================================================
 @  13.231,  14.167
     SIZE   1.500,  10.000
 Spacing:    5
```

```
Push Button Prompts:          (·) Horizontal    ( ) Vertical
                              [X] Terminating   <Spacing...>
\<Prior
                              Variable:

                              < Choose... >  m.lhPrior

                              Options:

                              [ ] When...     [ ] Comment...
                              [X] Valid...    [ ] Disabled
                              [ ] Message...

              «  OK  »     < Cancel >
MAC       RGB Color Scheme: (,,,,,)
MAC       Font: Geneva,    9
         Style: Bold
 Valid code above
*==============================================================
*  m.lhDone
*==============================================================
 @  13.231,  25.333
     SIZE   1.500,  10.000
 Spacing:    5
```

```
Push Button Prompts:           (·) Horizontal    ( ) Vertical
                               [X] Terminating  <Spacing...>
 \!\?\<Done
                              Variable:

                               < Choose... >  m.lhDone

                              Options:

                               [ ] When...       [ ] Comment...
                               [X] Valid...      [ ] Disabled
                               [ ] Message...


              «   OK   »    < Cancel >
```

```
MAC      RGB Color Scheme: (,,,,,)
MAC      Font: Geneva,   9
        Style: Bold
 Valid code above
*==============================================================
*  Line
*==============================================================
 @   0.308,   0.333
MAC      RGB Color Scheme: (130,130,130,130,130,130)
           Pen: 2
*==============================================================
*  Line
*==============================================================
 @   0.385,  57.833
MAC      RGB Color Scheme: (255,255,255,255,255,255)
           Pen: 1
*==============================================================
*  Line
*==============================================================
 @   0.308,   0.333
MAC      RGB Color Scheme: (130,130,130,130,130,130)
           Pen: 2
*==============================================================
*  Line
*==============================================================
 @  12.692,   0.500
MAC      RGB Color Scheme: (255,255,255,255,255,255)
           Pen: 1
*--------------------------------------------------------------
```

```
************************************************************
**--    ABOUTMEM.SCX - WINDOWS PLATFORM
************************************************************
```

```
( ) DeskTop                          (·) Window

Name:   wmAbout                      <Type...>
Title:
Footer:

Size:              Screen Code:

Height:   15.667   [X] Setup...
Width:    58.250   [ ] Cleanup & Procs...            «  OK  »

Position:          READ Clauses:                    < Cancel >

Row:        0.000  [ ] Activate...   [ ] Show...
Column:     0.000  [ ] Valid...      [ ] When...
[X] Center         [ ] Deactivate...

Environment:                           [X] Add alias

      Environment NOT saved with screen.
```

```
Type:      Dialog

Attributes:        Border:

[ ] Close          ( ) None
[X] Float          ( ) Single
[X] Shadow         (·) Double        «  OK  »
[ ] Minimize       ( ) Panel
                   ( ) System       < Cancel >

Color Schemes:

Primary:           Popup:
```

```
WINDOWS  RGB Fill Color Scheme: (192,192,192)
WINDOWS  Font: Terminal,   9
 Screen Setup code above
************************************************************
*--    G E T   O B J E C T S
************************************************************
*==========================================================
*
*==========================================================
 @   6.000,  31.500
```

```
 Field:
 ┌──────────────────────────────────────────────────┐
 │ (·) Say          ( ) Get          ( ) Edit       │
 └──────────────────────────────────────────────────┘

 <  Say...    > VAL(SYS(12))
                                                  «   OK   »
 < Format... > @B 999,999,999
                                                  < Cancel >
 Range:
 ┌──────────────────────────────────────────────────┐
 │ [ ] Upper...                    [ ] Lower...     │
 └──────────────────────────────────────────────────┘

 [ ] When...      [ ] Error...     [ ] Scroll bar
 [ ] Valid...     [ ] Comment...   [ ] Allow tabs
 [ ] Message...   [ ] Disabled     [ ] Refresh
```

```
WINDOWS  RGB Color Scheme: (,,,,,)
WINDOWS  Font: Terminal,   9
*============================================================
*
*============================================================
 @   7.667,  31.500
```

```
 Field:
 ┌──────────────────────────────────────────────────┐
 │ (·) Say          ( ) Get          ( ) Edit       │
 └──────────────────────────────────────────────────┘

 <  Say...    > VAL(SYS(23))*1024
                                                  «   OK   »
 < Format... > @B 999,999,999
                                                  < Cancel >
 Range:
 ┌──────────────────────────────────────────────────┐
 │ [ ] Upper...                    [ ] Lower...     │
 └──────────────────────────────────────────────────┘

 [ ] When...      [ ] Error...     [ ] Scroll bar
 [ ] Valid...     [ ] Comment...   [ ] Allow tabs
 [ ] Message...   [ ] Disabled     [ ] Refresh
```

```
WINDOWS  RGB Color Scheme: (,,,,,)
WINDOWS  Font: Terminal,   9
*============================================================
*
*============================================================
 @   4.667,  31.500
```

```
 Field:
 ┌───────────────────────────────────────────────┐
 │ (·) Say          ( ) Get          ( ) Edit     │
 └───────────────────────────────────────────────┘

 <  Say...    > VAL(SYS(1016))
                                               «   OK   »
 < Format... > @B 999,999,999
                                               < Cancel >
 Range:
 ┌───────────────────────────────────────────────┐
 │ [ ] Upper...                   [ ] Lower...    │
 └───────────────────────────────────────────────┘

 [ ] When...      [ ] Error...      [ ] Scroll bar
 [ ] Valid...     [ ] Comment...    [ ] Allow tabs
 [ ] Message...   [ ] Disabled      [ ] Refresh

WINDOWS  RGB Color Scheme: (,,,,,)
WINDOWS  Font: Terminal,   9
*=============================================================
*  Text: EMS Usage:
*=============================================================
 @   7.750,  18.750
WINDOWS  RGB Color Scheme: (,,,,,)
WINDOWS  Font: Terminal,   9
*=============================================================
*  Text: EMS Limit:
*=============================================================
 @   9.000,  18.750
WINDOWS  RGB Color Scheme: (,,,,,)
WINDOWS  Font: Terminal,   9
*=============================================================
*
*=============================================================
 @   8.917,  31.500

 Field:
 ┌───────────────────────────────────────────────┐
 │ (·) Say          ( ) Get          ( ) Edit     │
 └───────────────────────────────────────────────┘

 <  Say...    > VAL(SYS(24))
                                               «   OK   »
 < Format... > @BZ 999,999,999
                                               < Cancel >
 Range:
 ┌───────────────────────────────────────────────┐
 │ [ ] Upper...                   [ ] Lower...    │
 └───────────────────────────────────────────────┘

 [ ] When...      [ ] Error...      [ ] Scroll bar
 [ ] Valid...     [ ] Comment...    [ ] Allow tabs
 [ ] Message...   [ ] Disabled      [ ] Refresh

WINDOWS  RGB Color Scheme: (,,,,,)
```

```
WINDOWS  Font: Terminal,   9
*===========================================================
*
*===========================================================
 @  10.583,  31.500

   Field:
   ( ) Say          ( ) Get          ( ) Edit

   <  Say...   > SYS(17)
                                              «   OK   »
   < Format... >
                                              < Cancel >
   Range:
   [ ] Upper...                   [ ] Lower...

   [ ] When...     [ ] Error...     [ ] Scroll bar
   [ ] Valid...    [ ] Comment...   [ ] Allow tabs
   [ ] Message...  [ ] Disabled     [ ] Refresh

WINDOWS  RGB Color Scheme: (,,,,,)
WINDOWS  Font: Terminal,   9
*===========================================================
*  Text: Processor in Use:
*===========================================================
 @  10.667,  11.750
WINDOWS  RGB Color Scheme: (,,,,,)
WINDOWS  Font: Terminal,   9
*===========================================================
*
*===========================================================
 @   3.333,  31.500

   Field:
   ( ) Say          ( ) Get          ( ) Edit

   <  Say...   > VAL(SYS(1001))
                                              «   OK   »
   < Format... > @B 999,999,999
                                              < Cancel >
   Range:
   [ ] Upper...                   [ ] Lower...

   [ ] When...     [ ] Error...     [ ] Scroll bar
   [ ] Valid...    [ ] Comment...   [ ] Allow tabs
   [ ] Message...  [ ] Disabled     [ ] Refresh

WINDOWS  RGB Color Scheme: (,,,,,)
```

```
WINDOWS  Font: Terminal,   9
*==============================================================
*  Text: Object Memory (in use):
*==============================================================
 @   4.750,   5.750
WINDOWS  RGB Color Scheme: (,,,,,)
WINDOWS  Font: Terminal,   9
*==============================================================
*  Text: DOS Memory Available:
*==============================================================
 @   6.083,   7.750
WINDOWS  RGB Color Scheme: (,,,,,)
WINDOWS  Font: Terminal,   9
*==============================================================
*  Text: Total Memory:
*==============================================================
 @   3.417,  15.750
WINDOWS  RGB Color Scheme: (,,,,,)
WINDOWS  Font: Terminal,   9
*==============================================================
*  Text: Memory Configuration
*==============================================================
 @   1.417,  19.125
WINDOWS  RGB Color Scheme: (,,,,,)
WINDOWS  Font: Terminal,   9
*==============================================================
*  m.lhNext
*==============================================================
 @  13.250,  36.625
     SIZE   1.769,  10.000
 Spacing:    5
```

```
Push Button Prompts:        (·) Horizontal    ( ) Vertical
                            [X] Terminating   <Spacing...>
 \<Next
                           Variable:

                            < Choose... >  m.lhNext

                           Options:

                            [ ] When...      [ ] Comment...
                            [X] Valid...     [ ] Disabled
                            [ ] Message...

              «   OK   »     < Cancel >
```

```
WINDOWS  RGB Color Scheme: (,,,,,)
WINDOWS  Font: MS Sans Serif,   8
         Style: Bold
 Valid code above
*==============================================================
*  m.lhPrior
*==============================================================
 @  13.250,  14.125
     SIZE   1.769,  10.000
```

```
 Spacing:     5

┌─────────────────────────────────────────────────────────┐
│                                                         │
│  Push Button Prompts:       ┌─────────────────────────┐ │
│                             │ (·) Horizontal ( ) Vertical │
│  ┌──────────────────┐       │ [X] Terminating <Spacing...>│
│  │\<Prior           │       └─────────────────────────┘ │
│  │                  │       Variable:                   │
│  │                  │       ┌─────────────────────────┐ │
│  │                  │       │ < Choose... >  m.lhPrior │ │
│  │                  │       └─────────────────────────┘ │
│  │                  │       Options:                    │
│  │                  │       ┌─────────────────────────┐ │
│  │                  │       │ [ ] When...    [ ] Comment... │
│  │                  │       │ [X] Valid...   [ ] Disabled │
│  │                  │       │ [ ] Message...          │ │
│  └──────────────────┘       └─────────────────────────┘ │
│                                                         │
│               «   OK   »    < Cancel >                  │
│                                                         │
└─────────────────────────────────────────────────────────┘
WINDOWS  RGB Color Scheme: (,,,,,)
WINDOWS  Font: MS Sans Serif,    8
         Style: Bold
 Valid code above
*============================================================
*  m.lhDone
*============================================================
 @  13.250,   25.375
     SIZE   1.769,   10.000
 Spacing:     5

┌─────────────────────────────────────────────────────────┐
│                                                         │
│  Push Button Prompts:       ┌─────────────────────────┐ │
│                             │ (·) Horizontal ( ) Vertical │
│  ┌──────────────────┐       │ [X] Terminating <Spacing...>│
│  │\!\?\<Done        │       └─────────────────────────┘ │
│  │                  │       Variable:                   │
│  │                  │       ┌─────────────────────────┐ │
│  │                  │       │ < Choose... >  m.lhDone  │ │
│  │                  │       └─────────────────────────┘ │
│  │                  │       Options:                    │
│  │                  │       ┌─────────────────────────┐ │
│  │                  │       │ [ ] When...    [ ] Comment... │
│  │                  │       │ [X] Valid...   [ ] Disabled │
│  │                  │       │ [ ] Message...          │ │
│  └──────────────────┘       └─────────────────────────┘ │
│                                                         │
│               «   OK   »    < Cancel >                  │
│                                                         │
└─────────────────────────────────────────────────────────┘
WINDOWS  RGB Color Scheme: (,,,,,)
WINDOWS  Font: MS Sans Serif,    8
         Style: Bold
 Valid code above
*============================================================
*  Line
*============================================================
 @   0.333,   0.375
 Comment code above
<<tcPlatform>> RGB Color Scheme: <<jcFill>>
          Pen: <<pensize>>
```

```
*==============================================================
*  Line
*==============================================================
 @   0.417,  57.875
 Comment code above
<<tcPlatform>> RGB Color Scheme: <<jcFill>>
          Pen: <<pensize>>
*==============================================================
*  Line
*==============================================================
 @   0.333,   0.375
 Comment code above
<<tcPlatform>> RGB Color Scheme: <<jcFill>>
          Pen: <<pensize>>
*==============================================================
*  Line
*==============================================================
 @  12.667,   0.500
 Comment code above
<<tcPlatform>> RGB Color Scheme: <<jcFill>>
          Pen: <<pensize>>
```

Alert Dialog: ALERT.SCX

The DOS version of Alert() has not changed from the earlier *FoxPro Codebook*, Windows support, however, has been added by making use of FOXTOOLS.FLL (provided with FoxPro) and a call to the MSGBOX() function contained within it. Macintosh support has been added by making use of FOXTOOLS.MLB (provided with FoxPro for the Mac) and a call to the FxAlert() function contained within it.

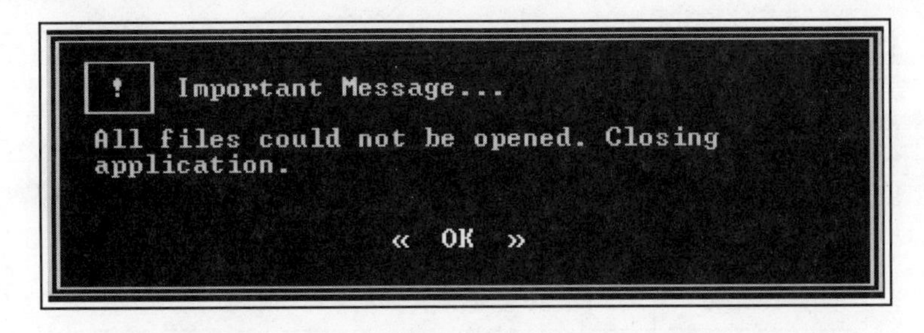

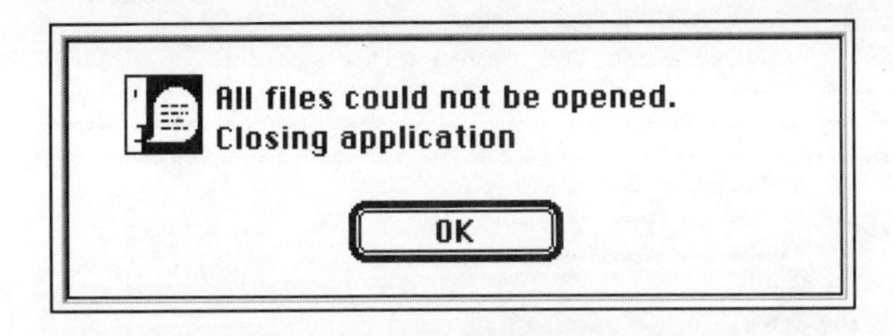

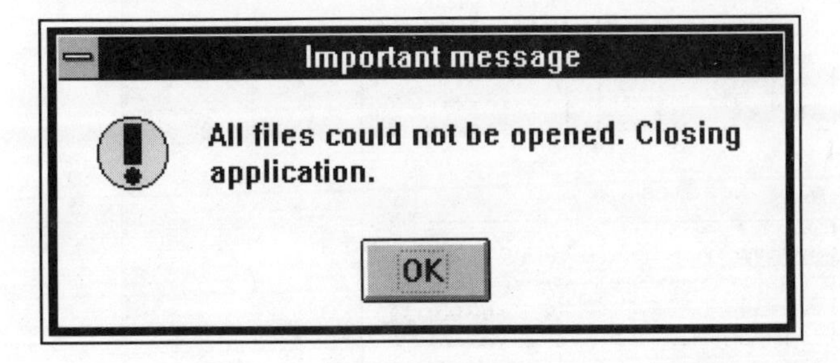

```
*-----------------------------------------------------------
************************************************************
**--    ALERT.SCX - DOS PLATFORM
************************************************************

 ( ) DeskTop                       (·) Window

 Name:                             <Type...>
 Title:
 Footer:

 Size:             Screen Code:

  Height:   11      [X] Setup...
  Width:    51      [X] Cleanup & Procs...          «   OK   »

 Position:         READ Clauses:                    < Cancel >

  Row:        0     [ ] Activate...   [ ] Show...
  Column:     0     [ ] Valid...      [ ] When...
  [X] Center        [ ] Deactivate...

 Environment:                         [ ] Add alias

        Environment NOT saved with screen.


  Type:        Alert

  Attributes:     Border:

   [ ] Close       ( ) None
   [X] Float       ( ) Single
   [X] Shadow      (·) Double      «   OK   »
   [ ] Minimize    ( ) Panel
                   ( ) System      < Cancel >

  Color Schemes:

   Primary:        Popup:

   Alerts          Alert Pops

************************************************************
*  SCREEN SETUP CODE
************************************************************
#SECT 1
*  Program..........: ALERT Screen
*  Author...........: yag
*  Project..........: COMMON
*  Created..........: 04/16/93
*  Copyright........: (c) Flash Creative Management, 1993
*) Description......: Alert Screen
```

```
*)                    : Standard alert window (! type)
*  Calling Samples...: DO Alert.spr WITH "Printer Not Available"
*  Parameter List....: lcString    -    Message text for dialog
*  Major change list.:
* Generic alert window
* -- "!" type of alert
PARAMETERS m.lcString
#SECT 2
REGIONAL m.llCursor, m.lhOK
DO CASE
   CASE _WINDOWS
      =msgbox(lcString,'Important message',48)
      RETURN
   CASE _MAC
      =fxalert(2,258,-1,-1,lcString)
      RETURN
ENDCASE

?? CHR(7)
IF SET("CURSOR") = "ON"
   m.llCursor = "ON"
   SET CURSOR OFF
ELSE
   m.llCursor = "OFF"
ENDIF
************************************************************
*--   G E T   O B J E C T S
************************************************************
*===========================================================
*
*===========================================================
 @   3,   2

   Field:

    (·) Say          ( ) Get          ( ) Edit

   <  Say...   > m.lcString
                                                  «   OK   »
   < Format... > @I
                                                  < Cancel >
   Range:

    [ ] Upper...                  [ ] Lower...

   [ ] When...       [ ] Error...      [ ] Scroll bar
   [ ] Valid...      [ ] Comment...    [ ] Allow tabs
   [ ] Message...    [ ] Disabled      [ ] Refresh

*===========================================================
*  m.lhOk
*===========================================================
 @   7,  20
 Spacing:    1
```

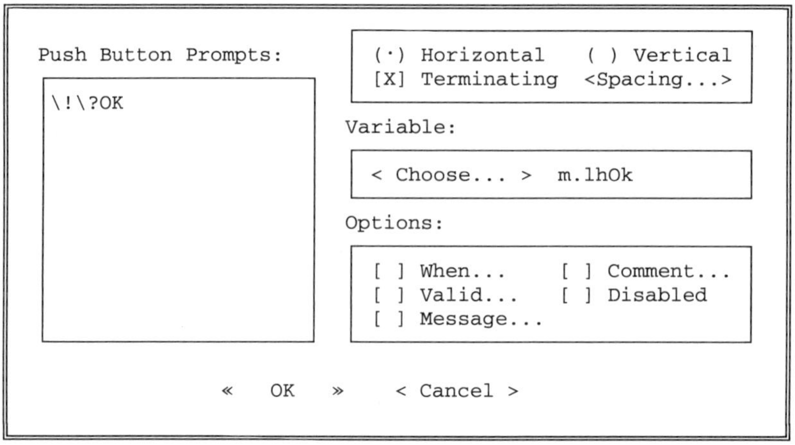

```
Push Button Prompts:        (·) Horizontal    ( ) Vertical
                            [X] Terminating  <Spacing...>
 \!\?OK
                           Variable:

                            < Choose... >  m.lhOk

                           Options:

                            [ ] When...      [ ] Comment...
                            [ ] Valid...     [ ] Disabled
                            [ ] Message...

              «   OK   »    < Cancel >
```

```
*============================================================
*  Text: !
*============================================================
 @   1,   3
*============================================================
*  Box
*============================================================
 @   0,   1
 SIZE   3,   5
*============================================================
*  Text: Important Message...
*============================================================
 @   1,   7
************************************************************
*--  SCREEN CLEANUP CODE
************************************************************
IF m.llCursor = "ON"
   SET CURSOR ON
ENDIF
*-----------------------------------------------------------
```

```
************************************************************
**--    ALERT.SCX - MAC PLATFORM
************************************************************
╔════════════════════════════════════════════════════════════════════════╗
║ ( ) DeskTop                          (·) Window                        ║
║                                                                        ║
║ Name:                                <Type...>                         ║
║ Title:                                                                 ║
║ Footer:                                                                ║
║                                                                        ║
║ Size:              Screen Code:                                        ║
║ ┌────────────────────┐ ┌──────────────────────────────────┐            ║
║ │ Height:    7.333   │ │ [X] Setup...                     │            ║
║ │ Width:    51.000   │ │ [X] Cleanup & Procs...           │  «  OK  »  ║
║ └────────────────────┘ └──────────────────────────────────┘            ║
║ Position:          READ Clauses:                           < Cancel >  ║
║ ┌────────────────────┐ ┌──────────────────────────────────┐            ║
║ │ Row:       0.000   │ │ [ ] Activate...     [ ] Show...  │            ║
║ │ Column:    0.000   │ │ [ ] Valid...        [ ] When...  │            ║
║ │ [X] Center         │ │ [ ] Deactivate...                │            ║
║ └────────────────────┘ └──────────────────────────────────┘            ║
║ Environment:                              [ ] Add alias                ║
║ ┌──────────────────────────────────────────────────────┐               ║
║ │        Environment NOT saved with screen.            │               ║
║ └──────────────────────────────────────────────────────┘               ║
╚════════════════════════════════════════════════════════════════════════╝
╔═══════════════════════════════════════════════════╗
║                                                   ║
║  Type:   ┌───────────────┐                        ║
║          │     Alert     │                        ║
║          └───────────────┘                        ║
║                                                   ║
║  Attributes:       Border:                        ║
║  ┌───────────────┐ ┌────────────┐                 ║
║  │ [ ] Close     │ │ ( ) None   │                 ║
║  │ [X] Float     │ │ ( ) Single │                 ║
║  │ [X] Shadow    │ │ (·) Double │   «   OK   »    ║
║  │ [ ] Minimize  │ │ ( ) Panel  │                 ║
║  └───────────────┘ │ ( ) System │   < Cancel >    ║
║                    └────────────┘                 ║
║  Color Schemes:                                   ║
║  ┌───────────────────────────────┐                ║
║  │ Primary:        Popup:        │                ║
║  │ ┌───────────┐   ┌───────────┐ │                ║
║  │ │           │   │           │ │                ║
║  │ └───────────┘   └───────────┘ │                ║
║  └───────────────────────────────┘                ║
╚═══════════════════════════════════════════════════╝
MAC      RGB Fill Color Scheme: (,,)
MAC      Font: Geneva,  10
 Screen Setup code above
************************************************************
*--    G E T    O B J E C T S
************************************************************
*===========================================================
*
*===========================================================
 @   2.167,   7.333
```

```
+--------------------------------------------------------------+
|                                                              |
|  Field:                                                      |
|  +------------------------------------------+                |
|  | (·) Say        ( ) Get        ( ) Edit   |                |
|  +------------------------------------------+                |
|                                                              |
|  <  Say...   > m.lcString                                    |
|                                              «   OK   »      |
|  < Format... >                                               |
|                                              < Cancel >      |
|  Range:                                                      |
|  +------------------------------------------+                |
|  | [ ] Upper...              [ ] Lower...    |                |
|  +------------------------------------------+                |
|                                                              |
|  [ ] When...     [ ] Error...     [ ] Scroll bar             |
|  [ ] Valid...    [ ] Comment...   [ ] Allow tabs             |
|  [ ] Message...  [ ] Disabled     [ ] Refresh                |
|                                                              |
+--------------------------------------------------------------+
MAC       RGB Color Scheme: (,,,,,)
MAC       Font: Terminal,   9
*=============================================================
*  m.lhOk
*=============================================================
 @   4.083,  20.000
     SIZE   1.917,  12.000
 Spacing:    2
+------------------------------------------------------------------+
|                                                                  |
|  Push Button Prompts:    +----------------------------------+    |
|                          | (·) Horizontal    ( ) Vertical   |    |
|  +--------------------+  | [X] Terminating  <Spacing...>    |    |
|  |\!\?OK              |  +----------------------------------+    |
|  |                    |  Variable:                               |
|  |                    |  +----------------------------------+    |
|  |                    |  | < Choose... >  m.lhOk            |    |
|  |                    |  +----------------------------------+    |
|  |                    |  Options:                                |
|  |                    |  +----------------------------------+    |
|  |                    |  | [ ] When...     [ ] Comment...   |    |
|  |                    |  | [ ] Valid...    [ ] Disabled     |    |
|  |                    |  | [ ] Message...                   |    |
|  +--------------------+  +----------------------------------+    |
|                                                                  |
|               «   OK   »    < Cancel >                           |
|                                                                  |
+------------------------------------------------------------------+
MAC       RGB Color Scheme: (,,,,,)
MAC       Font: Geneva,   9
         Style: Bold
*=============================================================
*  Text: !
*=============================================================
 @   1.083,    3.000
MAC       RGB Color Scheme: (,,,,,)
MAC       Font: Terminal,   9
         Style: Bold
*=============================================================
```

```
*  Box
*==============================================================
 @   0.583,   1.500
 SIZE   2.000,   3.667
MAC      RGB Color Scheme: (,,,,,)
           Pen: 1
*==============================================================
*  Text: Important Message...
*==============================================================
 @   1.083,   7.000
MAC      RGB Color Scheme: (,,,,,)
MAC      Font: Terminal,   9
        Style: Bold
 Screen Cleanup and Procedures code above
*--------------------------------------------------------------
**************************************************************
**--    ALERT.SCX - WINDOWS PLATFORM
**************************************************************
```

```
( ) DeskTop                           (·) Window

Name:                                 <Type...>
Title:
Footer:

Size:              Screen Code:

  Height:    7.333   [X] Setup...
  Width:    51.000   [X] Cleanup & Procs...          «   OK   »

Position:          READ Clauses:                     < Cancel >

  Row:       0.000   [ ] Activate...    [ ] Show...
  Column:    0.000   [ ] Valid...       [ ] When...
  [X] Center         [ ] Deactivate...

Environment:                          [ ] Add alias

        Environment NOT saved with screen.
```

```
Type:      Alert

Attributes:        Border:

  [ ] Close          ( ) None
  [X] Float          ( ) Single
  [X] Shadow         (·) Double     «   OK   »
  [ ] Minimize       ( ) Panel
                     ( ) System     < Cancel >

Color Schemes:

  Primary:          Popup:
```

```
WINDOWS  RGB Fill Color Scheme: (,,)
WINDOWS  Font: Terminal,   9
 Screen Setup code above
************************************************************
*--    G E T    O B J E C T S
************************************************************
*===========================================================
*
*===========================================================
 @   2.167,    7.250

  Field:
  ┌──────────────────────────────────────────┐
  │ (·) Say         ( ) Get         ( ) Edit │
  └──────────────────────────────────────────┘

  <  Say...    > m.lcString
                                              «    OK    »
  < Format... > @I
                                              < Cancel >
  Range:
  ┌──────────────────────────────────────────┐
  │ [ ] Upper...                [ ] Lower... │
  └──────────────────────────────────────────┘

  [ ] When...     [ ] Error...     [ ] Scroll bar
  [ ] Valid...    [ ] Comment...   [ ] Allow tabs
  [ ] Message...  [ ] Disabled     [ ] Refresh

WINDOWS  RGB Color Scheme: (,,,,,)
WINDOWS  Font: Terminal,   9
*===========================================================
*  m.lhOk
*===========================================================
 @   4.083,  20.000
     SIZE   1.923,  12.000
 Spacing:    2

  Push Button Prompts:     ┌────────────────────────────────┐
                           │ (·) Horizontal    ( ) Vertical │
  ┌──────────────────────┐ │ [X] Terminating  <Spacing...>  │
  │\!\?OK                │ └────────────────────────────────┘
  │                      │ Variable:
  │                      │ ┌────────────────────────────────┐
  │                      │ │ < Choose... >  m.lhOk          │
  │                      │ └────────────────────────────────┘
  │                      │ Options:
  │                      │ ┌────────────────────────────────┐
  │                      │ │ [ ] When...     [ ] Comment... │
  │                      │ │ [ ] Valid...    [ ] Disabled   │
  │                      │ │ [ ] Message...                 │
  └──────────────────────┘ └────────────────────────────────┘

               «   OK   »     < Cancel >

WINDOWS  RGB Color Scheme: (,,,,,)
```

```
WINDOWS  Font: MS Sans Serif,   8
        Style: Bold
*============================================================
*  Text: !
*============================================================
 @   1.083,   3.000
WINDOWS  RGB Color Scheme: (,,,,,)
WINDOWS  Font: Terminal,   9
        Style: Bold
*============================================================
*  Box
*============================================================
 @   0.583,   1.500
 SIZE   2.000,   3.625
WINDOWS  RGB Color Scheme: (,,,,,)
           Pen: 1
*============================================================
*  Text: Important Message...
*============================================================
 @   1.083,   7.000
WINDOWS  RGB Color Scheme: (,,,,,)
WINDOWS  Font: Terminal,   9
        Style: Bold
 Screen Cleanup and Procedures code above
```

FoxPro for Windows and FOXTOOLS.FLL

Microsoft Windows includes library functions for calling standard message box routines. Using FOXTOOLS.FLL, a library that ships with FoxPro/Windows, our applications can call these and other functions that are built into Windows Dynamic Link Libraries (DLLs).

Once we have linked FOXTOOLS.FLL into FoxPro via the SET LIBRARY TO command, we have access to a number of functions, including MSGBOX(). This function gives us access to the native Windows MESSAGEBOX function. MSGBOX() requires three parameters: the message text, the window title, and a number that designates what bitmap appears in the top left of the box, and what pushbuttons are used by the message box.

The available bitmaps include a stop sign, a question mark, an exclamation point and an international information symbol (the letter "i" in a blue circle). Each of these bitmaps is assigned a number, in increments of sixteen.

Stop	16
Question	32
Exclamation	48
Information	64

The pushbuttons are also assigned a number, in increments of one.

OK	0
OK/Cancel	1
Abort/Retry/Ignore	2
Yes/No/Cancel	3
Yes/No	4
Retry/Cancel	5

We decide what bitmaps and pushbuttons we want, and add the numbers together for the third parameter. For instance, if we want the following message box to appear, the code would read as follows:

```
SET LIBRARY TO sys(2004)+'foxtools.fll'
lcTitle = "Important Message"
lcText  = "This is an example of how FoxPro for Windows calls a DLL"
lcIconBut = 64
=msgbox(lcText, lcTitle, lcIconBut)
```

The MSGBOX() function returns a number that indicates which button was pressed. The button and the associated number are as follows:

OK	1
Cancel	2
Abort	3
Retry	4
Ignore	5
Yes	6
No	7

Using the native Windows functions for message boxes, can give our FoxPro for Windows applications a more Windows-like look and feel.

FoxPro for the Mac and FOXTOOLS.MLB

The Macintosh includes library functions for calling standard message box routines. Using FOXTOOLS.MLB, a library that ships with FoxPro for the Mac, our applications can call these and other functions that are built into the Macintosh toolbox.

Once we have linked FOXTOOLS.MLB into FoxPro via the SET LIBRARY TO command, we have access to a number of functions, including FxAlert(). This function gives us access to the native Macintosh alert functions. FxAlert() requires five parameters: bitmap, resource number, X-position, Y-position, first text field. It can take three additional optional text fields to display as well.

The bitmap parameter is a numeric parameter: Caution (0), Stop (1) or Note (2).

The resource number tells the Macintosh toolbox which pushbuttons to show and which one is the default pushbutton.

Resource #	**Pushbutton Options**	**Default**
257	Continue	Continue
258	OK	OK
259	Yes, No	Yes
260	Yes, No	No
261	Yes, No, Cancel	Yes
262	Yes, No, Cancel	No
263	Continue (bigger dialog)	Continue
264	OK (bigger dialog)	OK
265	Yes, No (bigger dialog)	Yes
266	Yes, No (bigger dialog)	No
267	Yes, No, Cancel (bigger dialog)	Yes
268	Yes, No, Cancel (bigger dialog)	No

The position parameters will typically be set to -1, -1 in order to default the dialog to the center.

FxAlert() returns the position of the selected button. In other words, if the pushbutton choices were Yes, No and Cancel, and No were selected, FxAlert() would return a 2.

Cross-Platform Alerts: Conclusion

Alert() and other reusable alert boxes have been modified to call the MSGBOX() or FxAlert() function in the Setup snippet and then to RETURN. This causes the rest of the code to only run during DOS applications. Again we have found an approach that allows our code to move seamlessly across platforms without having to recode the application.

Searching Dialog: APPSRCH.SCX

AppSrch is an enhanced version of the reusable screen that ships with FoxPro's FOXAPP application builder. The added enhancements hook it into our DataDict table and provide full field descriptions for the search criteria.

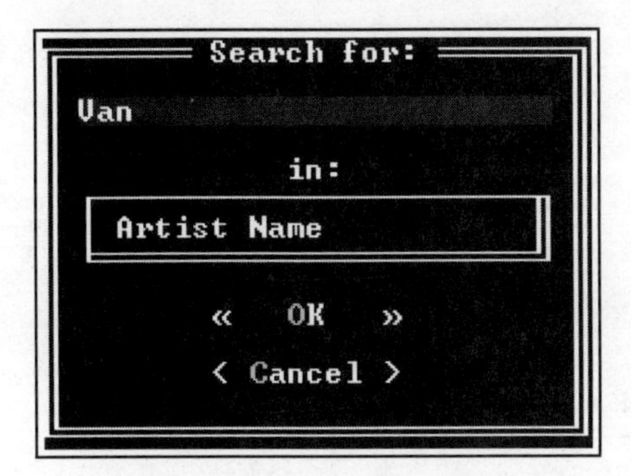

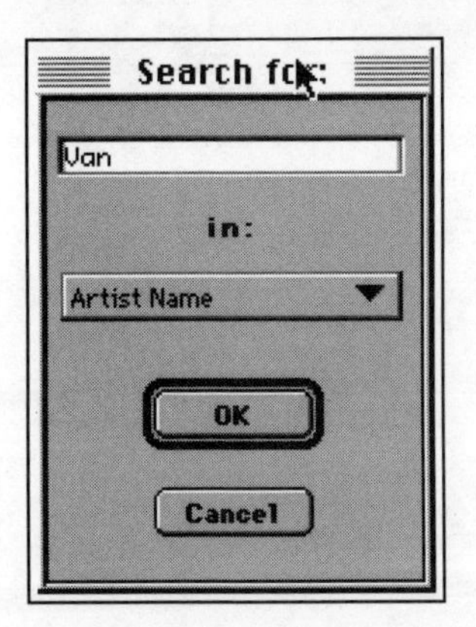

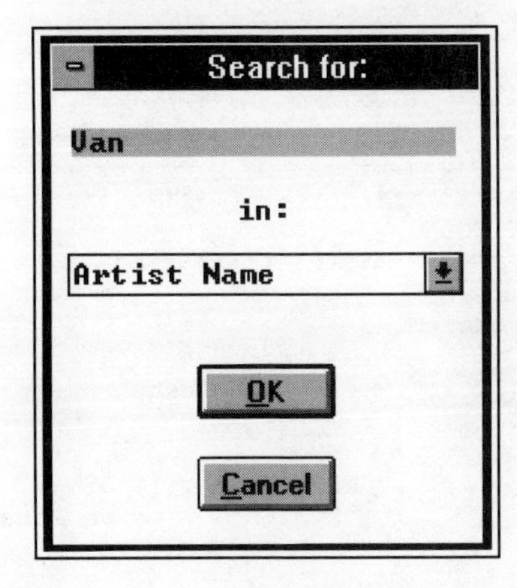

```
*-------------------------------------------------------------
**************************************************************
**--     APPSRCH.SCX - DOS PLATFORM
**************************************************************
```

```
( ) DeskTop                           (·) Window

Name:                                 <Type...>
Title:  Search for:
Footer:

Size:             Screen Code:

 Height:   14      [X] Setup...
 Width:    29      [X] Cleanup & Procs...          «   OK   »

Position:         READ Clauses:                   < Cancel >

 Row:       0      [X] Activate...    [ ] Show...
 Column:    0      [ ] Valid...       [ ] When...
 [X] Center        [X] Deactivate...

Environment:                     [ ] Add alias

      Environment NOT saved with screen.
```

```
Type:      Dialog

Attributes:       Border:

 [ ] Close         ( ) None
 [X] Float         ( ) Single
 [X] Shadow        (·) Double     «   OK   »
 [ ] Minimize      ( ) Panel
                   ( ) System     < Cancel >

Color Schemes:

 Primary:          Popup:

 Dialogs           Dialog Pop
```

```
**************************************************************
*  SCREEN SETUP CODE
**************************************************************
#SECTION 1
#WCLAUSES IN &gcMainWind
#section 2
*  Program...........: APPSRCH Screen
*  Author............: YAG
*  Project...........: COMMON
*  Created...........: 06/06/93  05:11:35
*  Copyright.........: (c) Flash Creative Management, 1993
```

```
*) Description.......: Modified from FOXAPP. Generic search
*)                   : routine, tied to <FIND> button. Uses
*)                   : Datadict.dbf if available.
*  Calling Samples...: DO AppSrch.spr
*  Parameter List....:
*  Major change list.:
PRIVATE lcSrchTerm, lnFldNum, lnFldCnt, i, lcOldOrd, lcOldAlias
PRIVATE lcCurOrd, lcOldCurs, lnColShow
m.lcSrchTerm = SPACE(60)
m.lnFldNum = 0
IF FILE("Datadict.dbf")
   IF !USED("Datadict")
      USE DATADICT IN SELECT(1)
   ENDIF
   IF FCOUNT("Datadict") = 8              && Codebook 2.0
      SELECT Field_Name, Field_type, Field_Len, Field_Dec, cTag ;
         FROM Datadict ;
       WHERE DBF_Name = ALIAS() ;
         INTO ARRAY laFields
   ELSE
      SELECT Field_Name, Field_type, Field_Len, Field_Dec, cTag ;
         FROM Datadict ;
       WHERE DBF_Name = ALIAS() ;
         AND lShow ;
         INTO ARRAY laFields
   ENDIF
   lnFldCnt = _tally
   lnColShow = 5
ELSE
   m.lnFldCnt = AFIELDS(laFields)
   lnColShow = 1
ENDIF
m.lcOldOrd = ORDER()
m.lcOldAlias = ALIAS()
m.lcCurOrd = ORDER()
IF EMPTY(m.lcCurOrd)
   SET ORDER TO 1
   m.lcCurOrd = ORDER()
ENDIF
FOR i = 1 TO FCOUNT()
   IF FIELDS(i) == m.lcCurOrd
      m.lnFldNum = i
   ENDIF
ENDFOR
IF m.lnFldNum > 0
   m.lcFldName = FIELDS(m.lnFldNum)
ELSE
   SET ORDER TO 1
   m.lnFldNum  = 1
   m.lcFldName = FIELDS(1)
ENDIF
IF FILE("Datadict.dbf")
   m.lnFldNum  = ASCAN(laFields,lcCurOrd)
   IF m.lnFldNum = 0
      m.lnFldNum = 1
   ELSE
      m.lnFldNum = ASUBSCRIPT(laFields,m.lnFldNum,1)
   ENDIF
   m.lcFldName = laFields[lnFldNum,1]
ENDIF
```

```
lcOldCurs = (UPPER(SET("CURSOR")) = "ON")
SET CURSOR ON
-------------------------------------------------------------
*-- READ Activate Clause
-------------------------------------------------------------
```

```
READ Activate

  (·) Procedure
  ( ) Expression
```

```
SELECT (m.lcOldAlias)
-------------------------------------------------------------
*-- READ Deactivate Clause
-------------------------------------------------------------
```

```
READ Deactivate

  (·) Procedure
  ( ) Expression
```

```
?? CHR(7)
RETURN .F.
*************************************************************
*--     G E T    O B J E C T S
*************************************************************
*============================================================
*  Text: in:
*============================================================
 @   3,  12
*============================================================
*  m.lcsrchterm
*============================================================
 @   1,   1
```

```
Field:

  ( ) Say          (·) Get          ( ) Edit

<  Get...    > m.lcsrchterm
                                               «   OK    »
< Format... > @S60
                                               < Cancel >
Range:

  [ ] Upper...                    [ ] Lower...

[X] When...      [ ] Error...     [ ] Scroll bar
[ ] Valid...     [ ] Comment...   [ ] Allow tabs
[ ] Message...   [ ] Disabled     [ ] Refresh
```

```
-------------------------------------------------------------
*-- m.lcsrchterm When Clause
-------------------------------------------------------------

 When
  (·) Procedure
  ( ) Expression

m.lcSrchTerm = PADR(m.lcSrchTerm,60)
SHOW GETS
*=============================================================
*  lnfldnum
*=============================================================
 @   4,   1

  ( ) List Popup          (·) Array Popup  laFields

                          Variable:
                           < Choose... > lnfldnum

                          Options:
                           [ ] When...     [ ] Comment...
                           [X] Valid...    [ ] Disabled
                           [ ] Message... [X] 1st Element...
                                           [ ] # Elements...

  Initial:                  «   OK   »    < Cancel >

-------------------------------------------------------------
*-- lnfldnum Valid Clause
-------------------------------------------------------------

 Valid
  (·) Procedure
  ( ) Expression

IF FILE("Datadict.dbf")
   SET ORDER TO (laFields[lnFldNum,1])
   m.lcFldName = laFields[lnFldNum,1]
ELSE
   m.lcFldName = FIELDS(m.lnFldNum)
   tagnum = gettag(m.lcFldName)     && tag number of tag with name
lcFldName
   IF tagnum > 0
      SET ORDER TO TAG(m.tagnum)
   ELSE
      SET ORDER TO 0
```

```
   ENDIF
ENDIF
SHOW GETS
------------------------------------------------------------
*-- lnfldnum 1st Element Clause
------------------------------------------------------------

  1st Element

    ( ) Procedure
    (·) Expression

1st Element:   lnColShow
*============================================================
*  lhok
*============================================================
 @   8,   8
 Spacing:    1

  Push Button Prompts:           (·) Horizontal    ( ) Vertical
                                 [ ] Terminating  <Spacing...>
  \!\<OK
                                Variable:

                                 < Choose... >  lhok

                                Options:

                                 [ ] When...     [ ] Comment...
                                 [X] Valid...    [ ] Disabled
                                 [ ] Message...

                   «   OK   »    < Cancel >
------------------------------------------------------------
*-- lhok Valid Clause
------------------------------------------------------------

  Valid

    (·) Procedure
    ( ) Expression

IF !EMPTY(m.lcSrchTerm)
   m.lcSrchTerm = ALLTRIM(m.lcSrchTerm)
   WAIT CLEAR
   m.tagnum = gettag(m.lcFldName)
   IF m.tagnum > 0
      SET ORDER TO TAG(m.tagnum)
   ELSE
```

```
      DO waitmsg   && warn user that this may take a while
    ENDIF
    m.thisrec = RECNO()
    DO CASE
    CASE TYPE("&lcFldName") $ "CM"     && character or memo field
       IF m.tagnum > 0
          SEEK ALLTRIM(m.lcSrchTerm)
          IF !FOUND()
             IF m.thisrec <= RECCOUNT() AND m.thisrec > 0
                GOTO m.thisrec
             ENDIF
             answer = .F.
*             DO doloc WITH m.lcSrchTerm, m.answer   && prompt for locate
          m.lcSrchText = "Could not find a record that begins " + ;
                      "with your search term. Do you want " + ;
                      "to search for the term anywhere in " + ;
                      "the field? This is a slower but more " + ;
                      "thorough method."
           m.Answer = AreUSure(m.lcSrchText)
             IF m.answer = .T.
                DO waitmsg
                GOTO TOP
                LOCATE FOR UPPER(m.lcSrchTerm) $ UPPER(&lcFldName)
             ENDIF
          ENDIF
       ELSE
          LOCATE FOR UPPER(m.lcSrchTerm) $ UPPER(&lcFldName)
       ENDIF
    CASE TYPE("&lcFldName") $ "FN"     && floating or numeric
       m.lcSrchTerm = CHRTRAN(m.lcSrchTerm,'"','')
       m.lcSrchTerm = CHRTRAN(m.lcSrchTerm,"'","")
       LOCATE FOR VAL(ALLTRIM(m.lcSrchTerm)) = &lcFldName
    CASE TYPE("&lcFldName") = "D"      && date
       m.lcSrchTerm = CHRTRAN(m.lcSrchTerm,'{}"()','')
       m.lcSrchTerm = CHRTRAN(m.lcSrchTerm,"'",'')
       m.lcSrchTerm = ALLTRIM(m.lcSrchTerm)
       LOCATE FOR CTOD(lcSrchTerm) = &lcFldName
    CASE TYPE("&lcFldName") = "L"      && logical
       IF "T" $ UPPER(m.lcSrchTerm)
          LOCATE FOR &lcFldName
       ELSE
          LOCATE FOR !&lcFldName
       ENDIF
    CASE TYPE("&lcFldName") = "U"      && unknown field type--should't
happen
       WAIT WINDOW "Field "+m.lcFldName+" not found"
    ENDCASE
    IF !FOUND()
       SET CURSOR OFF
       WAIT WINDOW "Not found" NOWAIT
       IF m.thisrec <= RECCOUNT() AND m.thisrec > 0
          GOTO m.thisrec
       ENDIF
    ELSE
       SET CURSOR OFF
       WAIT WINDOW "Found it!" NOWAIT
       CLEAR READ
    ENDIF
ENDIF
*============================================================
*  lhCancel
*============================================================
 @  10,   8
 Spacing:    1
```

```
Push Button Prompts:        (·) Horizontal    ( ) Vertical
                            [X] Terminating  <Spacing...>
\?\<Cancel
                            Variable:

                            < Choose... >  lhCancel

                            Options:

                            [ ] When...      [ ] Comment...
                            [X] Valid...     [ ] Disabled
                            [ ] Message...

              «   OK   »     < Cancel >
```

```
-------------------------------------------------------------
*-- lhCancel Valid Clause
-------------------------------------------------------------
```

```
Valid

  (·) Procedure
  ( ) Expression
```

```
SET ORDER TO (m.lcOldOrd)
*************************************************************
*--  SCREEN CLEANUP CODE
*************************************************************
IF lcOldCurs
   SET CURSOR ON
ELSE
   SET CURSOR OFF
ENDIF
*!*****************************************************************
*!
*!       Procedure: GETTAG
*!
*!*****************************************************************
FUNCTION gettag
*) Returns tag number corresponding to field "lcFldName", or 0 if there
*) is not tag with the same name as "lcFldName."
parameter tcfldname
PRIVATE ALL
m.tcfldname = UPPER(ALLTRIM(m.tcfldname))
i = 1
DO WHILE !EMPTY(TAG(i)) AND i < 1000
   IF UPPER(TAG(i)) == m.tcfldname
      RETURN i
   ENDIF
   i = i + 1
ENDDO
RETURN 0
```

```
*!*****************************************************************
*!
*!      Procedure: WAITMSG
*!
*!*****************************************************************
PROCEDURE waitmsg
IF RECCOUNT() > 1000
  WAIT WINDOW "Searching.  This may take a few moments." NOWAIT
ELSE
  WAIT WINDOW "Searching" NOWAIT
ENDIF
*-------------------------------------------------------------
**************************************************************
**--    APPSRCH.SCX - MAC PLATFORM
**************************************************************
```

```
 ( ) DeskTop                           (·) Window

 Name:                                 <Type...>
 Title:  Search for:
 Footer:

 Size:               Screen Code:

  Height:   15.909    [X] Setup...
  Width:    23.333    [X] Cleanup & Procs...          «   OK   »

 Position:           READ Clauses:                    < Cancel >

  Row:       0.000    [X] Activate...    [ ] Show...
  Column:    0.000    [ ] Valid...       [ ] When...
  [X] Center          [X] Deactivate...

 Environment:                      [ ] Add alias

       Environment NOT saved with screen.
```

```
 Type:        Dialog

 Attributes:        Border:

  [ ] Close          ( ) None
  [X] Float          ( ) Single
  [X] Shadow         (·) Double      «   OK   »
  [ ] Minimize       ( ) Panel
                     ( ) System      < Cancel >

 Color Schemes:

  Primary:          Popup:
```

```
MAC      RGB Fill Color Scheme: (,,)
MAC      Font: monaco,   9
 Screen Setup code above
 READ Activate code above
 READ Deactivate code above
************************************************************
*--    G E T    O B J E C T S
************************************************************
*===========================================================
*  Text: in:
*===========================================================
 @   3.727,    9.833
MAC      RGB Color Scheme: (,,,,,)
MAC      Font: Monaco,   9
        Style: Bold
*===========================================================
*  m.lcsrchterm
*===========================================================
 @   1.364,    1.167
```

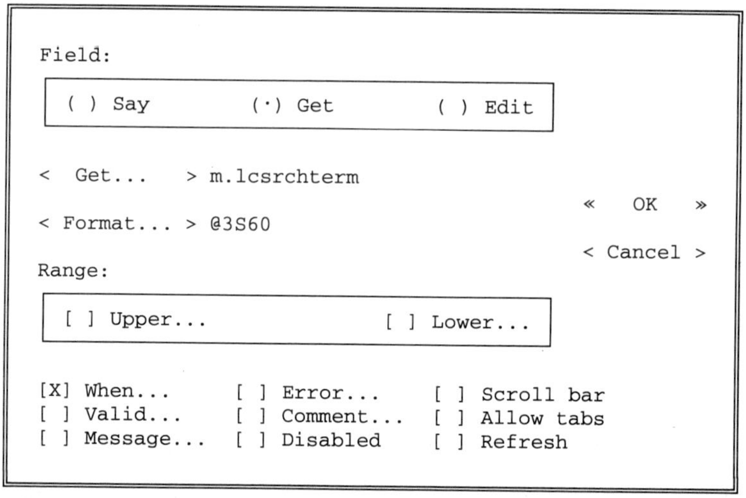

```
  Field:

  ( ) Say          (·) Get          ( ) Edit

  <  Get...   > m.lcsrchterm
                                                  «   OK   »
  < Format... > @3S60
                                                  < Cancel >
  Range:

  [ ] Upper...                   [ ] Lower...

  [X] When...      [ ] Error...      [ ] Scroll bar
  [ ] Valid...     [ ] Comment...    [ ] Allow tabs
  [ ] Message...   [ ] Disabled      [ ] Refresh
```

```
MAC      RGB Color Scheme: (,,,,,)
MAC      Font: monaco,   9
 When code above
*===========================================================
*  lnfldnum
*===========================================================
 @   5.727,    0.833
     SIZE   1.500,   25.800
```

```
  ( ) List Popup          (·) Array Popup  laFields
  +-----------------+
  |                 |     Variable:
  |                 |     +------------------------------+
  |                 |     | < Choose... > lnfldnum       |
  |                 |     +------------------------------+
  |                 |     Options:
  |                 |     +------------------------------+
  |                 |     | [ ] When...    [ ] Comment...  |
  |                 |     | [X] Valid...   [ ] Disabled    |
  |                 |     | [ ] Message... [X] 1st Element...|
  |                 |     |                [ ] # Elements...|
  +-----------------+     +------------------------------+

  Initial: [          ]     «  OK  »   < Cancel >

MAC      RGB Color Scheme: (,,,,,)
MAC      Font: Geneva,   9
 Valid code above
 1st Element code above
*==========================================================
*  lhok
*==========================================================
 @   9.636,   6.667
     SIZE   1.500,  10.000
 Spacing:    1

  Push Button Prompts:    +----------------------------------+
                          | (·) Horizontal    ( ) Vertical   |
  +-----------------+     | [ ] Terminating  <Spacing...>    |
  | \!\<OK          |     +----------------------------------+
  |                 |     Variable:
  |                 |     +----------------------------------+
  |                 |     | < Choose... >  lhok              |
  |                 |     +----------------------------------+
  |                 |     Options:
  |                 |     +----------------------------------+
  |                 |     | [ ] When...    [ ] Comment...    |
  |                 |     | [X] Valid...   [ ] Disabled      |
  |                 |     | [ ] Message...                   |
  +-----------------+     +----------------------------------+

                 «  OK  »   < Cancel >

MAC      RGB Color Scheme: (,,,,,)
MAC      Font: Geneva,   9
       Style: Bold
 Valid code above
*==========================================================
*  lhCancel
*==========================================================
 @  12.909,   6.667
     SIZE   1.500,  10.000
 Spacing:    1
```

```
 Push Button Prompts:          (·) Horizontal    ( ) Vertical
                               [X] Terminating   <Spacing...>
 \?\<Cancel
                               Variable:

                               < Choose... >  lhCancel

                               Options:

                               [ ] When...       [ ] Comment...
                               [X] Valid...      [ ] Disabled
                               [ ] Message...

              «   OK   »    < Cancel >

MAC       RGB Color Scheme: (,,,,,)
MAC       Font: Geneva,   9
         Style: Bold
 Valid code above
 Screen Cleanup and Procedures code above
*------------------------------------------------------------
*************************************************************
**--    APPSRCH.SCX - WINDOWS PLATFORM
*************************************************************

 ( ) DeskTop                          (·) Window

 Name:                                <Type...>
 Title:  Search for:
 Footer:

 Size:             Screen Code:

  Height:   15.917   [X] Setup...
  Width:    23.250   [X] Cleanup & Procs...            «   OK   »

 Position:         READ Clauses:                       < Cancel >

  Row:       0.000   [X] Activate...     [ ] Show...
  Column:    0.000   [ ] Valid...        [ ] When...
  [X] Center         [X] Deactivate...

 Environment:                       [ ] Add alias

       Environment NOT saved with screen.
```

```
 Type:   [  Dialog  ]

 Attributes:            Border:
 ┌─────────────────┐   ┌───────────────┐
 │ [ ] Close       │   │ ( ) None      │
 │ [X] Float       │   │ ( ) Single    │
 │ [X] Shadow      │   │ (·) Double    │   «  OK  »
 │ [ ] Minimize    │   │ ( ) Panel     │
 └─────────────────┘   │ ( ) System    │   < Cancel >
                       └───────────────┘
 Color Schemes:
 ┌──────────────────────────────────────┐
 │ Primary:          Popup:             │
 │ [          ]      [          ]       │
 └──────────────────────────────────────┘
WINDOWS  RGB Fill Color Scheme: (,,)
WINDOWS  Font: Terminal,    9
 Screen Setup code above
 READ Activate code above
 READ Deactivate code above
**********************************************************
*--   G E T   O B J E C T S
**********************************************************
*=========================================================
*  Text: in:
*=========================================================
 @   3.750,  10.125
WINDOWS  RGB Color Scheme: (,,,,,)
WINDOWS  Font: Terminal,   9
*=========================================================
*  m.lcsrchterm
*=========================================================
 @   1.333,   1.125

 Field:
 ┌────────────────────────────────────────────┐
 │ ( ) Say         (·) Get         ( ) Edit   │
 └────────────────────────────────────────────┘

 <  Get...   > m.lcsrchterm
                                                      «  OK  »
 < Format... > @S60
                                                      < Cancel >
 Range:
 ┌────────────────────────────────────────────┐
 │ [ ] Upper...                [ ] Lower...   │
 └────────────────────────────────────────────┘

 [X] When...      [ ] Error...      [ ] Scroll bar
 [ ] Valid...     [ ] Comment...    [ ] Allow tabs
 [ ] Message...   [ ] Disabled      [ ] Refresh
```

```
WINDOWS  RGB Color Scheme: (,,,,,)
WINDOWS  Font: Terminal,   9
 When code above
*===============================================================
*  lnfldnum
*===============================================================
 @   5.750,   0.875
     SIZE   1.500,  21.500

   ( ) List Popup              (·) Array Popup  laFields

                               Variable:

                               < Choose... > lnfldnum

                               Options:

                               [ ] When...      [ ] Comment...
                               [X] Valid...     [ ] Disabled
                               [ ] Message...   [X] 1st Element...
                                                [ ] # Elements...

   Initial:                       «  OK  »    < Cancel >

WINDOWS  RGB Color Scheme: (,,,,,)
WINDOWS  Font: Terminal,   9
 Valid code above
 1st Element code above
*===============================================================
*  lhok
*===============================================================
 @   9.667,   7.875
     SIZE   1.769,  10.000
 Spacing:    1

   Push Button Prompts:        (·) Horizontal    ( ) Vertical
                               [ ] Terminating   <Spacing...>
   \!\<OK
                               Variable:

                               < Choose... >  lhok

                               Options:

                               [ ] When...      [ ] Comment...
                               [X] Valid...     [ ] Disabled
                               [ ] Message...

               «  OK  »    < Cancel >

WINDOWS  RGB Color Scheme: (,,,,,)
WINDOWS  Font: MS Sans Serif,   8
       Style: Bold
```

```
 Valid code above
*==============================================================
*  lhCancel
*==============================================================
 @  12.917,    7.875
     SIZE   1.769,  10.000
 Spacing:    1
```

```
Push Button Prompts:        (·) Horizontal    ( ) Vertical
                            [X] Terminating  <Spacing...>
 \?\<Cancel
                           Variable:

                            < Choose... >  lhCancel

                           Options:

                            [ ] When...      [ ] Comment...
                            [X] Valid...     [ ] Disabled
                            [ ] Message...

                 «  OK  »    < Cancel >
```

```
WINDOWS  RGB Color Scheme: (,,,,,)
WINDOWS  Font: MS Sans Serif,   8
          Style: Bold
 Valid code above
 Screen Cleanup and Procedures code above
```

Confirmation Dialog: AREUSURE.SCX

AreUSure() is another example of using the MSGBOX() and FxAlert functions in FOXTOOLS.FLL and FOXTOOLS.MLB. For a more detailed explanation, please see the section titled *Alert Dialog—ALERT.SCX* earlier in this chapter.

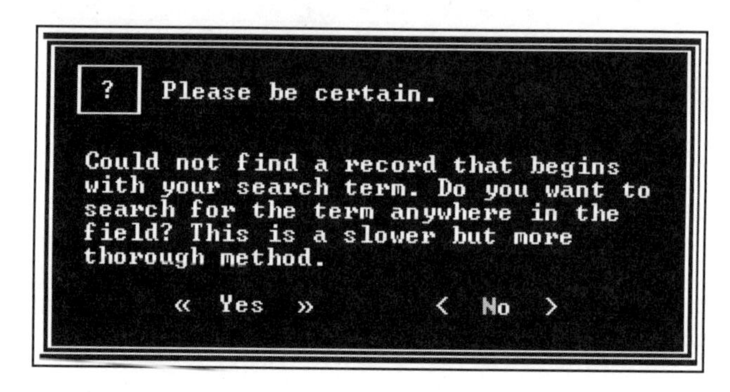

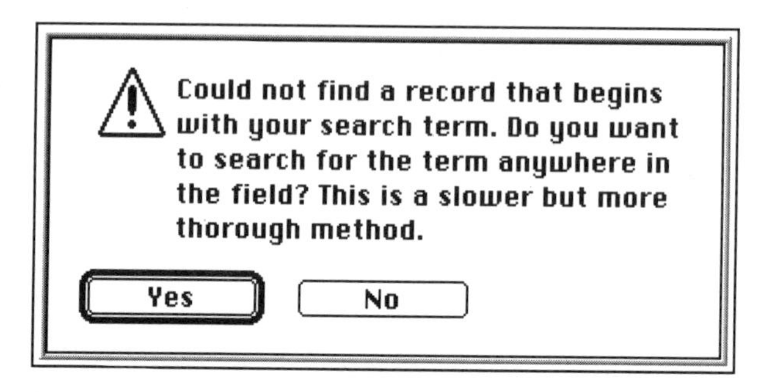

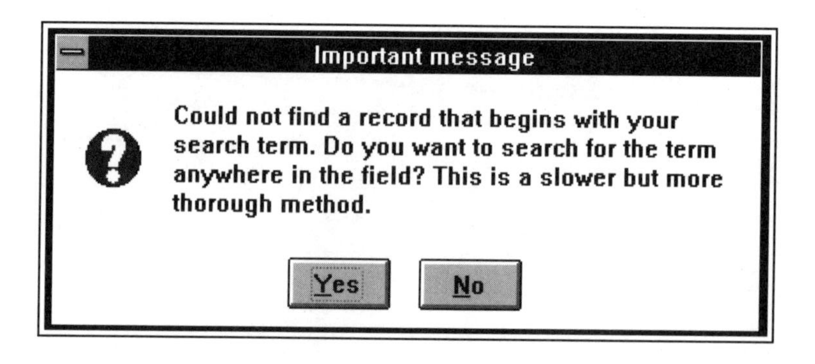

```
*-----------------------------------------------------------
************************************************************
**--    AREUSURE.SCX - DOS PLATFORM
************************************************************
```

```
( ) DeskTop                         (·) Window

Name:                               <Type...>
Title:
Footer:

Size:              Screen Code:
 Height:   14       [X] Setup...
 Width:    43       [X] Cleanup & Procs...          «   OK   »

Position:          READ Clauses:                  < Cancel >
 Row:       0       [ ] Activate...    [ ] Show...
 Column:    0       [ ] Valid...       [ ] When...
 [X] Center         [ ] Deactivate...

Environment:                      [X] Add alias
      Environment NOT saved with screen.
```

```
Type:      Dialog

Attributes:        Border:
 [ ] Close          ( ) None
 [X] Float          ( ) Single
 [X] Shadow         (·) Double      «   OK   »
 [ ] Minimize       ( ) Panel
                    ( ) System      < Cancel >

Color Schemes:
 Primary:          Popup:
  Dialogs           Dialog Pop
```

```
************************************************************
*  SCREEN SETUP CODE
************************************************************
#SECTION 1
*  Program...........: AREUSURE Screen
*  Author............: mb
*  Project...........: COMMON
*  Created...........: 04/16/93
*  Copyright.........: (c) Flash Creative Management, 1993
*) Description.......: Are You Sure Dialog
*)                   : Allows a passed message, and displays it in
```

```
*)                      : "?" type of dialog
*  Calling Samples...: IF AreUSure("Do you want to close the month?")
*  Parameter List....: lcMessage    -   Displayed message
*  Major change list.:
PARAMETER lcMessage
#SECTION 2
PRIVATE llRetVal
llRetVal = .T.
IF EMPTY(lcMessage)
  lcMessage = "Are you sure that you want to perform this action?"
ENDIF
DO CASE
   CASE _WINDOWS
      llRetVal = IIF(msgbox(lcMessage,'Important message',36)=6,.T.,.F.)
      RETURN llRetVal
   CASE _MAC
      llRetVal = IIF(fxalert(0,265,-1,-1,lcMessage) = 1, .T., .F.)
      RETURN llRetVal
ENDCASE
************************************************************
*--    G E T   O B J E C T S
************************************************************
*===========================================================
*  Text: ?
*===========================================================
 @   1,   3
*===========================================================
*  Box
*===========================================================
 @   0,   1
 SIZE   3,   5
*===========================================================
*
*===========================================================
 @   4,   2
```

```
 Field:
 ┌──────────────────────────────────────────────┐
 │ (·) Say          ( ) Get          ( ) Edit   │
 └──────────────────────────────────────────────┘

 <  Say...   > lcMessage
                                             «   OK   »
 < Format... > @I
                                             < Cancel >
 Range:
 ┌──────────────────────────────────────────────┐
 │ [ ] Upper...                   [ ] Lower...  │
 └──────────────────────────────────────────────┘

 [ ] When...      [ ] Error...      [ ] Scroll bar
 [ ] Valid...     [ ] Comment...    [ ] Allow tabs
 [ ] Message...   [ ] Disabled      [ ] Refresh
```

```
*===========================================================
*  Text: Please be certain.
*===========================================================
```

```
 @   1,   7
*==============================================================
*  lhYes
*==============================================================
 @  10,   8
 Spacing:    1
```

```
+----------------------------------------------------------------+
|                                                                |
|  Push Button Prompts:    +----------------------------------+  |
|                          | (·) Horizontal    ( ) Vertical   |  |
|  +--------------------+  | [X] Terminating  <Spacing...>    |  |
|  | \!\<Yes            |  +----------------------------------+  |
|  |                    | Variable:                              |
|  |                    | +----------------------------------+   |
|  |                    | | < Choose... >  lhYes             |   |
|  |                    | +----------------------------------+   |
|  |                    | Options:                               |
|  |                    | +----------------------------------+   |
|  |                    | | [ ] When...     [ ] Comment...   |   |
|  |                    | | [ ] Valid...    [ ] Disabled     |   |
|  |                    | | [ ] Message...                   |   |
|  +--------------------+ +----------------------------------+   |
|                                                                |
|              «   OK   »    < Cancel >                          |
|                                                                |
+----------------------------------------------------------------+
```

```
*==============================================================
*  lhNo
*==============================================================
 @  10,  25
 Spacing:    1
```

```
+----------------------------------------------------------------+
|                                                                |
|  Push Button Prompts:    +----------------------------------+  |
|                          | (·) Horizontal    ( ) Vertical   |  |
|  +--------------------+  | [X] Terminating  <Spacing...>    |  |
|  | \?\<No             |  +----------------------------------+  |
|  |                    | Variable:                              |
|  |                    | +----------------------------------+   |
|  |                    | | < Choose... >  lhNo              |   |
|  |                    | +----------------------------------+   |
|  |                    | Options:                               |
|  |                    | +----------------------------------+   |
|  |                    | | [ ] When...     [ ] Comment...   |   |
|  |                    | | [X] Valid...    [ ] Disabled     |   |
|  |                    | | [ ] Message...                   |   |
|  +--------------------+ +----------------------------------+   |
|                                                                |
|              «   OK   »    < Cancel >                          |
|                                                                |
+----------------------------------------------------------------+
```

```
--------------------------------------------------------------
*-- lhNo Valid Clause
--------------------------------------------------------------
```

```
Valid
 (·) Procedure
 ( ) Expression
```

```
llRetVal = .F.
************************************************************
*--  SCREEN CLEANUP CODE
************************************************************
RETURN llRetVal
*-----------------------------------------------------------
************************************************************
**--    AREUSURE.SCX - MAC PLATFORM
************************************************************
```

```
( ) DeskTop                        (·) Window

Name:                              <Type...>
Title:
Footer:

Size:            Screen Code:

 Height:   12.545   [X] Setup...
 Width:    43.000   [X] Cleanup & Procs...        «   OK   »

Position:        READ Clauses:                    < Cancel >

 Row:       0.000   [ ] Activate...   [ ] Show...
 Column:    0.000   [ ] Valid...      [ ] When...
 [X] Center         [ ] Deactivate...

Environment:                          [X] Add alias

      Environment NOT saved with screen.
```

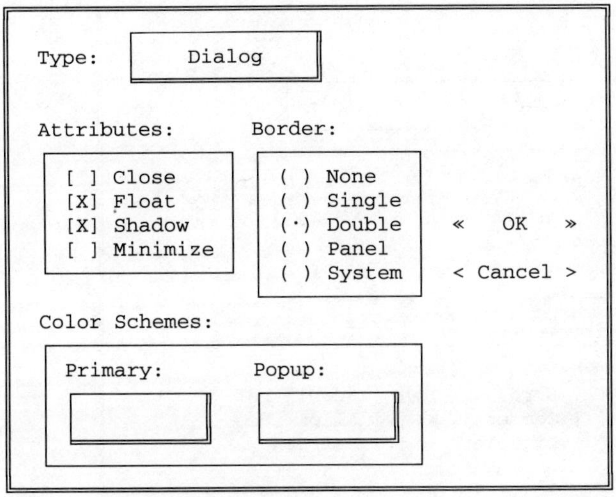

```
+--------------------------------------------------------+
|                                                        |
|  Type:    [      Dialog      ]                         |
|                                                        |
|  Attributes:       Border:                             |
|                                                        |
|  [ ] Close         ( ) None                            |
|  [X] Float         ( ) Single                          |
|  [X] Shadow        (·) Double       «   OK   »         |
|  [ ] Minimize      ( ) Panel                           |
|                    ( ) System       < Cancel >         |
|                                                        |
|  Color Schemes:                                        |
|                                                        |
|    Primary:        Popup:                              |
|    [          ]    [          ]                        |
|                                                        |
+--------------------------------------------------------+
MAC       RGB Fill Color Scheme: (,,)
MAC       Font: monaco,    9
 Screen Setup code above
***********************************************************
*--    G E T    O B J E C T S
***********************************************************
*==========================================================
*  Text: ?
*==========================================================
 @   1.091,    5.000
MAC       RGB Color Scheme: (,,,,,)
MAC       Font: Monaco,    9
         Style: Bold
*==========================================================
*  Box
*==========================================================
 @   0.545,    3.333
 SIZE   2.182,    3.833
MAC       RGB Color Scheme: (,,,,,)
            Pen: 2
*==========================================================
*
*==========================================================
 @   4.273,    3.167
```

```
+--------------------------------------------------------------+
|                                                              |
|  Field:                                                      |
|  +-------------------------------------------+               |
|  | (·) Say        ( ) Get         ( ) Edit   |               |
|  +-------------------------------------------+               |
|                                                              |
|  <  Say...   > lcMessage                                     |
|                                                « OK »       |
|  < Format... > @I                                            |
|                                              < Cancel >      |
|  Range:                                                      |
|  +-------------------------------------------+               |
|  | [ ] Upper...                 [ ] Lower... |               |
|  +-------------------------------------------+               |
|                                                              |
|  [ ] When...      [ ] Error...      [ ] Scroll bar           |
|  [ ] Valid...     [ ] Comment...    [ ] Allow tabs           |
|  [ ] Message...   [ ] Disabled      [ ] Refresh              |
|                                                              |
+--------------------------------------------------------------+
MAC      RGB Color Scheme: (,,,,,)
MAC      Font: monaco,   9
*==============================================================
*  Text: Please be certain.
*==============================================================
 @   1.091,   9.000
MAC      RGB Color Scheme: (,,,,,)
MAC      Font: Monaco,   9
        Style: Bold
*==============================================================
*  lhYes
*==============================================================
 @   9.091,   8.000
     SIZE   2.083,  13.500
 Spacing:    2
+------------------------------------------------------------------+
|                                                                  |
|  Push Button Prompts:       +----------------------------------+ |
|  +----------------------+   | (·) Horizontal    ( ) Vertical   | |
|  | \!\<Yes              |   | [X] Terminating   <Spacing...>   | |
|  |                      |   +----------------------------------+ |
|  |                      |   Variable:                            |
|  |                      |   +----------------------------------+ |
|  |                      |   | < Choose... >  lhYes             | |
|  |                      |   +----------------------------------+ |
|  |                      |   Options:                             |
|  |                      |   +----------------------------------+ |
|  |                      |   | [ ] When...     [ ] Comment...   | |
|  |                      |   | [ ] Valid...    [ ] Disabled     | |
|  |                      |   | [ ] Message...                   | |
|  +----------------------+   +----------------------------------+ |
|                                                                  |
|                  «  OK  »    < Cancel >                          |
|                                                                  |
+------------------------------------------------------------------+
MAC      RGB Color Scheme: (,,,,,)
MAC      Font: Geneva,   9
        Style: Bold
*==============================================================
```

```
*  lhNo
*==============================================================
 @   9.091,  25.000
     SIZE   2.083,  12.000
 Spacing:    2

 Push Button Prompts:        (·) Horizontal    ( ) Vertical
                             [X] Terminating  <Spacing...>
 \?\<No
                             Variable:

                             < Choose... >  lhNo

                             Options:

                             [ ] When...      [ ] Comment...
                             [X] Valid...     [ ] Disabled
                             [ ] Message...

                  «   OK   »    < Cancel >

MAC      RGB Color Scheme: (,,,,,)
MAC      Font: Geneva,    9
        Style: Bold
 Valid code above
 Screen Cleanup and Procedures code above
*--------------------------------------------------------------
***************************************************************
**--    AREUSURE.SCX - WINDOWS PLATFORM
***************************************************************

 ( ) DeskTop                        (·) Window

 Name:                              <Type...>
 Title:
 Footer:

 Size:            Screen Code:

  Height:   12.500   [X] Setup...
  Width:    43.000   [X] Cleanup & Procs...          «   OK   »

 Position:        READ Clauses:                      < Cancel >

  Row:       0.000   [ ] Activate...    [ ] Show...
  Column:    0.000   [ ] Valid...       [ ] When...
  [X] Center         [ ] Deactivate...

 Environment:                          [X] Add alias

      Environment NOT saved with screen.
```

```
Type:      Dialog

Attributes:          Border:

 [ ] Close            ( ) None
 [X] Float            ( ) Single
 [X] Shadow           (·) Double       «   OK   »
 [ ] Minimize         ( ) Panel
                      ( ) System       < Cancel >

Color Schemes:

 Primary:             Popup:
```

```
WINDOWS  RGB Fill Color Scheme: (,,)
WINDOWS  Font: Terminal,    9
 Screen Setup code above
************************************************************
*--    G E T    O B J E C T S
************************************************************
*===========================================================
*  Text: ?
*===========================================================
 @   1.083,    5.000
WINDOWS  RGB Color Scheme: (,,,,,)
WINDOWS  Font: Terminal,    9
        Style: Bold
*===========================================================
*  Box
*===========================================================
 @   0.500,    3.375
 SIZE   2.167,    3.875
WINDOWS  RGB Color Scheme: (,,,,,)
           Pen: 2
*===========================================================
*
*===========================================================
 @   4.250,    3.125
```

```
╔══════════════════════════════════════════════════════════╗
║                                                          ║
║  Field:                                                  ║
║  ┌────────────────────────────────────────┐              ║
║  │ (·) Say        ( ) Get        ( ) Edit │              ║
║  └────────────────────────────────────────┘              ║
║                                                          ║
║  <  Say...   > lcMessage                                 ║
║                                              «   OK   »  ║
║  < Format... > @I                                        ║
║                                              < Cancel >  ║
║  Range:                                                  ║
║  ┌────────────────────────────────────────┐              ║
║  │ [ ] Upper...              [ ] Lower... │              ║
║  └────────────────────────────────────────┘              ║
║                                                          ║
║  [ ] When...      [ ] Error...      [ ] Scroll bar       ║
║  [ ] Valid...     [ ] Comment...    [ ] Allow tabs       ║
║  [ ] Message...   [ ] Disabled      [ ] Refresh          ║
║                                                          ║
╚══════════════════════════════════════════════════════════╝
WINDOWS  RGB Color Scheme: (,,,,,)
WINDOWS  Font: Terminal,   9
*============================================================
*  Text: Please be certain.
*============================================================
 @   1.083,   9.000
WINDOWS  RGB Color Scheme: (,,,,,)
WINDOWS  Font: Terminal,   9
        Style: Bold
*============================================================
*  lhYes
*============================================================
 @   9.083,   8.000
    SIZE   2.077,  13.500
 Spacing:    2
╔══════════════════════════════════════════════════════════════╗
║                                                              ║
║  Push Button Prompts:     ┌───────────────────────────────┐  ║
║  ┌─────────────────────┐  │ (·) Horizontal   ( ) Vertical │  ║
║  │ \!\<Yes             │  │ [X] Terminating  <Spacing...> │  ║
║  │                     │  └───────────────────────────────┘  ║
║  │                     │  Variable:                          ║
║  │                     │  ┌───────────────────────────────┐  ║
║  │                     │  │ < Choose... >  lhYes          │  ║
║  │                     │  └───────────────────────────────┘  ║
║  │                     │  Options:                           ║
║  │                     │  ┌───────────────────────────────┐  ║
║  │                     │  │ [ ] When...     [ ] Comment...│  ║
║  │                     │  │ [ ] Valid...    [ ] Disabled  │  ║
║  │                     │  │ [ ] Message...                │  ║
║  └─────────────────────┘  └───────────────────────────────┘  ║
║                                                              ║
║               «   OK   »    < Cancel >                       ║
║                                                              ║
╚══════════════════════════════════════════════════════════════╝
WINDOWS  RGB Color Scheme: (,,,,,)
WINDOWS  Font: MS Sans Serif,   8
        Style: Bold
*============================================================
*  lhNo
```

```
*============================================================
 @   9.083,  25.000
     SIZE   2.077,  12.000
 Spacing:    2
╔════════════════════════════════════════════════════════════════╗
║                                                                ║
║  Push Button Prompts:       ┌────────────────────────────────┐ ║
║  ┌─────────────────────┐    │ (·) Horizontal   ( ) Vertical  │ ║
║  │\?\<No               │    │ [X] Terminating  <Spacing...>  │ ║
║  │                     │    └────────────────────────────────┘ ║
║  │                     │    Variable:                          ║
║  │                     │    ┌────────────────────────────────┐ ║
║  │                     │    │ < Choose... >  lhNo            │ ║
║  │                     │    └────────────────────────────────┘ ║
║  │                     │    Options:                           ║
║  │                     │    ┌────────────────────────────────┐ ║
║  │                     │    │ [ ] When...     [ ] Comment... │ ║
║  │                     │    │ [X] Valid...    [ ] Disabled   │ ║
║  │                     │    │ [ ] Message...                 │ ║
║  └─────────────────────┘    └────────────────────────────────┘ ║
║                                                                ║
║              «   OK   »     < Cancel >                         ║
║                                                                ║
╚════════════════════════════════════════════════════════════════╝
WINDOWS  RGB Color Scheme: (,,,,,)
WINDOWS  Font: MS Sans Serif,   8
         Style: Bold
 Valid code above
 Screen Cleanup and Procedures code above
```

Background Screen: BCKGRND.SCX

BckGrnd contains our Foundation READ. It is a good example of the capabilities of FoxPro's transporter. The character (DOS) version of the BckGrnd screen and the graphical (Windows, Macintosh) versions look nothing alike, yet they are all stored in the same .SCX file. The second illustration is used in both Windows and Macintosh.

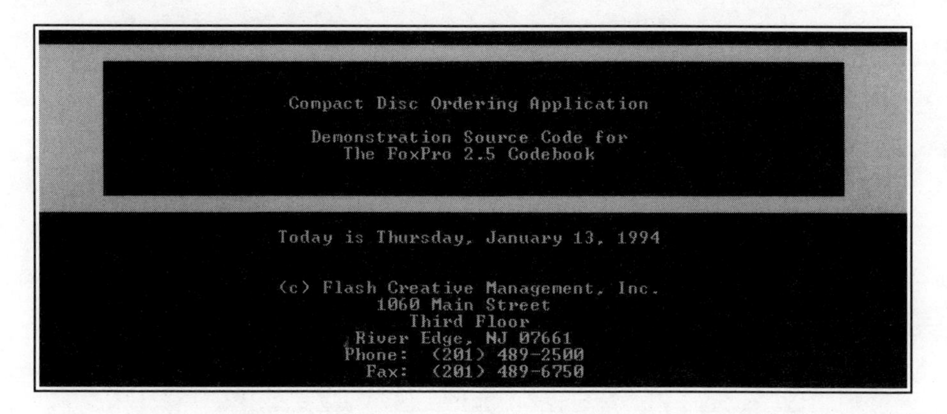

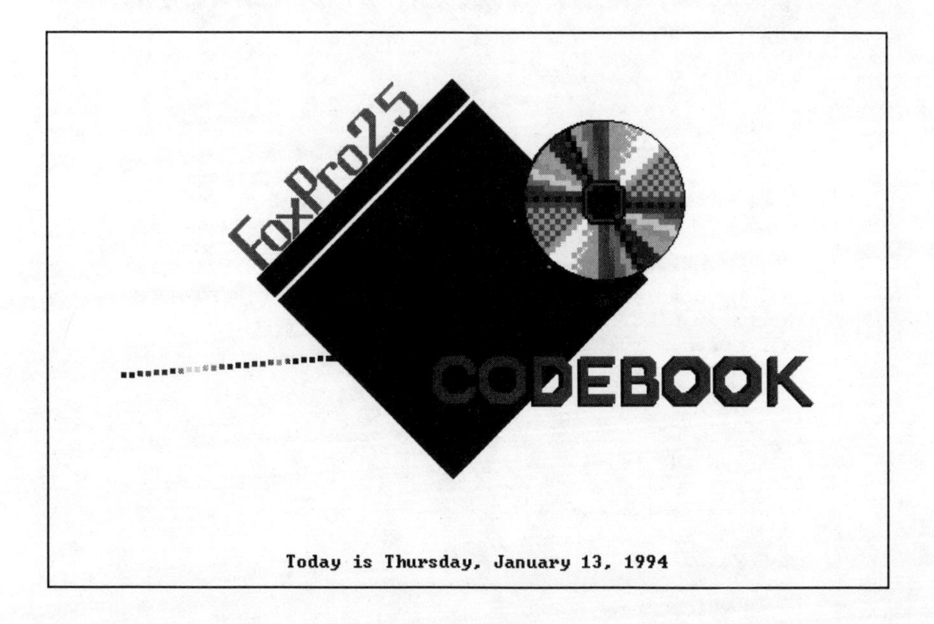

```
*----------------------------------------------------------------
******************************************************************
**--    BCKGRND.SCX - DOS PLATFORM
******************************************************************

 (·) DeskTop                          ( ) Window

 Name:                                <Type...>
 Title:
 Footer:

 Size:              Screen Code:

  Height:   26      [X] Setup...
  Width:    84      [ ] Cleanup & Procs...          «    OK    »

 Position:          READ Clauses:                   < Cancel >

  Row:        0     [ ] Activate...    [ ] Show...
  Column:     0     [X] Valid...       [ ] When...
  [ ] Center        [ ] Deactivate...

 Environment:                      [X] Add alias

       Environment NOT saved with screen.

******************************************************************
*  SCREEN SETUP CODE
******************************************************************
*  Program...........: BCKGRND Screen
*  Author............: yag
*  Project...........: COMMON
*  Created...........: 04/16/93
*  Copyright.........: (c) Flash Creative Management, 1993
*) Description.......: Background for all applications
*)                   : This screen contains the Foundation READ
*)                   : It uses info from SETUP.DBF to display
*)                   : application information
*  Calling Samples...: Called from traficop (DO BCKGRND.SPR)
*  Parameter List....:
*  Major change list.:
IF _windows OR _mac
   ZOOM WINDOW SCREEN MAX
ENDIF
----------------------------------------------------------------
*-- READ Valid Clause
----------------------------------------------------------------

  READ Valid

   ( ) Procedure
   (·) Expression

READ Valid:   myhandler()
```

```
***********************************************************
*--   G E T   O B J E C T S
***********************************************************
*==========================================================
*  Box
*==========================================================
 @   4,   0
 SIZE  10,  80
*==========================================================
*  Box
*==========================================================
 @   5,  77
 SIZE   8,   2
*==========================================================
*  Box
*==========================================================
 @   5,  76
 SIZE   8,   1
*==========================================================
*  Box
*==========================================================
 @   5,   2
 SIZE   8,   2
*==========================================================
*  Box
*==========================================================
 @   5,   1
 SIZE   8,   1
*==========================================================
*  Box
*==========================================================
 @   5,   4
 SIZE   8,   2
*==========================================================
*  Box
*==========================================================
 @   5,  74
 SIZE   8,   2
*==========================================================
*
*==========================================================
 @  15,   0

  Field:
  ┌──────────────────────────────────────────┐
  │ (·) Say        ( ) Get        ( ) Edit    │
  └──────────────────────────────────────────┘

  <  Say...   > PADC('Today is '+CDOW(DATE())+', '+CMONTH(
                                              «   OK   »
  < Format... >
                                              < Cancel >
  Range:
  ┌──────────────────────────────────────────┐
  │ [ ] Upper...              [ ] Lower...   │
  └──────────────────────────────────────────┘

  [ ] When...      [ ] Error...     [ ] Scroll bar
  [ ] Valid...     [ ] Comment...   [ ] Allow tabs
  [ ] Message...   [ ] Disabled     [ ] Refresh

*==========================================================
```

```
*
*==============================================================
 @   7,  20
╔══════════════════════════════════════════════════════════════╗
║                                                              ║
║  Field:                                                      ║
║  ┌──────────────────────────────────────────┐                ║
║  │ (•) Say         ( ) Get        ( ) Edit  │                ║
║  └──────────────────────────────────────────┘                ║
║                                                              ║
║  <  Say...    > setup.csystname                              ║
║                                               «   OK    »    ║
║  < Format... > @I                                            ║
║                                               < Cancel >     ║
║  Range:                                                      ║
║  ┌──────────────────────────────────────────┐                ║
║  │ [ ] Upper...               [ ] Lower...  │                ║
║  └──────────────────────────────────────────┘                ║
║                                                              ║
║  [ ] When...     [ ] Error...     [ ] Scroll bar             ║
║  [ ] Valid...    [ ] Comment...   [ ] Allow tabs             ║
║  [ ] Message...  [ ] Disabled     [ ] Refresh                ║
║                                                              ║
╚══════════════════════════════════════════════════════════════╝
*==============================================================
*
*==============================================================
 @   9,  20
╔══════════════════════════════════════════════════════════════╗
║                                                              ║
║  Field:                                                      ║
║  ┌──────────────────────────────────────────┐                ║
║  │ (•) Say         ( ) Get        ( ) Edit  │                ║
║  └──────────────────────────────────────────┘                ║
║                                                              ║
║  <  Say...    > setup.clongname1                             ║
║                                               «   OK    »    ║
║  < Format... > @I                                            ║
║                                               < Cancel >     ║
║  Range:                                                      ║
║  ┌──────────────────────────────────────────┐                ║
║  │ [ ] Upper...               [ ] Lower...  │                ║
║  └──────────────────────────────────────────┘                ║
║                                                              ║
║  [ ] When...     [ ] Error...     [ ] Scroll bar             ║
║  [ ] Valid...    [ ] Comment...   [ ] Allow tabs             ║
║  [ ] Message...  [ ] Disabled     [ ] Refresh                ║
║                                                              ║
╚══════════════════════════════════════════════════════════════╝
*==============================================================
*
*==============================================================
 @  10,  20
```

```
Field:

  (·) Say        ( ) Get        ( ) Edit

< Say...    > setup.clongname2
                                          «   OK   »
< Format... > @I
                                          < Cancel >
Range:

  [ ] Upper...                [ ] Lower...

[ ] When...      [ ] Error...      [ ] Scroll bar
[ ] Valid...     [ ] Comment...    [ ] Allow tabs
[ ] Message...   [ ] Disabled      [ ] Refresh
```

```
*============================================================
*
*============================================================
@ 18, 11
```

```
Field:

  (·) Say        ( ) Get        ( ) Edit

< Say...    > PADC('(c) '+m.gccompany,57)
                                          «   OK   »
< Format... > @I
                                          < Cancel >
Range:

  [ ] Upper...                [ ] Lower...

[ ] When...      [ ] Error...      [ ] Scroll bar
[ ] Valid...     [ ] Comment...    [ ] Allow tabs
[ ] Message...   [ ] Disabled      [ ] Refresh
```

```
*============================================================
*
*============================================================
@ 19, 11
```

```
╔══════════════════════════════════════════════════════════════╗
║                                                              ║
║  Field:                                                      ║
║  ┌──────────────────────────────────────────┐                ║
║  │ (•) Say        ( ) Get        ( ) Edit   │                ║
║  └──────────────────────────────────────────┘                ║
║                                                              ║
║  <  Say...   > PADC(m.gcaddress1,57)                         ║
║                                               «   OK    »    ║
║  < Format... > @I                                            ║
║                                               < Cancel >     ║
║  Range:                                                      ║
║  ┌──────────────────────────────────────────┐                ║
║  │ [ ] Upper...               [ ] Lower...  │                ║
║  └──────────────────────────────────────────┘                ║
║                                                              ║
║  [ ] When...     [ ] Error...     [ ] Scroll bar             ║
║  [ ] Valid...    [ ] Comment...   [ ] Allow tabs             ║
║  [ ] Message...  [ ] Disabled     [ ] Refresh                ║
║                                                              ║
╚══════════════════════════════════════════════════════════════╝
*============================================================
*
*============================================================
 @  20,  11
╔══════════════════════════════════════════════════════════════╗
║                                                              ║
║  Field:                                                      ║
║  ┌──────────────────────────────────────────┐                ║
║  │ (•) Say        ( ) Get        ( ) Edit   │                ║
║  └──────────────────────────────────────────┘                ║
║                                                              ║
║  <  Say...   > PADC(m.gcaddress2,57)                         ║
║                                               «   OK    »    ║
║  < Format... > @I                                            ║
║                                               < Cancel >     ║
║  Range:                                                      ║
║  ┌──────────────────────────────────────────┐                ║
║  │ [ ] Upper...               [ ] Lower...  │                ║
║  └──────────────────────────────────────────┘                ║
║                                                              ║
║  [ ] When...     [ ] Error...     [ ] Scroll bar             ║
║  [ ] Valid...    [ ] Comment...   [ ] Allow tabs             ║
║  [ ] Message...  [ ] Disabled     [ ] Refresh                ║
║                                                              ║
╚══════════════════════════════════════════════════════════════╝
*============================================================
*
*============================================================
 @  21,  11
```

```
Field:
 (·) Say          ( ) Get          ( ) Edit

<  Say...    > PADC(csz(m.gcCity,m.gcState,m.gcZip),57)
                                                 «   OK   »
< Format... > @I
                                                 < Cancel >
Range:
 [ ] Upper...                    [ ] Lower...

[ ] When...       [ ] Error...      [ ] Scroll bar
[ ] Valid...      [ ] Comment...    [ ] Allow tabs
[ ] Message...    [ ] Disabled      [ ] Refresh
```

```
*============================================================
*
*============================================================
 @  22,  36
```

```
Field:
 (·) Say          ( ) Get          ( ) Edit

<  Say...    > m.gcphone
                                                 «   OK   »
< Format... > @R (999) 999-9999
                                                 < Cancel >
Range:
 [ ] Upper...                    [ ] Lower...

[ ] When...       [ ] Error...      [ ] Scroll bar
[ ] Valid...      [ ] Comment...    [ ] Allow tabs
[ ] Message...    [ ] Disabled      [ ] Refresh
```

```
*============================================================
*  Text: Phone:
*============================================================
 @  22,  28
*============================================================
*  Text: Fax:
*============================================================
 @  23,  30
*============================================================
*
*============================================================
 @  23,  36
```

```
Field:
  (·) Say            ( ) Get             ( ) Edit

< Say...    > m.gcFax
                                                  «   OK   »
< Format... > @R (999) 999-9999
                                                  < Cancel >
Range:
  [ ] Upper...                    [ ] Lower...

[ ] When...      [ ] Error...      [ ] Scroll bar
[ ] Valid...     [ ] Comment...    [ ] Allow tabs
[ ] Message...   [ ] Disabled      [ ] Refresh
*-------------------------------------------------------------
**************************************************************
**--     BCKGRND.SCX - MAC PLATFORM
**************************************************************
(·) DeskTop                        ( ) Window

Name:                              <Type...>
Title:
Footer:

Size:              Screen Code:

  Height:    28.909    [X] Setup...
  Width:     92.500    [ ] Cleanup & Procs...           «   OK   »

Position:          READ Clauses:                        < Cancel >

  Row:         0.000   [ ] Activate...    [ ] Show...
  Column:      0.000   [X] Valid...       [ ] When...
  [ ] Center           [ ] Deactivate...

Environment:                       [X] Add alias

        Environment NOT saved with screen.

 Screen Setup code above
 READ Valid code above
**************************************************************
*--    G E T    O B J E C T S
**************************************************************
*=============================================================
*  BITMAP Object
*  File: ..\..\BOOK25\CD\BMPS\BCKGRND.BMP
*=============================================================
 @   1.091,   0.000
     SIZE  26.364,  91.833
```

```
  Screen Picture From:                              «   OK   »

   (·) File  : "..\..\BOOK25\CD\BMPS\BCKG
   ( ) Field :                                      < Cancel >

  If Picture And Frame Different Size:

   ( ) Clip Picture
   (·) Scale Picture - Retain Shape
   ( ) Scale Picture - Fill the Frame

   [ ] Center Picture          [ ] Refresh Output Field

   [ ] Comment

MAC      RGB Color Scheme: (,,,,,) Transparent
*------------------------------------------------------------
*************************************************************
**--     BCKGRND.SCX - WINDOWS PLATFORM
*************************************************************

 (·) DeskTop                          ( ) Window

 Name:                                <Type...>
 Title:
 Footer:

 Size:          Screen Code:

  Height:   40.000   [X] Setup...
  Width:    80.000   [ ] Cleanup & Procs...           «   OK   »

 Position:      READ Clauses:                         < Cancel >

  Row:       0.000   [ ] Activate...    [ ] Show...
  Column:    0.000   [X] Valid...       [ ] When...
   [ ] Center        [ ] Deactivate...

 Environment:                            [X] Add alias

        Environment NOT saved with screen.

 Screen Setup code above
 READ Valid code above
*************************************************************
*--    G E T    O B J E C T S
*************************************************************
*============================================================
*  BITMAP Object
*  File: \book25\cd\bmps\bckgrnd.bmp
*============================================================
 @    0.000,    4.375
    SIZE  25.000,  71.250
```

```
+--------------------------------------------------------------+
|                                                              |
|  Screen Picture From:                           «   OK   »    |
|                                                              |
|  +------------------------------------------+               |
|  | (·) File  : "\book25\cd\bmps\bckgrnd.b   |  < Cancel >   |
|  | ( ) Field :                              |               |
|  +------------------------------------------+               |
|                                                              |
|  If Picture And Frame Different Size:                        |
|                                                              |
|  +--------------------------------------+                   |
|  | (·) Clip Picture                     |                   |
|  | ( ) Scale Picture - Retain Shape     |                   |
|  | ( ) Scale Picture - Fill the Frame   |                   |
|  +--------------------------------------+                   |
|                                                              |
|    [ ] Center Picture          [ ] Refresh Output Field      |
|                                                              |
|    [ ] Comment                                               |
|                                                              |
+--------------------------------------------------------------+
WINDOWS  RGB Color Scheme: (,,,,,) Transparent
*=============================================================
*
*=============================================================
 @  28.417,    0.250
+--------------------------------------------------------------+
|                                                              |
|  Field:                                                      |
|                                                              |
|  +------------------------------------------+               |
|  | (·) Say          ( ) Get          ( ) Edit |               |
|  +------------------------------------------+               |
|                                                              |
|  <  Say...    > PADC('Today is '+CDOW(DATE())+',  '+CMONTH(  |
|                                                 «   OK   »    |
|  < Format... >                                               |
|                                                  < Cancel >   |
|  Range:                                                      |
|                                                              |
|  +------------------------------------------+               |
|  | [ ] Upper...                 [ ] Lower... |               |
|  +------------------------------------------+               |
|                                                              |
|  [ ] When...      [ ] Error...     [ ] Scroll bar            |
|  [ ] Valid...     [ ] Comment...   [ ] Allow tabs            |
|  [ ] Message...   [ ] Disabled     [ ] Refresh               |
|                                                              |
+--------------------------------------------------------------+
WINDOWS  RGB Color Scheme: (,,,,,)
WINDOWS  Font: Terminal,   9
```

Data-Driven Compression: DBFPACK.SCX

Our application allows the user to compress any memo fields being used. The user accesses this function by selecting Compress from the Database menu pad. This modal window allows the user to compress memo files for a specific database or for all of the application's databases. It uses the following code to move all the memo field files into an array, and displays the file name and size in a scrolling list.

```
=ADIR(laFptDir, '*.FPT')
lnAryLngth = ALEN(laFptDir,1)
DIMENSION laFptList(lnAryLngth)
FOR i = 1 TO lnAryLngth          && Create array with name/size
  laFptList(i) = PADR(laFptDir(i,1),18) + ;
                 STR(laFptDir(i,2),10,0)
ENDFOR
```

The first line shows FoxPro's ADIR() function. This places any file in the current directory that matches the second parameter ('*.FPT') into the array named in the first parameter (laFptDir). The second line uses the ALEN() function to determine the number of rows in the array, and the third line dimensions a new array to that length. A FOR command loops through all the array rows filling the new array with the name of the files and their sizes. This new array (laFptList) is used to create the scrolling list.

The rest of the screen is fairly straightforward. The llAll check box automatically highlights or dims the scrolling list of memo files using the SHOW GET <variable name> ENABLE/DISABLE command.

When <Compress> is selected, the Packaler() screen function is called. Packaler is a simple screen warning that the selected function may take some time. If the user elects to continue, the selected files are compressed using FoxPro's new PACK MEMO command.

The final item of interest is the use of the llCompress variable. It is set to TRUE only if the compression actually takes place. This allows the program to rerun the database-opening routine, Opendbf, only if we have actually had to close the databases in order to compress them.

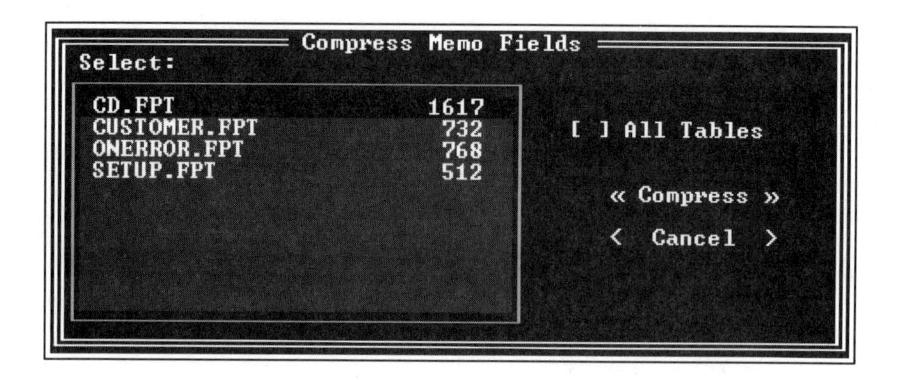
Compress Memo Fields
Select:
CD.FPT 1617
CUSTOMER.FPT 732
ONERROR.FPT 768
SETUP.FPT 512
[ ] All Tables
« Compress »
< Cancel >

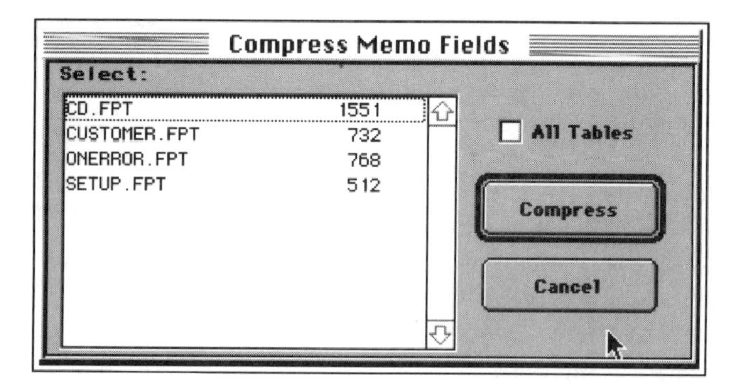
Compress Memo Fields
Select:
CD.FPT 1551
CUSTOMER.FPT 732
ONERROR.FPT 768
SETUP.FPT 512
All Tables
Compress
Cancel

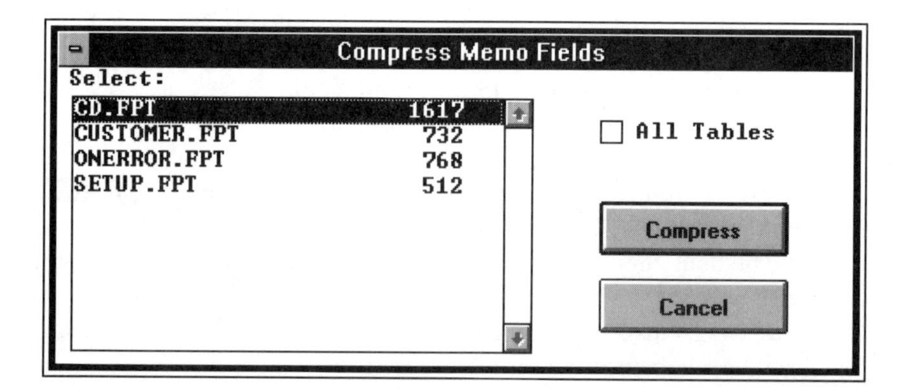
Compress Memo Fields
Select:
CD.FPT 1617
CUSTOMER.FPT 732
ONERROR.FPT 768
SETUP.FPT 512
All Tables
Compress
Cancel

```
*-----------------------------------------------------------------
******************************************************************
**--    DBFPACK.SCX - DOS PLATFORM
******************************************************************

 ( ) DeskTop                          (·) Window

 Name:                                <Type...>
 Title:  Compress Memo Fields
 Footer:

 Size:              Screen Code:

  Height:   15       [X] Setup...
  Width:    57       [ ] Cleanup & Procs...            «   OK   »

 Position:          READ Clauses:                      < Cancel >

  Row:          0    [ ] Activate...     [ ] Show...
  Column:       0    [ ] Valid...        [ ] When...
  [X] Center         [ ] Deactivate...

 Environment:                         [X] Add alias

         Environment NOT saved with screen.

  Type:       Dialog

  Attributes:       Border:

   [ ] Close         ( ) None
   [X] Float         ( ) Single
   [X] Shadow        (·) Double      «   OK   »
   [ ] Minimize      ( ) Panel
                     ( ) System      < Cancel >

  Color Schemes:

   Primary:          Popup:

   Dialogs           Dialog Pop

******************************************************************
*  SCREEN SETUP CODE
******************************************************************
*  Program...........: DBFPACK Screen
*  Author............: yag
*  Project...........: COMMON
*  Created...........: 04/16/93
*  Copyright.........: (c) Flash Creative Management, 1993
*) Description.......: This dialog allows the compression of any
*)                   : DBFs in the current directory.
*)                   : NOTE: This does a PACK MEMO, not a PACK.
*  Calling Samples...: DO DbfPack
```

```
*  Parameter List....:
*  Major change list.:
PRIVATE llCompress, llAll, lnPackThis, lhCompress, lcResource, lnPos, lnRow
STORE .F. TO llAll, llCompress
=ADIR(laFptDir, '*.FPT')
*-- Remove any active resource file...
lcResource = StripPat(StripExt(SET("RESOURCE",1)))
lnPos = ASCAN(laFptDir,lcResource+".FPT")
IF lnPos # 0
  lnRow = ASUBSCRIPT(laFptDir,lnPos,1)
  =ADEL(laFptDir,lnRow)
  DIME laFptDir[ALEN(laFptDir,1)-1,ALEN(laFptDir,2)]
ENDIF
*-- OK, back to work
lnAryLngth = ALEN(laFptDir,1)
DIMENSION laFptList(lnAryLngth)
FOR i = 1 TO lnAryLngth                   && Create array with name/size
  laFptList(i) = PADR(laFptDir(i,1),18) + STR(laFptDir(i,2),10,0)
ENDFOR
************************************************************
*--    G E T    O B J E C T S
************************************************************
*==========================================================
*  m.lnPackThis
*==========================================================
 @   1,   0
```

```
List Type:                                  Options:

 (•) From Array       laFptList              [ ] When...       [ ] Comment...
 ( ) From Popup                              [ ] Valid...      [ ] Disabled
 ( ) Prompt Structure                        [ ] Message...    [ ] 1st Element...
 ( ) Prompt Field                            [ ] Terminating   [ ] # Elements...
 ( ) Prompt Files

Variable:

 < Choose... > m.lnPackThis                      «   OK   »    < Cancel >
```

```
*==========================================================
*  m.llAll
*==========================================================
 @   3,  36
```

```
Check Box Prompt:
All Tables

Variable:                                        «   OK   »

 < Choose... > m.llAll                           < Cancel >

[ ] When...      [ ] Comment...
[X] Valid...     [ ] Disabled
[ ] Message...   [ ] Initially checked
```

```
-------------------------------------------------------------
*-- m.llAll Valid Clause
-------------------------------------------------------------

  Valid
    (·) Procedure
    ( ) Expression

IF m.llAll
  SHOW GET lnPackThis DISABLE
ELSE
  SHOW GET lnPackThis ENABLE
ENDIF
*=============================================================
*  m.lhCompress
*=============================================================
 @   6,  39
 Spacing:    1

  Push Button Prompts:      ( ) Horizontal   (·) Vertical
                            [ ] Terminating  <Spacing...>
   \!Compress
   \?Cancel                Variable:

                            < Choose... >  m.lhCompress

                           Options:

                            [ ] When...     [ ] Comment...
                            [X] Valid...    [ ] Disabled
                            [ ] Message...

              «   OK   »    < Cancel >

-------------------------------------------------------------
*-- m.lhCompress Valid Clause
-------------------------------------------------------------

  Valid
    (·) Procedure
    ( ) Expression

IF lhCompress = 1  && reindex
  IF packaler()
    llCompress = .T.
    CLOSE DATA
    IF !m.llAll
      IF OpenDB("EXCLUSIVE", STRIPEXT(laFptDir(lnPackThis,1)))
*         USE STRTRAN(laFptDir(lnPackThis,1),"FPT","DBF") EXCLUSIVE
```

```
          WAIT WINDOW "Now compressing:  " + laFptDir(lnPackThis,1) NOWAIT
          PACK MEMO
          USE
        ELSE
          DO Alert.spr WITH ;
             "File used by another. Cannot compress"
        ENDIF
    ELSE
      FOR i = 1 TO lnAryLngth
          IF OpenDB("EXCLUSIVE", STRIPEXT(laFptDir[i,1]))
*            USE STRTRAN(laFptDir(i,1),"FPT","DBF") EXCLUSIVE
             WAIT WINDOW "Now compressing:  " + laFptDir(i,1) NOWAIT
            PACK MEMO
            USE
        ELSE
          DO Alert.spr WITH ;
             "File used by another. Cannot compress"
          ENDIF
      ENDFOR
    ENDIF
  WAIT CLEAR
  ENDIF
ELSE
  CLEAR READ ALL
  IF llCompress
    DO opendbf IN main.mpr
  ENDIF
ENDIF
*============================================================
*  Text: Select:
*============================================================
 @   0,   1
*------------------------------------------------------------
************************************************************
**--    DBFPACK.SCX - MAC PLATFORM
************************************************************
```

```
( ) DeskTop                          (·) Window

Name:                                <Type...>
Title:  Compress Memo Fields
Footer:

Size:              Screen Code:

 Height:   13.636    [X] Setup...
 Width:    57.000    [ ] Cleanup & Procs...          «   OK   »

Position:          READ Clauses:                     < Cancel >

 Row:        0.000   [ ] Activate...    [ ] Show...
 Column:     0.000   [ ] Valid...       [ ] When...
 [X] Center          [ ] Deactivate...

Environment:                          [X] Add alias

        Environment NOT saved with screen.
```

```
+---------------------------------------------------------+
| Type:   [ Dialog ]                                      |
|                                                         |
| Attributes:        Border:                              |
|  [ ] Close          ( ) None                            |
|  [X] Float          ( ) Single                          |
|  [X] Shadow         (·) Double       «  OK  »           |
|  [ ] Minimize       ( ) Panel                           |
|                     ( ) System       < Cancel >         |
| Color Schemes:                                          |
|  Primary:          Popup:                               |
|  [        ]        [        ]                           |
+---------------------------------------------------------+
MAC      RGB Fill Color Scheme: (,,)
MAC      Font: monaco,   9
 Screen Setup code above
**********************************************************
*--    G E T    O B J E C T S
**********************************************************
*=========================================================
*  m.lnPackThis
*=========================================================
 @   1.364,   1.167
     SIZE  11.818,  34.667
+--------------------------------------------------------------------------+
| List Type:                          Options:                             |
|  (·) From Array      laFptList       [ ] When...        [ ] Comment...   |
|  ( ) From Popup                      [ ] Valid...       [ ] Disabled     |
|  ( ) Prompt Structure                [ ] Message...     [ ] 1st Element...|
|  ( ) Prompt Field                    [ ] Terminating    [ ] # Elements...|
|  ( ) Prompt Files                                                        |
|                                                                          |
| Variable:                                                                |
|  < Choose... > m.lnPackThis               «  OK  »     < Cancel >        |
+--------------------------------------------------------------------------+
MAC      RGB Color Scheme: (,,,,,)
MAC      Font: monaco,   9
*=========================================================
*  m.llAll
*=========================================================
 @   2.364,  40.000
     SIZE   1.417,  13.167
```

```
Check Box Prompt:
All Tables

Variable:                                        «   OK   »

< Choose... > m.llAll                            < Cancel >

[ ] When...     [ ] Comment...
[X] Valid...    [ ] Disabled
[ ] Message...  [ ] Initially checked

MAC      RGB Color Scheme: (,,,,,)
MAC      Font: Geneva,   9
        Style: Bold Transparent
 Valid code above
*==============================================================
*  m.lhCompress
*==============================================================
 @   5.455,  38.667
     SIZE   2.333,  15.500
 Spacing:    1

Push Button Prompts:       ( ) Horizontal   (·) Vertical
                           [ ] Terminating  <Spacing...>
\!Compress
\?Cancel                   Variable:

                           < Choose... >  m.lhCompress

                           Options:

                           [ ] When...     [ ] Comment...
                           [X] Valid...    [ ] Disabled
                           [ ] Message...

                  «   OK   »    < Cancel >

MAC      RGB Color Scheme: (,,,,,)
MAC      Font: Geneva,   9
        Style: Bold
 Valid code above
*==============================================================
*  Text: Select:
*==============================================================
 @   0.000,   1.000
MAC      RGB Color Scheme: (,,,,,)
MAC      Font: Monaco,   9
        Style: Bold
*--------------------------------------------------------------
```

```
************************************************************
**--    DBFPACK.SCX - WINDOWS PLATFORM
************************************************************

 ( ) DeskTop                        (·) Window

 Name:                              <Type...>
 Title:  Compress Memo Fields
 Footer:

 Size:           Screen Code:

  Height:   13.667   [X] Setup...
  Width:    57.000   [ ] Cleanup & Procs...        «   OK   »

 Position:       READ Clauses:                     < Cancel >

  Row:        0.000   [ ] Activate...    [ ] Show...
  Column:     0.000   [ ] Valid...       [ ] When...
  [X] Center          [ ] Deactivate...

 Environment:                      [X] Add alias

      Environment NOT saved with screen.

 Type:      Dialog

 Attributes:      Border:

  [ ] Close        ( ) None
  [X] Float        ( ) Single
  [X] Shadow       (·) Double      «   OK   »
  [ ] Minimize     ( ) Panel
                   ( ) System      < Cancel >

 Color Schemes:

  Primary:         Popup:

WINDOWS  RGB Fill Color Scheme: (,,)
WINDOWS  Font: Terminal,    9
 Screen Setup code above
************************************************************
*--   G E T   O B J E C T S
************************************************************
*===========================================================
*  m.lnPackThis
*===========================================================
 @   1.333,   1.125
    SIZE  11.667,  32.875
```

```
 List Type:                                     Options:

 (•) From Array        laFptList               [ ] When...        [ ] Comment...
 ( ) From Popup                                 [ ] Valid...       [ ] Disabled
 ( ) Prompt Structure                           [ ] Message...     [ ] 1st Element...
 ( ) Prompt Field                               [ ] Terminating    [ ] # Elements...
 ( ) Prompt Files

 Variable:

 < Choose... > m.lnPackThis                      «    OK    »      < Cancel >

WINDOWS  RGB Color Scheme: (,,,,,)
WINDOWS  Font: Terminal,   9
*==============================================================
*  m.llAll
*==============================================================
 @   2.167,  39.000
     SIZE   1.417,  12.875

 Check Box Prompt:
 All Tables

 Variable:                                       «    OK    »

 < Choose... > m.llAll                           < Cancel >

 [ ] When...      [ ] Comment...
 [X] Valid...     [ ] Disabled
 [ ] Message...   [ ] Initially checked

WINDOWS  RGB Color Scheme: (,,,,,)
WINDOWS  Font: Terminal,   9
 Valid code above
*==============================================================
*  m.lhCompress
*==============================================================
 @   6.083,  39.000
     SIZE   2.308,  18.000
 Spacing:    1
```

```
Push Button Prompts:          ( ) Horizontal    (·) Vertical
                              [ ] Terminating   <Spacing...>
 \!Compress
 \?Cancel                     Variable:

                              < Choose... >  m.lhCompress

                              Options:

                              [ ] When...      [ ] Comment...
                              [X] Valid...     [ ] Disabled
                              [ ] Message...

              «  OK  »    < Cancel >
```

```
WINDOWS  RGB Color Scheme: (,,,,,)
WINDOWS  Font: MS Sans Serif,   8
         Style: Bold
 Valid code above
*=============================================================
*  Text: Select:
*=============================================================
 @   0.000,   1.000
WINDOWS  RGB Color Scheme: (,,,,,)
WINDOWS  Font: Terminal,   9
```

Data-Driven Reindexing: DBFREIND.SCX

DBFReind() is a function that recreates the indices in a FoxPro table. As I explained in the original *FoxPro Codebook*, a common task in any FoxPro application is recreating any indexes that must be in place for an application to function. In order to achieve this aim, we create a screen called DBFREIND that will automatically select all database files associated with the current application, and will recreate any necessary indexes. If the indexing actually takes place, we will rerun our database opening routine, OPENDBF.

Note that we are *recreating* the index tags. We use the DELETE TAG ALL command to completely remove the existing index. This reduces fragmentation and index file bloat by deleting the entire CDX before recreating it. One new trick added to this version of DBFReind() is that the routine checks for a tag on DELETED() if SET DELETED is ON. FoxPro does not fully optimize a query if SET DELETED is ON unless you have an index tag on the DELETED() flag. Creating one reusable object that accomplishes this intelligent index creation would be very useful.

This screen must accomplish several different tasks. If we are prototyping an application, it will automatically build an index on every non-memo field in the database files that are in the application default directory (remember, that is where all user-modifiable database files are kept). Once the coding has commenced on an application, we will create a data dictionary database (called DATADICT.DBF) that will have the names of the specific index tags to create, and an easy to understand English description of each tag. The DBFREIND screen will automatically check to see if a data dictionary exists. If it does, it will use that dictionary to create only the necessary index tags, and will use the English descriptions to provide the user with an easy way of understanding what is happening.

Once again, we need only design this screen once, and it will work in all our applications, automatically. Adding a new index tag is simply a matter of adding a new record to the DATADICT database file.

This screen allows us to move seamlessly from the prototyping phase of our application development to the final coding phase of our application. The screen never changes. We simply add some records to a database to provide more functionality and ease-of-use to our users.

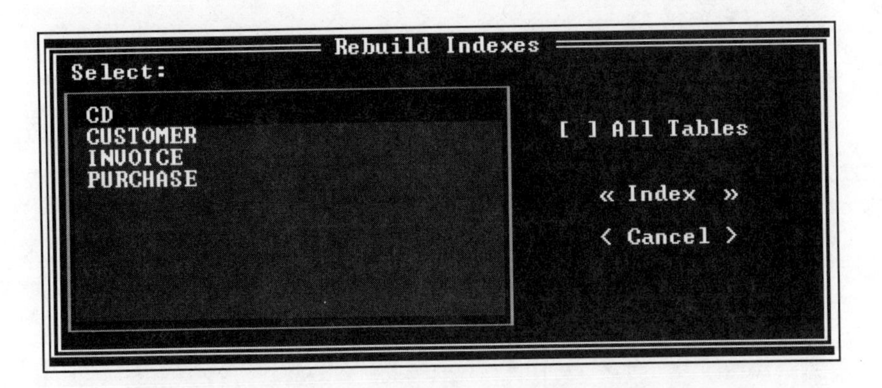
Rebuild Indexes
Select:
CD
CUSTOMER
INVOICE
PURCHASE
[ ] All Tables
« Index »
‹ Cancel ›

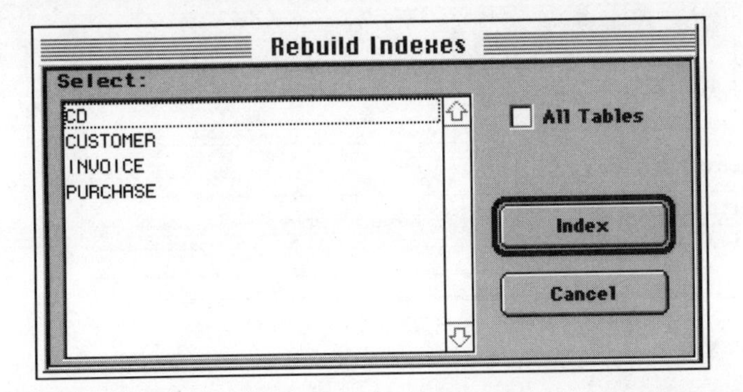
Rebuild Indexes
Select:
CD
CUSTOMER
INVOICE
PURCHASE
All Tables
Index
Cancel

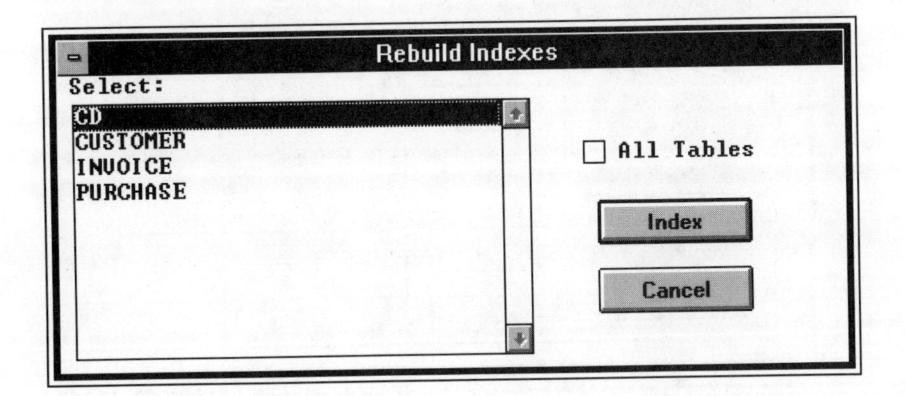
Rebuild Indexes
Select:
CD
CUSTOMER
INVOICE
PURCHASE
All Tables
Index
Cancel

```
*-----------------------------------------------------------
************************************************************
**--    DBFREIND.SCX - DOS PLATFORM
************************************************************
```

```
( ) DeskTop                           (·) Window

Name:                                 <Type...>
Title:  Rebuild Indexes
Footer:

Size:             Screen Code:

Height:   15      [X] Setup...
Width:    57      [X] Cleanup & Procs...              «  OK  »

Position:         READ Clauses:                       < Cancel >

Row:        0     [ ] Activate...    [ ] Show...
Column:     0     [ ] Valid...       [ ] When...
[X] Center        [ ] Deactivate...

Environment:                           [X] Add alias

      Environment NOT saved with screen.
```

```
Type:      Dialog

Attributes:       Border:

[ ] Close         ( ) None
[X] Float         ( ) Single
[X] Shadow        (·) Double      «  OK  »
[ ] Minimize      ( ) Panel
                  ( ) System      < Cancel >

Color Schemes:

Primary:          Popup:

Dialogs           Dialog Pop
```

```
************************************************************
*  SCREEN SETUP CODE
************************************************************
*  Program...........: DBFREIND Screen
*  Author............: yag
*  Project...........: COMMON
*  Created...........: 04/16/93
*  Copyright.........: (c) Flash Creative Management, 1993
*) Description.......: This dialog allows the reindexing of any or
*)                   : all dbfs in an application. If it finds a filled
*)                   : DATADICT.DBF, it uses that to determine what
```

```
*)                    : files can be indexed, and what indices to create.
*)                    : If DATADICT.DBF is not found, it defaults to
*)                    : files in the current directory, and indexes every
*)                    : field except for memo fields.
*  Calling Samples...: DO DbfReind.spr
*  Parameter List....:
*  Major change list.: 12/13/92    - If SET("DELETED")="ON", automatically
*                    :             INDEX ON DELETED() TAG Delrec
PRIVATE llIndexed, i, llAll
STORE .F. TO llAll, llIndexed
IF FILE("DATADICT.DBF")
  SELECT DISTINCT DBF_NAME FROM Datadict ;
    ORDER BY DBF_NAME INTO ARRAY laDBFList
  IF _tally = 0
    DIME laDBFList[1,1]
  ENDIF
ELSE
  DIMENSION laDBFList(1)
  =ADIR(laDBFList,"*.DBF")
  =ASORT(laDBFList)
ENDIF
************************************************************
*--   G E T   O B J E C T S
************************************************************
*===========================================================
*  lnIndxThis
*===========================================================
 @  1,   0
```

```
List Type:                              Options:

 (·) From Array       laDbfList         [ ] When...        [ ] Comment...
 ( ) From Popup                         [ ] Valid...       [ ] Disabled
 ( ) Prompt Structure                   [ ] Message...     [ ] 1st Element...
 ( ) Prompt Field                       [ ] Terminating    [X] # Elements...
 ( ) Prompt Files

Variable:

 < Choose... > lnIndxThis                  «  OK  »     < Cancel >
```

```
------------------------------------------------------------
*-- lnIndxThis # Elements Clause
------------------------------------------------------------
```

```
# Elements

 ( ) Procedure
 (·) Expression
```

```
# Elements:   sizearry(@ladbfList)
*===========================================================
*  m.llAll
```

```
*============================================================
 @   3,  36

  Check Box Prompt:
  All Tables

  Variable:                                    «   OK   »

  < Choose... > m.llAll                        < Cancel >

  [ ] When...     [ ] Comment...
  [X] Valid...    [ ] Disabled
  [ ] Message...  [ ] Initially checked

------------------------------------------------------------
*-- m.llAll Valid Clause
------------------------------------------------------------

  Valid

  (·) Procedure
  ( ) Expression

IF m.llAll
  SHOW GET lnIndxThis Disable
ELSE
  SHOW GET lnIndxThis Enable
ENDIF
*============================================================
*  m.lhIndex
*============================================================
 @   6,  39
 Spacing:    1

  Push Button Prompts:     ( ) Horizontal    (·) Vertical
                           [ ] Terminating   <Spacing...>
  \!Index
  \?Cancel                Variable:

                           < Choose... >  m.lhIndex

                          Options:

                           [ ] When...     [ ] Comment...
                           [X] Valid...    [ ] Disabled
                           [ ] Message...

                «   OK   »    < Cancel >

------------------------------------------------------------
```

```
*-- m.lhIndex Valid Clause
------------------------------------------------------------

  Valid

   (·) Procedure
   ( ) Expression

IF lhIndex = 1  && Reindex
  IF PACKALER()
    CLOSE DATA
    llIndexed = .T.
    IF !m.llAll
      =RNDX(laDBFList(lnIndxThis,1))    && Use the ,1 in case it's ADIR
      USE                               && Will still work w/ 1 dim. array
    ELSE
      PRIVATE lnDbfCnt
      FOR lnDbfCnt = 1 TO ALEN(laDbfList,1)
        =RNDX(laDbfList(lnDbfCnt,1))
        USE
      ENDFOR
    ENDIF
  ENDIF
ELSE
  CLEAR READ
  IF llIndexed
    DO opendbf IN main.mpr
  ENDIF
ENDIF
*============================================================
*  Text: Select:
*============================================================
 @   0,   1
************************************************************
*--  SCREEN CLEANUP CODE
************************************************************
FUNCTION RNDX
PARAMETER lcDBF
lcDBF = StripExt(lcDBF)
IF OpenDB('EXCLUSIVE',lcDbf,"RndxDBF")
*   USE (lcDBF) IN SELECT(1) ALIAS RndxDBF EXCLUSIVE
   SELECT RndxDBF
   DELETE TAG ALL                              && Remove the CDX
   IF FILE("DATADICT.DBF")                     && If DD exists, do it
      USE DataDict IN SELECT(1)
      SELECT DataDict
      SCAN FOR (DBF_NAME = lcDBF) .AND. (Datadict.lIndex)
         SELECT RndxDBF
         lcTempDesc = Datadict.cTag
         IF EMPTY(Datadict.Index_key)          && Structural
            STORE Datadict.Field_Name TO lcTempTag, lcTempFld
         ELSE                                  && Ad-Hoc
            lcTempFld = Datadict.Index_key
            lcTempTag = Datadict.Field_Name
         ENDIF
         WAIT WINDOW NOWAIT "Indexing field " +lcTempDesc +" of " +lcDBF
         INDEX ON &lcTempFld TAG &lcTempTag
```

```
      ENDSCAN
      USE
   ELSE        && No data dictionary, so INVERT database
      SELECT RndxDBF
      lnNumFields = FCOUNT("RndxDBF")
      PRIVATE lnFldCnt
      FOR lnFldCnt = 1 TO lnNumFields
         lcTempFld = FIELD(lnFldCnt,"RndxDBF")
         IF TYPE(lcTempFld) # "M"
            WAIT WINDOW NOWAIT "Indexing field " +lcTempFld +" of " +lcDBF
            INDEX ON &lcTempFld TAG &lcTempFld
         ENDIF
      ENDFOR
   ENDIF
   SELECT RndxDBF
   IF SET("DELETED") = "ON" AND NOT ISTAG("DelRec")
      INDEX ON DELETED() TAG DelRec
   ENDIF
   USE
ELSE
   DO Alert.spr WITH "File used by another. Cannot reindex"
ENDIF
WAIT CLEAR
RETURN .T.
*-------------------------------------------------------------
*************************************************************
**--    DBFREIND.SCX - MAC PLATFORM
*************************************************************
```

```
 ( ) DeskTop                            (·) Window

 Name:                                  <Type...>
 Title:  Rebuild Indexes
 Footer:

 Size:             Screen Code:

 Height:   13.636   [X] Setup...
 Width:    57.000   [X] Cleanup & Procs...              «   OK   »

 Position:         READ Clauses:                       < Cancel >

 Row:        0.000  [ ] Activate...    [ ] Show...
 Column:     0.000  [ ] Valid...       [ ] When...
 [X] Center         [ ] Deactivate...

 Environment:                          [X] Add alias

        Environment NOT saved with screen.
```

```
 Type:      Dialog

 Attributes:         Border:

  [ ] Close         ( ) None
  [X] Float         ( ) Single
  [X] Shadow        (·) Double      «   OK   »
  [ ] Minimize      ( ) Panel
                    ( ) System      < Cancel >

 Color Schemes:

  Primary:          Popup:

MAC       RGB Fill Color Scheme: (,,)
MAC       Font: monaco,   9
 Screen Setup code above
***********************************************************
*--   G E T   O B J E C T S
***********************************************************
*==========================================================
*  lnIndxThis
*==========================================================
 @   1.364,   1.167
     SIZE  11.818,  36.000

 List Type:                                Options:

  (·) From Array        laDbfList          [ ] When...       [ ] Comment...
  ( ) From Popup                           [ ] Valid...      [ ] Disabled
  ( ) Prompt Structure                     [ ] Message...    [ ] 1st Element...
  ( ) Prompt Field                         [ ] Terminating  [X] # Elements...
  ( ) Prompt Files

 Variable:

  < Choose... > lnIndxThis                      «   OK   »   < Cancel >

MAC       RGB Color Scheme: (,,,,,)
MAC       Font: monaco,   9
 # Elements code above
*==========================================================
*  m.llAll
*==========================================================
 @   1.727,  41.000
     SIZE   1.417,  13.167
```

```
 ┌──────────────────────────────────────────────────────────┐
 │                                                          │
 │  Check Box Prompt:                                       │
 │  All Tables                                              │
 │                                                          │
 │  Variable:                              «   OK   »       │
 │  ┌──────────────────────────────────┐                    │
 │  │ < Choose... > m.llAll            │   < Cancel >       │
 │  └──────────────────────────────────┘                    │
 │                                                          │
 │  [ ] When...     [ ] Comment...                          │
 │  [X] Valid...    [ ] Disabled                            │
 │  [ ] Message...  [ ] Initially checked                   │
 │                                                          │
 └──────────────────────────────────────────────────────────┘
MAC      RGB Color Scheme: (,,,,,)
MAC      Font: Geneva,   9
        Style: Bold Transparent
 Valid code above
*=============================================================
*  m.lhIndex
*=============================================================
 @   6.545,  40.000
     SIZE   1.917,  15.000
 Spacing:    1
 ┌──────────────────────────────────────────────────────────────────┐
 │                                                                  │
 │  Push Button Prompts:    ┌──────────────────────────────────┐    │
 │                          │ ( ) Horizontal   (·) Vertical    │    │
 │  ┌──────────────────┐    │ [ ] Terminating  <Spacing...>    │    │
 │  │\!Index           │    └──────────────────────────────────┘    │
 │  │\?Cancel          │    Variable:                               │
 │  │                  │    ┌──────────────────────────────────┐    │
 │  │                  │    │ < Choose... >  m.lhIndex         │    │
 │  │                  │    └──────────────────────────────────┘    │
 │  │                  │    Options:                                │
 │  │                  │    ┌──────────────────────────────────┐    │
 │  │                  │    │ [ ] When...     [ ] Comment...   │    │
 │  │                  │    │ [X] Valid...    [ ] Disabled     │    │
 │  │                  │    │ [ ] Message...                   │    │
 │  └──────────────────┘    └──────────────────────────────────┘    │
 │                                                                  │
 │               «   OK   »    < Cancel >                           │
 │                                                                  │
 └──────────────────────────────────────────────────────────────────┘
MAC      RGB Color Scheme: (,,,,,)
MAC      Font: Geneva,   9
        Style: Bold
 Valid code above
*=============================================================
*  Text: Select:
*=============================================================
 @   0.000,   1.000
MAC      RGB Color Scheme: (,,,,,)
MAC      Font: Monaco,   9
        Style: Bold
 Screen Cleanup and Procedures code above
*-------------------------------------------------------------
```

```
************************************************************
**--    DBFREIND.SCX - WINDOWS PLATFORM
************************************************************

( ) DeskTop                          (·) Window

Name:                                <Type...>
Title:  Rebuild Indexes
Footer:

Size:              Screen Code:

 Height:   13.667   [X] Setup...
 Width:    57.000   [X] Cleanup & Procs...          «   OK   »

Position:          READ Clauses:                    < Cancel >

 Row:        0.000  [ ] Activate...   [ ] Show...
 Column:     0.000  [ ] Valid...      [ ] When...
 [X] Center         [ ] Deactivate...

Environment:                            [X] Add alias

      Environment NOT saved with screen.


 Type:      Dialog

 Attributes:      Border:

  [ ] Close        ( ) None
  [X] Float        ( ) Single
  [X] Shadow       (·) Double      «   OK   »
  [ ] Minimize     ( ) Panel
                   ( ) System      < Cancel >

 Color Schemes:

  Primary:         Popup:


WINDOWS  RGB Fill Color Scheme: (,,)
WINDOWS  Font: Terminal,   9
 Screen Setup code above
************************************************************
*--   G E T   O B J E C T S
************************************************************
*===========================================================
*  lnIndxThis
*===========================================================
 @   1.333,   1.125
     SIZE  11.667,  32.875
```

```
List Type:                                    Options:
 ┌──────────────────────────────────────┐  ┌──────────────────────────────────────┐
 │ (·) From Array         laDbfList     │  │ [ ] When...        [ ] Comment...    │
 │ ( ) From Popup                       │  │ [ ] Valid...       [ ] Disabled      │
 │ ( ) Prompt Structure                 │  │ [ ] Message...     [ ] 1st Element...│
 │ ( ) Prompt Field                     │  │ [ ] Terminating    [X] # Elements... │
 │ ( ) Prompt Files                     │  └──────────────────────────────────────┘
 └──────────────────────────────────────┘

Variable:
 ┌──────────────────────────────────────┐
 │ < Choose... > lnIndxThis             │      «   OK   »     < Cancel >
 └──────────────────────────────────────┘
```

```
WINDOWS  RGB Color Scheme: (,,,,,)
WINDOWS  Font: Terminal,   9
 # Elements code above
*===========================================================
*  m.llAll
*===========================================================
 @   3.167,  38.000
     SIZE   1.417,  12.875
```

```
Check Box Prompt:
All Tables

Variable:                                       «   OK   »
 ┌──────────────────────────────────────────┐
 │ < Choose... > m.llAll                    │  < Cancel >
 └──────────────────────────────────────────┘

[ ] When...     [ ] Comment...
[X] Valid...    [ ] Disabled
[ ] Message...  [ ] Initially checked
```

```
WINDOWS  RGB Color Scheme: (,,,,,)
WINDOWS  Font: Terminal,   9
 Valid code above
*===========================================================
*  m.lhIndex
*===========================================================
 @   6.083,  39.000
     SIZE   1.923,  15.000
 Spacing:    1
```

```
 Push Button Prompts:          ( ) Horizontal    (·) Vertical
                               [ ] Terminating  <Spacing...>
  \!Index
  \?Cancel                    Variable:

                               < Choose... >  m.lhIndex

                              Options:

                               [ ] When...       [ ] Comment...
                               [X] Valid...      [ ] Disabled
                               [ ] Message...

                  «  OK  »    < Cancel >
WINDOWS  RGB Color Scheme: (,,,,,)
WINDOWS  Font: MS Sans Serif,   8
        Style: Bold
 Valid code above
*==============================================================
*  Text: Select:
*==============================================================
 @   0.000,    1.000
WINDOWS  RGB Color Scheme: (,,,,,)
WINDOWS  Font: Terminal,    9
 Screen Cleanup and Procedures code above
```

Prototyping without a Data Dictionary

In order to decide whether or not to use a data dictionary, the DBFREIND screen uses the FILE() function to see if a file called DATADICT.DBF exists. If it does not, it uses an ADIR() function to load all of the database files in the directory into the scrolling list. Once the files to be reindexed are selected (each file name is stored in RndxDBF), DBFREIND creates an index on every non-memo field by performing the following loop:

```
SELECT RndxDBF
 lnNumFields = FCOUNT("RndxDBF")
 FOR i = 1 TO lnNumFields
   lcTempFld = FIELD(i,"RndxDBF")
   IF TYPE(lcTempFld) # "M"
     WAIT WINDOW NOWAIT "Indexing field " +lcTempFld +" of " +lcDBF
     INDEX ON &lcTempFld TAG &lcTempFld
   ENDIF
 ENDFOR
```

The loop SELECTs the database that is to be reindexed and counts the number of fields in that database. It then goes through each field, and if the field is not of memo TYPE(), the routine flashes a message to the user, stating which field is being indexed, and INDEXes the field.

Using a Data Dictionary

If the FILE("DATADICT.DBF") function returns a true, the data dictionary file exists. DBFREIND then uses a SQL SELECT statement in order to fill the scrolling list. Once the file to be reindexed (DBFReind) has been selected, it performs the following routine:

```
USE DataDict in SELECT(1)
SELECT DataDict
SCAN FOR (DBF_NAME = lcDBF) .AND. (Datadict.lIndex)
  SELECT RndxDBF
  lcTempDesc = Datadict.cTag
  IF EMPTY(Datadict.Index_key)           && Structural
    STORE Datadict.Field_Name to lcTempTag, lcTempFld
  ELSE                                   && Ad-Hoc
    lcTempFld = Datadict.Index_key
    lcTempTag = Datadict.Field_Name
  ENDIF
  WAIT WINDOW NOWAIT "Indexing field " +lcTempDesc +" of " +lcDBF
  INDEX ON &lcTempFld TAG &lcTempTag
ENDSCAN
USE
```

The routine USEs the data dictionary and sets a filter so that only the TAGs to be created for the selected database are available to the routine. It then loops through the data dictionary, checking if there is an ad-hoc tag listed for the database. If an ad-hoc index is required, it stores the KEY and TAG of that index and uses those to create the index. If the index to be created is structural, the index KEY and TAG are the same. Finally, it places a message window on the screen that tells the user what is happening while the indexing takes place. This message uses the data dictionary to provide the user with a complete English description of the process.

Deletion Confirmation Dialog: DELREC.SCX

DelRec() is another of our platform-appropriate message dialogs.

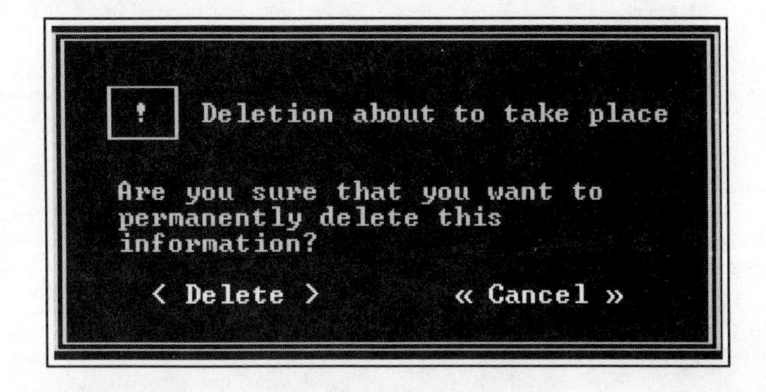

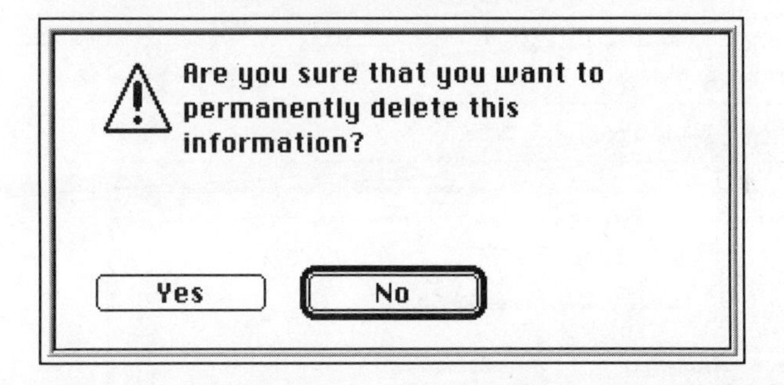

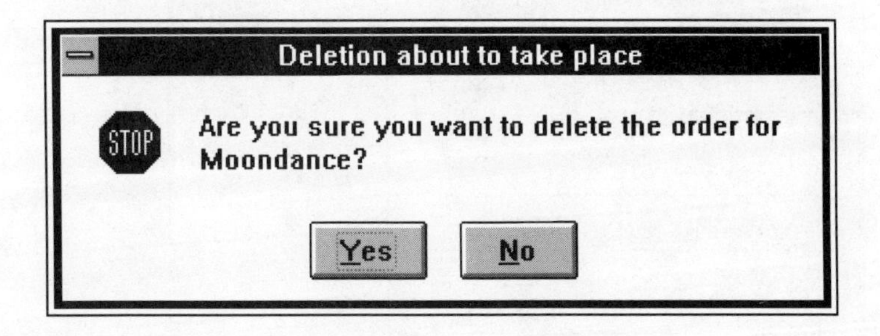

```
*-----------------------------------------------------------
************************************************************
**--    DELREC.SCX - DOS PLATFORM
************************************************************
```

```
( ) DeskTop                          (·) Window

Name:   wmDelRec                     <Type...>
Title:
Footer:

Size:              Screen Code:
 Height:   13       [X] Setup...
 Width:    40       [X] Cleanup & Procs...           «   OK   »

Position:          READ Clauses:                     < Cancel >
 Row:       0       [ ] Activate...    [ ] Show...
 Column:    0       [ ] Valid...       [ ] When...
 [X] Center         [ ] Deactivate...

Environment:                             [X] Add alias
       Environment NOT saved with screen.
```

```
 Type:        Alert

 Attributes:        Border:
  [ ] Close          ( ) None
  [X] Float          ( ) Single
  [ ] Shadow         (·) Double       «   OK   »
  [ ] Minimize       ( ) Panel
                     ( ) System       < Cancel >

 Color Schemes:
  Primary:          Popup:
   Alerts            Alert Pops
```

```
************************************************************
*  SCREEN SETUP CODE
************************************************************
#SECTION 1
PARAMETER lcMessage
#SECTION 2
IF EMPTY(lcMessage)
  lcMessage = ;
       "Are you sure that you want to permanently delete this information?"
ENDIF
DO CASE
```

```
   CASE _Windows
      PRIVATE lnRetVal
      lnRetVal=msgbox(lcMessage,"Deletion about to take place",20)
      RETURN IIF(lnRetVal=6,.T.,.F.)
   CASE _MAC
      PRIVATE lnRetVal
      lnRetVal = fxAlert(0,266,-1,-1,lcMessage)
      RETURN IIF(lnRetVal=2,.T.,.F.)
ENDCASE
PRIVATE llRetVal
llRetVal = .F.
************************************************************
*--   G E T   O B J E C T S
************************************************************
*==========================================================
*  Box
*==========================================================
 @   1,   2
 SIZE   3,   5
*==========================================================
*  Text: !
*==========================================================
 @   2,   4
*==========================================================
*  Text: Deletion about to take place
*==========================================================
 @   2,   8
*==========================================================
*
*==========================================================
 @   5,   3
```

```
  Field:
  ┌──────────────────────────────────────────┐
  │ (·) Say        ( ) Get        ( ) Edit   │
  └──────────────────────────────────────────┘

  <  Say...   > lcMessage
                                                  «   OK   »
  < Format... > @I
                                                  < Cancel >
  Range:
  ┌──────────────────────────────────────────┐
  │ [ ] Upper...              [ ] Lower...   │
  └──────────────────────────────────────────┘

  [ ] When...      [ ] Error...      [ ] Scroll bar
  [ ] Valid...     [ ] Comment...    [ ] Allow tabs
  [ ] Message...   [ ] Disabled      [ ] Refresh
```

```
*==========================================================
*  lhCancel
*==========================================================
 @   9,  23
 Spacing:    1
```

```
Push Button Prompts:        (·) Horizontal    ( ) Vertical
                            [X] Terminating   <Spacing...>
\!\?Cancel
                            Variable:

                            < Choose... >   lhCancel

                            Options:

                            [ ] When...      [ ] Comment...
                            [ ] Valid...     [ ] Disabled
                            [ ] Message...

              «  OK  »    < Cancel >
```

```
*===============================================================
*  lhDelete
*===============================================================
 @   9,   5
 Spacing:    1
```

```
Push Button Prompts:        (·) Horizontal    ( ) Vertical
                            [X] Terminating   <Spacing...>
Delete
                            Variable:

                            < Choose... >   lhDelete

                            Options:

                            [ ] When...      [ ] Comment...
                            [X] Valid...     [ ] Disabled
                            [ ] Message...

              «  OK  »    < Cancel >
```

```
----------------------------------------------------------------
*-- lhDelete Valid Clause
----------------------------------------------------------------
```

```
Valid

  (·) Procedure
  ( ) Expression
```

```
llRetVal = .T.
****************************************************************
*--  SCREEN CLEANUP CODE
****************************************************************
```

```
RETURN llRetVal
*----------------------------------------------------------------
*****************************************************************
**--    DELREC.SCX - MAC PLATFORM
*****************************************************************
```

```
( ) DeskTop                          (·) Window

Name:   wmDelRec                     <Type...>
Title:
Footer:

Size:              Screen Code:

 Height:   12.923   [X] Setup...
 Width:    53.000   [X] Cleanup & Procs...          «   OK   »

Position:          READ Clauses:                    < Cancel >

 Row:       0.000   [ ] Activate...   [ ] Show...
 Column:    0.000   [ ] Valid...      [ ] When...
 [X] Center         [ ] Deactivate...

Environment:                            [X] Add alias

      Environment NOT saved with screen.
```

```
Type:        Alert

Attributes:        Border:

 [ ] Close          ( ) None
 [X] Float          ( ) Single
 [ ] Shadow         (·) Double       «   OK   »
 [ ] Minimize       ( ) Panel
                    ( ) System       < Cancel >

Color Schemes:

 Primary:          Popup:
```

```
MAC      RGB Fill Color Scheme: (,,)
MAC      Font: Geneva,  10
 Screen Setup code above
*****************************************************************
*--    G E T   O B J E C T S
*****************************************************************
*================================================================
*  Box
*================================================================
 @   1.615,   2.500
 SIZE   2.000,   4.333
```

```
MAC      RGB Color Scheme: (,,,,,)
           Pen: 1
*============================================================
*  Text: !
*============================================================
 @   2.231,   4.000
MAC      RGB Color Scheme: (,,,,,)
MAC      Font: Terminal,   9
        Style: Bold
*============================================================
*  Text: Deletion about to take place
*============================================================
 @   2.231,   8.000
MAC      RGB Color Scheme: (,,,,,)
MAC      Font: Terminal,   9
        Style: Bold
*============================================================
*
*============================================================
 @   4.538,   2.500
```

```
+----------------------------------------------------------+
|                                                          |
|  Field:                                                  |
|  +-----------------------------------------+             |
|  |  (·) Say        ( ) Get        ( ) Edit |             |
|  +-----------------------------------------+             |
|                                                          |
|  <  Say...   > lcMessage                                 |
|                                             «   OK   »   |
|  < Format... >                                           |
|                                             < Cancel >   |
|  Range:                                                  |
|  +-----------------------------------------+             |
|  |  [ ] Upper...              [ ] Lower... |             |
|  +-----------------------------------------+             |
|                                                          |
|  [ ] When...      [ ] Error...     [ ] Scroll bar        |
|  [ ] Valid...     [ ] Comment...   [ ] Allow tabs        |
|  [ ] Message...   [ ] Disabled     [ ] Refresh           |
|                                                          |
+----------------------------------------------------------+
```

```
MAC      RGB Color Scheme: (,,,,,)
MAC      Font: Terminal,   9
        Style: Bold
*============================================================
*  lhCancel
*============================================================
 @   9.615,  30.500
    SIZE  1.500,  10.000
 Spacing:    1
```

```
 ┌────────────────────────────────────────────────────────────────┐
 │ Push Button Prompts:         (·) Horizontal    ( ) Vertical    │
 │                              [X] Terminating  <Spacing...>     │
 │ \!\?Cancel                                                     │
 │                             Variable:                          │
 │                              < Choose... >  lhCancel           │
 │                             Options:                           │
 │                              [ ] When...     [ ] Comment...    │
 │                              [ ] Valid...    [ ] Disabled      │
 │                              [ ] Message...                    │
 │                                                                │
 │                 «  OK  »     < Cancel >                        │
 └────────────────────────────────────────────────────────────────┘
MAC        RGB Color Scheme: (,,,,,)
MAC        Font: Geneva,   9
         Style: Bold
*============================================================
*  lhDelete
*============================================================
 @   9.615,  12.500
     SIZE   1.500,  10.000
 Spacing:    1
 ┌────────────────────────────────────────────────────────────────┐
 │ Push Button Prompts:         (·) Horizontal    ( ) Vertical    │
 │                              [X] Terminating  <Spacing...>     │
 │ Delete                                                         │
 │                             Variable:                          │
 │                              < Choose... >  lhDelete           │
 │                             Options:                           │
 │                              [ ] When...     [ ] Comment...    │
 │                              [X] Valid...    [ ] Disabled      │
 │                              [ ] Message...                    │
 │                                                                │
 │                 «  OK  »     < Cancel >                        │
 └────────────────────────────────────────────────────────────────┘
MAC        RGB Color Scheme: (,,,,,)
MAC        Font: Geneva,   9
         Style: Bold
 Valid code above
 Screen Cleanup and Procedures code above
*------------------------------------------------------------
```

```
***************************************************************
**--    DELREC.SCX - WINDOWS PLATFORM
***************************************************************

  ( ) DeskTop                          (•) Window

  Name:   wmDelRec                     <Type...>
  Title:
  Footer:

  Size:              Screen Code:

   Height:   12.923    [X] Setup...
   Width:    53.000    [X] Cleanup & Procs...          «   OK   »

  Position:          READ Clauses:                     < Cancel >

   Row:         0.000  [ ] Activate...    [ ] Show...
   Column:      0.000  [ ] Valid...       [ ] When...
   [X] Center          [ ] Deactivate...

  Environment:                             [X] Add alias

         Environment NOT saved with screen.


   Type:     Alert

   Attributes:       Border:

    [ ] Close         ( ) None
    [X] Float         ( ) Single
    [ ] Shadow        (•) Double       «   OK   »
    [ ] Minimize      ( ) Panel
                      ( ) System       < Cancel >

   Color Schemes:

    Primary:          Popup:

WINDOWS  RGB Fill Color Scheme: (,,)
WINDOWS  Font: MS Sans Serif,    8
        Style: Bold
 Screen Setup code above
***************************************************************
*--    G E T    O B J E C T S
***************************************************************
*==============================================================
*  Box
*==============================================================
 @   1.615,    2.500
 SIZE   2.000,    4.333
```

```
WINDOWS  RGB Color Scheme: (,,,,,)
            Pen: 1
*============================================================
*  Text: !
*============================================================
 @   2.231,   4.000
WINDOWS  RGB Color Scheme: (,,,,,)
WINDOWS  Font: Terminal,   9
         Style: Bold
*============================================================
*  Text: Deletion about to take place
*============================================================
 @   2.231,   8.000
WINDOWS  RGB Color Scheme: (,,,,,)
WINDOWS  Font: Terminal,   9
         Style: Bold
*============================================================
*
*============================================================
 @   4.538,   2.500
```

```
 Field:
 ┌──────────────────────────────────────────────┐
 │ (·) Say          ( ) Get          ( ) Edit   │
 └──────────────────────────────────────────────┘

 <  Say...    > lcMessage
                                               «   OK   »
 < Format... > @I
                                               < Cancel >
 Range:
 ┌──────────────────────────────────────────────┐
 │ [ ] Upper...                   [ ] Lower...  │
 └──────────────────────────────────────────────┘

 [ ] When...       [ ] Error...       [ ] Scroll bar
 [ ] Valid...      [ ] Comment...     [ ] Allow tabs
 [ ] Message...    [ ] Disabled       [ ] Refresh
```

```
WINDOWS  RGB Color Scheme: (,,,,,)
WINDOWS  Font: Terminal,   9
         Style: Bold
*============================================================
*  lhCancel
*============================================================
 @   9.615,  30.500
    SIZE   1.769,  10.000
 Spacing:    1
```

```
Push Button Prompts:        (·) Horizontal    ( ) Vertical
                            [X] Terminating  <Spacing...>
\!\?Cancel
                            Variable:

                            < Choose... >  lhCancel

                            Options:

                            [ ] When...      [ ] Comment...
                            [ ] Valid...     [ ] Disabled
                            [ ] Message...

              «   OK   »     < Cancel >
WINDOWS  RGB Color Scheme: (,,,,,)
WINDOWS  Font: MS Sans Serif,   8
        Style: Bold
*=============================================================
*  lhDelete
*=============================================================
 @   9.615,  12.500
     SIZE   1.769,  10.000
 Spacing:    1

Push Button Prompts:        (·) Horizontal    ( ) Vertical
                            [X] Terminating  <Spacing...>
Delete
                            Variable:

                            < Choose... >  lhDelete

                            Options:

                            [ ] When...      [ ] Comment...
                            [X] Valid...     [ ] Disabled
                            [ ] Message...

              «   OK   »     < Cancel >
WINDOWS  RGB Color Scheme: (,,,,,)
WINDOWS  Font: MS Sans Serif,   8
        Style: Bold
 Valid code above
 Screen Cleanup and Procedures code above
```

Active Index Selection: GETORDER.SCX

GetOrder has not changed greatly from the original *FoxPro Codebook*. It allows the user to select a new index order at any time. If the DataDict table exists, it is used to provide the user with an English description of the tags. The GetOrder window will now, however, only use tags marked with the lShow field.

Note how this is handled. The code that is dictionary dependent now contains an IF statement:

```
IF FCOUNT("DATADICT") = 8     && Codebook 2.0 Datadict
   SELECT DataDict.cTag,DataDict.Field_name ;
     FROM DataDict ;
     WHERE TRIM(DataDict.DBF_Name) = lcAlias ;
     AND !EMPTY(DataDict.cTag) ;
     AND lIndex ;
     ORDER BY DataDict.cTag ;
   INTO ARRAY laIndxTags
 ELSE        && Codebook 2.5
   SELECT DataDict.cTag,DataDict.Field_name ;
     FROM DataDict ;
     WHERE TRIM(DataDict.DBF_Name) = lcAlias ;
     AND !EMPTY(DataDict.cTag) ;
     AND lIndex ;
     AND lShow ;
     ORDER BY DataDict.cTag ;
   INTO ARRAY laIndxTags
ENDIF
```

We use the FCOUNT() function to see how many fields exist in the DataDict table. If there are eight fields, we know that we are using the original DataDict from the original *FoxPro Codebook*. If not, we are using the newer, enhanced DataDict table, and therefore use a different SQL SELECT statement. This is a very important technique for modifying reusable objects that are data driven. It allows you to continue working with your older applications, while enhancing the newer ones. We continue to call GetOrder, but we are now able to have it work correctly in any situation.

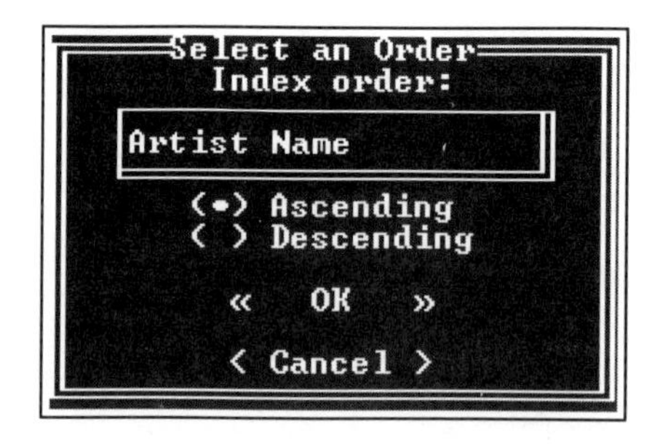
Select an Order
Index order:
Artist Name
(•) Ascending
( ) Descending
« OK »
< Cancel >

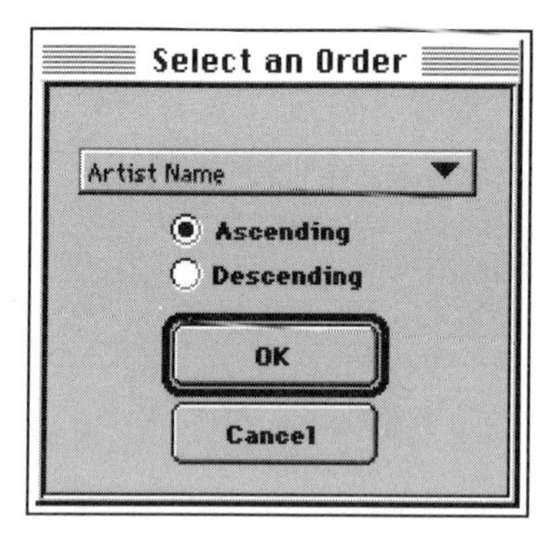
Select an Order
Artist Name
Ascending
Descending
OK
Cancel

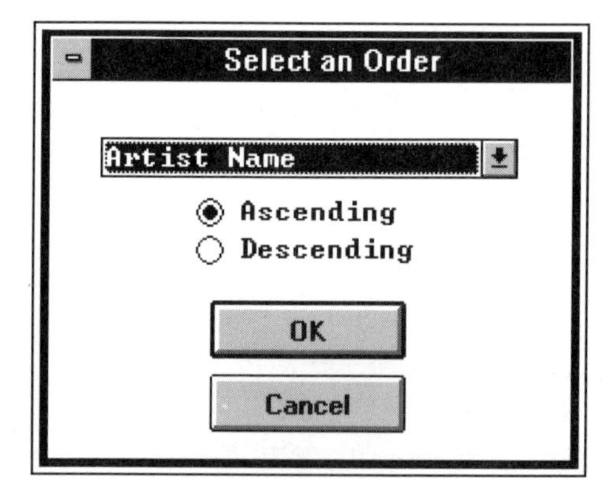
Select an Order
Artist Name
Ascending
Descending
OK
Cancel

```
*------------------------------------------------------------
*************************************************************
**--    GETORDER.SCX - DOS PLATFORM
*************************************************************
```

```
( ) DeskTop                         (·) Window

Name:                               <Type...>
Title:  Select an Order
Footer:

Size:            Screen Code:

 Height:   12     [X] Setup...
 Width:    28     [X] Cleanup & Procs...          «   OK   »

Position:        READ Clauses:                    < Cancel >

 Row:        0    [ ] Activate...    [ ] Show...
 Column:     0    [ ] Valid...       [ ] When...
 [X] Center       [ ] Deactivate...

Environment:                      [ ] Add alias

    Environment saved with this screen.
```

```
Type:      Dialog

Attributes:      Border:

 [ ] Close        ( ) None
 [X] Float        ( ) Single
 [X] Shadow       (·) Double     «   OK   »
 [ ] Minimize     ( ) Panel
                  ( ) System     < Cancel >

Color Schemes:

 Primary:         Popup:

 Dialogs          Dialog Pop
```

```
*************************************************************
*  SCREEN SETUP CODE
*************************************************************
*  Program...........: GETORDER Setup
*  Author............: Y. Alan Griver (YAG)
*  Project...........: Common
*  Created...........: 1/1/93
*  Copyright.........: (c) Flash Creative Management, 1993
*) Description.......: Allows the user to select any index order.
*)                   : If DATADICT.DBF exists, it uses that to display
*)                   : an English name for the index tags. If not,
*)                   : it uses the TAG() function to get the tag names.
```

```
*  Calling Samples...: DO GetOrder.spr
*  Parameter List....:
*  Major change list.: Menachem Bazian, CPA - March 31, 1993 - 20:13:29
*                    : Now returns the name of the index tag selected
*                    : if called as a UDF.
*                    :
*                    : yag - April 15, 1993
*                    : Added support for lShow field in Datadict
*                    : This field indicates what fields show in GETORDER
*                    : and in APPSRCH.
PRIVATE jcRetVal, lcAscDesc, lnOldTag, lcOldOrd, lcAlias
PRIVATE lnNumTags, lnTagNum
*-- CHANGE - Bill House - May 14, 1993 - 15:14:11
*-- Pre-initialized lnTagNum to zero
lnTagNum  = 0
lcAscDesc = "Ascending"
lnOldTag  = VAL(SYS(21))
lcOldOrd  = ORDER()
jcRetVal  = ""
IF FILE("DATADICT.DBF")
   lcAlias = ALIAS()
   IF !USED("Datadict")
      USE DATADICT IN SELECT(1)
   ENDIF
   IF FCOUNT("DATADICT") = 8                 && Codebook 2.0 Datadict
      SELECT DataDict.cTag,DataDict.Field_name ;
        FROM DataDict ;
        WHERE TRIM(DataDict.DBF_Name) = lcAlias ;
        AND !EMPTY(DataDict.cTag) ;
        AND lIndex ;
        ORDER BY DataDict.cTag ;
        INTO ARRAY laIndxTags
    ELSE                                               && Codebook 2.5
      SELECT DataDict.cTag,DataDict.Field_name ;
        FROM DataDict ;
        WHERE TRIM(DataDict.DBF_Name) = lcAlias ;
        AND !EMPTY(DataDict.cTag) ;
        AND lIndex ;
        AND lShow ;
        ORDER BY DataDict.cTag ;
        INTO ARRAY laIndxTags
   ENDIF
ELSE
   SET ORDER TO 0
   lnNumTags = 1
   DO WHILE "" <> TAG(lnNumTags)
      lnNumTags = lnNumTags + 1
   ENDDO
   DIMENSION laIndxTags(lnNumTags-1,1)
   i = 1
   DO WHILE i <= lnNumTags-1
      laIndxTags[i,1] = TAG(i)
      i = i + 1
   ENDDO
ENDIF
*-- CHANGE - Bill House - May 14, 1993 - 15:13:02
*-- Test for non-existent array and create dummy if not already existent
IF TYPE("laIndxTags") # "U"
   lnTagNum = ASCAN(laIndxTags,lcOldOrd)
```

```
ELSE
   ?? CHR(7)                                    && No TAGs available so quit
   WAIT WINDOW "No index available. No order can be set. Press any key..."
   RETURN jcRetVal
ENDIF
IF lnTagNum # 0
   lnTagNum = ASUBSCRIPT(laIndxTags,lnTagNum,1)
ENDIF

*************************************************************
*--    G E T    O B J E C T S
*************************************************************
*============================================================
*  Text: Index order:
*============================================================
 @   0,   7
*============================================================
*  lnTagNum
*============================================================
 @   1,   2
```

```
( ) List Popup              (·) Array Popup  laindxtags

                            Variable:
                            < Choose... > lnTagNum

                            Options:
                              [ ] When...      [ ] Comment...
                              [ ] Valid...     [ ] Disabled
                              [X] Message...   [ ] 1st Element...
                                               [ ] # Elements...

Initial:                       «  OK  »     < Cancel >
```

```
-------------------------------------------------------------
*-- lnTagNum Message Clause
-------------------------------------------------------------
```

```
Message
  ( ) Procedure
  (·) Expression
```

```
Message:   "Select the view order for the current data"
*============================================================
*  lcAscDesc
*============================================================
 @   4,   6
 Spacing:    0
```

```
Radio Button Prompts:              ( ) Horizontal   (·) Vertical
Ascending
Descending                         Variable:

                                   < Choose... > lcAscDesc

                                   Options:

                                   [ ] When...      [ ] Comment...
                                   [ ] Valid...     [ ] Disabled
                                   [ ] Message...

Initial:  Ascending                 «  OK  »    < Cancel >

*============================================================
*  lhOK
*============================================================
 @   7,   8
 Spacing:    1

Push Button Prompts:               ( ) Horizontal   (·) Vertical
                                   [X] Terminating  <Spacing...>
\!OK
                                   Variable:

                                   < Choose... >  lhOK

                                   Options:

                                   [ ] When...      [ ] Comment...
                                   [X] Valid...     [ ] Disabled
                                   [X] Message...

                    «  OK  »    < Cancel >

------------------------------------------------------------
*-- lhOK Valid Clause
------------------------------------------------------------

Valid

 (·) Procedure
 ( ) Expression

IF FILE("DATADICT.DBF")
  lcNewOrd = laIndxTags[lnTagNum,2]+" "+lcAscDesc
  jcRetVal = laIndxTags[lnTagNum,1]+" - "+IIF(lcAscDesc = 'Asc',"","")
ELSE
```

```
  lcNewOrd = TAG(lnTagNum)+" "+lcAscDesc
  jcRetVal = lcNewOrd
ENDIF
SET ORDER TO &lcNewOrd
------------------------------------------------------------
*-- lhOK Message Clause
------------------------------------------------------------
```

```
Message
  ( ) Procedure
  (·) Expression
```

```
Message:   "Select the above view order"
*============================================================
* lhCancel
*============================================================
 @   9,   8
 Spacing:    1
```

```
Push Button Prompts:      ( ) Horizontal    (·) Vertical
                          [X] Terminating  <Spacing...>
\?Cancel
                          Variable:
                          < Choose... >  lhCancel
                          Options:
                          [ ] When...     [ ] Comment...
                          [X] Valid...    [ ] Disabled
                          [X] Message...

          «   OK   »     < Cancel >
```

```
------------------------------------------------------------
*-- lhCancel Valid Clause
------------------------------------------------------------
```

```
Valid
  (·) Procedure
  ( ) Expression
```

```
SET ORDER TO TAG(lnOldTag)
------------------------------------------------------------
*-- lhCancel Message Clause
------------------------------------------------------------
```

```
Message

( ) Procedure
(·) Expression

Message:   "Do NOT change the view order"
*************************************************************
*--  SCREEN CLEANUP CODE
*************************************************************
RETURN jcRetVal
*-----------------------------------------------------------
*************************************************************
**--    GETORDER.SCX - MAC PLATFORM
*************************************************************

( ) DeskTop                          (·) Window

Name:                                <Type...>
Title:  Select an Order
Footer:

Size:                Screen Code:

Height:   14.000     [X] Setup...
Width:    30.000     [X] Cleanup & Procs...              «   OK   »

Position:            READ Clauses:                       < Cancel >

Row:        0.000    [ ] Activate...    [ ] Show...
Column:     0.000    [ ] Valid...       [ ] When...
[X] Center           [ ] Deactivate...

Environment:                         [ ] Add alias

        Environment saved with this screen.
```

```
Type:      Dialog

Attributes:         Border:

 [ ] Close          ( ) None
 [X] Float          ( ) Single
 [X] Shadow         (·) Double      «  OK  »
 [ ] Minimize       ( ) Panel
                    ( ) System      < Cancel >

Color Schemes:

 Primary:           Popup:

MAC        RGB Fill Color Scheme: (,,)
MAC        Font: monaco,      9
 Screen Setup code above
*************************************************************
*--    G E T    O B J E C T S
*************************************************************
*============================================================
*  lnTagNum
*============================================================
 @    2.091,    2.000
      SIZE    1.500,   31.200

 ( ) List Popup              (·) Array Popup  laindxtags

                             Variable:

                              < Choose... > lnTagNum

                             Options:

                              [ ] When...       [ ] Comment...
                              [ ] Valid...      [ ] Disabled
                              [X] Message...    [ ] 1st Element...
                                                [ ] # Elements...

 Initial:                      «  OK  »     < Cancel >

MAC        RGB Color Scheme: (,,,,,)
MAC        Font: Geneva,    9
 Message code above
*============================================================
*  lcAscDesc
*============================================================
 @    4.182,    8.000
      SIZE    1.417,   13.333
 Spacing:     0
```

```
  Radio Button Prompts:          ( ) Horizontal   (·) Vertical
  Ascending
  Descending                     Variable:
                                 < Choose... > lcAscDesc
                                 Options:
                                 [ ] When...      [ ] Comment...
                                 [ ] Valid...     [ ] Disabled
                                 [ ] Message...

  Initial: Ascending                « OK »    < Cancel >

MAC       RGB Color Scheme: (,,,,,)
MAC       Font: Geneva,   9
         Style: Bold Transparent
*============================================================
*  lhOK
*============================================================
 @   8.182,   8.167
     SIZE   2.000,  13.500
 Spacing:    1

  Push Button Prompts:           ( ) Horizontal   (·) Vertical
                                 [X] Terminating  <Spacing...>
  \!OK
                                 Variable:
                                 < Choose... >  lhOK
                                 Options:
                                 [ ] When...      [ ] Comment...
                                 [X] Valid...     [ ] Disabled
                                 [X] Message...

                       « OK »    < Cancel >

MAC       RGB Color Scheme: (,,,,,)
MAC       Font: Geneva,   9
         Style: Bold
 Valid code above
 Message code above
*============================================================
*  lhCancel
*============================================================
 @  10.909,   8.167
     SIZE   2.000,  13.500
 Spacing:    1
```

```
 ╔═══════════════════════════════════════════════════════════════╗
 ║ Push Button Prompts:     ( ) Horizontal    (·) Vertical       ║
 ║                          [X] Terminating   <Spacing...>       ║
 ║ \?Cancel                                                      ║
 ║                          Variable:                            ║
 ║                                                               ║
 ║                          < Choose... >  lhCancel              ║
 ║                                                               ║
 ║                          Options:                             ║
 ║                                                               ║
 ║                          [ ] When...     [ ] Comment...       ║
 ║                          [X] Valid...    [ ] Disabled         ║
 ║                          [X] Message...                       ║
 ║                                                               ║
 ║              «    OK    »    < Cancel >                       ║
 ╚═══════════════════════════════════════════════════════════════╝
MAC      RGB Color Scheme: (,,,,,)
MAC      Font: Geneva,    9
        Style: Bold
 Valid code above
 Message code above
 Screen Cleanup and Procedures code above
*------------------------------------------------------------
************************************************************
**--    GETORDER.SCX - WINDOWS PLATFORM
************************************************************
 ╔═══════════════════════════════════════════════════════════════════╗
 ║ ( ) DeskTop                        (·) Window                     ║
 ║                                                                   ║
 ║ Name:                              <Type...>                      ║
 ║ Title:  Select an Order                                           ║
 ║ Footer:                                                           ║
 ║                                                                   ║
 ║ Size:              Screen Code:                                   ║
 ║                                                                   ║
 ║  Height:   14.000   [X] Setup...                                  ║
 ║  Width:    30.000   [X] Cleanup & Procs...          «   OK   »    ║
 ║                                                                   ║
 ║ Position:          READ Clauses:                    < Cancel >    ║
 ║                                                                   ║
 ║  Row:       0.000   [ ] Activate...    [ ] Show...                ║
 ║  Column:    0.000   [ ] Valid...       [ ] When...                ║
 ║  [X] Center         [ ] Deactivate...                             ║
 ║                                                                   ║
 ║ Environment:                      [ ] Add alias                   ║
 ║                                                                   ║
 ║      Environment saved with this screen.                          ║
 ╚═══════════════════════════════════════════════════════════════════╝
```

```
Type:  Dialog

Attributes:        Border:

[ ] Close          ( ) None
[X] Float          ( ) Single
[X] Shadow         (·) Double      «  OK  »
[ ] Minimize       ( ) Panel
                   ( ) System      < Cancel >

Color Schemes:

Primary:           Popup:

WINDOWS  RGB Fill Color Scheme: (,,)
WINDOWS  Font: Terminal,   9
 Screen Setup code above
***********************************************************
*--    G E T    O B J E C T S
***********************************************************
*==========================================================
*  lnTagNum
*==========================================================
 @   2.083,   3.000
     SIZE   1.500,  24.000

( ) List Popup          (·) Array Popup  laindxtags

                        Variable:

                        < Choose... > lnTagNum

                        Options:

                        [ ] When...      [ ] Comment...
                        [ ] Valid...     [ ] Disabled
                        [X] Message...   [ ] 1st Element...
                                         [ ] # Elements...

Initial:                   «  OK  »   < Cancel >

WINDOWS  RGB Color Scheme: (,,,,,)
WINDOWS  Font: Terminal,   9
 Message code above
*==========================================================
*  lcAscDesc
*==========================================================
 @   4.167,   8.500
     SIZE   1.417,  12.875
```

```
 Spacing:    0
┌─────────────────────────────────────────────────────────────┐
│ Radio Button Prompts:         ( ) Horizontal    (·) Vertical │
│  Ascending                                                   │
│  Descending                   Variable:                      │
│                               < Choose... > lcAscDesc        │
│                               Options:                       │
│                               [ ] When...     [ ] Comment... │
│                               [ ] Valid...    [ ] Disabled   │ \
│                               [ ] Message...                 │
│                                                              │
│ Initial: Ascending            «   OK   »     < Cancel >      │
└─────────────────────────────────────────────────────────────┘
WINDOWS  RGB Color Scheme: (,,,,,)
WINDOWS  Font: Terminal,   9
*==========================================================
*  lhOK
*==========================================================
 @   8.167,   9.375
     SIZE   2.000,  15.000
 Spacing:    1
┌─────────────────────────────────────────────────────────────┐
│ Push Button Prompts:          ( ) Horizontal    (·) Vertical │
│                               [X] Terminating  <Spacing...>  │
│  \!OK                                                        │
│                               Variable:                      │
│                               < Choose... >  lhOK            │
│                               Options:                       │
│                               [ ] When...     [ ] Comment... │
│                               [X] Valid...    [ ] Disabled   │
│                               [X] Message...                 │
│                                                              │
│               «   OK   »    < Cancel >                       │
└─────────────────────────────────────────────────────────────┘
WINDOWS  RGB Color Scheme: (,,,,,)
WINDOWS  Font: MS Sans Serif,   8
        Style: Bold
 Valid code above
 Message code above
*==========================================================
*  lhCancel
*==========================================================
 @  10.917,   9.375
     SIZE   2.000,  15.000
 Spacing:    1
```

```
 Push Button Prompts:        ( ) Horizontal    (·) Vertical
                             [X] Terminating  <Spacing...>
 \?Cancel
                            Variable:

                             < Choose... >  lhCancel

                            Options:

                             [ ] When...      [ ] Comment...
                             [X] Valid...     [ ] Disabled
                             [X] Message...

              «   OK   »     < Cancel >
```

```
WINDOWS  RGB Color Scheme: (,,,,,)
WINDOWS  Font: MS Sans Serif,   8
        Style: Bold
 Valid code above
 Message code above
 Screen Cleanup and Procedures code above
```

Toolbar: MCONTROL.SCX

The toolbar created in Mcontrol is another excellent example of how a screen can perform the same function in multiple environments, and yet perform appropriately for each of them. Under DOS this window takes the form of a floating control panel, and under Windows and Macintosh it automatically becomes a toolbar that is fixed to a position just under the menu, as in many Windows or Macintosh applications.

This capability is accomplished by transporting the window from DOS to Windows or Macintosh, and changing the prompts from text prompts to graphical bitmaps. We use a standard bitmap size of 36 pixels by 36 pixels, with the graphic taking up to the top 22 pixels, and the text starting from the 24th pixel down. This allows us to provide both text and graphics on a bitmap, providing an understandable toolbar for everyone. Due to a bug in the first shipping version of FoxPro/Mac, the button bitmaps are created as two color black and white buttons. FoxPro/Mac will dim two color graphical buttons appropriately with a SHOW GET ... DISABLE command, but will incorrectly dim any other type of graphic.

The Setup code for this window contains an underdocumented transporter directive:

```
#TRAN SNIPPET ONLY
```

This directive tells FoxPro to only transport the window (header) snippet information, and not the rest of the information (including the window type, etc.). In this manner, we can transport this window even though we are using a different window type for each platform (DOS has a border, Windows and Macintosh do not).

In the graphical version of the toolbar, we add a single pixel line to the bottom of the window. This will provide definition, and separate the toolbar from the main application window area.

Finally, note that we have to do two other graphic platform specific pieces of code to enable the toolbar to work properly under Windows or the Macintosh. In the READ WHEN snippet, we issue the commands:

```
show get lhOops,1 ;
    prompt "\? Cancel1.BMP"
show get lhClose,1 ;
    prompt "\? Close1.BMP"
```

This code redraws our bitmaps for these buttons, and allows us to add in the "\?" necessary to map them to the escape key. FoxPro's tools do not allow us to assign these special characters to picture buttons, so we do that ourselves.

Additionally, the WHEN snippet of every tool has the following expression:

```
((_WINDOWS OR _MAC) AND MDOWN()) OR _DOS
```

This causes the tool to be available only by mouse-click in the Windows and Macintosh environments.

```
*-------------------------------------------------------------
**************************************************************
**--     MCONTROL.SCX - DOS PLATFORM
**************************************************************
```

```
( ) DeskTop                         (•) Window

Name:   WCMCONTROL                  <Type...>
Title:
Footer:

Size:              Screen Code:

 Height:     4     [X] Setup...
 Width:     72     [ ] Cleanup & Procs...          «   OK   »

Position:          READ Clauses:                   < Cancel >

 Row:       22     [ ] Activate...    [ ] Show...
 Column:     2     [ ] Valid...       [X] When...
 [X] Center        [ ] Deactivate...

Environment:                        [ ] Add alias

       Environment NOT saved with screen.
```

```
 Type:    [      User      ]

 Attributes:       Border:

  [ ] Close         ( ) None
  [X] Float         ( ) Single
  [ ] Shadow        ( ) Double      «   OK   »
  [ ] Minimize      ( ) Panel
                    (·) System      < Cancel >

 Color Schemes:

  Primary:          Popup:

  [Windows    ]     [Window Pop]
```

```
***********************************************************
*  SCREEN SETUP CODE
***********************************************************
*  Program...........: MCONTROL Screen
*  Author............: yag
*  Project...........: COMMON
*  Created...........: 04/16/93
*  Copyright.........: (c) Flash Creative Management, 1993
*) Description.......: Standard push buttons
*)                   : Meant to be added to "wr" screen sets
*  Calling Samples...:
*  Parameter List....:
*  Major change list.:
#TRAN SNIPPET ONLY
REGIONAL m.lhLastBtn
PRIVATE glQuitting
STORE SPACE(6) TO m.lhLastBtn
glQuitting = .F.
-----------------------------------------------------------
*-- READ When Clause
-----------------------------------------------------------
```

```
 READ When

  (·) Procedure
  ( ) Expression
```

```
DO CASE
CASE _WINDOWS       && Have to add \? to picture
   show get lhOops,1 ;
      prompt "\? Cancel1.BMP"
   show get lhClose,1 ;
      prompt "\? Close1.BMP"
ENDCASE
DO dimnavigat
*-- I'd like to have the above work for MAC also
```

```
*-- but FP/Mac doesn't find BMPs in an APP for some reason
**************************************************************
*--    G E T    O B J E C T S
**************************************************************
*=============================================================
*  m.lhAdd
*=============================================================
 @   0,   1
 Spacing:    2

 Push Button Prompts:      (·) Horizontal    ( ) Vertical
                           [ ] Terminating  <Spacing...>
 Add
                          Variable:

                           < Choose... >  m.lhAdd

                          Options:

                           [X] When...     [ ] Comment...
                           [X] Valid...    [ ] Disabled
                           [X] Message...

            «   OK   »    < Cancel >
-------------------------------------------------------------
*-- m.lhAdd When Clause
-------------------------------------------------------------

 When

   ( ) Procedure
   (·) Expression

When:   ((_WINDOWS OR _MAC) AND MDOWN()) OR _DOS
-------------------------------------------------------------
*-- m.lhAdd Valid Clause
-------------------------------------------------------------

 Valid

   (·) Procedure
   ( ) Expression

DO controlprc WITH "Add"
-------------------------------------------------------------
*-- m.lhAdd Message Clause
-------------------------------------------------------------
```

```
Message

  ( ) Procedure
  (·) Expression

Message:   "Add new information to the file"
*===========================================================
*  m.lhEdit
*===========================================================
 @   0,  13
 Spacing:    2

 Push Button Prompts:       (·) Horizontal    ( ) Vertical
                            [ ] Terminating  <Spacing...>
  Edit
                           Variable:

                            < Choose... >  m.lhEdit

                           Options:

                            [X] When...     [ ] Comment...
                            [X] Valid...    [ ] Disabled
                            [X] Message...

              «   OK   »    < Cancel >
-----------------------------------------------------------
*-- m.lhEdit When Clause
-----------------------------------------------------------

When

  ( ) Procedure
  (·) Expression

When:   ((_WINDOWS OR _MAC) AND MDOWN()) OR _DOS
-----------------------------------------------------------
*-- m.lhEdit Valid Clause
-----------------------------------------------------------

Valid

  (·) Procedure
  ( ) Expression

DO controlprc WITH "Edit"
```

```
------------------------------------------------------------
*-- m.lhEdit Message Clause
------------------------------------------------------------

  Message

   ( ) Procedure
   (•) Expression

Message:   "Enable editing of the current information"
*===========================================================
*  m.lhSave
*===========================================================
 @   0,  25
 Spacing:    2

  Push Button Prompts:      (•) Horizontal   ( ) Vertical
                            [ ] Terminating  <Spacing...>
   Save
                          Variable:

                            < Choose... >  m.lhSave

                          Options:

                            [X] When...     [ ] Comment...
                            [X] Valid...    [ ] Disabled
                            [X] Message...

                  «   OK   »    < Cancel >

------------------------------------------------------------
*-- m.lhSave When Clause
------------------------------------------------------------

  When

   ( ) Procedure
   (•) Expression

When:   ((_WINDOWS OR _MAC) AND MDOWN()) OR _DOS
------------------------------------------------------------
*-- m.lhSave Valid Clause
------------------------------------------------------------
```

```
 ╔══════════════════════════════════════════════╗
 ║                                              ║
 ║  Valid                                       ║
 ║  ┌────────────────────────────────────────┐  ║
 ║  │ (·) Procedure                          │  ║
 ║  │ ( ) Expression                         │  ║
 ║  └────────────────────────────────────────┘  ║
 ║                                              ║
 ╚══════════════════════════════════════════════╝
DO controlprc WITH "Save"
--------------------------------------------------------------
*-- m.lhSave Message Clause
--------------------------------------------------------------
 ╔══════════════════════════════════════════════╗
 ║                                              ║
 ║  Message                                     ║
 ║  ┌────────────────────────────────────────┐  ║
 ║  │ ( ) Procedure                          │  ║
 ║  │ (·) Expression                         │  ║
 ║  └────────────────────────────────────────┘  ║
 ║                                              ║
 ╚══════════════════════════════════════════════╝
Message:   "Save the information that is currently displayed"
*=============================================================
*  m.lhOops
*=============================================================
 @   0, 37
 Spacing:    2
 ╔══════════════════════════════════════════════════════════════════╗
 ║                                                                  ║
 ║  Push Button Prompts:     ┌────────────────────────────────────┐ ║
 ║  ┌──────────────────────┐ │ (·) Horizontal    ( ) Vertical     │ ║
 ║  │ \?Oops!              │ │ [ ] Terminating  <Spacing...>      │ ║
 ║  │                      │ └────────────────────────────────────┘ ║
 ║  │                      │ Variable:                              ║
 ║  │                      │ ┌────────────────────────────────────┐ ║
 ║  │                      │ │ < Choose... >  m.lhOops            │ ║
 ║  │                      │ └────────────────────────────────────┘ ║
 ║  │                      │ Options:                               ║
 ║  │                      │ ┌────────────────────────────────────┐ ║
 ║  │                      │ │ [X] When...      [ ] Comment...    │ ║
 ║  │                      │ │ [X] Valid...     [ ] Disabled      │ ║
 ║  │                      │ │ [X] Message...                     │ ║
 ║  └──────────────────────┘ └────────────────────────────────────┘ ║
 ║                                                                  ║
 ║                 «  OK  »     < Cancel >                          ║
 ║                                                                  ║
 ╚══════════════════════════════════════════════════════════════════╝
--------------------------------------------------------------
*-- m.lhOops When Clause
--------------------------------------------------------------
 ╔══════════════════════════════════════════════╗
 ║                                              ║
 ║  When                                        ║
 ║  ┌────────────────────────────────────────┐  ║
 ║  │ ( ) Procedure                          │  ║
 ║  │ (·) Expression                         │  ║
 ║  └────────────────────────────────────────┘  ║
 ║                                              ║
 ╚══════════════════════════════════════════════╝
When:   ((_WINDOWS OR _MAC) AND MDOWN()) OR _DOS OR (LASTKEY() = 27)
```

```
------------------------------------------------------------
*-- m.lhOops Valid Clause
------------------------------------------------------------

 Valid

  (·) Procedure
  ( ) Expression

DO controlprc WITH "Oops!"
------------------------------------------------------------
*-- m.lhOops Message Clause
------------------------------------------------------------

 Message

  ( ) Procedure
  (·) Expression

Message:   "Cancel all modifications that have been made.  Do NOT save any
information"
*============================================================
*  m.lhClose
*============================================================
 @   0,  49
 Spacing:    2

 Push Button Prompts:      (·) Horizontal    ( ) Vertical
                           [ ] Terminating  <Spacing...>
  \?Close
                          Variable:

                           < Choose... >  m.lhClose

                          Options:

                           [X] When...      [ ] Comment...
                           [X] Valid...     [ ] Disabled
                           [X] Message...

                  «   OK   »    < Cancel >
------------------------------------------------------------
*-- m.lhClose When Clause
------------------------------------------------------------
```

```
When

  ( ) Procedure
  (·) Expression

When:    ((_WINDOWS OR _MAC) AND MDOWN()) OR _DOS OR (LASTKEY() = 27)
--------------------------------------------------------------
*-- m.lhClose Valid Clause
--------------------------------------------------------------

Valid

  (·) Procedure
  ( ) Expression

DO controlprc WITH "Close"
--------------------------------------------------------------
*-- m.lhClose Message Clause
--------------------------------------------------------------

Message

  ( ) Procedure
  (·) Expression

Message:    "Remove this window from the screen"
*=============================================================
*  m.lhTop
*=============================================================
 @   1,    1
 Spacing:    2

Push Button Prompts:        (·) Horizontal    ( ) Vertical
                            [ ] Terminating  <Spacing...>
Top
                           Variable:

                            < Choose... >  m.lhTop

                           Options:

                            [X] When...      [ ] Comment...
                            [X] Valid...     [ ] Disabled
                            [X] Message...

             «   OK   »     < Cancel >
```

```
------------------------------------------------------------
*-- m.lhTop When Clause
------------------------------------------------------------

    When
        ( ) Procedure
        (·) Expression

When:   ((_WINDOWS OR _MAC) AND MDOWN()) OR _DOS
------------------------------------------------------------
*-- m.lhTop Valid Clause
------------------------------------------------------------

    Valid
        (·) Procedure
        ( ) Expression

DO controlprc WITH "Top"
------------------------------------------------------------
*-- m.lhTop Message Clause
------------------------------------------------------------

    Message
        ( ) Procedure
        (·) Expression

Message:   "Go to the first piece of information available"
*===========================================================
*  m.lhPrior
*===========================================================
 @   1,  13
 Spacing:    2
```

```
    Push Button Prompts:          (·) Horizontal    ( ) Vertical
                                  [ ] Terminating  <Spacing...>
     Prior
                                 Variable:

                                   < Choose... >  m.lhPrior

                                 Options:

                                   [X] When...       [ ] Comment...
                                   [X] Valid...      [ ] Disabled
                                   [X] Message...

                   «   OK   »    < Cancel >
------------------------------------------------------------
*-- m.lhPrior When Clause
------------------------------------------------------------

    When

      ( ) Procedure
      (·) Expression

When:   ((_WINDOWS OR _MAC) AND MDOWN()) OR _DOS
------------------------------------------------------------
*-- m.lhPrior Valid Clause
------------------------------------------------------------

    Valid

      (·) Procedure
      ( ) Expression

DO controlprc WITH "Prior"
------------------------------------------------------------
*-- m.lhPrior Message Clause
------------------------------------------------------------

    Message

      ( ) Procedure
      (·) Expression

Message:   "Show the previous information"
*===========================================================
*   m.lhNext
```

```
*==============================================================
 @   1,  25
 Spacing:    2
+------------------------------------------------------------+
|                                                            |
|  Push Button Prompts:    +----------------------------------+
|                          | (·) Horizontal    ( ) Vertical   |
| +--------------------+   | [ ] Terminating  <Spacing...>    |
| |Next                |   +----------------------------------+
| |                    |   Variable:
| |                    |   +----------------------------------+
| |                    |   | < Choose... >  m.lhNext          |
| |                    |   +----------------------------------+
| |                    |   Options:
| |                    |   +----------------------------------+
| |                    |   | [X] When...      [ ] Comment...  |
| |                    |   | [X] Valid...     [ ] Disabled    |
| |                    |   | [X] Message...                   |
| +--------------------+   +----------------------------------+
|                                                            |
|             «   OK   »     < Cancel >                       |
+------------------------------------------------------------+
--------------------------------------------------------------
*-- m.lhNext When Clause
--------------------------------------------------------------
+---------------------------------------------+
|                                             |
|  When                                       |
|  +---------------------------------------+  |
|  | ( ) Procedure                         |  |
|  | (·) Expression                        |  |
|  +---------------------------------------+  |
|                                             |
+---------------------------------------------+
When:   ((_WINDOWS OR _MAC) AND MDOWN()) OR _DOS
--------------------------------------------------------------
*-- m.lhNext Valid Clause
--------------------------------------------------------------
+---------------------------------------------+
|                                             |
|  Valid                                      |
|  +---------------------------------------+  |
|  | (·) Procedure                         |  |
|  | ( ) Expression                        |  |
|  +---------------------------------------+  |
|                                             |
+---------------------------------------------+
DO controlprc WITH "Next"
--------------------------------------------------------------
*-- m.lhNext Message Clause
--------------------------------------------------------------
+---------------------------------------------+
|                                             |
|  Message                                    |
|  +---------------------------------------+  |
|  | ( ) Procedure                         |  |
|  | (·) Expression                        |  |
|  +---------------------------------------+  |
|                                             |
+---------------------------------------------+
```

```
Message:   "Show the next record"
*==============================================================
*  m.lhBottom
*==============================================================
 @   1,  37
 Spacing:    2

╔════════════════════════════════════════════════════════════╗
║                                                            ║
║ Push Button Prompts:      ┌─────────────────────────────┐  ║
║                           │ (·) Horizontal   ( ) Vertical│  ║
║ ┌──────────────────────┐  │ [ ] Terminating <Spacing...>│  ║
║ │Bottom                │  └─────────────────────────────┘  ║
║ │                      │  Variable:                        ║
║ │                      │  ┌─────────────────────────────┐  ║
║ │                      │  │ < Choose... >  m.lhBottom   │  ║
║ │                      │  └─────────────────────────────┘  ║
║ │                      │  Options:                         ║
║ │                      │  ┌─────────────────────────────┐  ║
║ │                      │  │ [X] When...    [ ] Comment...│  ║
║ │                      │  │ [X] Valid...   [ ] Disabled │  ║
║ │                      │  │ [X] Message...              │  ║
║ └──────────────────────┘  └─────────────────────────────┘  ║
║                                                            ║
║                 «   OK   »    < Cancel >                   ║
║                                                            ║
╚════════════════════════════════════════════════════════════╝
--------------------------------------------------------------
*-- m.lhBottom When Clause
--------------------------------------------------------------

╔══════════════════════════════════════════╗
║                                          ║
║ When                                     ║
║                                          ║
║ ┌──────────────────────────────────────┐ ║
║ │ ( ) Procedure                        │ ║
║ │ (·) Expression                       │ ║
║ └──────────────────────────────────────┘ ║
║                                          ║
╚══════════════════════════════════════════╝
When:    ((_WINDOWS OR _MAC) AND MDOWN()) OR _DOS
--------------------------------------------------------------
*-- m.lhBottom Valid Clause
--------------------------------------------------------------

╔══════════════════════════════════════════╗
║                                          ║
║ Valid                                    ║
║                                          ║
║ ┌──────────────────────────────────────┐ ║
║ │ (·) Procedure                        │ ║
║ │ ( ) Expression                       │ ║
║ └──────────────────────────────────────┘ ║
║                                          ║
╚══════════════════════════════════════════╝
DO controlprc WITH "Bottom"
--------------------------------------------------------------
*-- m.lhBottom Message Clause
--------------------------------------------------------------

╔══════════════════════════════════════════╗
║                                          ║
║ Message                                  ║
║                                          ║
║ ┌──────────────────────────────────────┐ ║
║ │ ( ) Procedure                        │ ║
║ │ (·) Expression                       │ ║
║ └──────────────────────────────────────┘ ║
║                                          ║
╚══════════════════════════════════════════╝
```

```
Message:   "Show the last record available"
*===============================================================
*  m.lhList
*===============================================================
 @   1,  49
 Spacing:    2
```

```
Push Button Prompts:        (·) Horizontal    ( ) Vertical
                            [ ] Terminating  <Spacing...>
 List
                           Variable:

                            < Choose... >  m.lhList

                           Options:

                            [X] When...      [ ] Comment...
                            [X] Valid...     [ ] Disabled
                            [X] Message...

              «   OK   »    < Cancel >
```

```
---------------------------------------------------------------
*-- m.lhList When Clause
---------------------------------------------------------------
```

```
When

  ( ) Procedure
  (·) Expression
```

```
When:    ((_WINDOWS OR _MAC) AND MDOWN()) OR _DOS
---------------------------------------------------------------
*-- m.lhList Valid Clause
---------------------------------------------------------------
```

```
Valid

  (·) Procedure
  ( ) Expression
```

```
DO controlprc WITH "List"
---------------------------------------------------------------
*-- m.lhList Message Clause
---------------------------------------------------------------
```

```
Message

  ( ) Procedure
  (·) Expression

Message:   "List all records available.  Allow the selection of any record"
*==============================================================
*  lhFind
*==============================================================
 @  1,  61
 Spacing:    1

 Push Button Prompts:        (·) Horizontal    ( ) Vertical
                             [ ] Terminating  <Spacing...>
  Find
                            Variable:

                             < Choose... >  lhFind

                            Options:

                             [X] When...      [ ] Comment...
                             [X] Valid...     [ ] Disabled
                             [X] Message...

                 «   OK   »    < Cancel >
--------------------------------------------------------------
*-- lhFind When Clause
--------------------------------------------------------------
When

  ( ) Procedure
  (·) Expression

When:    ((_WINDOWS OR _MAC) AND MDOWN()) OR _DOS
--------------------------------------------------------------
*-- lhFind Valid Clause
--------------------------------------------------------------
Valid

  (·) Procedure
  ( ) Expression

DO ControlPrc WITH "Find"
```

```
-------------------------------------------------------------
*-- lhFind Message Clause
-------------------------------------------------------------
```

```
Message

  ( ) Procedure
  (·) Expression
```

```
Message:   "Search for a specific record"
*------------------------------------------------------------
*************************************************************
**--    MCONTROL.SCX - MAC PLATFORM
*************************************************************
```

```
( ) DeskTop                          (·) Window

Name:   WCMCONTROL                   <Type...>
Title:
Footer:

Size:              Screen Code:

 Height:    4.167   [X] Setup...
 Width:   109.333   [ ] Cleanup & Procs...         «   OK   »

Position:          READ Clauses:                   < Cancel >

 Row:       0.000   [ ] Activate...    [ ] Show...
 Column:    0.000   [ ] Valid...       [X] When...
 [ ] Center         [ ] Deactivate...

Environment:                        [ ] Add alias

        Environment NOT saved with screen.
```

```
Type:    User

Attributes:       Border:

 [ ] Close         (·) None
 [ ] Float         ( ) Single
 [ ] Shadow        ( ) Double      «   OK   »
 [ ] Minimize      ( ) Panel
                   ( ) System      < Cancel >

Color Schemes:

 Primary:         Popup:
```

```
MAC      RGB Fill Color Scheme: (197,197,197)
MAC      Font: Geneva,  10
 Screen Setup code above
 READ When code above
************************************************************
*--   G E T    O B J E C T S
************************************************************
*==========================================================
*  Line
*==========================================================
 @   3.583,   0.000
MAC      RGB Color Scheme: (,,,,,)
           Pen: 1
*==========================================================
*  m.lhTop
*==========================================================
 @   0.000,   0.000
     SIZE   3.500,   7.000
 Spacing:    2

 Push Button Prompts:         (·) Horizontal    ( ) Vertical
                              [ ] Terminating  <Spacing...>
  ..\BMPS\FIRST1.BMP
                             Variable:

                              < Choose... >  m.lhTop

                             Options:

                              [X] When...     [ ] Comment...
                              [X] Valid...    [ ] Disabled
                              [X] Message...

                  «   OK   »    < Cancel >

   List of Push Button Prompts:
      ..\BMPS\FIRST1.BMP

MAC      RGB Color Scheme: (,,,,,)
MAC      Font: Geneva,  10
 When code above
 Valid code above
 Message code above
*==========================================================
*  m.lhPrior
*==========================================================
 @   0.000,   7.167
     SIZE   3.500,   7.000
 Spacing:    2
```

```
 Push Button Prompts:              (·) Horizontal    ( ) Vertical
                                   [ ] Terminating  <Spacing...>
 ..\BMPS\PREV1.BMP
                                  Variable:

                                   < Choose... >  m.lhPrior

                                  Options:

                                   [X] When...      [ ] Comment...
                                   [X] Valid...     [ ] Disabled
                                   [X] Message...

                   «   OK   »    < Cancel >

  List of Push Button Prompts:
     ..\BMPS\PREV1.BMP

MAC      RGB Color Scheme: (,,,,,)
MAC      Font: Geneva,  10
 When code above
 Valid code above
 Message code above
*==============================================================
*  m.lhNext
*==============================================================
 @   0.000,  14.333
     SIZE   3.500,   7.000
 Spacing:    2

 Push Button Prompts:              (·) Horizontal    ( ) Vertical
                                   [ ] Terminating  <Spacing...>
 ..\BMPS\NEXT1.BMP
                                  Variable:

                                   < Choose... >  m.lhNext

                                  Options:

                                   [X] When...      [ ] Comment...
                                   [X] Valid...     [ ] Disabled
                                   [X] Message...

                   «   OK   »    < Cancel >

  List of Push Button Prompts:
     ..\BMPS\NEXT1.BMP

MAC      RGB Color Scheme: (,,,,,)
MAC      Font: Geneva,  10
 When code above
 Valid code above
```

```
 Message code above
*==========================================================
*  m.lhBottom
*==========================================================
 @   0.000,  21.500
     SIZE   3.500,   7.000
 Spacing:    2

  Push Button Prompts:      (·) Horizontal   ( ) Vertical
                            [ ] Terminating  <Spacing...>
   ..\BMPS\LAST1.BMP
                           Variable:

                            < Choose... >  m.lhBottom

                           Options:

                            [X] When...     [ ] Comment...
                            [X] Valid...    [ ] Disabled
                            [X] Message...

                 «   OK   »    < Cancel >

  List of Push Button Prompts:
     ..\BMPS\LAST1.BMP

MAC      RGB Color Scheme: (,,,,,)
MAC      Font: Geneva,  10
 When code above
 Valid code above
 Message code above
*==========================================================
*  m.lhList
*==========================================================
 @   0.000,  30.833
     SIZE   3.500,   7.000
 Spacing:    2

  Push Button Prompts:      (·) Horizontal   ( ) Vertical
                            [ ] Terminating  <Spacing...>
   ..\BMPS\LIST1.BMP
                           Variable:

                            < Choose... >  m.lhList

                           Options:

                            [X] When...     [ ] Comment...
                            [X] Valid...    [ ] Disabled
                            [X] Message...

                 «   OK   »    < Cancel >
```

```
  List of Push Button Prompts:
     ..\BMPS\LIST1.BMP

MAC      RGB Color Scheme: (,,,,,)
MAC      Font: Geneva,  10
 When code above
 Valid code above
 Message code above
*==============================================================
*  lhFind
*==============================================================
 @   0.000,  38.000
     SIZE   3.500,   7.000
 Spacing:    1
```

```
 Push Button Prompts:          (·) Horizontal    ( ) Vertical
                               [ ] Terminating  <Spacing...>
 ..\BMPS\FIND1.BMP
                              Variable:

                               < Choose... >  lhFind

                              Options:

                               [X] When...     [ ] Comment...
                               [X] Valid...    [ ] Disabled
                               [X] Message...

                 «   OK   »    < Cancel >
```

```
  List of Push Button Prompts:
     ..\BMPS\FIND1.BMP

MAC      RGB Color Scheme: (,,,,,)
MAC      Font: Geneva,  10
 When code above
 Valid code above
 Message code above
*==============================================================
*  m.lhAdd
*==============================================================
 @   0.000,  47.833
     SIZE   3.500,   7.000
 Spacing:    2
```

```
  Push Button Prompts:            (·) Horizontal    ( ) Vertical
                                  [ ] Terminating   <Spacing...>
   ..\BMPS\NEW1.BMP
                                 Variable:

                                  < Choose... >  m.lhAdd

                                 Options:

                                  [X] When...     [ ] Comment...
                                  [X] Valid...    [ ] Disabled
                                  [X] Message...

                 «   OK   »    < Cancel >

  List of Push Button Prompts:
     ..\BMPS\NEW1.BMP

MAC       RGB Color Scheme: (,,,,,)
MAC       Font: Geneva,  10
 When code above
 Valid code above
 Message code above
*==============================================================
*  m.lhEdit
*==============================================================
 @   0.000,  55.000
     SIZE   3.500,   7.000
 Spacing:    2

  Push Button Prompts:            (·) Horizontal    ( ) Vertical
                                  [ ] Terminating   <Spacing...>
   ..\BMPS\EDIT1.BMP
                                 Variable:

                                  < Choose... >  m.lhEdit

                                 Options:

                                  [X] When...     [ ] Comment...
                                  [X] Valid...    [ ] Disabled
                                  [X] Message...

                 «   OK   »    < Cancel >

  List of Push Button Prompts:
     ..\BMPS\EDIT1.BMP

MAC       RGB Color Scheme: (,,,,,)
MAC       Font: Geneva,  10
 When code above
 Valid code above
 Message code above
```

```
*==============================================================
*  m.lhSave
*==============================================================
 @   0.000,  64.000
     SIZE   3.500,   7.000
 Spacing:    2

  Push Button Prompts:        (·) Horizontal   ( ) Vertical
                              [ ] Terminating  <Spacing...>
  ..\BMPS\SAVE1.BMP
                             Variable:

                              < Choose... >  m.lhSave

                             Options:

                              [X] When...     [ ] Comment...
                              [X] Valid...    [ ] Disabled
                              [X] Message...

               «   OK   »    < Cancel >

  List of Push Button Prompts:
     ..\BMPS\SAVE1.BMP

MAC      RGB Color Scheme: (,,,,,)
MAC      Font: Geneva,  10
 When code above
 Valid code above
 Message code above
*==============================================================
*  m.lhOops
*==============================================================
 @   0.000,  71.167
     SIZE   3.500,   7.000
 Spacing:    2

  Push Button Prompts:        (·) Horizontal   ( ) Vertical
                              [ ] Terminating  <Spacing...>
  ..\BMPS\CANCEL1.BMP
                             Variable:

                              < Choose... >  m.lhOops

                             Options:

                              [X] When...     [ ] Comment...
                              [X] Valid...    [ ] Disabled
                              [X] Message...

               «   OK   »    < Cancel >
```

```
 List of Push Button Prompts:
    ..\BMPS\CANCEL1.BMP

MAC      RGB Color Scheme: (,,,,,)
MAC      Font: Geneva,  10
 When code above
 Valid code above
 Message code above
*==============================================================
*  m.lhClose
*==============================================================
 @   0.000,  80.167
     SIZE   3.500,   7.000
 Spacing:    2
```

```
+------------------------------------------------------------------+
|                                                                  |
|  Push Button Prompts:      | (·) Horizontal    ( ) Vertical   |  |
|  +---------------------+   | [ ] Terminating  <Spacing...>    |  |
|  | ..\BMPS\CLOSE1.BMP  |                                         |
|  |                     |   Variable:                             |
|  |                     |   | < Choose... >  m.lhClose         |  |
|  |                     |                                         |
|  |                     |   Options:                              |
|  |                     |   | [X] When...      [ ] Comment...  |  |
|  |                     |   | [X] Valid...     [ ] Disabled    |  |
|  |                     |   | [X] Message...                   |  |
|  +---------------------+                                         |
|                                                                  |
|                 «  OK  »    < Cancel >                           |
+------------------------------------------------------------------+
```

```
 List of Push Button Prompts:
    ..\BMPS\CLOSE1.BMP

MAC      RGB Color Scheme: (,,,,,)
MAC      Font: Geneva,  10
 When code above
 Valid code above
 Message code above
*--------------------------------------------------------------
```

```
***********************************************************
**--    MCONTROL.SCX - WINDOWS PLATFORM
***********************************************************

 ( ) DeskTop                        (·) Window

 Name:   WCMCONTROL                 <Type...>
 Title:
 Footer:

 Size:              Screen Code:

  Height:    3.833   [X] Setup...
  Width:    86.750   [ ] Cleanup & Procs...          «  OK  »

 Position:          READ Clauses:                   < Cancel >

  Row:       0.000   [ ] Activate...   [ ] Show...
  Column:    0.000   [ ] Valid...      [X] When...
  [ ] Center         [ ] Deactivate...

 Environment:                          [ ] Add alias

        Environment NOT saved with screen.


 Type:     User

 Attributes:      Border:

  [ ] Close        (·) None
  [ ] Float        ( ) Single
  [ ] Shadow       ( ) Double       «  OK  »
  [ ] Minimize     ( ) Panel
                   ( ) System      < Cancel >

 Color Schemes:

  Primary:        Popup:

WINDOWS  RGB Fill Color Scheme: (192,192,192)
WINDOWS  Font: Terminal,   9
 Screen Setup code above
 READ When code above
***********************************************************
*--    G E T    O B J E C T S
***********************************************************
*==========================================================
*  Line
*==========================================================
 @   3.583,   0.125
WINDOWS  RGB Color Scheme: (,,,,,)
```

```
          Pen: 1
*============================================================
*  m.lhTop
*============================================================
 @   0.000,   0.000
     SIZE   3.500,   5.250
 Spacing:    2
```

```
+------------------------------------------------------------+
|                          +-------------------------------+ |
|  Push Button Prompts:    | (·) Horizontal    ( ) Vertical| |
|  +-------------------+   | [ ] Terminating  <Spacing...> | |
|  |..\BMPS\FIRST1.BMP |   +-------------------------------+ |
|  |                   |   Variable:                         |
|  |                   |   +-------------------------------+ |
|  |                   |   | < Choose... >  m.lhTop        | |
|  |                   |   +-------------------------------+ |
|  |                   |   Options:                          |
|  |                   |   +-------------------------------+ |
|  |                   |   | [X] When...     [ ] Comment...| |
|  |                   |   | [X] Valid...    [ ] Disabled  | |
|  |                   |   | [X] Message...                | |
|  +-------------------+   +-------------------------------+ |
|                                                            |
|              «   OK   »     < Cancel >                     |
+------------------------------------------------------------+
```

```
   List of Push Button Prompts:
      ..\BMPS\FIRST1.BMP

WINDOWS  RGB Color Scheme: (,,,,,)
WINDOWS  Font: Terminal,    9
 When code above
 Valid code above
 Message code above
*============================================================
*  m.lhPrior
*============================================================
 @   0.000,   5.375
     SIZE   3.500,   5.250
 Spacing:    2
```

```
+------------------------------------------------------------+
|                          +-------------------------------+ |
|  Push Button Prompts:    | (·) Horizontal    ( ) Vertical| |
|  +-------------------+   | [ ] Terminating  <Spacing...> | |
|  |..\BMPS\PREV1.BMP  |   +-------------------------------+ |
|  |                   |   Variable:                         |
|  |                   |   +-------------------------------+ |
|  |                   |   | < Choose... >  m.lhPrior      | |
|  |                   |   +-------------------------------+ |
|  |                   |   Options:                          |
|  |                   |   +-------------------------------+ |
|  |                   |   | [X] When...     [ ] Comment...| |
|  |                   |   | [X] Valid...    [ ] Disabled  | |
|  |                   |   | [X] Message...                | |
|  +-------------------+   +-------------------------------+ |
|                                                            |
|              «   OK   »     < Cancel >                     |
+------------------------------------------------------------+
```

```
  List of Push Button Prompts:
     ..\BMPS\PREV1.BMP

WINDOWS  RGB Color Scheme: (,,,,,)
WINDOWS  Font: Terminal,   9
 When code above
 Valid code above
 Message code above
*=============================================================
*  m.lhNext
*=============================================================
 @   0.000,  10.750
     SIZE   3.500,   5.250
 Spacing:    2
```

```
 Push Button Prompts:          (·) Horizontal    ( ) Vertical
                               [ ] Terminating  <Spacing...>
 ..\BMPS\NEXT1.BMP
                              Variable:

                               < Choose... >  m.lhNext

                              Options:

                               [X] When...     [ ] Comment...
                               [X] Valid...    [ ] Disabled
                               [X] Message...

              «  OK  »    < Cancel >
```

```
  List of Push Button Prompts:
     ..\BMPS\NEXT1.BMP

WINDOWS  RGB Color Scheme: (,,,,,)
WINDOWS  Font: Terminal,   9
 When code above
 Valid code above
 Message code above
*=============================================================
*  m.lhBottom
*=============================================================
 @   0.000,  16.125
     SIZE   3.500,   5.250
 Spacing:    2
```

```
 Push Button Prompts:          (·) Horizontal    ( ) Vertical
                               [ ] Terminating  <Spacing...>
 ..\BMPS\LAST1.BMP
                              Variable:

                               < Choose... >  m.lhBottom

                              Options:

                               [X] When...     [ ] Comment...
                               [X] Valid...    [ ] Disabled
                               [X] Message...

              «   OK   »    < Cancel >
```

```
 List of Push Button Prompts:
    ..\BMPS\LAST1.BMP

WINDOWS  RGB Color Scheme: (,,,,,)
WINDOWS  Font: Terminal,   9
 When code above
 Valid code above
 Message code above
*============================================================
*  m.lhList
*============================================================
 @   0.000,  23.125
     SIZE   3.500,   5.250
 Spacing:   2
```

```
 Push Button Prompts:          (·) Horizontal    ( ) Vertical
                               [ ] Terminating  <Spacing...>
 ..\BMPS\LIST1.BMP
                              Variable:

                               < Choose... >  m.lhList

                              Options:

                               [X] When...     [ ] Comment...
                               [X] Valid...    [ ] Disabled
                               [X] Message...

              «   OK   »    < Cancel >
```

```
 List of Push Button Prompts:
    ..\BMPS\LIST1.BMP

WINDOWS  RGB Color Scheme: (,,,,,)
WINDOWS  Font: Terminal,   9
 When code above
 Valid code above
 Message code above
```

```
*==============================================================
*  lhFind
*==============================================================
 @   0.000,  28.500
     SIZE   3.500,   5.250
 Spacing:    1

  Push Button Prompts:         (·) Horizontal    ( ) Vertical
                               [ ] Terminating  <Spacing...>
  ..\BMPS\FIND1.BMP
                              Variable:

                               < Choose... >  lhFind

                              Options:

                               [X] When...     [ ] Comment...
                               [X] Valid...    [ ] Disabled
                               [X] Message...

              «   OK   »    < Cancel >

  List of Push Button Prompts:
     ..\BMPS\FIND1.BMP

WINDOWS  RGB Color Scheme: (,,,,,)
WINDOWS  Font: Terminal,   9
 When code above
 Valid code above
 Message code above
*==============================================================
*  m.lhAdd
*==============================================================
 @   0.000,  35.500
     SIZE   3.500,   5.250
 Spacing:    2

  Push Button Prompts:         (·) Horizontal    ( ) Vertical
                               [ ] Terminating  <Spacing...>
  ..\BMPS\NEW1.BMP
                              Variable:

                               < Choose... >  m.lhAdd

                              Options:

                               [X] When...     [ ] Comment...
                               [X] Valid...    [ ] Disabled
                               [X] Message...

              «   OK   »    < Cancel >
```

```
 List of Push Button Prompts:
   ..\BMPS\NEW1.BMP

WINDOWS  RGB Color Scheme: (,,,,,)
WINDOWS  Font: Terminal,   9
 When code above
 Valid code above
 Message code above
*===========================================================
*  m.lhEdit
*===========================================================
 @   0.000,  40.875
     SIZE   3.500,   5.250
 Spacing:    2
```

```
 Push Button Prompts:       (·) Horizontal   ( ) Vertical
                            [ ] Terminating  <Spacing...>
 ..\BMPS\EDIT1.BMP
                           Variable:

                            < Choose... >  m.lhEdit

                           Options:

                            [X] When...    [ ] Comment...
                            [X] Valid...   [ ] Disabled
                            [X] Message...

              «  OK  »    < Cancel >
```

```
 List of Push Button Prompts:
   ..\BMPS\EDIT1.BMP

WINDOWS  RGB Color Scheme: (,,,,,)
WINDOWS  Font: Terminal,   9
 When code above
 Valid code above
 Message code above
*===========================================================
*  m.lhSave
*===========================================================
 @   0.000,  47.875
     SIZE   3.500,   5.250
 Spacing:    2
```

```
Push Button Prompts:            (•) Horizontal   ( ) Vertical
                                [ ] Terminating  <Spacing...>
..\BMPS\SAVE1.BMP
                                Variable:

                                < Choose... >  m.lhSave

                                Options:

                                [X] When...      [ ] Comment...
                                [X] Valid...     [ ] Disabled
                                [X] Message...

              «  OK  »    < Cancel >

  List of Push Button Prompts:
     ..\BMPS\SAVE1.BMP

WINDOWS  RGB Color Scheme: (,,,,,)
WINDOWS  Font: Terminal,   9
 When code above
 Valid code above
 Message code above
*==============================================================
*  m.lhOops
*==============================================================
 @   0.000,  53.250
     SIZE   3.500,   5.250
 Spacing:    2

Push Button Prompts:            (•) Horizontal   ( ) Vertical
                                [ ] Terminating  <Spacing...>
..\BMPS\CANCEL1.BMP
                                Variable:

                                < Choose... >  m.lhOops

                                Options:

                                [X] When...      [ ] Comment...
                                [X] Valid...     [ ] Disabled
                                [X] Message...

              «  OK  »    < Cancel >

  List of Push Button Prompts:
     ..\BMPS\CANCEL1.BMP

WINDOWS  RGB Color Scheme: (,,,,,)
WINDOWS  Font: Terminal,   9
 When code above
 Valid code above
```

```
 Message code above
*================================================================
*  m.lhClose
*================================================================
 @    0.000,  60.250
      SIZE   3.500,    5.250
 Spacing:      2
╔══════════════════════════════════════════════════════════════╗
║                                                              ║
║  Push Button Prompts:       ┌───────────────────────────────┐ ║
║                             │ (·) Horizontal   ( ) Vertical │ ║
║  ┌─────────────────────┐    │ [ ] Terminating  <Spacing...> │ ║
║  │ ..\BMPS\CLOSE1.BMP  │    └───────────────────────────────┘ ║
║  │                     │    Variable:                         ║
║  │                     │    ┌───────────────────────────────┐ ║
║  │                     │    │ < Choose... >  m.lhClose      │ ║
║  │                     │    └───────────────────────────────┘ ║
║  │                     │    Options:                          ║
║  │                     │    ┌───────────────────────────────┐ ║
║  │                     │    │ [X] When...     [ ] Comment...│ ║
║  │                     │    │ [X] Valid...    [ ] Disabled  │ ║
║  │                     │    │ [X] Message...                │ ║
║  └─────────────────────┘    └───────────────────────────────┘ ║
║                                                              ║
║                «    OK    »     < Cancel >                    ║
║                                                              ║
╚══════════════════════════════════════════════════════════════╝
   List of Push Button Prompts:
      ..\BMPS\CLOSE1.BMP

WINDOWS  RGB Color Scheme: (,,,,,)
WINDOWS  Font: Terminal,    9
 When code above
 Valid code above
 Message code above
```

Multi-Row Selection: MOVER.SCX

Mover is discussed in Chapter 7, *Mover—a Sample Reusable Object.*

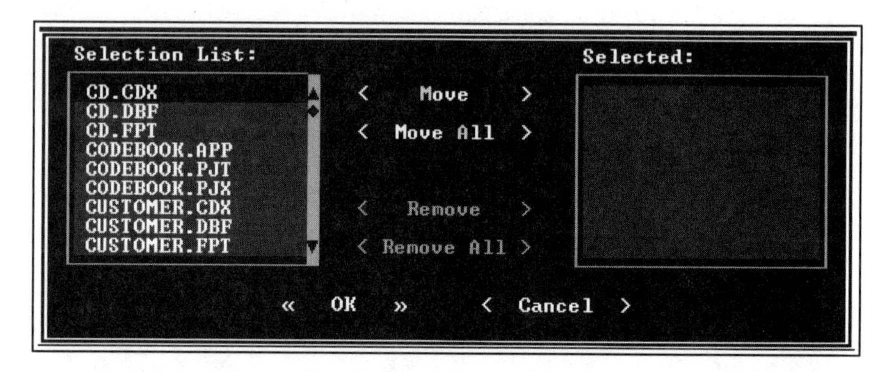

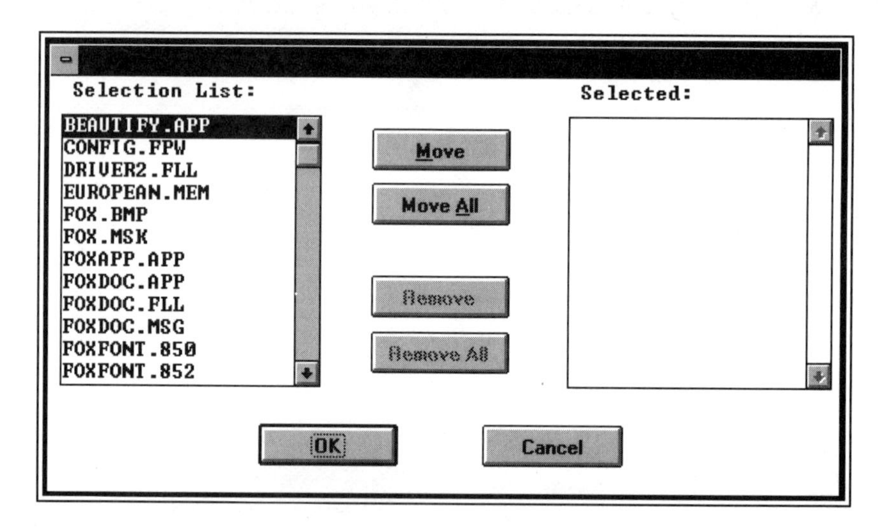

```
*-------------------------------------------------------------
**************************************************************
**--    MOVER.SCX - DOS PLATFORM
**************************************************************

( ) DeskTop                          (·) Window

Name:                                <Type...>
Title:
Footer:

Size:            Screen Code:

  Height:   17     [X] Setup...
  Width:    66     [X] Cleanup & Procs...              «   OK   »

Position:        READ Clauses:                         < Cancel >

  Row:       0     [X] Activate...      [ ] Show...
  Column:    0     [ ] Valid...         [ ] When...
  [X] Center       [ ] Deactivate...

Environment:                          [ ] Add alias

       Environment saved with this screen.


  Type:        Dialog

  Attributes:       Border:

   [ ] Close         ( ) None
   [X] Float         ( ) Single
   [X] Shadow        (·) Double      «   OK   »
   [ ] Minimize      ( ) Panel
                     ( ) System      < Cancel >

  Color Schemes:

   Primary:          Popup:

   Dialogs           Dialog Pop

**************************************************************
*   SCREEN SETUP CODE
**************************************************************
#SECTION 1
*   Program..........: MOVER Screen
*   Author...........: yag
*   Project..........: COMMON
*   Created..........: 04/16/93
*   Copyright........: (c) Flash Creative Management, 1993
*)  Description......: Mover dialog.
*)                   : Accepts two arrays, and allows the user
*)                   : to move items from one to the other.
```

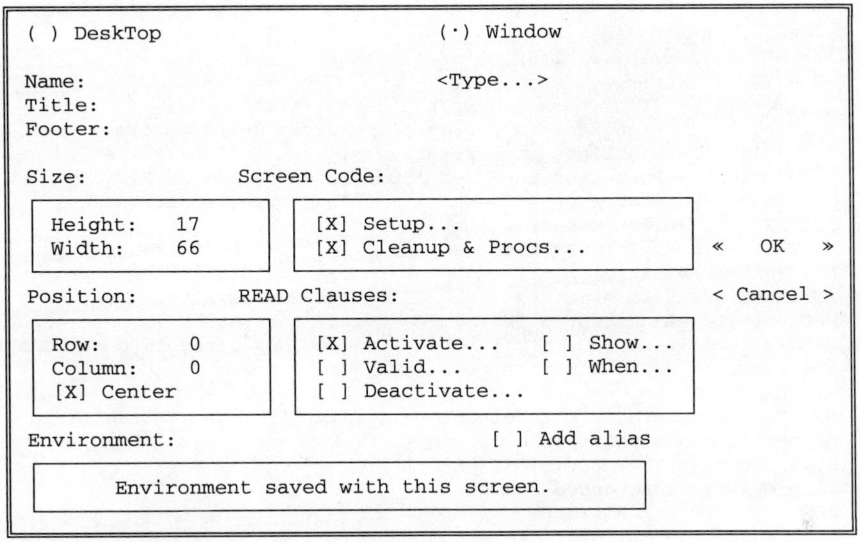

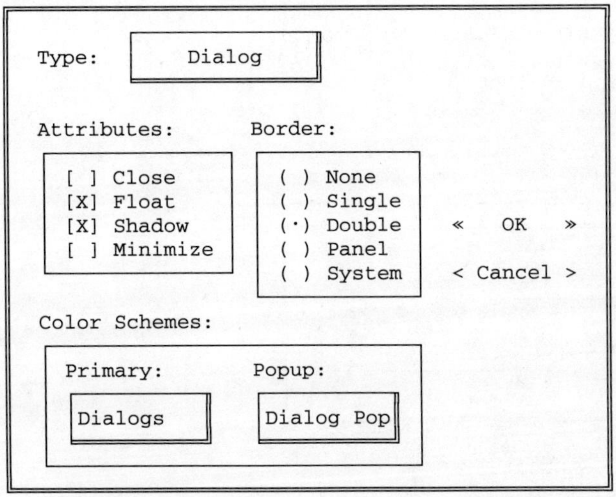

```
*)                    : This dialog displays the arrays vertically.
*  Calling Samples...: =mover(@laFull, @laSelect)
*  Parameter List....: laFullList -   The list of all possible items
*                    : laSeleList -   The list of selected items
*                    : llNoSort   -   If .T. the select list isn't sorted
*  Major change list.:
PARAMETER laFullList, laSeleList, llNoSort
#SECTION 2
* llNoSort   - If .T. don't sort the select list.
* lnSelect   - Highlight on currently selected Selected List item
* lnFull     - Highlight on currently selected Full List item
* lnFullCnt - Number of un-moved items (used to dim MOVE)
* lnSeleCnt - Number of selected items (used to dim REMOVE)
PRIVATE m.lnSelect, m.lnFull, m.lnFullCnt
PRIVATE m.lnSeleCnt, laOrigList
EXTERNAL ARRAY laFullList               && The complete listing
EXTERNAL ARRAY laSeleList               && The selected items
=ACOPY(laSeleList,laOrigList)           && Copy array in case <CANCEL>
=ACOPY(laFullList,laOrigFull)           && Copy array in case <CANCEL>
lcOldExact = SET("EXACT")
SET EXACT ON
STORE 1 TO m.lnFull, m.lnSelect         && highlight initial selections
m.lnFullCnt = sizearry(@laFullList)
m.lnSeleCnt = SizeArry(@laSeleList)
*- Dim already selected items
FOR i = 1 TO m.lnSeleCnt
  lnFound = ASCAN(laFullList,laSeleList[i,1])
  IF lnFound # 0
    lnFound = ASUBSCRIPT(laFullList,lnFound,1)
    laFullList[lnFound,1] = "\"+laFullList[lnFound,1]
    m.lnFullCnt = m.lnFullCnt - 1
  ENDIF
ENDFOR
------------------------------------------------------------
*-- READ Activate Clause
------------------------------------------------------------
```

```
READ Activate

  (·) Procedure
  ( ) Expression
```

```
IF EMPTY(laFullList)
   SHOW GETS ONLY DISABLE
   SHOW GET lhCancel ENABLE
ENDIF
IF EMPTY(laSeleList)
    SHOW GET m.lhRemove DISABLE
    SHOW GET m.lhRemoveAll DISABLE
ENDIF
************************************************************
*--    G E T    O B J E C T S
************************************************************
*===========================================================
*  Text: Selection List:
```

```
*==========================================================
 @   0,   2
*==========================================================
*  Text: Selected:
*==========================================================
 @   0,  43
*==========================================================
*  m.lnFull
*==========================================================
 @   1,   1

  List Type:                            Options:

   (·) From Array         lafulllist    [ ] When...      [ ] Comment...
   ( ) From Popup                       [X] Valid...     [ ] Disabled
   ( ) Prompt Structure                 [ ] Message...   [X] 1st Element...
   ( ) Prompt Field                     [ ] Terminating  [X] # Elements...
   ( ) Prompt Files

  Variable:

   < Choose... > m.lnFull                   «   OK   »     < Cancel >

----------------------------------------------------------
*-- m.lnFull Valid Clause
----------------------------------------------------------

  Valid

   (·) Procedure
   ( ) Expression

lnLastKey = LASTKEY()
=ValMover()
IF lnLastKey = 13
  _CUROBJ = OBJNUM(m.lnFull)
ENDIF
----------------------------------------------------------
*-- m.lnFull 1st Element Clause
----------------------------------------------------------

  1st Element

   ( ) Procedure
   (·) Expression

1st Element:   1
----------------------------------------------------------
*-- m.lnFull # Elements Clause
----------------------------------------------------------
```

```
 # Elements

 ( ) Procedure
 (·) Expression

# Elements:   sizearry(@laFullList)
*===========================================================
*  m.lhMove
*===========================================================
 @   2,  25
 Spacing:    1

 Push Button Prompts:      ( ) Horizontal   (·) Vertical
                           [ ] Terminating  <Spacing...>
 \<Move
                          Variable:

                           < Choose... >  m.lhMove

                          Options:

                           [ ] When...     [ ] Comment...
                           [X] Valid...    [ ] Disabled
                           [ ] Message...

               «   OK   »    < Cancel >
-----------------------------------------------------------
*-- m.lhMove Valid Clause
-----------------------------------------------------------

 Valid

 (·) Procedure
 ( ) Expression

  DO ValMover
*===========================================================
*  m.lhRemove
*===========================================================
 @   8,  25
 Spacing:    0
```

```
Push Button Prompts:          ( ) Horizontal    (·) Vertical
                              [ ] Terminating  <Spacing...>
\<Remove
                              Variable:

                              < Choose... >  m.lhRemove

                              Options:

                              [ ] When...      [ ] Comment...
                              [X] Valid...     [ ] Disabled
                              [ ] Message...

              «   OK   »    < Cancel >
-------------------------------------------------------------
*-- m.lhRemove Valid Clause
-------------------------------------------------------------

  Valid

   (·) Procedure
   ( ) Expression

DO ValRemove
*=============================================================
*  m.lnSelect
*=============================================================
 @   1,  42

  List Type:                               Options:

   (·) From Array        laSeleList     [ ] When...        [ ] Comment...
   ( ) From Popup                       [X] Valid...       [ ] Disabled
   ( ) Prompt Structure                 [ ] Message...     [X] 1st Element...
   ( ) Prompt Field                     [ ] Terminating    [X] # Elements...
   ( ) Prompt Files

  Variable:

   < Choose... > m.lnSelect                 «   OK   »    < Cancel >
-------------------------------------------------------------
*-- m.lnSelect Valid Clause
-------------------------------------------------------------
```

```
 ┌──────────────────────────────────────┐
 │                                      │
 │  Valid                               │
 │   ┌────────────────────────────────┐ │
 │   │ (·) Procedure                  │ │
 │   │ ( ) Expression                 │ │
 │   └────────────────────────────────┘ │
 │                                      │
 └──────────────────────────────────────┘
lnLastKey = LASTKEY()
=ValRemove()
IF lnLastKey = 13
  _CUROBJ = OBJNUM(m.lnSelect)
ENDIF
-------------------------------------------------------------
*-- m.lnSelect 1st Element Clause
-------------------------------------------------------------
 ┌──────────────────────────────────────┐
 │                                      │
 │  1st Element                         │
 │   ┌────────────────────────────────┐ │
 │   │ ( ) Procedure                  │ │
 │   │ (·) Expression                 │ │
 │   └────────────────────────────────┘ │
 │                                      │
 └──────────────────────────────────────┘
1st Element:   1
-------------------------------------------------------------
*-- m.lnSelect # Elements Clause
-------------------------------------------------------------
 ┌──────────────────────────────────────┐
 │                                      │
 │  # Elements                          │
 │   ┌────────────────────────────────┐ │
 │   │ ( ) Procedure                  │ │
 │   │ (·) Expression                 │ │
 │   └────────────────────────────────┘ │
 │                                      │
 └──────────────────────────────────────┘
# Elements:   SizeArry(@laSeleList)
*============================================================
*  lhOk
*============================================================
 @  13,  19
 Spacing:    9
```

```
 Push Button Prompts:         (·) Horizontal   ( ) Vertical
                              [X] Terminating  <Spacing...>
 \!OK
                             Variable:

                              < Choose... >  lhOk

                             Options:

                              [ ] When...     [ ] Comment...
                              [ ] Valid...    [ ] Disabled
                              [ ] Message...

               «   OK   »    < Cancel >
```

```
*==============================================================
*  m.lhMoveAll
*==============================================================
 @   4,  25
 Spacing:    1
```

```
 Push Button Prompts:         ( ) Horizontal   (·) Vertical
                              [ ] Terminating  <Spacing...>
 Move \<All
                             Variable:

                              < Choose... >  m.lhMoveAll

                             Options:

                              [ ] When...     [ ] Comment...
                              [X] Valid...    [ ] Disabled
                              [ ] Message...

               «   OK   »    < Cancel >
```

```
--------------------------------------------------------------
*-- m.lhMoveAll Valid Clause
--------------------------------------------------------------
```

```
 Valid

   (·) Procedure
   ( ) Expression
```

```
FOR i = 1 TO sizearry(@laFullList)
  IF LEFT(laFullList[i,1],1) # "\"    && If not dimmed
    laFullList[i,1] = "\"+laFullList[i,1]
   ENDIF
ENDFOR
```

```
DIMENSION laSeleList[ALEN(laOrigFull,1),ALEN(laOrigFull,2)]
=ACOPY(laOrigFull,laSeleList)
lnSeleCnt = sizearry(@laSeleList)
lnFullCnt = 0
m.lnSelect = m.lnSelect
IF NOT llNoSort
   =ASORT(laSeleList,1,lnSeleCnt)
ENDIF
SHOW GET m.lnSelect
SHOW GET m.lnFull
SHOW GET m.lhMove DISABLE
SHOW GET m.lhMoveAll DISABLE
SHOW GET m.lhRemove ENABLE
SHOW GET m.lhRemoveAll ENABLE
*============================================================
*  m.lhRemoveAll
*============================================================
 @  10,  25
 Spacing:    1
```

```
Push Button Prompts:        ( ) Horizontal   (·) Vertical
                            [ ] Terminating  <Spacing...>
Remo\<ve All
                           Variable:

                            < Choose... >  m.lhRemoveAll

                           Options:

                            [ ] When...     [ ] Comment...
                            [X] Valid...    [ ] Disabled
                            [ ] Message...

                 «  OK  »    < Cancel >
```

```
------------------------------------------------------------
*-- m.lhRemoveAll Valid Clause
------------------------------------------------------------
```

```
Valid

  (·) Procedure
  ( ) Expression
```

```
laSeleList = .F.
m.lnSeleCnt = 0
m.lnSelect = 0
m.lnFullCnt = sizearry(@laFullList)
FOR i = 1 TO m.lnFullCnt
  IF LEFT(laFullList[i,1],1) = "\"
    laFullList[i,1] = RIGHT(laFullList[i,1],LEN(laFullList[i,1])-1)
  ENDIF
ENDFOR
```

```
SHOW GET m.lnSelect
SHOW GET m.lnFull
SHOW GET m.lhMove ENABLE
SHOW GET m.lhMoveAll ENABLE
SHOW GET m.lhRemove DISABLE
SHOW GET m.lhRemoveAll DISABLE
*============================================================
*  lhCancel
*============================================================
 @  13,  35
 Spacing:    7
```

```
  Push Button Prompts:         (·) Horizontal    ( ) Vertical
                               [X] Terminating  <Spacing...>
  \?Cancel
                              Variable:

                               < Choose... >  lhCancel

                              Options:

                               [ ] When...     [ ] Comment...
                               [X] Valid...    [ ] Disabled
                               [ ] Message...

                 «   OK   »    < Cancel >
```

```
------------------------------------------------------------
*-- lhCancel Valid Clause
------------------------------------------------------------
```

```
  Valid

    (·) Procedure
    ( ) Expression
```

```
=ACOPY(laOrigList,laSeleList)
************************************************************
*--  SCREEN CLEANUP CODE
************************************************************
SET EXACT &lcOldExact
=ACOPY(laOrigFull,laFullList)
RETURN
FUNCTION ValMover
IF (m.lnFull # 0) AND (LEFT(laFullList[m.lnFull,1],1) # "\")
  IF m.lnSeleCnt+1 > ALEN(laSeleList,1)
    DIMENSION laSeleList[m.lnSeleCnt+1,ALEN(laFullList,2)]
  ENDIF
  FOR i = 1 TO ALEN(laFullList,2)       && Fill all columns
     laSeleList[m.lnSeleCnt+1,i] = laFullList[m.lnFull,i]
  ENDFOR
  laFullList[m.lnFull,1] = "\"+laFullList[m.lnFull,1]
  m.lnSeleCnt = m.lnSeleCnt + 1
  m.lnFullCnt = m.lnFullCnt - 1
```

```
  m.lnSelect = m.lnSeleCnt
  IF NOT llNoSort
    =ASORT(laSeleList,1,lnSeleCnt)
  ENDIF
  SHOW GET m.lnSelect
  SHOW GET m.lnFull
  SHOW GET m.lhRemove ENABLE
  IF m.lnFullCnt = 0
     SHOW GET m.lhMove DISABLE
  ENDIF
ENDIF
RETURN .T.
FUNCTION ValRemove
IF m.lnSelect # 0
  lnFound = ASCAN(laFullList,"\"+laSeleList[m.lnSelect,1])
  IF lnFound # 0
    lnFound = ASUBSCRIPT(laFullList,lnFound,1)
    laFullList[lnFound,1] = ;
      SUBSTR(laFullList[lnFound,1],2)
     m.lnFullCnt = m.lnFullCnt + 1
  ENDIF
   =ADEL(laSeleList, m.lnSelect)
   m.lnSeleCnt = m.lnSeleCnt - 1
   m.lnSelect = m.lnSeleCnt
   IF m.lnSeleCnt = 0
      SHOW GET m.lhRemove DISABLE
   ENDIF
   IF m.lnFullCnt > 0
     SHOW GET m.lhMove ENABLE
  ENDIF
   SHOW GET m.lnSelect
   SHOW GET m.lnFull
ENDIF
RETURN .T.
*------------------------------------------------------------
************************************************************
**--    MOVER.SCX - MAC PLATFORM
************************************************************
```

```
( ) DeskTop                          (·) Window

Name:                                <Type...>
Title:
Footer:

Size:              Screen Code:

 Height:   21.545   [X] Setup...
 Width:    63.833   [X] Cleanup & Procs...           «   OK   »

Position:          READ Clauses:                     < Cancel >

 Row:       0.000   [X] Activate...    [ ] Show...
 Column:    0.000   [ ] Valid...       [ ] When...
 [X] Center         [ ] Deactivate...

Environment:                             [ ] Add alias

      Environment saved with this screen.
```

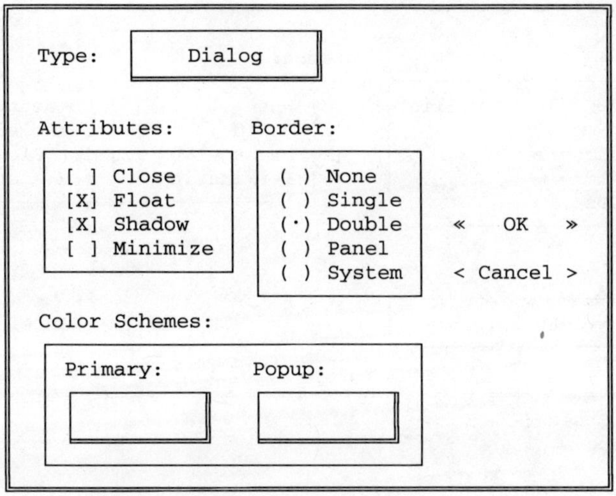

```
┌─────────────────────────────────────────────┐
│                                             │
│  Type:      [   Dialog   ]                  │
│                                             │
│  Attributes:      Border:                   │
│   ┌──────────────┐ ┌────────────┐           │
│   │ [ ] Close    │ │ ( ) None   │           │
│   │ [X] Float    │ │ ( ) Single │           │
│   │ [X] Shadow   │ │ (·) Double │  «  OK  » │
│   │ [ ] Minimize │ │ ( ) Panel  │           │
│   └──────────────┘ │ ( ) System │ < Cancel >│
│                    └────────────┘           │
│  Color Schemes:                             │
│   ┌────────────────────────────┐            │
│   │ Primary:      Popup:       │            │
│   │ [          ]  [          ] │            │
│   └────────────────────────────┘            │
└─────────────────────────────────────────────┘
MAC      RGB Fill Color Scheme: (,,)
MAC      Font: monaco,   9
 Screen Setup code above
 READ Activate code above
************************************************************
*--    G E T    O B J E C T S
************************************************************
*===========================================================
*  Text: Selection List:
*===========================================================
 @   0.273,   2.000
MAC      RGB Color Scheme: (,,,,,)
MAC      Font: Monaco,   9
       Style: Bold
*===========================================================
*  Text: Selected:
*===========================================================
 @   0.273,  43.000
MAC      RGB Color Scheme: (,,,,,)
MAC      Font: Monaco,   9
       Style: Bold
*===========================================================
*  m.lnFull
*===========================================================
 @   2.000,   1.000
    SIZE  14.182,  21.000
```

```
 List Type:                                    Options:
 ┌──────────────────────────────────────┐    ┌──────────────────────────────────────────┐
 │ (·) From Array        lafulllist     │    │ [ ] When...        [ ] Comment...        │
 │ ( ) From Popup                       │    │ [X] Valid...       [ ] Disabled          │
 │ ( ) Prompt Structure                 │    │ [ ] Message...     [X] 1st Element...    │
 │ ( ) Prompt Field                     │    │ [ ] Terminating    [X] # Elements...     │
 │ ( ) Prompt Files                     │    └──────────────────────────────────────────┘
 └──────────────────────────────────────┘

 Variable:
 ┌──────────────────────────────────────┐
 │ < Choose... > m.lnFull               │        «  OK  »     < Cancel >
 └──────────────────────────────────────┘

MAC      RGB Color Scheme: (,,,,,)
MAC      Font: monaco,   9
 Valid code above
 1st Element code above
 # Elements code above
*============================================================
*  m.lhMove
*============================================================
 @   2.636,  24.500
     SIZE   2.000,  14.833
 Spacing:    1

 Push Button Prompts:      ┌───────────────────────────────────┐
                           │ ( ) Horizontal    (·) Vertical    │
 ┌────────────────────┐    │ [ ] Terminating   <Spacing...>    │
 │\<Move              │    └───────────────────────────────────┘
 │                    │    Variable:
 │                    │    ┌───────────────────────────────────┐
 │                    │    │ < Choose... >  m.lhMove           │
 │                    │    └───────────────────────────────────┘
 │                    │    Options:
 │                    │    ┌───────────────────────────────────┐
 │                    │    │ [ ] When...      [ ] Comment...   │
 │                    │    │ [X] Valid...     [ ] Disabled     │
 │                    │    │ [ ] Message...                    │
 └────────────────────┘    └───────────────────────────────────┘

              «  OK  »     < Cancel >

MAC      RGB Color Scheme: (,,,,,)
MAC      Font: Geneva,   9
         Style: Bold
 Valid code above
*============================================================
*  m.lhRemove
*============================================================
 @  10.364,  24.500
     SIZE   2.000,  14.833
 Spacing:    1
```

```
╔══════════════════════════════════════════════════════════════╗
║  Push Button Prompts:     ┌──────────────────────────────┐   ║
║                           │ ( ) Horizontal   (·) Vertical│   ║
║  ┌────────────────────┐   │ [ ] Terminating <Spacing...> │   ║
║  │\<Remove            │   └──────────────────────────────┘   ║
║  │                    │   Variable:                          ║
║  │                    │   ┌──────────────────────────────┐   ║
║  │                    │   │ < Choose... >  m.lhRemove    │   ║
║  │                    │   └──────────────────────────────┘   ║
║  │                    │   Options:                           ║
║  │                    │   ┌──────────────────────────────┐   ║
║  │                    │   │ [ ] When...    [ ] Comment...│   ║
║  │                    │   │ [X] Valid...   [ ] Disabled  │   ║
║  │                    │   │ [ ] Message...               │   ║
║  └────────────────────┘   └──────────────────────────────┘   ║
║                                                              ║
║              «   OK   »    < Cancel >                        ║
╚══════════════════════════════════════════════════════════════╝
MAC       RGB Color Scheme: (,,,,,)
MAC       Font: Geneva,   9
         Style: Bold
 Valid code above
*===========================================================
*  m.lhMoveAll
*===========================================================
 @   5.545,  24.500
     SIZE   2.000,  14.833
 Spacing:    1
╔══════════════════════════════════════════════════════════════╗
║  Push Button Prompts:     ┌──────────────────────────────┐   ║
║                           │ ( ) Horizontal   (·) Vertical│   ║
║  ┌────────────────────┐   │ [ ] Terminating <Spacing...> │   ║
║  │Move \<All          │   └──────────────────────────────┘   ║
║  │                    │   Variable:                          ║
║  │                    │   ┌──────────────────────────────┐   ║
║  │                    │   │ < Choose... >  m.lhMoveAll   │   ║
║  │                    │   └──────────────────────────────┘   ║
║  │                    │   Options:                           ║
║  │                    │   ┌──────────────────────────────┐   ║
║  │                    │   │ [ ] When...    [ ] Comment...│   ║
║  │                    │   │ [X] Valid...   [ ] Disabled  │   ║
║  │                    │   │ [ ] Message...               │   ║
║  └────────────────────┘   └──────────────────────────────┘   ║
║                                                              ║
║              «   OK   »    < Cancel >                        ║
╚══════════════════════════════════════════════════════════════╝
MAC       RGB Color Scheme: (,,,,,)
MAC       Font: Geneva,   9
         Style: Bold
 Valid code above
*===========================================================
*  m.lhRemoveAll
*===========================================================
 @  13.273,  24.500
     SIZE   2.000,  14.833
 Spacing:    1
```

```
Push Button Prompts:          ( ) Horizontal    (·) Vertical
                              [ ] Terminating   <Spacing...>
Remo\<ve All
                              Variable:

                              < Choose... >  m.lhRemoveAll

                              Options:

                              [ ] When...      [ ] Comment...
                              [X] Valid...     [ ] Disabled
                              [ ] Message...

                 «   OK   »     < Cancel >
```

```
MAC      RGB Color Scheme: (,,,,,)
MAC      Font: Geneva,   9
        Style: Bold
 Valid code above
*==============================================================
*  m.lnSelect
*==============================================================
 @   2.000,  42.000
     SIZE  14.182,  21.000
```

```
List Type:                                  Options:

  (·) From Array       laSeleList           [ ] When...        [ ] Comment...
  ( ) From Popup                            [X] Valid...       [ ] Disabled
  ( ) Prompt Structure                      [ ] Message...     [X] 1st Element...
  ( ) Prompt Field                          [ ] Terminating    [X] # Elements...
  ( ) Prompt Files

Variable:

  < Choose... > m.lnSelect                      «   OK   »     < Cancel >
```

```
MAC      RGB Color Scheme: (,,,,,)
MAC      Font: monaco,   9
 Valid code above
 1st Element code above
 # Elements code above
*==============================================================
*  lhOk
*==============================================================
 @  18.091,  17.333
     SIZE   2.000,  15.000
 Spacing:    9
```

```
 ┌──────────────────────────────────────────────────────────┐
 │ Push Button Prompts:     (·) Horizontal    ( ) Vertical  │
 │                          [X] Terminating  <Spacing...>   │
 │  \!OK                                                    │
 │                          Variable:                       │
 │                                                          │
 │                           < Choose... >  lhOk            │
 │                                                          │
 │                          Options:                        │
 │                                                          │
 │                           [ ] When...     [ ] Comment... │
 │                           [ ] Valid...    [ ] Disabled   │
 │                           [ ] Message...                 │
 │                                                          │
 │              «   OK   »    < Cancel >                    │
 └──────────────────────────────────────────────────────────┘
MAC       RGB Color Scheme: (,,,,,)
MAC       Font: Geneva,   9
         Style: Bold
*==============================================================
*  lhCancel
*==============================================================
 @  18.091,  35.333
     SIZE   2.000,  15.000
 Spacing:     9
 ┌──────────────────────────────────────────────────────────┐
 │ Push Button Prompts:     (·) Horizontal    ( ) Vertical  │
 │                          [X] Terminating  <Spacing...>   │
 │  \?Cancel                                                │
 │                          Variable:                       │
 │                                                          │
 │                           < Choose... >  lhCancel        │
 │                                                          │
 │                          Options:                        │
 │                                                          │
 │                           [ ] When...     [ ] Comment... │
 │                           [X] Valid...    [ ] Disabled   │
 │                           [ ] Message...                 │
 │                                                          │
 │              «   OK   »    < Cancel >                    │
 └──────────────────────────────────────────────────────────┘
MAC       RGB Color Scheme: (,,,,,)
MAC       Font: Geneva,   9
         Style: Bold
 Valid code above
 Screen Cleanup and Procedures code above
*--------------------------------------------------------------
```

```
************************************************************
**--     MOVER.SCX - WINDOWS PLATFORM
************************************************************
  ( ) DeskTop                        (·) Window

  Name:                              <Type...>
  Title:
  Footer:

  Size:             Screen Code:

   Height:   21.583    [X] Setup...
   Width:    63.750    [X] Cleanup & Procs...          «   OK   »

  Position:         READ Clauses:                      < Cancel >

   Row:        0.000   [X] Activate...     [ ] Show...
   Column:     0.000   [ ] Valid...        [ ] When...
   [X] Center          [ ] Deactivate...

  Environment:                          [ ] Add alias

        Environment saved with this screen.

  Type:       Dialog

  Attributes:       Border:

   [ ] Close         ( ) None
   [X] Float         ( ) Single
   [X] Shadow        (·) Double      «   OK   »
   [ ] Minimize      ( ) Panel
                     ( ) System      < Cancel >

  Color Schemes:

   Primary:          Popup:

WINDOWS  RGB Fill Color Scheme: (,,)
WINDOWS  Font: Terminal,   9
 Screen Setup code above
 READ Activate code above
************************************************************
*--    G E T   O B J E C T S
************************************************************
*===========================================================
*  Text: Selection List:
*===========================================================
 @   0.250,   2.000
WINDOWS  RGB Color Scheme: (,,,,,)
```

```
WINDOWS  Font: Terminal,   9
*============================================================
*  Text: Selected:
*============================================================
 @   0.250,  43.000
WINDOWS  RGB Color Scheme: (,,,,,)
WINDOWS  Font: Terminal,   9
*============================================================
*  m.lnFull
*============================================================
 @   2.000,   1.000
     SIZE  14.000,  21.000

  List Type:                              Options:

   (·) From Array        lafulllist        [ ] When...       [ ] Comment...
   ( ) From Popup                          [X] Valid...      [ ] Disabled
   ( ) Prompt Structure                    [ ] Message...   [X] 1st Element...
   ( ) Prompt Field                        [ ] Terminating  [X] # Elements...
   ( ) Prompt Files

  Variable:

   < Choose... > m.lnFull                    «   OK   »    < Cancel >

WINDOWS  RGB Color Scheme: (,,,,,)
WINDOWS  Font: Terminal,   9
 Valid code above
 1st Element code above
 # Elements code above
*============================================================
*  m.lhMove
*============================================================
 @   2.667,  26.250
     SIZE   2.000,  14.833
 Spacing:    1

  Push Button Prompts:       ( ) Horizontal    (·) Vertical
                             [ ] Terminating   <Spacing...>
   \<Move
                            Variable:

                             < Choose... >  m.lhMove

                            Options:

                             [ ] When...     [ ] Comment...
                             [X] Valid...    [ ] Disabled
                             [ ] Message...

                  «   OK   »    < Cancel >

WINDOWS  RGB Color Scheme: (,,,,,)
```

```
WINDOWS  Font: MS Sans Serif,   8
        Style: Bold
 Valid code above
*============================================================
*  m.lhRemove
*============================================================
 @  10.333,  26.250
     SIZE   2.000,  14.833
 Spacing:    1
```

```
 Push Button Prompts:        ( ) Horizontal   (·) Vertical
                             [ ] Terminating  <Spacing...>
 \<Remove
                            Variable:

                             < Choose... >  m.lhRemove

                            Options:

                             [ ] When...    [ ] Comment...
                             [X] Valid...   [ ] Disabled
                             [ ] Message...

              «   OK   »    < Cancel >
```

```
WINDOWS  RGB Color Scheme: (,,,,,)
WINDOWS  Font: MS Sans Serif,   8
        Style: Bold
 Valid code above
*============================================================
*  m.lhMoveAll
*============================================================
 @   5.500,  26.250
     SIZE   2.000,  14.833
 Spacing:    1
```

```
 Push Button Prompts:        ( ) Horizontal   (·) Vertical
                             [ ] Terminating  <Spacing...>
 Move \<All
                            Variable:

                             < Choose... >  m.lhMoveAll

                            Options:

                             [ ] When...    [ ] Comment...
                             [X] Valid...   [ ] Disabled
                             [ ] Message...

              «   OK   »    < Cancel >
```

```
WINDOWS  RGB Color Scheme: (,,,,,)
WINDOWS  Font: MS Sans Serif,   8
```

```
        Style: Bold
 Valid code above
*==============================================================
*  m.lhRemoveAll
*==============================================================
 @  13.250,  26.250
    SIZE  2.000,  14.833
 Spacing:   1
```

```
+------------------------------------------------------------------+
|                                                                  |
|  Push Button Prompts:      | ( ) Horizontal    (·) Vertical   |  |
|                            | [ ] Terminating  <Spacing...>    |  |
|  | Remo\<ve All        |                                       |
|  |                     |   Variable:                           |
|  |                     |   | < Choose... >  m.lhRemoveAll |    |
|  |                     |                                       |
|  |                     |   Options:                            |
|  |                     |   | [ ] When...     [ ] Comment... |  |
|  |                     |   | [X] Valid...    [ ] Disabled   |  |
|  |                     |   | [ ] Message...                 |  |
|                                                                  |
|                  «  OK  »    < Cancel >                          |
+------------------------------------------------------------------+
```

```
WINDOWS  RGB Color Scheme: (,,,,,)
WINDOWS  Font: MS Sans Serif,   8
        Style: Bold
 Valid code above
*==============================================================
*  m.lnSelect
*==============================================================
 @   2.000,  42.000
    SIZE  14.000,  21.000
```

```
+--------------------------------------------------------------------------------+
|                                                                                |
|  List Type:                              Options:                              |
|  | (·) From Array       laSeleList |     | [ ] When...        [ ] Comment...     |
|  | ( ) From Popup                  |     | [X] Valid...       [ ] Disabled       |
|  | ( ) Prompt Structure            |     | [ ] Message...     [X] 1st Element... |
|  | ( ) Prompt Field                |     | [ ] Terminating    [X] # Elements...  |
|  | ( ) Prompt Files                |                                           |
|                                                                                |
|  Variable:                                                                     |
|  | < Choose... > m.lnSelect        |         «  OK  »    < Cancel >           |
|                                                                                |
+--------------------------------------------------------------------------------+
```

```
WINDOWS  RGB Color Scheme: (,,,,,)
WINDOWS  Font: Terminal,    9
 Valid code above
 1st Element code above
 # Elements code above
```

```
*==============================================================
*  lhOk
*==============================================================
 @  18.083,  17.250
      SIZE   2.000,  15.000
 Spacing:     9
```

```
  Push Button Prompts:        (·) Horizontal    ( ) Vertical
                              [X] Terminating   <Spacing...>
  \!OK
                             Variable:

                              < Choose... >  lhOk

                             Options:

                              [ ] When...     [ ] Comment...
                              [ ] Valid...    [ ] Disabled
                              [ ] Message...

                 «   OK   »    < Cancel >
```

```
WINDOWS  RGB Color Scheme: (,,,,,)
WINDOWS  Font: MS Sans Serif,   8
        Style: Bold
*==============================================================
*  lhCancel
*==============================================================
 @  18.083,  35.250
      SIZE   2.000,  15.000
 Spacing:     9
```

```
  Push Button Prompts:        (·) Horizontal    ( ) Vertical
                              [X] Terminating   <Spacing...>
  \?Cancel
                             Variable:

                              < Choose... >  lhCancel

                             Options:

                              [ ] When...     [ ] Comment...
                              [X] Valid...    [ ] Disabled
                              [ ] Message...

                 «   OK   »    < Cancel >
```

```
WINDOWS  RGB Color Scheme: (,,,,,)
WINDOWS  Font: MS Sans Serif,   8
        Style: Bold
 Valid code above
 Screen Cleanup and Procedures code above
```

Error Dialog: ONERROR.SCX

OnError() is a very generic error handler. It allows you to record the data from an error and provides the user with the capability of continuing or exiting from the application.

```
*-----------------------------------------------------------
************************************************************
**--     ONERROR.SCX - DOS PLATFORM
************************************************************

 ( ) DeskTop                          (·) Window

 Name:                                <Type...>
 Title:  Error Message
 Footer:

 Size:              Screen Code:

  Height:   12       [X] Setup...
  Width:    54       [ ] Cleanup & Procs...             «   OK   »

 Position:          READ Clauses:                       < Cancel >

  Row:       0       [ ] Activate...    [ ] Show...
  Column:    0       [ ] Valid...       [X] When...
  [X] Center         [ ] Deactivate...

 Environment:                            [X] Add alias

        Environment NOT saved with screen.


  Type:       Alert

  Attributes:        Border:

   [ ] Close          ( ) None
   [X] Float          ( ) Single
   [X] Shadow         (·) Double       «   OK   »
   [ ] Minimize       ( ) Panel
                      ( ) System       < Cancel >

  Color Schemes:

   Primary:          Popup:

   Alerts            Alert Pops

************************************************************
*  SCREEN SETUP CODE
************************************************************
```

```
#SECTION 1
*  Program...........: ONERROR Setup
*  Author............: yag
*  Project...........: COMMON
*  Created...........: 04/16/93
*  Copyright.........: (c) Flash Creative Management, 1993
*) Description.......: Simple error handler
*  Calling Samples...: ON ERROR DO Onerror WITH ;
*                    :   MESSAGE, MESSAGE(1), PROC(), LINENO(), ERROR()
*  Parameter List....:
*  Major change list.:
PARAMETER lcMessage, lcMessage1, lcProc, lnLineNo, lnError
#SECTION 2
------------------------------------------------------------
*-- READ When Clause
------------------------------------------------------------
```

```
READ When

  (•) Procedure
  ( ) Expression
```

```
?? CHR(7)
INSERT ;
  INTO OnError ;
  (mMessage,mMessage1,mProc,nLineNo,nError,dDate,cTime) ;
  VALUES ;
  (lcMessage,lcMessage1,lcProc,lnLineNo,lnError,DATE(),TIME())
************************************************************
*--    G E T    O B J E C T S
************************************************************
*===========================================================
*  Box
*===========================================================
 @   0,   5
 SIZE   3,   5
*===========================================================
*  Text: !
*===========================================================
 @   1,   7
*===========================================================
*  Text: A system error has been detected.
*===========================================================
 @   1,  12
*===========================================================
*  Text: saved for support personnel use.  Please call
*===========================================================
 @   5,   2
*===========================================================
*  Text: support.
*===========================================================
 @   6,   2
*===========================================================
*  m.lhQuit
*===========================================================
 @   8,  29
```

```
Spacing:    1

Push Button Prompts:          (·) Horizontal    ( ) Vertical
                              [ ] Terminating   <Spacing...>
\<Quit
                              Variable:

                              < Choose... >  m.lhQuit

                              Options:

                              [ ] When...      [ ] Comment...
                              [X] Valid...     [ ] Disabled
                              [X] Message...

            «   OK   »    < Cancel >
--------------------------------------------------------------
*-- m.lhQuit Valid Clause
--------------------------------------------------------------

  Valid

    (·) Procedure
    ( ) Expression

QUIT
--------------------------------------------------------------
*-- m.lhQuit Message Clause
--------------------------------------------------------------

  Message

    ( ) Procedure
    (·) Expression

Message:   "Emergency quit from the application"
*=============================================================
*  lhResume
*=============================================================
 @   8,  15
 Spacing:    1
```

```
Push Button Prompts:          (·) Horizontal    ( ) Vertical
                              [X] Terminating  <Spacing...>
 \<Resume
                             Variable:

                              < Choose... >  lhResume

                             Options:

                              [ ] When...      [ ] Comment...
                              [ ] Valid...     [ ] Disabled
                              [X] Message...

              «  OK  »     < Cancel >
------------------------------------------------------------
*-- lhResume Message Clause
------------------------------------------------------------

  Message

   ( ) Procedure
   (·) Expression

Message:   "Continue working with this program"
*============================================================
*  Text: A copy of the current system information is being
*============================================================
 @   4,   2
*------------------------------------------------------------
```

```
************************************************************
**--    ONERROR.SCX - MAC PLATFORM
************************************************************
```

```
( ) DeskTop                         (·) Window

Name:                               <Type...>
Title:  Error Message
Footer:

Size:          Screen Code:

 Height:   12.364    [X] Setup...
 Width:    54.500    [ ] Cleanup & Procs...          «   OK   »

Position:      READ Clauses:                        < Cancel >

 Row:        0.000   [ ] Activate...    [ ] Show...
 Column:     0.000   [ ] Valid...       [X] When...
 [X] Center          [ ] Deactivate...

Environment:                          [X] Add alias

      Environment NOT saved with screen.
```

```
Type:    Alert

Attributes:      Border:

 [ ] Close        ( ) None
 [X] Float        ( ) Single
 [X] Shadow       (·) Double      «   OK   »
 [ ] Minimize     ( ) Panel
                  ( ) System      < Cancel >

Color Schemes:

 Primary:        Popup:
```

```
MAC      RGB Fill Color Scheme: (,,)
MAC      Font: monaco,    9
 Screen Setup code above
 READ When code above
************************************************************
*--    G E T   O B J E C T S
************************************************************
*===========================================================
*  Box
*===========================================================
 @   0.545,   7.667
 SIZE   2.455,   4.167
MAC      RGB Color Scheme: (,,,,,)
```

```
            Pen: 2
*================================================================
*  Text: !
*================================================================
 @   1.273,    9.167
MAC       RGB Color Scheme: (,,,,,)
MAC       Font: Monaco,    9
         Style: Bold
*================================================================
*  Text: A system error has been detected.
*================================================================
 @   1.273,  12.500
MAC       RGB Color Scheme: (,,,,,)
MAC       Font: monaco,    9
*================================================================
*  Text: A copy of the current system information is being
*================================================================
 @   3.909,    2.000
MAC       RGB Color Scheme: (,,,,,)
MAC       Font: monaco,    9
*================================================================
*  m.lhQuit
*================================================================
 @   9.182,  29.667
     SIZE   2.273,  13.167
 Spacing:     1
```

```
  Push Button Prompts:        (·) Horizontal     ( ) Vertical
                              [ ] Terminating   <Spacing...>
  \<Quit
                             Variable:

                              < Choose... >  m.lhQuit

                             Options:

                              [ ] When...      [ ] Comment...
                              [X] Valid...     [ ] Disabled
                              [X] Message...

                     «  OK  »     < Cancel >
```

```
MAC       RGB Color Scheme: (,,,,,)
MAC       Font: monaco,    9
 Valid code above
 Message code above
*================================================================
*  lhResume
*================================================================
 @   9.182,  15.333
     SIZE   2.273,  13.167
 Spacing:     1
```

```
Push Button Prompts:          (·) Horizontal    ( ) Vertical
                              [X] Terminating  <Spacing...>
 \<Resume
                             Variable:

                              < Choose... >  lhResume

                             Options:

                              [ ] When...      [ ] Comment...
                              [ ] Valid...     [ ] Disabled
                              [X] Message...

               «   OK   »    < Cancel >
```

```
MAC      RGB Color Scheme: (,,,,,)
MAC      Font: monaco,   9
 Message code above
*================================================================
*  Text: saved for support personnel use.  Please call
*================================================================
 @   5.000,   2.000
MAC      RGB Color Scheme: (,,,,,)
MAC      Font: monaco,   9
*================================================================
*  Text: support.
*================================================================
 @   6.000,   2.000
MAC      RGB Color Scheme: (,,,,,)
MAC      Font: monaco,   9
*----------------------------------------------------------------
*****************************************************************
**--     ONERROR.SCX - WINDOWS PLATFORM
*****************************************************************
```

```
( ) DeskTop                          (·) Window

Name:                                <Type...>
Title:  Error Message
Footer:

Size:              Screen Code:

 Height:   12.167   [X] Setup...
 Width:    55.000   [ ] Cleanup & Procs...          «   OK   »

Position:          READ Clauses:                    < Cancel >

 Row:        0.000  [ ] Activate...    [ ] Show...
 Column:     0.000  [ ] Valid...       [X] When...
 [X] Center         [ ] Deactivate...

Environment:                          [X] Add alias

       Environment NOT saved with screen.
```

```
Type:   [ Alert ]

Attributes:        Border:

[ ] Close          ( ) None
[X] Float          ( ) Single
[X] Shadow         (·) Double      «  OK  »
[ ] Minimize       ( ) Panel
                   ( ) System      < Cancel >

Color Schemes:

Primary:           Popup:
[        ]         [        ]
```

```
WINDOWS  RGB Fill Color Scheme: (,,)
WINDOWS  Font: Terminal,   9
 Screen Setup code above
 READ When code above
************************************************************
*--    G E T    O B J E C T S
************************************************************
*===========================================================
*  Box
*===========================================================
 @   0.500,   7.500
 SIZE   2.333,   4.250
WINDOWS  RGB Color Scheme: (,,,,,)
           Pen: 2
*===========================================================
*  Text: !
*===========================================================
 @   1.250,   9.125
WINDOWS  RGB Color Scheme: (,,,,,)
WINDOWS  Font: Terminal,   9
*===========================================================
*  Text: A system error has been detected.
*===========================================================
 @   1.250,  12.500
WINDOWS  RGB Color Scheme: (,,,,,)
WINDOWS  Font: Terminal,   9
*===========================================================
*  Text: A copy of the current system information is being
*===========================================================
 @   3.917,   2.000
WINDOWS  RGB Color Scheme: (,,,,,)
WINDOWS  Font: Terminal,   9
*===========================================================
*  m.lhQuit
*===========================================================
 @   9.167,  29.625
    SIZE   2.077,  13.167
 Spacing:    1
```

```
+----------------------------------------------------------------+
| Push Button Prompts:     (·) Horizontal    ( ) Vertical         |
|                          [ ] Terminating  <Spacing...>          |
| \<Quit                                                          |
|                          Variable:                              |
|                          < Choose... >  m.lhQuit                |
|                          Options:                               |
|                          [ ] When...      [ ] Comment...        |
|                          [X] Valid...     [ ] Disabled          |
|                          [X] Message...                         |
|                                                                 |
|              «  OK  »    < Cancel >                            |
+----------------------------------------------------------------+
WINDOWS  RGB Color Scheme: (,,,,,)
WINDOWS  Font: MS Sans Serif,   8
         Style: Bold
 Valid code above
 Message code above
*=============================================================
*  lhResume
*=============================================================
 @   9.167,  15.375
     SIZE   2.077,  13.167
 Spacing:    1
+----------------------------------------------------------------+
| Push Button Prompts:     (·) Horizontal    ( ) Vertical         |
|                          [X] Terminating  <Spacing...>          |
| \<Resume                                                        |
|                          Variable:                              |
|                          < Choose... >  lhResume                |
|                          Options:                               |
|                          [ ] When...      [ ] Comment...        |
|                          [ ] Valid...     [ ] Disabled          |
|                          [X] Message...                         |
|                                                                 |
|              «  OK  »    < Cancel >                            |
+----------------------------------------------------------------+
WINDOWS  RGB Color Scheme: (,,,,,)
WINDOWS  Font: MS Sans Serif,   8
         Style: Bold
 Message code above
*=============================================================
*  Text: saved for support personnel use.  Please call
*=============================================================
 @   5.000,   2.000
WINDOWS  RGB Color Scheme: (,,,,,)
WINDOWS  Font: Terminal,   9
*=============================================================
```

```
*  Text: support.
*============================================================
 @   6.000,   2.000
WINDOWS  RGB Color Scheme: (,,,,,)
WINDOWS  Font: Terminal,   9
```

Lengthy Process Warning: PACKALER.SCX

PackAler() is an alert window that alerts the user to the fact that the coming operation may take some time.

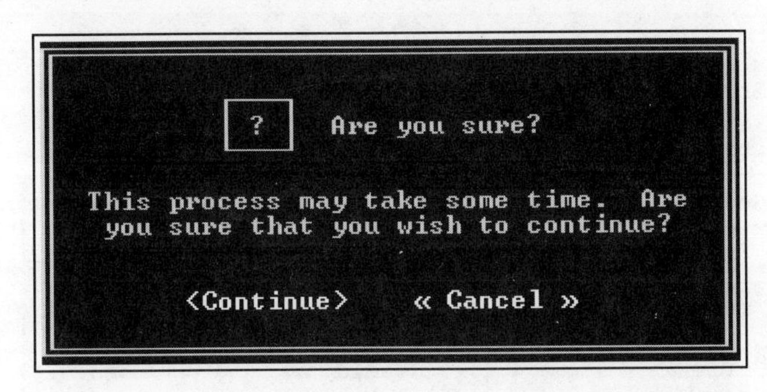

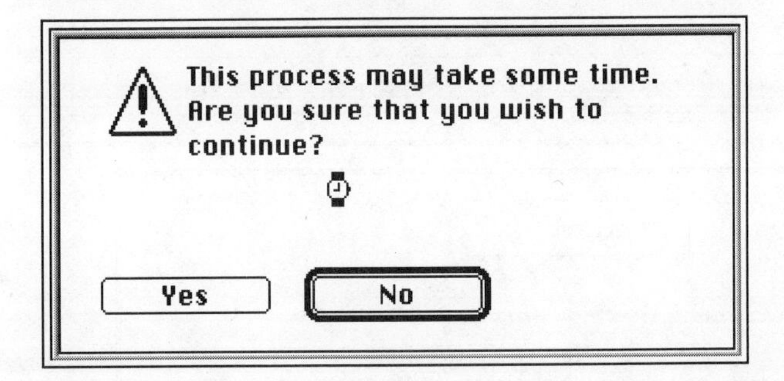

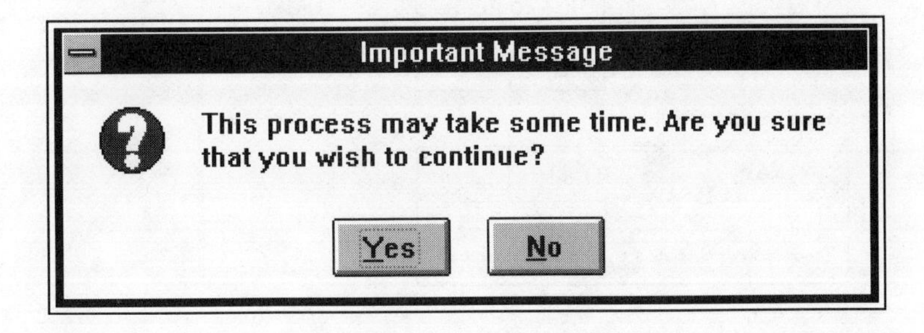

```
*---------------------------------------------------------------
****************************************************************
**--    PACKALER.SCX - DOS PLATFORM
****************************************************************

 ( ) DeskTop                           (·) Window

 Name:                                 <Type...>
 Title:
 Footer:

 Size:            Screen Code:

  Height:   13     [X] Setup...
  Width:    43     [X] Cleanup & Procs...          «   OK   »

 Position:        READ Clauses:                    < Cancel >

  Row:       0     [ ] Activate...    [ ] Show...
  Column:    0     [ ] Valid...       [ ] When...
  [X] Center       [ ] Deactivate...

 Environment:                          [X] Add alias

        Environment NOT saved with screen.


  Type:       Alert

  Attributes:      Border:

   [ ] Close        ( ) None
   [X] Float        ( ) Single
   [X] Shadow       (·) Double       «   OK   »
   [ ] Minimize     ( ) Panel
                    ( ) System       < Cancel >

  Color Schemes:

   Primary:          Popup:

   Alerts            Alert Pops

****************************************************************
*  SCREEN SETUP CODE
****************************************************************
*  Program..........: PACKALER Setup
*  Author...........: yag
*  Project..........: COMMON
*  Created..........: 04/16/93
*  Copyright........: (c) Flash Creative Management, 1993
*) Description......: Questioning dialog - this may take some time...
*  Calling Samples...: IF PackAler()
*  Parameter List....:
```

```
*  Major change list.:
PRIVATE llDoIt
llDoIt = .F.                              && Default to <CANCEL>
DO CASE
   CASE _WINDOWS
      RETURN IIF(msgbox('This process may take some time. ' + ;
         'Are you sure that you wish to continue? ', ;
         'Important Message',36)=6,.T.,.F.)
   CASE _MAC
      RETURN IIF(fxAlert(0,266,-1,-1,"This process may take some time. " +
;
         'Are you sure that you wish to continue? ') = 1,.F.,.T.)
ENDCASE
************************************************************
*--    G E T    O B J E C T S
************************************************************
*===========================================================
*  lhContinue
*===========================================================
 @   9,   8
 Spacing:    5

  Push Button Prompts:        (·) Horizontal    ( ) Vertical
                              [X] Terminating  <Spacing...>
  Continue
                             Variable:

                              < Choose... >  lhContinue

                             Options:

                              [ ] When...      [ ] Comment...
                              [X] Valid...     [ ] Disabled
                              [X] Message...

                 «  OK  »    < Cancel >
------------------------------------------------------------
*-- lhContinue Valid Clause
------------------------------------------------------------

  Valid

    (·) Procedure
    ( ) Expression

llDoIt = .T.
------------------------------------------------------------
*-- lhContinue Message Clause
------------------------------------------------------------
```

```
Message

  ( ) Procedure
  (·) Expression

Message:   "Run the selected procedure"
*==============================================================
*  lhCancel
*==============================================================
 @   9,  22
 Spacing:    5

Push Button Prompts:         (·) Horizontal   ( ) Vertical
                             [X] Terminating  <Spacing...>
\?\!Cancel                  Variable:

                             < Choose... >  lhCancel

                            Options:

                             [ ] When...     [ ] Comment...
                             [ ] Valid...    [ ] Disabled
                             [X] Message...

                 «   OK   »    < Cancel >
--------------------------------------------------------------
*-- lhCancel Message Clause
--------------------------------------------------------------

Message

  ( ) Procedure
  (·) Expression

Message:   "Do NOT run the procedure"
*==============================================================
*  Box
*==============================================================
 @   1,  10
 SIZE   3,   5
*==============================================================
*  Text: ?
*==============================================================
 @   2,  12
*==============================================================
*  Text: Are you sure?
*==============================================================
```

```
 @   2,  17
*===========================================================
*  Text: This process may take some time.  Are
*===========================================================
 @   5,   2
*===========================================================
*  Text: you sure that you wish to continue?
*===========================================================
 @   6,   3
************************************************************
*--  SCREEN CLEANUP CODE
************************************************************
RETURN llDoIt
*-----------------------------------------------------------
************************************************************
**--    PACKALER.SCX - MAC PLATFORM
************************************************************
```

```
( ) DeskTop                          (·) Window

Name:                                <Type...>
Title:
Footer:

Size:              Screen Code:

  Height:   13.455    [X] Setup...
  Width:    49.000    [X] Cleanup & Procs...              «   OK   »

Position:          READ Clauses:                          < Cancel >

  Row:       0.000    [ ] Activate...    [ ] Show...
  Column:    0.000    [ ] Valid...       [ ] When...
  [X] Center          [ ] Deactivate...

Environment:                          [X] Add alias

        Environment NOT saved with screen.
```

```
Type:       Alert

Attributes:       Border:

  [ ] Close         ( ) None
  [X] Float         ( ) Single
  [X] Shadow        (·) Double      «   OK   »
  [ ] Minimize      ( ) Panel
                    ( ) System      < Cancel >

Color Schemes:

  Primary:          Popup:
```

```
MAC      RGB Fill Color Scheme: (255,255,255)
```

```
MAC      Font: monaco,   9
 Screen Setup code above
************************************************************
*--    G E T    O B J E C T S
************************************************************
*===========================================================
*  lhContinue
*===========================================================
 @   9.636,  11.833
     SIZE   2.417,  10.000
 Spacing:    5

  Push Button Prompts:        (·) Horizontal    ( ) Vertical
                              [X] Terminating  <Spacing...>
  Continue
                             Variable:

                              < Choose... >  lhContinue

                             Options:

                              [ ] When...     [ ] Comment...
                              [X] Valid...    [ ] Disabled
                              [X] Message...

                 «   OK   »    < Cancel >

MAC      RGB Color Scheme: (,,,,,)
MAC      Font: Geneva,   9
        Style: Bold
 Valid code above
 Message code above
*===========================================================
*  lhCancel
*===========================================================
 @   9.818,  26.833
     SIZE   2.417,  10.000
 Spacing:    5

  Push Button Prompts:        (·) Horizontal    ( ) Vertical
                              [X] Terminating  <Spacing...>
  \?\!Cancel
                             Variable:

                              < Choose... >  lhCancel

                             Options:

                              [ ] When...     [ ] Comment...
                              [ ] Valid...    [ ] Disabled
                              [X] Message...

                 «   OK   »    < Cancel >

MAC      RGB Color Scheme: (,,,,,)
MAC      Font: Geneva,   9
```

```
        Style: Bold
 Message code above
*==========================================================
*  Box
*==========================================================
 @   1.818,   3.833
 SIZE   2.182,   2.833
MAC      RGB Color Scheme: (,,,,,)
           Pen: 1
*==========================================================
*  Text: ?
*==========================================================
 @   2.545,   4.833
MAC      RGB Color Scheme: (,,,,,)
MAC      Font: Monaco,   9
        Style: Bold
*==========================================================
*  Text: Are you sure?
*==========================================================
 @   2.545,   8.167
MAC      RGB Color Scheme: (,,,,,)
MAC      Font: Monaco,   9
        Style: Bold
*==========================================================
*  Text: This process may take some time.  Are
*==========================================================
 @   5.818,   3.500
MAC      RGB Color Scheme: (,,,,,)
MAC      Font: Monaco,   9
        Style: Bold
*==========================================================
*  Text: you sure that you wish to continue?
*==========================================================
 @   7.000,   4.333
MAC      RGB Color Scheme: (,,,,,)
MAC      Font: Monaco,   9
        Style: Bold
 Screen Cleanup and Procedures code above
*----------------------------------------------------------
***********************************************************
**--    PACKALER.SCX - WINDOWS PLATFORM
***********************************************************
```

```
( ) DeskTop                          (·) Window

Name:                                <Type...>
Title:
Footer:

Size:             Screen Code:

  Height:   13.583    [X] Setup...
  Width:    39.889    [X] Cleanup & Procs...           «  OK  »

Position:         READ Clauses:                        < Cancel >

  Row:       0.000    [ ] Activate...     [ ] Show...
  Column:    0.000    [ ] Valid...        [ ] When...
  [X] Center          [ ] Deactivate...

Environment:                           [X] Add alias

        Environment NOT saved with screen.
```

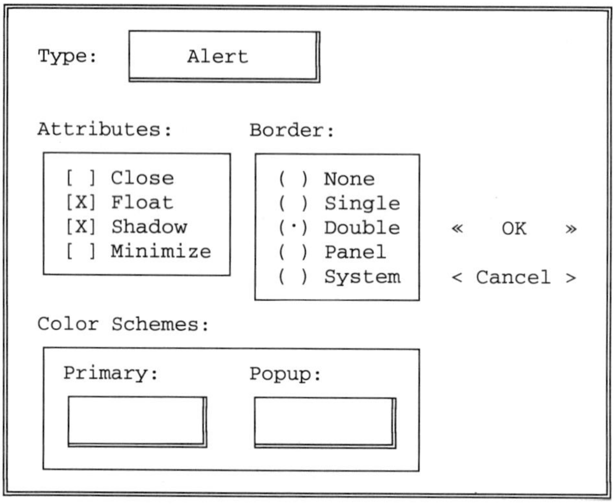

```
Type:  Alert

Attributes:        Border:
 [ ] Close          ( ) None
 [X] Float          ( ) Single
 [X] Shadow         (·) Double      «  OK  »
 [ ] Minimize       ( ) Panel
                    ( ) System      < Cancel >
Color Schemes:
 Primary:          Popup:

WINDOWS  RGB Fill Color Scheme: (255,255,255)
WINDOWS  Font: Terminal,   9
        Style: Bold
 Screen Setup code above
**************************************************************
*--    G E T    O B J E C T S
**************************************************************
*=============================================================
*  lhContinue
*=============================================================
 @   9.667,  11.889
     SIZE   2.385,  10.000
 Spacing:    5

Push Button Prompts:     (·) Horizontal    ( ) Vertical
                         [X] Terminating  <Spacing...>
 Continue
                        Variable:
                         < Choose... >  lhContinue
                        Options:
                         [ ] When...      [ ] Comment...
                         [X] Valid...     [ ] Disabled
                         [X] Message...

            «  OK  »     < Cancel >

WINDOWS  RGB Color Scheme: (,,,,,)
WINDOWS  Font: MS Sans Serif,   8
        Style: Bold
 Valid code above
 Message code above
*=============================================================
```

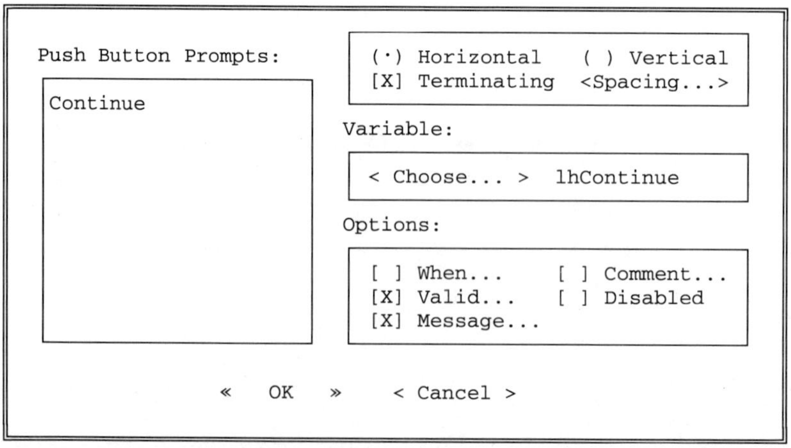

```
*  lhCancel
*==========================================================
 @   9.667,  21.222
     SIZE   2.385,  10.000
 Spacing:    5

  Push Button Prompts:      (·) Horizontal    ( ) Vertical
                            [X] Terminating  <Spacing...>
  \?\!Cancel
                           Variable:

                            < Choose... >  lhCancel

                           Options:

                            [ ] When...     [ ] Comment...
                            [ ] Valid...    [ ] Disabled
                            [X] Message...

               «   OK   »    < Cancel >

WINDOWS  RGB Color Scheme: (,,,,,)
WINDOWS  Font: MS Sans Serif,   8
        Style: Bold
 Message code above
*==========================================================
*  Box
*==========================================================
 @   1.833,    3.778
 SIZE   2.167,    2.889
WINDOWS  RGB Color Scheme: (,,,,,)
           Pen: 1
*==========================================================
*  Text: ?
*==========================================================
 @   2.500,    4.778
WINDOWS  RGB Color Scheme: (,,,,,)
WINDOWS  Font: Terminal,   9
*==========================================================
*  Text: Are you sure?
*==========================================================
 @   2.500,    8.111
WINDOWS  RGB Color Scheme: (,,,,,)
WINDOWS  Font: Terminal,   9
*==========================================================
*  Text: This process may take some time.  Are
*==========================================================
 @   5.833,    3.444
WINDOWS  RGB Color Scheme: (,,,,,)
WINDOWS  Font: Terminal,   9
*==========================================================
*  Text: you sure that you wish to continue?
*==========================================================
 @   7.000,    4.333
WINDOWS  RGB Color Scheme: (,,,,,)
WINDOWS  Font: Terminal,   9
 Screen Cleanup and Procedures code above
```

Reusable Screen: REPORTS.SCX

A common requirement for database applications is the generation of reports. It is possible to design a standard report selection window that can be used to select the report to be run.

The report window in the sample application is an example of a window that is "data driven." In other words, the window look remains static, but the capabilities of the window changes depending on the database that drives it. In this application, REPOLIST.DBF drives the report screen.

The report selections appear in the scrolling window. The report window compares the cWindShow field to the first four characters of the calling menu to decide which reports should be shown at the time. If a report is of a "List" or "Labe" (Label) type, a simple REPORT FORM or LABEL FORM is performed on the database stored in the cSelect field. If a "Repo" type is selected, a .QPR file with the same name as the report file is run. This file will typically contain a SQL query, but can also contain FoxPro code that lets the user modify the WHEN clause of the query. The REPORT FORM command is the run against the output of the query. Double clicking on a report (or pressing <Enter>) will run the report as well. This is accomplished by calling the reporting function in the VALID of the scrolling list snippet.

The "To Screen" selection does not use FoxPro's PREVIEW enhancement. The original version of this window did use this feature. However, we prefer to allow the user to move about both backwards and forwards through the report. PREVIEW does not allow this. The solution that we used of sending the report to a file, and using MODIFY COMMAND NOMODIFY on that file solves this issue. It would also allow us to add a Find menu option, allowing the user to search for a key word in the report. Note that we used MODIFY COMMAND, and not MODIFY FILE. MODIFY FILE defaults to wrapping text, MODIFY COMMAND does not. This makes MODIFY COMMAND more suitable to reports that are over 80 characters in length.

Note that this object is geared towards running DOS reports. Reports created under the Windows environment are graphical and can not be sent to a file. Therefore, we create reports using FoxPro/DOS and run them under Windows. If you wish to create graphical reports, you will have to change the code that performs a MODI COMM to either use REPORT FORM ... PREVIEW under Windows and Macintosh, or have your code do a SQL SELECT to a temporary FRX for every record that has its platform set to DOS, and report off of that temporary report file.

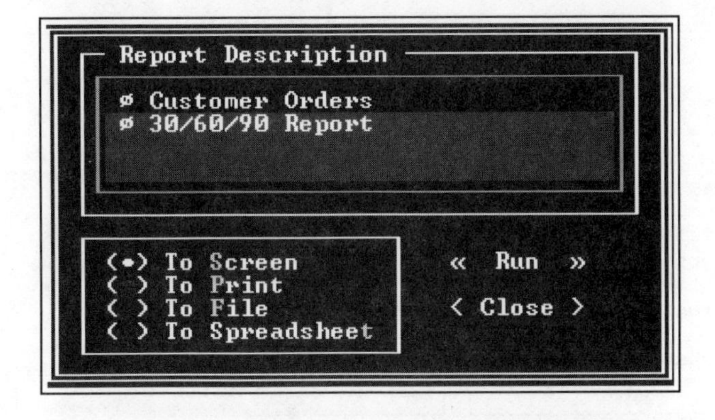
Report Description
ø Customer Orders
ø 30/60/90 Report
(•) To Screen
( ) To Print
( ) To File
( ) To Spreadsheet
« Run »
< Close >

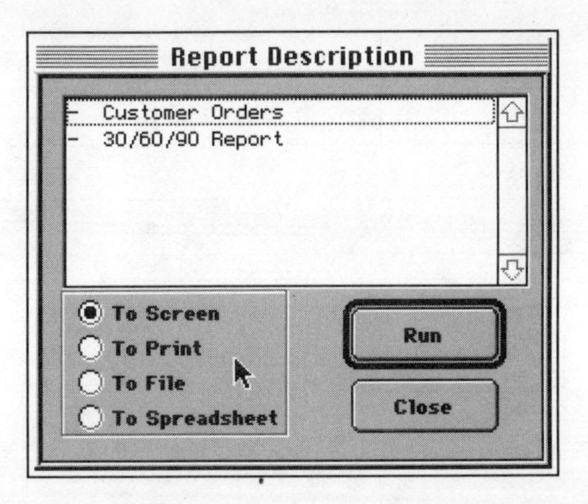
Report Description
- Customer Orders
- 30/60/90 Report
To Screen
To Print
To File
To Spreadsheet
Run
Close

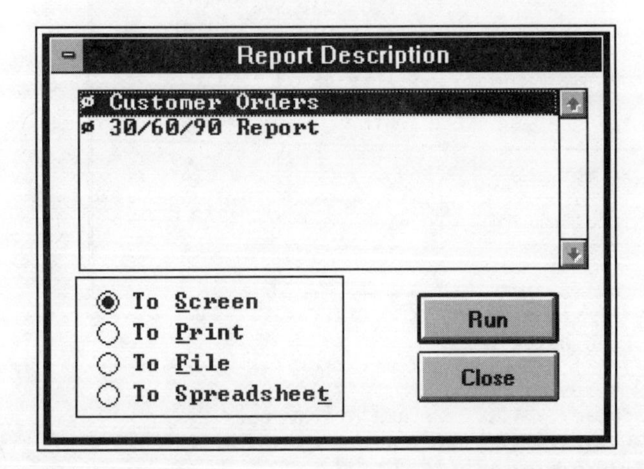
Report Description
ø Customer Orders
ø 30/60/90 Report
To Screen
To Print
To File
To Spreadsheet
Run
Close

```
*----------------------------------------------------------------
******************************************************************
**--    REPORTS.SCX - DOS PLATFORM
******************************************************************

 ( ) DeskTop                         (·) Window

 Name:   WRreports                   <Type...>
 Title:
 Footer:

 Size:              Screen Code:

  Height:   16       [X] Setup...
  Width:    42       [X] Cleanup & Procs...          «  OK  »

 Position:          READ Clauses:                    < Cancel >

  Row:        1      [ ] Activate...    [ ] Show...
  Column:     1      [ ] Valid...       [ ] When...
  [X] Center         [ ] Deactivate...

 Environment:                         [ ] Add alias

        Environment NOT saved with screen.


  Type:      Dialog

  Attributes:      Border:

   [ ] Close        ( ) None
   [X] Float        ( ) Single
   [X] Shadow       (·) Double      «  OK  »
   [ ] Minimize     ( ) Panel
                    ( ) System      < Cancel >

  Color Schemes:

   Primary:        Popup:

    Dialogs         Dialog Pop

******************************************************************
*  SCREEN SETUP CODE
******************************************************************
#TRAN SNIPPETS ONLY
*  Program...........: REPORTS Screen
*  Author............: yag
*  Project...........: COMMON
*  Created...........: 04/16/93
*  Copyright.........: (c) Flash Creative Management, 1993
*) Description.......: Standard Reporting Engine
*)                   : Requires use of REPOLIST.DBF
```

```
*  Calling Samples...: DO Reports.spr
*  Parameter List....:
*  Major change list.:
PRIVATE m.lcOutPut, m.lcFileName, m.lhOK, ;
   m.lnReport, laReps, m.lcSaveArea, m.lnCount, ;
   m.lnSaveRec, m.lcSeleRepo, m.lcRepoType
m.lhOK   = ""
m.lcOutPut   = "To Screen"
m.lcFileName = SPACE(8)
m.lnReport   = 1
m.lcSaveArea = SELECT()
m.lnSaveRec  = IIF(EOF() OR BOF(),-1,RECNO())
DIMENSION Rtags[1]             && Initialize "Order" popup
m.Rtags = ""
lcRepoType = LEFT(PROMPT(),4)
SELECT RepoList.cDosName, "  "+Repolist.cFullName, ;
  RepoList.lEditable, RepoList.cSelect, RepoList.cType FROM RepoList ;
  WHERE RepoList.cWindShow =lcRepoType ;
  INTO ARRAY laReps
SELECT RepoList
COUNT FOR ALLTRIM(cWindShow) = lcRepoType TO m.lnCount
IF EMPTY(m.lnCount)
  WAIT WINDOW "None available" NOWAIT
  USE
  SELECT (m.lcSaveArea)
  RELEASE WINDOW wrReports
  RETURN
ENDIF
FOR i = 1 TO m.lnCount       && Disable missing reports
   IF NOT FILE(laReps[i,1]+".FRX")
      laReps[i,2] = "\"+laReps[i,2]
   ENDIF
   IF !laReps[i,3]             && Not editable
     laReps[i,2] = STUFF(laReps[i,2],1,1,"-")
   ENDIF
   laReps[i,4] = ALLTRIM(laReps[i,4])
ENDFOR
************************************************************
*--   G E T   O B J E C T S
************************************************************
*===========================================================
*  Box
*===========================================================
 @   0,   1
 SIZE   8,  38
------------------------------------------------------------
*--  Comment Clause
------------------------------------------------------------
```

```
+------------------------------------------+
|                                          |
|  Comment                                 |
|  +------------------------------------+  |
|  | ( ) Procedure                      |  |
|  | ( ) Expression                     |  |
|  +------------------------------------+  |
|                                          |
+------------------------------------------+
```

```
Comment:   #DOSOBJ
*===========================================================
*  m.lnReport
```

```
*============================================================
 @   1,   2

   List Type:                        Options:

    (·) From Array      laReps        [ ] When...      [ ] Comment...
    ( ) From Popup                    [X] Valid...     [ ] Disabled
    ( ) Prompt Structure              [ ] Message...   [X] 1st Element...
    ( ) Prompt Field                  [ ] Terminating  [X] # Elements...
    ( ) Prompt Files

   Variable:

    < Choose... > m.lnReport               «   OK   »    < Cancel >

------------------------------------------------------------
*-- m.lnReport Valid Clause
------------------------------------------------------------

   Valid

    (·) Procedure
    ( ) Expression

DO RunRepo
------------------------------------------------------------
*-- m.lnReport 1st Element Clause
------------------------------------------------------------

   1st Element

    ( ) Procedure
    (·) Expression

1st Element:   2
------------------------------------------------------------
*-- m.lnReport # Elements Clause
------------------------------------------------------------

   # Elements

    ( ) Procedure
    (·) Expression

# Elements:   m.lnCount
*============================================================
```

```
*  m.lcoutput
*==============================================================
 @   9,   3
 Spacing:    0

 Radio Button Prompts:            ( ) Horizontal   (·) Vertical

  To \<Screen                     Variable:
  To \<Print
  To \<File                       < Choose... > m.lcoutput
  To Spreadshee\<t
                                  Options:

                                  [ ] When...     [ ] Comment...
                                  [ ] Valid...    [ ] Disabled
                                  [ ] Message...

 Initial:  To \<Screen                «   OK   »    < Cancel >

*==============================================================
*  m.lhRun
*==============================================================
 @   9,  26
 Spacing:    1

 Push Button Prompts:             ( ) Horizontal   (·) Vertical
                                  [ ] Terminating  <Spacing...>
  \!Run
                                  Variable:

                                  < Choose... >  m.lhRun

                                  Options:

                                  [ ] When...     [ ] Comment...
                                  [X] Valid...    [ ] Disabled
                                  [ ] Message...

                «   OK   »    < Cancel >

--------------------------------------------------------------
*-- m.lhRun Valid Clause
--------------------------------------------------------------

 Valid

  (·) Procedure
  ( ) Expression

DO RunRepo
```

```
*==============================================================
*  Text:  Report Description
*==============================================================
 @   0,   3
--------------------------------------------------------------
*--  Comment Clause
--------------------------------------------------------------
```

```
Comment

 ( ) Procedure
 ( ) Expression
```

```
Comment:   #DOSOBJ
*==============================================================
*  Box
*==============================================================
 @   8,   1
 SIZE   6,  22
*==============================================================
*  lhClose
*==============================================================
 @  11,  26
 Spacing:    1
```

```
Push Button Prompts:      (·) Horizontal   ( ) Vertical
                          [X] Terminating  <Spacing...>
\?Close
                         Variable:

                          < Choose... >  lhClose

                         Options:

                          [ ] When...     [ ] Comment...
                          [ ] Valid...    [ ] Disabled
                          [ ] Message...

               «   OK   »    < Cancel >
```

```
**************************************************************
*--  SCREEN CLEANUP CODE
**************************************************************
IF USED(m.lcSaveArea)
   SELECT (m.lcSaveArea)
   IF m.lnSaveRec <= 0
      GO TOP
   ELSE
      GO m.lnSaveRec
   ENDIF
ENDIF
*************************************************
PROCEDURE RunRepo
```

```
*************************************************
*) Procedure.........: RunRepo
*  Author............: yag
*  Project...........: COMMON
*  Created...........: 04/29/1993  15:25:17
*  Copyright.........: (c) Flash Creative Management, 1993
*) Description.......: Actually runs the selected report
*  Calling Samples...: DO RunRepo
*  Parameter List....:
*  Major change list.:
PRIVATE lnRepoTally
lnRepoTally = -1
IF m.lnReport = 0
   WAIT WINDOW "Report not available" NOWAIT
   RETURN
ENDIF
IF laReps[m.lnReport,5] = "Labe"
   lcSeleRepo = ALLTRIM(laReps[m.lnReport,1])+".LBX"
   m.lcCommand = "LABEL "
ELSE
   lcSeleRepo = ALLTRIM(laReps[m.lnReport,1])+".FRX"
   m.lcCommand = "REPORT "
ENDIF
IF laReps[m.lnReport,5] = "Repo"      && Run Query for OK or Modify
   SET TALK WINDOW
   SET TALK ON
   DO ALLTRIM(laReps[m.lnReport,1])+".QPR"
   lnRepoTally = _TALLY
   SET TALK NOWINDOW
   SET TALK OFF
ELSE
   IF USED(laReps[m.lnReport,4])
      SELECT laReps[m.lnReport,4]
   ELSE
      SELECT 0
      USE (laReps[m.lnReport,4])
   ENDIF
   lnListRec = IIF(EOF() OR BOF(),-1,RECNO())
ENDIF
IF lnRepoTally # 0
   IF NOT FILE(lcSeleRepo)
      WAIT WINDOW "Report not found" NOWAIT
      RETURN
   ENDIF
   DO CASE
      CASE m.lcOutPut = "To Screen"
         *[ CHANGE - Ari Neugroschl - August 24, 1993 - 19:14:52
         *[ SYS(2015) returns 10 characters, a DOS file only wants 8
         *[ Added SUBSTR(1,8)
         lcFileName = SUBSTR(SYS(2015),1,8) + ".REP"
         *[ CHANGE - Menachem Bazian, CPA - 08/27/93
         *[ Added code to clear out PDSETUP for report
         *[ to screen and file
         _PDSETUP = ""
         &lcCommand FORM &lcSeleRepo ;
            TO FILE (lcFileName) ENVIRONMENT NOCONSOLE
         ACTI &gcMainWind
         DO CASE
            CASE _DOS OR _UNIX
               DEFINE WINDOW wcSHOWIT ;
```

```
                IN &gcMainWind ;
                AT 1,0 SIZE WROWS()-4,WCOLS()-6 ;
                TITLE " Arrow Keys to Move, <ESC> to Exit " ;
                SYSTEM CLOSE ZOOM FLOAT GROW COLOR SCHEME 8
        CASE _WINDOWS
            DEFINE WINDOW wcSHOWIT ;
                IN &gcMainWind ;
                AT 1,0 SIZE WROWS()-4,WCOLS()-6 ;
                FONT "Terminal",9 ;
                TITLE " Arrow Keys to Move, <ESC> to Exit " ;
                SYSTEM CLOSE ZOOM FLOAT GROW COLOR SCHEME 8
        CASE _MAC
            DEFINE WINDOW wcSHOWIT ;
                IN &gcMainWind ;
                AT 1,0 SIZE WROWS()-10,WCOLS()-45 ;
                FONT "FoxFont",12 ;
                TITLE " Arrow Keys to Move, <ESC> to Exit " ;
                SYSTEM CLOSE ZOOM FLOAT GROW COLOR SCHEME 8
    ENDCASE
    MOVE WINDOW wcShowIt CENTER
    MODI COMM (lcFileName) NOMODIFY WINDOW wcSHOWIT
    RELEASE WINDOW wcShowit
    ERASE (lcFileName)
CASE m.lcOutPut = "To Print"
    IF PRINTSTATUS()
        *[ CHANGE - Menachem Bazian, CPA - 08/27/93
        *[ Added PDSETUP Keyword.
        *? Note: We need to make this a report by report
        *? option in REPOLIST and we need to allow the
        *? developer to turn off PDSETUP from SETUP.
        *?
        *? As per discussion with Yair...
        &lcCommand FORM &lcSeleRepo ;
            TO PRINTER ENVIRONMENT NOCONSOLE PDSETUP
        CLEAR READ
    ELSE
        DO alert.spr WITH "Printer not ready"
    ENDIF
CASE m.lcOutPut = "To File"
    lcRepoOut = PUTFILE("Save report to:","","PRT")
    IF !EMPTY(strippat(lcRepoOut))
        *[ CHANGE - Menachem Bazian, CPA - 08/27/93
        *[ Added code to clear out PDSETUP for report
        *[ to screen and file
        _PDSETUP = ""
        &lcCommand FORM &lcSeleRepo ;
            TO FILE (lcRepoOut) NOCONSOLE
    ELSE
        DO alert.spr WITH "No output file selected"
    ENDIF
CASE m.lcOutput = "To Spreadsheet"
    PRIVATE lcCommand
    #DEFINE dnWkshtNam   1
    #DEFINE dnWkShtTyp   2
    #DEFINE dnWkShtOpn   3
    #DEFINE dnSheetInf   3
    DIMENSION laSheetInf[1,dnSheetInf]
    =GetSheet(@laSheetInf)
    lcRepoOut = TRIM(laSheetInf[1,dnWkshtNam])
```

```
        IF NOT EMPTY(STRIPPAT(lcRepoOut))
           COPY TO (lcRepoOut) TYPE &laSheetInf[1,dnWkShtTyp]
        ELSE
           DO alert.spr WITH "No output file selected"
        ENDIF
        IF laSheetInf[1,dnWkshtOpn]
           IF !EMPTY(gcSpread)
              DO CASE
                 CASE _DOS
                    lcCommand = 'RUN /0 ' + gcSpread + ' ' + ;
                       lcRepoOut
                    &lcCommand
                 CASE _WINDOWS
                    PRIVATE lnChannel
                    =DDESetoption("SAFETY",.F.)
                    m.lnChannel = DDEinitiate("Excel","System")
                    IF m.lnChannel < 0
                       lcCommand = 'RUN /N ' + gcSpPath-gcSpread + ' ' + ;
                          lcRepoOut
                       &lcCommand
                    ELSE
                       =ddeexecute(lnChannel,'[OPEN("' ;
                          + lcRepoOut + ;
                          '")]')
                       =DDEexecute(lnChannel,'[APP.ACTIVATE()]')
                       =DDEexecute(lnChannel,'[APP.MAXIMIZE()]')
                    ENDIF
                    =DDETerminate(lnChannel)
              ENDCASE
           ELSE
              DO Alert.spr WITH 'No default spreadsheet specified'
           ENDIF
        ENDIF
   ENDCASE
   *-- Fox bug, this doesn't work, so we do a workaround...
   *   IF FILE(STRIPEXT(lcSeleRepo)+".QPC")
   PRIVATE lcOldErr, lcTmpQPC
   lcTmpQPC = STRIPEXT(lcSeleRepo)+".QPC"
   lcOldErr = ON("ERROR")
   ON ERROR *
   DO (lcTmpQPC)
   ON ERROR &lcOldErr
   IF laReps[m.lnReport,5] = "Repo"         && Get rid of CURSOR
      USE
   ELSE
      IF lnListRec <= 0
         GO TOP
      ELSE
         GO lnListRec
      ENDIF
   ENDIF
ELSE
   ?? CHR(7)
   WAIT WINDOW "No Records Matched Criteria" TIMEOUT 5
ENDIF
*-------------------------------------------------------------
```

```
*************************************************************
**--    REPORTS.SCX - MAC PLATFORM
*************************************************************

 ( ) DeskTop                         (·) Window

 Name:   WRreports                   <Type...>
 Title:  Report Description
 Footer:

 Size:             Screen Code:

  Height:   16.818   [X] Setup...
  Width:    41.500   [X] Cleanup & Procs...         «   OK   »

 Position:         READ Clauses:                    < Cancel >

  Row:       1.000   [ ] Activate...   [ ] Show...
  Column:    1.000   [ ] Valid...      [ ] When...
  [X] Center         [ ] Deactivate...

 Environment:                        [ ] Add alias

       Environment NOT saved with screen.


 Type:    Dialog

 Attributes:      Border:

  [ ] Close        ( ) None
  [X] Float        ( ) Single
  [X] Shadow       (·) Double      «   OK   »
  [ ] Minimize     ( ) Panel
                   ( ) System      < Cancel >

 Color Schemes:

  Primary:         Popup:

MAC      RGB Fill Color Scheme: (,,)
MAC      Font: monaco,    9
 Screen Setup code above
*************************************************************
*--    G E T   O B J E C T S
*************************************************************
*============================================================
*  m.lnReport
*============================================================
 @   0.727,   1.667
     SIZE   8.273,   38.333
```

```
List Type:                                  Options:

 (·) From Array        laReps                [ ] When...        [ ] Comment...
 ( ) From Popup                              [X] Valid...       [ ] Disabled
 ( ) Prompt Structure                        [ ] Message...     [X] 1st Element...
 ( ) Prompt Field                            [ ] Terminating    [X] # Elements...
 ( ) Prompt Files

Variable:

 < Choose... > m.lnReport                      «   OK   »     < Cancel >
```

```
MAC       RGB Color Scheme: (,,,,,)
MAC       Font: monaco,    9
 Valid code above
 1st Element code above
 # Elements code above
*============================================================
*  m.lcoutput
*============================================================
 @   9.636,   3.000
     SIZE   1.417,  17.833
 Spacing:    0
```

```
 Radio Button Prompts:            ( ) Horizontal   (·) Vertical

 To \<Screen                     Variable:
 To \<Print
 To \<File                        < Choose... > m.lcoutput
 To Spreadshee\<t
                                 Options:

                                  [ ] When...    [ ] Comment...
                                  [ ] Valid...   [ ] Disabled
                                  [ ] Message...

 Initial:  To \<Screen            «   OK   »    < Cancel >
```

```
MAC       RGB Color Scheme: (,,,,,)
MAC       Font: Geneva,    9
         Style: Bold Transparent
*============================================================
*  m.lhRun
*============================================================
 @  10.182,  25.667
     SIZE   2.167,  12.333
 Spacing:    1
```

```
 Push Button Prompts:          ( ) Horizontal    (·) Vertical
                               [ ] Terminating   <Spacing...>
 \!Run
                              Variable:

                               < Choose... >  m.lhRun

                              Options:

                               [ ] When...       [ ] Comment...
                               [X] Valid...      [ ] Disabled
                               [ ] Message...

              «   OK   »    < Cancel >
MAC       RGB Color Scheme: (,,,,,)
MAC       Font: Geneva,   9
         Style: Bold
 Valid code above
*==============================================================
*  Box
*==============================================================
 @   9.364,   1.500
 SIZE   6.545,  19.000
MAC       RGB Color Scheme: (,,,,,)
            Pen: 2
*==============================================================
*  lhClose
*==============================================================
 @  13.364,  25.667
     SIZE   2.167,  12.333
 Spacing:    2

 Push Button Prompts:          (·) Horizontal    ( ) Vertical
                               [X] Terminating   <Spacing...>
 \?Close
                              Variable:

                               < Choose... >  lhClose

                              Options:

                               [ ] When...       [ ] Comment...
                               [ ] Valid...      [ ] Disabled
                               [ ] Message...

              «   OK   »    < Cancel >
MAC       RGB Color Scheme: (,,,,,)
MAC       Font: Geneva,   9
         Style: Bold
 Screen Cleanup and Procedures code above
```

```
*-------------------------------------------------------------
**************************************************************
**--    REPORTS.SCX - WINDOWS PLATFORM
**************************************************************

 ( ) DeskTop                              (·) Window

 Name:   WRreports                        <Type...>
 Title:  Report Description
 Footer:

 Size:              Screen Code:

  Height:   16.667    [X] Setup...
  Width:    39.250    [X] Cleanup & Procs...          «   OK   »

 Position:          READ Clauses:                     < Cancel >

  Row:       1.000    [ ] Activate...    [ ] Show...
  Column:    1.000    [ ] Valid...       [ ] When...
  [X] Center          [ ] Deactivate...

 Environment:                         [ ] Add alias

       Environment NOT saved with screen.


  Type:        Dialog

  Attributes:      Border:

   [ ] Close        ( ) None
   [X] Float        ( ) Single
   [X] Shadow       (·) Double      «   OK   »
   [ ] Minimize     ( ) Panel
                    ( ) System      < Cancel >

  Color Schemes:

   Primary:         Popup:


WINDOWS  RGB Fill Color Scheme: (,,)
WINDOWS  Font: Terminal,    9
 Screen Setup code above
**************************************************************
*--    G E T    O B J E C T S
**************************************************************
*=============================================================
*  m.lnReport
*=============================================================
 @   0.750,   2.000
     SIZE   8.167,  36.000
```

```
╔══════════════════════════════════════════════════════════════════════╗
║                                                                      ║
║  List Type:                          Options:                        ║
║  ┌───────────────────────────────┐  ┌──────────────────────────────┐ ║
║  │ (·) From Array       laReps   │  │ [ ] When...      [ ] Comment...  │ ║
║  │ ( ) From Popup                │  │ [X] Valid...     [ ] Disabled    │ ║
║  │ ( ) Prompt Structure          │  │ [ ] Message...   [X] 1st Element...│ ║
║  │ ( ) Prompt Field              │  │ [ ] Terminating  [X] # Elements... │ ║
║  │ ( ) Prompt Files              │  └──────────────────────────────┘ ║
║  └───────────────────────────────┘                                   ║
║                                                                      ║
║  Variable:                                                           ║
║  ┌───────────────────────────────┐                                   ║
║  │ < Choose... > m.lnReport      │     «   OK   »     < Cancel >     ║
║  └───────────────────────────────┘                                   ║
║                                                                      ║
╚══════════════════════════════════════════════════════════════════════╝
WINDOWS  RGB Color Scheme: (,,,,,)
WINDOWS  Font: Terminal,   9
 Valid code above
 1st Element code above
 # Elements code above
*===========================================================
*  m.lcoutput
*===========================================================
 @   9.833,   3.250
     SIZE   1.417,  16.875
 Spacing:     0
╔══════════════════════════════════════════════════════════════╗
║                                                              ║
║  Radio Button Prompts:     ┌────────────────────────────────┐║
║  ┌─────────────────────┐   │ ( ) Horizontal   (·) Vertical  │║
║  │To \<Screen          │   └────────────────────────────────┘║
║  │To \<Print           │   Variable:                         ║
║  │To \<File            │   ┌────────────────────────────────┐║
║  │To Spreadshee\<t     │   │ < Choose... > m.lcoutput       │║
║  │                     │   └────────────────────────────────┘║
║  │                     │   Options:                          ║
║  │                     │   ┌────────────────────────────────┐║
║  │                     │   │ [ ] When...     [ ] Comment... │║
║  │                     │   │ [ ] Valid...    [ ] Disabled   │║
║  │                     │   │ [ ] Message...                 │║
║  └─────────────────────┘   └────────────────────────────────┘║
║                                                              ║
║  Initial: ┌────────────┐                                     ║
║           │To \<Screen │      «   OK   »     < Cancel >      ║
║           └────────────┘                                     ║
╚══════════════════════════════════════════════════════════════╝
WINDOWS  RGB Color Scheme: (,,,,,)
WINDOWS  Font: Terminal,   9
*===========================================================
*  m.lhRun
*===========================================================
 @  10.167,  26.000
     SIZE   2.154,  13.500
 Spacing:     1
```

```
 ┌──────────────────────────────────────────────────────────────┐
 │ Push Button Prompts:    ( ) Horizontal   (·) Vertical        │
 │                         [ ] Terminating  <Spacing...>        │
 │ \!Run                                                        │
 │                         Variable:                            │
 │                         < Choose... >  m.lhRun               │
 │                                                              │
 │                         Options:                             │
 │                         [ ] When...      [ ] Comment...      │
 │                         [X] Valid...     [ ] Disabled        │
 │                         [ ] Message...                       │
 │                                                              │
 │              «   OK   »    < Cancel >                        │
 └──────────────────────────────────────────────────────────────┘
WINDOWS  RGB Color Scheme: (,,,,,)
WINDOWS  Font: MS Sans Serif,   8
        Style: Bold
 Valid code above
*============================================================
*  Box
*============================================================
 @   9.333,   1.750
 SIZE   6.500,  19.000
WINDOWS  RGB Color Scheme: (,,,,,)
            Pen: 1
*============================================================
*  lhClose
*============================================================
 @  12.833,  26.000
    SIZE   2.154,  13.500
 Spacing:    2
 ┌──────────────────────────────────────────────────────────────┐
 │ Push Button Prompts:    (·) Horizontal   ( ) Vertical        │
 │                         [X] Terminating  <Spacing...>        │
 │ \?Close                                                      │
 │                         Variable:                            │
 │                         < Choose... >  lhClose               │
 │                                                              │
 │                         Options:                             │
 │                         [ ] When...      [ ] Comment...      │
 │                         [ ] Valid...     [ ] Disabled        │
 │                         [ ] Message...                       │
 │                                                              │
 │              «   OK   »    < Cancel >                        │
 └──────────────────────────────────────────────────────────────┘
WINDOWS  RGB Color Scheme: (,,,,,)
WINDOWS  Font: MS Sans Serif,   8
        Style: Bold
 Screen Cleanup and Procedures code above
```

A Splash Screen: STARTUP.SCX

In graphical environments, it is often important to provide a splash screen that appears while an application is being initialized. The most important thing to note is that the READ WHEN returns a false, allowing the screen to be shown and then having the rest of the code continue.

```
*------------------------------------------------------------
*************************************************************
**--    STARTUP.SCX - MAC PLATFORM
*************************************************************

( ) DeskTop                          (·) Window

Name:   wsStartup                    <Type...>
Title:
Footer:

Size:          Screen Code:

 Height:   26.083   [X] Setup...
 Width:    64.167   [ ] Cleanup & Procs...          «   OK   »

Position:      READ Clauses:                        < Cancel >

 Row:        0.000   [ ] Activate...   [ ] Show...
 Column:     0.000   [ ] Valid...      [X] When...
 [X] Center          [ ] Deactivate...

Environment:                          [X] Add alias

     Environment NOT saved with screen.


 Type:       User

 Attributes:     Border:

  [ ] Close       (·) None
  [ ] Float       ( ) Single
  [ ] Shadow      ( ) Double      «   OK   »
  [ ] Minimize    ( ) Panel
                  ( ) System      < Cancel >

 Color Schemes:

  Primary:        Popup:


MAC      RGB Fill Color Scheme: (194,194,194)
MAC      Font: Geneva,  10
*************************************************************
*  SCREEN SETUP CODE
*************************************************************
#WCLAUSE IN DESKTOP      && Force it to Windows Desktop
-------------------------------------------------------------
*-- READ When Clause
-------------------------------------------------------------
```

```
READ When

 ( ) Procedure
 (·) Expression
```

```
READ When:    .f.
**************************************************************
*--    G E T    O B J E C T S
**************************************************************
*============================================================
*  Line
*============================================================
 @   0.250,  53.500
MAC       RGB Color Scheme: (255,255,255,255,255,255)
            Pen: 1
*============================================================
*  Box
*============================================================
 @   1.000,   3.167
 SIZE  23.083,  57.000
MAC       RGB Color Scheme: (255,255,255,,,)
            Pen: 1
*============================================================
*  BITMAP Object
*  File: ..\BMPS\STARTUP.BMP
*============================================================
 @   1.917,   8.333
     SIZE  20.833,  47.500
```

```
Screen Picture From:                                  «   OK   »

 (·) File  : "..\BMPS\STARTUP.BMP"
 ( ) Field :                                          < Cancel >

If Picture And Frame Different Size:

 (·) Clip Picture
 ( ) Scale Picture - Retain Shape
 ( ) Scale Picture - Fill the Frame

 [ ] Center Picture              [ ] Refresh Output Field

 [ ] Comment
```

```
MAC       RGB Color Scheme: (,,,,,) Transparent
*============================================================
*  Box
*============================================================
 @   1.083,   3.333
 SIZE  22.917,  56.667
MAC       RGB Color Scheme: (,,,,,)
```

```
          Pen: 1
*===========================================================
*  Line
*===========================================================
 @   0.000,   0.000
MAC       RGB Color Scheme: (255,255,255,255,255,255)
          Pen: 4
*===========================================================
*  Line
*===========================================================
 @  25.750,   3.667
MAC       RGB Color Scheme: (130,130,130,130,130,130)
          Pen: 4
*===========================================================
*  Line
*===========================================================
 @   0.000,   0.000
MAC       RGB Color Scheme: (255,255,255,255,255,255)
          Pen: 4
*===========================================================
*  Line
*===========================================================
 @   0.000,  63.333
MAC       RGB Color Scheme: (130,130,130,130,130,130)
          Pen: 4
*===========================================================
*  Line
*===========================================================
 @  25.750,   0.667
MAC       RGB Color Scheme: (130,130,130,130,130,130)
          Pen: 1
*===========================================================
*  Line
*===========================================================
 @   1.833,  48.000
MAC       RGB Color Scheme: (,,,,,)
          Pen: 1
*===========================================================
*  Line
*===========================================================
 @   1.833,  48.000
MAC       RGB Color Scheme: (,,,,,)
          Pen: 1
*===========================================================
*  Line
*===========================================================
 @  25.833,   0.333
MAC       RGB Color Scheme: (130,130,130,130,130,130)
          Pen: 1
*===========================================================
*  Line
*===========================================================
 @   0.000,  59.167
MAC       RGB Color Scheme: (255,255,255,255,255,255)
          Pen: 1
*===========================================================
*  Line
*===========================================================
 @  25.917,   0.167
MAC       RGB Color Scheme: (130,130,130,130,130,130)
```

```
           Pen: 1
*============================================================
*  Line
*============================================================
 @  26.000,   0.000
MAC      RGB Color Scheme: (130,130,130,130,130,130)
           Pen: 1
*============================================================
*  Line
*============================================================
 @   0.083,  59.000
MAC      RGB Color Scheme: (255,255,255,255,255,255)
           Pen: 1
*============================================================
*  Line
*============================================================
 @   0.083,   0.000
MAC      RGB Color Scheme: (130,130,130,130,130,130)
           Pen: 1
*============================================================
*  Line
*============================================================
 @   0.000,   0.167
MAC      RGB Color Scheme: (130,130,130,130,130,130)
           Pen: 1
*============================================================
*  Line
*============================================================
 @   0.167,  58.667
MAC      RGB Color Scheme: (255,255,255,255,255,255)
           Pen: 1
*------------------------------------------------------------
*************************************************************
**--    STARTUP.SCX - WINDOWS PLATFORM
*************************************************************
```

```
( ) DeskTop                          (·) Window

Name:   wsStartup                    <Type...>
Title:
Footer:

Size:            Screen Code:

 Height:   22.462    [X] Setup...
 Width:    59.600    [ ] Cleanup & Procs...           «  OK  »

Position:        READ Clauses:                        < Cancel >

 Row:       0.000    [ ] Activate...    [ ] Show...
 Column:    0.000    [ ] Valid...       [X] When...
 [X] Center          [ ] Deactivate...

Environment:                         [X] Add alias

      Environment NOT saved with screen.
```

```
 Type:   [    User     ]

 Attributes:        Border:
  [ ] Close          (·) None
  [ ] Float          ( ) Single
  [ ] Shadow         ( ) Double     «   OK   »
  [ ] Minimize       ( ) Panel
                     ( ) System     < Cancel >

 Color Schemes:
  Primary:          Popup:
  [          ]      [          ]

WINDOWS  RGB Fill Color Scheme: (192,192,192)
WINDOWS  Font: MS Sans Serif,   8
 Screen Setup code above
 READ When code above
************************************************************
*--   G E T   O B J E C T S
************************************************************
*===========================================================
*  Box
*===========================================================
 @   1.000,   3.200
 SIZE  20.385,  53.000
WINDOWS  RGB Color Scheme: (255,255,255,,,)
         Pen: 1
*===========================================================
*  BITMAP Object
*  File: ..\BMPS\STARTUP.BMP
*===========================================================
 @   1.385,   2.000
     SIZE  19.231,  53.000

  Screen Picture From:                                  «   OK   »

   (·) File  : "..\BMPS\STARTUP.BMP"
   ( ) Field :                                          < Cancel >

  If Picture And Frame Different Size:

   (·) Clip Picture
   ( ) Scale Picture - Retain Shape
   ( ) Scale Picture - Fill the Frame

   [ ] Center Picture             [ ] Refresh Output Field

   [ ] Comment
```

```
WINDOWS  RGB Color Scheme: (,,,,,) Transparent
*============================================================
*  Box
*============================================================
 @   1.077,   3.400
 SIZE  20.385,  53.000
WINDOWS  RGB Color Scheme: (,,,,,)
           Pen: 1
*============================================================
*  Line
*============================================================
 @   0.000,   0.000
WINDOWS  RGB Color Scheme: (255,255,255,255,255,255)
           Pen: 4
*============================================================
*  Line
*============================================================
 @  22.154,   0.000
WINDOWS  RGB Color Scheme: (128,128,128,128,128,128)
           Pen: 4
*============================================================
*  Line
*============================================================
 @   0.000,   0.000
WINDOWS  RGB Color Scheme: (255,255,255,255,255,255)
           Pen: 4
*============================================================
*  Line
*============================================================
 @   0.000,  58.800
WINDOWS  RGB Color Scheme: (128,128,128,128,128,128)
           Pen: 4
*============================================================
*  Line
*============================================================
 @  22.154,   0.600
WINDOWS  RGB Color Scheme: (128,128,128,128,128,128)
           Pen: 1
*============================================================
*  Line
*============================================================
 @   1.846,  48.000
WINDOWS  RGB Color Scheme: (,,,,,)
           Pen: 1
*============================================================
*  Line
*============================================================
 @   1.846,  48.000
WINDOWS  RGB Color Scheme: (,,,,,)
           Pen: 1
*============================================================
*  Line
*============================================================
 @  22.231,   0.400
WINDOWS  RGB Color Scheme: (128,128,128,128,128,128)
           Pen: 1
*============================================================
*  Line
*============================================================
```

```
 @   0.000,  54.600
WINDOWS  RGB Color Scheme: (255,255,255,255,255,255)
           Pen: 1
*============================================================
*  Line
*============================================================
 @  22.308,   0.200
WINDOWS  RGB Color Scheme: (128,128,128,128,128,128)
           Pen: 1
*============================================================
*  Line
*============================================================
 @  22.385,   0.000
WINDOWS  RGB Color Scheme: (128,128,128,128,128,128)
           Pen: 1
*============================================================
*  Line
*============================================================
 @   0.077,  54.400
WINDOWS  RGB Color Scheme: (255,255,255,255,255,255)
           Pen: 1
*============================================================
*  Line
*============================================================
 @   0.154,  54.200
WINDOWS  RGB Color Scheme: (255,255,255,255,255,255)
           Pen: 1
*============================================================
*  Line
*============================================================
 @   0.231,  54.000
WINDOWS  RGB Color Scheme: (255,255,255,255,255,255)
           Pen: 1
*============================================================
*  Line
*============================================================
 @   0.000,   0.000
WINDOWS  RGB Color Scheme: (128,128,128,128,128,128)
           Pen: 1
*============================================================
*  Line
*============================================================
 @   0.000,   0.000
WINDOWS  RGB Color Scheme: (128,128,128,128,128,128)
           Pen: 1
```

A Look-Up Window: STATES.SCX

One of the most common validation techniques involves validating two-character state abbreviations entered by the user against a list of valid state abbreviations. It is straightforward to write a generic pop-up that will appear if an invalid state abbreviation is entered. The popup consists of the full state names, allowing the user to easily select the desired state.

Since this state array is commonly in use throughout tour application, we declare it once, and make it a global array with the name gaStates. It is now a simple matter to create a screen set saved as a file called STATES.PRG. The screen set takes two parameters (using the ubiquitous #SECTION generator directive) that determine the row and column where the pop-up will appear.

The program now returns the row in the array where the selected state exists.

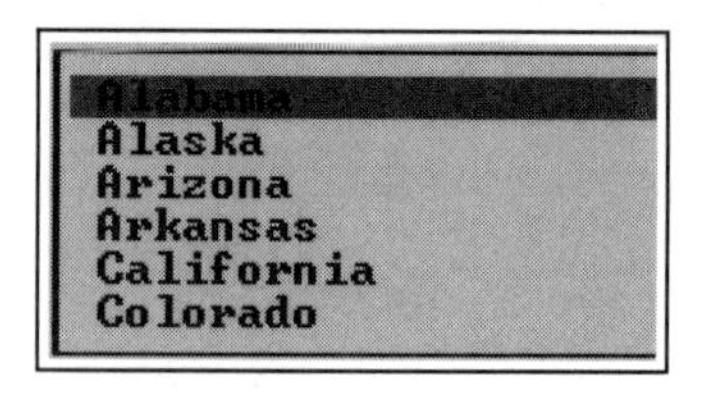

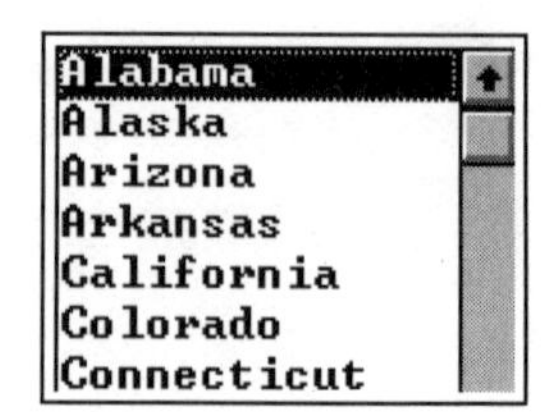

```
*-----------------------------------------------------------
************************************************************
**--    STATES.SCX - DOS PLATFORM
************************************************************

 ( ) DeskTop                          (·) Window

 Name:   wrStates                     <Type...>
 Title:  State Lookup
 Footer:

 Size:              Screen Code:

  Height:   10       [X] Setup...
  Width:    24       [X] Cleanup & Procs...          «    OK    »

 Position:          READ Clauses:                    < Cancel >

  Row:        0      [ ] Activate...    [ ] Show...
  Column:     0      [ ] Valid...       [ ] When...
  [X] Center         [ ] Deactivate...

 Environment:                         [X] Add alias

         Environment NOT saved with screen.


  Type:       User


  Attributes:      Border:

    [ ] Close       (·) None
    [ ] Float       ( ) Single
    [X] Shadow      ( ) Double       «    OK    »
    [ ] Minimize    ( ) Panel
                    ( ) System       < Cancel >

  Color Schemes:

    Primary:        Popup:

    User Winds      User Menus

************************************************************
*  SCREEN SETUP CODE
************************************************************
#SECTION 1
*  Program...........: STATES Screen
*  Author............: yag
*  Project...........: COMMON
*  Created...........: 04/16/93
*  Copyright.........: (c) Flash Creative Management, 1993
*) Description.......: Pop up of full state names
*)                   : Pass it the row and column, and it pops up.
*  Calling Samples...: =states(ROW(),COL())
```

```
*  Parameter List....: lnRow    -    Top left Row
*                    : lnCol    -    Top left Column
*  Major change list.:
PARAMETER lnRow, lnCol
#SECTION 2
DEFINE WINDOW wrStates FROM lnRow, lnCol TO lnRow+7, lnCol+21 ;
  FLOAT ;
  SHADOW ;
  NONE
************************************************************
*--    G E T    O B J E C T S
************************************************************
*==========================================================
*  lnStates
*==========================================================
 @   0,   0
```

```
List Type:                                  Options:

 (·) From Array        gaStates             [ ] When...       [ ] Comment...
 ( ) From Popup                             [ ] Valid...      [ ] Disabled
 ( ) Prompt Structure                       [ ] Message...    [X] 1st Element...
 ( ) Prompt Field                           [ ] Terminating   [ ] # Elements...
 ( ) Prompt Files

Variable:

 < Choose... > lnStates                        «   OK   »     < Cancel >
```

```
----------------------------------------------------------
*-- lnStates 1st Element Clause
----------------------------------------------------------
```

```
1st Element

 ( ) Procedure
 (·) Expression
```

```
1st Element:   2
************************************************************
*--  SCREEN CLEANUP CODE
************************************************************
RETURN lnStates
*---------------------------------------------------------
```

```
************************************************************
**--    STATES.SCX - MAC PLATFORM
************************************************************

 ( ) DeskTop                          (·) Window

 Name:    wrStates                    <Type...>
 Title:   State Lookup
 Footer:

 Size:              Screen Code:

   Height:    9.500   [X] Setup...
   Width:    16.500   [X] Cleanup & Procs...        «   OK   »

 Position:          READ Clauses:                   < Cancel >

   Row:       0.000   [ ] Activate...    [ ] Show...
   Column:    0.000   [ ] Valid...       [ ] When...
   [X] Center         [ ] Deactivate...

 Environment:                          [X] Add alias

        Environment NOT saved with screen.


  Type:        User

  Attributes:     Border:

   [ ] Close       (·) None
   [ ] Float       ( ) Single
   [X] Shadow      ( ) Double      «   OK   »
   [ ] Minimize    ( ) Panel
                   ( ) System      < Cancel >

  Color Schemes:

   Primary:        Popup:


MAC      RGB Fill Color Scheme: (,,)
MAC      Font: monaco,    9
 Screen Setup code above
************************************************************
*--    G E T    O B J E C T S
************************************************************
*==========================================================
*  lnStates
*==========================================================
 @   0.083,   0.125
     SIZE   9.333,  16.250
```

```
List Type:                                   Options:

 (·) From Array        gaStates               [ ] When...       [ ] Comment...
 ( ) From Popup                               [ ] Valid...      [ ] Disabled
 ( ) Prompt Structure                         [ ] Message...    [X] 1st Element...
 ( ) Prompt Field                             [ ] Terminating   [ ] # Elements...
 ( ) Prompt Files

Variable:

 < Choose... > lnStates                        «   OK   »     < Cancel >

MAC      RGB Color Scheme: (,,,,,)
MAC      Font: monaco,   9
 1st Element code above
 Screen Cleanup and Procedures code above
*-------------------------------------------------------------
**************************************************************
**--    STATES.SCX - WINDOWS PLATFORM
**************************************************************

( ) DeskTop                          (·) Window

Name:   wrStates                     <Type...>
Title:  State Lookup
Footer:

Size:             Screen Code:

 Height:    9.500   [X] Setup...
 Width:    16.500   [X] Cleanup & Procs...          «   OK   »

Position:         READ Clauses:                     < Cancel >

 Row:       0.000   [ ] Activate...    [ ] Show...
 Column:    0.000   [ ] Valid...       [ ] When...
 [X] Center         [ ] Deactivate...

Environment:                          [X] Add alias

      Environment NOT saved with screen.
```

```
  Type:    [     User     ]

  Attributes:        Border:
  [ ] Close          (·) None
  [ ] Float          ( ) Single
  [X] Shadow         ( ) Double      «  OK  »
  [ ] Minimize       ( ) Panel
                     ( ) System      < Cancel >

  Color Schemes:
    Primary:         Popup:
    [        ]       [        ]
WINDOWS  RGB Fill Color Scheme: (,,)
WINDOWS  Font: Terminal,   9
 Screen Setup code above
************************************************************
*--   G E T   O B J E C T S
************************************************************
*===========================================================
*  lnStates
*===========================================================
 @   0.083,   0.125
     SIZE   9.333,  16.250

  List Type:                              Options:
    (·) From Array       gaStates         [ ] When...       [ ] Comment...
    ( ) From Popup                        [ ] Valid...      [ ] Disabled
    ( ) Prompt Structure                  [ ] Message...    [X] 1st Element...
    ( ) Prompt Field                      [ ] Terminating   [ ] # Elements...
    ( ) Prompt Files

  Variable:
    < Choose... > lnStates                       «  OK  »   < Cancel >
WINDOWS  RGB Color Scheme: (,,,,,)
WINDOWS  Font: Terminal,   9
 1st Element code above
 Screen Cleanup and Procedures code above
```

A Cross-Tab View: YEARSHOW.SCX

YearShow is a reusable window that handles displaying year to date information. It is usually called after issuing a cross tab to divide information by months. You can pass YearShow a parameter which will appear on top of the window (in our application, that parameter is the name of a customer).

Note that the setting of CURSOR is saved, modified and reset. Also, note that we initialize all of our memory variables to 0.00 just in case we have no information for a particular month. In that case, the cross tab will not create a field for us. The SCATTER MEMVAR overwrites any memory variables with the information that exists in the cross tab.

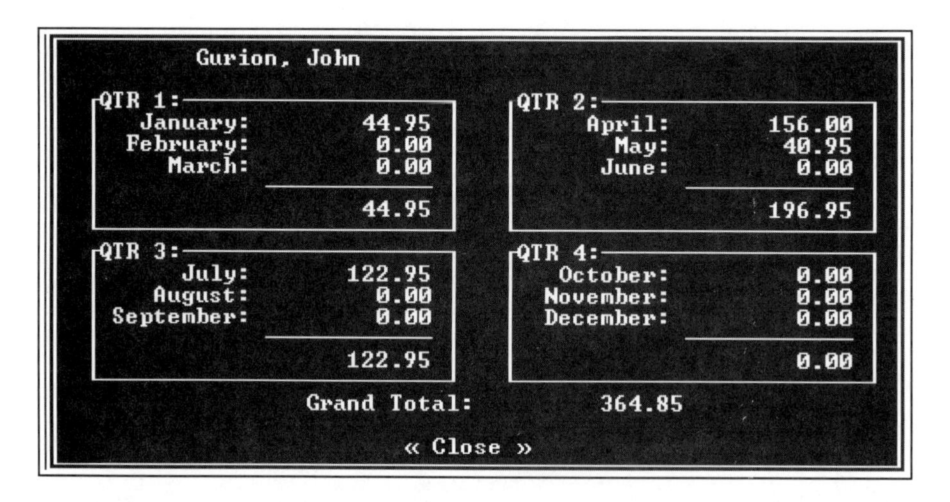

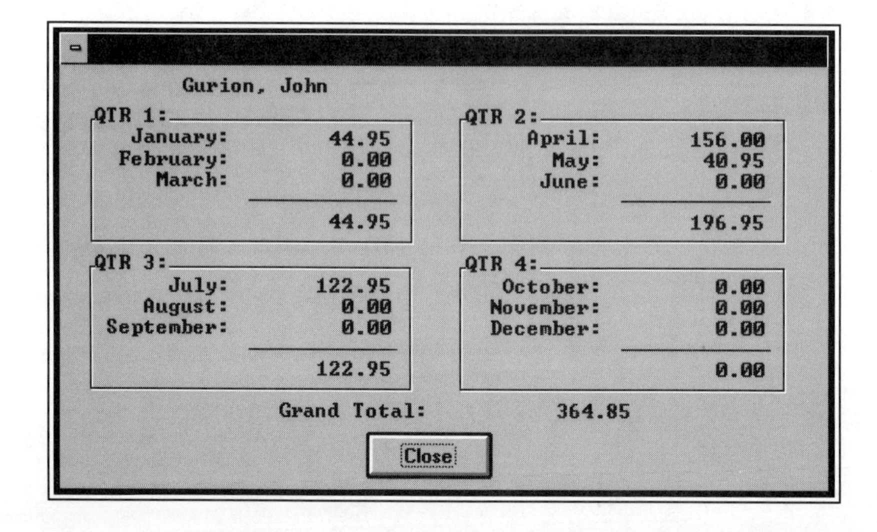

```
*------------------------------------------------------------
*************************************************************
**--    YEARSHOW.SCX - DOS PLATFORM
*************************************************************

 ( ) DeskTop                          (·) Window

 Name:                                <Type...>
 Title:
 Footer:

 Size:              Screen Code:

   Height:   21       [X] Setup...
   Width:    62       [X] Cleanup & Procs...              «   OK   »

 Position:          READ Clauses:                         < Cancel >

   Row:        0      [ ] Activate...    [ ] Show...
   Column:     0      [ ] Valid...       [ ] When...
   [X] Center         [ ] Deactivate...

 Environment:                             [X] Add alias

        Environment NOT saved with screen.


  Type:        Dialog

  Attributes:        Border:

    [ ] Close          ( ) None
    [X] Float          ( ) Single
    [X] Shadow         (·) Double        «   OK   »
    [ ] Minimize       ( ) Panel
                       ( ) System        < Cancel >

  Color Schemes:

    Primary:           Popup:

     Dialogs            Dialog Pop

*************************************************************
*  SCREEN SETUP CODE
*************************************************************
#SECTION 1
*  Program...........: YEARSHOW Screen
*  Author............: YAG
*  Project...........: COMMON
*  Created...........: 06/06/93  05:10:06
*  Copyright.........: (c) Flash Creative Management, 1993
*) Description.......: Show a years worth of data. Typically
*)                   : from a SQL SELECT and XTAB
*  Calling Samples...: DO YearShow WITH m.lcCustName
```

```
*  Parameter List....: tcName - A name to show at the top of the form
*  Major change list.:
PARAMETER tcName
#SECTION 2
lcOldCurs = SET("CURSOR")
SET CURSOR OFF
IF EMPTY(tcName)
   tcName = ""
ENDIF
STORE 0.00 TO m.january, m.february, m.march, m.april, ;
                m.may, m.june, m.july, m.august, m.september, ;
                m.october, m.november, m.december

SCATTER MEMVAR
************************************************************
*--    G E T   O B J E C T S
************************************************************
*==========================================================
*  Box
*==========================================================
 @   2,  32
 SIZE   7,  27
*==========================================================
*
*==========================================================
 @   0,  10
```

```
  Field:
  ┌──────────────────────────────────────────┐
  │ (·) Say          ( ) Get          ( ) Edit │
  └──────────────────────────────────────────┘

  <  Say...    > m.tcname
                                             «   OK   »
  < Format... > @I
                                             < Cancel >
  Range:
  ┌──────────────────────────────────────────┐
  │ [ ] Upper...                [ ] Lower... │
  └──────────────────────────────────────────┘

  [ ] When...     [ ] Error...     [ ] Scroll bar
  [ ] Valid...    [ ] Comment...   [ ] Allow tabs
  [ ] Message...  [ ] Disabled     [ ] Refresh
```

```
*==========================================================
*  Box
*==========================================================
 @   6,  15
 SIZE   1,  12
*==========================================================
*  Text: January:
*==========================================================
 @   3,   6
*==========================================================
*  Text: February:
*==========================================================
```

```
 @   4,   5
*==============================================================
*  Text: March:
*==============================================================
 @   5,   8
*==============================================================
*  Text: April:
*==============================================================
 @   3,  38
*==============================================================
*  Text: May:
*==============================================================
 @   4,  40
*==============================================================
*  Text: June:
*==============================================================
 @   5,  39
*==============================================================
*  Box
*==============================================================
 @   6,  45
 SIZE   1,  12
*==============================================================
*
*==============================================================
 @   3,  16
```

```
Field:

 (·) Say          ( ) Get          ( ) Edit

<  Say...    > m.january
                                          «    OK    »
< Format... >
                                          < Cancel >
Range:

 [ ] Upper...                 [ ] Lower...

[ ] When...      [ ] Error...      [ ] Scroll bar
[ ] Valid...     [ ] Comment...    [ ] Allow tabs
[ ] Message...   [ ] Disabled      [ ] Refresh
```

```
*==============================================================
*
*==============================================================
 @   3,  46
```

```
Field:
 ( ) Say          ( ) Get          ( ) Edit

< Say...   > m.april
                                             «   OK   »
< Format... >
                                             < Cancel >
Range:
 [ ] Upper...                   [ ] Lower...

[ ] When...      [ ] Error...     [ ] Scroll bar
[ ] Valid...     [ ] Comment...   [ ] Allow tabs
[ ] Message...   [ ] Disabled     [ ] Refresh
```

```
*==============================================================
*
*==============================================================
 @   4,  16
```

```
Field:
 ( ) Say          ( ) Get          ( ) Edit

< Say...   > m.february
                                             «   OK   »
< Format... >
                                             < Cancel >
Range:
 [ ] Upper...                   [ ] Lower...

[ ] When...      [ ] Error...     [ ] Scroll bar
[ ] Valid...     [ ] Comment...   [ ] Allow tabs
[ ] Message...   [ ] Disabled     [ ] Refresh
```

```
*==============================================================
*
*==============================================================
 @   4,  46
```

```
╔══════════════════════════════════════════════════════════════╗
║                                                              ║
║  Field:                                                      ║
║  ┌──────────────────────────────────────────┐                ║
║  │ (•) Say        ( ) Get        ( ) Edit   │                ║
║  └──────────────────────────────────────────┘                ║
║                                                              ║
║  <  Say...   > m.may                                         ║
║                                                 «  OK  »     ║
║  < Format... >                                               ║
║                                               < Cancel >     ║
║  Range:                                                      ║
║  ┌──────────────────────────────────────────┐                ║
║  │ [ ] Upper...               [ ] Lower...  │                ║
║  └──────────────────────────────────────────┘                ║
║                                                              ║
║  [ ] When...     [ ] Error...     [ ] Scroll bar             ║
║  [ ] Valid...    [ ] Comment...   [ ] Allow tabs             ║
║  [ ] Message...  [ ] Disabled     [ ] Refresh                ║
║                                                              ║
╚══════════════════════════════════════════════════════════════╝
*============================================================
*
*============================================================
 @   5,  16
╔══════════════════════════════════════════════════════════════╗
║                                                              ║
║  Field:                                                      ║
║  ┌──────────────────────────────────────────┐                ║
║  │ (•) Say        ( ) Get        ( ) Edit   │                ║
║  └──────────────────────────────────────────┘                ║
║                                                              ║
║  <  Say...   > m.march                                       ║
║                                                 «  OK  »     ║
║  < Format... >                                               ║
║                                               < Cancel >     ║
║  Range:                                                      ║
║  ┌──────────────────────────────────────────┐                ║
║  │ [ ] Upper...               [ ] Lower...  │                ║
║  └──────────────────────────────────────────┘                ║
║                                                              ║
║  [ ] When...     [ ] Error...     [ ] Scroll bar             ║
║  [ ] Valid...    [ ] Comment...   [ ] Allow tabs             ║
║  [ ] Message...  [ ] Disabled     [ ] Refresh                ║
║                                                              ║
╚══════════════════════════════════════════════════════════════╝
*============================================================
*
*============================================================
 @   5,  46
```

```
 Field:
 ( ) Say          ( ) Get          ( ) Edit

 <  Say...    > m.june
                                                   «    OK    »
 < Format... >
                                                   < Cancel >
 Range:
 [ ] Upper...                   [ ] Lower...

 [ ] When...      [ ] Error...     [ ] Scroll bar
 [ ] Valid...     [ ] Comment...   [ ] Allow tabs
 [ ] Message...   [ ] Disabled     [ ] Refresh

*=============================================================
*
*=============================================================
 @    7,   15

 Field:
 ( ) Say          ( ) Get          ( ) Edit

 <  Say...    > m.january + m.february + m.march
                                                   «    OK    »
 < Format... >
                                                   < Cancel >
 Range:
 [ ] Upper...                   [ ] Lower...

 [ ] When...      [ ] Error...     [ ] Scroll bar
 [ ] Valid...     [ ] Comment...   [ ] Allow tabs
 [ ] Message...   [ ] Disabled     [ ] Refresh

*=============================================================
*
*=============================================================
 @    7,   45
```

```
Field:
  (·) Say          ( ) Get          ( ) Edit

<  Say...    > m.april + m.may + m.june
                                                 «    OK    »
< Format... >
                                                 < Cancel >
Range:
  [ ] Upper...                   [ ] Lower...

[ ] When...       [ ] Error...      [ ] Scroll bar
[ ] Valid...      [ ] Comment...    [ ] Allow tabs
[ ] Message...    [ ] Disabled      [ ] Refresh

*==============================================================
*
*==============================================================
 @  10,  16

Field:
  (·) Say          ( ) Get          ( ) Edit

<  Say...    > m.july
                                                 «    OK    »
< Format... >
                                                 < Cancel >
Range:
  [ ] Upper...                   [ ] Lower...

[ ] When...       [ ] Error...      [ ] Scroll bar
[ ] Valid...      [ ] Comment...    [ ] Allow tabs
[ ] Message...    [ ] Disabled      [ ] Refresh

*==============================================================
*
*==============================================================
 @  10,  46
```

```
Field:
  (·) Say          ( ) Get          ( ) Edit

<  Say...   > m.october
                                          «   OK    »
< Format... >
                                          < Cancel >
Range:
  [ ] Upper...                  [ ] Lower...

[ ] When...     [ ] Error...     [ ] Scroll bar
[ ] Valid...    [ ] Comment...   [ ] Allow tabs
[ ] Message...  [ ] Disabled     [ ] Refresh
```

```
*==============================================================
*
*==============================================================
 @  11,  16
```

```
Field:
  (·) Say          ( ) Get          ( ) Edit

<  Say...   > m.august
                                          «   OK    »
< Format... >
                                          < Cancel >
Range:
  [ ] Upper...                  [ ] Lower...

[ ] When...     [ ] Error...     [ ] Scroll bar
[ ] Valid...    [ ] Comment...   [ ] Allow tabs
[ ] Message...  [ ] Disabled     [ ] Refresh
```

```
*==============================================================
*
*==============================================================
 @  11,  46
```

```
 Field:
 ( ) Say         ( ) Get         ( ) Edit

 <  Say...    > m.november
                                          «   OK   »
 < Format... >
                                          < Cancel >
 Range:
 [ ] Upper...                 [ ] Lower...

 [ ] When...      [ ] Error...      [ ] Scroll bar
 [ ] Valid...     [ ] Comment...    [ ] Allow tabs
 [ ] Message...   [ ] Disabled      [ ] Refresh

*=============================================================
*
*=============================================================
 @  12,  16

 Field:
 ( ) Say         ( ) Get         ( ) Edit

 <  Say...    > m.september
                                          «   OK   »
 < Format... >
                                          < Cancel >
 Range:
 [ ] Upper...                 [ ] Lower...

 [ ] When...      [ ] Error...      [ ] Scroll bar
 [ ] Valid...     [ ] Comment...    [ ] Allow tabs
 [ ] Message...   [ ] Disabled      [ ] Refresh

*=============================================================
*
*=============================================================
 @  12,  46
```

```
Field:
 ┌──────────────────────────────────────────────┐
 │ (·) Say          ( ) Get          ( ) Edit    │
 └──────────────────────────────────────────────┘

< Say...   > m.december
                                                   «   OK   »
< Format... >
                                                   < Cancel >
Range:
 ┌──────────────────────────────────────────────┐
 │ [ ] Upper...                   [ ] Lower...   │
 └──────────────────────────────────────────────┘

[ ] When...     [ ] Error...     [ ] Scroll bar
[ ] Valid...    [ ] Comment...   [ ] Allow tabs
[ ] Message...  [ ] Disabled     [ ] Refresh
```

```
*==============================================================
*  Text: July:
*==============================================================
 @  10,   9
*==============================================================
*  Text: August:
*==============================================================
 @  11,   7
*==============================================================
*  Text: September:
*==============================================================
 @  12,   4
*==============================================================
*  Box
*==============================================================
 @  13,  15
 SIZE   1,  12
*==============================================================
*  Box
*==============================================================
 @  13,  45
 SIZE   1,  12
*==============================================================
*
*==============================================================
 @  14,  15
```

```
┌──────────────────────────────────────────────────────────┐
│                                                          │
│  Field:                                                  │
│  ┌────────────────────────────────────────────┐          │
│  │ (·) Say         ( ) Get         ( ) Edit    │          │
│  └────────────────────────────────────────────┘          │
│                                                          │
│  <  Say...   > m.july + m.august + m.september           │
│                                           «    OK    »   │
│  < Format... >                                           │
│                                           < Cancel >     │
│  Range:                                                  │
│  ┌────────────────────────────────────────────┐          │
│  │ [ ] Upper...                [ ] Lower...    │          │
│  └────────────────────────────────────────────┘          │
│                                                          │
│  [ ] When...      [ ] Error...      [ ] Scroll bar       │
│  [ ] Valid...     [ ] Comment...    [ ] Allow tabs       │
│  [ ] Message...   [ ] Disabled      [ ] Refresh          │
│                                                          │
└──────────────────────────────────────────────────────────┘
*============================================================
*
*============================================================
 @  14,  45
┌──────────────────────────────────────────────────────────┐
│                                                          │
│  Field:                                                  │
│  ┌────────────────────────────────────────────┐          │
│  │ (·) Say         ( ) Get         ( ) Edit    │          │
│  └────────────────────────────────────────────┘          │
│                                                          │
│  <  Say...   > m.october + m.november + m.december       │
│                                           «    OK    »   │
│  < Format... >                                           │
│                                           < Cancel >     │
│  Range:                                                  │
│  ┌────────────────────────────────────────────┐          │
│  │ [ ] Upper...                [ ] Lower...    │          │
│  └────────────────────────────────────────────┘          │
│                                                          │
│  [ ] When...      [ ] Error...      [ ] Scroll bar       │
│  [ ] Valid...     [ ] Comment...    [ ] Allow tabs       │
│  [ ] Message...   [ ] Disabled      [ ] Refresh          │
│                                                          │
└──────────────────────────────────────────────────────────┘
*============================================================
*  Text: October:
*============================================================
 @  10,  36
*============================================================
*  Text: November:
*============================================================
 @  11,  35
*============================================================
*  Text: December:
*============================================================
 @  12,  35
*============================================================
*  Box
```

```
*=============================================================
 @   2,   2
 SIZE   7,  27
*=============================================================
*  Box
*=============================================================
 @   9,  32
 SIZE   7,  27
*=============================================================
*  Box
*=============================================================
 @   9,   2
 SIZE   7,  27
*=============================================================
*  Text: QTR 2:
*=============================================================
 @   2,  33
*=============================================================
*  Text: QTR 1:
*=============================================================
 @   2,   3
*=============================================================
*  Text: QTR 3:
*=============================================================
 @   9,   3
*=============================================================
*  Text: QTR 4:
*=============================================================
 @   9,  33
*=============================================================
*  Text: Grand Total:
*=============================================================
 @  16,  18
*=============================================================
*
*=============================================================
 @  16,  31

  Field:
   (·) Say          ( ) Get          ( ) Edit

  <  Say...   > m.january + m.february + m.march + m.april
                                                  «   OK   »
  < Format... >
                                                  < Cancel >
  Range:
   [ ] Upper...                    [ ] Lower...

  [ ] When...      [ ] Error...      [ ] Scroll bar
  [ ] Valid...     [ ] Comment...    [ ] Allow tabs
  [ ] Message...   [ ] Disabled      [ ] Refresh

*=============================================================
```

```
*  lhClose
*==============================================================
 @  18,  25
 Spacing:    1

 Push Button Prompts:        (·) Horizontal    ( ) Vertical
                             [X] Terminating  <Spacing...>
 \?\!Close
                             Variable:
                             < Choose... >  lhClose
                             Options:
                             [ ] When...     [ ] Comment...
                             [ ] Valid...    [ ] Disabled
                             [ ] Message...

               «   OK   »    < Cancel >

*************************************************************
*--  SCREEN CLEANUP CODE
*************************************************************
SET CURSOR &lcOldCurs
*------------------------------------------------------------
*************************************************************
**--    YEARSHOW.SCX - MAC PLATFORM
*************************************************************

 ( ) DeskTop                   (·) Window

 Name:                         <Type...>
 Title:
 Footer:

 Size:           Screen Code:

 Height:   22.000   [X] Setup...                      «  OK  »
 Width:    62.000   [X] Cleanup & Procs...

 Position:       READ Clauses:                       < Cancel >

 Row:       0.000   [ ] Activate...     [ ] Show...
 Column:    0.000   [ ] Valid...        [ ] When...
 [X] Center         [ ] Deactivate...

 Environment:                   [X] Add alias

     Environment NOT saved with screen.
```

```
Type:    [ Dialog ]

Attributes:          Border:

[ ] Close            ( ) None
[X] Float            ( ) Single
[X] Shadow           (·) Double       «   OK   »
[ ] Minimize         ( ) Panel
                     ( ) System       < Cancel >

Color Schemes:

  Primary:           Popup:
  [          ]       [          ]
```

```
MAC      RGB Fill Color Scheme: (194,194,194)
MAC      Font: monaco,   9
 Screen Setup code above
*************************************************************
*--    G E T    O B J E C T S
*************************************************************
*============================================================
*  Box
*============================================================
 @  10.364,  32.333
 SIZE   6.455,  26.167
MAC      RGB Color Scheme: (255,255,255,,,)
           Pen: 2
*============================================================
*  Box
*============================================================
 @  10.364,   2.333
 SIZE   6.455,  26.167
MAC      RGB Color Scheme: (255,255,255,,,)
           Pen: 2
*============================================================
*  Box
*============================================================
 @   2.727,   2.333
 SIZE   6.455,  26.167
MAC      RGB Color Scheme: (255,255,255,,,)
           Pen: 2
*============================================================
*
*============================================================
 @   0.545,  10.167
```

```
Field:
  (·) Say        ( ) Get        ( ) Edit

< Say...   > m.tcname
                                       «  OK  »
< Format... > @I
                                       < Cancel >
Range:
  [ ] Upper...              [ ] Lower...

[ ] When...      [ ] Error...      [ ] Scroll bar
[ ] Valid...     [ ] Comment...    [ ] Allow tabs
[ ] Message...   [ ] Disabled      [ ] Refresh
```

```
MAC      RGB Color Scheme: (,,,,,)
MAC      Font: monaco,  9
*============================================================
*  Line
*============================================================
 @   7.000,  15.500
MAC      RGB Color Scheme: (,,,,,)
           Pen: 1
*============================================================
*  Text: January:
*============================================================
 @   3.273,   6.000
MAC      RGB Color Scheme: (,,,,,)
MAC      Font: Monaco,   9
        Style: Bold
*============================================================
*  Text: February:
*============================================================
 @   4.455,   5.000
MAC      RGB Color Scheme: (,,,,,)
MAC      Font: Monaco,   9
        Style: Bold
*============================================================
*  Text: March:
*============================================================
 @   5.545,   8.000
MAC      RGB Color Scheme: (,,,,,)
MAC      Font: Monaco,   9
        Style: Bold
*============================================================
*  Text: April:
*============================================================
 @   3.273,  38.000
MAC      RGB Color Scheme: (,,,,,)
MAC      Font: Monaco,   9
        Style: Bold
*============================================================
*  Text: May:
*============================================================
```

```
 @   4.455,  40.000
MAC      RGB Color Scheme: (,,,,,)
MAC      Font: Monaco,   9
        Style: Bold
*==========================================================
*  Text: June:
*==========================================================
 @   5.545,  39.000
MAC      RGB Color Scheme: (,,,,,)
MAC      Font: Monaco,   9
        Style: Bold
*==========================================================
*  Line
*==========================================================
 @   7.000,  45.500
MAC      RGB Color Scheme: (,,,,,)
          Pen: 1
*==========================================================
*
*==========================================================
 @   3.364,  16.167
```

```
Field:

 (·) Say          ( ) Get          ( ) Edit

< Say...   > m.january
                                          «   OK   »
< Format... >
                                          < Cancel >
Range:

 [ ] Upper...                  [ ] Lower...

[ ] When...     [ ] Error...     [ ] Scroll bar
[ ] Valid...    [ ] Comment...   [ ] Allow tabs
[ ] Message...  [ ] Disabled     [ ] Refresh
```

```
MAC      RGB Color Scheme: (,,,,,)
MAC      Font: monaco,   9
*==========================================================
*
*==========================================================
 @   3.364,  46.167
```

```
╔══════════════════════════════════════════════════════════════════╗
║                                                                  ║
║  Field:                                                          ║
║   ┌──────────────────────────────────────────────┐               ║
║   │ (·) Say        ( ) Get        ( ) Edit       │               ║
║   └──────────────────────────────────────────────┘               ║
║                                                                  ║
║  <  Say...   > m.april                                           ║
║                                              «   OK   »          ║
║  < Format... >                                                   ║
║                                              < Cancel >          ║
║  Range:                                                          ║
║   ┌──────────────────────────────────────────────┐               ║
║   │ [ ] Upper...                 [ ] Lower...    │               ║
║   └──────────────────────────────────────────────┘               ║
║                                                                  ║
║   [ ] When...      [ ] Error...     [ ] Scroll bar               ║
║   [ ] Valid...     [ ] Comment...   [ ] Allow tabs               ║
║   [ ] Message...   [ ] Disabled     [ ] Refresh                  ║
║                                                                  ║
╚══════════════════════════════════════════════════════════════════╝
MAC      RGB Color Scheme: (,,,,,)
MAC      Font: monaco,   9
*===============================================================
*
*===============================================================
 @   4.455,  16.167
╔══════════════════════════════════════════════════════════════════╗
║                                                                  ║
║  Field:                                                          ║
║   ┌──────────────────────────────────────────────┐               ║
║   │ (·) Say        ( ) Get        ( ) Edit       │               ║
║   └──────────────────────────────────────────────┘               ║
║                                                                  ║
║  <  Say...   > m.february                                        ║
║                                              «   OK   »          ║
║  < Format... >                                                   ║
║                                              < Cancel >          ║
║  Range:                                                          ║
║   ┌──────────────────────────────────────────────┐               ║
║   │ [ ] Upper...                 [ ] Lower...    │               ║
║   └──────────────────────────────────────────────┘               ║
║                                                                  ║
║   [ ] When...      [ ] Error...     [ ] Scroll bar               ║
║   [ ] Valid...     [ ] Comment...   [ ] Allow tabs               ║
║   [ ] Message...   [ ] Disabled     [ ] Refresh                  ║
║                                                                  ║
╚══════════════════════════════════════════════════════════════════╝
MAC      RGB Color Scheme: (,,,,,)
MAC      Font: monaco,   9
*===============================================================
*
*===============================================================
 @   4.455,  46.167
```

```
      Field:
      ( ) Say          ( ) Get          ( ) Edit

      <  Say...    > m.may
                                                 «   OK    »
      < Format... >
                                                 < Cancel >
      Range:
      [ ] Upper...                  [ ] Lower...

      [ ] When...     [ ] Error...     [ ] Scroll bar
      [ ] Valid...    [ ] Comment...   [ ] Allow tabs
      [ ] Message...  [ ] Disabled     [ ] Refresh
MAC       RGB Color Scheme: (,,,,,)
MAC       Font: monaco,   9
*============================================================
*
*============================================================
 @   5.545,  16.167

      Field:
      ( ) Say          ( ) Get          ( ) Edit

      <  Say...    > m.march
                                                 «   OK    »
      < Format... >
                                                 < Cancel >
      Range:
      [ ] Upper...                  [ ] Lower...

      [ ] When...     [ ] Error...     [ ] Scroll bar
      [ ] Valid...    [ ] Comment...   [ ] Allow tabs
      [ ] Message...  [ ] Disabled     [ ] Refresh
MAC       RGB Color Scheme: (,,,,,)
MAC       Font: monaco,   9
*============================================================
*
*============================================================
 @   5.545,  46.167
```

```
  Field:
  ( ) Say        ( ) Get        ( ) Edit

  <  Say...   > m.june
                                          «   OK   »
  < Format... >
                                          < Cancel >
  Range:
  [ ] Upper...                  [ ] Lower...

  [ ] When...      [ ] Error...      [ ] Scroll bar
  [ ] Valid...     [ ] Comment...    [ ] Allow tabs
  [ ] Message...   [ ] Disabled      [ ] Refresh

MAC      RGB Color Scheme: (,,,,,)
MAC      Font: monaco,   9
*============================================================
*
*============================================================
 @   7.636,  15.167

  Field:
  ( ) Say        ( ) Get        ( ) Edit

  <  Say...   > m.january + m.february + m.march
                                          «   OK   »
  < Format... >
                                          < Cancel >
  Range:
  [ ] Upper...                  [ ] Lower...

  [ ] When...      [ ] Error...      [ ] Scroll bar
  [ ] Valid...     [ ] Comment...    [ ] Allow tabs
  [ ] Message...   [ ] Disabled      [ ] Refresh

MAC      RGB Color Scheme: (,,,,,)
MAC      Font: monaco,   9
*============================================================
*
*============================================================
 @   7.636,  45.167
```

```
Field:
  (·) Say          ( ) Get          ( ) Edit

< Say...    > m.april + m.may + m.june
                                                   «   OK    »
< Format... >
                                                   < Cancel >
Range:
  [ ] Upper...                    [ ] Lower...

[ ] When...      [ ] Error...      [ ] Scroll bar
[ ] Valid...     [ ] Comment...    [ ] Allow tabs
[ ] Message...   [ ] Disabled      [ ] Refresh

MAC       RGB Color Scheme: (,,,,,)
MAC       Font: monaco,    9
*============================================================
*
*============================================================
 @  11.000,  16.167

Field:
  (·) Say          ( ) Get          ( ) Edit

< Say...    > m.july
                                                   «   OK    »
< Format... >
                                                   < Cancel >
Range:
  [ ] Upper...                    [ ] Lower...

[ ] When...      [ ] Error...      [ ] Scroll bar
[ ] Valid...     [ ] Comment...    [ ] Allow tabs
[ ] Message...   [ ] Disabled      [ ] Refresh

MAC       RGB Color Scheme: (,,,,,)
MAC       Font: monaco,    9
*============================================================
*
*============================================================
 @  11.000,  46.167
```

```
 Field:
 (·) Say        ( ) Get        ( ) Edit

 <  Say...   > m.october
                                          «   OK   »
 < Format... >
                                          < Cancel >
 Range:
 [ ] Upper...                [ ] Lower...

 [ ] When...     [ ] Error...     [ ] Scroll bar
 [ ] Valid...    [ ] Comment...   [ ] Allow tabs
 [ ] Message...  [ ] Disabled     [ ] Refresh

MAC       RGB Color Scheme: (,,,,,)
MAC       Font: monaco,   9
*============================================================
*
*============================================================
 @  12.091,  16.167

 Field:
 (·) Say        ( ) Get        ( ) Edit

 <  Say...   > m.august
                                          «   OK   »
 < Format... >
                                          < Cancel >
 Range:
 [ ] Upper...                [ ] Lower...

 [ ] When...     [ ] Error...     [ ] Scroll bar
 [ ] Valid...    [ ] Comment...   [ ] Allow tabs
 [ ] Message...  [ ] Disabled     [ ] Refresh

MAC       RGB Color Scheme: (,,,,,)
MAC       Font: monaco,   9
*============================================================
*
*============================================================
 @  12.091,  46.167
```

```
 Field:
 ┌──────────────────────────────────────────────┐
 │ (·) Say          ( ) Get          ( ) Edit   │
 └──────────────────────────────────────────────┘

 <  Say...   > m.november
                                               «   OK   »
 < Format... >
                                               < Cancel >
 Range:
 ┌──────────────────────────────────────────────┐
 │ [ ] Upper...                [ ] Lower...     │
 └──────────────────────────────────────────────┘

 [ ] When...      [ ] Error...      [ ] Scroll bar
 [ ] Valid...     [ ] Comment...    [ ] Allow tabs
 [ ] Message...   [ ] Disabled      [ ] Refresh

MAC       RGB Color Scheme: (,,,,,)
MAC       Font: monaco,    9
*============================================================
*
*============================================================
 @  13.182,  16.167

 Field:
 ┌──────────────────────────────────────────────┐
 │ (·) Say          ( ) Get          ( ) Edit   │
 └──────────────────────────────────────────────┘

 <  Say...   > m.september
                                               «   OK   »
 < Format... >
                                               < Cancel >
 Range:
 ┌──────────────────────────────────────────────┐
 │ [ ] Upper...                [ ] Lower...     │
 └──────────────────────────────────────────────┘

 [ ] When...      [ ] Error...      [ ] Scroll bar
 [ ] Valid...     [ ] Comment...    [ ] Allow tabs
 [ ] Message...   [ ] Disabled      [ ] Refresh

MAC       RGB Color Scheme: (,,,,,)
MAC       Font: monaco,    9
*============================================================
*
*============================================================
 @  13.182,  46.167
```

```
Field:
 ┌──────────────────────────────────────────────┐
 │ (·) Say        ( ) Get         ( ) Edit      │
 └──────────────────────────────────────────────┘

 <  Say...    > m.december
                                            «   OK    »
 < Format... >
                                            < Cancel >
 Range:
 ┌──────────────────────────────────────────────┐
 │ [ ] Upper...                [ ] Lower...     │
 └──────────────────────────────────────────────┘

 [ ] When...      [ ] Error...      [ ] Scroll bar
 [ ] Valid...     [ ] Comment...    [ ] Allow tabs
 [ ] Message...   [ ] Disabled      [ ] Refresh
```

```
MAC       RGB Color Scheme: (,,,,,)
MAC       Font: monaco,   9
*=============================================================
*  Text: July:
*=============================================================
 @  11.000,   9.000
MAC       RGB Color Scheme: (,,,,,)
MAC       Font: Monaco,   9
         Style: Bold
*=============================================================
*  Text: August:
*=============================================================
 @  12.091,   7.000
MAC       RGB Color Scheme: (,,,,,)
MAC       Font: Monaco,   9
         Style: Bold
*=============================================================
*  Text: September:
*=============================================================
 @  13.182,   4.000
MAC       RGB Color Scheme: (,,,,,)
MAC       Font: Monaco,   9
         Style: Bold
*=============================================================
*  Line
*=============================================================
 @  14.727,  15.500
MAC       RGB Color Scheme: (,,,,,)
            Pen: 1
*=============================================================
*  Line
*=============================================================
 @  14.727,  45.500
MAC       RGB Color Scheme: (,,,,,)
            Pen: 1
*=============================================================
*
*=============================================================
 @  15.364,  15.167
```

```
   Field:
   ┌──────────────────────────────────────────────┐
   │ (·) Say          ( ) Get          ( ) Edit  │
   └──────────────────────────────────────────────┘

   <  Say...   > m.july + m.august + m.september
                                                 «   OK   »
   < Format... >
                                                 < Cancel >
   Range:
   ┌──────────────────────────────────────────────┐
   │ [ ] Upper...                 [ ] Lower...    │
   └──────────────────────────────────────────────┘

   [ ] When...      [ ] Error...     [ ] Scroll bar
   [ ] Valid...     [ ] Comment...   [ ] Allow tabs
   [ ] Message...   [ ] Disabled     [ ] Refresh

MAC      RGB Color Scheme: (,,,,,)
MAC      Font: monaco,   9
*==============================================================
*
*==============================================================
 @  15.364,  45.167

   Field:
   ┌──────────────────────────────────────────────┐
   │ (·) Say          ( ) Get          ( ) Edit  │
   └──────────────────────────────────────────────┘

   <  Say...   > m.october + m.november + m.december
                                                 «   OK   »
   < Format... >
                                                 < Cancel >
   Range:
   ┌──────────────────────────────────────────────┐
   │ [ ] Upper...                 [ ] Lower...    │
   └──────────────────────────────────────────────┘

   [ ] When...      [ ] Error...     [ ] Scroll bar
   [ ] Valid...     [ ] Comment...   [ ] Allow tabs
   [ ] Message...   [ ] Disabled     [ ] Refresh

MAC      RGB Color Scheme: (,,,,,)
MAC      Font: monaco,   9
*==============================================================
*  Text: October:
*==============================================================
 @  11.000,  36.000
MAC      RGB Color Scheme: (,,,,,)
MAC      Font: Monaco,   9
         Style: Bold
*==============================================================
*  Text: November:
```

```
*==============================================================
 @  12.091,  35.000
MAC       RGB Color Scheme: (,,,,,)
MAC       Font: Monaco,   9
         Style: Bold
*==============================================================
*  Text: December:
*==============================================================
 @  13.182,  35.000
MAC       RGB Color Scheme: (,,,,,)
MAC       Font: Monaco,   9
         Style: Bold
*==============================================================
*  Box
*==============================================================
 @   2.727,  32.333
 SIZE   6.455,  26.167
MAC       RGB Color Scheme: (,,,,,)
            Pen: 2
*==============================================================
*  Text: QTR 2:
*==============================================================
 @   2.182,  33.000
MAC       RGB Color Scheme: (,,,,,)
MAC       Font: Monaco,   9
         Style: Bold
*==============================================================
*  Text: QTR 1:
*==============================================================
 @   2.182,   3.000
MAC       RGB Color Scheme: (,,,,,)
MAC       Font: Monaco,   9
         Style: Bold
*==============================================================
*  Text: QTR 3:
*==============================================================
 @   9.818,   3.000
MAC       RGB Color Scheme: (,,,,,)
MAC       Font: Monaco,   9
         Style: Bold
*==============================================================
*  Text: QTR 4:
*==============================================================
 @   9.818,  33.000
MAC       RGB Color Scheme: (,,,,,)
MAC       Font: Monaco,   9
         Style: Bold
*==============================================================
*  Text: Grand Total:
*==============================================================
 @  17.545,  18.000
MAC       RGB Color Scheme: (,,,,,)
MAC       Font: Monaco,   9
         Style: Bold
*==============================================================
*
*==============================================================
 @  17.545,  32.333
```

```
+-------------------------------------------------------------------+
|  Field:                                                           |
|  +--------------------------------------------+                  |
|  | (·) Say        ( ) Get        ( ) Edit     |                  |
|  +--------------------------------------------+                  |
|                                                                   |
|  <  Say...   > m.january + m.february + m.march + m.april         |
|                                                 «   OK   »        |
|  < Format... >                                                    |
|                                                 < Cancel >        |
|  Range:                                                           |
|  +--------------------------------------------+                  |
|  | [ ] Upper...                [ ] Lower...    |                  |
|  +--------------------------------------------+                  |
|                                                                   |
|  [ ] When...      [ ] Error...      [ ] Scroll bar                |
|  [ ] Valid...     [ ] Comment...    [ ] Allow tabs                |
|  [ ] Message...   [ ] Disabled      [ ] Refresh                   |
+-------------------------------------------------------------------+
MAC      RCB Color Scheme: (,,,,,)
MAC      Font: monaco,   9
*=============================================================
*  lhClose
*=============================================================
 @  19.545,  25.000
     SIZE   1.750,  13.500
 Spacing:    2
+-------------------------------------------------------------------+
|  Push Button Prompts:      +-----------------------------------+  |
|                            | (·) Horizontal    ( ) Vertical    |  |
|  +----------------------+  | [X] Terminating   <Spacing...>    |  |
|  | \?\!Close            |  +-----------------------------------+  |
|  |                      |  Variable:                              |
|  |                      |  +-----------------------------------+  |
|  |                      |  | < Choose... >  lhClose            |  |
|  |                      |  +-----------------------------------+  |
|  |                      |  Options:                               |
|  |                      |  +-----------------------------------+  |
|  |                      |  | [ ] When...      [ ] Comment...   |  |
|  |                      |  | [ ] Valid...     [ ] Disabled     |  |
|  |                      |  | [ ] Message...                    |  |
|  +----------------------+  +-----------------------------------+  |
|                                                                   |
|               «   OK   »     < Cancel >                           |
+-------------------------------------------------------------------+
MAC      RGB Color Scheme: (,,,,,)
MAC      Font: Geneva,   9
        Style: Bold
 Screen Cleanup and Procedures code above
*-------------------------------------------------------------
```

```
************************************************************
**--    YEARSHOW.SCX - WINDOWS PLATFORM
************************************************************

 ( ) DeskTop                          (·) Window

 Name:                                <Type...>
 Title:
 Footer:

 Size:              Screen Code:

  Height:   22.000   [X] Setup...
  Width:    62.000   [X] Cleanup & Procs...             «   OK   »

 Position:          READ Clauses:                       < Cancel >

  Row:        0.000  [ ] Activate...     [ ] Show...
  Column:     0.000  [ ] Valid...        [ ] When...
  [X] Center         [ ] Deactivate...

 Environment:                         [X] Add alias

        Environment NOT saved with screen.

  Type:        Dialog

  Attributes:        Border:

   [ ] Close          ( ) None
   [X] Float          ( ) Single
   [X] Shadow         (·) Double        «   OK   »
   [ ] Minimize       ( ) Panel
                      ( ) System        < Cancel >

  Color Schemes:

   Primary:          Popup:

WINDOWS  RGB Fill Color Scheme: (192,192,192)
WINDOWS  Font: Terminal,   9
 Screen Setup code above
************************************************************
*--    G E T    O B J E C T S
************************************************************
*===========================================================
*  Box
*===========================================================
 @   2.833,  32.625
 SIZE   6.417,  26.125
WINDOWS  RGB Color Scheme: (255,255,255,,,)
          Pen: 1
```

```
*==============================================================
*  Box
*==============================================================
 @  10.583,  32.625
 SIZE   6.417,  26.125
WINDOWS  RGB Color Scheme: (255,255,255,,,)
           Pen: 1
*==============================================================
*  Box
*==============================================================
 @  10.583,   2.625
 SIZE   6.417,  26.125
WINDOWS  RGB Color Scheme: (255,255,255,,,)
           Pen: 1
*==============================================================
*  Box
*==============================================================
 @   2.917,   2.750
 SIZE   6.417,  26.125
WINDOWS  RGB Color Scheme: (255,255,255,,,)
           Pen: 1
*==============================================================
*
*==============================================================
 @   0.583,  10.125
```

```
Field:

 (·) Say          ( ) Get          ( ) Edit

< Say...   > m.tcname
                                              «   OK   »
< Format... > @I
                                              < Cancel >
Range:

 [ ] Upper...                 [ ] Lower...

[ ] When...      [ ] Error...      [ ] Scroll bar
[ ] Valid...     [ ] Comment...    [ ] Allow tabs
[ ] Message...   [ ] Disabled      [ ] Refresh
```

```
WINDOWS  RGB Color Scheme: (,,,,,)
WINDOWS  Font: Terminal,   9
*==============================================================
*  Line
*==============================================================
 @   7.000,  15.500
WINDOWS  RGB Color Scheme: (,,,,,)
           Pen: 1
*==============================================================
*  Text: January:
*==============================================================
 @   3.250,    6.000
WINDOWS  RGB Color Scheme: (,,,,,)
```

```
WINDOWS  Font: Terminal,    9
*==============================================================
*  Text: February:
*==============================================================
 @   4.417,   5.000
WINDOWS  RGB Color Scheme: (,,,,,)
WINDOWS  Font: Terminal,    9
*==============================================================
*  Text: March:
*==============================================================
 @   5.500,   8.000
WINDOWS  RGB Color Scheme: (,,,,,)
WINDOWS  Font: Terminal,    9
*==============================================================
*  Text: April:
*==============================================================
 @   3.250,  38.000
WINDOWS  RGB Color Scheme: (,,,,,)
WINDOWS  Font: Terminal,    9
*==============================================================
*  Text: May:
*==============================================================
 @   4.417,  40.000
WINDOWS  RGB Color Scheme: (,,,,,)
WINDOWS  Font: Terminal,    9
*==============================================================
*  Text: June:
*==============================================================
 @   5.500,  39.000
WINDOWS  RGB Color Scheme: (,,,,,)
WINDOWS  Font: Terminal,    9
*==============================================================
*  Line
*==============================================================
 @   7.000,  45.500
WINDOWS  RGB Color Scheme: (,,,,,)
          Pen: 1
*==============================================================
*
*==============================================================
 @   3.333,  16.125
```

```
  Field:
   ┌────────────────────────────────────────────┐
   │ (·) Say         ( ) Get          ( ) Edit  │
   └────────────────────────────────────────────┘

  <  Say...   > m.january
                                              «    OK    »
  < Format... >
                                              < Cancel >
  Range:
   ┌────────────────────────────────────────────┐
   │ [ ] Upper...                [ ] Lower...   │
   └────────────────────────────────────────────┘

   [ ] When...       [ ] Error...      [ ] Scroll bar
   [ ] Valid...      [ ] Comment...    [ ] Allow tabs
   [ ] Message...    [ ] Disabled      [ ] Refresh
```

```
WINDOWS  RGB Color Scheme: (,,,,,)
WINDOWS  Font: Terminal,   9
*==============================================================
*
*==============================================================
 @   3.333,  46.125
```

```
  Field:
  ( ) Say          ( ) Get          ( ) Edit

  <  Say...    > m.april
                                            «    OK    »
  < Format... >
                                            < Cancel >
  Range:
  [ ] Upper...                  [ ] Lower...

  [ ] When...      [ ] Error...     [ ] Scroll bar
  [ ] Valid...     [ ] Comment...   [ ] Allow tabs
  [ ] Message...   [ ] Disabled     [ ] Refresh
```

```
WINDOWS  RGB Color Scheme: (,,,,,)
WINDOWS  Font: Terminal,   9
*==============================================================
*
*==============================================================
 @   4.417,  16.125
```

```
  Field:
  ( ) Say          ( ) Get          ( ) Edit

  <  Say...    > m.february
                                            «    OK    »
  < Format... >
                                            < Cancel >
  Range:
  [ ] Upper...                  [ ] Lower...

  [ ] When...      [ ] Error...     [ ] Scroll bar
  [ ] Valid...     [ ] Comment...   [ ] Allow tabs
  [ ] Message...   [ ] Disabled     [ ] Refresh
```

```
WINDOWS  RGB Color Scheme: (,,,,,)
WINDOWS  Font: Terminal,   9
*==============================================================
*
*==============================================================
```

```
 @   4.417,  46.125
+--------------------------------------------------------------------+
|                                                                    |
|  Field:                                                            |
|  +----------------------------------------------+                  |
|  | (·) Say         ( ) Get          ( ) Edit    |                  |
|  +----------------------------------------------+                  |
|                                                                    |
|  <  Say...    > m.may                                              |
|                                                    «   OK   »      |
|  < Format... >                                                     |
|                                                    < Cancel >      |
|  Range:                                                            |
|  +----------------------------------------------+                  |
|  | [ ] Upper...                  [ ] Lower...   |                  |
|  +----------------------------------------------+                  |
|                                                                    |
|  [ ] When...      [ ] Error...     [ ] Scroll bar                  |
|  [ ] Valid...     [ ] Comment...   [ ] Allow tabs                  |
|  [ ] Message...   [ ] Disabled     [ ] Refresh                     |
|                                                                    |
+--------------------------------------------------------------------+
WINDOWS  RGB Color Scheme: (,,,,,)
WINDOWS  Font: Terminal,    9
*==============================================================
*
*==============================================================
 @   5.500,  16.125
+--------------------------------------------------------------------+
|                                                                    |
|  Field:                                                            |
|  +----------------------------------------------+                  |
|  | (·) Say         ( ) Get          ( ) Edit    |                  |
|  +----------------------------------------------+                  |
|                                                                    |
|  <  Say...    > m.march                                            |
|                                                    «   OK   »      |
|  < Format... >                                                     |
|                                                    < Cancel >      |
|  Range:                                                            |
|  +----------------------------------------------+                  |
|  | [ ] Upper...                  [ ] Lower...   |                  |
|  +----------------------------------------------+                  |
|                                                                    |
|  [ ] When...      [ ] Error...     [ ] Scroll bar                  |
|  [ ] Valid...     [ ] Comment...   [ ] Allow tabs                  |
|  [ ] Message...   [ ] Disabled     [ ] Refresh                     |
|                                                                    |
+--------------------------------------------------------------------+
WINDOWS  RGB Color Scheme: (,,,,,)
WINDOWS  Font: Terminal,    9
*==============================================================
*
*==============================================================
 @   5.500,  46.125
```

```
Field:
 (·) Say          ( ) Get          ( ) Edit

< Say...    > m.june
                                          «   OK   »
< Format... >
                                          < Cancel >
Range:
 [ ] Upper...                  [ ] Lower...

[ ] When...      [ ] Error...     [ ] Scroll bar
[ ] Valid...     [ ] Comment...   [ ] Allow tabs
[ ] Message...   [ ] Disabled     [ ] Refresh

WINDOWS  RGB Color Scheme: (,,,,,)
WINDOWS  Font: Terminal,   9
*============================================================
*
*============================================================
 @   7.667,  15.125

Field:
 (·) Say          ( ) Get          ( ) Edit

< Say...    > m.january + m.february + m.march
                                          «   OK   »
< Format... >
                                          < Cancel >
Range:
 [ ] Upper...                  [ ] Lower...

[ ] When...      [ ] Error...     [ ] Scroll bar
[ ] Valid...     [ ] Comment...   [ ] Allow tabs
[ ] Message...   [ ] Disabled     [ ] Refresh

WINDOWS  RGB Color Scheme: (,,,,,)
WINDOWS  Font: Terminal,   9
*============================================================
*
*============================================================
 @   7.667,  45.125
```

```
Field:
   (·) Say          ( ) Get          ( ) Edit

< Say...    > m.april + m.may + m.june
                                                  «   OK   »
< Format... >
                                                  < Cancel >
Range:
   [ ] Upper...                    [ ] Lower...

[ ] When...       [ ] Error...      [ ] Scroll bar
[ ] Valid...      [ ] Comment...    [ ] Allow tabs
[ ] Message...    [ ] Disabled      [ ] Refresh

WINDOWS  RGB Color Scheme: (,,,,,)
WINDOWS  Font: Terminal,   9
*==============================================================
*
*==============================================================
 @  11.000,  16.125

Field:
   (·) Say          ( ) Get          ( ) Edit

< Say...    > m.july
                                                  «   OK   »
< Format... >
                                                  < Cancel >
Range:
   [ ] Upper...                    [ ] Lower...

[ ] When...       [ ] Error...      [ ] Scroll bar
[ ] Valid...      [ ] Comment...    [ ] Allow tabs
[ ] Message...    [ ] Disabled      [ ] Refresh

WINDOWS  RGB Color Scheme: (,,,,,)
WINDOWS  Font: Terminal,   9
*==============================================================
*
*==============================================================
 @  11.000,  46.125
```

Field:

(·) Say ( ) Get ( ) Edit

< Say... > m.october

« OK »

< Format... >

< Cancel >

Range:

[ ] Upper... [ ] Lower...

[ ] When... [ ] Error... [ ] Scroll bar
[ ] Valid... [ ] Comment... [ ] Allow tabs
[ ] Message... [ ] Disabled [ ] Refresh

WINDOWS RGB Color Scheme: (,,,,,)
WINDOWS Font: Terminal, 9
*==
*
*==
@ 12.083, 16.125

Field:

(·) Say ( ) Get ( ) Edit

< Say... > m.august

« OK »

< Format... >

< Cancel >

Range:

[ ] Upper... [ ] Lower...

[ ] When... [ ] Error... [ ] Scroll bar
[ ] Valid... [ ] Comment... [ ] Allow tabs
[ ] Message... [ ] Disabled [ ] Refresh

WINDOWS RGB Color Scheme: (,,,,,)
WINDOWS Font: Terminal, 9
*==
*
*==
@ 12.083, 46.125

```
+-------------------------------------------------------------+
|                                                             |
| Field:                                                      |
| +------------------------------------------+                |
| | (·) Say        ( ) Get        ( ) Edit   |                |
| +------------------------------------------+                |
|                                                             |
| <  Say...   > m.november                                    |
|                                              «   OK   »     |
| < Format... >                                               |
|                                              < Cancel >     |
| Range:                                                      |
| +------------------------------------------+                |
| | [ ] Upper...             [ ] Lower...    |                |
| +------------------------------------------+                |
|                                                             |
| [ ] When...      [ ] Error...      [ ] Scroll bar           |
| [ ] Valid...     [ ] Comment...    [ ] Allow tabs           |
| [ ] Message...   [ ] Disabled      [ ] Refresh              |
|                                                             |
+-------------------------------------------------------------+
WINDOWS  RGB Color Scheme: (,,,,,)
WINDOWS  Font: Terminal,   9
*============================================================
*
*============================================================
 @  13.167,  16.125
+-------------------------------------------------------------+
|                                                             |
| Field:                                                      |
| +------------------------------------------+                |
| | (·) Say        ( ) Get        ( ) Edit   |                |
| +------------------------------------------+                |
|                                                             |
| <  Say...   > m.september                                   |
|                                              «   OK   »     |
| < Format... >                                               |
|                                              < Cancel >     |
| Range:                                                      |
| +------------------------------------------+                |
| | [ ] Upper...             [ ] Lower...    |                |
| +------------------------------------------+                |
|                                                             |
| [ ] When...      [ ] Error...      [ ] Scroll bar           |
| [ ] Valid...     [ ] Comment...    [ ] Allow tabs           |
| [ ] Message...   [ ] Disabled      [ ] Refresh              |
|                                                             |
+-------------------------------------------------------------+
WINDOWS  RGB Color Scheme: (,,,,,)
WINDOWS  Font: Terminal,   9
*============================================================
*
*============================================================
 @  13.167,  46.125
```

```
Field:
 ┌──────────────────────────────────────────────────┐
 │ (·) Say          ( ) Get          ( ) Edit      │
 └──────────────────────────────────────────────────┘

< Say... > m.december
                                                  «   OK   »
< Format... >
                                                  < Cancel >
Range:
 ┌──────────────────────────────────────────────────┐
 │ [ ] Upper...                     [ ] Lower...   │
 └──────────────────────────────────────────────────┘

[ ] When...      [ ] Error...      [ ] Scroll bar
[ ] Valid...     [ ] Comment...    [ ] Allow tabs
[ ] Message...   [ ] Disabled      [ ] Refresh
```

```
WINDOWS  RGB Color Scheme: (,,,,,)
WINDOWS  Font: Terminal,   9
*============================================================
*  Text: July:
*============================================================
 @  11.000,   9.000
WINDOWS  RGB Color Scheme: (,,,,,)
WINDOWS  Font: Terminal,   9
*============================================================
*  Text: August:
*============================================================
 @  12.083,   7.000
WINDOWS  RGB Color Scheme: (,,,,,)
WINDOWS  Font: Terminal,   9
*============================================================
*  Text: September:
*============================================================
 @  13.167,   4.000
WINDOWS  RGB Color Scheme: (,,,,,)
WINDOWS  Font: Terminal,   9
*============================================================
*  Line
*============================================================
 @  14.750,  15.500
WINDOWS  RGB Color Scheme: (,,,,,)
           Pen: 1
*============================================================
*  Line
*============================================================
 @  14.750,  45.500
WINDOWS  RGB Color Scheme: (,,,,,)
           Pen: 1
*============================================================
*
*============================================================
 @  15.333,  15.125
```

```
      Field:
      ┌─────────────────────────────────────────────────┐
      │ (·) Say           ( ) Get           ( ) Edit    │
      └─────────────────────────────────────────────────┘

      <  Say...    > m.july + m.august + m.september
                                                  «   OK   »
      < Format... >
                                                  < Cancel >
      Range:
      ┌─────────────────────────────────────────────────┐
      │ [ ] Upper...                   [ ] Lower...     │
      └─────────────────────────────────────────────────┘

      [ ] When...       [ ] Error...      [ ] Scroll bar
      [ ] Valid...      [ ] Comment...    [ ] Allow tabs
      [ ] Message...    [ ] Disabled      [ ] Refresh

WINDOWS  RGB Color Scheme: (,,,,,)
WINDOWS  Font: Terminal,   9
*==============================================================
*
*==============================================================
 @  15.333,  45.125

      Field:
      ┌─────────────────────────────────────────────────┐
      │ (·) Say           ( ) Get           ( ) Edit    │
      └─────────────────────────────────────────────────┘

      <  Say...    > m.october + m.november + m.december
                                                  «   OK   »
      < Format... >
                                                  < Cancel >
      Range:
      ┌─────────────────────────────────────────────────┐
      │ [ ] Upper...                   [ ] Lower...     │
      └─────────────────────────────────────────────────┘

      [ ] When...       [ ] Error...      [ ] Scroll bar
      [ ] Valid...      [ ] Comment...    [ ] Allow tabs
      [ ] Message...    [ ] Disabled      [ ] Refresh

WINDOWS  RGB Color Scheme: (,,,,,)
WINDOWS  Font: Terminal,   9
*==============================================================
*  Text: October:
*==============================================================
 @  11.000,  36.000
WINDOWS  RGB Color Scheme: (,,,,,)
WINDOWS  Font: Terminal,   9
*==============================================================
*  Text: November:
*==============================================================
 @  12.083,  35.000
```

```
WINDOWS  RGB Color Scheme: (,,,,,)
WINDOWS  Font: Terminal,   9
*============================================================
*  Text: December:
*============================================================
 @  13.167,  35.000
WINDOWS  RGB Color Scheme: (,,,,,)
WINDOWS  Font: Terminal,   9
*============================================================
*  Box
*============================================================
 @   2.833,   2.625
 SIZE   6.417,  26.125
WINDOWS  RGB Color Scheme: (,,,,,)
           Pen: 1
*============================================================
*  Box
*============================================================
 @   2.750,  32.500
 SIZE   6.417,  26.125
WINDOWS  RGB Color Scheme: (,,,,,)
           Pen: 1
*============================================================
*  Box
*============================================================
 @  10.500,  32.500
 SIZE   6.417,  26.125
WINDOWS  RGB Color Scheme: (,,,,,)
           Pen: 1
*============================================================
*  Box
*============================================================
 @  10.500,   2.500
 SIZE   6.417,  26.125
WINDOWS  RGB Color Scheme: (,,,,,)
           Pen: 1
*============================================================
*  Text: QTR 2:
*============================================================
 @   2.167,  33.000
WINDOWS  RGB Color Scheme: (,,,,,)
WINDOWS  Font: Terminal,   9
*============================================================
*  Text: QTR 1:
*============================================================
 @   2.167,   3.000
WINDOWS  RGB Color Scheme: (,,,,,)
WINDOWS  Font: Terminal,   9
*============================================================
*  Text: QTR 3:
*============================================================
 @   9.833,   3.000
WINDOWS  RGB Color Scheme: (,,,,,)
WINDOWS  Font: Terminal,   9
*============================================================
*  Text: QTR 4:
*============================================================
 @   9.833,  33.000
WINDOWS  RGB Color Scheme: (,,,,,)
WINDOWS  Font: Terminal,   9
```

```
*==============================================================
*  Text: Grand Total:
*==============================================================
 @  17.500,  18.000
WINDOWS  RGB Color Scheme: (,,,,,)
WINDOWS  Font: Terminal,   9
*==============================================================
*
*==============================================================
 @  17.500,  32.375

  Field:
   (·) Say          ( ) Get          ( ) Edit

  <  Say...   > m.january + m.february + m.march + m.april
                                               «   OK   »
  < Format... >
                                               < Cancel >
  Range:
   [ ] Upper...                      [ ] Lower...

  [ ] When...      [ ] Error...      [ ] Scroll bar
  [ ] Valid...     [ ] Comment...    [ ] Allow tabs
  [ ] Message...   [ ] Disabled      [ ] Refresh

WINDOWS  RGB Color Scheme: (,,,,,)
WINDOWS  Font: Terminal,   9
*==============================================================
*  lhClose
*==============================================================
 @  19.083,  25.000
    SIZE   2.231,  13.500
 Spacing:    2

  Push Button Prompts:           (·) Horizontal    ( ) Vertical
                                 [X] Terminating  <Spacing...>
   \?\!Close
                                Variable:
                                 < Choose... >  lhClose

                                Options:
                                 [ ] When...      [ ] Comment...
                                 [ ] Valid...     [ ] Disabled
                                 [ ] Message...

                 «   OK   »    < Cancel >

WINDOWS  RGB Color Scheme: (,,,,,)
WINDOWS  Font: MS Sans Serif,   8
       Style: Bold
 Screen Cleanup and Procedures code above
```

Appendix A

Cross-Platform Tips and Tricks

General Advice

It is always easiest to move up from the lowest common denominator. This leads to a number of tips:

- If your application is to work in both character- and graphic-mode environments, start with the character-mode version of the application, then transport it to the graphical platforms. If the application is to work only in a graphical environment, pick whichever you feel more comfortable in.
- In graphical environments, select fonts that will work across platforms. For Windows development, use TrueType fonts in order to get maximum scalability across video modes.

Use the most recent version of GENSCRN, GENMENU and TRANSPRT. At this writing, that version is the one that ships with FoxPro 2.6. Simply copy these files to the home directories of your other platforms.

Reports

Many developers dislike using FoxPro's native PREVIEW capability for graphic reports because you can't show an entire page on the screen at once. The common workaround is to send the results to a file and then to MODI COMM that file, allowing your user maximum flexibility in moving through the file. Unfortunately, FoxPro will not let you send a Windows- or Macintosh-created report to a file. Thankfully, FoxPro will use the DOS version of the report if that is the only version available. Therefore, we need to have FoxPro report from a character mode report. Two techniques are available to the developer:

- Create your reports in DOS and never transport them to the other platforms. If they are accidentally transported, USE the FRX, and DELETE FOR Platform # "DOS" and you will be set.
- Create DOS versions of your reports, transport them to other platforms, but if the user chooses to print to the screen, USE the FRX, and COPY TO a temporary file FOR Platform = "DOS". Do the reporting off the temporary file and FoxPro will invoke its DOS reporting engine.

Menus

FoxPro's Menu Builder is the only one of the metafile-driven tools that does not transport from one platform to another. FoxPro uses the same menu across all platforms. This can lead to problems when you want to give your users platform-correct menus. As I discuss in the book, if you are writing a cross-platform application that will be the only application that your users run, and minimizing training costs is more important than platform correctness, this issue won't affect you. If you do need to have a platform-correct menu, however, here are two ways of accomplishing this:

- Create one menu that includes platform-correct bars for all three platforms. In the CLEANUP snippet of the menu, simply add platform-specific code that removes the bars that do not apply to the current platform. This technique is easiest to use with the Windows standard menu for DOS and Windows, and simply delete the About... option from the Help pad on the Macintosh (being sure to add it to the Apple Menu with the SET APLABOUT and ON APLABOUT commands).
- Create three separate menus, one for each platform. Then have your program call the appropriate one for the current platform. This technique requires that you put little code in the menus because you would have to duplicate any corrections and enhancements across all three.

Screens

Remember that Window Footers are only available in FoxPro for DOS. Do not use them if you plan on going multiplatform.

Use the #DOSOBJ, #WINOBJ, #MACOBJ screen generator directives to make sure that platform-specific objects are not transported. They will show up in the transporter, which can be annoying, but will not be moved over.

If you have written a reusable screen that will always be modal, add the generator directive #READCLAUSE MODAL to the SETUP snippet. This will ensure that the screen remains modal, even if it is automatically added to your project and you don't select that option from the generate options window.

Macintosh

DOS and Windows cross-platform capabilities are mainly hampered by the move from character- to graphic-mode screens. Adding the Macintosh to the mix adds the issue of different pathing and file naming capabilities. The following are some tips to minimize these platform differences:

- Use DOS naming conventions on the Macintosh.
- Use FoxPro for the Mac's SET VOLUME command to give your Macintosh drive a DOS drive name. This works particularly well on a network. For instance, if I have mapped drive H: to F:\USERS\HOME\YAG, and the Macintosh has the network mapped as Volume 2, issuing

  ```
  SET VOLUME H: TO "Volume 2:USERS:HOME:YAG"
  ```

  will allow me to work on a project from either a PC or a Macintosh and call it with the same reference. This will prevent FoxPro from thinking that a project has been moved.

There are also a number of behavioral changes that affect FoxPro for the Mac.

- A Menu Pad's SKIP FOR clause doesn't work. The SKIP FOR works fine on Menu Bars, however, allowing you to work around this problem by duplicating the SKIP FOR code in each bar of the Menu Pad.
- If you want bitmaps to properly dim when you issue a SHOW GET...DISABLE, you must use only two-color bitmaps. Sixteen-color bitmaps will not be dimmed properly.
- If you reference a bitmap in code, that bitmap must be shipped separately with the APP/EXE. FoxPro will not find it in the project.

Appendix B

Converting from Codebook 2.0

For those of you who have been working with applications based on the original *FoxPro Codebook*, this appendix describes the steps you have to take to move your application into the approach that I describe in this book. Please note that your preexisting *Codebook* applications will transport and run in FoxPro 2.6, but moving them over to this approach will allow you the benefits of the object-oriented types of capabilities described, as well as the enhanced platform-correct user interface.

Readying Your Project

Back up all your files.

Point all COMMON files to your new 2.6 COMMON files. One way to do this is to USE your PJX file and make a note of how it records the path to your COMMON directory. For instance, it may say:

```
..\COMMON\PROGS\SETSETS.PRG
```

on one of the lines. Assuming that you have installed your new COMMON files in:

```
C:\COMMON26
```

you can change all of your files by typing:

```
REPLACE ALL Name WITH ;
       STRTRAN(Name,"..\COMMON","C:\COMMON26")
```

This will change all references that pointed to your old COMMON code so that they will now point to your new COMMON code.

Close the PJX file.

Add the following COMMON files to the project:

File	Comments
STARTUP.SCX	Turn off [ ]Release Windows.
METHODS.PRG	Set as MAIN program.
GETSHEET.SCX	Set output as GETSHEET.PRG, make it a [X]Modal window, and arrange it as a Centered window.
FOXTOOLS.FLL FOXTOOLS.MLB	Add this as a Library using FoxPro for Windows or FoxPro for the Mac as appropriate.
AREUSURE.SCX	Set output as AREUSURE.PRG and make it a [X]Modal window.

File	Comments
ABOUTCOM.SCX	Turn off [ ]Define Windows and [ ]Release Windows.
INTSETUP.DBF	Change the information in this table so that it contains your company information.

If you are working in FoxPro for Windows or FoxPro for the Mac, create an icon with the same name as the shortname that you have assigned your application (in the Setup table) and add this icon file to your project.

Modifying Tables

Modify SETUP.DBF and add the field CSESSIONID (C:4) to the table.

Modifying the Menu: MAIN.MNX

Menu Option	Comments
System/About	Take out the .SPR from the command line so that it reads: DO ABOUT WITH Setup.cSystName
Database/Reindex	Change the SKIP FOR to: `RDLEVEL() # 1`
Database/Compress	Change the SKIP FOR to: `RDLEVEL() # 1`

Modifying "WR" Screens

Target Platform	Action to Take
Windows/ Macintosh	Transport the "WR" screen set and arrange it so that the "WR" window is centered and the control window is at 0,0.
DOS	Transport the "WR" screen set. The arrangement can remain as in 2.0.

Target Platform	Action To Take
All	Add the following to #SECTION 1 in the SETUP snippet: `#WCLAUSES IN &gcMainWind.`
ALL	If there are no objects that are always available (even when NOT glEditable), add an invisible button called "li" + the screen set name. For example, CD.SPR would have an invisible button called "liCD."

Completing the Move

Build the application; when you are asked for a bitmap, you can Locate it in the COMMON\BMPS directory.

That's it! You now have a basically functioning cross-platform application. You can now add more features, like object orientation and state saving, when you are ready for them; simply emulate the *Codebook 2.6* screens.

Index

Boldface page numbers indicate definitions and principal discussions of topics. *Italic* page numbers indicate illustrations.

Numbers and Symbols

A

B

C

D

E

F

G

H

I

K

L

M

N

O

P

Q

R

S

T

U

V

W

Y

Z

The FoxPro 2.6 Codebook

GET A FREE CATALOG JUST FOR EXPRESSING YOUR OPINION.

Help us improve our books and get a ***FREE*** full-color catalog in the bargain. Please complete this form, pull out this page and send it in today. The address is on the reverse side.

Name ______________________ **Company** ______________________

Address ______________________ **City** __________ **State** ____ **Zip** ______

Phone ( ) ______________

1. How would you rate the overall quality of this book?

- ❑ Excellent
- ❑ Very Good
- ❑ Good
- ❑ Fair
- ❑ Below Average
- ❑ Poor

2. What were the things you liked most about the book? (Check all that apply)

- ❑ Pace
- ❑ Format
- ❑ Writing Style
- ❑ Examples
- ❑ Table of Contents
- ❑ Index
- ❑ Price
- ❑ Illustrations
- ❑ Type Style
- ❑ Cover
- ❑ Depth of Coverage
- ❑ Fast Track Notes

3. What were the things you liked *least* about the book? (Check all that apply)

- ❑ Pace
- ❑ Format
- ❑ Writing Style
- ❑ Examples
- ❑ Table of Contents
- ❑ Index
- ❑ Price
- ❑ Illustrations
- ❑ Type Style
- ❑ Cover
- ❑ Depth of Coverage
- ❑ Fast Track Notes

4. Where did you buy this book?

- ❑ Bookstore chain
- ❑ Small independent bookstore
- ❑ Computer store
- ❑ Wholesale club
- ❑ College bookstore
- ❑ Technical bookstore
- ❑ Other ______________

5. How did you decide to buy this particular book?

- ❑ Recommended by friend
- ❑ Recommended by store personnel
- ❑ Author's reputation
- ❑ Sybex's reputation
- ❑ Read book review in ________
- ❑ Other ______________

6. How did you pay for this book?

- ❑ Used own funds
- ❑ Reimbursed by company
- ❑ Received book as a gift

7. What is your level of experience with the subject covered in this book?

- ❑ Beginner
- ❑ Intermediate
- ❑ Advanced

8. How long have you been using a computer?

years ______________

months ______________

9. Where do you most often use your computer?

- ❑ Home
- ❑ Work
- ❑ Both
- ❑ Other ______________

10. What kind of computer equipment do you have? (Check all that apply)

- ❑ PC Compatible Desktop Computer
- ❑ PC Compatible Laptop Computer
- ❑ Apple/Mac Computer
- ❑ Apple/Mac Laptop Computer
- ❑ CD ROM
- ❑ Fax Modem
- ❑ Data Modem
- ❑ Scanner
- ❑ Sound Card
- ❑ Other ______________

11. What other kinds of software packages do you ordinarily use?

- ❑ Accounting
- ❑ Databases
- ❑ Networks
- ❑ Apple/Mac
- ❑ Desktop Publishing
- ❑ Spreadsheets
- ❑ CAD
- ❑ Games
- ❑ Word Processing
- ❑ Communications
- ❑ Money Management
- ❑ Other ______________

12. What operating systems do you ordinarily use?

- ❑ DOS
- ❑ OS/2
- ❑ Windows
- ❑ Apple/Mac
- ❑ Windows NT
- ❑ Other ______________

13. **On what computer-related subject(s) would you like to see more books?**

14. **Do you have any other comments about this book? (Please feel free to use a separate piece of paper if you need more room)**

PLEASE FOLD, SEAL, AND MAIL TO SYBEX

SYBEX INC.
Department M
2021 Challenger Drive
Alameda, CA
94501

About the Authors

Menachem Bazian, CPA, who contributed to the chapters on Windows Dynamic Data Exchange, is a senior consultant at Flash Creative Management. Menachem is a well known software developer and author in the FoxPro community. He has recently completed Volume # 5 of *The Pros Talk Fox* series. His years of experience in both accounting and systems analysis and design have earned him a reputation as a leading authority on FoxPro programming and Accounting Software. He has written for many publications including *Data Based Advisor*, *FoxTalk*, *The IDBUG Journal*, and *New Accountant*. Mr. Bazian has also been a featured speaker at the Fox Developer's Conference, DBExpo, The FAE Accounting Show, the New York State Society of CPAs (NYSSCPA) Evening Technical Sessions, and the first FoxPro Televideo Conference. Mr. Bazian also currently serves as a member of the NYSSCPA Committee on Management Advisory Services, Practice Administration and Structure.

David Blumenthal, who contributed to the chapters on organizational design and management, is President of Flash Creative Management. David's background includes an MBA in Organizational Development and Personnel Management. He has spoken at various user groups and national developers conferences on managing technical groups and integrating teams to improve corporate-wide performance, effectiveness and efficiency. David's articles have been published in *Data Based Advisor*.

Before founding Flash, David served with various companies where he managed a nationwide sales force, customer support teams, documentation groups and was responsible for implementing organizational changes.

Yair Alan Griver is a principal in Flash Creative Management, a consulting and software development firm in River Edge, New Jersey. A contributing editor to *Data Based Advisor* and *FoxPro Advisor*, Alan has written articles and been quoted in many industry publications. He has spoken at the Fox Developers Conference, DB/Expo, Database World, Windows & OS/2 World, and numerous video conferences, in addition to providing training around the world.

Bill House, a Senior Consultant at Flash Creative Management, contributed to the chapter on FoxPro and Object Orientation. Bill House is co-author of the *FoxPro 2.0 Programmer's Reference* and a frequent contributor to *Data Based Advisor* and *FoxPro Advisor*. Bill has extensive knowledge of FoxPro, C, and other Xbase dialects, and has written a variety of applications for the TV, film, and advertising industries. He is a founder and member of the ANSI X3J19 Xbase Language Standards Committee and has sold his memo-indexing technology, Hbase, to such organizations as KPMG Peat Marwick and the US Geological Service. Bill is the lead developer of the Flash Tools for Collaborative Programming, a suite of FoxPro development products.

The *FoxPro 2.6 Codebook* Program Disk Order Form

☐ Please send me a disk containing the programs from the *FoxPro 2.6 Codebook* by Y. Alan Griver. Enclosed is a check for $24.95 OR I have included credit card information below ($26.70 for New York and New Jersey residents; *residents outside the U.S., add appropriate shipping costs*).

☐ Please send me a FREE subscription to the *Flash Consultant*, a newsletter containing programming tips and techniques along with the latest information about Flash Creative Management.

☐ Please send me information about other Flash Creative Management development tools and services.

Name: ______________________________

Company Name: ______________________________

Address: ______________________________

City/State/Zip Code: ______________________________

Phone/Fax Numbers: ______________________________

CompuServe I.D.: ______________________________

If you would prefer to pay by credit card, please include the following:

Credit Card Information: ☐ Visa ☐ MasterCard ☐ American Express

Name (as it appears on the card): ____________________

Card Number: ____________________

Expiration Date: ____________________

Please make checks payable to *Flash Creative Management, Inc.*, and mail to:

Flash Creative Management
1060 Main Street, Third Floor
River Edge, NJ 07661

Phone: (201) 489-2500
Fax: (201) 489-6750

CompuServe: 71756,2444

Get More FoxPro Help Right Away

Alan Griver, author of this book, offers additional resources for users of FoxPro. Alan is a partner in Flash Creative Management, a consulting and training firm specializing in providing information solutions to your organization's business needs.

The *FoxPro 2.6 Codebook* Diskette

All the source code examples from this book with all the reusable objects are ready for you to use in your applications. The *FoxPro Codebook* 2.6 Source Code Disk is available from Flash Creative Management for only $24.95. Simply return the program disk order form on the next page.

Flash Tools for Collaborative Development

Flash Creative Management believes that efficient development arises from a scientific approach to programming. This approach, which is outlined in *The FoxPro 2.6 Codebook*, seeks to eliminate any duplication of code by the developer, which not only eases the programming process, but prevents many problems from ever occurring. Flash Creative Management offers a collection of software tools that embody the Flash Creative Management approach to quickly developing easily maintainable applications in FoxPro. These tools include Technical Standards and Guidelines manual and utilities disk, a Multiuser Project Builder, a link to version-control systems, and more!

Video

On June 9, 1993, Alan Griver delivered a videoconference on application development from the ground up using his modeless, event-driven methodology. The complete conference—approximately seven hours—is now available on videocassette for those who missed the conference or want to review the material.

Training

Flash Creative Management is one of the pre-eminent software-training firms in the country. Flash offers on-site and in-house training on Xbase data-management systems and other leading software packages, including many commonly (and not so commonly) used programs.

Consulting and Development

The best computer software is only as good as its ability to solve problems and enhance your business. Flash Creative Management maximizes your ability to use microcomputer technology effectively by working with you to create innovative, flexible solutions to business information needs. Flash combines top technical expertise with a pragmatic, quality-oriented approach, creating computer systems and software that are maintainable, expandable, and ready to respond to rapidly changing needs.

The *Flash Consultant*

The *Flash Consultant* is a free newsletter that Flash Creative Management makes available to members of the Xbase community. It includes programming tips and tricks, as well as information about upcoming events and new products. To start your subscription, simply return the form on the previous page.

To learn more about Flash Creative Management's services, return the form or call Flash at (201) 489-2500.

Flash Creative Management
1060 Main Street, Third Floor
River Edge, NJ 07661

Phone: (201) 489-2500
Fax: (201) 489-6750

CompuServe:

Product Information: 71756,2444—Avi Greengart
Codebook Questions: 71541,3150—Yair Alan Griver

The Event Handler

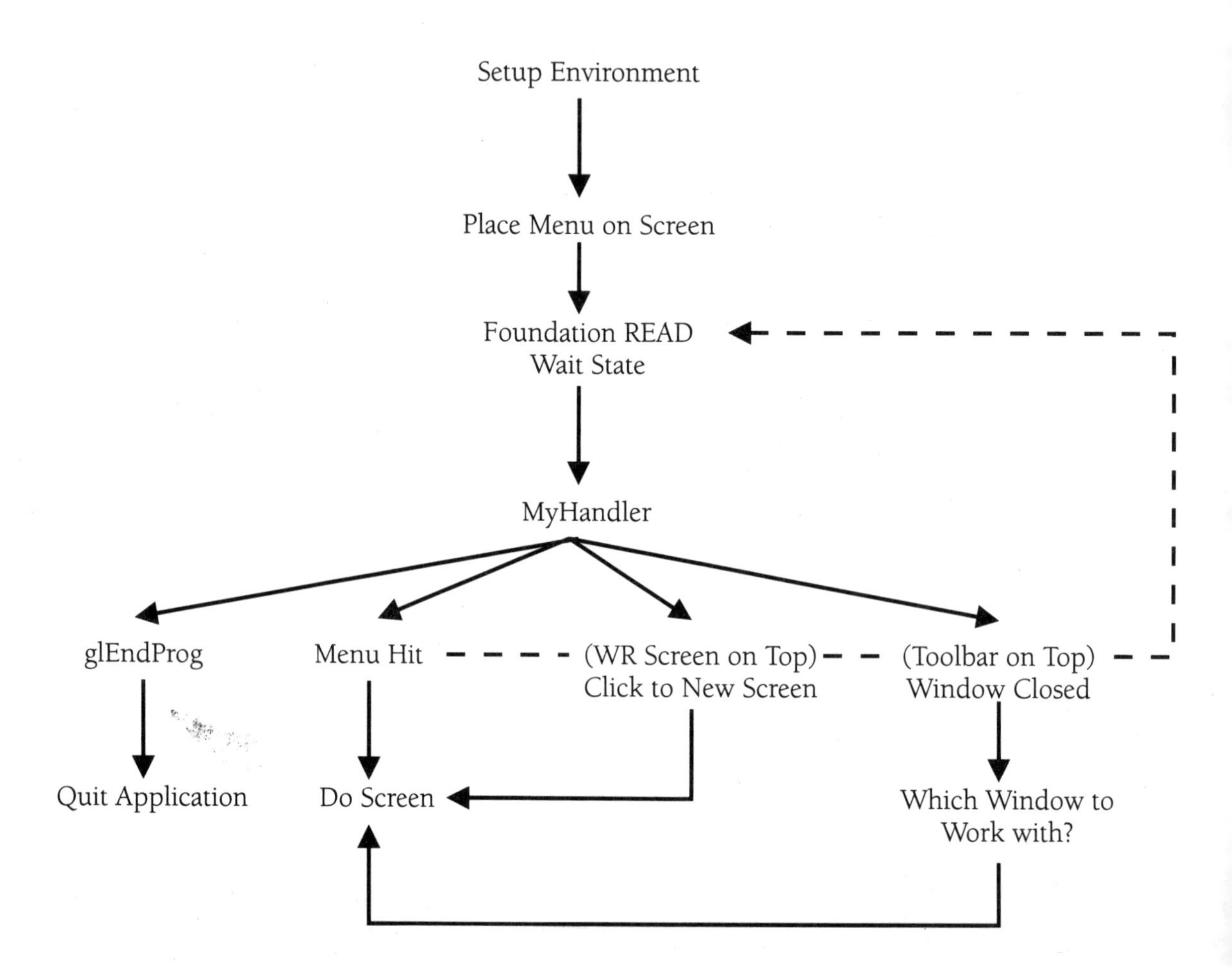